PUBLICATIONS OF THE NEW CHAUCER SOCIETY

THE NEW CHAUCER SOCIETY

Studies in the Age of Chaucer, the yearbook of The New Chaucer Society, is published annually. Each issue contains substantial articles on all aspects of Chaucer and his age, book reviews, and an annotated Chaucer bibliography. Manuscripts, in duplicate, accompanied by return postage, should follow the *Chicago Manual of Style,* 14th edition. Unsolicited reviews are not accepted. Authors receive free twenty offprints of articles and ten of reviews. All correspondence regarding manuscript submissions should be directed to the Editor, Frank Grady, Department of English, University of Missouri-St. Louis, 8001 Natural Bridge Road, St. Louis, MO 63121. Subscriptions to The New Chaucer Society and information about the Society's activities should be directed to David Lawton, Department of English, Washington University, CB 1122, One Brookings Drive, St. Louis, MO 63130. Back issues of the journal may be ordered from The University of Notre Dame Press, Chicago Distribution Center, 11030 South Langley Avenue, Chicago, IL 60628; phone: 800-621-2736; fax: 800-621-8476, from outside the United States: phone: 773-702-7000; fax: 773-702-7212.

Studies in the Age of Chaucer

Studies in the Age of Chaucer

Volume 28
2006

EDITOR

FRANK GRADY

PUBLISHED ANNUALLY BY THE NEW CHAUCER SOCIETY
WASHINGTON UNIVERSITY IN ST. LOUIS

The frontispiece design, showing the Pilgrims at the Tabard Inn, is adapted from the woodcut in Caxton's second edition of *The Canterbury Tales*.

ISBN 0-933784-30-9
ISSN 0190-2407

CONTENTS

CONTENTS

REVIEWS

CONTENTS

Studies in the Age of Chaucer

"Paths of Long Study":

Reading Chaucer and Christine de Pizan in Tandem

Theresa Coletti
University of Maryland

Consider the following. Thomas Hoccleve translated Christine de Pizan's *L'Epistre au dieu d'Amours* into Middle English as the *Letter of Cupid,* a poem that invoked Geoffrey Chaucer's literary authority and circulated alongside his courtly writings in important fifteenth-century anthologies such as Bodleian Library MSS Fairfax 16 and Tanner 346. Despite its clear debt to Christine's poem, Hoccleve's *Letter* found its way into the Chaucer apocrypha and subsequently appeared in Renaissance editions of the poet's collected works.[1] The triangulation of texts and writers illustrated by the case of the *Epistre* and the *Letter of Cupid* instances a pattern that elsewhere marks the relationship of Chau-

Earlier versions of this essay were presented at the Biennial Conference of the New Chaucer Society, University of Colorado, Boulder; the Center for Renaissance and Baroque Studies, University of Maryland; the University of Pennsylvania; and the University of Michigan. I am grateful to my interlocutors at all these venues for their helpful commentary. I also want to thank Anne Coldiron, Richard Emmerson, Lynn Staley, and Sarah Stanbury for their suggestions and encouragement and Frank Grady for astute editorial advice.

[1] For editions of the two poems, see *Poems of Cupid, God of Love,* ed. and trans. Thelma S. Fenster and Mary Carpenter Erler (Leiden: E. J. Brill, 1990). An early discussion by J. A. Burrow treats Hoccleve's *Letter* solely in terms of homage to Chaucer and *The Legend of Good Women,* but a more recent analysis corrects the prior neglect of Hoccleve's source text. See "Hoccleve and Chaucer," in *Chaucer Traditions: Studies in Honour of Derek Brewer,* ed. Ruth Morse and Barry Windeatt (Cambridge: Cambridge University Press, 1990), pp. 54–55; and "Hoccleve and the Middle French Poets," in *The Long Fifteenth Century: Essays for Douglas Gray,* ed. Helen Cooper and Sally Mapstone (Oxford: Clarendon Press, 1997), p. 36. For detailed considerations of this triangle of authors, see Roger Ellis, "Chaucer, Christine de Pizan, and Hoccleve: The *Letter of Cupid,*" in *Essays on Thomas Hoccleve,* ed. Catherine Batt (Turnhout: Brepols, 1996), pp. 29–54; and Ethan Knapp, *The Bureaucratic Muse: Thomas Hoccleve and the Literature of Late Medieval England* (University Park: Pennsylvania State University Press, 2001), pp. 45–75.

1

cer and Christine de Pizan in late medieval England. Two important texts of the Chaucer apocrypha, the anonymous *Assembly of Ladies* and *The Flower and the Leaf*, exhibit thematic and narrative features that point to the influence of Christine de Pizan's *Dit de la Rose* and *Livre de la Cité des Dames*.[2] A shared commitment to promoting the good wife's prudent counsel produces complex textual connections between Chaucer's *Tale of Melibee*, Philippe de Mézières's *Le Livre de la vertu du sacrement de mariage*, and Christine's *Livre des Trois Vertus*.[3] In 1526 Richard Pynson decisively linked the woman writer and the English laureate: his edition of *The Boke of Fame, made by Geffray Chaucer: with Dyuers other of his Workes* included in that diversity Anthony Woodville's fifteenth-century translation of Christine de Pizan's *Proverbes moraulx*.

The texts and careers of Geoffrey Chaucer and Christine de Pizan crisscross each other with dizzying complexity. Although the woman writer holds a place in the reigning critical narrative of Chaucer's relationships to his literary influences and his contemporaries, she has yet to lay claim to the prominent position in it that is warranted, I contend, by her extensive rhetorical, historical, and cultural affiliations with the English poet.[4] This essay sketches a provisional map of those affiliations.

[2] Jane Chance, "Christine de Pizan as Literary Mother: Woman's Authority and Subjectivity in 'The Floure and the Leafe' and 'The Assembly of Ladies,'" in *The City of Scholars: New Approaches to Christine de Pizan,* ed. Margarete Zimmerman and Dina De Rentiis (Berlin: Walter de Gruyter, 1994), pp. 245–59.

[3] See Carolyn P. Collette, "Chaucer and the French Tradition Revisited: Philippe de Mézières and the Good Wife," in *Medieval Women: Texts and Contexts in Late Medieval Britain,* ed. Jocelyn Wogan-Browne et al. (Turnhout: Brepols, 2000), pp. 151–68; and "Heeding the Counsel of Prudence: A Context for the *Melibee,*" *ChauR* 29 (1995): 416–33.

[4] Inscribing Christine's prominent connections with the work of Chaucer can also prompt fuller investigation of her relationships to his contemporaries. The woman writer's moralized reflections on the hierarchical body politic, for example, strike a chord with central preoccupations of John Gower, whose *vox clamantis* finds its counterpart in Christine's "povre voix criant en ce royaume." See Josette A. Wisman, ed. and trans., *Christine de Pizan: The Epistle of the Prison of Human Life, with an Epistle to the Queen of France and Lament on the Evils of the Civil War* (New York: Garland, 1984), p. 94; quoted in Renate Blumenfeld-Kosinski, "Christine de Pizan and the Political Life in Late Medieval France," in *Christine de Pizan: A Casebook,* ed. Barbara K. Altmann and Deborah L. McGrady (New York: Routledge, 2003), p. 18. With John Lydgate, Christine de Pizan shared both a well-advertised dependence on aristocratic patronage and a penchant for prolix allegorical narrative. Her elaborate autobiographical portraiture, across a range of her works, rivals Thomas Hoccleve's self-referentiality in the *Regement of Princes* and *The Series.* Christine de Pizan and the translator of her *Epistre au dieu d'Amours* were also both deeply engaged—as copyists, arrangers, and editors—in the physical production of their own texts. See James Laidlaw, "Christine and the Manuscript Tradition," in *Casebook,* pp. 231–49; Catherine Batt, "Introduction," in *Essays on Thomas Hoccleve,* pp.

Whereas comparative literary analyses of these two writers' intersections up to now have focused primarily on Chaucer's *Legend of Good Women* and Christine's *Livre de la cité des dames,* their mutual investment in medieval discourses that defamed and defended women is but a single aspect of a far deeper engagement with the same set of cultural materials.[5] The so-called father of English poetry and medieval Europe's first professional woman writer operated within the same literary system, yet they responded to—and made their marks upon—that system by exercising very different formal and ideological options. My investigation centers on texts whose deployment of identical literary sources points to an elaborate intertextual conversation about authorship, poetics, and the politics of representation: Chaucer's *House of Fame* and Christine's *Livre de Chemin de long estude.* Reading these dream visions in tandem, this essay analyzes how Chaucer and Christine draw on the same literary traditions to make different aesthetic and political moves. What factors account for these differences? How do gender categories frame the ideological and literary positions exhibited in their texts? Granting Christine de Pizan full admission into the circle of Chaucer's contemporaries provides an opportunity to revisit late medieval constructions of authorship in the context of a broadly configured, international literary history.[6] This augmented narrative of Chaucer's literary

7–8; and Roger Ellis's "Introduction" to his edition of Hoccleve, *"My Compleinte" and Other Poems* (Exeter: University of Exeter, 2001), pp. 10–28.

[5] See Sheila Delany, "Rewriting Women Good: Gender and the Anxiety of Influence in Two Late-Medieval Texts," in *Chaucer and the Eighties,* ed. Julian N. Wasserman and Robert J. Blanch (Syracuse: Syracuse University Press, 1986), pp. 75–92; and *The Naked Text: Chaucer's Legend of Good Women* (Berkeley and Los Angeles: University of California Press, 1994), pp. 93–100; A. J. Minnis, with V. J. Scattergood and J. J. Smith, *Oxford Guides to Chaucer: The Shorter Poems* (Oxford: Clarendon Press, 1995), pp. 377–78, 427–30; Alcuin Blamires, *The Case for Women in Medieval Culture* (Oxford: Clarendon Press, 1997), pp. 199–230; Carol Meale, "Legends of Good Women in the European Middle Ages," *Archiv für Studium der neueren Sprachen und Literaturen* 229 (1992): 55–70; and Judith Laird, "Good Women and *Bonnes Dames:* Virtuous Females in Chaucer and Christine de Pizan," *ChauR* 30 (1995): 58–70. Christine de Pizan scholarship rarely entertains Chaucer's texts and preoccupations. Maureen Quilligan occasionally invokes Chaucer to elucidate Christine's texts; *The Allegory of Female Authority: Christine de Pizan's "Cité des Dames"* (Ithaca: Cornell University Press, 1991). A more wide-ranging exception to these emphases is provided by Robert Meyer-Lee, "Christine de Pizan and the Beginning of the English Poetic Tradition," paper delivered at the International Congress on Medieval Studies, Western Michigan University, 2004.

[6] The list of "Chaucer and . . ." studies is long. For example, see Piero Boitani, *Chaucer and Boccaccio,* MÆ Monographs, n.s. 8 (Oxford: Society for the Study of Mediaeval Languages and Literature, 1977); Boitani, ed., *Chaucer and the Italian Trecento* (Cambridge: Cambridge University Press, 1983); David Wallace, *Chaucer and the Early Writings of Boccaccio* (Woodbridge, Suffolk: D. S. Brewer, 1985); Robert R. Edwards,

3

relationships also furnishes a new purchase on a subject that of late has attracted much critical attention: the convergence of the literary identities of Geoffrey Chaucer and Christine de Pizan in late medieval and early Tudor England.

I

It is not surprising that works by Chaucer and Christine de Pizan were conflated with each other or that texts written by one were printed in a collection devoted to the other. Many points of contact between the two figures made such literary mix-ups inevitable.[7] Although neither Chaucer nor Christine was of noble birth, their respective social locations on the periphery of court culture significantly shape their individual development as writers, enhancing their exposure to and participation in an international, predominantly French, discourse of courtly letters.[8]

Chaucer and Boccaccio: Antiquity and Modernity (Basingstoke, Hampshire: Palgrave, 2002); Warren Ginsberg, *Chaucer's Italian Tradition* (Ann Arbor: University of Michigan Press, 2002); James I. Wimsatt, *Chaucer and the French Love Poets* (Chapel Hill: University of North Carolina Press, 1968); Wimsatt, *Chaucer and His French Contemporaries: Natural Music in the Fourteenth Century* (Toronto: University of Toronto Press, 1991); R. F. Yeager, ed., *Chaucer and Gower: Difference, Mutuality, Exchange,* English Literary Studies 51 (Victoria, B.C.: University of Victoria, 1991); J. Allen Mitchell, *Ethics and Exemplary Narrative in Chaucer and Gower* (Cambridge: D. S. Brewer, 2004); George Kane, *Chaucer and Langland* (Berkeley and Los Angeles: University of California Press, 1989); Derek Pearsall, "Chaucer and Lydgate," in *Chaucer Traditions,* pp. 39–53.

[7] Where the repetition of the full name Christine de Pizan would be cumbersome, I have opted frequently for the shortened "Christine." Instead of reinforcing the gender bias of speaking of men by their surnames and women by first names, this choice, I believe, is justified in Christine's case. She took delight in her given name, which she expressed not only through her anagrams and signatures ("Je, Christine") but also by declaring herself the namesake of Saint Christine and Christ.

[8] For basic overviews of Chaucer's response to French literary culture, see James I. Wimsatt, "Chaucer and French Poetry," in *Geoffrey Chaucer,* ed. Derek Brewer (Athens: Ohio University Press, 1975), pp. 109–36; Richard Firth Green, *Poets and Princepleasers: Literature and the English Court in the Late Middle Ages* (Toronto: University of Toronto Press, 1980); and Elizabeth Salter, "Chaucer and Internationalism," *SAC* 2 (1980): 71–79. More recent considerations of the issue include Wimsatt, *Chaucer and His French Contemporaries;* Helen Phillips, "Frames and Narrators in Chaucerian Poetry," in *Long Fifteenth Century,* pp. 71–97; William Calin, *The French Tradition and the Literature of Medieval England* (Toronto: University of Toronto Press, 1994); and important essays by Ardis Butterfield, "Chaucer's French Inheritance," in *The Cambridge Companion to Chaucer,* ed. Piero Boitani and Jill Mann, 2nd ed. (Cambridge: Cambridge University Press, 2003), pp. 20–35; and "French Culture and the Richardian Court," in *Essays on Ricardian Literature in Honour of J. A. Burrow,* ed. A. J. Minnis, Charlotte C. Morse, and Thorlac Turville-Petre (Oxford: Clarendon Press, 1997), p. 86. For an overview of Christine's court-centered life and work, see Charity Cannon Willard, *Christine de Pizan: Her Life and Works* (New York: Persea Books, 1984).

Encounters with courtly culture initiate comparable trajectories for the careers of both, involving especially their sustained reflections on the *Roman de la Rose,* a generative text for major works by each writer.[9] Although courtliness is a great enabler of their literary efforts, each perceives the problems that courtly paradigms pose for society and cultural production. From different perspectives, Chaucer and Christine mount critiques of courtly values and bear witness to courtly discourse's negative impact on women and gender relationships. Rejecting the role of courtly maker, both writers eventually direct their ambitions to prospects for inclusion among the ranks of poets.[10] Chaucer and Christine work in the same genres, writing love lyrics, allegorical dream visions, discourses of consolation, and treatises of advice for princes. They both recast classical mythology to mount a defense of women and advance critiques of the chivalric ethos. They make use of the same literary mentors (Machaut, Deschamps),[11] draw upon the same literary influences

---

[9] Derek Pearsall observes that the *Roman* "became part of . . . [Chaucer's] mentality, perhaps more part of his experience than the experience of life itself"; *The Life of Geoffrey Chaucer* (Oxford: Blackwell, 1992), p. 80. Among the many commentaries on Chaucer's probable translation and reworking of the *Roman,* Charles Muscatine's *Chaucer and the French Tradition* (Berkeley and Los Angeles: University of California Press, 1957) remains a foundational text. Renate Blumenfeld-Kosinski says that "the *Roman de la Rose* is ever present as a kind of foil or counterpoint" in Christine's writings; "Christine de Pizan and the Misogynistic Tradition," in *The Selected Writings of Christine de Pizan,* ed. Blumenfeld-Kosinski; trans. Blumenfeld-Kosinski and Kevin Brownlee (New York: W. W. Norton, 1997), p. 308. See also Kevin Brownlee, "Discourses of the Self: Christine de Pizan and the *Romance of the Rose,*" in *Rethinking the "Romance of the Rose": Text, Image, Reception,* ed. Brownlee and Sylvia Huot (Philadelphia: University of Pennsylvania Press, 1992), pp. 234–61. Christine de Pizan's participation in the *querelle de la Rose* is also relevant here; see Rosalind Brown-Grant, *Christine de Pizan and the Moral Defence of Women: Reading beyond Gender* (Cambridge: Cambridge University Press, 1999), pp. 7–51; and Alastair Minnis, *Magister Amoris: The "Roman de la Rose" and Vernacular Hermeneutics* (Oxford: Oxford University Press, 2001).

[10] Glending Olson, "Making and Poetry in the Age of Chaucer," *CL* 31 (1979): 272–90; see also Lee Patterson, *Chaucer and the Subject of History* (Madison: University of Wisconsin Press, 1991), pp. 49–61. Chaucer's ultimate rejection of the "poetic" ideal is further analyzed by Patterson, "'What Man Artow?' Authorial Self-Definition in *The Tale of Sir Thopas* and *The Tale of Melibee,*" *SAC* 11 (1989): 117–75. Although Christine wrote many of her later works in prose, she and her readers nonetheless would have considered them under the rubric of "poetry," which has as much to do with figurative language and subject matter as it does verse. See her preface to *L'Avision-Christine,* ed. and trans. Christine Reno, "The Preface to the *Avision-Christine* in ex-Phillips 128," in *Reinterpreting Christine de Pizan,* ed. Earl Jeffrey Richards, with Joan Williamson, Nadia Margolis, and Christine Reno (Athens: University of Georgia Press, 1992), pp. 208–9.

[11] See Wimsatt, *Chaucer and His French Contemporaries;* Willard, *Christine de Pizan,* p. 44; and Barbara K. Altmann, "Reopening the Case: Machaut's *Jugement* Poems as a Source in Christine de Pizan," in *Reinterpreting Christine de Pizan,* pp. 137–56.

(Boethius, Dante, Boccaccio),[12] and, at least in late medieval England, share some of the same readers.[13]

Chaucer and Christine de Pizan further contribute to the cases of mistaken identity attending the circulation of their texts by employing similar rhetorical tools and topoi to fashion their self-image as writers. Their literary personae, figured as readers, enact the powerful impact of books on individual experience and regularly exploit their distance from centers of cultural authority.[14] For Christine, lack of access to learning and detachment from social and political power are always functions of gender, yet from her various self-positionings as the outsider, the stranger, and the little lone woman, she paradoxically lays claim to a space from which she can speak. Chaucer's personae are more notoriously marginalized. Whereas his earlier poems underscore their narrators' detachment from experience of love, Chaucer figures the persona of the *Canterbury Tales* as removed from literary and other forms of cultural competence. In their textual self-presentations, both Chaucer and Christine engage in literary cross-dressing. Chaucer's extraordinary efforts to ventriloquize female voices and occupy feminine positions can be paralleled to Christine's experiments in writing the masculine voice in works such as her *Cent ballades d'amant et de dame, Le livre du duc des vrais amans,* and *L'Epistre au dieu d'amours.*[15] Christine outdoes the English poet,

---

[12] In a sense, Christine's debt to Boethius in works such as *L'Avision Christine* and *Le chemin de long estude* makes her, like Chaucer, a translator of the *Consolation of Philosophy.* David Lawton calls Boethianism an important attribute of fifteenth-century poetry; "Dullness and the Fifteenth Century," *ELH* 54 (1987): 761–99. On Chaucer's debts to Italian writers, see the works cited in note 6. Boccaccio's impact on Christine's writing is most evident in the *Cité des dames;* see Patricia A. Phillippy, "Establishing Authority: Boccaccio's *De Claris Mulieribus* and Christine de Pizan's *Le livre de la cité des dames,*" in *Selected Writings of Christine de Pizan,* pp. 329–61. Petrarch's influence on Christine is less commonly observed; see Earl Jeffrey Richards, "Christine, the Conventions of Courtly Diction, and Italian Humanism," in *Reinterpreting Christine de Pizan,* pp. 257–62.

[13] An inventory of books owned by fifteenth-century Norfolk gentleman John Paston records his copies of Chaucer's *Troilus and Criseyde* and *Legend of Good Women* and Christine de Pizan's *Epistre d'Othéa.* See G. A. Lester, "The Books of a Fifteenth-Century English Gentleman, John Paston," *NM* 88 (1987): 200–217.

[14] Laurel Amtower, *Engaging Words: The Culture of Reading in the Later Middle Ages* (New York: Palgrave, 2000), p. 10; Marilynn Desmond, "Introduction," *Christine de Pizan and the Categories of Difference,* ed. Desmond (Minneapolis: University of Minnesota Press, 1998), p. xii. Susan Schibanoff discusses the importance of Chaucer's reader-narrators; see "The New Reader and Female Textuality in Two Early Commentaries on Chaucer," in *Writing After Chaucer: Essential Readings in Chaucer and the Fifteenth Century,* ed. Daniel J. Pinti (New York: Garland, 1998), p. 62.

[15] Nadia Margolis, "Clerkliness and Courtliness in the Complaintes of Christine de Pizan," in *Christine de Pizan and the Medieval French Lyric,* ed. Earl Jeffrey Richards (Gainesville: University Press of Florida, 1998), pp. 135–54. On Christine's "intellectual

though; in *Le Livre de la mutacion de Fortune,* she declares that Fortune transformed her from a woman to a man.

Recent scholarship has emphasized common efforts by Chaucer and Christine de Pizan to expand the resources and influence of vernacular writing. The international literary culture embraced by both writers saw the development of the vernacular as a medium for instruction as well as courtly entertainment, part of a broader, late medieval cultural movement characterized by increasing "self-consciousness about language, political identity, and intellectual achievement." Glending Olson posits that Chaucer's effort to foster "English participation in contemporary European letters" drew inspiration from his exposure, in several visits during the 1370s, to the learned values of the court of Charles V—the very place that the young Christine de Pizan called home.[16] Influenced by her early contacts with this milieu, Christine established her vernacular scholarly credentials through her contributions to the *Querelle de la Rose,* as well as many texts and translations that rendered classical and other learned sources for ethical and political purposes serving monarchical interests.[17]

Were it not for the crucial fact that echoes of Chaucerian genres and themes in Christine's works can be attributed to these two writers' common literary influences and participation in late medieval international courtly and humanist culture, we might speculate that a volume or two of Geoffrey Chaucer must have been among the books that so regularly surround Christine in the manuscript portraits whose production she supervised.[18] The possibility that the woman writer at least knew of

---

cross-dressing," see Jane Chance, "Speaking *In Propria Persona:* Authorizing the Subject as a Political Act in Late Medieval Feminine Spirituality," in *New Trends in Feminine Spirituality: The Holy Women of Liège,* ed. Juliette Dor, Lesley Johnson, and Jocelyn Wogan-Browne (Turnhout: Brepols, 1999), p. 279.

[16] Glending Olson, "Geoffrey Chaucer," in *The Cambridge History of Medieval English Literature,* ed. David Wallace (Cambridge: Cambridge University Press, 1999), p. 580. See also Willard, *Christine de Pizan,* pp. 20–31.

[17] See Thelma Fenster, "'Perdre son latin': Christine de Pizan and Vernacular Humanism," in *Christine de Pizan and the Categories of Difference,* pp. 91–107; Lori Walters, "'Translating' Petrarch: *Cité des dames* II.7.1, Jean Daudin, and Vernacular Authority," in *Christine de Pizan 2000,* ed. John Campbell and Nadia Margolis (Amsterdam: Rodopi, 2000), pp. 283–97, 347–50; Walters, "Christine de Pizan as Translator and Voice of the Body Politic," in *Casebook,* pp. 25–41.

[18] Julia Boffey observes that the Chaucerian cast of the English poems of Charles of Orleans illustrates the complex intertextualities that characterize literary relations in a "war-torn but culturally homogeneous community of readers." See "Charles of Orleans Reading Chaucer's Dream Visions," in *Mediaevalitas: Reading the Middle Ages,* ed. Piero Boitani and Anna Torti (Cambridge: D. S. Brewer, 1996), pp. 43–62, at 62.

Chaucer surely can be entertained.[19] Both writers lavishly praised Oton de Granson, the poet-knight who was a familiar of Chaucer during his long period of service in England; both entered into poetic communication with Eustache Deschamps, who extolled Chaucer as "the God of earthly Love in Albion" ("d'Amours mondains Dieux en Albie") and "grand translateur" of French culture into English and praised Christine for her "great philosophy" and her dedication to teaching and study.[20] A well-documented narrative records the two writers intersecting personal fortunes through their common associations with the Earl of Salisbury, John Montagu, and Henry IV, who brought Christine's son Jean de Castel into his home after Montagu's execution and invited the mother to join him.[21]

[19] See Delany, "Rewriting Women Good," pp. 89–90 n. 3; Ellis, "Chaucer, Christine de Pizan, and Hoccleve," pp. 38–40; and Dhira B. Mahoney, "Middle English Regenderings of Christine de Pizan," in *The Medieval Opus: Imitation, Rewriting, and Transmission in the French Tradition,* ed. Douglas Kelly (Amsterdam: Rodopi, 1996), p. 414. S. H. Rigby evaluates assertions by Jane Chance and Sheila Delany that Christine knew works by Chaucer and Gower; "The Wife of Bath, Christine de Pizan, and the Medieval Case for Women," *ChauR* 35 (2000): 139. I've encountered nothing that suggests Christine de Pizan could read English. Christine did not consistently acknowledge her debts to male writers, as Josette Wisman explains in her account of Christine's significant borrowing from Jacques Legrand's *Livre de bonnes meurs* in her *Epistre de la prison de vie humaine;* "Jacques Legrand, Christine de Pizan, et la question de la 'nouveleté,'" *MÆ* 63 (1994): 75–83.

[20] On Chaucer, Christine, and Granson, see Wimsatt, *Chaucer and His French Contemporaries,* pp. 210–41. Chaucer invokes Granson in "The Complaint of Venus," line 82; *The Riverside Chaucer,* gen. ed. Larry D. Benson (Boston: Houghton Mifflin, 1987). Christine praises Granson in *L'Epistre au dieu d'Amours* (2.8, lines 233–44) and *Le Debat de deux Amans* (2.97, lines 1615–18). Citations refer to *Oeuvres Poétiques de Christine de Pisan,* ed. Maurice Roy, 3 vols. Société des Anciens Texts Français (1884; repr. New York: Johnson, 1965). Eustache Deschamps, *Oeuvres complètes de Eustache Deschamps,* ed. Le Marquis de Queux de Saint-Hilaire and Gaston Raynaud, 11 vols. Société des Anciens Textes Français (Paris: Firmin Didot, 1878–1904), 2:138–40, no. 138 (Chaucer); 6:251–52, no. 1242 (Christine). For an English translation of Deschamps's poem to Chaucer, see Derek Brewer, ed., *Chaucer: The Critical Heritage,* 2 vols. (London: Routledge and Kegan Paul, 1978), 1:40–41. See also Wimsatt, *Chaucer and His French Contemporaries,* pp. 248–52. Christine's poem to Deschamps appears in *Oeuvres Poétiques,* 2:295–301. For English translations of her poem and Deschamps's reply, see Blumenfeld-Kosinski, *Selected Writings of Christine de Pizan,* pp. 109–13. Lori Walters discusses Christine's relationship to Deschamps; "Fathers and Daughters: Christine de Pizan as Reader of the Male Tradition of *Clergie* in the *Dit de la Rose,*" in *Reinterpreting Christine de Pizan,* pp. 63–76. Olson notes resemblances between Deschamps's two poems to these literary interlocutors; "Geoffrey Chaucer," p. 578.

[21] On Montagu and the Chaucer circle, see Paul Strohm, "Chaucer's Fifteenth-Century Audience and the Narrowing of the 'Chaucer Tradition,'" *SAC* 4 (1982): 9–11; Pearsall, *Life of Geoffrey Chaucer,* pp. 181–82. See also P. G. C. Campbell, "Christine de Pisan en Angleterre," *Revue de littérature comparée* 5 (1925): 659–70; and J. C. Laidlaw,

If Christine de Pizan had been introduced to Chaucer's work or met the poet himself, what would she have thought of him?[22] No stranger to the instability of aristocratic patronage, she may have sympathized with Chaucer's readiness to ally himself with the new English prince whose kingship "by lyne and free eleccion" (23) garnered the poet's encomium in "The Complaint to his Purse" (23).[23] Christine de Pizan had more important philosophical and literary reasons, though, to be at odds with the English poet whom Deschamps had christened "Ovides grans en ta poëterie." In work after work, she labored to ameliorate the negative effects of courtly ideology on women *and* men, the very thing that Deschamps had praised "the God of earthly love in Albion" for perpetuating.[24] For the woman writer, those dangers were epitomized by the amorous verses of Ovid and his medieval literary offspring, Jean de Meun, the principal targets of her critique of courtly misogyny in the *Epistre au dieu d'Amour* and her contributions to the *Querelle de*

"Christine de Pizan, the Earl of Salisbury, and Henry IV," *French Studies* 36 (1982): 129–43. Christine relates the story of her son's sojourn in England and her response to political events there in *Lavision-Christine,* ed. Sister Mary Louis Towner (1932; repr: New York: AMS Press, 1969). For a modern English translation, see Christine de Pizan, *Christine's Vision,* trans. Glenda K. McLeod (New York: Garland, 1993). Royal marriage arrangements provided occasions for potential literary contacts. Montagu was sent to France in 1398 to discourage a marriage between the future Henry IV and Marie, daughter of the Duke of Berry. Gontier Col, one of Christine's interlocutors in the *Querelle de la Rose,* was involved in negotiations to return Isabella of France to her home after the death of Richard II; see Willard, *Christine de Pizan,* pp. 164–65, 78. In a stunning historical coincidence, Thomas Montagu, the young son of the Earl of Salisbury for whom Christine's Jean was sent to England as a companion, grew up to become the second husband of Alice Chaucer, the English poet's granddaughter and one of late medieval England's most influential owners of works by Christine de Pizan. See Carol Meale, "Reading Women's Culture in Fifteenth-Century England: The Case of Alice Chaucer," in *Mediaevalitas,* pp. 87–95.

[22] Rigby hypothesizes Christine's reading of the Wife of Bath and her tale; "Wife of Bath, Christine de Pizan, and the Medieval Case for Women," 154–56.

[23] *The Riverside Chaucer,* p. 656. Christine knew how to work both sides of the political fence, accepting commissions from both Burgundian and Armagnac factions during the French civil wars. See Charity Cannon Willard, "Christine de Pizan: From Poet to Political Commentator," in *Politics, Gender, and Genre: The Political Thought of Christine de Pizan,* ed. Margaret Brabant (Boulder: Westview Press, 1992), pp. 17–32.

[24] Christine's responses to the ethical problems of courtliness and women's harmful relationship to courtly culture are discussed by Roberta Krueger, *Women Readers and the Ideology of Gender in Old French Verse Romance* (Cambridge: Cambridge University Press, 1993), pp. 217–46; Kevin Brownlee, "Rewriting Romance: Courtly Discourse and Auto-Citation in Christine de Pizan," in *Gender and Text in the Later Middle Ages,* ed. Jane Chance (Gainesville: University Press of Florida, 1996), pp. 172–94; and Sandra Hindman and Stephen Perkinson, "Insurgent Voices: Illuminated Versions of Christine de Pizan's *Le Livre du Duc des vrais amans,*" in *City of Scholars,* pp. 221–31.

la Rose.[25] By aligning Chaucer with this troubled masculine genealogy, Deschamps had identified the English poet with the very literary discourses whose harm to women and society Christine sought to expose in her poetic and humanist epistles.[26]

The ideological tensions that might be elicited from this imaginary encounter have parallels in the fundamentally different approaches that Geoffrey Chaucer and Christine de Pizan exhibit toward the personal and public politics of the literary vocation. Christine's texts are regularly punctuated by autobiographical record and commentary, a topic on which Chaucer is exceptionally reticent.[27] Compared to the woman writer's frequent self-credentialing and advertisement of her royal commissions and would-be patrons, Chaucer's notice of his own noble contacts is spare indeed.[28] Whereas Chaucer comments only obliquely about personal engagement with his work, Christine regularly articulates what writing as a woman signifies for her, reinforcing her authorial presence with her famous signature, "Je, Christine."[29] If Chaucer cultivated a

[25] On Christine's negative assessment of Ovidian writing, see Earl Jeffrey Richards, "Rejecting Essentialism and Gendered Writing: The Case of Christine de Pizan," in *Gender and Text in the Later Middle Ages,* pp. 96–131; Judith Kellogg, "Transforming Ovid: The Metamorphosis of Female Authority," in *Christine de Pizan and the Categories of Difference,* pp. 181–94; and Brownlee, "Discourses of the Self."

[26] On Chaucer as an Ovidian poet, see John Fyler, *Chaucer and Ovid* (New Haven: Yale University Press, 1979); Helen Cooper, "Chaucer and Ovid: A Question of Authority," in *Ovid Renewed: Ovidian Influences in Literature and Art from the Middle Ages to the Twentieth Century,* ed. Charles Martindale (Cambridge: Cambridge University Press, 1988), pp. 71–81, 263–65; and Michael A. Calabrese, *Chaucer's Ovidian Arts of Love* (Gainesville: University Press of Florida, 1994).

[27] Important discussions of Christine's self-portraiture include Quilligan, *Allegory of Female Authority,* pp. 11–68; Jacqueline Cerquiglini, "The Stranger," in *Selected Writings of Christine de Pizan,* pp. 265–74; Roberta Krueger, "Christine's Anxious Lessions: Gender, Morality, and the Social Order from the *Enseignemens* to the *Avision,*" in *Christine de Pizan and the Categories of Difference,* pp. 16–40; and the following essays in *Au champ des escriptures, IIIe colloque international sur Christine de Pizan,* ed. Eric Hicks (Paris: Honoré Champion, 2000): Kevin Brownlee, "Le projet 'autobiographique' de Christine de Pizan: Histoires et fables du moi," pp. 5–23; Anne Paupert, "'La narracion de mes aventures': Des premiers poèmes à *L'Advision,* L'élaboration d'une écriture autobiographique dans l'oeuvre de Christine de Pizan," pp. 51–71; and Patrizia Romagnoli, "Les formes de la voix: Masques et dédoublements du moi dans l'oeuvre de Christine de Pizan," pp. 73–90.

[28] Seth Lerer, *Chaucer and His Readers* (Princeton: Princeton University Press, 1994), p. 17; Spearing discusses this Chaucerian reticence; "Father Chaucer," in *Writing After Chaucer,* pp. 158–60.

[29] These divergent approaches to literary vocation have a codicological parallel: Christine's well-documented involvement with the production of her texts, her industrious self-assertion as copyist, reviser, editor, and publicist, could not be further removed from Chaucer's silence about the material aspects of textual production. On Christine's activities, see these essays by Laidlaw, "Christine and the Manuscript Tradition," in

notorious detachment from the pressing issues of his day, Christine threw herself into the literary and political fray. She engaged humanist scholars and clerics in a heated epistolary exchange over the immorality of the *Roman*, was appointed official biographer of Charles V, appealed to the nobility to show wise governance of France, and championed the cause of Joan of Arc.[30]

Chaucer and Christine de Pizan articulate rhetorical constructions of authorship and exhibit material investments in their respective textual legacies that inversely mirror the social and political opportunities that grounded their work as writers. As courtier, diplomat, and civil servant, Chaucer acquired both international and local exposure to a public life that provided him ample opportunity to observe and participate in that world's complexities and dangers at close range. His social position and the personal connections that accompanied it at times must have given him cause for concern. Helen Cooper's notice that Chaucer "kept his head on by keeping it down" invites speculation about precisely what and whom he may have tried to avoid, in his public service and his poetry; his infamous reticence on all fronts frustrates expectations that his activities will have inflected the products of his other, poetic vocation.[31] Christine de Pizan's exclusion from the prominent spheres of cultural activity frequented by Chaucer doubtless had its positive side, sheltering her from the personal and political risks that the English poet must have sidestepped. But the woman writer's willingness to show her

---

Casebook, pp. 231–49; "Christine de Pizan—An Author's Progress," *MLR* 78 (1983): 532–50; and "Christine de Pizan—A Publisher's Progress," *MLR* 82 (1987): 35–75. See also Sandra Hindman, *Christine de Pizan's "Epistre Othéa": Painting and Politics at the Court of Charles VI* (Toronto: Pontifical Institute of Medieval Studies, 1986); and Marilynn Desmond and Pamela Sheingorn, *Myth, Montage, and Visuality in Late Medieval Manuscript Culture* (Ann Arbor: University of Michigan Press, 2003). On Chaucer's, see Stephen Partridge, "Questions of Evidence: Manuscripts and the Early History of Chaucer's Works," in *Writing After Chaucer*, pp. 1–26; and Lerer, *Chaucer and His Readers*, p. 8. See also Linne R. Mooney's important identification of the Hengwrt and Ellesmere scribe as Adam Pinkhurst; "Chaucer's Scribe," *Speculum* 81 (2006): 97–138.

[30] See Eric Hicks, "The Political Significance of Christine de Pizan," in *Politics, Gender, and Genre*, pp. 7–15; and Renata Blumenfeld-Kosinski, "Christine de Pizan and the Political Life in Medieval France," in *Casebook*, pp. 9–24. On Christine's evolution as a political thinker and woman writer, see Margaret W. Ferguson, *Dido's Daughters: Literacy, Gender, and Empire in Early Modern England and France* (Chicago: University of Chicago Press, 2003), pp. 181–85.

[31] Helen Cooper, "After Chaucer," *SAC* 25 (2003): 16. What was at stake is indicated by the fate of Thomas Usk; see Paul Strohm, "Politics and Poetics: Usk and Chaucer in the 1380s," in *Literary Practice and Social Change in Britain, 1380–1530*, ed. Lee Patterson (Berkeley and Los Angeles: University of California Press, 1990), pp. 83–112.

political hand ironically underscores how she, by virtue of her gender, could not be taken for a player in those worldly arenas.[32] Because she could not ever be a diplomat, she would write like one. Different relationships to cultural institutions, official discourses, and social and political authority are implicit in the gendered social locations of Chaucer and Christine de Pizan. These differences parallel responses to the common literary culture that they inscribe in their encounters with the dream vision.

II

No two texts better illustrate these writers' common literary inheritance and profound poetic and philosophical differences than Chaucer's *House of Fame* and Christine's *Livre du chemin de long estude*.[33] Mutually indebted to the *Aeneid* and *The Divine Comedy,* both works are considered pivotal in their authors' subsequent development as vernacular authors. Yet these poems engage the epic grandeur and visionary illumination of their predecessors for distinctly different ends. In *The House of Fame,* Chaucer explores the possibilities for writing an authoritative English poetry in a textual world riven by suspect truth claims; his persona's chatty and breathless narrative articulates the frustration and exhilaration of an English author trying to craft high-minded verse after exposing the instabilities of classical literary tradition.[34] In the *Chemin,* Christine de Pizan rewrites the journeys of her most important poetic countrymen and, from her perspective as a woman writer, for the first time in her career undertakes visionary and philosophical commentary

---

[32] See Kate Langdon Forhan, *The Political Theory of Christine de Pizan* (Aldershot, Hampshire: Ashgate, 2001); Karen Green and Constant J. Mews, eds., *Healing the Body Politic: The Political Thought of Christine de Pizan* (Turnhout: Brepols, 2005).

[33] The *Livre du chemin de long estude* was composed for Charles VI and dedicated to the Dukes of Berry, Burgundy, and Orleans. Nine manuscript copies survive; manuscript traditions of the poem suggest that the text probably evolved under Christine's supervision. See J. C. Laidlaw, "How Long Is the *Livre du chemin de long estude?*" in *The Editor and the Text,* ed. Philip E. Bennett and Graham A. Runnalls (Edinburgh: Edinburgh University Press, 1990), pp. 83–95. On the three manuscripts of *The House of Fame,* see *The Riverside Chaucer,* p. 1139.

[34] Helen Cooper discusses the poem's poetic theory in light of its Ovidian debts; see "Chaucer and Ovid." For recent studies detailing *The House of Fame*'s conversation with native textual traditions, see Frank Grady, "Chaucer Reading Langland: *The House of Fame,*" *SAC* 18 (1996): 3–23; and Ruth Evans, "Chaucer in Cyberspace," *SAC* 23 (2001): 54–56.

for ethical and political purposes.[35] The respective uses to which Chaucer and Christine put literary tradition in *The House of Fame* and the *Chemin de long estude* signal important differences in their approaches to vernacular writing and their self-conception as authors and also adumbrate the trajectories of their literary careers. Whereas Christine increasingly pursued history and philosophy in moral treatise and social critique, Chaucer embraced a commitment to represent and address the world through multileveled fictions.

Because Christine's poem in particular may be less familiar to readers of Chaucer, I want to review evidence for my claim that these texts illuminate each other. For both authors, these poems are early works; *The House of Fame* was written c. 1380 and the *Chemin* during the period of explosive productivity that Christine experienced from 1399 to 1405.[36] These dream visions in octosyllabic couplets invoke the genre of the intellectual quest as celestial journey, classical and medieval counterparts of which include Cicero's *Somnium Scipionis,* Alan de Lille's *Anticlaudianus,* Martianus Capella's *De nuptiis Mercurii et Philologiae,* and Dante's *Commedia.*[37] Both visionary journeys are undertaken by a solitary and reclusive persona. Whereas Christine's autobiographically-identified narrator bemoans the loss of husband and marital comfort that has rendered her "often alone and thoughtful" ("[s]ouvent seulete et pensive" [68]), Chaucer's Geffrey suffers a more general detachment

[35] Helen Solterer, *The Master and Minerva: Disputing Women in French Medieval Culture* (Berkeley and Los Angeles: University of California Press, 1995), p. 164; Willard, *Christine de Pizan,* pp. 105–6. For another comparative analysis of the *Chemin* with interesting implications for Christine's relationship to Chaucer, see Andrea Tarnowski, "Christine, Philippe, and the Search for Solace," in *Au champ des escriptures,* pp. 325–33. On Christine's experiments with authoritative roles before writing the *Chemin,* see Tarnowski, "The Lessons of Experience and the *Chemin de long estude,*" in *Casebook,* pp. 181–97.

[36] *The House of Fame* in *The Riverside Chaucer,* p. 347; all citations refer to this edition, hereafter cited as *HF.* Christine de Pizan, *Le Chemin de longue étude,* ed. Andrea Tarnowski (Paris: Librairie Générale Français, 2000). Tarnowski provides an edition of the text from British Library MS Harley 4431 and a modern French translation. All quotations and line numbers refer to this edition, hereafter cited as *CLE.* Wherever possible, I cite Kevin Brownlee's partial English translation of the *Chemin* in *Selected Writings of Christine de Pizan,* pp. 59–87. Otherwise, translations are my own.

[37] On the *Chemin's* debt to twelfth-century neoplatonic mythography, see Anna Slerca, "Le *Livre du chemin de long estude* (1402–1403): Christine au pays des merveilles," in *Sur le chemin de longue étude . . . : Actes du colloque d'Orléans Juillet 1995, Étude Christiniennes* 3, ed. Bernard Ribémont (Paris: Honoré Champion, 1998), pp. 135–47. Minnis's discussion of generic counterparts of *The House of Fame* applies just as readily to the *Chemin;* see *Shorter Poems,* p. 183. Because Minnis's commentary on Chaucer's poem is also a kind of variorum, I occasionally rely on its summary characterization of critical perspectives on this text.

from human contact and communication. Deprived of "tydynges / Of Loves folk," he sits at home like a hermit, "domb as any stoon," "daswed" in countenance (644–45; 655–59).[38] As is typical of the genre, dreams arouse these personae from their respective social and psychological conditions, offering journeys toward knowledge that will amend the dilemmas from which they suffer. Geffrey's eagle-guide promises him the "disport and game" of a trip to the House of Fame in recompense for his unrequited labors and devotion to Cupid (661–68). Christine is likewise rewarded for past effort: because she has been "more devoted to study than other people" ("car a ta parue / Me sembles trop plus diligent / D'estre a l'estude qu'entre gent" [640–42]), the guide of her dream promises an expansion of her intellectual powers as antidote to her personal suffering and the disturbances of a conflict-ridden world (648–58).

The narrators of the two poems punctuate their journeys with similar observations and experiences. In the manner of French courtly poetry, both record the date on which their visionary journeys occur: Geffrey's on December 10 (111), Christine's on October 5, 1402 (185–87).[39] Although the narrators' paths and methods of transport are different—Christine's traverses earth before setting out for heavenly realms and moves on foot rather than in the "sharpe nayles longe" (542) of a soaring eagle—both speakers acknowledge the anxieties of celestial travel. Initially, Geffrey is rendered insensate by his upward journey (541–53), and Christine feels the fear that accompanies bearing her material body to places it was never intended to go (1717–21). Both glance back at a diminutive earth from the heavenly heights. For Geffrey that world seems "[n]o more . . . than a prikke" (907); for Christine, "like a little sphere, as round as a ball" ("Que toute la terre veoye / Comme une petite pellote / Aussi ronde que une balote" [1702–4].[40] Both celestial travelers recall the fate of Icarus; whereas the eagle proudly acknowledges that the mythic boy and his father, Daedalus, had not soared as high as Geffrey (913–24), Christine simply identifies with the boy's falling (1725–33). Both travelers invoke the muses; and both come to a resting place before the visionary figure of an enthroned goddess—Fame

---

[38] Cf. *CLE:* "Si fus de grief dueil confuse / Et devins comme recluse" (lines 119–20).

[39] On dating in courtly poetry, see Minnis, *Shorter Poems,* p. 168.

[40] The glance back to earth has precedents in Cicero's *Somnium Scipionis* through Macrobius and Dante (*Paradiso,* 22.134–35 and 27.78–87); see *Selected Writings of Christine de Pizan,* p. 81 n. 2.

and Reason—whose role it is to adjudicate matters of central importance to their respective poems.[41]

The *House of Fame* and the *Chemin de long estude* display an energetic
command of learned discourses and authorities. Both poems are deeply
indebted to the *Consolation of Philosophy.* Boethius's text provides inspiration for narrator Christine's dream, which is preceded by a lengthy meditation on the impact of Fortune on her own life and the larger society.
The *Consolation* furnishes the source for some of Chaucer's descriptions
in *Fame* and informs that poem's reflections on reputation and loss.[42]
The *Chemin* incorporates lengthy rehearsals of learning and copiously
cites classical and Christian authorities; *The House of Fame*'s garrulous
eagle holds forth on "physics, metaphysics, astronomy/astrology, grammar, music, rhetoric, [and] poetics."[43] Bernard Ribémont's notice that
Christine's presentation of such learning employs an "enumerative language" that has citation, not explanation, as its goal aptly describes the
narrative technique of *The House of Fame* as well.[44] The most important
moment in each poem's exhibition of learning involves its narrator's
encounter with ancient poets. Christine finds Virgil, Homer, Ovid, and
Horace among the classical philosophers who inhabit the most beautiful
paths on Parnassus (1007–66); atop the pillars that line the House of
Fame, Geffrey discerns Josephus, Statius, Homer, Virgil, Ovid, and
Lucan, struggling to bear up the weight of their famous stories (1429–
1512). Yet the narratives of both works break off before their travelers
attain the goal toward which these learned journeys tend: for Geffrey,

---

[41] *HF,* 520–22; *CLE,* 977–96. See Mary Weitzel Gibbons, *"The Bath of the Muses* and
Visual Allegory in the *Chemin de long estude,"* in *Christine de Pizan and the Categories of
Difference,* pp. 128–45. For the descriptions of Fame and Reason, see *HF,* 1360–406,
and *CLE,* 2515–58.

[42] Piero Boitani, *Chaucer and the Imaginary World of Fame* (Cambridge: D. S. Brewer,
1984), pp. 45–47; Minnis, *Shorter Poems,* pp. 187, 188–90.

[43] This list is from Minnis, who calls *HF* "the most bookish of Chaucer's books";
Shorter Poems, p. 183. Boitani analyzes the convergence of learned traditions in Chaucer's
poem; *Chaucer and the Imaginary World of Fame.* Helen Solterer describes *CLE* as a kind
of florilegium; *Master and Minerva,* p. 171. Authorities cited by Christine in *CLE* include
Augustine, Jerome, Alain de Lille, Aristotle, Cato, Cicero, Chrysostom, Claudian, Ful-
gentius, Juvenal, Seneca, John of Salisbury, Vegetius, Valerius Maximus, and Suetonius.
Andrea Tarnowski discusses Christine's references to authorities in *CLE,* observing—in
a felicitous invocation of Chaucer's poem—that mentioning learned sources "adds another pillar to the structure of the poem, supporting the verses and lending them solid-
ity." See "The Lessons of Experience and the *Chemin de long estude,"* p. 192.

[44] Bernard Ribémont, "Entre espace scientifique et espace imaginé," in *Sur le chemin
de longue étude,"* p. 255.

receipt of long-deferred tidings of love; for Christine, conclusion to an allegorical debate intended to select the perfect prince.[45]

Although framed by similar narrative gestures and shadowed by the same authoritative texts, the accounts of celestial travel in *The House of Fame* and the *Chemin de long estude* also negatively mirror each other. For example, the poems' narrators react very differently to their encounters with extraordinary sights and sounds. From the prospect of the firmament (the fifth heaven—as high as she as is permitted to go), Christine's narrator experiences a spectacle of blinding yet beautiful light. Led on by this light, she longs to be turned completely into eyes, burning "with desire to understand" ("toute de desir ardoie / De comprendre" [1984–85]) everything that she can see of the heavens. This perception prompts detailed astrological observations as she contemplates the planets, stars, sun and moon, the two hemispheres of the sky, and the Milky Way. Her visual pleasure is matched by the aural delight provided by the "calm, measured and perfect" sound ("un doulx son . . . / Amesuré et parfait" [2004–5]) of the moving celestial spheres, "the sovereign music that contains all the perfect chords" ("la souveraine musique / Ou sont tous les parfais accors" [2006–7]).[46]

Nothing could be further from Geffrey's experience in the heavenly regions than this. Rather than celestial harmonies, he encounters a "grete soun . . . that rumbleth up and doun" (1025–26), tidings that produce a "grete swogh" (1031), a wall of noise. Instead of Christine's "well-defined circles" ("cercles mesurez" [2001]) of the heavenly

[45] Christine may have derived the central political idea of the *Chemin* from secretary and counselor to Louis d'Orléans, Ambrogio Migli. See Gilbert Ouy and Christine M. Reno, "Où mène le *Chemin de long estude*? Christine de Pizan, Ambrogio Migli, et les ambitions impériales de Louis d'Orléans (A propos du ms. BNF fr. 1643)," in *Christine de Pizan 2000*, pp. 177–95, 325–28.

[46] Here I summarize *CLE*, 1785–2020. At one point Christine's astrological encounter takes in a shining white circle that the poets call "the Galaxy: it is grand and beautiful and wide. Many have called it the Milky Way because of its whiteness" ("Galace est cellui appellez, / Qui moult est grant et beaulx et lez. / Cercle de lait mains l'appellerent, / Pour sa blancheur" [lines 1921–24]). After observing the positions of the signs of the zodiac, the planets, and the paths of the sun and moon, Christine describes the movements of the sun figured as four "beloved horses" that maintain the sun's chariot; one of these is Phaeton, "red and blazing" (*CLE*, 1969–79); *Selected Writings of Christine de Pizan*, pp. 84–85). Christine's account of her astrological observations echoes a terser sequence in *The House of Fame*, in which the eagle invites Geffrey to look up and "Se yonder, loo, the Galaxie, / Which men clepeth the Milky Wey / For hit ys whit (and somme, parfey, / Kallen hyt Watlynge Strete), / That ones was ybrent with hete, / Whan the sonnes sone the rede, / That highte Pheton, wolde lede / Algate hys fader carte, and gye" (lines 936–43).

spheres, he confronts the incessant whirling, squeaking, creaking, blowing, and jangling of Domus Dedaly, the House of Rumor made of twigs (1916–76). Afforded opportunities for astrological learning and visual pleasure, Geffrey rejects both. When the eagle encourages him to learn something of the stars, his refusal is unambiguous. The eagle's offer to show Geoffrey astral positions about which the traveler "redest [in] poetrie" (1001) draws the same response. "'No fors,'" he protests, ironically declaring a preference for authority over experience: "'hyt is no nede. / I leve as wel, so God me spede, / Hem that write of this matere, / As though I knew her places here'" (1011–14)—an odd position in view of the poem's suspicions about the reliability of "hem that write." Exhibiting none of Christine's visual desire, he complains about stars so bright that "'[h]yt shulde shenden al my syghte / To loke on hem'" (1016–17).

The distance between the visionary paths traversed by these two narrators is epitomized in the endings of their respective poems, both of which focus on the transmittal of news and information. The troublesome conclusion to *The House of Fame* promises that "man of gret auctorite" who at long last will articulate "tydyings" of love and other things whose unsolicited pursuit has motivated Geffrey's visionary travels. But the ambiguous man of authority does not deliver, and the poem's final vista is one of "[c]urrours, and eke messagers" (2128) bearing packs full of lies, more unreliable tidings to join the other suspect forms of verbal communication invoked in the poem, including that of the ancient poets, whose words, though plentiful, only produce "a ful confus matere" (1517). Grinding to a halt with this perception of both the excess and inadequacy of human verbal communication, the poem leaves unresolved all the issues regarding textual authority and truth that the journey to and sojourn with Fame have introduced. The resources of comedy may help to avert epistemological and semiotic meltdown, but the fortunes of "art poetical" (1095) are raked over the coals by recognition of the vulnerability of the poetic medium to falsification, transience, and misreading, that is, to the fundamental problems of verbal representation, spoken and written, embraced by the ambivalent trope of Fame.[47]

The *Chemin* likewise draws to a close with the anticipation of an authoritative message. After a leisurely exposition of learned authority that

---

[47] For a useful summary of critical opinion about the larger issues tackled in the poem, see Minnis, *Shorter Poems*, pp. 216–51.

consumes over half of the poem, the ladies Noblesse, Richesse, Chevalerie, and Sagesse conclude their allegorical debate regarding the qualities that the perfect prince should possess—the prince that the world, by Christine's assessment, desperately needs. But Reason's Court is unable to decide who such a person might be; the sole point of agreement is that the choice should be referred to the princes of France, whose "court is sovereign, and whose reputation is know[n] throughout the entire world" ("dont la court / Est souveraine, et de qui court / Le renom par l'univers monde" [6261–63]). Who would be an appropriate messenger for such an assignment? The Sibyl immediately volunteers her new disciple, enumerating her qualifications for this honored position (6283–309). Thus Christine's *chemin de long estude*—the journey and the poem—reaches for closure as the narrator casts herself in the role of the person "of great authority," someone "wise and well spoken," "good and appropriate" ("stilé et sage"; "couvenable et bonne" [6278, 6288]) to bear tidings of immense import to France and humankind. Ever the diligent student, Christine quickly resolves Reason's quandary regarding how all the terms of the aforementioned debate may be put into writing.[48] Not to worry; in the most impressive instance of note-taking in Western literature, Christine has already written everything down (6357–60). Reviewing her writing, Reason attests that the narrator's rendering of what she has witnessed is without fault: "there were no corrections to be made" ("il n'y avoit riens a redire" [6368]). Her message now authenticated, Christine sets off to deliver it. Demonstrating her command of the learning that she is selected to communicate, the *Chemin* by its very existence registers the fulfillment of the mission with which its narrator is charged.[49]

At least some of the resemblances just noted between *The House of Fame* and the *Chemin de long estude* can be attributed to these poems' common debt to Dante's *Commedia*. If, as Lydgate's *Fall of Princes* suggests, *The House of Fame* is "Dante in Inglissh," then the *Chemin de long*

---

[48] *CLE:* "si soit quis / Ainçois qui sache tous les termes / De ce debat bien mettre en termes / Et par escript tout mettre en ordre / Si bien qu'il n'y ait que remordre" (lines 6348–52). For translations in this paragraph, see *Selected Writings of Christine de Pizan,* pp. 86–87.

[49] On the poem's ending, see Bärbel Zühlke, "Christine de Pizan—Le 'moi' dans le texte et l'image," in *City of Scholars,* p. 234. Tarnowski comments on the linkage between Christine's visionary journey and the production of her poem and compares the *Chemin* to the *Dit de la Rose,* another work in which Christine depicts her narrator as messenger; "Introduction," *Chemin de long estude,* pp. 22, 24–25.

estude is "Dante in French."[50] Each poem is, with respect to vernacular writing, the first such effort of its kind.[51] Chaucer's debt to Dante in *The House of Fame* has been the subject of extensive commentary, ranging from the cautious assessment that the poem was written "with the *Comedy* in mind," to the proposition that the encounter with the Italian poet recorded in *Fame* was the decisive event in the formation of Chaucer's vernacular "art poetical."[52] Dante's poem clearly inspired specific passages and motifs in *The House of Fame,* as well as its three-part structure; but Chaucer's dialogue with Dante in his challenging dream vision encompasses far more than these specific borrowings. Helen Cooper's recent contention about this Chaucerian debt is especially relevant to this analysis of the *Chemin*'s implicit conversation with *Fame.* Chaucer, she asserts, recognized Dante's brilliance yet thought that the Italian's view of the poet's divine omniscience "was *wrong.*"[53] This provocative characterization once more renders *The House of Fame* as negative mirror of Christine's *Chemin,* but now at the level of conception and purpose rather than detail. For Christine's poem is her unambiguous *hommage* to the premier poet of her native Italy. The work's very title derives from Dante's plea that Virgil assist him in recognition of the "lungo studio"

---

[50] *Lydgate's Fall of Princes,* ed. Henry Bergen, EETS, e.s. 121–24, 4 vols. (London: Oxford University Press, 1924–27), 1: Prologue 302–3. Kevin Brownlee calls the *Chemin* "in part a 'translation' of Dante's *Commedia* into French"; "Literary Genealogy and the Problem of the Father: Christine de Pizan and Dante," in *Dante Now: Current Trends in Dante Studies,* ed. Theodore J. Cachey Jr. (Notre Dame: University of Notre Dame Press, 1995), p. 227. David Wallace observes that *The House of Fame* "acts out and meditates upon" Chaucer's discovery of Dante; "Chaucer's Continental Inheritance: The Early Poems and *Troilus and Criseyde,*" in *The Cambridge Chaucer Companion,* ed. Piero Boitani and Jill Mann (Cambridge: Cambridge University Press, 1986), pp. 19–37, at 21.

[51] R. A. Shoaf explores pre-Chaucerian evidence of the use of Dante by the *Pearl*-poet; "'Noon Englissh Digne': Dante in Late Medieval England," in *Dante Now,* 189–203. In France, Philippe de Mézières was the first to refer to Dante, but Christine was the first to incorporate elements of the *Commedia* into her own texts; Earl Jeffrey Richards, "Christine de Pizan and Dante: A Reexamination," *Archiv* 222 (1985): 100–111, at 100.

[52] The poem's debt to the *Divine Comedy* is summarized in the Riverside edition's textual notes (977). The understatement in this sentence is from Minnis, *Shorter Poems,* p. 49; see also pp. 172–83, 201–3, 227–32, 247–51 and works cited therein. The more expansive view is summarized by Wallace, "Chaucer's Continental Inheritance." See also Karla Taylor, *Chaucer Reads "The Divine Comedy"* (Stanford: Stanford University Press, 1989), pp. 20–49; Helen Cooper, "The Four Last Things in Dante and Chaucer: Ugolino in the House of Rumour," *New Medieval Literatures* 3 (1999): 39–66; and Glenn A. Steinberg, "Chaucer in the Field of Cultural Production: Humanism, Dante, and the *House of Fame,*" *ChauR* 35 (2000): 182–203.

[53] Helen Cooper, "After Chaucer," 12.

19

that he has devoted to the master's work; the *Chemin* invokes the opening to the *Inferno* as the sanction and model for its author-narrator's visionary quest.[54] Christine's reliance on Dante in the *Chemin* is inseparable from her poem's equally important debt to Virgil. In fact, the fortunes of the *Aeneid* in *The House of Fame* and the *Chemin de long estude* further clarify the respective uses that Chaucer and Christine made of Dante's *Commedia*.

By focusing on the narrator's rapt encounter with the Dido and Aeneas plot—indeed by grounding the dream vision in that act of empathic reading—Chaucer's poem renders the Virgilian epic of *pietas* and divine destiny as an exemplary instance of Ovidian female complaint. Virgil provides the test case for the literary and philosophical project of Chaucer's poem. *The House of Fame* decenters Virgil's epic narrative and demonstrates its availability to other hermeneutic paradigms, thereby dislodging Virgil from his position of cultural authority and exposing the vulnerability of not only Virgil's but all poetic "truth" to the accidents and arbitrariness of the verbal and epistemological chaos that Chaucer identifies with Fame.[55]

Christine de Pizan could not entertain such a treatment of Virgil. Her reading of the *Aeneid* also fixates on one of its female figures, but in the *Chemin* it is the Cumaean Sibyl who takes center stage; Dido is nowhere in sight.[56] Christine borrows Aeneas's guide through the underworld and makes the prophetess her mentor as she translates the "path of long study" on which Virgil led Dante.[57] The Sibyl is crucial to Christine's

---

[54] *Inferno* 1.83; *CLE*, 1109–52. On Christine's use of Dante in the *Chemin*, see Brownlee, "Literary Genealogy"; Richards, "Christine de Pizan and Dante"; and in *City of Scholars*, see Dina De Rentiis, " 'Sequere me': 'Imitatio' dans la *Divine Comédie* et dans le *Livre du Chemin de long estude*," pp. 31–42; and Zühlke, "Christine de Pizan—le 'moi' dans le texte et l'image," pp. 232–41.

[55] See Cooper, "Four Last Things in Dante and Chaucer," pp. 55–56.

[56] Later in the *Chemin*, Noblesse gives a capsule summary of the *Aeneid*, noting that lineage served as guarantor of Aeneas's success in Italy; she makes no mention of Dido; *CLE*, 3551–68. Although the Dido of *Aeneid*, Book 4, and Ovid's *Heroides* is absent from Christine's visionary efforts here, Dido's importance for the woman writer's oeuvre is well established. Christine elaborated Dido's story in the *Cité des Dames*, where her role as a city-builder, as Margaret Ferguson observes, makes her a "cultural mother for the woman writer aspiring to appropriate textual territory for political purposes"; *Dido's Daughters*, p. 21; see also pp. 186–90. Kevin Brownlee relates Christine's self-portraiture as a widow to her role as a "corrected Dido"; "Widowhood, Sexuality, and Gender in Christine de Pizan," *Romanic Review* 86 (1995): 340–53. See also Marilynn Desmond, *Reading Dido: Gender, Textuality, and the Medieval Aeneid*, pp. 195–224.

[57] Christine's initial encounter with the Sibyl in the *Chemin* has a Dantesque echo: "I do not possess enough knowledge for my understanding to be worthy of your benevo-

ambitions in and for the *Chemin,* and her role in this poem signals the woman writer's fascination with the feminine prophetic authority that is also an explicit theme of later works such as the *Livre de la Cité des dames* and the *Ditié de Jehanne d'Arc.*[58] As the repository of ancient wisdom ("femme moult senee") and the figure who prophesied the coming of Christ, the Cumaean Sibyl importantly melds classical and Christian traditions; in the *Chemin,* she explicitly identifies Christine as one worthy of sharing—and carrying on—her vatic wisdom: "I love you and want you to learn part of my secret knowledge before I leave you" ("Je t'aim, et vueil faire a savoir / De mes secrés une partie / Ains que de toy soie partie" [500–502]).[59] The Sibyl is an apt mentor for Christine because, as Solterer notes, "her prophetic powers are linked expressly to governance" and because she is a writer (541–42).[60] Thus it is under the Sibyl's influence that a quest which begins for Christine's persona with a generalized lament about human misery and discord evolves into a visionary debate at the Court of Reason about the qualities that the ideal ruler of humanity should possess. Over the course of their journey together, the woman writer's identity—and voice—slide into those of

---

lent offer to guide me as you did him whom it pleased you to show the painful spectacle of hell, where you were willing to lead the noble knight Aeneas" ("je n'en [savoir] puis pas tant avoir / Que soit mon entendement digne / Que vostre voulenté benigne / Me doye a cil accompaigner / A qui il vous plot a daigner / Monster enfer le douleureux, / Ou le noble, chevalereux / Eneas vous voltes conduire" [lines 678–85]); *Selected Writings of Christine de Pizan,* p. 69. Christine invokes *Inferno* 2.32–33 more explicitly when she responds to the directive from Reason, Rectitude, and Justice to construct a refuge for women in the *Cité des Dames:* "How will such grace be bestowed on me that I will receive the boon . . . to build and construct in the world from now on a new city? I am not Saint Thomas the Apostle, who through divine grace built a rich palace in heaven for the king of India, and my feeble sense does not know the craft, or the measures, or the study, or the science, or the practice of construction"; *The Book of the City of Ladies,* trans. Earl Jeffrey Richards (New York: Persea Books, 1982), p. 15. Richards finds an echo of this Dantean moment at the beginning of Christine's *Livre de la Mutacion de Fortune;* "Christine de Pizan and Sacred History," in *City of Scholars,* p. 24. Christine also invokes a Dantean visionary authority in *L'Avision-Christine;* see Benjamin Semple, "A Critique of Knowledge as Power: The Limits of Philosophy and Theology in Christine de Pizan," in *Christine de Pizan and the Categories of Difference,* p. 116.

[58] In her *Epistre d'Othéa* (1399), Christine makes the Cumaean Sibyl the subject of the one-hundredth and final allegory, using as her text the Sibyl's reprimand of Augustus Caesar for letting himself be worshiped; *Epistre d'Othéa,* ed. Gabriella Parussa (Geneva: Droz, 1999), p. 341.

[59] *Selected Writings of Christine de Pizan,* p. 66. For the Sibyl's introductory speech, see *CLE,* 490–658. Zühlke discusses depictions of Christine and the Sibyl in illuminated manuscripts of the *Chemin;* "Christine de Pizan—Le 'moi' dans le texte et l'image."

[60] Solterer, *Master and Minerva,* pp. 166–67, at 166; DeRentiis, "'Sequere me,'" pp. 41–42. On the Sibyl as a writer, see Ribémont, "Entre espace scientifique et espace imaginé," p. 248.

the Sibyl; under her tutelage—and legitimized by her Italian masters—Christine acquires the knowledge needed to become a prophet for France.

The *Chemin* is Christine de Pizan's implicit rejoinder to the poetics and philosophical vision articulated in *The House of Fame;* the poem's commitment to prophecy, exemplified in the role of the Sibyl, renders it a reverse image of the work that A. C. Spearing has called an "anti-oraculum."[61] Chaucer's *House of Fame,* as much commentary has noted, subverts epic aspirations and eschews the vatic role in self-parody. Unlike his Dantean model, the narrator refigures his famous rejection of visionary privilege—" 'I neyther am Ennok, ne Elye, / Ne Romulus, ne Ganymede / That was ybore up, as men rede, / To heven with daun Jupiter' " (588–91)—in the chaotic disposition of his entire celestial voyage. If *The House of Fame* elaborates the transient and unstable authority of verbal representation, the *Chemin* argues that learned discourses are neither gratuitous nor "self-engrossing."[62] The outcomes of the poems' respective journeys underscore Christine's allegiance to dominant discursive traditions in rhetoric and philosophy, politics and poetry, and mark Chaucer's ambivalence toward all cultural gestures that would authorize these discourses.

These divergent perspectives on the purpose and use of their writing are grounded in different approaches to the politics of representation. Christine addressed that subject head-on in the *Querelle de la Rose,* her early fifteenth-century epistolary exchange with Jean de Montreuil and Gontier and Pierre Col. At the center of the *Querelle* was an argument about the uses of poetry that pitted the humanists' support for the autonomy of poetic form against Christine's pursuit of a "socially profitable language."[63] The woman writer challenged defenders of the aesthetic of Jean de Meun's poem by debating the signifying capacities of poetic language, the ground of textual interpretation, the purposes of fiction, and the ethical responsibilities of the writer.[64] Her contributions

[61] A. C. Spearing, *Medieval Dream Poetry* (Cambridge: Cambridge University Press, 1976), p. 11.

[62] Solterer, *Master and Minerva,* p. 171.

[63] On Christine's critique of the fictive nature of poetic discourse in relation to the civic good, see Solterer, *Master and Minerva,* pp. 158–62, at 161.

[64] Eric Hicks, ed., *Le Débat sur le Roman de la Rose,* Bibliothèque du Xve siècle 43 (Paris: Honoré Champion, 1977); Joseph L. Baird and John R. Kane, trans., *La Querelle de la Rose,* North Carolina Studies in the Romance Languages and Literatures, 199 (Chapel Hill: University of North Carolina Department of Romance Languages, 1978). For recent discussions, see Marilynn Desmond, "The *Querelle de la Rose* and the Ethics of Reading," in *Casebook,* pp. 167–80; Rosalind Brown-Grant, "A New Context for Read-

to the *Querelle* disputed the literary authority of the *Roman de la Rose,* the master-text for vernacular, courtly writers, by exposing the ills that its poetic language perpetrated on woman specifically and society generally.[65] "[W]omen," remarks Earl Jeffrey Richards, "paid the price" for the poem's "aesthetic gratuity," the artful linguistic play, promotion of indeterminacy, and refusal of referentiality that Christine identified in the work of Jean de Meun.[66] In Dante, whose *Commedia* reinforced her conviction that literary writing could be undertaken for the common good, she found a model of vernacular eloquence that neither slandered women nor cultivated ambiguity.[67] When Christine made the production of such writing the aim of her own literary vocation, she turned, not surprisingly, to her countryman's precedent and example. Solterer posits the *Chemin de long estude* as Christine's answer to the hermeneutic impasse of the *Querelle.* Trading epistolary polemics for the vatic mode of the allegorical poem, Christine in that poem engaged sapiential discourses for the benefit of all citizens of the polis.[68]

It is precisely a vexed refusal of such instrumentality that most distinctly marks Chaucer's departure from the moral and social concerns that motivate the writings of Christine de Pizan.[69] As important critical

---

ing the 'Querelle de la Rose': Christine de Pizan and Medieval Literary Theory," in *Au champ des escriptures,* pp. 581–95.

[65] Sylvia Huot discusses Christine's critique of the poetic values of Jean de Meun, with important implications for the woman writer's differences from Chaucer; see "Seduction and Sublimation: Christine de Pizan, Jean de Meun, and Dante," *Romance Notes* 25 (1985): 361–73.

[66] Richards, "Rejecting Essentialism and Gendered Writing: The Case of Christine de Pizan," p. 100.

[67] See Richards, "Christine de Pizan and Sacred History," p. 17; and "Rejecting Essentialism and Gendered Writing," pp. 99, 115–16. Christine's commitment to the instrumentality of the political and philosophical writings that dominated her work after 1405 is illuminated by her allegiance to ideas of vernacular eloquence within Italian humanism; see Richards, "Christine de Pizan, the Conventions of Courtly Diction, and Italian Humanism," pp. 256–62.

[68] Solterer, *Master and Minerva,* pp. 164–67. In responding to the linguistic and social ills that she attributed to the *Roman,* Christine also embraced a view of allegory that enabled her to retain an idea of the literal sense and historical truth, against the *Roman*'s celebration of poetic fable; see Richards, "Christine de Pizan and Sacred History," pp. 19–21; and "Rejecting Essentialism and Gendered Writing." See also Andrea N. Tarnowski, "Perspectives on the *Advision,*" in *Christine de Pizan* 2000, pp. 105–14, 317–18.

[69] Maureen Quilligan discusses Christine's positioning of her texts to achieve "historical instrumentality"; *Allegory of Female Authority,* p. 282. Carol Meale formulates the difference between Chaucer's and Christine's treatment of female legends in terms of their respective emphases on representation and politics; "Legends of Good Women," 69–70. Renata Blumenfeld-Kosinski discusses Christine's engagement with history and politics across the many genres in which she worked and the many rhetorical positions that she occupied; "Christine de Pizan and the Political Life in Late Medieval France."

work has recently argued, efforts to characterize a Chaucerian politics of representation must grapple with the poet's insistence on literary writing autonomous "from both ideological programs and social appropriations," and his preference for inscribing his responses to social and political issues through the generic, formal, and thematic intricacies of his texts.[70] If Chaucer experienced a crisis of authorial identity, such as the one that Patterson suggests he stages through his pilgrim narrator in the *Canterbury Tales,* the poet articulated it only through his fictions. Chaucer's "investment in the power of the fictive" marks his allegiance to the poetic camp of Jean de Meun, whose text and poetic techniques he manipulates throughout his work, thereby signaling his affinity with the very ambiguities and evasions that Christine excoriated in the *Roman de la Rose.*[71] In view of their clear differences on this issue, it is noteworthy that responses by Chaucer and Christine to Jean de Meun's poem fixate on the same issues—for example, the authority and gendering of clerkly discourse, the semiotic operations of poetic language represented in the *Roman*'s "cullions" and "relics"—so much so that Christine's contributions to the *Querelle* at moments seem to echo some of Chaucer's rhetorical maneuvers in the *Canterbury Tales.* As is typical of Chaucer's refusal to acknowledge directly his poetry's encounter with the political and historical world, however, his invocation of Jean de Meun's slippery signifiers involves no comparable indignation at their dangerous implications for women or society (he leaves that critique for the God of Love in his *Legend of Good Women*). The distinctive receptions of the *Roman de la Rose* by Chaucer and Christine thus provide a critical genealogy for the conflicting visionary poetics of *The House of Fame* and the *Chemin de long estude.*[72]

Christine fictionalized herself as a writer but withdrew from fictionalized representation; see Thelma Fenster, "Who's a Heroine?" in *Casebook,* p. 123.

[70] See Patterson, " 'What Man Artow?' " 173. Spearing frames the issue in terms of the metaphor of textuality; "Father Chaucer," p. 160.

[71] Patterson, " 'What Man Artow?' " 128.

[72] Space does not permit me to consider how Christine's *L'Avision* pursues a key issue of Chaucer's poem through the figure of Dame Opinion, an unstable source of information analogous to Chaucer's Rumor. For Christine the untruths of defamation and the vulnerability of reputation to defamatory language parallel dangers of fictive literary representation. See Rosalind Brown-Grant, "*L'Avision Christine:* Autobiographical Narrative or Mirror for Prince," in *Politics, Gender, and Genre,* pp. 95–111; Lori S. Walters, "Constructing Reputations: *Fama* and Memory in Christine de Pizan's *Charles V* and *L'Advision Christine,*" in *Fama: The Politics of Talk and Reputation in Medieval Europe,* ed. Thelma Fenster and David Lord Smail (Ithaca: Cornell University Press, 2003), pp. 118–42; and Thelma Fenster, "La *fama,* la femme, et la Dame de la Tour: Christine de Pizan et la médisance," in *Au champ des escriptures,* pp. 461–77.

The divergent literary ideologies that comparative reading of these dream visions enables us to map, however, are not relentlessly oppositional. Despite the confidence that the *Chemin* expresses about the possibilities for prophecy and the truth claims of poetry, in works such as the *Epistre au dieu d'Amours* and the *Cité des Dames,* as well as her contributions to the *Querelle de la Rose,* Christine de Pizan also articulates her awareness of the social and ideological contingencies of knowledge and authority. Her political and philosophical works do not lack self-consciousness regarding the textual and royal politics of their own cultural production. Nor is she reluctant, in the *Chemin,* to qualify her own vision's conformity with dominant ideologies of politics and letters. Seen from a different perspective, the ending of that poem is nearly as inconclusive as that of *The House of Fame;* no person of "great authority" speaks, and the allegorical debate about kingship is left unresolved—whom would the princes of France choose?[73] I have emphasized Christine's confidence in the moral probity of the message to be delivered; yet we should also recognize how, as her poem draws to a close, the author-narrator expresses more optimism about her own role as messenger than she does about any prospects for the debate's salutary outcome. In this light, the ending of the *Chemin* offers an important instance of what Roberta Krueger terms Christine's "thematics of failure," her tendency to articulate doubt about enactment of the moral principles that her work inscribes.[74] Inspired by the Sibyl, Christine's persona may adopt the vatic profile, but she does so through the side door: she makes herself the copyist of all that has been spoken, grounding her prophetic role in a service function that Christine the author had actually performed. Furthermore, the woman writer's notice in the poem's final lines that she was awakened from her dream by her mother, who expressed surprise that she was still asleep, anchors her sublime effort to fashion the perfect prince within the domestic realm, bringing with it a hint of

---

[73] Rather than produce a man of great authority at this point in her poem, Christine instead introduces "maistre Avis," who might be seen as a refugee from *The House of Fame* (lines 6139–225). Dressed like an "avocat" (line 6229), he advises that Reason not show favoritism; he then offers the Judgment of Paris as a cautionary tale illustrating how weighty decisions among supernatural beings are best referred to the judgment of wise courtly people on earth. Since the wisdom of ancient Greece and Rome is now long past, he avers, the place to which such a judgment is transferred should be chosen carefully; *CLE,* 6137–245. On this point, see Tarnowski, "Lessons of Experience," p. 193.

[74] Krueger, "Christine's Anxious Lessons," pp. 36, 23.

parental disapproval that calls to mind the personal touches with which Chaucer also punctuates his dream visions.[75]

On several other key points, *The House of Fame* and the *Chemin de long estude* display more congruence than difference. Both poems are resolutely secular in perspective, refusing any transcendent purchase on the dilemmas they describe. Despite their oppositional constructions of textual authority, *The House of Fame* and the *Chemin* articulate complementary understandings of the situated reader whose responsibility it is to sort out and act on authoritative communications. Christine's commitment to sapiential and prophetic writing in the *Chemin* directs attention away from the medium of representation to focus instead on how—and by whom—messages are received and used. The poem stakes a claim for the salutary impact of learning and persuasion on individual human beings and on the capacity of speech and writing to inspire wisdom and prudence. As is typical of Christine's didactic works in which ideas of reform involve individual morality rather than recommendations for social change, the *Chemin* leaves its allegorical debate unresolved in order to "appeal to the moral judgment of the *reader*" regarding the "quality most important for the king."[76] Chaucer's poem scarcely invokes an analogous program for reform, yet *The House of Fame* nonetheless provides one of his most powerful statements on the capacities and limitations of the reader: the problems of its narrator-protagonist focus fundamentally on the individual's reception and interpretation of verbal messages.[77] Whereas Chaucer emphasizes the dilemmas faced by a reader confronting written and spoken discourses unmoored from any stable authority, Christine articulates a faith in the efficacy of ethical words for the discerning recipient. Yet both writers reinforce the semiotic and epistemological labor of the interpreting subject.

Important contexts for these writers' literary production offer rationales for the conflicting poetic ideologies and the tactical resemblances

[75] On Christine's mother, see Quilligan, *Allegory of Female Authority;* and Blumenfeld-Kosinski, "Christine de Pizan and the Misogynistic Tradition," pp. 304–8. The sheer garrulity of Christine's allegorical ladies, especially Sagesse (she talks for several thousand lines), introduces ironic undertones to the debate by invoking traditions of commentary on women's excessive speech. Christine's poem is also immensely self-flattering, since the forms of knowledge that she praises are those that she demonstrates. On Christine's identification with Sagesse, see Andrea Tarnowski, "Pallas Athena, la science et la chevalerie," in *Sur le chemin de longue étude,* p. 156.

[76] Krueger, "Christine's Anxious Lessons," p. 23 (her emphasis).

[77] Laurel Amtower, "Authorizing the Reader in Chaucer's *House of Fame,*" *PQ* 79 (2000): 273–91.

that we have been tracking. Although Chaucer and Christine de Pizan both practiced their craft in political environments divided by dynastic struggles, in a more fundamental sense they inhabited very different political cultures. Lynn Staley has recently formulated this difference in terms of distinctive English and French languages of regal power. Whereas late fourteenth-century Valois France successfully promoted a mystique of sacral kingship and the hierarchically ordered society that followed from its just rule, England under Richard II sought by various means, and with only mixed results, to fashion commensurately authoritative ideals of monarchy and community. Staley's observation that Chaucer's household literature "creates questions" from what are "assertions" in its French textual counterparts aptly characterizes the different ideological climates in which Chaucer and Christine wrote—and the directions that they pursue in *The House of Fame* and the *Chemin de long estude*.[78] As a familiar of the Valois household in her youth and the hand-picked biographer of Charles V, Christine had reason to be more comfortable with the idea of monarchical authority, even as she petitioned princes of the realm to act more responsibly toward each other and France's people. Chaucer's obliquity on comparably urgent issues implicitly assesses the kinds of discourse that he thought possible—or desirable—in English political culture.

The aspiring French prophetess's commitment to poetic knowledge and the English poet's equivocation before the radical contingency of all verbal traditions of authority are also illuminated by the cultural capital of the respective vernaculars within which these writers worked. Chaucer labored within a linguistic medium that lacked prestige; his narrator in *The House of Fame* seems both excited by and wary of that fact: "Now herkeneth every maner man / That Englissh understonde kan / And listeth of my drem to lere" (509–11). Christine de Pizan worked within a viable vernacular tradition, even if she was alienated from it by gender.[79] Her efforts "to install French as a language of learning" in a new "hybrid culture that brought together the closed world of masculine Latin letters and the more open and accessible arena of vernacular schol-

---

[78] Lynn Staley, *Languages of Power in the Age of Richard II* (University Park: Pennsylvania State University Press, 2005), chaps. 1 and 3; quotation at 327.

[79] I am indebted to Thomas Hahn for this distinction; "Chaucer's Sister: Gender, Language, and Literary Ambition in Late Medieval Vernacular Culture," paper delivered at the Biennial Conference of the New Chaucer Society, University of Colorado, Boulder, July 2002.

arship" drew sanction and support from earlier vernacular translations of learned texts commissioned by Charles V.[80] However unique her efforts to bring a gendered idiom to vernacular literary culture, from a linguistic perspective she was not improvising to the degree that Chaucer must have thought he was.

III

The implicit dialogue between Geoffrey Chaucer and Christine de Pizan posited in this essay becomes explicit in late medieval and early Tudor England, when the reception of these two writers was provocatively intertwined. Indeed, Christine emerges as England's most celebrated woman writer in the very era that Chaucer achieves preeminence as the English laureate whose influence would register across succeeding poetic generations.[81] Whereas the implicit textual dialogue between these writers concentrates on poetic authority and epistemologies, the conversation attested by literary history takes a different turn, as we shall see, concentrating on the rhetorical and gendered positions that effectively ground writings on love and morality.

Recent approaches to the reception of Christine's works in late medieval and early Tudor England have focused on the transformations wrought upon her identity as a woman writer by the translators, printers, and patrons responsible for introducing her work to English readers. This critical narrative contends that the translation of Christine's texts into English involved suppression of her identity and authority as a woman writer and appropriation of her desirable intellectual attributes

---

[80] On the program of vernacular translation, see Willard, *Christine de Pizan*, pp. 21–22, 126–28. The quotation in this sentence is from Fenster, "Perdre son latin," p. 91.

[81] Between 1402 and 1521, Christine's *L'Epistre au dieu d'amours, L'Epistre d'Othéa, Livre des fais d'armes et de chevalrie, Proverbes moraulx, Livre du corps de policie,* and *Livre de la Cité des dames* were all translated into English. Two of these translations were published by Caxton, Anthony Woodville's *Morall Proverbes* (1478) and the printer's own rendering of the *Book of Fayttes of Armes and of Chyualrye* (1489). Fifteenth-century English aristocratic audiences also acquired luxury French manuscripts such as the famous collected works of Christine in British Library MS Harley 4431, which the Duke of Bedford brought to England from France. John Talbot bestowed MS Royal 15.E.VI, an anthology containing Christine's *Livre des fais d'armes et de chevalrie* upon Margaret Anjou to celebrate her marriage to Henry VI. See Willard, *Christine de Pizan*, p. 214; Michel-André Bossy, "Arms and the Bride: Christine de Pizan's Military Treatise as a Wedding Gift for Margaret of Anjou," in *Christine de Pizan and the Categories of Difference*, pp. 236–56; Summit, *Lost Property*, pp. 69–70.

by the gentlemen scholars and bureaucrats who made her work available.[82] Jennifer Summit's important contribution to this account focuses on the relationship between the Englishing of Christine and the construction of Chaucer's identity as English laureate, parallel processes that are seen to converge with the inclusion of Christine's *Morall Prouerbes* (*Proverbes moraulx*) in Richard Pynson's 1526 edition of *The Boke of Fame, made by Geffray Chaucer: with Dyuers other of his Workes*. In Pynson's collection, Summit argues, Christine de Pizan's authorial identity is absorbed by that of Chaucer, who needed the woman writer's self-constructed role as public teacher and prudent counselor—a role that the *Chemin de long estude* had first established for her—to bolster an identity as moralist that had been attenuated by his more prominent reputation as a love poet.[83] I want to pursue alternative explanations for this textual convergence, taking into account the overlapping literary careers and parallel poetic self-fashionings that we have been tracking.

Late medieval and Tudor traditions of anthologizing Chaucerian and other texts in manuscript and print culture, translation practices, and the exigencies and economics of Tudor printing can account in part for the inclusion of Christine's *Morall Prouerbes* in Pynson's *Boke of Fame*.[84] As Kathleen Forni and Anne Coldiron independently have noted, although the *Morall Prouerbes* is integrated into Pynson's anthology under the rubric of Chaucerian authorship, the text nonetheless is specifically

[82] See Mahoney, "Middle English Regenderings of Christine de Pizan"; Jane Chance, "Gender Subversion and Linguistic Castration in Fifteenth-Century English Translations of Christine de Pizan," in *Violence Against Women in Medieval Texts,* ed. Anna Roberts (Gainesville: University Press of Florida, 1998), pp. 161–94; Laurie Finke, *Women's Writing in English: Medieval England* (London: Longman, 1999), pp. 197–217; and Jennifer Summit, *Lost Property,* pp. 61–107, 226–41.

[83] Summit, *Lost Property,* pp. 81–93. The alternative explanation that I offer for the convergence of Chaucer and Christine in Pynson's edition is nonetheless indebted to Summit's fine scholarship on this subject.

[84] Kathleen Forni, "Richard Pynson and the Stigma of the Chaucerian Apocrypha," *ChauR* 34 (2000): 428–36; Martha Driver, "Christine de Pisan and Robert Wyer: The .C. Hystoryes of Troye, or L'Epistre d'Othéa Englished," *Gutenberg Jarhbuch* 72 (1997): 125–39; Dana M. Symons, ed., *Chaucerian Dream Visions and Complaints* (Kalamazoo: Medieval Institute Publications, 2004), pp. 10–17; A. E. B. Coldiron, "Taking Advice from a Frenchwoman: Caxton, Pynson, and Christine de Pizan's *Moral Proverbs*," in *Caxton's Trace: Studies in the History of English Printing,* ed. William Kuskin (Notre Dame: University of Notre Dame Press, 2005), pp. 127–66; and Coldiron, "Christine de Pizan and Translation: A Woman Writer's Authority in Early English Print," in *Gender, Translation, and Print Poetics, 1476–1558: French Poems in Early Modern England* (Aldershot, Hampshire: Ashgate), forthcoming. I am grateful to Professor Coldiron for sharing this work in advance of its publication.

designated as that "of Christyne."[85] Pynson's treatment of Christine's translated text is consistent with his book's representation of other translations and apocryphal attributions; male writers and translators are also elided or rendered ambiguous to enable Pynson's assemblage of these works as Chaucerian. For example, the translation of Alain Chartier's *La belle dame sans mercy,* identified as the work of "Master Aleyne . . . chefe secratorie with the kyng of France," is assimilated to Chaucer, "flour of poets in our mother tong" (sig. Dii[v]); there is no mention of Richard Roos, its actual translator. Anthony Woodville's identity as the translator of Christine's text is similarly eliminated to make way for the association of the *Morall Prouerbes* with Chaucer, although Woodville's effort and Christine's authorship are both acknowledged in Caxton's version, which was Pynson's source. The final work in *The Boke of Fame,* Lydgate's *Consulo Quisquis Eris,* is presented, without further gloss, under the rubric "Prouerbes by Lydgate," thereby producing the same confusion about authorship that results from identifying the woman writer's text as "morall prouerbes of Christine."

The acts of appropriation that align Christine's *Prouerbes* with other texts by and attributed to Chaucer in Pynson's *Boke* may also be situated in the shared literary system and cultures of reading that connected the lives and literary preoccupations of the two writers. From this perspective, the convergence of authorial identities represented by the appearance of Christine's text in Pynson's *Boke of Fame* is less an outcome of Chaucer's conflicted image than of these writers' historically parallel construction of authorial identity. As we have seen, Chaucer and Christine de Pizan occupy analogous, if distinct, positions in a shared literary culture, and they posed similar challenges and questions to that culture's textual traditions. Among their tendencies to articulate rhetorical and epistemological issues in similar terms, Chaucer and Christine especially employ gender as an analytic category to shape their self-conceptions as writers and frame broader meditations on literary authority and tradition. The enduring experiments with gendered speaking positions that are a signature of both writers' texts mark their mutual participation in a late medieval literature culture that privileged such

---

[85] Coldiron analyzes how Christine's *Proverbes moraulx* was positioned and transformed in its three different late medieval English incarnations: the French text in B.L. MS Harley 4431, brought to England by the Duke of Bedford; Caxton's imprint of Anthony Woodville's translation; and Pynson's *Boke of Fame.* In each case Christine retains her authoritative role as adviser; see "Taking Advice from a French Woman."

rhetorical moves.[86] Gendered performances are an important facet of Pynson's edition, then, at least in part because they are central to these authors' rhetorical manipulations of poetic authority.

Christine labored consistently to construct a discursive persona and occupy a rhetorical position whose authority was "beyond gender."[87] She stressed that the effective voice of counsel should be determined by learning and qualities of character rather than birth because "good words and good teaching are praiseworthy for whoever may have said them" ("bonne parole et bon enseignement font a louer de quelconques personne que ilz soient dis").[88] She pitched her arguments on gender-related questions in ethical terms relevant not just to women but all humanity.[89] Yet Christine always writes from within her gendered, feminine "fable of self-definition" even as she strategically occupies masculine rhetorical positions.[90] Paradoxically, the motivation to establish this gender-neutral rhetorical persona was predicated, first, on the idiosyncrasy of a woman writer very publicly linking her literary efforts to a struggle for economic self-sufficiency; and, second, on the ideological anomaly of her desire to be a female counselor to princes, a counselor whose words of advice were grounded in a textual tradition that had established authorship and moral and political authority as masculine preserves. Christine's regular pronouncements on her participation in these spheres underscore the sheer novelty of her act.[91] In work after work, her detailed reporting of the personal and political implications of her endeavor to transform gendered textual traditions—and the social and cultural institutions that they influenced—secures her historical and literary identity as champion of feminine authorship.

Chaucer's textual portrayals of his writing self articulate no comparable ambitions, in part because authorship is naturalized for him in a way

---

[86] See Knapp, *Bureaucratic Muse*, pp. 57–60.

[87] Here I invoke Brown-Grant's phrase; *Christine de Pizan and the Moral Defence of Women: Reading Beyond Gender*.

[88] *Epistre d'Othéa*, p. 341; *Selected Writings of Christine de Pizan*, p. 40.

[89] Brown-Grant, *Christine de Pizan and the Moral Defence of Women;* Richards, "Christine de Pizan and Sacred History," p. 16.

[90] Brownlee, "Literary Genealogy and the Problem of the Father," p. 206.

[91] In *L'Avision*, Christine remarks that her noble patrons graciously received her literary offerings "more I think for the novelty of a woman who could write (since that had not occurred for some time) than for any worth there might be in them" ("et plus comme ie tiens pour la chose non usagee que femme escripse comme pieca ne avenist que pour dignete qui y soit"); *Lavision-Christine*, p. 165; *Christine's Vision*, p. 120. Patrizia Romagnoli observes Christine's "singularité irréductible"; "Les formes de la voix," p. 74.

it could never be for Christine. Yet, as many readers have observed, Chaucer was also deeply invested in exploring the crucial role that gender played in constructions of authorship available to him. From his troubled personae in the *Legend of Good Women* and the *Troilus,* to the conflicted representations of masculinity offered by his pilgrim narrator in the tales of *Sir Thopas* and *Melibee,* to his brilliant manipulations of the gendered voices of textual authority in the words of the Wife of Bath, Chaucer reveals his consistent preoccupation with the gender of the voice that speaks and writes. Jennifer Summit has argued that feminine voices provide the context in which Chaucer explores challenges encountered in the formation of his poetic identity. The representations of writing women—Criseyde, Dido, Anelida—who occupy prominent positions in his classical texts, she observes, signify his awareness of the contingencies and instabilities of writing in a vernacular with no literary tradition of any recognizable prestige.[92] These plaintive images of female authorship articulate Chaucer's distance from authoritative traditions of antiquity and figure his anxieties about the transience of his poetic identity and his texts.[93] If the poet's textual occupation of such feminine positions signifies the linguistic and cultural constraints that he faced as a vernacular writer, however, it also constitutes an important rehearsal of a representational strategy that he devised to overcome them: his habit of ventriloquizing the voice of the other, his abiding attraction, in Marshall Leicester's phrase, to an "impersonated" artistry.[94] The dedication of Chaucerian poetics to representing all human verbal acts—even those of revered textual traditions—as the utterances of inevitably situated and contingent perspectives constitutes part of the poet's response to the problem of writing in the long shadow cast by ancient authorities and rival traditions. *The Boke of Fame*'s rendering of other masculine and feminine voices, including Christine's, as Chaucerian thus reproduces a rhetorical self-characterization in which the poet was deeply invested.

[92] Summit, *Lost Property,* pp. 23–59, 217–26.

[93] Ruth Evans has argued recently that Chaucer feminizes the vernacular archive and its writer in *The House of Fame;* her invocation of the vernacular's familiar gendered symbolism usefully allows an analogy between the subaltern efforts of the insecure English author and the alienated female French writer; "Chaucer in Cyberspace," pp. 57–59, 63–67. Marilynn Desmond alternatively contends that Chaucer's use and treatment of the *Aeneid* in *The House of Fame* place gender issues at that heart of his poem, where the very invocation of the epic constitutes a performance of masculine reading practices within an intellectual culture dominated by masculine technologies of rhetoric and memory; *Reading Dido,* pp. 128–51.

[94] Marshall Leicester, "The Art of Impersonation: A General Prologue to the *Canterbury Tales,*" *PMLA* 95 (1980): 213–24.

Julia Boffey's analysis of *The Boke of Fame* establishes the complex influences that shaped Pynson's collection, ranging from the printer's opportunistic inclusion of works already available in print to evidence suggesting that the volume was compiled according to a purposeful design. In this "exemplary anthology of early echoes of Chaucer's works and of attempts to emulate them," as Boffey points out, the apocryphal texts are all related to the concerns of the canonical works. For example, *Morall Prouerbes* and Lydgate's *Consulo Quisquis Eris* "reiterate and amplify the advice encapsulated in *Truth*"; *La Belle Dame sans Mercy* addresses the debate about earthly love pursued in *The House of Fame* and *The Parliament of Fowls*.[95] The collection's apocryphal works (except *Morall Prouerbes)* are all written in rhyme royal or ballade stanzas—the preferred forms for courtly verse in England—yet *The Book of Fame* as a whole is stamped by a "pattern of exemplary moral instruction."[96] This pattern encompasses not only explicitly edifying works such as *Truth* and the *Morall Prouerbes,* but also the monitory envoy to the *La Belle Dame sans Mercy* and the translator's prologue and envoy to the *Letter of Dido.* Moralizing texts, Chaucer's *Truth* and Christine's *Prouerbes,* constitute a structural if not physical center of the *Boke;* they are framed by love poems—*House of Fame, Parliament of Fowls,* and *La Belle Dame* on one end, the *Lamentation of Mary Magdalene* and *Letter of Dido* on the other—that focus on complaint, especially female complaint. Toward the conclusion of the volume, Dido's *Letter* echoes part one of Chaucer's dream vision.[97] Voices of amorous complaint, admonished to "[B]eware of love," seek only lovers who are "secrete, stedfast and true," and "neuer consent / To do þe thing whiche folkes may reproue," are a dominant rhetorical feature of the collection.[98] These alternating rhetorics of love complaint and admonition shed light on early Tudor reception of *The House of Fame,* suggesting how the example of the sorrowful, jilted Dido may have encouraged the poem's construal as a "morally instructive"

---

[95] Julia Boffey, "Richard Pynson's *Book of Fame* and the *Letter of Dido*," *Viator* 19 (1988): 340–41. The works in Pynson's book appear in this order: *House of Fame, Parliament of Fowls, La Belle Dame sans Mercy, Truth, Morall Prouerbes,* the *Lamentacyon,* or *Complaint of Mary Magdalene,* the *Letter of Dido,* and Lydgate's *Consulo Quisquis Eris.*

[96] Boffey, "Richard Pynson's *Book of Fame*," p. 341, quotation at 352; and *Manuscripts of English Courtly Love Lyrics in the Later Middle Ages* (Woodbridge, Suffolk: D. S. Brewer, 1985), pp. 104–5. The only other work in the volume not written in one of these stanzas is *The House of Fame.*

[97] Boffey, "Richard Pynson's *Book of Fame*," p. 341.

[98] From the *Letter of Dido, Boke of Fame, STC* 5088, sig. Fv^r.

text.[99] Editorial comment appended to the conclusion of the poem solic-
its precisely such an edifying reading: this "worke . . . is craftely made /
and digne to be writen & knowen: for . . . [Chaucer] toucheth in it right
great wysedome and subtell understandyng / and so in all his workes he
excelleth in myn opinyon / all other writers in Englysshe / for he writeth
no voyde wordes / but all his mater is full of hye & quicke sentence."[100]
   The image of the laureate's "great wysedome and subtell understanding" is a far remove from the poetics that so distinguishes *The House of
Fame* from Christine's *Chemin*. Yet this description defines a mode of
reading the dream vision that illuminates the inclusion of Christine's
Prouerbes in *The Boke of Fame* by underscoring the congruence of the
edition's emphases with those of Chaucer's late medieval and early
Tudor reception. Audiences for the poet in the generations after his
death were not especially drawn to the formal complexities and intricate
ironies that have inspired more modern appreciations of his literary
achievements. This "narrowing of the Chaucer tradition" in the fifteenth
century involved a demonstrated preference for the poet's courtly and
moral works.[101] Chaucer's fifteenth-century scribes and imitators, as
Seth Lerer notes, constructed "a Chaucer of political advice and lyric
virtuosity."[102] This poetic identity is evidenced in manuscript traditions
that show widespread anthologizing of those *Canterbury Tales* with an

---

   [99] Boffey, "Richard Pynson's *Book of Fame*," p. 352. The issue of the poem's sixteenth-
century reception raises important questions about how, or whether, the ambiguous and
ironic Chaucer so congenial to modern perspectives would have been construed by
Tudor and Elizabethan readers. Carol A. N. Martin observes that "the depth of Renaissance discomfort" with *The House of Fame* stems from the poem's hermeneutic openness
and skepticism about authoritative truth. Speght's 1598 edition of Chaucer's collected
works, she argues, "deliberately muted" that ambivalence. See "Authority and the Defense of Fiction: Renaissance Poetics and Chaucer's *House of Fame*," in *Refiguring Chaucer
in the Renaissance,* ed. Theresa M. Krier (Gainesville: University Press of Florida, 1998),
pp. 40–65, quotes at 46 and 41. Speght's indexing of "sentences and proverbs" in
Troilus and Criseyde demonstrates the editor's tendency to decontextualize sententiae so
as to misrepresent central issues of the poem. Claire Kinney argues that this method
imposes a univocality on the text that resists its narrative's errancies and imposes an
order consistent with humanist practice of assembling proverbial wisdom. See "Thomas
Speght's Renaissance Chaucer and the *solaas* of *sentence* in *Troilus and Criseyde*," in *Refiguring Chaucer in the Renaissance,* pp. 66–84.
   [100] *Boke of Fame*, sig. Ciii^r. Pynson takes this comment, as he did his text, from Caxton's 1483 edition, *The book of fame made by Gefferey Chaucer*, STC 5087.
   [101] Strohm, "Chaucer's Fifteenth-Century Audience and the Narrowing of the 'Chaucer Tradition'"; Spearing, "Father Chaucer"; Lerer, *Chaucer and His Readers;* Lawton,
"Dullness and the Fifteenth Century," 779–81.
   [102] Lerer, *Chaucer and His Readers,* pp. 7–8; see also Strohm, "Chaucer's Fifteenth-
Century Audience," 18–23.

edifying bent and the collecting of Chaucer's courtly writings with those of his contemporaries and the courtly makers who tried to emulate him.[103] Manuscripts from the period further reveal a pattern of misattribution that turned Chaucer into a "relentlessly . . . moralizing figure, cited as a fount of proverbial wisdom."[104] Fifteenth-century readers' inclination to promote a sagacious Chaucer may have derived its warrant from the poet's manipulations of that very identity. Lee Patterson argues that the *Melibee* represents Chaucer's effort to associate his narrator with a form of prudential discourse whose philosophical commonplaces were targeted for instruction of the young, a genre of late medieval writing that included texts such as Christine de Pizan's *Enseignemens* and *Proverbes moraulx*. Patterson's notice of this coincidence suggests that the sagacious aspect of Chaucer's authorial identity later concretized in Pynson's anthologizing of Christine's text was already under construction in the *Canterbury Tales*.[105]

As the earlier example of the Findern manuscript (MS Cambridge University Library Ff. 1.6) suggests, *The Boke of Fame*'s association of Chaucer with the feminine voices of Dido, Mary Magdalene, and Christine and its use of female-voiced love poetry for affective and edifying ends reinforces an image of the poet that late medieval readers seem to have considered Chaucerian.[106] At the same time, though, this associa-

---

[103] Lerer, *Chaucer and His Readers*, pp. 57–84.

[104] Julia Boffey, "Proverbial Chaucer and the Chaucer Canon," in *Reading from the Margins: Textual Studies, Chaucer, and Medieval Literature*, ed. Seth Lerer (San Marino, Calif.: Huntington Library, 1996), p. 44.

[105] Patterson, "'What Man Artow?'" pp. 146–49. Chaucer's image as a poet of love *and* morality endures in the sixteenth-century editions of his collected works; the forty-eight apocryphal texts in these editions exhibit a preponderance of "moral, allegorical . . . [and] amorous" writing. See Alice Miskimin, *Renaissance Chaucer* (New Haven: Yale University Press, 1975), pp. 242–47, at 245. On the complex Tudor dissemination of Chaucer's texts and image, see John Watkins, "'Wrastling for this world': Wyatt and the Tudor Canonization of Chaucer," in *Refiguring Chaucer in the Renaissance*, pp. 21–39.

[106] Recognized for its unique collection of female-voiced (and perhaps female-authored) lyrics, MS Cambridge University Library Ff.1.6 is an important anthology of courtly poems by Chaucer and his contemporaries and imitators. Like the *Boke of Fame*, it contains the *Parliament of Fowls* and *La Belle Dame sans Mercy;* the manuscript's focus on female-voiced complaint is represented by Chaucer's *Legend of Thisbe* from the *Legend of Good Women*, the *Complaint of Venus*, and *Anelida's Complaint*. The manuscript also contains Hoccleve's *Letter of Cupid* and excerpts from Gower's *Confessio Amantis*. See Kate Harris, "The Origins and Make-up of Cambridge University Library MS Ff.1.6," *Transations of the Cambridge Bibliographical Society* 8 (1983): 299–333; Sarah McNamer, "Female Authors, Provincial Setting: The Re-versing of Courtly Love in the Findern Manuscript," *Viator* 22 (1991): 279–310; and Ashby Kinch, "'A Woman Can and Dar as Well as He': Chaucerian Imitation and the Female Voices of the Findern Lyrics," paper delivered at the Biennial Conference of the New Chaucer Society, University of

tion complicates the rhetorical function of the *Morall Prouerbes* in Pynson's anthology, especially because the articulation of "proverbs" by a "Christine" offers a counterpoint to other female voices in the book. The voice of the proverbs is not a voice of complaint but of wisdom, speaking from inside discursive traditions with which "proverbial" Chaucer had long been identified, and from a position of feminine counsel that held exceptional fascination for the poet. Thus the transformations wrought upon Christine by Pynson's *Boke of Fame* follow from the two writers' reception as well as their common participation in an international literary culture that privileged traditions of moral discourse and gender performance that they both manipulated for their individual ends

With respect to this international literary culture, the shared rhetorical location of the father of English poetry and Europe's first professional woman writer deserves more attention than it has received. In an important exception, Ethan Knapp includes Chaucer and Christine de Pizan among the cohort of lay administrators and secretaries whose textual services to aristocratic communities contributed to the expanded authority of vernacular writing under the auspices of a "bureaucratic muse."[107] The late medieval European cultural formation that Knapp analyzes has been identified in numerous contexts; it is anticipated in the Latin writings on political counsel that Albertano of Brescia addressed to thirteenth-century Italian urban society and extends to public officials in government, royal service, and great households whom David Lawton credits with producing a markedly "dull" fifteenth-century English literature.[108] The efforts of these writers mark the definition and valorization of a new conception of the literate, lay counselor, who derived social

---

Colorado, Boulder, 2002. On the prominence of female complaint in Chaucer, see also Phillips, "Frames and Narrators in Chaucer's Poetry," p. 88.

[107] Knapp, *The Bureaucratic Muse,* pp. 6, 30. See also Burrow, "Hoccleve and the Middle French Poets," p. 45.

[108] Lawton, "Dullness and the Fifteenth Century"; see also David Wallace, *Chaucerian Polity: Absolutist Lineages and Associational Forms in England and Italy* (Stanford: Stanford University Press, 1997), pp. 213–21. In summarizing the major characteristics of this development in late medieval literary culture, I do not mean to elide historical differences over several centuries and between specific social and geographical contexts. Chaucer's relationship to this emergent concept was complex, since some of his administrative appointments were not directly implicated in his pursuit of a career in letters. His attitude toward that enterprise displays an ambivalent embrace and disavowal of the available cultural models for literary activity; see Patterson, "'What Man Artow?'" and "'Thirled with the Poynt of Remembraunce': Memory and Modernity in Chaucer's Poetry," in *Modernité au moyen âge: Le défi du passé,* ed. Brigitte Cazelles and Charles Méla (Geneva: Librairie Droz, 1990), pp. 113–51.

and literary identity from sources of authority other than *clergie* and *chevalrie,* the dominant cultural institutions for masculine intellectual and social accomplishment. Under the auspices of royal, governmental, and aristocratic sponsorship, these lay counselors promoted the value of reading and writing outside traditional university and monastic settings and shifted ideals of praiseworthy masculine activity from chivalric to rhetorical performance. Embodying a political and social conception of a civil, secularized profession of letters, these "new men" championed vernacular eloquence in the service of the public good.[109] Christine de Pizan contributed brilliantly to this cultural formation by recognizing in the ideal of the literate, lay counselor an ideological opportunity to anchor her intellectual aspirations and authorial identity as a woman writer.[110] The learning, moral integrity, and eloquence that authorized the lay counselor were precisely the qualities that Christine invoked to articulate her self-conception. Reversing the gender transformation she announces in the *Livre de Mutacion de Fortune,* Christine de Pizan made the "new man" into a woman.[111]

[109] See Anne Middleton's well-known essays, "Chaucer's 'New Men' and the Good of Literature in the *Canterbury Tales,*" in *Literature and Society, Selected Papers from the English Institute,* ed. Edward Said (Baltimore: Johns Hopkins University Press, 1980), pp. 15–56; and "The Idea of Public Poetry in the Reign of Richard II," *Speculum* 53 (1978): 94–114. On "new men," see also Wallace, *Chaucerian Polity,* pp. 220–21. The summary in this paragraph also relies on Knapp, *Bureaucratic Muse,* pp. 1–9; Summit, *Lost Property,* pp. 66–81; and Carolyn Collette, "Chaucer and the French Tradition Revisited." See also Joel Blanchard, "'Vox poetica, vox politica': The Poet's Entry into the Political Arena in the Fifteenth Century," trans. Renate Blumenfeld-Kosinski, in *Selected Writings of Christine de Pizan,* pp. 362–71; and Katherine Kerby-Fulton and Steven Justice, "Langlandian Reading Circles and the Civil Service in London and Dublin, 1380–1427," in *New Medieval Literatures* 1 (1997): 59–83.

[110] I want to clarify my difference from Summit on this point (*Lost Property,* pp. 67–71). Summit posits that Christine de Pizan was a generative force in inventing and modeling a new identity for the secular literary community of fifteenth-century England. I emphasize that the secular, prudential, public terms of Christine's authorial self-construction were already available as rhetorical and ethical positions when the woman writer transformed them by recognizing their aptness for a female speaker. Without denying Christine's literary agency, I stress its location in a broader, international system of literary discourse.

[111] Michael Hanly's analysis of interactions among lettered French and English courtiers who account for the northwestward transmission of themes and texts of Italian humanism—Philippe de Mézières, Oton de Granson, Eustache Deschamps, Gontier and Pierre Col, Jean de Montreuil, Lewis Clifford, and John Clanvowe—reads like a list of Christine de Pizan's and Chaucer's most important literary contacts and influences; see "Courtiers and Poets: An International System of Literary Exchange in Late Fourteenth-Century Italy, France, and England," *Viator* 28 (1997): 305–32. Hanly's portrait of this "framework of intellectual contacts centered around books" (327–28) underscores the exclusively masculine nature of these exchanges among lettered courtiers and diplomats, thereby showing exactly what Christine de Pizan was up against. On the "male-

David Lawton observes that "[f]ifteenth-century writing is to a great extent the literature of public servants . . . [who] were adroit survivors . . . and politically expert."[112] Even though Christine de Pizan, unlike other members of her literary cohort, did not have a "day job," Lawton's notice of the public preoccupations, survival skills, and political expertise of these fifteenth-century poets furnishes an apt description of the woman writer as well.[113] His characterization of the politically engaged yet precarious position of these writers also illuminates several important moments in late medieval Anglo-French literary culture when the texts and authorial identities of Chaucer and Christine intersect. Translating Christine's *L'Epistre au dieu d'Amours,* Hoccleve's *Letter of Cupid* invokes its author's complex relationship to both writers. Hoccleve makes himself heir and subject to Chaucer, but he models the construction of his authorial identity after that of Christine: as writers, both are situated outside the dominant cultural traditions that granted authority to literary activity—she because of gender, he because of class.[114] More closely intertwined are the threads connecting Chaucer and Christine on the subject of counsel, which they both enlist to explore the rhetorical complexities of speaking truth to princes. Their pronouncements on this subject share a debt to Renaud de Louens's *Livre de Melibee et Dame Prudence,* the French translation of Albertano of Brescia's *Liber consolationis et consilii* that furnished Chaucer's direct source for the *Tale of Melibee.* In Pierpont Morgan Library MS Morgan M 39, another Melibee text, the fifteenth-century *Le roman de Melibee et de Prudence* appears alongside excerpts from Chaucer's *Tale;* the Morgan *Melibee* is mistakenly attributed to Christine de Pizan, an attribution that makes perfect

---

bonding" that must have occurred in reading circles based on bureaucratic service in England, see Kerby-Fulton and Justice, "Langlandian Reading Circles," 62.

[112] Lawton, "Dullness and the Fifteenth Century," 788.

[113] Helen Solterer labels Christine's role as woman of letters in this culture of bureaucratic humanists as that of the "freelancer"; "Fiction versus Defamation: The Quarrel over *The Romance of the Rose,*" *Medieval History Journal* 2 (1999): 111–41. On the woman writer's necessarily hybrid literary identity, see also Louise D'Arcens, "Her Own *Maistress?* Christine de Pizan the Professional Amateur," in *Maistress of My Wit: Medieval Women, Modern Scholars,* ed. Louise D'Arcens and Juanita Feros Ruys (Turnhout: Brepols, 2004), pp. 119–45.

[114] Knapp, *Bureaucratic Muse,* pp. 45–75. The unusual mix of autobiography, complaint, and political analysis in Christine's *L'Avision* calls to mind the complex rhetorical modes of Hoccleve's works. See Liliane Dulac, "Themes et variations du *Chemin de long estude* à *L'Advision Christine:* Remarques sur un itinéraire," *Sur le chemin de longue étude,* pp. 77–86.

sense in view of Christine's actual authorship of *Le livre de prudence.*[115] The ideal of feminine sagacity, which Christine also promoted in works such as the *Epistre Othea,* has a long history in which she and Chaucer are mutually implicated.

If Christine de Pizan's contribution to the making of her authorial identity in late medieval and early Tudor England involved her embodiment of this ideal of literate female counsel, Chaucer's unwitting role in that endeavor arose from his obvious affinities for the rhetorical and gendered role that the woman writer claimed for herself, an attraction that is registered in the poet's "dedication to exploring the domestic dynamics and political efficacy of female eloquence." David Wallace identifies "[e]loquent wives who influence or determine the outcome of events" as "the most singular aspect of his oeuvre."[116] Focusing on a prominent illustration of this Chaucerian preoccupation, Carolyn Collette analyzes correspondences between the *Tale of Melibee* and a French literary tradition that promoted the good wife as an exemplar of prudence whose moral and rhetorical influence in the domestic sphere resonated in the public realm. This is the tradition on which Christine de Pizan importantly draws for her portraits of wifely prudence and eloquence in *Le Livre des Trois Vertus* and the *Cité des Dames.*[117] Christine's capacity to speak from within the sphere of wifely eloquence was complicated by Boethian fortunes that made her a widow not long after making her a wife. Yet we might see her regular reminiscences of her marriage not only as complex autobiographical acts of self-definition but as efforts to situate herself within the discursive tradition that promoted the contributions of wifely eloquence to a particular kind of polity—that is, to derive claims for the authority of her good counsel from the domestic and experiential as well as the learned spheres. However widely she ranged in intellectual terms, Christine never relinquished her claim to the domestic, often grounding her articulation of her most im-

---

[115] Summit, *Lost Property,* pp. 105–7. See also Christine Reno, "Le *Livre de Prudence* / *Livre de la Prod'hommie de l'homme:* Nouvelles perspectives," in *Une femmes de lettres au Moyen Âge: Études autour de Christine de Pizan,* ed. Liliane Dulac and Bernard Ribémont (Orléans: Paradigme, 1995), pp. 25–37; and Collette, "Heeding the Counsel of Prudence."

[116] Wallace, *Chaucerian Polity,* pp. 376–77.

[117] Collette, "Heeding the Counsel of Prudence"; and "Chaucer and the French Tradition Revisited." Collette identifies de Mézières's *Le Livre de la vertu du sacrement de mariage* (1384–89) as a likely source for Chaucer, who probably knew the French writer. Christine was a familiar of Philippe, selling to him a property she inherited from her father; see Willard, *Christine de Pizan,* p. 23.

portant political and ethical pronouncements in that realm.[118] It is little wonder then that the voices and texts of Chaucer and Christine de Pizan cohabit in *The Boke of Fame* to be read in tandem with each other. Had Christine performed such an act of reading across the Chaucer canon, that is, had she participated in the poet's late medieval reception, she would have discovered his compelling exploration of the rhetorical, social, and ethical role that she independently adopted for herself.

From similar positions on the periphery of their respective courts, within a shared Anglo-French literary culture, Geoffrey Chaucer and Christine de Pizan crafted comparably wide-ranging careers and tackled commensurately ambitious rhetorical, aesthetic, and political issues. Gender differences, social and rhetorical, were a defining element of their careers and their reading of the issues; their works consistently demonstrate the textual play of gender with other political and literary ideologies and discourses. Over the course of their careers, Chaucer and Christine conducted a sustained if necessarily implicit dialogue about matters that were crucial to their respective textual enterprises: the truth of literary language, the relationship of experience and authority, the counselor's role in the delivery of counsel. The canonical status of these two writers and nationalist preoccupations of literary history have muted terms of that conversation which fifteenth- and sixteenth-century audiences would have found more familiar. The political commitments of a feminist critique dedicated to lauding the singularity of Christine de Pizan's achievements have also played their part in turning down the volume on this important late medieval exchange. Eavesdropping on this still engaging conversation produces new perspectives on gender's significance for late medieval Anglo-French literary relations and the national literary histories with which these relationships intersect. Encountering the father of English poetry and the "mother to think back through" on our path of long study, we can be confident that parts of their imaginative journey, and ours, still lie ahead.[119]

---

[118] On Christine's reliance on experience to support authority, see Tarnowski, "The Lessons of Experience and the *Chemin de long estude*"; and Angela Jane Wiesl, "The Widow as Virgin: Desexualized Narrative in Christine de Pizan's *Livre de la Cité des Dames*," in *Constructions of Widowhood and Virginity in the Middle Ages*, ed. Cindy L. Carlson and Angela Jane Weisl (New York: St. Martin's Press, 1999), pp. 49–62.

[119] My description of Christine invokes Sheila Delany's famous essay, "'Mothers to Think Back Through': Who Are They? The Ambiguous Example of Christine de Pizan," in *Selected Writings of Christine de Pizan*, pp. 312–28.

Narrative Artistry in *St. Erkenwald* and the *Gawain*-Group:

The Case for Common Authorship Reconsidered

Marie Borroff
Yale University

DID THE *GAWAIN*-POET also write *St. Erkenwald?* The question is important, bearing as it does on the creative legacy of a major poet of the late Middle English period, the author of the acknowledged masterpieces *Sir Gawain and the Green Knight* and *Pearl*. And the saint's legend stands up well under comparative scrutiny, for its author was both a superb storyteller and a master of the craft of alliterative verse.

Beginning almost immediately after *St. Erkenwald* was published for the first time in the late nineteenth century,[1] a series of scholars propounded the view that it should be added to the *Gawain*-group[2]—that

---

I am indebted to Frank Grady for his closely attentive editing; my essay in its present form has benefited greatly from his labors.

[1] "De Erkenwalde," in *Altenglische Legenden: Neue Folge, mit Einleitung und Anmerkungen* (Heilbronn, 1881), pp. 265–74. Since then, the following editions have appeared: Israel Gollancz, *St. Erkenwald (Bishop of London 675–693), An Alliterative poem, written about 1386* . . . (London: Oxford University Press, 1922); Henry L. Savage, *St. Erkenwald: A Middle English Poem* (New Haven: Yale University Press, 1926); Ruth Morse, *St. Erkenwald* (Cambridge: D. S. Brewer, 1975); Clifford Peterson, *Saint Erkenwald* (Philadelphia: University of Pennsylvania Press, 1977); Thorlac Turville-Petre, in *Alliterative Poetry of the Later Middle Ages* (Washington, D.C.: Catholic University of America Press, 1989; originally published by Routledge [London, 1989]), pp. 101–19; and J. A. Burrow and Thorlac Turville-Petre, *A Book of Middle English* (Oxford: Blackwell, 1992), pp. 199–212. Throughout this essay, I quote *St. Erkenwald* from Peterson's edition.

[2] Moritz Trautmann, in *Anglia* 5 (1882): 21–25, stated that the authorship of *St. Erkenwald* could be assigned with great exactitude ("mit grosser bestimmtheit") to the poet who wrote *Pearl, Cleanness,* and *Patience* (p. 23). In the Introduction to his edition, Savage, a proponent of common authorship, gave a history of the controversy to 1926, with full documentation and a detailed account of the supporting evidence presented by previous scholars. Peterson continued the historical account: "A general acceptance of the attribution, or at least the possibility of attribution, of *Erkenwald* to the *Pearl*-poet has been the situation until fairly recently. . . . But there have long been dissenters

is, to the four poems modern editors call *Pearl, Cleanness* or *Purity, Patience,* and *Sir Gawain and the Green Knight,* found, in that order, in the late fourteenth-century MS. Cotton Nero A. X., and only there.[3] But though the single manuscript containing *St. Erkenwald,* Ms. Harley 2250, is now thought to be virtually the same in geographical provenance, the poem was copied about seventy-five years later.[4] The presumption of shared authorship established by contiguity for the *Gawain*-group is lacking for the fifth poem, and the case for attribution must be made on internal evidence.

What kind of evidence can these poems be expected to yield? As readers of late Middle English alliterative verse know, the "long alliterative line" in which four of them are written[5] is the vehicle of a wholly conventional narrative style inherited by the poets from their predecessors and used by all alike. Moreover, the alliterative school flourished at a time when authors for the most part remained anonymous and the verbal originality we so prize today was not thought important. One

---

from the consensus" (p. 16). As one of the dissenters, he names Larry Benson, whose essay arguing against common authorship I discuss on pp. 44–45 below. Peterson then presents a body of external evidence connecting the manuscripts of *St. Erkenwald* and the *Gawain*-group with the name Massey, which "was a common one in Cheshire and southern Lancashire from at least the twelfth century" (p. 20). A poem by Thomas Hoccleve praises a man skilled in rhetoric whom he calls "maister Massey"; it is reasonably certain that a version of this poem was sent by Hoccleve to John of Lancaster, that is, John of Gaunt, before 1414. A John Massey of Cotton meets the "limiting criteria" for authorship of the *Gawain*-group. In conclusion, Peterson states his own view: that "the question of whether John Massey of Cotton wrote *St. Erkenwald*—and *Gawain and the Green Knight* and perhaps all the Cotton Nero poems—is a very live one" (pp. 19–23).

[3] See Malcolm Andrew and Ronald Waldron, *The Poems of the Pearl Manuscript,* rev. ed. (Exeter: University of Exeter Press, 1987, 1996), Introduction, p. 15. Throughout this essay, I quote the poems of the *Gawain*-group from Andrew and Waldron's edition.

[4] See Peterson, *Saint Erkenwald,* pp. 1–2. For the provenance of the manuscript, see "Key map 2" in *A Linguistic Atlas of Late Medi;aeval English,* ed. Angus McIntosh, M. L. Samuels, and Michael Benskin et al. (Aberdeen: University of Aberdeen Press, 1986), 4:335, where Cotton Nero A.x and Harley 2250, numbered 26 and 419, respectively, are located in east Cheshire, close to the Staffordshire border. Professor Samuels, in a private communication, has kindly supplemented the information on the map, stating that the slight differences between the scribal dialects represented by the two have led "to their being placed a mere seven miles apart." Lists of the distinctive forms found in the two manuscripts are given on pages 45–46 of volume 3 of the *Atlas* (for Harley 2250) and pages 37–38 (for Cotton Nero A x). See also, in Peterson's edition, "Dialect," pp. 23–26.

[5] *Pearl* is written in rhymed verse and "mixed" meter. See "Rhymed Verse," in Marie Borroff, *Sir Gawain and the Green Knight, Patience, Pearl, Verse Translations* (New York: W. W. Norton, 2001), pp. 174–80. However, the lines of the poem contain many ornamental alliterating phrases, some of which are found also in alliterative verse.

poet reading another would have felt free to take over a phrase or line he found useful for his own purposes. A search for authorial individuality in poems whose metrical patterns, vocabulary, phrasal combinations, syntactic patterns, and descriptive topoi are shared with other poems might seem doomed from the outset. Nevertheless, advocates of common authorship thought for over fifty years that they had found signs of it in the form of a body of words and phrases present in both *St. Erkenwald* and the Cotton Nero poems, and peculiar (as it seemed at the time) to them.[6] Especially conspicuous among these was a set of expressions called the "periphrases for God," exemplified by "He that on hyghe syttes"[7] (*Gawain* 256; cf. *Gawain* 2441–42, *Cleanness* 552, 1498, and *Patience* 261) and "the prince that paradis weldes" (*Erkenwald* 161; cf. *Cleanness* 195 and *Gawain* 2473 "the Prynce of paradise").[8] As late as 1935, "the prince that paradis weldes" was quoted, among other words and phrases, in J. P. Oakden's *Alliterative Poetry in Middle English,* as evidence of "the close connection that undoubtedly exists among the five poems."[9]

---

[6] Savage lists forty-four words believed by Trautmann to have been "more frequently used in the same sense by the *Gawain*-poet than by the other poets of the [alliterative] school" and eight words "common only to *Erkenwald* and the four poems of the Cotton MS," but added that "an examination of [*OED*] reduces that number to 5" and that "further examination serves also to reduce the value of certain words and expressions which Trautmann adduced as evidence of common authorship" (pp. liv–lv and nn. 17 and 18).

[7] In all quotations from Middle English, I have modernized the alphabet, substituting *z, y,* or *gh* for yogh, *u* for *v, v* for *u,* and *j* for *i* in accordance with modern English spelling. I have also substituted *and* for ampersand in the text of *Cleanness,* as edited by Gollancz, and in several other editions of the alliterative poems.

[8] I take these examples from the Introduction to Robert J. Menner's edition of *Purity* (New Haven: Yale University Press, 1920). Menner discusses the periphrases chiefly in relation to the authorship of the *Gawain*-group. He lists a number of examples noted by Trautmann, and later by Friedrich Knigge in *Die Sprache des Dichters von Sir Gawain and the Green Knight, der sogenannten Early English Alliterative Poems, und de Erkenwalde* (Marburg, 1885), p. 6, crediting Knigge as having first singled them out as a distinctive feature of the language of the five poems. Menner notes that Knigge used "the prince that paradis weldes" as "an argument for considering *Erkenwald* one of the group," but this was the only example he cited from the fifth poem, and could perhaps be explained as a borrowing from the *Gawain*-poet (xvi n. 2). For further discussion of the distribution of this phrase, see note 12, below. Savage, citing Menner, treats the periphrases briefly as a stylistic mannerism or habit (pp. lxii–iii).

[9] Oakden's pathbreaking study was originally published by Manchester University Press in two volumes, subtitled *The Dialectical and Metrical Survey* (1930) and *A Survey of the Traditions* (1935). Both have since been reprinted in one volume by Archon Books (1968). I quote above from volume 2, p. 93. Earlier in that volume, Oakden had said that "[t]ests of vocabulary, metre, style and artistic merit appear to justify the theory that the author of *St. Erkenwald* also wrote the poems of the Cotton MS. Nero A.X., but

The evidence that had been compiled in support of the theory of common authorship was examined in detail in 1965, and largely discredited, by Professor Larry Benson.[10] Benson began by noting that the work of scholars such as Oakden had brought about a full recognition of "the traditional nature of the style of alliterative verse, . . . and its dependence on formulas," and that previously unavailable data on word distribution had been appearing in the *Middle English Dictionary* (p. 144). (The publication of the *MED* in successive fascicles began in 1952 and continued through 1996.) As a result, the list of words formerly thought to be found only in the *Gawain*-group and *St. Erkenwald* had dwindled to almost nothing.[11] Turning to the periphrases for God, which had "seemed the most striking confirmation of the attribution [of *St. Erkenwald* to the *Gawain*-poet]," Benson presented a sizable anthology of such expressions assembled from some fifteen alliterative poems by authors other than the *Gawain*-poet, as well as from the works of Chaucer and others who used end-rhyme rather than alliteration (pp. 148–52).[12] In a second line of argument, he pointed out that the author

---

it is not insignificant that all five poems are indelibly stamped with the same distinctive personality" (p. 78).

[10] "The Authorship of *St. Erkenwald*," *JEGP* 64 (1965): 393–405, reprinted "with minor corrections" in *Contradictions: From Beowulf to Chaucer* (Aldershot, England, and Brookfield, Vt.: Scolar Press, 1995), pp. 141–54.

[11] Two such words have not yet been eliminated. The verb *norne*, which seems to have the general meaning "to offer" (usually with reference to speech), appears eleven times in *Erkenwald* and the *Gawain*-group (*Cleanness* 65, 669, 803, *Erkenwald* 101, 152, 195, *Gawain* 1661, 1669, 1771, 1823, 2443), and nowhere else. In addition, the verb whose forms are spelled *glewed* in *Patience* "uchon glewed on his god" (164) and *glow* in *Erkenwald* "glow on goure Godde" (171) is apparently found only in these two poems in the sense "call (upon) in prayer." See the entries in *MED* s.v. *nornen* v. and *gleuen* v. (1), sense 3, which contain only the lines listed above. The evidence that survives, though meager, remains significant.

[12] For example, Benson adds, "For his luf that heghe in hevene sittez" from *Morte Arthure* 1261 to the previously identified periphrases using that verb (p. 149). Menner had previously cited "that hathill at ("that") on highe sittis" from *Wars of Alexander* 4518 (numbered 4647 in Hoyt N. Duggan and Thorlac Turville-Petre's edition of the poem [Oxford: Early English Text Society, s.s. 10, 1989]). In Menner's view, this represents a borrowing from the *Gawain*-poet, "a relationship that the late date of *The Wars,* which there is no good reason for doubting, would in any case require" (p. xxvi). Benson notes that a variant with *wroghte* of "The prince that paradis weldes" appears in line 296 of *Winner and Waster,* the composition of which can safely be assigned to the mid-fourteenth century (see Turville-Petre, *Alliterative Poetry,* Introduction to the poem, p. 38), and that the periphrasis is also found in line 13 of *Death and Life,* an alliterative poem surviving only in the mid-seventeenth century "Percy Folio" MS., which is thought to have been composed in the late fourteenth or fifteenth century. (See the Introduction to *Death and Liffe,* ed. Joseph M. P. Donatelli [Cambridge, Mass.: The Medieval Academy of America, Speculum Anniversary Monographs Fifteen, 1989], pp. 1, 17.) Benson posits for this phrase "a complicated chain of borrowing" (p. 27 and n.

of *St. Erkenwald,* in contrast to the author of the *Gawain*-group, used "a small and conventional vocabulary" of appellations for God and Jesus Christ, and referred to the main characters of his story by a few reiterative and synonymous designations (152–53). He concluded that "the author of the saint's legend was not the *Gawain*-poet nor even one who imitated his style closely" (154).

Since the publication of Benson's essay, the negative view has established itself by default. When, for example, the question of the authorship of *St. Erkenwald* was discussed in the *Companion to the Gawain-Poet,* published in 1997, Benson was referred to without further discussion as having given it the definitive answer.[13] I submit, however, that Benson's evidence for the negative judgment is no more conclusive than the old evidence for the positive judgment. Although words and phrases formerly thought distinctive to the four poems of *Gawain*-group and *St. Erkenwald* turn out to have been used also by other poets, this in itself does not rule out the possibility that all five are the sole surviving works of a single author. Nor is common authorship ruled out by the differences between them in the content of the periphrases, or in their ways of referring to God and the main human characters of their stories: a skilled author may use different descriptive techniques at different

---

27). He further observes that "original" (that is, uniquely occurring) periphrases were devised by poets other than the author or authors of the *Gawain*-group and *St. Erkenwald*—e.g., "He that stighe ("climbed") to the sternes ("stars")" (*Morte Arthure* 3617), and "A king that kid ("renowned") is in blisse" (*Alexander and Dindimus* 431) (p. 151). He sees the *Gawain*-poet as "evidently a creator rather than a borrower, for his poems contain a great many periphrases that are apparently his own inventions. Likewise, in *St. Erkenwald* one finds not only the common "Prince that Paradis weldith" but four other periphrases, none of which appears in the Cotton Nero manuscript (pp. 147–48); these "emphasize almost exclusively God's role as Judge of man . . . an aspect of God that never appears in the Cotton Nero poems . . . and that is relatively rare in the tradition as a whole" (p. 151).

[13] Ed. Derek Brewer and Jonathan Gibson (Cambridge: D. S. Brewer, 1997). In the chapter entitled "Theories of Authorship" (pp. 23–33), Malcolm Andrew states that "since c.1950, the theory [of common authorship] has lost ground rapidly. It is reviewed in a scholarly and judicious article by Larry D. Benson, who finds the case unconvincing" (p. 28). Thorlac Turville-Petre, in the Introduction to his edition of *St. Erkenwald* in *Alliterative Poetry of the Later Middle Ages,* holds that "[t]he earlier view that the *Gawain* poet also wrote *St. Erkenwald,* while not demonstrably wrong, has nothing to support it; see Benson (1965)" (p. 102). However, T. McAlindon, in a detailed and deeply appreciative essay on the poem published in 1970, explicitly took issue with Benson: "For reasons which I hope to develop elsewhere, I cannot accept [his] conclusion that the theory of common authorship is fallacious" ("Hagiography into Art: A Study of *St. Erkenwald,*" *SP* 67 [1970]: 472–94, 475 n. 7). So far as I am aware, McAlindon has published no further account of his views on this matter.

times. The question is, What criteria can yield a valid judgment of authorial individuality in a body of works representing a shared literary tradition?

In his concluding paragraph, Benson said that "usually stylistic tests are of only secondary value; on the basis of style alone, no one would conclude that the *Miller's Tale* and the *Parson's Tale* are the work of a single author. In the case of *Erkenwald* a supposed resemblance in style is the only basis for the theory of the *Gawain*-poet's authorship. In the light of our present knowledge of alliterative style and of the style of the *Cotton Nero* poems we can now reject that theory" (154). These remarks imply what might be called, echoing Benson, a secondary conception of style, as in a reference, say, to "the style of the English Renaissance sonnet." Style so conceived is constituted by the mere presence in language of words, phrases, and syntactic formulations: raw lexicographical data that can be observed and counted. In this sense, all of the alliterative poets used the same "style" in describing the characters, settings, and actions of their narratives. Benson's achievement was to clear the way for an approach to attribution in which lexicographical research, having accomplished all it could, would be subordinated to an investigation of style in the fullest sense of that word, as the distinctive power acquired by language in the hands of the gifted poet. Individuality would be sought in the way items in a shared vocabulary and phraseology become charged with expressive force as devices contributing to the portrayal of human experience. It is fair to ask why, given that the periphrases for God occur throughout late Middle English poetry, it was the periphrases in the *Gawain*-group and *St. Erkenwald,* rather than the periphrases in other poems, that attracted the attention and interest of scholars. The explanation can only be that they acquire in these poems a saliency they lack elsewhere. In this essay, I shall investigate the expressive values acquired by certain of the periphrases and other features of language in context in one or another of the five narratives. These investigations, I hope, will support the conclusion that the poems are linked by particular and profound imaginative affinities, whose presence can be sensed beyond doubt even though it cannot be established by lexicographical evidence.[14]

---

[14] Paradoxically, my studies have yielded in the end a small body of data of the lexicographical sort (see the Appendixes below). I am grateful to Curtis M. Perrin and Jennifer L. Sisk for their assistance in my research. Ms. Sisk has kindly checked my manuscript for typographical errors and accuracy of documentation.

In making periphrastic references to God, the *Gawain*-poet drew on an aspect of the alliterative tradition that I call the "descriptive style" of the poems. It consists—to use the most general terms possible—of ways of rendering the events making up a given narrative into successive lines of alliterative verse, that is, of transforming summaries into fully realized accounts. It provided the poets with repertoires of alternative ways of expressing the traditional subject matter of the poems. It was also a mnemonically transmitted system, consisting of a limited number of items having multiple affiliations of content, vocabulary, and syntax. Within this system, the periphrases for God are linked with other, equally traditional, kinds of detail. By themselves they form a subset of the set of expressions serving in the poems to refer to God and the Redeemer. On a wider scale, they are linked by wording and syntax with the larger set of expressions used to refer to human as well as divine beings. And they are linked by metrical structure with a still larger body of descriptive details, variable in form and adapted in content to the requirements of a given narrative at a given point, in which certain verbs occupy final position in the line. The verbs used in this way belong to a traditional vocabulary consisting of words "common" in two senses: in their ordinary rather than distinctively poetic value as diction, and in the frequency of their use. These words differ in stylistic value and metrical function from an equally traditional vocabulary of distinctively poetic words. The common words were used both within the line in alliterating combinations and in nonalliterating position at the end of the line; the poetic words were used in alliterating combinations only. The traditional synonyms for "man" (which were also used to refer to God) included sets of words of both kinds.[15] The poetic vocabulary contained other sets

---

[15] In an important article entitled "Oral-Formulaic Technique and Middle English Alliterative Poetry" (*Speculum* 32 [1957]: 792–804), Ronald A. Waldron showed that the repetitiveness of the traditional descriptive style did not consist in words alone. He pointed out the presence throughout the alliterative poems of "'empty' rhythmical-syntactical 'moulds,' ready to be filled with meaning," such as "*the first* (NOUN) *that he* (VERB)" (pp. 798–99 and n. 14). (He cites *Gawain* 224 "the fyrst word that he warp," and refers, among other parallels, to *Cleanness* 377 "Fyrst feng to the flyght" and *Erkenwald* 331 "The fyrst slent that on me slode.") I find questionable in Waldron's discussion not this useful finding, but the appropriateness to his material of the terms "formula" and "formulaic." As originally conceived, and applied to Homeric epic, the "formula" was a group of words, of fixed form and descriptive content, recurrently used as a metrical unit of the line in a body of narrative verse belonging to a particular tradition. "As the worlde askes," discussed by Waldron as the basis of "one formulaic system in the second half-line" (p. 797), and cited from *Gawain* 530, *Morte Arthure* 2187, and *Death and Life* 5, is a formula in this specific sense. The "formulaic system" to which

of synonyms for subjects often referred to in the traditional stories—nouns meaning "battle" and "steed," adjectives meaning "brave" and "comely," and verbs meaning "speak" and "go." Since the members of such sets began with a variety of letters and could be used interchangeably to alliterate with words having no readily available synonyms, they were a technical aid to the poet in the process of translating narrative content into lines of verse. The poetic words died out with the alliterative tradition; most of the common words are still in use.

For the sake of economy, and to facilitate comparison with poems by other authors,[16] I shall largely restrict my discussion of the *Gawain*-poet's use of the traditional descriptive style to three verbs belonging to the common vocabulary as described above: *to sit, to lie,* and *to stand,* discussing the first two at some length and the third more briefly. The periphrases for God containing the verb *to sit* provide a natural point of departure. In calling the expression "He that on hyghe syttes" periphrastic, we are saying that it is a "roundabout" (Greek *peri-*, around, + *phrasos,* speech) way of referring to a being who could have been designated by a single word. The experienced reader recognizes it as a literary device taking the form of a definition in which an attribute (here, an activity in a given location) serves as "differentia" for the

---

Waldron assigns it includes such variations as "as the dede askez" (*Gawain* 1327) and "when the tyme asket" (*Destruction of Troy* 10787). He is able to include in a single diagram all the variant wordings of the formula that he found in the sixteen poems he examined. But he then goes on to say that this system, in turn, is "only part of a wider system of second half-lines ending in *askes,"* in some of which *askes* means not "asks" but "ashes" (ibid.). The permutations and combinations of such a "system" are virtually limitless; were additional poems representing the tradition to come to light, further variants would no doubt be found. It has thus seemed to me preferable to describe the various kinds of repetition exemplified by the traditional descriptive style in more general terms. Given the fact that "formulas," properly so called, rarely appear in it, the term "formulaic" can be applied to it only loosely.

I am in full agreement with Waldron's view of the relation between Old English and Middle English alliterative poetry: "It seems beyond doubt that there was some sort of continuity in the use of alliterative meter between the eleventh and the fourteenth century, although there are virtually no written records. The most convincing evidence of this is that the meter developed in just the direction and to just the extent that one would have expected if it had been in use all the time" (p. 793).

[16] I am deeply indebted to Professor Hoyt N. Duggan for his generosity in making available to me an electronic database stored with the texts of the major poems of the "alliterative school," and thus enabling me to track selected words in the works of the *Gawain*-poet's fellow poets. I obtained similar data for the Cotton Nero poems and *St. Erkenwald* from *A Concordance to Five Middle English Poems,* ed. Barnet Kottler and Alan M. Markman (Pittsburgh, Pa.: University of Pittsburgh Press, 1966).

"genus" expressed by the noun:[17] the Christian God is the male person (*he, prince*, etc.) whose seat of authority is located in Heaven. In this and other such clauses, the verb imputes dominion rather than physical posture.[18] It also appears in the alliterative poems in expressions of analogous meaning describing pagan deities and secular authorities such as kings. With reference to human as opposed to divine beings, its sphere of reference is sometimes physical rather than social: it may signify simply the occupation of a seat in a certain place at a certain time. The author of *Wars of Alexander* uses *to sit* in all these ways. It appears, as noted earlier, in a periphrasis for the Christian God in line 4647 "that hathill at ("that") on highe sittis."[19] It refers to the pagan God Serapis in line 161 "Sire Sirraphis at sittis in his trone," and to King Darius when he describes himself, at the opening of a letter to Alexander, as "The kynge . . . of kyngis all othire, . . . / The soverayne sire of my soyle that sittis in my trone" (lines 1845, 1848). But in lines 47–48, "Emang his duykis on a day, as he [Anectanabus] on dese ("dais") syttis, / Than was him bodword ("a message") unblyth broght to the sale," and line 792, "Than strenys he [Alexander] hys steropes and streght up [he] sittes [on Bucephalus]," the verb has the meaning relevant to physical position. The *Gawain*-poet, too, uses *to sit* in clauses signifying position in the physical sense, at table or elsewhere, for example, in *Gawain*, line 110, "Agravayn a la dure mayn on that other syde [of Sir Gawain] sittes [at King Arthur's feast]," and *Cleanness*, lines 1499–1500, "Now a boster on benche [Balthasar] bibbes ("drinks") thereof [from the holy vessels] / Tyl he be dronkken as the devel and dotes ther he sittes."

These clauses, taken together, exemplify a contrast between two kinds of detail that I will call "definitional" and "expository." Details of the former kind, as I said, express characteristic actions or inherent attributes enabling a knowledgeable reader to identify the referent. Details

---

[17] Periphrasis is defined in *The New Princeton Encyclopedia of Poetry and Poetics* (ed. Alex Preminger and T. V. F. Brogan [Princeton: Princeton University Press, 1993] as "a roundabout expression" interpreted via "a culturally perceived relationship"; its history is traced from classical Greek and Latin poetry, through Old English and other Germanic poetic traditions, to "its occasional appearance in the work of modernists such as T. S. Eliot" (p. 896).

[18] The relevant definition of *sitten* v. in *MED* is "to sit enthroned in Heaven" (sense 3[f]).

[19] I quote the edition of *Wars* by Hoyt Duggan and Thorlac Turville-Petre (Early English Text Society, 1989).

of the latter kind provide information that elaborates the ongoing narrative line. The two differ in that the actions or attributes signified by the former are abstracted from, and those of the latter kind located in, ongoing time—one is timeless, the other time-bound. In the periphrasis "He that on hyghe sittez," referring to God, the meaning of *sittez* is like that of the meaning of *rises* in "The Mississippi River rises in northern Minnesota"; both clauses are definitional, and hold true without temporal limitation. In details referring to earthly sovereigns that impute power or a claim to power, the attribute is similarly conceived. But when the verb simply signifies the occupation of a seat on a particular occasion, the clause containing it is expository, and furthers the action by telling us something new.

The grammatical terms "stative" and "dynamic" express a distinction corresponding, by and large, to this distinction between kinds of meaning. To quote *A Comprehensive Grammar of the English Language*,[20] "stative situation types," as expressed by finite verbs, include "[q]ualities," or "relatively permanent . . . properties of the subject referent" ("Mary has blue eyes") and "states" ("Mary has a bad cold"). Verbs expressing qualities and states "[n]ormally . . . do not occur with the progressive [aspect]" (ibid.). Thus, the class to which a verb in a given sentence belongs can be determined by recasting it in the progressive: it is stative if the sentence, so translated, changes in meaning.[21] When Darius's description of himself in *Wars of Alexander*, line 1848, is restated as "the sovereign sire that *is sitting* on my throne," the verb changes from stative to dynamic and the clause becomes expository rather than definitional. We then take it to mean that Darius is holding power only temporarily, or that he has taken his place on the throne on a certain occasion. In clauses whose content is expository, the verbs are dynamic, and translations into the progressive aspect are understood as equivalent in force to the originals: Anectanabus *is sitting* on the dais on a certain day, Agravayn *is sitting* on the other side of Sir Gawain, Balthasar *is sitting* drunken at the feast.[22]

[20] Ed. Randolph Quirk et al. (London and New York: Longman, 1985), 4.28.

[21] "If sentences such as ["Mary has blue eyes" and "Mary has a bad cold"] do occur with the progressive, it is a sign that they have been in some sense reinterpreted as containing a dynamic predication" (ibid.).

[22] What is true of *sittez* in the periphrases for God is true for other periphrases containing verbs in the present tense. Those containing verbs in the past tense, such as "the wyghe that al wroght" and "the renk that on the rode dyed" (see note 12 above), refer to actions that are part of salvation history. Though their verbs do not express "definitional," i.e., unchanging, attributes, they resemble definitional verbs in that the actions they signify are conceived of as accomplished facts rather than as taking place

I said above that the meaning of *sittez* in the periphrases for God is "regularly definitional" in that the action it signifies, like the deity himself, is conceived of in abstraction from ongoing time. I must now qualify this generalization. It does indeed seem to hold true for all such expressions in poems other than those in MS. Cotton Nero (as it happens, no periphrases for God containing forms of *to sit* appear in *St. Erkenwald*). But a variant of the stock expression in *Patience* presents a striking, and significant, exception to the rule. After the prophet Jonah has heard God command him to go to Niniveh, the poet has him rationalize his refusal to obey as follows:

"Oure Syre syttes," he says, "on sege so hyghe
In his glowande glorye, and gloumbes ful lyttel ("feels little sorrow")
Thagh I be nummen ("captured") in Nunnive and naked dispoyled,
On rode rwly ("grievously") torent with rybaudes mony."

(93–96)

A translation of *sittes* into the progressive aspect reveals that its meaning has taken on, in context, a dynamic component. God "is sitting," the prophet thinks, enthroned in his heavenly glory, and will "be feeling" little sorrow if he falls into enemy hands and is roughly treated. In these lines, the poet adapts an item from the repertoire of periphrases describing God in such a way as to enlarge definitional with what I have called expository force, placing what is normally timeless in the temporal continuity of human experience as imagined in the narration. When we examine further the use of the traditional descriptive style in the other poems of the *Gawain*-group and *St. Erkenwald,* we will repeatedly see signs of this same preoccupation with time-located and temporary circumstances.

---

in ongoing time. The statements containing them would change in meaning, taking on circumstantial force, if they were translated into the progressive aspect. "Christ died on the cross" states a fact; "Christ was dying on the cross" sounds like part of a narrative: "While Christ was dying on the cross, the soldiers cast lots for his garments." See the discussion of "Event, state, and habit in the past" in Quirk et al., *Comprehensive Grammar*, 4.14 and 4.15. The factual statement "Christ died on the cross" signifies, in their terminology, "a happening in the past [considered] as a complete unit, with a beginning and an end" (4.15). It is significant that, among the periphrases cited by Benson from works not attributed to the *Gawain*-poet, verbs in the past tense outnumber verbs in the present tense by about two to one. Among the periphrases cited from the Cotton Nero poems and *St. Erkenwald,* the opposite is true. This poet, or poets, knew of and acknowledged God's actions as facts located in the past, but preferred to imagine Him in the present. See below.

Two other verbs in *Patience,* in an expansion of the biblical story original with the *Gawain*-poet, are modified in the same way as *sittes.* After Jonah has embarked for Tarshish, the narrator dismisses him with contempt for having foolishly disregarded God's omnipotence and omnipresence. He does not fear the consequences of his action, but he will soon be brought up short, because God has means of accomplishing things in the world he "planted" (111) that he can call on whenever he wishes to: "at wylle hatz he slyghtes" (130). The noun phrase that anticipates *he* in this line consists of an appellation for God, "the Welder ("wielder") of wyt" (129), perhaps original with the poet, followed by two periphrastic relative clauses describing him:

> the Welder of wyt that wot alle thynges,
> That ay ("ever") wakes and waytes ("watches"), at wylle hatz he slyghtes.
> (129–30)

God is by definition always "awake," and he has by definition a comprehensive awareness of human history, past, present, and future, but he is also imagined by the narrator of the passage as "staying awake" and "watching" as Jonah sets sail from Joppa.

Eternity is similarly brought into the earthly time of the narrative, with the addition of a dynamic meaning to a statement that is normally definitional, in *St. Erkenwald.* The passage in question concerns not the divine ruler but the life of the heavenly realm, represented, by an important concept in Christian doctrine, as a feast in which the souls of the blessed participate. The appeal of this symbol to the imagination of the *Gawain*-poet is shown by his use of it in *Cleanness* and *Pearl.* Its most important biblical source is a parable found in somewhat different forms in Matthew 22 and Luke 14. In *Cleanness,* the poet cites and follows the version in Matthew, which tells of a king who holds a feast to celebrate the marriage of his son, first narrating the story (51–160), then summarizing Christ's interpretation of it (161–64).

In *Pearl,* the symbol of the heavenly banquet is invoked through a play on two Middle English words. When the maiden describes to the dreamer the life she leads with her companions as brides of the Lamb, she tells him that "the Lombe . . . myrthez ("gives joy to") uus alle at uch a mes" (861–62).[23] *Mes* here means both "a meal or feast" (*mes*

---

[23] I quote from *Pearl,* ed. E. V. Gordon (Oxford: Clarendon Press, 1953).

n.[2], sense 3, in *MED*) and "the celebration . . . of the Eucharistic service" (*messe* n.[1] sense 1a). This latter is also, of course, a kind of anticipatory feast celebrated in the mortal realm, at which the body and blood of Christ are consumed, in the form of consecrated bread and wine, by the priest or the communicants present, or both.[24]

In *St. Erkenwald,* we hear of the heavenly banquet in the words of the body of the pagan judge when, animated temporarily by God (191), it responds to Bishop Erkenwald's exhortation to reveal its worldly identity and its situation in the afterlife (179–88). It says that because the judge lived too early to know of the Redemption, his soul "sits" (293) in the limbo from which Christ rescued the patriarchs, exiled from

> that soper, that solempne fest
> Ther richely hit arne refetyd ("refreshed") that after right hungride.
>
> (303–4)

"Hungrie in-wyt helle-hole," the soul may "herken after meeles ("meals") / Long er ho that soper se ("sees that supper") other segge hyr to lathe ("or anyone invites her to it")" (307–8). After a tear fallen from the eyes of the compassionate bishop has baptized it, the body announces that its soul has been transported to heaven, and "ryght now to soper . . . is sette at the table" in "the cenacle[25] . . . ther soupen alle trew" (332, 336). This last clause ("where all the faithful dine") has a definitional meaning in Christian doctrine: heaven is a banquet hall where the faithful feast eternally. But in *St. Erkenwald,* the body has been speaking of its soul as existing continuously, "sitting" in limbo, and "harkening" to the sounds of the heavenly feast beyond the darkness that encompasses it. Given the fact that the soul "ryght now . . . is sette at the table," *soupen* permits of translation into "are dining," just

---

[24] In Section XIX, at the climactic point of his vision, the dreamer watches the activity of Heaven in process, describing it in verbs that consistently have dynamic force; the members of the procession, *moving* along with great delight, seem to him "as mylde as maydenez . . . at mas" (1115). Though the procession is surreal—those who participate in it are simultaneously departing, moving forward, and arriving—the dreamer experiences it as taking place in earthly time. See "The Many and the One: Contrasts and Complementarities in the Design of *Pearl,*" in Marie Borroff, *Traditions and Renewals* (New Haven: Yale University Press, 2003), pp. 136–37.

[25] The term *cenacle* is metaphorically transferred by the poet to the heavenly banquet hall from the *cenaculum* or "dining-room" of Acts 2 in the Latin Vulgate Bible (cf. 1.13), where the Holy Spirit descended to the disciples at Pentecost. I discuss this detail further below.

as *sittes* in *Patience,* line 93, and *wakes* and *waytes* in line 130 permit of translation into "is sitting," "is staying awake," and "is watching." The author of *Erkenwald,* like the author of the Cotton Nero poems, imagines the divine sovereign and the divine realm as existing at once eternally and in a temporal continuity projected from human experience.

I turn now to details containing the verb *to sit* that refer to human rather than divine actions. Of these, a relative clause describing the hero in Part I of *Sir Gawain and the Green Knight* is of particular interest. Sir Gawain is first mentioned in the poem in an account of the knights and other notables, including the queen, who are present at King Arthur's New Year's Day feast. The adjective modifying the proper name used as an appellation by the poet at that point—"gode Gawain" (109)—reappears throughout the poem with the value of an epithet (like "Odysseus of many stratagems" or "pious Aeneas") signifying the virtuousness intrinsic to the hero: he is essentially and always "good." More than two hundred lines later, after the Green Knight has challenged the court to play the Beheading Game with him, he enters the action of the poem. The narrator introduces him thus:

> Gawan, that sate by the quene,
> To the kyng he can enclyne ("bow"),
> (339–40)

In this detail, the poet confers on the hero an identity that is not intrinsic but might rather be called accidental or incidental, constituted by his occupancy at a certain moment in the narrative of a certain position in the scene. The combination of name and relative clause resembles a periphrasis;[26] if it were changed to "He that sat by the queen," it would become one, and we would interpret it, as we interpret "He that died on the cross," on the basis of our knowledge—here, knowledge we have derived from the poem itself. I shall call this sort of descriptive detail an "embedded periphrasis"; we will meet other examples of it in the other

---

[26] I disregard here and elsewhere a distinction irrelevant to my argument: in true periphrases, as defined earlier, the referent of the relative clause is a noun or pronoun rather than a proper name. The presence of a name makes it unnecessary to deduce the identity of the person referred to in traditional fashion. A further difference between these constructions and periphrases of the traditional sort should also be noted: their verbs, in grammatical terminology, are not stative but dynamic: "Gawain, who sat by the queen" is equivalent to "Gawain, who was sitting by the queen."

poems of the *Gawain*-group and *St. Erkenwald*, but I have found none in the rest of the alliterative corpus.[27]

Gawain's literal position, of course, has social implications as well: it bespeaks his high status at court as the king's nephew. And beyond that, it has implications for his state of mind, as we learn from the speech he makes after bowing to the king. He wishes to act in response to the Green Knight's challenge, and he believes that he is entitled to take the king's place, but he feels bound to remain on "this benche" (344) until he has permission to rise. The detail is of minor importance and can easily go unnoticed; I discuss it at some length because it is a sign of an important tendency or bias in the poet's way of imagining narrative material that is akin to the tendency I noted earlier in his treatment of the periphrases for God, in which he brings the timeless realm of the divine into the imagined human realm of temporal process. His description of Sir Gawain, once the Green Knight has issued his challenge, as the knight sitting next to the queen who bows to the king and asks his permission to leave his place, shows this same interest in the time-located and the temporary. He fixes our attention on the hero as he responds to a situation at a particular moment in the unfolding drama, within limits imposed by his relationships to others in the scene and his sense of duty as a knight—his "position" in every sense. Throughout the narratives recounted in the *Gawain*-group and *St. Erkenwald*, we see the characters whose fortunes centrally concern us in situations defined by temporary physical "positions" whose social and psychological implications affect their experiences and govern their actions.

The *Gawain*-poet's well-known interest in ceremonial protocol is shown by his use of the verb *to sit*. Forms of this verb appear in his works in passages, such as we do not find in other alliterative poems, describing the relative placement of guests at a banquet in accordance with social status. In *Sir Gawain*, in the account of the New Year's feast at Camelot, we are told that the members of the court take their places after they have washed, "[t]he best burne ay abof, as hit best semed" (73). At Hautdesert, the narrator says that the "old ancient lady," who will turn out to be Morgan le Fay, sits "highest," in the place of honor,

---

[27] I list examples from these poems in Appendix 1(a), below at the end of this essay. In Appendix 1(b) I list examples of another kind of embedded periphrasis equally distinctive to the five poems: details in which a relative clause describes something that has happened to a character, or an action he has performed, in the immediate past.

with Lord Bertilak at her side, and that Gawain and Bertilak's wife sit together in the middle of the high table (see, in Norman Davis's revised edition of the poem[28] the note on lines 1003ff.). The food is brought first to these four; then "uche grome ("man") at his degré ("according to his rank") graythely ("properly") watz served" (1001–6). Here, Gawain's placement at the table enables the chatelaine to continue the intimate conversations she has initiated each morning, thus intensifying his uneasiness as he tries to ward off her advances without discourtesy. In *Cleanness,* the guests arriving at the wedding-feast are shown to their places at the table by a marshal; each is assigned a seat "[a]s he watz dere ("noble") of degré" (92). In *St. Erkenwald,* though the seating arrangements at the heavenly feast are not described, the narrator pays attention in similar fashion to comparative degrees of rank in his account of the bishop's passage from the cathedral to the tomb. Lords bow to him as he passes along the aisle, and those who accompany him are mentioned in order of status: barons walk beside him, followed by the mayor, who is attended by citizens of importance and by bearers of the mace, symbolizing high office (138, 142–43). At the end of the poem, a marshal reminiscent of the marshal in *Cleanness* ceremoniously escorts the redeemed soul of the pagan judge to its assigned space, a "room of its own" in heaven (337–38).

I turn next to the verb *to lie.* As used in the alliterative tradition, this verb is almost always expository in force and "dynamic" in the grammatical sense I explained above; that is, it elaborates the action via a detail signifying a changeable, time-bound state, as it does in *Wars of Alexander,* line 4902, "The kyng in his caban ("tent") with his knightis ligis ("lies/is lying")".[29] The verb seems to have been associated in Middle English, more than it is at present, with incapacitation and misfortune (cf. *MED,* senses 1, 3, and 4). When battles are described in alliterative verse, the verb appears frequently, referring to those who have fallen wounded or dead, as in *Morte Arthure,* lines 1372–73, "The gome and the grette horse at ("on") the grounde lyggez / Full gryselyche gronande, for grefe of his woundez." The *Gawain*-poet uses it similarly in *Cleanness,* line 1792, "Now is a dogge also ("as") dere [as Balthasar] that in a dych lygges," that is, "lies dead."

As with *to sit,* the position literally signified by *to lie* in certain details

[28] *Sir Gawain and the Green Knight,* ed. J. R. R. Tolkien and E. V. Gordon, 2nd ed., rev. Norman Davis (Oxford: Clarendon Press, 1967), p. 103.
[29] I quote the edition of *Wars* by Duggan and Turville-Petre (see above, note 12).

in the five poems takes on a more than literal significance. In pointing out this kind of enhancement of meaning, I begin with a statement about Sir Gawain made by the poet at the beginning of the first bed-room scene. It immediately follows a description of the departure of Lord Bertilak from Hautdesert, with a hundred companions, on the morning of the deer-hunt, a passage packed with details vividly expressive of motion and commotion. Its concluding "wheel," or four-line stanza, describes the lord as "carried away with joy," spending the day in free and vigorous activity in an arena affording his prowess full scope:

> The lorde, for blys abloy,
> Ful oft con launce and lyght,[30]
> And drof that day wyth joy
> Thus to the derk nyght.
> (1174–77)

The verse-paragraph that immediately follows begins,

> Thus laykez ("disports himself") this lorde by lynde-wodez evez
> ("linden-woood borders"),
> And Gawayn the god mon in gay bed lygez.
> (1178–79)

In these two lines, a contrast between two physical actions or states, enhanced by syntactic parallelism, is epitomized by the alliterating verbs *laykes* and *lygez*. Although the narrator makes explicit the feelings of the lord as he "disports himself," he remains silent about the inner state of the man who lies in the gay bed. But we can and should infer it from our knowledge of Gawain's plight at this point in the story: he is "on hold" on the way to an encounter that may well result in his death, but that he cannot avoid without forsaking the "trouthe," symbolized, among other virtues, by his emblematic pentangle (625–26). He stays where he is, even though sunlight is shining on the walls of his room (1180), because he is a "god mon," and therefore obedient to his tempo-rary lord, the host who has ordered him to sleep late (1039–40, 1071–

---

[30] Lines 1174–75 are translated in the notes to Davis's revised edition of *Sir Gawain* as "the lord, carried away with joy, often galloped and dismounted." (Cf. *MED abloi* ppl.)

72, 1096). This psychological constraint is made literally heavier by his material surroundings: we are told that he lies covered by costly bed-clothes within a curtain (1181). We see from his point of view the lady's entrance into the room (we do not learn who has entered until Gawain lifts the curtain and peers out), and her subsequent intrusion into the private space that encloses him. Her presence, as readers of the poem well know, constrains him still further, exerting pressure on him socially and psychologically. His helplessness in the situation is intensified by the lady's playful announcement that she has taken him captive and intends to bind him in his bed (1210–11). Reading the account as presented by the poet, we are drawn as if into a three-dimensional scene within which we share imaginatively in the experience of the hero.

The poet uses the same verb in the same way in his account of the second morning, again presenting a contrast between the free activity of Lord Bertilak and the virtual immobility of his guest (1468–69). It makes its final appearance in a relative clause describing Sir Gawain as he spends his last night at Lord Bertilak's castle before being escorted to the Green Chapel. "Wylde wederez ('weathers')" awaken in the world outside, and the "snittering" snow whose sharp crystals afflict the wild beasts is piled into great drifts by the "warbling" north wind (2000–2005).

> The leude ("man") lystened ful wel, that legh in his bedde,
> Thagh he lowkez ("locks") his liddez ful lyttel he slepes;
>
> (2006–7)

"The leude . . . that legh in his bedde," like "Gawan, that sate by the quene," is what I called earlier an "embedded periphrasis." The detail presents no new information; the narrator has already told us that Gawain is lying in bed (cf. 1989–90, 1994). It further implies the tendency I consider distinctive on the part of this poet, to confer on the central characters of his unfolding narratives, and focus our attention on, a temporally located identity. And here again, a temporarily occupied physical position has psychological implications we are made vividly aware of, though, or rather because, the narrator keeps them implicit and leads us to infer them.[31]

---

[31] Another embedded periphrasis containing the verb *to lie* appears in *Cleanness* in the episode describing God's visit to Abraham in threefold human form. In the heat of the sun, Abraham has sought the shade of an oak tree (lines 601–4). Referring to him as he rises and hastens toward his approaching guests, the narrator calls him "the lede that ther laye the levez anunder" (609).

In *St. Erkenwald,* as in the poems of the *Gawain*-group, descriptive details containing the verbs *to sit* and *to lie* describe the central characters of the narrative *mutatis mutandis,* in the same way and with the same kind of effect. Two such details appear in a passage I have discussed above, the account given by the pagan judge's dead body of the plight of its soul. Unredeemed because ignorant of the Redemption (285–89), consigned eternally to the limbo from which Christ rescued the Old Testament patriarchs when He harrowed hell (291–92), the soul is forever encompassed by a darkness beyond which it may not see:

And ther sittes my soule, that se may no fyrre ("farther"),
Dwynande ("pining away") in the derke dethe that dyght us our
    fader ("that our father prepared for us").
                                                            (293–94)

So situated, it is exiled from the endless banquet of the saved,

                        that solemn fest
Ther richely hit arne refetyd ("refreshed") that after right hungride.
                                                            (298–99)

It may "sitte ther in sorow, . . . Hungrie in-wyt helle-hole, and herken after meeles ("harken after meals"), / Longe er ho that soper se other segge hyr to lathe"—"long before she [the soul] sees that supper, or anyone invites her to it" (305, 307–8). In this passage, the poignant plight of the conscious soul, situated in an eternal darkness from within whose boundary it can actually hear the festivities taking place in the bright banquet hall of heaven—in the next room, so to speak—is one we can readily imagine in earthly terms. No such description is found in the poem's many analogues.

Forms of *to lie* appear in *St. Erkenwald* twelve times in the 320 lines that follow the 32-line prologue. In all but one of them, they signify the state of the body in the tomb, and thus take on the specific meaning "to lie dead." They appear twice in embedded periphrases of the kind I have identified in *Sir Gawain* and *Cleanness,* signifying redundantly, and thus again drawing our attention to, a positional detail we have already been informed of. In line 281, the poet refers to the body as "he that ther lay"; when Bishop Erkenwald first exhorts the body to speak, he addresses it as "lykhame ("corpse") that thus lies" (179). The verb appears in two lines in succession in the passage in which the bishop exhorts the body to tell him and the other witnesses

> "In worlde quat weghe thou was and quy thow thus ligges,
> How longe thou has layne here and quat laghe thou usyt."
> (186–87)

Shortly thereafter, though without repeating the verb, the poet again
mentions the dead body's location, calling it "the bryght body in the
buryñes" (190). Later, he describes the bishop as bending over "the liche
("corpse") ther hit lay" (314). Both of these references are redundant.

In the narration of the first bedroom scene in *Sir Gawain* and the
body's description of the plight of its soul in *St. Erkenwald,* the "situations" of the characters who concern us are spatially defined: enclosing
curtains, a visually impermeable wall or curtain separating darkness
from brightness. Readers of the *Gawain*-group will also recall the description of the bower built by Jonah in *Patience,* "happed ("enclosed")
upon ayther half," with "a nos ("opening") on the north syde and nowhere non ellez" (450–51), and of the deluge in *Cleanness,* in which
waters from above and below join to force all living creatures upward
into steadily diminishing space (363–406). The action of greatest importance in *St. Erkenwald,* too, takes place within clearly signified spatial
limits. The bishop, after celebrating mass, goes to the enclosure containing the tomb accompanied by "barones" and "the maire ("mayor")
with mony maghti men (that is, important citizens) and macers ("macebearers") before hym" (142–43). The gathering, as it enters, is shown
pressing against spatial limits: "pyne wos wyt the grete prece ("[there]
was difficulty [in finding space] for the great crowd)[32] that passyd hym
after" (141). These people stand around the bishop within this limited
space as witnesses and auditors of his conversation with the corpse, and
the poet more than once reminds us of their presence. Before addressing
the body, the bishop says that "we all" must turn to God and abandon
the attempt to understand the mystery by "at oure self ("by ourselves")"

---

[32] This line is cited by *MED* s.v. *pine* n.(1) sense 4, "difficulty, exertion." The word is
used to the same effect in *Gawain* 122–24, also cited by *MED,* where the poet says that
so many dishes were served at Arthur's New Year's feast that "pine to fynde the place
the peple biforne / For to sette the sylveren that sere sewes ("different dishes") halden /
On clothe." In both *Gawain* and *St. Erkenwald,* the word bespeaks the poet's tendency
to crowd a limited space, thus sacrificing a more traditional grandiosity of description
in favor of a stereoscopic vividness.

(170–71); during the ensuing dialogue between body and bishop, "the pepulle" stand still and listen, many of them weeping (219–20); hearing the body's lament over the situation of its soul, "alle wepyd for woo" (310).

Despite the fact that the plots of the two poems are completely different in content, the descriptive details I have cited from *St. Erkenwald* resemble those I discussed earlier in *Sir Gawain and the Green Knight* in that they enhance our vicarious experience of constraints, at once physical and psychological, affecting the central characters. In the bedroom scenes in *Gawain,* the limited space in which the hero entertains the lady enhances an anxiety we understand and sympathetically share. In *St. Erkenwald,* constraint takes the form of urgency, the compelling need felt by the bishop, once the presence of the body lying in its casket is thrust inescapably upon him, to solve without delay the baffling mysteries of its anonymity and perfectly preserved state.[33] The anxiety we sense in him, and vicariously share, is intensified by his and our awareness of his responsibility, *as* bishop, for the spiritual welfare of his flock.

My third verb, *to stand,* belongs to the same component of the traditional descriptive style as *to sit* and *to lie:* an inherited vocabulary of common verbs susceptible of use in both alliterating and final position in the long line. In alliterative poetry generally, as in present-day English, the verb either signifies upright posture or places something or someone in a scene via an expository detail.[34] But it is used in *Sir Gawain,* as it is not used in poems by other authors, to signify the presence during an event of "bystanders" in the literal sense, persons unimportant in themselves who surround an action as "supers" or "extras" do on a stage, and thus provide it with a spatial frame. These include the knights other than the hero who are present at, but take no part in, the

---

[33] Monika Otter has aptly described the impression produced by the poem as "one of tremendous nervous energy, . . . and, perhaps even more strongly, a general mood of wonder and questioning: it is as if a big question mark hangs over the entire poem." "'Newe Werke': St. Erkenwald, St. Albans, and the Medieval Sense of the Past," *Journal of Medieval and Renaissance Studies* 24 (1994): 387–414, at 404.

[34] In *The Parliament of the Three Ages,* line 289, for example, the verb refers to Elde, who says that he cannot "stale stonden ("stand up") one my fete bot ("unless") I my staffe have" ; in *Cleanness* 984, to Lot's wife, who, after her metamorphosis, becomes "Al so salt as ani se—and so ho yet standez"; in *Wars of Alexander* to the "governour of Grece, who "tas ("takes") a torche fra a tulke that ("who") by the table standis" (lines 3092, 3096). I quote *The Parliament* as edited by Thorlac Turville-Petre in *Alliterative Poetry,* pp. 67–100. For the meaning of "stale stonden" in line 289, see *stonden* in Turville-Petre's Glossary.

encounter with the Green Knight at Arthur's New Year's Feast: "Al studied *that ther stod* and stalked hym nerre ("stepped nearer to him")" (237); cf. "And runyschly ("mysteriously") he [the Green Knight] raght out *thereas renkkez stoden*" (432). (Italics added in these and other quoted lines.) (In this last line, the fact of standing takes on insidious suggestions of a cowardly reluctance to act, reminding us of the Green Knight's contemptuous statement that "al dares ("cower") for drede withoute dynt schewed!" (315). When, in the second hunt, the boar is brought to bay, the poet says that "with hym [toward the boar] then irked ("felt annoyance")[35] / Alle the burnez so bolde *that hym by stoden*" (1573–74). Again, these bold retainers do not act; it is Lord Bertilak who rides up, dismounts, and makes the kill (1581ff.). Details containing verbs other than *to stand* sometimes signify, in similar fashion, the presence of witnesses to an action, for example, lines 1171–72: "the grehoundez . . . / . . . hem tofylched ("pulled the deer down") as fast *as frekez myght loke.*" (Cf. *Cleanness* 1529: "Forthy a ferly bifel *that fele folk seghen.*") In *St. Erkenwald,* the presence of observers is of course emphasized throughout; among the details mentioning them, I consider "wehes ("men") *that stoden,*" referring to people other than the bishop who surrounded the tomb as its lid was laid aside (73), a particularly telling sign of common authorship.[36] These details, like those cited above containing the verbs *to sit* and *to lie,* locate the actions in question both in narrative time and within a bounded space.[37]

I have been discussing selected details based on the traditional descriptive style of alliterative poetry in the *Gawain*-group and *St. Erkenwald*

[35] *Irken* v. in this line is cited in *MED* under sense 2(a), "to . . . be unwilling or reluctant (to do something)." This meaning, however, would be redundant in a way uncharacteristic of the poet, for he tells us in the next line that "neghe hym non durst ("none dared approach him") / For wothe ("danger")" (lines 1575–76). It therefore seems to me to belong under sense 2(b), to . . . dislike." Cf. *irk(e* adj. sense 2(c), "troublesome, difficult, annoying."

[36] Another formulation to the same effect, telling of the reactions of "many" bystanders to an action or circumstance, is exemplified by *Gawain* 1442, "Ful grymme qhen he [the boar] gronyed ("grunted"); thenne greved mony ("many were dismayed")." Lines so formulated appear a number of times in the Cotton Nero poems and *St. Erkenwald* but not, with one exception, in the rest of the alliterative corpus. I list its occurrences, and discuss the exception, in Appendix 2 at the end of this essay.

[37] Cf. McAlindon, "Hagiography into Art," pp. 480–81: "After the vivid opening passage, . . . there are numerous, brief place-references which serve to give to the action that spatial definition which is conspicuously absent from most religious legend and romance. . . . One of the salient effects of the story [is] that of a confined space overflowing with life and significance."

as they reflect a distinctive imaginative bias whose signs I see in all five poems. Together with others, they remind us, in a given narrative, of the spatial, moral, and social constraints and limitations—most generally, the circumstances—within which the characters who most interest us act from moment to moment. This awareness leads us to understand their inner life and identify with them emotionally. "Iche tolke mon do as he is tan," says Sir Gawain, when he excuses himself to the lady for not presenting her with a love-gift—literally, "Each man must do as he is taken" (1811). A freer and fuller translation speaks more directly to the conception of human experience I see realized in the language of the Cotton Nero poems and *St. Erkenwald:* "Each man must act in accordance with the situation in which he finds himself." Each of the five poems conveys to us a vision of human experience in process, hedged about by circumstances that define its quality and influence its course.

I now turn to the second line of argument presented by Larry Benson to differentiate *St. Erkenwald* from the poems of the *Gawain*-group (see pp. 44–45 above), rephrasing each of its two branches as a question. First, why would an author who used a number of the traditional poetic words meaning "(male) person" (that is, *burne, wyghe, tulk,* and *hathel*) as appellations for God in the four poems generally attributed to him use none of these in a fifth poem? Second, why would this same author, having deployed a variety of appellations for the central characters of the four poems, use reiterative ones for the central characters of a fifth? My answer to the first and more important of these questions depends on the fact that *St. Erkenwald* differs from the other four poems in its representation of divinity as posited in Christian doctrine, with respect both to what aspect of it is represented and to how that aspect is characterized, as indeed the other four poems differ among themselves. This point will be clarified by the discussion that follows.

We obviously expect that God alone, as distinct from the other two members of the Holy Trinity, will participate in narratives set in the time frame of the Old Testament. So it is with the Jonah story in *Patience* (61–524) (though "the Master," that is, Christ, figures in the prologue [10]), and in the Old Testament stories in *Cleanness* that make up more than three quarters of the poem. But the two portrayals of God differ from each other. In both poems, he is presented as the creator of the world (Jonah, in *Patience* 206, calls him "that Wyghe . . . that wroght alle thynges," and the narrator of *Cleanness* refers to him at the beginning of the poem via the same periphrasis [5]). But in *Cleanness,* where the narratives are dominated by the poet's idiosyncratic conception of purity, he is also portrayed as the lord of a heavenly court modeled on the great courts on earth (17–20). And the poet emphasizes a trait in him that the God of *Patience* does not possess: he is "scoymus," that is, "squeamish or fastidious" (21), nauseated as well as offended by evil (305–6). Christ, as well as God, appears in *Cleanness;* he is the subject of a long passage connecting the story of the destruction of Sodom with that of the Chaldean conquest of Jerusalem, in which the Virgin Mary appears as well, exemplifying spiritual and physical purity. In *Pearl,* as I have argued at length elsewhere, Christ predominates over God in the symbolic forms of the Lamb and the Pearl,[38] and the Virgin Mary is invoked by the maiden as Empress over the 144,000 queens who are seen following the Lamb in the penultimate section of the poem. *Sir Gawain* is unique in being a secular, though in part surreal, drama. We see the divine from the point of view of human society in religious observances at Camelot and Hautdesert, in the role of the Virgin as Gawain's patroness and protector, and in the speech of the characters *passim,* as when, replying to Lord Bertilak's statement that he is pleased to be visited by Sir Gawain "at Goddez awen fest" (1035), the hero replies "al the honour is your awen—the heghe Kyng yow yelde!" (1038). It is not surprising that only in *Sir Gawain* does a periphrasis for God contain the word *mensk.* At the end of the encounter at the Green Chapel, Gawain expresses the hope that "He . . . that yarkkez ("confers") al menskes" will repay Lord Bertilak for his invitation to return to Hautdesert (2410). *MED* translates the word in this line as "kindness" or "humaneness" (s.v. *mensk(e* n. sense 2[a]). Of these the second is the more apposite, for *mensk* is cognate with Old Icelandic *mennska* "human nature" (ibid.).

In *St. Erkenwald,* on the other hand, the supernal presence of greatest importance is the Holy Spirit, the member of the Holy Trinity least accessible to the human imagination. It enters the action explicitly when, after Erkenwald has prayed "welnyghe al the nyght" (119) to be allowed to clarify the mystery presented by the perfectly preserved body, he is granted "[a]n ansuare of the Holy Goste" (127). That morning, he

---

[38] "[His] presence . . . underlies the changing content of the successive sections as a ground bass in music underlies a series of changing melodies and harmonizations." "The Many and the One: Contrasts and Complementarities in the Design of *Pearl,*" in Marie Borroff, *Traditions and Renewals: Chaucer, the Gawain-Poet, and Beyond* (New Haven: Yale University Press, 2003), pp. 124–62, at 148.

conducts in the cathedral a "masse . . . / Of *Spiritus Domini*" (131–32); though scholars differ as to the exact identity of this mass,[39] we understand that the bishop, in celebrating it, is invoking the divine being through whose agency God's grace has come to him. Moreover, the speech addressed by Erkenwald to the crowd in the enclosure under the cathedral contains two allusions to the Holy Spirit, which the poet would have been conscious of, and which would have been recognized by most members, if not all, of a late fourteenth-century audience. Responding to the Dean's account of the mystery that neither he nor any of his colleagues can solve (146–58) with a curt "Thu says sothe" (159), he proceeds to draw a devastating comparison between the limited scope of human understanding and the "providens of the prince that paradis weldes" (161).[40] From this he concludes that when men's intellectual powers are at a loss, they must turn to "the comforthe of the creatore" (167) whose grace, when sought, unstintingly provides "counselle and comforthe" (172). "Comforter" was and is a name for the Holy Spirit.[41] In addition, in saying that God has no difficulty in "releasing with a finger" what human hands are powerless to control, he alludes to a traditional image of the Spirit as "finger of God."[42]

But in a more profound sense, the power of the Holy Spirit underlies

[39] McAlindon identifies "the masse . . . of *Spiritus Domini*" as "the mass of Pentecost Sunday" (p. 488), a view with which Peterson concurs (p. 48). But Gordon Whatley, in "The Middle English *St. Erkenwald* and Its Liturgical Context" (*Mediaevalia* 8 [1982], pp. 277–306), argues convincingly against this identification: "the mass of *Spiritus Domini* is best taken as the votive mass, *Missa de Sancto Spiritu*. The latter . . . is appropriate in the context because it is a formal liturgical invocation of the power of the Holy Spirit for special occasions, such as here where there is an immediate need to promote the Bishop's and the people's *spede* in their encounter with the dead. Moreover it appears to have been closely associated with the legal profession and the civil government, since it was the mass that the judges attended at the beginning of each law term both in England and France" (pp. 278–79).

[40] Peterson describes Erkenwald's reply as "gently undercut[ting] pompous ecclesiasts who overstate the obvious" (p. 19). His point about the Dean's speech is well taken, but the bishop's words sound to me loftily dismissive rather than "gentle."

[41] See *MED* s.v. *comfortour* n. sense 1(a), "Of the Holy Ghost, Jesus, the Virgin: one who gives spiritual strength or solace." The word *comforter* continues in use today in John 14.16 and other relevant verses in the Authorized Version.

[42] See *MED* s.v. *finger* n. sense 2, "*finger of God,* a designation of the Holy Spirit or of the power and working of God through the Holy Spirit." The third stanza of the famed ninth-century hymn "Veni, Creator Spiritus" invokes the Holy Spirit as "dextrae dei tu digitus" (quoted in Frederick Raby, *A History of Christian-Latin Poetry* [Oxford: Clarendon Press, 1927], p. 183). I suspect that the poet's statement that the Dean of the cathedral pointed with a finger ("wyt fynger he mynte" 145) in speaking of the body carries an ironic suggestion of the divine agency he and his colleagues have ignored in their scholarly research.

the whole poem. The word *cenacle,* used by the body in its concluding speech to refer to the place to which its soul has been translated (336), alludes, as I said earlier, to an event of crucial importance in the early history of the Christian church, recounted in chapter 2 of Acts: the descent of the Holy Spirit on the disciples as they shared a meal in a *coenaculum* (l.13) or dining room at Pentecost. The gift of tongues conferred on them on this occasion enabled them to preach the gospel in all the languages of the "Jews, devout men out of every nation under heaven," who were then living in Jerusalem (2.5–6). As the primary agency of conversion, the Holy Spirit was operative in the westward progress of the Christian faith, which eventually extended to England; the poem begins with an account of the conversion of the Anglo-Saxons under the aegis of Saint Augustine.

The main theme of the poem has been variously identified by various scholars, most recurrently as some form of conversion or transformation.[43] But I argue elsewhere that a theme of even greater importance is that of confirmation in the specifically Christian sense of the word[44]—a theme whose presence has been alluded to in passing in the scholarly literature (for example, by McAlindon, p. 477), but, so far as I am aware, not adequately acknowledged. As conceived of in Christian doctrine, confirmation was and is "the rite whereby the grace of the Holy Spirit is conveyed in a new or fuller way to those who have already received it . . . at Baptism;" it can be administered only by a bishop (*Oxford Dictionary of the Christian Church,* 3rd ed., 1997, s.vv. *confirmation,*

---

[43] According to McAlindon, "the legend contains three themes: perversion and conversion . . . ; human and divine wisdom; worldly and spiritual royalty. . . . These themes are interdependent" ("Hagiography into Art," p. 476). Lester L. Faigley finds that the "motif [of] transformation, anchored within historical time near Christ's immolation [in lines 1–32], establishes the tone and theme of the legend that follows" ("Typology and Justice in *St. Erkenwald,*" *American Benedictine Review* 29 [1978]: 381–90, p. 383). Vincent F. Petronella sees the poem as unified partly "through the theme of transformation," identifying as "other unifying features of the poem: first, references to words denoting labor, . . . and the use of a particular word, "name," and, second, descriptions which appeal to the aural sense" ("*St. Erkenwald:* Style as the Vehicle for Meaning," *JEGP* 66 [1967]: 532–40, p. 537). For Russell A. Peck, "*St. Erkenwald* is fundamentally about baptism and regeneration. The poet unfolds his plot through three analogous and concentric events, all of which describe new beginnings out of old failures" ("Number Structure in *St. Erkenwald,*" *Annuale Mediaevale* 14 [1973]: 9–21, p. 13).

[44] "*St. Erkenwald:* Narrative and Narrative Art," forthcoming in 2005 in *Spirited Thought in Late Medieval Literature: Essays in Honor of Elizabeth Kirk,* ed. Bonnie Wheeler (New York: Palgrave Macmillan).

bishop).[45] What takes place in the enclosure below St. Paul's Cathedral, as those standing there witness the conversation between Erkenwald and the dead body and the miraculous baptism that follows, is in effect a ceremony designed to confirm the faith of the congregation, as the bishop himself indicates when he tells the assembly that God will send his comfort and counsel "in fastynge ("strengthening, confirming") of your faithe" (173). (See *MED* s.v. *fasten* v. [1] senses 7a and b.)

The implicit foregrounding of the Holy Spirit throughout *St. Erkenwald* partly accounts for what Benson thought implied an author other than the *Gawain*-poet: the absence from the poem of periphrases for God containing poetic words for man, such as appear in the Cotton Nero group.[46] But their absence is also due to an aspect of the poem's dramatic structure that I have not mentioned so far. The first eighty lines, or about one-fourth, of the story proper, extending from Erkenwald's assumption of Saint Augustine's episcopal office in London (33–34) to his return from Essex to St. Paul's (113), contain no references whatever to the Christian divinity in any of its forms. The subject matter of this part of the poem is wholly secular. The narrator describes in specific and, where appropriate, concrete detail the engagement of a series of groups of people in various kinds of worldly "busy-ness:" the masons hewing hard stones "wyt eggit ("edged") toles" (40), the "grubber in grete ("grit")"(41) searching the cathedral foundations; the clerks with their shaven crowns (55) vainly attempting to pronounce the bright gold letters of the inscription and decipher their meaning; the "mony hundrid" Londoners, meticulously categorized by status and occupation, flocking to St. Paul's (57–64); the mayor arriving with his retinue and consulting with the sexton (65–66); the lifting of the tomb's heavy marble lid by "wyght werke-men" using "prises ("levers")" and "crowes of yrne" (69–70); the cathedral clerics searching all available records day after day in the best scholarly fashion for some reference

---

[45] A quotation from the works of John Drury dated c. 1434 in *MED* s.v. *confirmacioun* n., sense 4, "the sacrament or rite of confirmation," reads "The sacrament of confirmacion mynystrid be bischopis handis confermyd the holy gost in the persone baptyzid."

[46] Peterson explains the absence of such periphrases as due to "the poetic necessities of the work. . . . In a very short poem, the poet must make it clear that God is spiritual and that his spiritual quality is to be contrasted to the mere physical qualities of miracles. . . . To describe God as a *tulk,* or a *wygh* (misprinted *wyght*), or a *hathel* would only blur the distinction between God and man" (Introduction, p. 18). The general point made by these comments seems to me valid, and useful, but I would emphasize the implicit presence of the Holy Spirit throughout the narrative rather than the "spiritual quality" of God Himself.

to the evidently royal personage buried below (101–4). The throng of Londoners converging on the cathedral behaves as if responding to the news of an amazing act in a traveling circus; the clerics treat the mystery as a problem that can be solved by research in a library. The shift from this confidence in human agency to the bishop's dismissal of it enacts a dramatic contrast of great power.

Accordingly, the periphrases for God contained in the poem appear only after the secular phase of the action has ended. What is of most importance at that point, given the situation as the poet dramatizes it, is the contrast between God's power and human helplessness. This accounts for the fact the nouns in expressions referring to him signify his sovereignty, rather than his imagined identity as a male being in general. Bishop Erkenwald calls Him "the *prince* that paradis weldes" (161), and the body, explaining that its exemption from decay was a reward from God for the unswerving righteousness of the judge on earth, calls Him "the riche *kynge* . . . that ryght ever alowes" (267). (*Alowes,* translated "accepts, approves" in Peterson's note, must rather mean "rewards"; *MED* s.v. *allouen* v. sense 5[a] "to . . . reward [good deeds, etc.]" cites *Pearl* 634, where the maiden, referring to the fact that those who came latest to the vineyard are paid the same by the owner as the others, asks "Why schulde he not her labour alow?"[47] The next line is "Yys, and pay hym at the fyrst fyne?")

The above analysis shows that whoever wrote *St. Erkenwald* was an artist of the first order, an opinion I am by no means the first to express.[48] What is more to my purpose, however, is that in the fleshing out of the story, as I have analyzed it, we see at work the same circumstantial bent, the same focus on the situation of the central characters of the drama from moment to moment, that I described above as distinctive in the imagination of the *Gawain*-poet. It should not surprise us to find that the reiterations noted somewhat dismissively by Ben-

---

[47] Two other periphrases have pronouns as subjects. The body refers to God as "He . . . that loves ryght best" (line 272). Erkenwald echoes this description when he questions the body about the judge's soul, saying that "He that rewardes uche a renke as he has right servyd / Myght evel forgo the ("thee") to gyfe of His grace summe brawnche" (lines 275–76).

[48] McAlindon eloquently describes *St. Erkenwald* as a "beautiful and wholly successful poem by any standards. . . . In a reading of this poem the hagiographical context alerts us to the presence of a talent sufficiently bold and original to succeed in an extremely conventionalized narrative tradition" (p. 472). Its author "was expert in the specifically narrative art of exciting expectations which are fulfilled in a wholly unexpected manner" (p. 475).

son[49]—of *body* (twelve times), plus the synonyms *corce* (once), *liche* (once), and *lykhame* (twice) in referring to the occupant of the tomb, and of *bishop* (fifteen times), *prelate* (twice), and *primate* (once), as well as *segge* (twice) and *lede* (once) in referring to Erkenwald himself—are in fact strategic, working to underscore what is central to the role of each of his two main actors. The poet's repetition of the word *body* and its synonyms, like his repetitive use of the verb *to lie,* keeps impressing on our attention the presence of the enigmatic shape in the tomb.[50] His avoidance of both the common and the poetic words for male person in referring to the body also shows his awareness that what lies before the spectators, its soul being absent, is not a man.[51] Compelling evidence for this is provided by a change in verbal tactics, as inconspicuous as it is momentous, that takes place immediately after one of the tears the bishop is shedding on the tomb falls on the body's face. At that point, the narrator, in saying that "the freke syked ("sighed") (323), refers to the dead judge for the first time as a human being.[52] Its miraculous exemption from physical change having come to an end, it has reentered

---

[49] "The author of *St. Erkenwald* uses a small and conventional vocabulary [in referring to God]. . . . [He] employs as small a vocabulary for designating his saintly hero as for God. . . . His hero is almost invariably 'Erkenwald,' 'biscop,' 'prelate,' or 'primate,' and the pagan judge is usually 'body,' 'mon,' or 'cors' " (pp. 152–53).

[50] McAlindon puts it thus: "By continually designating Erkenwald's interlocutor as 'the corpse' and 'the body' . . . [the poet] keeps the central, amazing fact in the foreground of consciousness" (p. 483).

[51] William A. Quinn presents a helpful account of the body's state as it would have been understood in the poet's time in "The Psychology of *St Erkenwald*" (*MÆ* 53 [1984]: 180–93). Having quoted Saint Thomas Aquinas's definition of life as "the body's union with the soul," Quinn goes on to say, "The *Erkenwald*-poet apparently refuses to acknowledge that this composite of body and soul has been fully effected by the miracle of the judge's reanimation. The form of the mere corpse (distinguishable as such from the form of a human being) can theoretically endure indefinitely as something else (and in *St. Erkenwald* it does), but not as the *corpus* of the judge. Therefore, even after the corpse's *animation* all narrative references to the judge in *St. Erkenwald* are either simply pronominal or impersonal: *this ilke body, that body, the liche.* . . . His *soul,* it seems, remains distinguishable from 'some ghost' and remains elsewhere apart from these physical remains" (pp. 184–85).

[52] The nicety with which the poet deploys appellations is also evident in the first episode of *Sir Gawain.* When the Green Knight appears in Arthur's court, he is so outlandish that his worldly status, if any, is unclear. The narrator first calls him "an aghlich ("fearful") mayster" (136), then a "gome" (151, 178, 179), a "freke" (196), a "hathel" (221), and a "wyghe" (249). He is first addressed by Arthur as "wyghe" (252), then, after he explains that he has armor and weapons at home but has chosen not to wear them, as "Sir cortays knyght" (276). Only after the "covenant" has been agreed on, and the visitor makes clear that he has a place of residence and a name (408), does the narrator refer to him as "the Green Knight" (417).

the realm of human mortality.[53] Once it has joyfully reported that its soul has been translated from limbo to heaven, it turns to dust.[54]

In accounting for the poet's reiterative designation of Erkenwald as a bishop or prelate, I begin with the observation I made earlier that no references to the divine in any aspect appear in the first quarter of the narrative. Once Erkenwald arrives at St. Paul's, a turn of major importance takes place as emphasis shifts from the secular to the sacred. In subsequent references to him, the words *bishop* and *prelate* recurrently insist on his high status as church official. When, in response to the Dean's presentation, he launches into his eloquent description of God's beneficence and power, the elaborately formal periphrasis the poet uses in referring to him—"the segge that sacrid ("consecrated") was byschop" (159)—speaks to the authority vested in him by the ecclesiastical establishment. The words he addresses to God and the spectators at the tomb make clear his realization that the faith of the people in his charge urgently needs the revitalizing, the confirming, that he prays to be allowed to accomplish. In every aspect of its presentation, then, the story as dramatized by this poet would seem to stress the indispensable functions in society of the church and its high officers, who do or should manifest a personal sanctity befitting their worldly eminence.[55] This is

[53] "By baptism, therefore, the pagan judge is—if not biologically, then psychologically—born again in *St Erkenwald,* and the narrator acknowledges him as a person (*freke*) for the first time only in line 323" (Quinn, "The Psychology of *St Erkenwald,*" p. 188).

[54] Morse comments insightfully on the meaning of this change: "It is a splendid touch that salvation is immediately followed by bodily dissolution: everyone had thought that the preservation of the 'ferly' was the miracle, but the true miracle was the salvation of the heathen, to which the wonder was the means" (p. 39).

[55] Though I have not attempted in this study to place *St. Erkenwald* in its historical context, I believe that William Kamowski is right in thinking that "the poem—in its perspectives on baptism, on justice and mercy, and on the temporal and spiritual powers of the Church—constitutes an argument against major Wycliffite challenges to the efficacy and authority of the established Church at the end of the fourteenth century" ("*Saint Erkenwald* and the Inadvertent Baptism," p. 6). Kamowski points out that "the poem specifically extols the necessity and virtues of three sacraments whose necessity and efficacy Wyclif questioned: the Eucharist, baptism and holy orders." He argues that in making sure that the full ceremonial formula is pronounced by a bishop, who then casts water on the face of the candidate, the *Erkenwald*-poet implicitly expresses his disagreement with the views of Wyclif, who regarded "baptism . . . of fire (or of the spirit)" as "the essence of the sacrament," and believed that "baptism of spirit, rather than of sacramental form with water, was the only necessity" (p. 12). Kamowski recognizes that the poem's "celebration of earthly splendor" contrasts with "Wyclif's political perspectives on the relationship between wealth and temporal or spiritual authority. . . . Moreover, in the inherent comparisons between the empowered bishop and the helpless judge . . . the poem images the efficacy of spiritual authority and power at the expense of civil authority" (p. 17). There is also good reason to link the composition of *St. Erkenwald* with certain late fourteenth-century events in which the saint figured, spe-

not the message of any of the other poems, but neither does anything in them contradict it.

A. C. Spearing has said of the *Gawain*-poet that he "is notoriously one with a passion for pattern, a rage for order," who "also possesses a willingness to confront, immerse himself in and express disorder."[56] The latter part of this thematic opposition is especially conspicuous, as Spearing says, in "the violent and vengeful destructiveness with which God punishes human transgression" in *Purity* (p. 188) and in "the great storm that first threatens shipwreck to the vessel in which Jonah has embarked" in *Patience* (p. 191). Spearing sees an obvious manifestation of the poet's love of pattern in the "numerological and metrical architecture" (ibid.) of *Sir Gawain* and *Pearl*, to which pair of poems *St. Erkenwald* (assuming now that the same poet wrote it) may be added.[57] While

---

cifically, "the elevation of the two feasts of Erkenwald (with those of Saint Paul) to first-class status by Bishop Braybrooke in 1386, and . . . the annual processions of the clergy of the diocese (in full dress) in honor of Erkenwald which Braybrooke instituted a few years later" (Peterson, Introduction, p. 38). The poet may have been inspired by these events; it is even possible that he was asked, in connection with them, to write a celebratory poem. The assertion of ecclesiastical authority in *St. Erkenwald* need not, however, be thought of as representing the poet's definitive view on the relation between temporal and spiritual. I described *Sir Gawain and the Green Knight* above as "a secular drama," and have argued at length elsewhere that "the poem . . . anticipates . . . the passing of judgment from the divine to the earthly realm" ("Sir Gawain and the Green Knight: The Passing of Judgment," in *Traditions and Renewals*, pp. 97–113, at 111). It seems plausible that the richly sophisticated (though religiously observant) worldliness represented in *Sir Gawain* should have succeeded the doctrinal preoccupations central to the other poems of the *Gawain*-group and *St. Erkenwald*.

[56] See the chapter entitled "*Purity* and Danger" in his *Readings in Medieval Poetry* (Cambridge: Cambridge University Press, 1987), pp. 173–94, at 191.

[57] The subject of numerical symbolism lies beyond the scope of this essay, and I can give it no more than momentary attention here. As is well known, *Sir Gawain* is built around the number 5 (it has 2525 + 5 lines, and the pentangle that symbolizes the hero's ostensible human perfection is a five-pointed star, each point of which has a fivefold symbolic value). See Kent Hieatt, "*Sir Gawain*: Pentangle, *Luf-lace*, Numerical Structure," in *Silent Poetry: Essays on Numerological Analysis*, ed. Alastair Fowler (London: Routledge, 1970), pp. 116–40. The corresponding number in *Pearl* is 12; the poem is 1212 lines long, and the first three digits of 144,000, the number of innocents in the procession in the Celestial Jerusalem, are the square of 12. See Borroff, "Contrasts and Complementarities," in *Traditions and Renewals*, p. 155. Maren-Sofie Røstvig presents a more elaborate analysis in "Numerical Composition in *Pearl*: A Theory," *ES* 48 (1967): 326–32. In *St. Erkenwald*, the key-number is 8. In "Number Structure in *St. Erkenwald*," Russell Peck points out that the poem is 352 lines long, or 88 × 4; it begins and ends with sections 32 lines long, or 8 × 4, and it is divided in half by a rubricated initial at line 177. The number 8 is associated with baptism and with Pentecost, both of which figure importantly in the poem. Peck further observes that, since the Dean reports that he and the other clerics have searched the records for seven days, the baptism is imagined as occurring on the eighth day (p. 11).

I find Spearing's interpretation convincing and useful, I believe that pattern also figures in the works of the *Gawain*-poet in a thematic opposition as important as, and in fact more pervasive than, the opposition between pattern and violence—an opposition according to which pattern is understood as timelessness and its opposite is process, that is, the passing of time. The numerological architecture representing pattern in Spearing's duality represents abstraction from the temporal sequence of the unfolding narrative in mine. In addition, our awareness of it as knowledgeable readers is abstract in that we do not experience it at any particular moment or moments. We simply know that it is present, as we know while reading a sonnet that it conforms to a fourteen-line limit. Numerical design is associated with timelessness in another way: the particular numbers chosen by the poet for his designs signify aspects of the perfect and changeless heavenly kingdom posited by Christian doctrine. The invisible presence of numbers governing the length of a verse-narrative can thus be thought of as bringing the perfection of eternity to bear on the temporal realm of mortality, sinfulness, and death. In each of the five poems, human beings, individually or in social groups, are shown falling short of perfection as they are tested in various ways by changing circumstances. In *Sir Gawain,* the hero fails to live up to the human ideal symbolized by the five fives of the pentangle. In *Pearl,* the dreamer fails to arrive at the visionary union with the Lamb toward which the maiden has been leading him. In *St. Erkenwald,* even the one person whose faith is adequate to the situation does not fully understand God's providential plan, the "quontyse strange" or "strange wisdom"[58] that is beyond the reach of those who first see the body (73–74), though he is unwittingly led to fulfill it at the end. *Cleanness* and *Patience,* though they seem not to be numerically structured, also exhibit this relationship.[59] In *Patience,* Jonah is unable to emulate or accept the

---

[58] Peterson's note on line 74 reads "*quontyse:* 'marvel,' and is so glossed by editors; but the poet may be referring to an armorial device." I believe this interpretation is erroneous, and associate the word rather with Gordon's emendation, following Bradley, of *Pearl* 690, where *kyntly,* in the manuscript, is replaced by *Koyntise* and translated "Wisdom" (so also Andrew and Waldron). The fact that the passage alludes to the Book of Wisdom validates Gordon's interpretation, since Wisdom in that book was thought to be a personification of God. See Gordon's note on the line, and *MED* s.v. *queintis(e* (n.) sense 1(a), "wisdom, intelligence, skill." The phrase "koyntyse of clergye" (*Gawain* 2447) is cited in the *MED* entry and glossed "knowledge."

[59] The disparity between *Cleanness* and *Patience* and the other three poems may conceivably have resulted from the order in which they were composed, though this is a matter about which we can do no more than speculate. My own hypothesis, for what it is worth, is that *Cleanness,* the least satisfactory in terms of formal and thematic structure, was written first, when the poet's artistry had not yet matured. For a cogent

infinite and eternal patience of God, which leads Him to spare the sinful (via the earthly agency of the church) once they have repented and done penance. In *Cleanness,* human beings deviate in various ways from the divinely instituted order of nature, or *kynde,* which includes the bliss attendant on sexual relations between loving males and females in mutual commitment. The daughters of men mate with fallen angels; men engage in sexual relations with other men; men worship idols instead of God and drink from God's holy vessels in profane banquets.

Whatever the poet's views as a Christian believer may have been concerning fallen human nature, with its incessant lapses from virtue, minor and major, his dealings with it as a narrative poet bespeak an engagement with it at once intimate and sympathetic. His achievement was to take a traditional style originally developed for use in transmitting legends about heroes defined as invulnerable in strength and unimpeachable in virtue, and adapt it for portraying the predicament of the mortal being, beset from moment to moment by constraining circumstances and led to perform actions having unforeseen consequences. The representation of human experience in his poems continues to captivate us today. Although, in the words of the narrator of *Sir Gawain,* "the forme to the fynisment foldez ful selden" (499), I suspect that it will not captivate us less in the future.

I have attempted in this essay to show that *St. Erkenwald* is linked by deep-seated and pervasive affinities to the poems of the *Gawain*-group. For those who see these affinities as implying a single author, the five poems taken together yield a many-faceted and in some ways problematic portrait of the man who created them. He was a Cheshireman who had some connection with St. Paul's Cathedral in London; his learning

---

critique of the poem as a whole expressing a negative judgment, see Elizabeth B. Keiser, *Courtly Desire and Medieval Homophobia: The Legitimation of Sexual Pleasure in Cleanness and Its Contexts* (New Haven: Yale University Press, 1997), chap. 8, "Theopoetic Coherence: *Cleanness* among Its Manuscript Companions," pp. 201–24. I believe that *Patience,* a shorter poem with a simple but clear design, was written next. Of the four sections marked by large capitals in the manuscript that follow the introduction, two correspond to the chapter divisions in the Book of Jonah in the modern Bible. The poem as a whole must originally have been 532, not 531, lines long (see Borroff, *Sir Gawain and the Green Knight, Patience, Pearl,* 134 n. 8). Of these two numbers, 532, which is divisible by 2, 4, 7, and 14, would seem to lend itself a good deal more readily to analysis in terms of numerical patterning than 531, which is divisible only by 3. But I have no particular pattern to propose for *Patience.* By the time the poet wrote *Pearl, St. Erkenwald,* and *Sir Gawain* (in that order, according to my hypothesis), he had become interested in numerologically governed composition, and fully capable of writing long poems in which elaborate numerical patterns are inconpicuously present.

in Christian doctrine and disputation befits a cleric, perhaps a priest, yet he lost an infant daughter and mourned her death in a solitary vision that brought him out of despair; in his best-known poem, he revealed an intimate knowledge of the conduct of life in great houses as he told of a scion of the knightly nobility who, having committed a minor fault out of love of life, was forgiven by an older member of his profession; in a hagiographical legend of his own contriving, he affirmed the importance of ecclesiastical authority in a London strangely devoid of men.[60] For their part, those who continue to think that *St. Erkenwald* and the *Gawain*-group were written by different authors are willing to believe that two extraordinarily gifted men wrote poems using the same traditional style in the same way, in the same part of England, within a seventy-five-year time span. As between the two, I find the hypothesis of a single author, with all its complications, the more plausible one. I hope that my account of him here will find a sympathetic audience among those who know and prize the five poems that are his lasting legacy.

Appendix:
Distinctive Features Shared by *St. Erkenwald* with the Poems of the *Gawain*-group

1. "Embedded periphrases" (see page 54 above)
(a) Periphrases identifying persons in terms of their occupancy of a certain location at a certain moment.
In *Sir Gawain:*
Gawan, that sate by the quene (339)
The leude . . . that legh in his bedde (2006)
In *Cleanness:*
The lede [Abraham] that ther laye the levez an-under
In *St. Erkenwald:*
"Lykhame that thus lies" (1789)
He that ther lay [the body in the tomb] (281)

(b) Periphrases in which a relative clause implies a character's emotional state by describing an action he has recently performed, or something that has just happened to him.
In *Sir Gawain:*

[60] Morse makes this observation in her note to lines 59–64.

[Gawain], that the grace hade geten of his lyve (2480)
The bores hed watz borne bifore the burnes selven
That him forferde in the forthe thurgh forse of his honde
   So stronge. (1616–18)
In *Patience:*
Jonas . . . [t]hat the daunger of Dryghtyn so derfly ascaped (110–11)
In *Cleanness:*
The kyng [Balthasar,] . . .
That watz so doghty that day and drank of the vessayl (1789, 1791)
In *St. Erkenwald:*
Ser Erkenwolde . . .
That welneghe al the nyght hade naityd his houres (118–19).

2. Lines ending in the word *many* in which the second half describes the reactions of onlookers to some circumstance or event mentioned in the first half.
In *Cleanness:*
In the anger of His [God's] ire, that arghed ("frightened") mony (572)
Fast fayled hem the fode, enfamined monie (1194)
The candelstik . . . watz cayred ("brought") thider sone,
Upon the pyleres apiked ("adorned"), that praysed hit mony (1478–79)
This cry watz upcaste, and ther comen mony (1575)
Ascry ("outcry") scarred on the scue ("rose (?) to the sky"†), that scom-
   fyted mony (1784)
†See Menner's Glossary
In *Sir Gawain and the Green Knight:*
Ful grymme quen he [the boar] gronyed ("grunted"); thenne greved
   mony (1442)
In *St. Erkenwald:*
Fulle verray were the vigures ("letters [of the inscription]"); ther avisyde
   hom mony (53)
Bot al as stille as the ston stoden and listonde
Wyt meche wonder forwrast, and wepid ful mony (219–20)

A similarly constructed line appears in the B-text of *Piers Plowman* in the story of the raising of Lazarus. The poet says that, seeing the sorrow of Mary, sister of Lazarus, and the Jews, "[Jesus] wepte water with hise eighen; ther seighen it manye" (116) (cf. John 33.35). Here, however, the witnesses in question are important in themselves, whereas the presence of those mentioned in the lines cited from the *Gawain* group serves simply to frame, and thus provide a periphery for, the action or event in question. In the passage in *Piers,* the spectators are part of the continuing story: "some" are convinced that Jesus is "leche of life and lord of heigh hevene" (118), whereas Jewish judges among them accuse him of practicing witchcraft with the aid of the devil (120).

I have also found a similar line in *Wars of Alexander* 611: "His [Alexander's] stevyn ("voice") stiffe ("loud") was and steryn ("stern"), that stonayid ("astounded") mony." But there is a crucial difference between this detail and those cited from the *Gawain*-group. The latter refer to reactions confined to a moment or limited period of narrative time. The line from *Wars of Alexander* states a fact that is part of a description. The relative clause refers to the way people always reacted to the king's voice, rather than their reaction to it on a particular occasion; its verb is thus definitional. "The Knyght of the Grene Chapel men knowen me mony" (*Gawain* 454) is similarly ineligible for my list; here, too, the clause states a fact rather than describing an event.

Povre Griselda and the All-Consuming *Archewyves*

Andrea Denny-Brown

University of California–Riverside

T HE LATE MEDIEVAL FASCINATION with naked Griselda and her changes of clothing is at its heart, according to modern critical discussion, a fascination with translation. Most influential in this respect have been the studies of Chaucer's *Clerk's Tale* by Carolyn Dinshaw and David Wallace, which have deepened our comprehension of Griselda's sartorial symbolism through an understanding of her figure in relation to masculine hermeneutics, her role as a text undressed and dressed, or read and "translated" by educated men, often for sociopolitical purposes.[1] As these and other studies have shown, each new translation of the Griselda tale—from Boccaccio's original through Petrarch, Philippe de Mézières and the anonymous French translations, Christine de Pizan, Chaucer, and forward to the early modern renditions—revised not only the interpretative adornment of the challenging tale but also the descriptions

My heartfelt thanks to Frank Grady and the anonymous readers of *SAC* for their helpful comments on this essay.

[1] Carolyn Dinshaw's influential chapter "Griselda Translated" examines the tale through Jerome's image of the allegorical text as veiled captive women, focusing primarily on the double valence of the Clerk's *translatio* to both eliminate and restore the feminine. Dinshaw, *Chaucer's Sexual Poetics* (Madison: University of Wisconsin Press, 1989), pp. 32–55. David Wallace, in his chapter " 'Whan She Translated Was': Humanism, Tyranny, and the Petrarchan Academy," explores the tale from a similar perspective of masculine rhetorical control over the female body, but his greater objective concerns the uses of this rhetoric to further the interests of tyrannical "Lumbardye." Wallace, *Chaucerian Polity* (Stanford: Stanford University Press, 1997), pp. 261–98. Although both of these studies, and especially Dinshaw's, address *The Clerk's Tale*'s emphasis on clothing, their interest lies primarily in the symbolism of the clothing as veiled allegorical woman (esp. Dinshaw, 144–48) and/or as masculine adornment and insight (esp. Wallace, pp. 284–86).

of Griselda's clothes themselves.[2] The readings of Griselda's sartorial "translations" have varied over the years: while earlier studies tended to concentrate on Griselda's allegorical and spiritual translations,[3] more recent readings have focused on ritualized investitures, the social performances involved in marriage, divorce, and (in the early modern period) guild membership.[4] Yet, as I will argue in this essay, Griselda is not merely *translated;* rather, as Chaucer's text states, she is translated "in swich richesse" (*Clerk's Tale*, 385).[5] This often-overlooked adverbial

[2] Dinshaw's statement that "the Clerk is made to fashion his narrative around Griselda's changes of clothes" (p. 144), for example, could very easy apply to all the poets who translate Griselda's tale. See J. Burke Severs, *The Literary Relationships of Chaucer's Clerk's Tale* (Hamden, Conn.: Archon Books, 1972), pp. 215–50; Roberta L. Kreuger, "Uncovering Griselda: Christine de Pizan, 'une seule chemise,' and the Clerical Tradition: Boccaccio, Petrarch, Philippe de Mézières, and the Ménagier de Paris," in *Medieval Fabrications: Dress, Textiles, Cloth Work, and Other Cultural Imaginings,* ed. E. Jane Burns (New York: Palgrave Macmillan, 2004), pp. 71–88. Helen Cooper, *Oxford Guides to Chaucer: The Canterbury Tales* (Oxford: Oxford University Press, 1989), pp. 189–90. On the specific theme of interpretation, see also Kevin Brownlee, "Commentary and the Rhetoric of Exemplarity: Griseldis in Petrarch, Philippe de Mézières, and the *Estoire,*" *SAQ* 91:4 (1992): 865–90; and Emma Campbell, "Sexual Poetics and the Politics of Translation in the Tale of Griselda," *CL* 55:3 (2003): 191–216.

[3] See Dudley David Griffith, *The Origin of the Griselda Story* (Seattle: University of Washington Press, 1931), esp. pp. 92–93; Elizabeth Salter, *Chaucer: The Knight's Tale and the Clerk's Tale* (London: Edward Arnold, 1962), pp. 47–48; John P. McCall, "The Clerk's Tale and the Theme of Obedience," *MLQ* 27 (1966): 260–69; and Dolores Warwick Frese, "Chaucer's *Clerk's Tale:* The Monsters and the Critics Reconsidered," *ChauR* 8 (1973): 133–46.

[4] Susan Crane has recently illuminated the historicity of Griselda's sartorial symbolism, pointing out the way her re-clothing by Walter and Janicula spoke to fourteenth-century court rituals of marriage and divorce in *The Performance of Self: Ritual, Clothing, and Identity During the Hundred Years' War* (Philadelphia: University of Pennsylvania Press, 2002), pp. 21–38. Christiane Klapisch-Zuber has found that the popularity of the Griselda theme in the art and literature of Renaissance Florence coincided with rituals of marriage and the steady erosion of women's property rights in "The Griselda Complex: Dowry and Marriage Gifts in the Quattrocento," in *Women, Family, and Ritual in Renaissance Italy,* trans. Lydia Cochrane (Chicago: University of Chicago Press, 1985), pp. 213–46. Ann Rosalind Jones and Peter Stallybrass describe the use of guild liveries as a type of "translation" of Griselda in the early modern dramatic versions of the tale in *Renaissance Clothing and the Materials of Memory* (Cambridge: Cambridge University Press, 2000), pp. 220–44. In a more general sense, my current understanding of Griselda's related social and sartorial translations is also indebted to the substantial scholarly work on medieval society and subjectivity, including but not limited to Paul Strohm's *Social Chaucer* (Cambridge, Mass.: Harvard University Press, 1989) and *Hochon's Arrow: The Social Imagination of Fourteenth-Century Texts* (Princeton: Princeton University Press, 1992); David Aers's *Community, Gender, and Individual Identity* (New York: Routledge, 1988); Lee Patterson's *Chaucer and the Subject of History* (Madison: University of Wisconsin Press, 1991); and Peggy Knapp's *Chaucer and the Social Contest* (New York: Routledge, 1990).

[5] *The Riverside Chaucer,* 3rd ed., gen. ed. Larry D. Benson (Boston: Houghton Mifflin, 1987). All subsequent quotations of Chaucer will be from this edition.

phrase is a vital and underdiscussed element of Griselda's figuration, whose linguistic purpose can serve as momentary metaphor for the critical shift this study follows. I would like to extend our attention outward from the actions performed on Griselda's body—the verbal translating, stripping, and testing—to include the objects modifying these actions: the riches, gems, clothes, and rags that materialize the changing world and changing perceptions around her.

In a basic sense this essay will attempt to take Griselda's clothes at face value, to understand the text's obsession with changing clothes as just that—an obsession with changing clothes.[6] But, *whose* obsession? Griselda's own lack of attachment to the goods that adorn her body, her stability in the face of extreme misfortune and fortune—literal rags and riches—seems to dismiss the possibility that the tale holds a lesson about material desires. Yet Griselda's sartorial stoicism implicitly evokes a desiring audience; her own indeterminate or utterly absent reactions to her clothes serve to emphasize the overt reactions of the people around her. This heightened audience reception and perception of Griselda's alternatively rich and rude clothes in Chaucer's work reveals the type of classifying of consumption and objectification that Pierre Bourdieu defines as the "distinction" of cultural tastes, or "the social relations objectified in familiar objects, in their luxury or poverty, their 'distinction' or 'vulgarity,' their 'beauty' or 'ugliness.'"[7] Further, the consumer categories associated with clothing are manipulated and appropriated in, Chaucer's tale. Whereas garments hold the power to transform peasant

---

[6] This "obsession" has quantifiable evidence: Griselda is stripped of her clothes three times, she wears five apparently different garments (her garments of "richesse" at her wedding, her smock when cast out of Walter's palace, her "olde coote" when she returns to her father's house, her "rude and somdeel eek torent" clothing when waiting on Walter and his new bride-to-be, and her "clooth of gold" when Walter reconciles with her), and the word "array" is used seventeen times in the tale. The most extensive study regarding this amplification of the theme of array is still that of Kristine Gilmartin Wallace, who suggests that the tale's important expansion of the theme both distinguishes it from its sources and reveals Chaucer's attention to the realistic "psychological coherence" of Walter and Griselda's marriage. Kristine Gilmartin Wallace, "Array as Motif in the *Clerk's Tale*," *Rice University Studies* 62 (1976): 99.

[7] *Distinction: A Social Critique of the Judgement of Taste*, trans. Richard Nice (London: Routledge, 1984), p. 53. Related to this is Bourdieu's concept of symbolic capital, which he describes as "a transformed and thereby disguised form of physical, 'economic' capital, [which] produces its proper effect inasmuch, and only inasmuch, as it conceals the fact that it originates in 'material' forms of capital which are also, in the last analysis, the source of its effects." *Outline of a Theory of Practice*, trans. Richard Nice (Cambridge: Cambridge University Press, 1977), pp. 171–83, at 183; and *The Logic of Practice*, trans. Richard Nice (Stanford: Stanford University Press, 1990), pp. 112–21.

social status and sway bourgeois public perception, for example, they hold no apparent appeal for the "serious" and "insightful" aristocratic eye of Walter. As I will discuss, while the Clerk may condemn Walter's tyrannical testing of Griselda,[8] he celebrates his prudential ability to see through rude material surfaces to inner beauty and virtue. In contrast, he identifies and targets those who are seduced by aesthetic beauty and the cultural capital behind it, ultimately aligning superfluity, frivolity, and love of novelty with not only the common "peple" of his tale but also the *nouveaux riches* merchant class and its spendthrift "arch" wives.

Reading against the grain of the poem, I will explore how this rhetorical offensive against conspicuous consumers grows out of the potential of sartorial consumption as a new form of cultural resistance, an example of what Michel de Certeau calls the "tactics" that consumers use to get around the "strategies" of disciplinary forces.[9] In a world in which the problem of status-blurring garments and ever-changing, ever-more exorbitant fashions was fast becoming one of the most prominent social concerns, the *Clerk's Tale* situates itself at the very crux of the debate: the sartorial basis of social change and public perception.[10] By underscoring the disparity between a woman who remains exactly the same whether in rags or riches and the public's constantly changing perception of her, the tale not only invokes what Lee Patterson calls the "quintessentially bourgeois" appropriation and dislocation of social val-

[8] See, for example, lines 456–62 and 621–23.

[9] Michel de Certeau, *The Practice of Everyday Life,* trans. Steven F. Rendall (Berkeley and Los Angeles: University of California Press, 1984), pp. xix, 29–42.

[10] On sumptuary concerns in this period, see Claire Sponsler, *Drama and Resistance: Bodies, Goods, and Theatricality in Late Medieval England* (Minneapolis: University of Minnesota Press, 1997), and "Narrating the Social Order: Medieval Clothing Laws," *CLIO* 21 (1992): 265–83; Stella Mary Newton, *Fashion in the Age of the Black Prince* (Rochester, N.Y.: Boydell Press, 1980); Diane Owen Hughes, "Regulating Women's Fashions," in *A History of Women: Silences of the Middle Ages,* ed. Christiane Klapisch-Zuber (Cambridge, Mass.: Belknap Press of Harvard University Press, 1992), and "Sumptuary Law and Social Relations in Renaissance Italy," in *Disputes and Settlements: Law and Human Relations in the West,* ed. John Bossy (Cambridge: Cambridge University Press, 1983); Susan Mosher Stuard, "Gravitas and Consumption," in *Conflicted Identities and Multiple Masculinities: Men in the Medieval West,* ed. Jacqueline Murray (New York: Garland, 1999), pp. 215–42; and Carole Collier Frick, *Dressing Renaissance Florence: Families, Fortunes, and Fine Clothing* (Baltimore: John Hopkins University Press, 2002). On Chaucer's sumptuary discourses, see Margaret Hallissy, *Clean Maids, True Wives, Steadfast Widows: Chaucer's Women and Medieval Codes of Conduct* (Westport, Conn.: Greenwood Press, 1993), pp. 113–34; and Laura F. Hodges, *Chaucer and Costume: The Secular Pilgrims in the General Prologue* (Cambridge: D. S. Brewer, 2000), and *Chaucer and Clothing: Clerical and Academic Costume in the General Prologue to the Canterbury Tales* (Cambridge: D. S. Brewer, 2005).

ues (here aristocratic *gentillesse*),[11] but also comments on that process, putting into question the very apparatus of that dislocation (here clothing) in the medieval imaginary. Griselda's lack of material appetite is thus inseparable from the importance Walter and his subjects (and we the readers) give to array and appearance, and ultimately from the moral judgment the Clerk renders on this mistaken importance.

It is within this latter textual presence—that is, the nuanced style, terminology, and object(s) of the Clerk's moralizing rhetoric—that I have found the strongest evidence for this materialist reading. While much of the sumptuary detail in *The Clerk's Tale* and *Envoy* is undoubtedly generated by the repressed sociohistorical materials that Paul Strohm calls the "textual unconscious,"[12] *The Clerk's Tale*'s profound interest in comparing spiritual and material interpretation, and the placement of these concerns in the mouth of the logician Clerk, leads to a significant amount of what appears to be aesthetic (or anti-aesthetic) "intent" on the Clerk's part. As I will argue, it is specifically through the Clerk's self-conscious insistence on rhetorical and material frugality, coupled with his open address to the sumptuous material world of the Wife of Bath and "al hire secte" (1171), that this tale links larger gendered and hegemonic formulations of marriage, authority, and feudal subjectivity to the more immediate problem of the influence of material goods on the medieval worldview. In its attempt to shape audience interpretation according to class and gender, the text grapples intently with the different lenses through which Griselda might be seen, aligning the seemingly divergent but equally illogical forces of tyranny, temptation, and fashion, for example, and it does this through a figure, I will argue, whose own frugality betrays an excessiveness equal to the superficies that he shuns.

Griselda's *Richesse*

Stylistically, *The Clerk's Tale,* like the Clerk himself, is stripped of almost all ornament and color, pared down well beyond the simple to the plain.[13] Yet, despite—or as I will suggest, because of—its divestiture of

---

[11] Patterson, *Chaucer and the Subject of History*, p. 324.

[12] Paul Strohm, *Theory and the Premodern Text* (Minneapolis: University of Minnesota Press, 2000), p. xvi.

[13] "There are only four images of color in the entire poem," Charles Muscatine declares in his influential study of Chaucerian style, *Chaucer and the French Tradition* (Berkeley and Los Angeles: University of California Press, 1969), p. 192.

the type of sumptuous detail found in, say, the clothing descriptions of the Wife of Bath or Prioress in the *General Prologue*, or the delectably decorated Alisoun of *The Miller's Tale*, *The Clerk's Tale* is more profoundly invested in the implications of material ornament than perhaps any of the other *Tales*. The first pivotal moment for this reading is the scene of Griselda's translation into *richesse* (IV.372–85):

> And for that no thyng of hir olde geere
> She sholde brynge into his hous, he bad
> That wommen sholde dispoillen hire right theere;
> Of which thise ladyes were nat right glad
> To handle hir clothes, wherinne she was clad.
> But nathelees, this mayde bright of hewe
> Fro foot to heed they clothed han al newe.
>
> Hir heris han they kembd, that lay untressed
> Ful rudely, and with hir fyngres smale
> A corone on hire heed they han ydressed,
> And sette hire ful of nowches gret and smale.
> Of hire array what sholde I make a tale?
> Unnethe the peple hir knew for hire fairnesse
> Whan she translated was in swich richesse.

The question directed in the Clerk's own voice toward the listener or reader in line 383 represents Chaucer's most dramatic addition to this scene, parts of which he borrows from both Petrarch's version of the tale and the anonymous French *Le Livre Griseldis*.[14] While this type of editorial comment is far from unusual for Chaucer or his sources, its unique

---

[14] Many of the details in Chaucer's clothing descriptions are taken from *Le Livre Griseldis*, the French translation of Petrarch's version, known for its realism in comparison to Petrarch's allegory. These details include the discussion of the unwearability of Griselda's old robe and the revulsion of the ladies to touching Griselda's old clothing when they are instructed by Walter to strip her and dress her in finery. Chaucer himself added the details of the cloth of gold and the jeweled crown in which Griselda is clothed at the end of the tale. Chaucer takes the greater plot explanations—such as Walter's wanting her to bring "no thynge of hir olde geere" into his house—from Petrarch. See Severs, *The Literary Relationships of Chaucer's Clerk's Tale*, pp. 3–37, 135–80, 190–211; and Severs, "The Clerk's Tale," in *Sources and Analogues of Chaucer's Canterbury Tales*, ed. W. F. Bryan and Germaine Dempster (Chicago: University of Chicago Press, 1941), pp. 288–331. See also Dinshaw, *Chaucer's Sexual Politics*, p. 144; Gilmartin Wallace, "Array as Motif in the Clerk's Tale," pp. 100–101; and Cooper, *Oxford Guides to Chaucer*, pp. 189–90.

placement here introduces and even publicizes the Clerk's complicated interest in the subject of clothing. For one, the contradiction that lies at the heart of the *occupatio* form itself—a device that purports to draw the reader away from a specific subject and toward a larger narrative purpose, even as it effectively highlights that subject with its rhetorical intercession—also lies at the heart of the Clerk's rhetorical question: How can one simultaneously address and refute the subject of "array"?

Ascetic simplicity in both speech and clothing were expected characteristics of young scholars in Chaucer's time,[15] and for this reason the Clerk's pronounced position on vestimentary goods at first appears merely to be consistent with his overall soberness and place in life. On the surface his indifference to all and any ornamentation, what Charles Muscatine calls his spurning of poetry's "ordinary riches" and readers' corresponding "extravagant taste,"[16] also seems in keeping with the "pleyn" tale that the Host requests of him so that he and the other pilgrims "may understonde what ye seye" (*Clerk's Prologue,* 19, 20). I would argue, however, that through implied comparisons to the secular, worldly, commercial members of his audience, the Clerk's careful sartorial and rhetorical austerity speaks *about* the untutored masses as much as *for* them.[17] For instance, while on the one hand his portrait in the *General Prologue* appears to present an "ideal" and ascetic Clerk,[18] this idealization is primarily presented in terms of its contrasting relation to consumption and exchange. To begin, while his garment is "ful thredbar," it is also a "courtepy," or a short, secular tunic that would have been considered part of the "new" fashion of the period.[19] This

---

[15] Jill Mann, *Chaucer and Medieval Estates Satire* (Cambridge: Cambridge University Press, 1973), pp. 74–85.

[16] Muscatine, *Chaucer and the French Tradition,* p. 191.

[17] The curious tension between the tale's high style and apparent simplicity has generated divergent readings of the Clerk's overall style. While Muscatine states that "the poem has a fine astringency, an austerity that will not appeal to the untutored" (p. 191), Wallace discusses the same quality in terms of the tale's "policy of removing obstacles that stand between the story and the common reader" (p. 286). My own opinion is that, like his garments, he gives the appearance of rhetorical simplicity while still indulging in a sophisticated rhetoric of his own, "above the heads" of the secular pilgrims.

[18] Mann, *Chaucer and Medieval Estates Satire,* p. 74.

[19] On fourteenth-century discourses about the "new" and "old" fashion aesthetic, see Newton, *Fashion in the Age of the Black Prince,* pp. 14–18, 38, and my discussion on pages 95-96 below. Hodges has recently offered a more thorough argument that the Clerk's garment as "social mirror" counters, or at least complicates, the "ideal" figure he has been supposed to present. Citing contemporary debates over proper clerkly attire, the problematic symbolism of "thredbar" garments (worn at times by both Avarice and Coveitise), and the Clerk's potential for the vice of *curiositas,* or excessive desire for

shabby yet once fashionable garment is but one example among manifold other consumer analogies in the Clerk's description, which together reveal a surprisingly consistent economics of self-mortification: leanness discussed in terms of being "nat right fat" (288), philosophy in terms of "litel gold in cofre" (298), education in terms of borrowed money "spente" (300), desire for purchasing books in terms of shunning "robes riche" (296), and poverty in terms of his refusal of secular or "worldly" employment (292). Just as this subtext of his *General Prologue* portrait suggests the interface between Chaucer the narrator's (and other pilgrims') worldly, commercial perspective and the Clerk's own performed (and possibly exaggerated) asceticism, so the Clerk's meta-textual dismissal of "array" in Griselda's first clothing scene speaks to the greater interaction between the moral lesson embedded in his rhetorical performance and the reception of his audience. The Host demands, for the pleasure of the listening audience, not only a plain tale but also a cheerful, or "myrie tale" (9) that does not cause the pilgrims to lament about their vices (12–13); technically the Clerk delivers this, but solely on the surface: his is a deceptively simple tale whose comedic cheer lies only in its basic premise (it is about a peasant girl who becomes marchioness, after all), and in which, as I will discuss, he encodes not only moral lessons, but moral lessons shrewdly directed back at his pilgrim audience. Like his hero Walter, the Clerk gives all the appearance of complying with the wishes of the people (or in this case, their secular representative, the Host), but in fact acts on his own terms and even at their expense.

Indeed, the Clerk's question about array not only inherently brings to the forefront the presence of his audience, but also invites the reader to contemplate the audience's own desires—for the "riches" of literary-cultural entertainment, for protracted descriptions of attire, and, arguably, for luxurious attire itself.[20] Despite the fact that it is a rhetorical question and thus not meant to be answered, for instance, there are some ostensibly obvious answers to the question of why an educated narrator like the Clerk would "make a tale" of array, most of which have

---

knowledge, Hodges comes to the conclusion that his garment displays the precarious balance of his current life situation. See Hodges, *Clerical and Academic Costume,* 160–98.

[20] See Patricia J. Eberle's argument that Chaucer expected his audience to have "a lively interest in the world of getting and spending money, the world of commerce," in "Commercial Language and Commercial Outlook in the *General Prologue,*" *ChauR* 18:2 (1983): 161–74, at 163.

to do with medieval literary theories on audience reception of fictional material: Macrobius's influential concept of *narratio fabulosa,* for example, describes fiction as the veil or dress necessary to express the most serious of philosophical or sacred truths (a device one would think especially pertinent to the Clerk's own ultimate allegorical leanings).[21] Geoffrey of Vinsauf's popular *Poetria nova* also encourages lengthy passages describing women's attire as part of "the food and ample refreshment of the mind" that is *descriptio.*[22] Chaucer of course knew both of these texts, and his most popular work creates its own type of sartorial presence; as Laura F. Hodges has pointed out, the *Canterbury Tales* provides readers with "the widest range (quality and value) of contemporary fabric names in a single English literary work in the Middle Ages."[23]

Importantly, however, within this larger sartorial inventory in the *Tales,* Chaucer seems to associate clothing *descriptio* at least in part with lower-class or bourgeois (versus aristocratic) tastes; for it is only in the Miller's "nyce" or silly tale (*Reeve's Prologue,* 3855), heartily enjoyed by all but the Reeve, that we find the type of lavish head-to-toe clothing description suggested in Vinsauf.[24] If, therefore, Chaucer's Clerk refuses to divulge sartorial details, perhaps it is in part to distinguish his tale and its heroine from the type of conspicuously ornamented object of desire such as Alisoun, whose trappings proclaim, for all to see, the newfound wealth of her carpenter husband's (and miller narrator's) social class. Moreover, if we consider that the Host's opening comment to the Clerk—that he appears like a new bride at a feast, or "sittynge at the bord" (*Clerk's Prologue,* 2–3)—works not merely as a slight about the properly modest demeanor of a clerk,[25] but also as a reminder of the highly charged culture of consumption that makes up the tale-telling competition, in which both tales and tale-tellers, and both men and women, are continually evaluated and assessed by the other pilgrims, as

[21] Macrobius, *Commentary on the Dream of Scipio,* trans. William Harris Stahl (New York: Columbia University Press, 1990), 1.2.11.
[22] Geoffrey of Vinsauf, *Poetria Nova,* trans. Margaret F. Nims (Toronto: Pontifical Institute, 1967), p. 36. Quoted in Robert P. Miller, *Chaucer: Sources and Backgrounds* (New York: Oxford University Press, 1977), pp. 67–68.
[23] Hodges, *The Secular Pilgrims,* p. 233.
[24] I borrow this latter point from Benson, who suggests that Chaucer thought this type of *descriptio* was old-fashioned, which is why he used it in *The Miller's Tale.* "Rhetorical Descriptions of Beautiful People: *Poetria Nova, Romance of the Rose,* and Guy of Warwick," *The Harvard Chaucer Website,* May 12, 2000. <http://www.courses.fas.harvard.edu/~chaucer/special/litsubs/style/vins-de s.htm> (September 3, 2003).
[25] Benson, "Explanatory Notes," *The Riverside Chaucer,* p. 879.

metaphorical "feasts" offered up by the Host, then we can also see the Clerk's tale as a repudiation of and comment on that culture. Further underscoring this reading is the way the Clerk's question marks a thematic shift in the passage from describing how the "ladyes" dress Griselda to how "the peple" see her, from the courtly "dressing" of her crown and "setting" of her jewels to the public's "knowing" of her: "Of hire array what sholde I make a tale? / Unnethe the peple hir knew for hire fairnesse" (383–84). The question behind the question is perhaps not *whether* or *why* array belongs in tale-telling, but *how* it belongs.[26]

In the rest of the passage dealing with Griselda's first sartorial transformation, the Clerk maintains this uneasy balance between seeming to avoid sartorial detail and seeming to emphasize, through culturally charged terms, the public's use, abuse, and perception of her sartorial goods. Although we are clearly made to focus on the *fact* that Griselda is re-clothed "fro foot to heed" (378), for example, we hear nothing about the color, material, style, or embroidery of her attire. This dearth of detail goes against not only literary tradition but also the long tradition of elaborate clothing symbolism and ritual in royal marriages, which used investiture as a way of performing, through careful color, embroidery, and livery symbols, the social, political, and economic import of the new alliance.[27] It also distinguishes itself from the extensive detail of contemporary homiletic and legislative discourses, which, as Claire Sponsler has pointed out, often "acted unwittingly as shopping lists for would-be consumers, laying out all the wares available for (forbidden) consumption."[28] Instead, the Clerk gives his audience a list of base generalities devoid of color, ornament, or detail: "olde geere" and "clothes" for her former peasant attire, and "corone" and "nowches" for her new courtly clothes.

These apparently generic accounts are thus easily (and I would suggest deliberately) overshadowed by the reactions they invoke. In addition to the Clerk's own reaction to the scene in the form of his *occupatio*, and the aforementioned reaction of "the peple" who "hardly" recognize

---

[26] Lynn Staley makes a similar point in a different context: "How can her clothes mean? If Griselda's new clothes signify her translation from commoner to queen, her marriage to the husband of all souls, why are we not distraught when she puts them off?" In David Aers and Lynn Staley, *The Powers of the Holy: Religion, Politics, and Gender in Late Medieval English Culture* (University Park: Pennsylvania State University Press, 1996), p. 238.

[27] See, for example, Crane, *The Performance of Self*, pp. 21–29.

[28] Sponsler, *Drama and Resistance*, p. 23.

her, for example, we also have Chaucer's enhancement of the response to her peasant garments by the court ladies, who are "nat right glad / To handle hir clothes" (375–76). In contrast to this threefold response, Griselda's own reaction is duly absent; this scene is rather about the perception of the people around her to the clothes that she wears. Griselda merely forms the backdrop: she is never specifically named or even made physically visible in the passage. Instead, she becomes the blank material to be adorned with the jewels of human artifice, literally "sette . . . ful of nowches gret and smale" (382),[29] and the passage's running references to *hir, she,* and *this mayde* become the general field against which the "wommen," "the peple," and the narrative "I" gauge their own prejudices and ideas about the garments. The Clerk effectively strips the marriage ritual down to its basic structural purpose—the control of audience perception by ceremonial material goods—without appearing to indulge in those material goods himself. In the end the combination of the colorless clothing descriptions and the dramatic reactions of the people to them powerfully enlists the reader's own imagination to fill in the narrative and aesthetic gaps regarding Griselda's clothing—one reason, perhaps, for the heightened critical interest in hermeneutics and the word *translated* in this passage. Yet I would argue that it is in the last words of the passage—that she was translated "in swich richesse" (385)—that much of the interpretive weight of the description lies.

Chaucer uses the word *richesse,* meaning primarily "riches," "wealth," or "abundance," sparingly yet purposefully in his *Tales,* almost always invoking "temporeel richesses," or the Boethian sense of false riches of Fortune's material goods.[30] The Parson describes "richesses" as the first of three main categories of earthly pleasures (along with "honours" and "delices" [185]) that require penance, and states that those who enjoy such wealth while alive will suffer a painful fourfold poverty in hell: poverty of treasure, of meat and drink, of clothing, and of friends (191–99). *Richesse* represents a fantasy that embodies the uncertainty and changeability of both life and its trappings; as the Parson states, "alle the / Richesses in this world ben in aventure, and / Passen as a shadwe on the wal" (1068–70). In Chaucer's *Tale of Melibee,* Prudence likewise

---

[29] Here Griselda seems to echo the gems "set" in gold that Walter had made for her prior to meeting her (line 254). *MED,* s.v. "richesse."
[30] *MED,* s.v. "swich." Adj. 3a.

condemns the "sweete temporeel richesses, and delices and honours of this world" (1410) that have skewed Melibee's perception away from God. That examples of worldly *richesse* as materialistic, corrupting, and ungodly are expressed by the Parson as well as Prudence in the *Melibee*, the two most morally upright (and excessively didactic) of Chaucer's characters in the *Tales*, is especially enlightening, for they seem to correspond quite accurately to the Clerk's own abstemious performance and moralizing perspective. Indeed, even in his strict economy the Clerk is careful to emphasize that the garments clothing Griselda are extreme: she is not simply translated into riches, but into *"swich* richesse" (385, italics mine).[31]

By far the most thorough discussion of *richesse* in Chaucer's works and the clear source of much of the rhetoric of *richesse* in the *Tales* is his translation of Boethius's *Consolation of Philosophy*. The word *rychesses* dominates Philosophie's discussion of "the yiftes of Fortune" (4–5) in Book II Prosa 5 of the *Boece*. Here *richesses* concern not only questions of false "beaute" and "bountee" (40) but also the excesses of "superfluyte" (78), "covetyse" (123), and the "anguysschous love of havynge" (Metrum [5] 30). Like most of her teachings, Philosophie's discussion of *richesse* quickly becomes a question about mortal self-knowledge: " 'Richesses ben they preciouse by the nature of hemself, or elles by the nature of the?' " (8–10), she asks Boethius. She interrogates the poet's and reader's understanding of *richesse* by revealing the buried foundations of human investments in material goods: the false sense of importance, value, and beauty they bestow, the hunger for power they induce. To Philosophie, *richesse* represents only misunderstanding and transgression—the "errour" and "folie" (158) of humans, whose desire for "diverse clothynge" (86) and "straunge apparailementz" (160–61) condemns them to bestial ignorance about themselves and the world. Moreover, lastly and ironically, *richesse* also brings destitution. When in the form of money, *richesse* gains its true worth only in exchange: when it is " 'transferred fro o man to an othir' " (18–19), and more important, in the context of Griselda, " 'whan it is translated' " (20–21). Because it cannot be shared without its value diminishing, and because the *richesse* of one brings poverty to so many others, Philosophie depicts wealth itself as abject: " 'O streyte and nedy clepe I this richesse' " (33).

[31] Griselda, however, is also named three times in the *Envoy*, which brings her entire total to thirty-one. Walter, by comparison, is named ten times throughout the tale.

In light of Chaucer's uses of the concept, Griselda's sartorial transformation into *richesse* has intriguing moral implications specifically
linked to her new rich clothing. Like the description of *richesse* in the
Boece, Griselda's transformation into "swich richesse" could test her
own potential for pride and greed; as in the *Boece,* it could test her self-
knowledge and possible artifice; as in the *Boece,* it could test her value
as a possession transferred and "translated"; and finally, as in the *Boece,*
her transformation could be seen to test the very notion of good fortune,
illustrating through Walter's sadistic tests the abject side of *richesse.* Its
consistent use by the moral figures of the Parson, Prudence, and Philosophy further suggests that the word's placement at such a crucial moment in *The Clerk's Tale* could be meant to trigger personal meditation
on the dangers of material goods and the beauty and power they bestow.
Griselda's story certainly depicts the cyclical nature of *temporeal richesses:*
the arbitrary gaining and losing of material goods at the whim of Fortune, with whom Walter is repeatedly associated throughout the tale
(69, 756, 812).

But importantly, although she acts as the didactic vessel, Griselda is
not the recipient of the lesson of *richesse.* Like so much about Griselda,
her clothing symbolism gains the necessary clarity only through comparison. The moral targets another vital character in the tale: "the
peple" who gaze at her "fairnesse / Whan she translated was in swich
richesse" (384–85), and who are mentioned no less than twenty-eight
times throughout the tale (the exact number, incidentally, that Griselda
herself is named).[32] The "peple" of *The Clerk's Tale* represent a significant
elaboration on Chaucer's part that subtly transforms the tale's social
framework; as Lynn Staley has pointed out, Chaucer's creation of "a
single force, point of view, and voice that he designates as 'the people'"
diverges substantially from the representative mix of lesser nobles and
courtiers in Petrarch's tale.[33] Susan Yager also argues that the distinction
between the terms "peple" and "folk" in this tale forms part of Chaucer's larger exploration of intellectual, behavioral, and class differences
between the ignorant many and the refined and knowledgeable few.[34]

[32] In Aers and Staley, *The Powers of the Holy,* p. 236. See also Lynn Staley Johnson,
"The Prince and His People: A Study of the Two Covenants in the Clerk's Tale," ChauR
10:1 (Summer 1975): 17–29.
[33] Susan Yager, "Chaucer's *Peple* and *Folk,*" *JEGP* 100:1 (April 2001): 211–23.
[34] Ibid., p. 221. See also Paul Strohm's discussion of the "swarm of 'folk'" who gape
at the marvelous gifts in *The Squire's Tale,* in *Social Chaucer* (Cambridge, Mass.: Harvard
University Press, 1989), p. 170; and David Aers's discussion of "the people" as Mede's
followers in *Piers Plowman,* in *"Vox populi* and the Literature of 1381," in *The Cambridge*

Unlike Griselda, the Clerk's "peple" are ripe for a lesson on the dangers of temporal riches. For one, their collective desire maintains a formidable presence throughout this poem, from their initial request of Walter that he "hastily to wyve" (140), which spurs the central action of the poem, to Walter's own repeated assertions to Griselda that his (monstrous) actions toward her are not his, but his people's wishes— "Nat as I wolde, but as my peple leste" (490). Yet even more palpable than the people's desire, or "poeplissh appetit" as Yager calls it,[35] is their *observing* and *watching* of Griselda: they witness nearly every narrated action between Walter and Griselda, beginning with the moment Walter enters Janicula's house to ask for her hand, and even those things that they do not literally witness, such as Walter's "murdering" of his children, eventually come "to the peples ere" (727).[36] Essential to the related themes of desire and surveillance is the people's collective gaze at Griselda's array, which first emerges in this scene of her translation into *richesse* and grows increasingly significant with each subsequent scene of sartorial consequence. As we ultimately find out, while Walter does not marry Griselda for her *richesse* (795), it seems that "the peple" do.

Griselda's *Rudenesse*

The problematic material subtext of Griselda's *richesse* accrues its full weight only when compared to her corresponding aesthetic of *rudenesse*. The Clerk describes Griselda as born and raised in "rudenesse" (397), an attribute that manifests itself physically first in her "rudely" unkempt hair (380) when Walter first has her transformed into *richesse,* and later in the old "rude" cloth (916) that her father places on her shoulders after her exile. The latter is a garment so wrought with holes that, again according to Chaucer's elaboration of his sources, it has lost its fundamental purpose of concealing her body (IV.913–17):

> And with hire olde coote, as it myghte be
> He covered hire, ful sorwefully wepyng.

History of Medieval Literature, ed. David Wallace (Cambridge: Cambridge University Press, 1999), pp. 432–53, esp. 439.
[35] For additional ramifications of this public gaze, see Sarah Stanbury, "Regimes of the Visual in Premodern England: Gaze, Body, and Chaucer's *Clerk's Tale,*" NLH 28:2 (1997): 261–89.
[36] Muscatine, *Chaucer and the French Tradition,* p. 192.

But on hire body myghte he it nat brynge,
For rude was the clooth, and moore of age
By dayes fele than at hire mariage.

This torn garment is arguably the most memorable image in *The Clerk's Tale*.[37] Ostensibly it is a symbol of pared-down simplicity like the Clerk's own threadbare garments, used to counter the *richesse* in which Walter had clothed her and of which he had her stripped. Griselda's stoic bearing of her ragged clothing can thus be said to embody a lesson about the false importance of material goods and clothing in itself. But it is the Clerk's almost obsessive reiteration and visualization of this "rude" attire that seems to encompass a most fascinating moral directive, for Griselda's torn garments are continually and repeatedly mentioned in a way her garments of *richesse* are not. In fact, between the moment in which she dons the *olde coote* and the moment she reconciles with Walter, Griselda's decrepit garments are described no less than nine times: her clothing is of "rude . . . clooth" and of great "age" (916); "badde" and "yvel" (965); "rude" and "eek torent" (1012); "povre" (1020); "poverliche" (1055); and once again, "rude" (1116).

The prominent aesthetic of this garment in a tale that goes out of its way to strip itself of imagery, and the tale's blunt insistence that we re-imagine Griselda's rags over and over, work to implicate and then appropriate visual as well as material modes of consumption. For while *The Clerk's Tale's* exploration of *gentillesse* endeavors to compare moral and material treasures more broadly, the Clerk's careful handling of Griselda's appearance serves to specifically highlight and categorize the way people perceive and desire material ornament and especially clothing. When he first introduces his heroine, the Clerk takes care to emphasize how others view her low socioeconomic status: her father is not merely poor, he is the person that even the "povre folk" (204) hold to be "the povrest of hem alle" (205); correspondingly, it is upon Griselda as a "povre creature" (232) that Walter first literally and metaphorically "sette his ye" (233). Furthermore, while the Clerk makes an initial gesture toward Griselda's physical attractiveness to others—she is "fair ynogh to sighte" (209)—he immediately and somewhat self-consciously

---

[37] According to the *MED*, the word "likerous" was used to connote both lasciviousness and luxuriousness, with the common theme being excess or self-indulgent desire, pride, or way of living.

channels this into a description of *moral* rather than physical "beautee" (IV.211–14):

> But for to speke of vertuous beautee,
> Thanne was she oon the faireste under sonne;
> For povreliche yfostred up was she,
> No likerous lust was thurgh hire herte yronne.

Yet even when he purports to avoid material description here, he includes a significant sumptuary detail: unlike the Miller's bourgeois Alisoun, who has a "likerous ye" (*Miller's Tale*, 3244) to go with her eye-catching clothing, Griselda's poor upbringing ensures that she carries no greedy desire or "likerous lust" in her heart.[38] In the Clerk's view, Griselda's own lack of desire is inversely proportionate to her beauty and "fairness"—a "fairnesse," we remember, that "the peple" can only see after her transformation into *richesse*.

Indeed, according to the Clerk, to recognize (Griselda's) true value one must have the ability not only to look through rhetorical artifice (as he makes clear in his allegorical interpretation of Griselda at the end of the tale), but also through *artifi*cial trappings, which ultimately Walter can do but his "peple" cannot. The Clerk takes the time to clarify, for instance, that when Walter gazes at peasant Griselda before choosing her as his wife, he does not look at her with lascivious or foolish intentions, but in a serious manner (IV.235–38):

> And whan it fil that he myghte hire espye,
> He noght with wantown lookyng of folye
> His eyen caste on hire, but in sad wyse
> Upon hir chiere he wolde hym ofte avyse.

The Clerk further presents Walter's clear-sightedness in direct contrast with the flawed or absent "insight" of the people (IV.242–45):

> For thogh the peple have no greet insight
> In vertu, he considered ful right

---

[38] According to the Parson, the first finger of the hand of lechery is "the fool lookynge of the fool womman and of the fool man; that sleeth, right as the basilicok sleeth folk by the venym of his sighte, for the coveitise of eyen folweth the coveitise of the herte" (*The Parson's Tale*, line 852).

> Hir bountee, and disposed that he wolde
> Wedde hire oonly, if evere he wedde sholde.

Just as Walter's "sad," or serious way of looking corresponds to his keen perception of Griselda's value despite her rude clothing, so the people's lack of "insight"—literally, their inability to see *into,* or beyond, the surface—corresponds to their ultimate "[u]nsad" nature (995) and their superficial attachment to her *richesse.* The people's perception thus by default seems to be identified with the "wantown lookyng of folye" that Walter avoids. This problematic looking evokes what Chaucer's Parson elsewhere calls people's "coveitise of eyen" (852)—namely, the obsessive gazing at the opposite sex that both incites and is incited by conspicuous consumption. The Parson specifically links wasteful consumption and "fool lookynge" (852) under the sin of *luxuria,* denouncing men and especially women whose lechery causes them to "dispenden . . . hir catel and substaunce" on the opposite sex (848).[39] In *The Clerk's Tale,* the people's impaired (in)sight means they literally cannot understand who or even what Griselda is when she returns to her *rudenesse:* "they wondren what she myghte bee / That in so povre array was for to see" (1019–20).

Hence it is the literal sight of copious luxurious clothes that makes the people finally betray Griselda for (what they think is) her younger, richer replacement. When Walter's "newe markysesse" (942) arrives with her brother, the people interpret her superior worth solely upon her sumptuous appearance, and for the first time they begin to question Griselda's own merit (IV.983–87):

> For which the peple ran to seen the sighte
> Of hire array, so richely biseye;
> And thanne at erst amonges hem they seye
> That Walter was no fool, thogh that hym leste
> To chaunge his wyf, for it was for the beste.

The repeated emphasis on seeing in this passage, the twofold *seen the sighte* followed by *biseye,* "splended to look at," further underscores the people's voracity for sartorial riches and changes. Griselda, whose rude clothes are correspondingly "yvel biseye" (965), and who even in her

---

[39] See John M. Ganim, "The Noise of the People," in *Chaucerian Theatricality* (Princeton: Princeton University Press, 1990), pp. 108–20.

former role as Walter's wife displayed "[n]o pompe, no semblant of roialtee" (928), cannot compare, in the public's view, to "swich pompe and richesse" (943), an exhibition so grand that, as the Clerk states, "nevere was ther seyn with mannes ye / So noble array in al West Lumbardye" (944–45). Regardless of her dutiful and beneficial service as their marchioness, her promotion of the "commune profit" (431) and her devotion to "[p]eple to save and every wrong t'amende" (441), like the "olde" rags that she wears, Griselda is cast away by the fickle public in favor of "newe" array and *richesse*.

Moreover, just in case his audience missed the moral, the Clerk explicitly emphasizes the people's fickleness in the following outburst about their changefulness and vulnerability to novelty, which does not exist in Chaucer's sources (IV.995–98):

> O stormy peple! Unsad and evere untrewe!
> Ay undiscreet and chaungynge as a fane!
> Delitynge evere in rumbul that is newe,
> For lyk the moone ay wexe ye and wane!"

It is in this turbulent fickleness that we find the closest correlation between the "peple" of *The Clerk's Tale* and the social disruption that John M. Ganim finds associated with the "peple" in Chaucer's other work.[40] Yet here the Clerk provides his statement with extra authority by placing it in the mouths of some of the "folk" themselves, thus dividing the public according to whether they are "unsad" or "sadde," frivolous and serious, unstable or stable (1002–5). While the "[u]nsad" people gaze voraciously "up and doun" at the "newe lady," the "sadde folk," like "sad" Walter earlier (237), have the ability to see more clearly and thus avoid the allure of "noveltee" (1004).

In this focus on the seductive powers of material novelty and its link to changefulness, *The Clerk's Tale* suggests a more direct relation to contemporary discourses about clothing and consumption. The fourteenth-century preacher John Bromyard, for example, discusses the restless change of current fashions and the incitement of the public gaze in similar terms:

---

[40] John Bromyard's *Summa Predicantium* (*SP*), quoted by G. R. Owst in *Literature and Pulpit in Medieval England* (Oxford: Basil Blackwell, 1966), pp. 407–8.

From day to day the desire and appetite for elegance, singularity and vanity in all outward adornment, whether of hair or clothing, meets the eye. So it befalls that amongst such folk no fashion pleases them for long; because, inasmuch as that piece of singularity or elegance which originally was but rarely seen begins to be used and seen by many, it begins to displease them when the cause of its singularity and vanity ceases along with the admiration of men. . . . Whence it comes about that they devise some new piece of foppery to make men gaze at them in wonderment anew.[41]

The contemporary denigration of new and changing fashions took many forms; according to a popular satire on manners and costume written in the same decade as *The Clerk's Tale,* the "new faccion" in this period is not only "now shorte and now longe" but "now is here, now goon."[42] The short/long dialectic was part of a larger discourse that emerged earlier in the century and which articulated courtly fashion as a choice between two aesthetics: that of the new style [*de novo modo*] and that of the old style [*de antiquo modo*].[43] Thus, like his use of *richesse,* the Clerk's descriptions of Griselda's clothes as either "al newe" (378) or "olde" (913), and his subsequent condemnation of "the peple" who allow their loyalty to be purchased by "noveltee," work simultaneously as deceptively simple descriptions that correlate to his seemingly "pleyn" style and as phrases that would have carried strong moral and material resonance in Chaucer's world.

Chaucer's broader use of the word "newe" in his *Tales* underscores this ostensible purpose in *The Clerk's Tale* and also suggests more specifically which Canterbury pilgrims the Clerk's fickle, materially inclined "peple" most closely resemble. The word most often appears to describe the intersecting arenas of fashion and commerce. Lexically, the "newe world" (*GP,* 176) that the pleasure-loving Monk admires and the new style, or "newe jet" (*GP,* 682), that the corrupt Pardoner thinks he performs is that embodied by the liveried guildsmen, with their instruments arrayed "[f]ul fressh and newe" (*GP,* 365), and by the wealthy, cloth-making Wife of Bath in her "ful moyste and newe" shoes (*GP,* 457). Such "newe" purchases resonate not only with English commercial

---

[41] From lines 133, 167, 123, respectively, in the 1388 poem "A Satire on Manners and Costume," in Thomas Wright, *Political Poems and Songs* (London: Longman, Green, Longman, and Roberts, 1859), 1.2.270–78.

[42] Newton, *Fashion in the Age of the Black Prince,* pp. 14–18, 38.

[43] Grant McCracken, *Culture and Consumption: New Approaches to the Symbolic Character of Consumer Goods and Activities* (Bloomington: Indiana University Press, 1990), p. 117.

enterprise but also with the uniqueness of foreign goods, for in *The Man of Law's Tale,* it is the novelty of "newe" Eastern goods—specifically "[c]lothes of gold, and satyns riche of hewe" (137)—that both instills the Western desire for commercial exchange and enriches Eastern merchants (138–40). Such references to the desire for and aesthetic of "newe" things can be found in various forms throughout the *Tales;* even Griselda, who verbalizes her opinion so rarely, declares when Walter exiles her that "[l]ove is noght oold as whan that it is newe" (*Clerk's Tale,* 857). However, although many types of pilgrims wear fashions that can and should be perceived as novel—the Merchant and the Squire to name a few—Chaucer's specific use of the word "newe" in relation to material goods, like his use of sartorial *descriptio,* appears primarily in connection with the lower classes or the newly-rich bourgeoisie (here the guildsmen and the Wife of Bath). Even peasants obtain cherished "newe" objects; in *The Friar's Tale,* for example, it is out of protection for her "newe panne" (1614) that the old peasant woman finally curses (and thus condemns) the fraudulent summoner to his infernal fate. In this way the "newe" object, with its self-conscious link to purchasing, spending, and exchanging, can be seen to carry with it an oblique class indicator, or "distinction," in Bourdieu's sense, whether it implies a coveted necessity (the old peasant's pan) or conspicuous consumption (the Wife's shoes).

In describing consumer appetite, Grant McCracken identifies goods as "bridges to displaced meaning," or as a way to recover individual and cultural hopes and ideals: coveted goods represent, he says, "not who we are, but who we wish we were."[44] As medieval historians have pointed out, one curious aspect of medieval English merchants is that in this period of burgeoning mercantile growth, they allocated their newfound wealth toward consumption rather than investment, choosing to imitate the aristocracy rather than expanding their commercial businesses.[45] Thus, rather than using their powers of consumption to create

---

[44] See Lillian M. Bisson, "All that Glitters: Trade, Industry, and the Money Economy," in *Chaucer and the Late Medieval World* (New York: St. Martin's Press, 1998), p. 169; and J. L. Bolton, *The Medieval English Economy, 1150–1500* (London: Dent, 1985), pp. 144, 285.

[45] Hence, while the middling classes actually dress themselves in "newe" garments, Chaucer once again reserves for the educated aristocracy the potential for insight into such material performances. The Knight subtly undercuts the value of novelty, nostalgically claiming that all new fashions simply recycle old ones: "Ther is no newe gyse that it nas old" (*KT* 125). His son the Squire has a more problematic statement on innovation, first proclaiming humankind's natural love of novelty (line 610), but then, as if to

a new, mercantile identity, they attempted to purchase social status, to use their goods as a "bridge" to the social performance of the aristocracy. Chaucer's aligning of "newness" with the middling and lower classes reveals a possible cultural reaction to this new type of spending, in that it attempts to shift the meaning of sartorial riches (traditionally associated with aristocracy), re-ascribing them as mercantile fodder, and ascribing the hunger for things that medieval moralists found so disturbing to superficial social aspiration.[46]

In this context Walter's lavish production of his fictional marriage to a "newe lady" (1005)—which the Clerk points out is "gretter of costage" than his original marriage (1126–27)—can be understood as a theatrical display of the "emptiness" of such material novelty; a "revelation" about the level of public seduction and deception that money and costume can accomplish. Walter is again the only one who knows the "truth" behind the dazzling surface, behind the material dramatics of "pompe and richesse" into which the frivolous "peple" have bought. Ironically, his last-minute substitution of "povre" Griselda in her "rude" "olde coote" for the "newe lady" whose array is "so richely biseye" enacts the type of false advertising and bait-and-switch mercantile tactics deplored in Chaucer's London.[47] Yet unlike these commercial practices, Walter's manipulation of material goods strives not to fool the people into thinking that what is "olde" is "newe," but rather once again to reevaluate the terms of their (visual) consumption, so that *rudenesse* supplants *richesse* as the figurehead of pomp and circumstance, and as the focus of spectacle and celebration. Just as the Clerk links new *richesse* with changeability, deception, and the fickleness of the commons, so he claims old *rudenesse* as a marker of the beauty, prosperity, and nobility of virtuous constancy.

---

counter any existing claims that state otherwise, later declaring that even noble blood cannot prevent this love of novelty (lines 619–20). Like his father's own stance on novelty and fashion, the Squire's defense of "novelries" simultaneously discloses his own worldview and positions himself in contrast to (and in competition with) the more traditional ways of his father. However, it also reveals the timeliness and complexity of "newfangelnesse" as a subject in Chaucer's world: by explicitly arguing that novelty seduces all classes, *including* the aristocracy, the Squire in effect highlights the ubiquity of the unspoken opposite argument: that change and newness are endemic only to the middle and lower classes.

[46] Owst, *Literature and Pulpit,* pp. 355, 396.

[47] The others being the silent Dyer, Weaver, Haberdasher, and Tapestry-Weaver of *The General Prologue.* We know the Merchant deals with trade of wool and cloth because of his reference to "the passage between Middleburg and Orwell, the Netherlands and East Anglia, through which much of the English trade in wool and cloth passed from the 1380's onwards" (Cooper, *Oxford Guides to Chaucer,* p. 42).

In the end the Clerk's inversion of the cultural categories of new and old, *richesse* and *rudenesse* in his tale do more than invoke the "poverty of riches" theme of his Christian asceticism. In its aligning of material comprehension according to sociopolitical status—Walter's superb insight regarding Griselda's garments versus the people's faulty sight, which is underscored by the larger divide between aristocratic and middle-class relationships to newness in the *Tales*—*The Clerk's Tale* reveals a more particular investment in the material status of its listeners. We are invited to compare Griselda's *rude* garments not only to her former *richesse* and to the *richesse* of Walter's fictional new wife, but to the new *richesse* of the listening audience—Walter's, the Clerk's, and Chaucer's. It is no accident, once again, that the two pilgrims with whom the Clerk and his tale most closely interact are the *nouveaux riches* Merchant and Wife of Bath, whose own lavish attire proclaims their positions as the *Tales'* most prominent representatives of England's burgeoning cloth trade and rising mercantile classes.[48] In direct opposition to the threadbare frugality of the Clerk and his *povre* Griselda, the *General Prologue* descriptions of the Merchant and the Wife are laden with references to sartorial wealth: in addition to her moist "newe" shoes (*GP* 457), at church the Wife wears many layers of "fyne" coverchiefs, and "fyn" red hose (*GP* 453, 456), while the Merchant wears a Flemish beaver hat, fashionable polychrome "mottelee" clothes, and "bootes clasped faire and fetisly" (*GP* 271–73).[49] The Merchant's lucrative financial dealings—his "bargaynes" and "chevyssaunce" (*GP* 282)—and the Wife's role as a rich widow and successful cloth-maker tie their sumptuary excesses to the expansive influence of mercantile wealth in fourteenth-century culture.

To put it briefly, the connections between the Clerk and these two figures of mercantile *richesse* go beyond simple contrasting aesthetics. In their corresponding themes of perspectives skewed by material wealth, penetrating insight versus superficial sight, and the eroticization of newness—new spouses, new clothes, and even new bodies (in the case of the Wife's old crone)—the three tales suggest a larger dialectic between the literary and the material, with the ultimate effect of unsettling the Clerk's spiritual allegory of his tale and underscoring its more material

---

[48] Hodges *Secular Pilgrims*, argues that a few of the Merchant's garments are "neither as expensive nor as flagrant a sign of wealth as critics have supposed" (p. 86).

[49] See Patterson, *Chaucer and the Subject of History,* p. 344; and Bisson, "All that Glitters," pp. 169–70.

themes. The desireless Griselda might be seen as the antitype to the appetitive May and Alisoun of Bath, and the more general "bourgeois" predicament of a husband not prepared for an equal partner who can both assert her own desires and manipulate her reality to satiate them,[50] but she is also a comment *on* them, and thus cannot be understood in isolation from them. As I will discuss in the next section, this is especially true for the mercantile, domineering Wife of Bath and her "secte" of material women.

All-Consuming *Archewyves*

While throughout his tale the Clerk positions Griselda's fluctuating sartorial symbolism more generally in relation to the shallow gaze of the "peple" and their implied pilgrim contingent, in the final words of his tale and in the subsequent *Envoy* he explicitly narrows the tale's directive into a practical, material interpretation for a more specific type of practical, material listener: the Wife of Bath "and al hire secte" (1170–71).[51] Whether this "secte" carries its sexual or legal meaning, or whether it refers to the Wife's materialist *cause célèbre*,[52] it finally makes overt the heretofore veiled gendering of the Clerk's antimaterialism. This gendering is partly, but not wholly, a response to the Wife of Bath and her

---

[50] Considering the long-standing critical discourse on the ironic function of the *Envoy*, I feel I should point out that the larger themes of the *Envoy* as I discuss them here support the case that the *Envoy* was indeed meant as an address by the Clerk himself, though always with the underlying resonance of his own creator, Chaucer. On this critical debate, see George Lyman Kittredge, *Chaucer and His Poetry* (Cambridge Mass.: Harvard University Press, 1915), pp. 199–200; Michael D. Cherniss, "The *Clerk's Tale* and *Envoy*, the Wife of Bath's Purgatory, and the *Merchant's Tale*," *ChauR* 6 (1972): 235–54; Dolores Warwick Frese, "Chaucer's *Clerk's Tale:* The Monsters and the Critics Reconsidered," *ChauR* 8 (1973): 133–46; Thomas J. Farrell, "The 'Envoy de Chaucer' and the *Clerk's Tale*," *ChauR* 24 (1990): 329–36; John M. Ganim, "Carnival Voices in the Clerk's *Envoy*,"in *Chaucerian Theatricality* (Princeton: Princeton University Press, 1990), pp. 79–91; Howell Chickering, "Form and Interpretation in the *Envoy* to the *Clerk's Tale*," *ChauR* 29 (1995): 352–72.

[51] See Paul A. Olson's reading of this passage as the Clerk's attempt to associate the Wife with the flagrant materialism of the Epicurean sect, in *The Canterbury Tales and the Good Society* (Princeton: Princeton University Press, 1986), pp. 235–75. On the possible legal meaning of "secte" in this passage, see Joseph L. Baird, "The 'Secte' of the Wife of Bath," *ChauR* 2 (1968): 188–90, and "*Secte* and *Suite* Again: Chaucer and Langland," *ChauR* 6 (1971): 117–19, and Lillian Herlands Hornstein, "The Wyf of Bathe and the Merchant: From Sex to 'Secte,'" *ChauR* 3 (1968): 65–67.

[52] See, for example, Chaucer's lyric "Against Women Unconstant," which associates a women's desire for "newefangelnesse" in lovers with the changing color of her dress (*The Riverside Chaucer*, p. 657).

particular form of bourgeois materialism and marital economics. In a larger sense it taps into the moralizing sumptuary discourses of Chaucer's world, in which the category of person most associated with changeability and material desires, and thus that most likely to be the implied target of these themes in *The Clerk's Tale*, is the medieval woman or wife.[53] Tellingly, as a temptation in the human stages in life, *richesse* was thought to be especially pertinent for women—women being, in Diane Owen Hughes's words, the "ultimate symbol of a too transitory material world, corrupted initially by Eve's sin."[54]

The medieval tradition of seeing Griselda as a type of mirror for women underscores the Clerk's own possible objective in this regard. Roberta L. Krueger has recently outlined the trope of "impossibility" through which Boccaccio and Petrarch compare Griselda to contemporary wives, a theme reformulated into Griselda's role as a "biau mirror," or beautiful mirror for wives in the French translations by Philippe de Mézières and the *Le Ménagier de Paris,* and then later challenged by Christine de Pizan in her *Cité des Dames.*[55] Susan Crane has likewise pointed to "the reorientation toward exemplarity for women" in Chaucer's own version and in his anonymous French source, *Le Livre Griseldis,* which states in its preface that it has been created "a l'exemplaire des femmes mariees et toutes autres" [as an example for married women and all other women].[56]

When read with an eye toward the Clerk's acknowledged female audience, and within the larger context of the Griselda tale as a mirror for women, the Clerk's use of sartorial symbols suggests even stronger comparisons to "real" wives and their sumptuary excesses. In particular, his gendered allusions to attire highlight the substantial sumptuary component of marital conflict in this period. When placed in the context of contemporary women's marital rights, for example, the "smok" that Griselda requests of Walter at the dissolution of their marriage can be seen as a barbed reminder to English wives of their absolute lack of personal property rights. On the one hand, Griselda's smock works as a moral exemplum against women's attachment to their finery, the literal manifestation of the sartorial humility the Wife of Bath lacks: " 'In habit

[53] Hughes, "Regulating Women's Fashions," p. 144.
[54] Kreuger, "Uncovering Griselda," esp. pp. 76–81.
[55] Severs, *The Literary Relationships of Chaucer's Clerk's Tale*, p. 255 (line 2); Crane, *The Performance of Self,* p. 30.
[56] Klapisch-Zuber, *A History of Women,* esp. pp. 228–29.

maad with chastitee and shame / Ye wommen shul apparaille yow,'" the Wife quotes one husband as saying, "'And noght in tressed heer and gay perree, / As perles, ne with gold, ne clothes riche'" (*WOB Prologue,* 342–45). On the other hand, the scene is steeped in a commercial rhetoric that locates the smock in the realm of marital sexual and economic exchange: Griselda pointedly returns to Walter "*your* clothyng . . . *your* weddyng ryng,*" and "*youre* jueles" (867–69), and demands the smock in clear terms of compensatory payment "in gerdon of *my* maydenhede" and "to *my* meede" (883, 885, italics mine).

Importantly, while Chaucer in large part inherits these themes from his sources, he also enhances the material reality of the scene by adding Walter's reply to Griselda that she may have "the smok . . . that thou hast on thy bak" (890). In the same way that Italian audiences would have recognized the vesting and divesting of Griselda as part of the social practices around their marriage rituals, as Christiane Klapisch-Zuber has discussed,[57] English audiences would have recognized this sole garment "on thy bak" as the one personal item that a husband was legally required to bestow to his wife on his death. Despite Chaucer's depiction of the widow of Bath as gaining much wealth through the gifts "yeven" to her by her rich, old husbands (*WOB Prologue,* 631),

[57] Unlike any other item a wife might inherit from her husband, this garment "on her back" could not be claimed by creditors. See Frederick Pollock and Frederic Maitland, *The History of English Law,* vol. 2, 2nd ed. (Cambridge: Cambridge University Press, 1923), pp. 427–30. According to Janet S. Loengard, this does not mean that this garment was the only thing that married women received when their husbands died; in parts of England they received "dower," or life interest in land, and in some areas "thirds," and were even sometimes executors to the will. What the *paraphernalia* law represents is "the personal property [women] got as of right everywhere in England, with no gift from the husband—indeed, sometimes in spite of his wishes" (personal email, 27 April 2003). Much of Loengard's current work on the subject of paraphernalia rights has been presented in conference-paper form: "(Some of) the Clothes on Her Back: Widows, Personal Property, and Paraphernalia in Late Medieval England," 36th International Congress on Medieval Studies, Kalamazoo, Michigan, 2001; "Wills, Wives, and Chattels: Husbands' Attitudes to Household Property in Late-Medieval England," Medieval Academy of America Conference, Minneapolis, 2003. A related essay is her "'Plate, good stuff, & household things': Husbands, Wives, and Chattels in England at the End of the Middle Ages," in *Tant d'Emprises—So Many Undertakings: Essays in Honour of Anne F. Sutton,* ed. Livia Visser-Fuchs, *The Ricardian,* vol. 13 (2003). See also Maryanne Kowaleski's discussion of the difference between *common law,* under which women were "mere adjuncts" of their husbands, and *commercial law* (or law merchant), under which women could be considered "femme sole" if she traded separately from her husband, and under which men were not necessarily responsible for their wives' trading debts. Kowaleski, "Women's Work in a Market Town: Exeter in the Late Fourteenth Century," in *Women and Work in Pre-Industrial Europe,* ed. Barbara A. Hanawalt (Bloomington: Indiana University Press, 1986), pp. 145–64, at 146.

according to English common law, the husband, who owned outright all of the couple's personal property, was not legally required to return a woman's dowry or any other private item, with one exception: according to the law of *paraphernalia* rights, the woman had to be allowed one piece of "necessary" clothing.[58] In stipulating that Griselda, like a "wydwe" (836), leaves the marriage with only the garment on her back, and returns all other personal items to Walter, the Clerk emphasizes women's own meager legal status regarding the goods and clothes with which they adorn themselves.

Chaucer's most significant addition to Griselda's wardrobe, the "clooth of gold that brighte shoon" (1117) in which she is dressed after her third and final stripping, also extends the Clerk's rhetoric against ostentatious wives. On the surface the garment represents the long-overdue end to Griselda's suffering; after proving herself worthy, she, like Job, has her fortunes restored and receives her rightful place according to her *gentillesse* and humility. In late medieval Europe, "clooth of gold" was a specific and highly coveted material good; the pinnacle of sumptuous display, it was usually worn and exchanged by nobility and the very elite of the social strata. By the late fourteenth century, however, sumptuary legislation barring such material from lower and middle classes suggests that it had become problematically accessible.[59] "Clothes of gold," we remember, top the list of the "newe" vestimentary commodities that the wealthy Syrian merchants of *The Man of Law's Tale* bring for trading (137). The immorality of such clothing became a favorite topic of sermonizers; the fourteenth-century preacher Thomas Wimbleton, for example, explicitly uses the Job passage referred to in *The Clerk's Tale* to condemn gold clothes and other riches: "For we beþ / nouȝt gete wiþ riche cloþis, neiþer bore wiþ gold ne wiþ / siluer. Ynakid he bryngeþ vs in to þe world, nedy of mete, / cloþynge and drynke."[60]

Moreover, a few stanzas after describing Griselda's superior garment, the Clerk offers a contrasting image in the impure metaphorical "gold"

---

[58] See, for example, "A Statute Concerning Diet and Apparel," 37 Edwardi III (1363), *Statutes of the Realm* (*SR*) (London: Dawsons, 1963), I.380–81. On Italian Renaissance legislations of gold clothing and other luxuries, see studies by Hughes, Stuard, and Frick in n. 10 above.

[59] *Wimbleton's Sermon "Redde Rationem Villicationis tue": A Middle English Sermon of the Fourteenth Century,* ed. Ione Kemp Knight (Pittsburgh, Pa.: Duquesne University Press, 1967), lines 523–26. Quoted and discussed in Sponsler, *Drama and Resistance,* p. 7.

[60] Goldsmiths were included in the 1363 English sumptuary law, in which they are legally required to have surveyors make an "Assay" of their "Allay." See *SR* I.380.

of contemporary wives, which, he says, would not hold up under testing the way Griselda did: "The gold of hem hath now so badde alayes / With bras, that thogh the coyne be fair at ye, / It wolde rather breste a-two than plye" (1166–69).[61] Griselda's pure gold clothing works nicely to contrast the flashy but substandard gold of contemporary women, yet it still presents a problem with regard to the Clerk's larger rhetorical project: that is, how can he reward Griselda's humility with gold clothing without engaging in and encouraging the very artifice and covetousness that he shuns? Once again, the Clerk seems to find an answer to this dilemma in the material consciousness of his ever-present, ever-watching—and this time, explicitly gendered—fictional audience. Until this moment women have interacted with Griselda's clothing only as vehicles for Walter's power: Walter oversees the measurement of Griselda's first set of clothes on a "mayde lyk to hire stature" (257), and, as we have seen, before his first marriage he orders "the women" to strip her of her *rude* clothes and dress her in *richesse*. In regard to her gold clothing, however, for the first time Walter does not instigate Griselda's change of clothes. *The Clerk's Tale* makes no indication that Walter decrees or even knows in advance about Griselda's final "clooth of gold"; rather, it is a group of anonymous watchful "ladyes" (perhaps the same aforementioned women) who discretely take her away to strip and reclothe her when they see the right moment in the festivities: "whan that they hir tyme say" (1114). While, as Susan Crane has pointed out, the women's actions effectively condone Walter's treatment of his wife and even "remake" their marriage,[62] the implications of the scene seem more complicated than this. Why would this text, which has gone out of its way to locate the power of women's clothing symbolism in the hands of recognized patriarchal figures (husband, ruler, father), and thus also to keep true to its source texts, now in its final hour place Griselda's ultimate sartorial transformation entirely in the hands of anonymous female revelers? Is it really an accident that our first real glimpse at female agency in this tale concerns a socially savvy and upwardly-mobile costume change? Why is this particular moment allocated as women's "tyme" to step forward and intervene in the presentation of *povre* Griselda?

While the text does not give easy answers to these questions, it does

---

[61] Crane, *The Performance of Self,* p. 36.
[62] Wife of Bath's *Prologue,* lines 253–56, 265–70; and *Roman de la rose,* lines 8587–92, 8597–600.

seem telling that the Clerk would suddenly leave open the question of exactly who has power over Griselda's sartorial symbolism—which, despite his opening rhetoric of dismissal, he has repeatedly shown to hold immense social, political, economic, and even spiritual importance. Have these women usurped or been given some control here, and, if so, what does it mean? Could this final and unusual scene of private stripping and public acceptance (versus her heretofore public stripping and private acceptance) mean, for instance, that Griselda in some way finally *owns* the clothes on her body? Although I may be belaboring the point here, these questions gain real currency when we consider the subtext of marital ownership of material goods in this tale and *Envoy,* and the lengths to which the Clerk seems willing to go to conceal any potential for real resistance here from his listeners. As if on cue, for example, the sartorial transformation brought about by these women triggers the beginning of the end of the tale, for the following stanza initiates a temporal and spatial retreat into rhetorical synopsis and completion: "Thus hath this pitous day a blisful ende" (1121), concludes the Clerk, a remark that swiftly unites Griselda's final clothing transformation, the joyful "murthe and revel" (1123) of the people, and the ensuing, two-stanza happy ending of his Griselda narrative. The actions of "these ladies" thus mark an important shift in the tale, for the Clerk's apparent transfer of the sartorial matter from serious Walter to the reveling women, and his related move from "pitous" to "blisful," foreshadow the larger shift the Clerk makes in and around his *Envoy* a few stanzas later, when he loosens his formal structure and tone and appears to embrace the perspective of the Wife of Bath "and al hire secte": "I wol with lusty herte, fresshe and grene, / Seyn yow a song to glade yow, I wene" (1173–74). Not surprisingly, however, his apparent (and I might add, rather late) appeal to the pleasure of his listeners comes with its own inherent reproach, for in order to present this "glad" song, he says, he must "stynte of ernestful matere" (1175). Thus, as the Clerk constructs it, the *Envoy* in honor of all that is new, desirous, and entertaining (or "fressh and grene," "lusty," and "glad"), not to mention in honor of the "maistrie" of women, is frivolous and superfluous: an unnecessary, if popular and fashionable, new adornment to his heretofore "ernestful" tale.

As part of his strategy of undercutting the ornamental, the pleasurable, the popular, and the feminine, the Clerk situates his *Envoy* in the belief that men's and women's modes and materials of interpretation dramatically differ, for his shift from addressing "lordynges" (1163) to addressing "noble wyves" (1183) crucially coincides with his shift from insisting that the tale should be read as allegory for the trials of the Christian soul (1142–48) to his ultimate suggestion that the tale pertains to the material reality of contemporary "archewyves" (1195). This is especially clear at the end of the *Envoy*, when the Clerk adopts the language of the Wife of Bath (who adopted the language of the *Roman de la rose*) to advise women on how to manipulate their material performances for social gain:[63]

> If thou be fair, ther folk been in presence,
> Shewe thou thy visage and thyn apparaille;
> If thou be foul, be fre of thy dispence;
> To gete thee freendes ay do thy travaille;
> Be ay of chiere as light as leef on lynde,
> And lat hym care, and wepe, and wrynge, and waille!
> (1207–10)

This final stanza positions Griselda most clearly as the unstated counterexample to contemporary women's production of self-presentation. While she was "ay oon in herte and in visage" (711), for example, here we have the womanly manipulation of both "visage" and "apparaille." *Visage* in particular, with its correlation to falsity and deception, suggests the negative implications of women's control over their appearances.[64] Moreover, while Griselda exhibited no emotion when repeatedly stripped and dressed by her spouse, contemporary women almost inadvertently bring their spouses to dramatic displays of weeping with their consumption and ostentation. And finally, while Griselda worked untiringly with little interest in clothes or *richesse*, here contemporary women's work, or *travaille, is* their exuberant dressing and spending.[65] This

---

[63] *MED*, s.v. "visage," esp. 3b. In a related scene in *The Merchant's Tale*, May's predicament provokes the goddess Proserpine to bestow on all women the gift of cunning doubleness of "visage" (2272–75).

[64] On the various types of expenditure that this word expressed in this period, see *MED*, s.v. "dispence."

[65] See de Certeau, *The Practice of Everyday Life,* pp. xii–xx, 39–42, esp. 40–41. The Clerk's sarcastic reference to women's sumptuary "work" also invites correlation with a key aspect of what Thorstein Veblen termed "vicarious consumption," that is, the process in which women's association with consumption as a type of "work" coincides with their ultimate exclusion from economically productive, "public" work. See Thorstein Veblen, *The Theory of the Leisure Class* (1899; New York: Viking Press, 1967,), p. 81). Such a reading has obvious ramifications in this period, in which women's numerous

crucial troping of consumers as workers taps into what de Certeau has described as the active processes of consumption, by which consumption itself becomes not only a type of production but also a practice or method of resistance for the repressed. This type of resistance informs the sum and substance of the *Envoy,* in which women's "work" of *apparaille* and *dispence* determines not only their marital relationships but also women's roles in the greater community and even their reception of fictional tales like Griselda's.

The *Envoy*'s anonymous archwives obviously get much of their general momentum from their explicit association with the rebellious Wife of Bath. One specific and underexamined similarity is that the Wife's *Tale* also ends in a fervent state of conflict between husbands' general niggardliness and wives' love of *dispence.* For while she humorously draws her tale to a close by imagining a world in which Christ sends to women "Housbondes meeke, yonge, and fressh abedde" (1259) with which to live their long, ever-joyous lives, Alisoun actually ends on a much angrier and arguably more revealing note, in which she curses "olde and angry nygardes of dispence," asking God to cut short their lives with the "verray pestilence" (1263–64). After the extended talk about sexual, rhetorical, social, and intellectual "sovereignty" throughout her *Prologue* and *Tale,* then, the Wife chooses as her ultimate word on the subject *consumer* sovereignty.[66] Despite the Wife of Bath's jolly resistance to her various husbands' attempts to curb her sartorial spending and display in her *Prologue* ("Thou shalt nat bothe, thogh that thou were wood, / Be maister of my body and of my good," she declares [313–14]), it seems she cannot encompass these misers neatly into her fantasy of feminine dominance, and the undisguised resentment they bring out in the normally humorous if histrionic Wife lingers after her own formidable verbal performance has ended.

Considering the Clerk's larger rhetoric of sartorial *richesse* and *rudenesse*

---

positions in post-plague market production heightened anxiety about socioeconomic gender roles, and, moreover, which directly preceded women's relative exclusion from the workforce in the Early Modern period. See Martha C. Howell, *Women, Production, and Patriarchy in Late Medieval Cities* (Chicago: University of Chicago Press, 1986), esp. pp. 182–83.

[66] A corresponding focus on marital *dispence* exists in *The Shipman's Tale,* which critical tradition surmises probably originated as a tale for the Wife. This tale's exploration of the themes of marital, sexual, and financial spending, exchanging, and debt echoes the Wife's own; indeed, as in the Wife's *Prologue,* in this tale marital *dispence,* though technically the responsibility of husbands, is ultimately controlled through manipulation by wives. See esp. lines 1–19.

and his overt address to the Wife of Bath, it is no coincidence that this theme of *dispence* reemerges at the end of his *Envoy.* In fact, from its inception, the *Envoy* seems to frame its marital concerns as sumptuary concerns. The Clerk's reference to Griselda at the beginning of the *Envoy*—his last mention of her—asks us to envision her not only "deed" and buried in Italy (1177–78), but as the potential victim of a curiously literal mode of consumption—that is, in the entrails of that fabled ingester of patient wives, Chichevache:

> O noble wyves, ful of heigh prudence,
> Lat noon humylitee youre tonge naille,
> Ne lat no clerk have cause or diligence
> To write of yow a storie of swich mervaille
> As of Grisildis pacient and kynde,
> Lest Chichevache yow swelwe in hire entraille!
> (*Envoy,* 1183–88)

This striking depiction of the public reception of stories as a feminine cow that eats patient wives has one target and one immediate parallel: the "noble wyves" to whom these words are addressed, and who have at this moment received the Clerk's tale of Griselda.[67] Yet this is not merely about a cannibalistic feminine that "consumes" both masculine writing and a favorite subject of masculine writing, feminine patience. Rather, these lines form part of a greater context of consumption in the *Envoy* that harnesses more traditional misogynist themes of female oral rapaciousness and verbosity to contemporary material modes of consumption, women's *apparaille* and *dispence.*

The legend of Chichevache comes from the French *Chicheface,* and while it is often translated as lean-cow or lean-face, a more literal interpretation would be "miser-cow."[68] Chichevache signifies one of the few

---

[67] Lydgate's later poem about Chichevache offers just such a vision; in it, the emaciated cow mourns Griselda as her "oone" and only meal long gone, and prepares to give up on her life's search because "Wymmen haue made hem self so stronge" with their "cruweltee" and "violence." John Lydgate, "Bycorne and Chychevache," in *The Minor Poems of John Lydgate II,* ed. Henry Noble MacCracken, EETS, e.s. 107 (London: Oxford University Press, 1934), pp. 433–38; lines 99, 122, 121, 126.

[68] A *chiche* or *chinche* in Middle English means a rich person who is stingy or greedy; it is associated with *coveitise,* and the hording of *richesse* (*MED,* "chinche"). On the names of these beasts, see Eleanor Prescott Hammond, *English Verse Between Chaucer and Surrey* (Durham, N.C.: Duke University Press, 1927), pp. 113–15. See also Malcolm Jones, "Monsters of Misogyny: Bigorne and Chichevache—Suite et Fin?" in *Marvels, Monsters, and Miracles: Studies in Medieval and Early Modern Imaginations,* ed. Timothy S. Jones and

fabled monsters of medieval origin—she emerges for the first time in fourteenth-century French and English texts—and she is a paradoxical figure. She is a beast both monstrous and pitiful, whose only food consists of patient and virtuous wives, and thus who almost dies of starvation from lack thereof. While her gender is usually designated as feminine, a clear tradition of associating the beast with the abused husband exists; Jehan le Fèvre's fourteenth-century *Lamentations de Mathéolus,* for example (a text Chaucer most likely knew, and which may have been the model for Jankyn's book of wicked wives), positions *himself* as the poor beast, monstrously shrunken and emasculated by his proud beast of a wife.[69] The idea that Chichevache might represent piteous, feminized husbands starved of their capacity to "consume" their wives, and the corresponding aesthetic of the emaciated miser-husband consumed by proud, horned, ostentatious wives (in the figure of Chichevache's mate, Bicorn), fits very easily into the larger network of sartorial discourses that underline the Clerk's dialectic of marital rivalry in his *Envoy.*

Women's attire in late medieval Europe was said to metaphorically "consume" men in various ways, from the ravishment men experienced by looking at women's clothing, to the entrapment of their souls by women "wantonly adorned," to the ruination of husbands' fortunes by wives' lavish spending on attire.[70] England's own growing cultural concern about material property and subjectivity took on special meaning with regard to lower- and middle-class women for several reasons,

---

David A. Sprunger (Kalamazoo: Western Michigan University, 2002), pp. 203–21; and Steven M. Taylor, "Monsters of Misogyny: The Medieval French 'Dit de Chincheface' and the 'Dit de Bigorne,'" in *Allegorica* 5:2 (Winter 1980): 99–124. See also Lydgate's poem "Bycorne and Chychevache" in his *Minor Poems,* pp. 433–37. I explore the fable of Chichevache and Bicorn more thoroughly in my forthcoming article "Lydgate's Golden Cows: Appetite and Avarice in *Bycorne and Chichevache,*" in *Poetry and Material Culture in the Fifteenth Century,* ed. Lisa H. Cooper and Andrea Denny-Brown (New York: Palgrave MacMillen, 2007).

[69] "Je suy comme une chicheface, Maigre par dessoubs ma peaucelle" ["I am like a Chicheface, meager beneath my skin"]. Jehan le Fèvre, *Les Lamentations de Matheolus et Le Livre de Leesce de Jehan le Fèvre,* ed. A. G. Van Hamel (Paris: Émile Bouillon, 1892), 3.3320–21, mistakenly numbered as line 3220 in the edition of text and subsequent citations.

[70] On "wantonly adorned" women who capture souls and deceive men, see Owst, *Literature and Pulpit,* pp. 390–404, at 395. On the preambles of sumptuary laws that agonize over women's "excessive expenditures on wicked and impractical" attire that "consumes their husbands and sons," see Stanley Chojnaki, "The Power of Love: Wives and Husbands in Late Medieval Venice," in *Women and Power in the Middle Ages,* ed. Mary Erler and Maryanne Kowaleski (Athens: University of Georgia Press, 1988), p. 131.

among them, women's symbolic status as commodities, their traditional role as figures for men's adornment, and their new importance in post-plague market production, all of which played important roles in the cultural inscription of conspicuous consumption on the female body.[71] Indeed, although medieval European sumptuary laws show substantial variation in their targets and objectives, most sumptuary historians agree that the shift in sumptuary laws to focus more on women's dress coincided with the growth of the urban mercantile class.[72] In England in particular, legislation of women's sartorial choices was tied closely to their subordinate cultural status. Following what Claire Sponsler has described as the "imaginary pattern of social relations" constructed by sumptuary laws, for instance, women's attire and consumption privileges were governed almost completely by the socioeconomic status of their father or husband.[73] Related to this is the aforementioned ongoing dispute, starting in the mid-fourteenth century, between the ecclesiastical and secular courts in England about whether a woman's clothing and jewelry—her *paraphernalia* in medieval legalese—were her very own (*sua propria*) or, like the rest of her land and goods, under the control of her husband. In the words of Pollock and Maitland's eminent *History of English Law*, "[t]he idea that the ornaments of the wife's person are specially her own seems to struggle for recognition in England" in this period.[74] Control over the resources of a woman's appearance and self-presentation became central to late medieval identity constructions, manifesting itself not only in sumptuary and property laws but also in the performance of gender and marital subject positions. At its heart was a growing recognition among men that women could use the very material of masculine adornment to accrue their own material and symbolic capital; that is, they could transform commodities to be their own and thus maneuver around the strategies of masculine disciplining forces.[75]

---

[71] On the new status of women in market production challenging "male preserves" and helping to form a new gender identity, see Howell, *Women, Production, and Patriarchy in Late Medieval Cities,* esp. pp. 182–83.

[72] Alan Hunt, *Governance of the Consuming Passions: A History of Sumptuary Law* (New York: St. Martin's Press, 1996), p. 235.

[73] Sponsler, *Drama and Resistance,* p. 17.

[74] Pollock and Maitland, *The History of English Law,* p. 430. See my discussion on pp. 101–02 above.

[75] Boccaccio illuminates this process in his description of women's post-marriage power grab: "Thinking they have climbed to a high station, though they know they were born to be servants, they at once take hope and whet their appetite for mastery;

Chaucer's Clerk situates the disparity between his *Tale* and *Envoy* precisely in this site of contention. As we remember, Griselda's marriage is based on her abdication of her right to choose: her choice is *not* to choose, her response is *not* to respond, and this lack of choice manifests itself in her vacillating sartorial *richesse* and *rudenesse*. In direct contrast to this, the Clerk positions the archwives as rulers in the act of decision-making: praising, albeit ironically, the women's "heigh prudence" (1183) and offering to "consaille" the women's "governaille" (1200). Underlying these general themes of marital and political control are further examples of a concerted focus on economic control over commodities and consumption. For example, when the Clerk tells the *noble wyves* that in order to take on themselves the "governaille" (1192), they must "evere answereth at the countretaille" (1190), he alludes to wives' general garrulousness, but also to their consumer profligacy.[76] Literally the other half of a tally kept by the creditor and presented for payment, a counter-tally was often used as a pun that linked material and sexual debt, as in *The Shipman's Tale,* in which a wife explains how she will pay her merchant husband for the debt she accrued with her new clothing ("I am youre wyf," she says, "score it upon my taille" [416]). This pun also invokes a popular conceit that portrays women as serpents or scorpions, who flatter with their heads so they can sting with their sexual and sumptuary "tail," a conceit that Chaucer elsewhere explicitly associates with the dangers of the "monstre" Fortune and her false goods.[77]

This association of a wife's defiant "reply" to her husband with monstrous or devilish sumptuary resistance was part of the larger moral discourse in which fashionable women were identified as the devil's army,

---

and while pretending to be meek, humble, and obedient, they beg from their wretched husbands the crowns, girdles, cloths of gold, ermines, the wealth of clothes, and the various other ornaments in which they are seen resplendent every day; the husband does not perceive that all these are weapons to combat his mastery and vanquish it. The women, no longer servants but suddenly equals . . . contrive with all their might to seize control." Giovanni Boccaccio, *Corbaccio,* trans. Anthony K. Cassell (Urbana: University of Illinois Press, 1975), p. 24. Quoted in Hallissy, *Clean Maids, True Wives, Steadfast Widows,* p. 127. See also David Wallace, *Chaucerian Polity,* 19.

[76] See, for example, Benson's gloss on this word, which identifies both meanings (p. 153).

[77] See *The Merchant's Tale,* lines 2057–62; quotation at 2062. "A scorpion that maketh fair semblaunt with the face and pricketh with the tail; so a wickid woman draweth by flatteryngis, and prickith til deth"; Gloss from Ecclesiasticus 8.10 in the Wycliffite Bible, as quoted in Bartlett J. and Helen W. Whiting, *Proverbs, Sentences, and Proverbial Phrases from English Writings Mainly Before 1500* (Cambridge, Mass.: Belknap Press of Harvard University Press, 1968), S96. See also Benson, "Explanatory Notes," p. 972.

which was "armed for every sin, having, for their helmet, horns and head-dresses and frontlets, and likewise with the rest of their armor, so that from the sole of their foot to the crown of their head you will find nothing save the Devil's sharpest arrows in them . . . to wound the heart of the beholder."[78] Men, moreover, were taught to defend themselves from this vestimentary attack: Saint Bernadino of Siena, for example, advises that a husband should counter his spouse's vestimentary excesses by "beating a wife 'with feet and fists.' "[79] The Clerk also taps into this discourse with his reference to *archewyves* who "stondeth at defense," as "strong as is a greet camaille" (1195–96). Here he appears to be using a pun on the word "camaille" as both the desert beast and a piece of knightly armor called a "camel," thus implying that not only were these wives unnaturally strong in particularly alien ways, but that they were literally armored in response to the "housbonde armed . . . in maille," with which it rhymes in the next stanza (1202).[80] These armored wives use their "arwes of . . . crabbed eloquence" (1203) to pierce a husband's "brest and eek his aventaille" (1204).

While the rhetoric of armored women or amazons that persisted as a popular image of female rebelliousness in late medieval sermons and literature was in part informed by the ancient literary fascination with amazons, in the fourteenth century there were also new material considerations behind such rhetoric. For among the striking changes in attire in fourteenth-century Europe was a widespread shift toward a more militaristic appearance in both male and female dress. The most dramatic changes in fashions in this period not only followed the cut-to-fit tailoring of knightly doublets or pourpoints, the padded garments worn under plate armor, but also took on a distinctly armored aesthetic, with the surface of clothing "punctuated by decorative accents produced by pointed daggers, the sharp metal points of laces and conspicuous buckles."[81] In addition to fictional women such as the Wife of Bath, who wears a hat "[a]s brood as is a bokeler or a targe" and "spores sharpe" on her feet (*General Prologue* 471, 473), in the fourteenth century there were well-known stories about "actual" women publicly donning male

---

[78] Bromyard, "Bellum," *Summa Predicantium* [*SP*], British Library, MS Royal 7 E IV, quoted in Owst, *Literature and Pulpit*, p. 393.

[79] Angela M. Lucas, *Women in the Middle Ages: Religion, Marriage, and Letters* (New York: St. Martin's Press, 1983), p. 127. Quoted in Hallissy, *Clean Maids, True Wives, Steadfast Widows*, p. 119.

[80] See Benson, "Explanatory Notes," p. 884.

[81] Newton, *Fashion in the Age of the Black Prince*, p. 8.

attire or knightly armor. Henry Knighton's *Chronicon,* for example, describes the growing problem of large groups of women attending tournaments dressed in masculine attire, with daggers slung low on their hips.[82] Such stories have led at least one historian to surmise that discourses about women's rebelliousness in attire might be indicative of a greater and recognized "feminist movement" in this period.[83]

Griselda as Sumptuary Model

The questions of materialism that develop in *The Clerk's Tale* and *Envoy,* and especially the sartorial particulars of these questions, leave us looking on some level for material interpreters. Chaucer offers two immediate examples in the Host and the Merchant, both of whom relate the tale, against the apparent directive of the Clerk, to their own wives.[84]

Looking beyond the pilgrim audience, however, one can see that while Chaucer's Clerk addresses his own sumptuary reading of Griselda to contemporary "archewyves," it is another avid clerkly reader who responds. Nearly half a century after Chaucer's death, the monk and poet John Lydgate writes a poem addressed to "Noble pryncessis," in which he decries women's fashionable headdresses—dubbed "horns" by moralists—and implored women to "cast away" such unnatural attire:

> Clerkys recorde, by gret auctoryte,
> Hornes wer yove to bestys ffor dyffence—
> A thyng contrarie to ffemynyte,
> To be maad sturdy of resystence.
> But arche wives, egre in ther vyolence,
> Fers as tygre ffor to make affray,
> They haue despit, and ageyne concyence,
> Lyst nat of pryde, ther hornes cast away.
>
> (33–40)[85]

---

[82] Knighton's *Chronicle 1137–1396,* ed. and trans. G. H. Martin (Oxford: Clarendon Press, 1995), pp. 92–95. See also Newton's discussion of Galvano della Flamma's descriptions of Milanese amazons in golden girdles (pp. 10–11).

[83] Newton, *Fashion in the Age of the Black Prince,* p. 19.

[84] While the Host wishes aloud that his wife could have heard the tale (1212b–e), the Merchant aligns his own "wepyng and waylyng" (*Prologue* 1213) with those husbands of the *Envoy* beaten down by their profligate arch-wives; she would "overmacche" (1220) the devil, he says, with her "passyng crueltee" (1225) and her "cursednesse" (1239). On Chaucer's likely canceling of the Host's stanza, see Benson, "Explanatory Notes," p. 884.

[85] Lydgate, "A dyte of womenhis hornys," entitled "Horns Away," in *Minor Poems,* pp. 662–65.

As this passage suggests, Lydgate effectively adopts the vocabulary of the Clerk's *Envoy* and the Wife of Bath's *Prologue* to explore the issue of women's sartorial extravagance. In addition to hailing clerkly "auctoryte," for example, Lydgate describes how "experyence" proves that beauty prevails despite elaborate fashions (7–8), and how nature has "souereynte" over crafted appearance (2–3). As in the Clerk's *Envoy*, Lydgate's true target is not specifically the Wife of Bath, but the greater general population of "arche wives" that she exemplifies; while Chaucer's Clerk states "Ye archewyves, stondeth at defense, / . . . egre as is a tygre yond in Ynde" (1195, 1199), Lydgate's likewise declares them "arche wives, egre in ther vyolence, / Fers as tygre ffor to make affray."

In addition to the overt lexical borrowings from the *Envoy*, Lydgate invokes Griselda as the sartorial counterexample in various subtle ways. While Griselda remains "ay oon in herte and in visage" (711) throughout all of Walter's attempts to "assaye" her "variance" (710), Lydgate decries the "counterfet" aspects of contemporary women's attire (22), focusing on the "foreyn apparence" of elaborate fashions and the accompanying implications of duplicity in the wearer (2). Like the attractive but impure gold alloy of the Clerk's contemporary women (1167–69), Lydgate declares that in the world of fashion "[t]hyng counterfeet wol faylen at assay" (14). More specifically like the Clerk, Lydgate uses the metaphor of amalgamated gold to describe women's deceptive appearance, stating that "trewe metall requeryth noon allay" (6). Generally speaking, Lydgate addresses the pretences of high fashion more directly, pushing his sartorial metaphors even further than Chaucer's Clerk, such as when he contrasts "pure" gold with the golden cloth that women wear: "Tween gold and gossomer is greet dyfference" (5).[86] Within this framework Lydgate formulates a clear sartorial binary construction from the vocabulary of *The Clerk's Tale* and *Envoy,* and specifically from the contrasting attributes of the ostentatious Wife of Bath and naked Griselda: on the one hand are the "arche wives," whose "counterfeet" fashions ally them with "Crafft," "richesse," "dyffence," "vyolence," "resystence," and "thyng contrarie to ffemynyte," and on the other are the "wyves trewe," whose "natural" kerchiefs characterize their associations with "Nature," God-given "bewte," "prudence," "humylyte," "chast

---

[86] Lydgate often uses the term *gossamer,* a specific type of gauzy gold material popular for decoration in the Middle Ages, to contrast with simpler material. In his satirical poem "The Order of Fools," for example, he twice compares gossamer to wool, in *Minor Poems,* pp. 449–55; lines 63–64, 137–38.

innocence," and of course, "pacyence." In the end, Lydgate summons this final and most famous attribute of Griselda to entreat women to strip themselves of their finery: "Vnder support of your pacyence," he pleads, "Yeveth example hornes to cast away" (47–48).

In addressing women's horned headdresses, this poem tackles one of the most common and most dramatic examples of late medieval women's fashion rebellion, and one that certainly would have informed the sartorial subtext of the Clerk's *Envoy*. Fourteenth- and fifteenth-century sermons and poems cite women's horned headdresses as the epitome of fashion's unnaturalness, violent disobedience, and ornamental extremes.[87] The homiletic tradition associates a woman wearing a horned headdress with the violent ox of Exodus 21.28–29, who kills innocent people when its master fails to restrain it.[88] One early fourteenth-century French poem likewise founds its objections to women's horns on the fact that women wear such clothes "por tuer les hommes," to kill the men.[89] The way to counter this rebellion, the sermonizer Bromyard suggests, is to strip the women bald of their headdresses and other adornments in an Isaiah-like (and Walter-like) purging of prideful adornment: "The Lord will make bald the crown of the head of the daughters of Sion, and will strip their hair."[90] The biblical passage he cites was a favorite of moralists in this period, and it revels in the endless possibilities of stripping away women's finery:

In that day the Lord will take away the ornaments of shoes, and little moons, / And chains and necklaces, and bracelets, and bonnets, / And bodkins, and ornaments of the legs, and tablets, and sweet balls, and earrings, / And rings, and jewels hanging on the forehead, / And changes of apparel, and short cloaks, and fine linen, and crisping pins, / And looking glasses, and lawns, and headbands, and fine veils. (Isaiah 3:18–23)

---

[87] Owst, *Literature and Pulpit,* pp. 393–96.

[88] Bromyard, "Ornatus," *SP,* quoted in ibid., p. 403. Men can also be seen defending themselves with a sword and shield from a woman wearing a horned headdress in a medieval misericord in a parish church of Ludlow, reproduced in Francis Bond, *Wood Carvings in English Churches I: Misericords* (Oxford: Henry Frowde, 1910), p. 180.

[89] Line 22 of "Des Cornetes," in Frederick W. Fairholt, *Satirical Songs and Poems on Costume* (London: Percy Society, 1849), pp. 29–39. According to the poem, this marital conflict is encouraged by the Bishop of Paris, who will give ten days' pardon to anyone who condemns horned ladies in public with the phrase "push, ram," in reference to the Exodus passage.

[90] Bromyard, "Ornatus," *SP,* quoted in Owst, *Literature and Pulpit,* p. 403.

Considering this larger context, while Lydgate's incorporation of the Clerk's *Envoy* into his own contemporary fashion debates on women's horned headdresses may suggest a certain level of effectiveness of Chaucer's sumptuary discourses, it also attests to the moralized and popularized appeal throughout the last centuries of the Middle Ages for women to "cast away" their finery, and the corresponding attractiveness of the figure of Griselda as a contemporary sartorial model for that appeal. The Clerk's antimaterialism is steeped in this particular moral discourse about material goods, which targets the disparity between the spiritual abjection such goods expose and the cultural capital they bestow. While the Clerk may dismiss the frivolity of materialistic, untutored "interpreters" in his dress, his rhetoric, and in his final words, his larger sartorial dialectic between *richesse* and *rudenesse*, his link between Griselda's sartorial transformations and the worldly, changing "peple," and his final address to the consuming *archevyves* of the world, all suggest that his asceticism hides an unspoken apprehension about, and fascination with, worldly, material aesthetics.

The Parson's Predilection for Pleasure

Nicole D. Smith
University of North Texas

F ASHIONABLE DRESS tended to outrage clerics in the fourteenth century.[1] While aristocrats and the upwardly mobile donned luxurious garments to signal wealth and beauty, churchmen railed against these stylish wares as marks of vainglory and invitations to lust. It is thus not surprising that Chaucer's Parson condemns the excesses of fashion under the rubric of pride in his vernacular penitential, a guide that outlines the seven deadly sins and further instructs clerics and laity in the arts of contrition, confession, and satisfaction of sin.[2] Ostentatious notching of sleeves and hemlines, undulating stripes, and folded decorative borders are understood as unnecessary sartorial additions that waste precious cloth and convey the proud individual's tendency toward excess. Such "wast of clooth in vanitee" (X.417) is furthermore evident, according to the Parson, in gowns of superfluous length, which become "consumed, thredbare, and rotten with donge" when trailed through mire (X.419), and in ornamental cut-outs of dagged designs, which are not only ex-

I am grateful to Susan Crane, Stacy Klein, Frank Grady, and the anonymous readers of *SAC* for their valuable comments at various stages in the development of this essay.

[1] For a general overview of clerical opinions of dress in the fourteenth century, see G. R. Owst, *Literature and Pulpit in Medieval England* (New York: Barnes and Noble, 1961), pp. 390–414.

[2] Lee Patterson's "The 'Parson's Tale' and the Quitting of the 'Canterbury Tales,'" *Traditio* 34 (1978): 331–80, establishes the genre of the *Tale* as a penitential manual with a "tripartite structure to match the three parts of penance": contrition in the heart, confession by mouth, and satisfaction through penitential deeds (p. 339). For the critical debate over the *Tale*'s genre prior to Patterson, see Coolidge O. Chapman, "The Parson's Tale: A Medieval Sermon," *MLN* 43 (1928): 229–34; H. G. Pfander, "Some Medieval Manuals of Religious Instruction in England and Observations on Chaucer's Parson's Tale," *JEGP* 35 (1936): 243–58; and Siegfried Wenzel, "Notes on the *Parson's Tale*," *ChauR* 16:3 (1982): 237–56, esp. pp. 248–49. For a more recent critical inquiry into the influence of meditative literature on *The Parson's Tale*, see Thomas H. Bestul, "Chaucer's *Parson's Tale* and the Late-Medieval Tradition of Religious Meditation," *Speculum* 64:3 (1989): 600–619.

travagant but also impractical: punching holes in garments and slitting them with shears results in apparel that fails to provide adequate protection from inclement weather.

In a sharp turn from "to muche superfluite" (X.415) in dress, the Parson looks to the demerits of scant of attire in such a way that invites further consideration:

Upon that oother side, to speken of the horrible disordinat scantnesse of clothyng, as been thise kutted sloppes, or haynselyns, that thurgh hire shortnesse ne covere nat the shameful membres of man, to wikked entente. / Allas, somme of hem shewen the boce of hir shap, and the horrible swollen membres, that semeth lik the maladie of hirnia, in the wrappynge of hir hoses; / and eek the buttokes of hem faren as it were the hyndre part of a she-ape in the fulle of the moone. / And mooreover, the wrecched swollen membres that they shewe thurgh disgisynge, in departynge of hire hoses in whit and reed, semeth that half hir shameful privee membres weren flayne. / And if so be that they departen hire hoses in othere colours, as is whit and blak, or whit and blew, or blak and reed, and so forth, / thanne semeth it, as by variaunce of colour, that half the partie of hire privee membres were corrupt by the fir of Seint Antony, or by cancre, or by oother swich meschaunce. / Of the hyndre part of hir buttokes, it is ful horrible for to see. For certes, in that partie of hir body ther as they purgen hir stynkynge ordure, / that foule partie shewe they to the peple prowdly in despit of honestitee, which honestitee that Jhesu Crist and his freendes observede to shewen in hir lyve. / Now, as of the outrageous array of women, God woot that though the visages of somme of hem seme ful chaast and debonaire, yet notifie they in hire array of atyr likerousnesse and pride. (X.422–30)[3]

Here the message is clear: men who wear short, fitted jackets and tight hose act sinfully because they "shewe to the peple" the contours of their "horrible swollen membres." Likewise, women display vices of lechery and pride in their "outrageous array" of attire. Both are guilty of partaking in what the Parson describes as "the synful costlewe array of clothynge, and, namely, in to muche superfluite" (a nod to the women) "or elles in to desordinat scantnesse" (a gesture to the men) (X.415).

It has been well over a century since Mark Liddell first observed the passage's similarity to a thirteenth-century French sermon, which states

---

[3] Quotations are from *The Riverside Chaucer,* 3rd ed., gen. ed. Larry D. Benson (New York: Houghton Mifflin, 1987).

that one sins through pride by wearing clothing that is either too short and revealing or too luxurious in length and style.[4] Liddell explains that the preacher of MS Bodley 90 "presents his bill of particulars with the same vindictiveness that is found in Chaucer" when addressing the men in his audience: "knights, valets, squires, clerics, laity, and secular folk, . . . take pains to ornament, adorn, and reveal [them]selves in garments too tightly tailored in front at the breast and [too tightly] brought together at the rear."[5] Both the French sermon and *The Parson's Tale* are concerned with the excessive shortness and superfluity in prideful apparel,[6] and both call attention to bodies that "shewe" themselves.[7] But while Liddell notes that the French sermon treats women's extravagance at great length, the consideration of women and their fineries in *The Parson's Tale* is at best anticlimactic.[8] The Parson's rendition instead elaborates quite extensively on the contours of the male body clad in couture. This is a somewhat surprising rhetorical decision and one that merits renewed consideration because the more common clerical position, as the Wife of Bath reminds us in her *Prologue,* would be to condemn women for making themselves "gay with clothyng" (III.337–38).

---

[4] Mark Liddell provides selected excerpts from the French sermon of MS Bodley 90, fol. 3a, in his "The Source of Chaucer's 'Person's Tale' II," *The Academy* 1259 (June 20, 1896): 509. "De fet pecche home par orgoil . . . in uesture des robes, sicome en robes trop preciouses selonc son estat, ou trop lunges, ou trop curtes, . . . ou par orgoil taillez, ou estreitment recoillez, ou attornez, ou trop deliciouses, ou a superfluite, ceo est trop larges ou trop lunges, e ausi en chaucure ou en cheuals" [Concerning deed, man sins through pride . . . in clothing of men's dress, as in garments that are too precious for one's estate, or too long, or too short, . . . or cut pridefully, or assembled tightly, or adorned, or too sumptuous, or excessive, that is to say too wide or too long, and also in shoes and in horses]. The omissions are Liddell's; English translations here and elsewhere are mine unless otherwise specified. Liddell provides information on the dating of the sermon in "The Source of Chaucer's 'Person's Tale,'" *The Academy* 1256 (May 30, 1896): 447–48.

[5] "Aus cheualers, uallez, esquires, clers e lais, seculers, ke tant de peine metez de vus acemer e aorner, e en robes trop queintement taillez vus atorner e deuant au peitrin e a reredos recoillees," in Liddell, "The Source of Chaucer's 'Person's Tale' II," p. 509.

[6] For similarities between MS Bodley 90, fol. 3a, and *The Parson's Tale,* see Liddell, "A New Source of the Parson's Tale," in *An English Miscellany* (Oxford: Clarendon Press, 1901), pp. 255–77; Siegfried Wenzel, "The Source for Chaucer's Seven Deadly Sins," *Traditio* 30 (1974): 351–78; Wenzel, "The Source for the 'Remedia' of the Parson's Tale," *Traditio* 27 (1971): 433–53; and Patterson, "The 'Parson's Tale,'" p. 340 n. 29.

[7] In the French sermon, the verbs *aorner, acesmer,* and *atorner* all imply that one dresses oneself in order to be shown ("se parer" would be the modern French equivalent). See Algirdas Julien Greimas, *Dictionnaire de l'ancien français* (Paris: Larousse, 2001).

[8] Liddell, "The Source of Chaucer's 'Person's Tale' II," p. 509; see also John Finlayson, "The Satiric Mode and the *Parson's Tale,*" *ChauR* 6 (1971): 94–116, at 115.

What we have in the Parson's diatribe on dress seems to be a rare example of original Chaucerian invention, which stands in sharp contrast to the rest of the largely translated tale.[9]

Such an observation is hardly new.[10] Many deem the Parson's commentary on prideful dress noteworthy because of its vivid imagery; it has been described as "some lively turns of phrase and pungent descriptive writing,"[11] "savagely humorous," and "sexually titillating."[12] Yet critics have not hitherto considered the sexual and social implications of having the Parson voice more concern over proud fashionable men than their equally sinful female counterparts.[13] Indeed, the renewed critical atten-

---

[9] Derrick G. Pitard has described *The Parson's Tale* as being the "least vernacular" tale in the *Canterbury* collection because of its status as a largely translated text. See his "Sowing Difficulty: *The Parson's Tale*, Vernacular Commentary, and the Nature of Chaucerian Dissent," *SAC* 26 (2004): 299–330, at 299. Kate Oelzner Petersen establishes in *The Sources of the Parson's Tale* (Boston: Aethenaeum Press, 1901) that lines 80–386 and lines 958–1080 of the *Tale* are derived from the chapter "De paenitentiis et remissionibus" in Raymond of Pennafort's *Summa de paenitentia*, written between 1225 and 1227 and reworked in 1235–36. Chaucer drew a larger part of his treatment of the seven deadly sins and their remedies from William Peraldus's *Summa de vitiis et virtutibus*, which was circulated widely in 1249–50. Both Pennafort and Peraldus composed their penitential tracts in order to promote penitential and pastoral reforms of the Fourth Lateran Council in 1215, which required annual auricular confession. For introductory material on Pennafort and Peraldus in relation to *The Parson's Tale*, see Richard Newhauser's entry in *Sources and Analogues of the Canterbury Tales*, vol. 1, ed. Robert M. Correale and Mary Hamel (Cambridge: D. S. Brewer, 2002), pp. 529–614.

[10] For Chaucer's treatment of fashion as original invention, see Albert E. Hartung, "'The Parson's Tale' and Chaucer's Penance," in *Literature and Religion in the Later Middle Ages* (Binghamton: Medieval and Renaissance Texts and Studies, 1995), pp. 61–80, at 71; D. Biggins, in "*Canterbury Tales* X (I) 424: 'The Hyndre Part of a She-Ape in the Fulle of the Moone,'" *MÆ* 33:3 (1964): 200–203; Wenzel, "The Source for Chaucer's Seven Deadly Sins," p. 377; Wenzel, "The Source for the 'Remedia' of the Parson's Tale," p. 453; and Patterson, "The 'Parson's Tale,'" p. 340 n. 29.

[11] Derek Pearsall, *The Canterbury Tales* (London: George Allen, 1985), p. 289.

[12] Finlayson, "The Satiric Mode and the *Parson's Tale*," p. 116. David Aers sees "the erotic as a degraded area" in *The Parson's Tale*, but not because of sexual innuendo. Rather, Aers finds eroticism corrupt because the Parson neglects to incorporate love into the practices of marital sex; see his *Chaucer, Langland, and the Creative Imagination* (London: Routledge, 1980), p. 110. For a reading that elides eroticism in *The Parson's Tale*, see Anne Laskaya, *Chaucer's Approach to Gender in the Canterbury Tales* (Cambridge: D. S. Brewer, 1995), pp. 128–30.

[13] Beryl Rowland highlights the relationship between the sartorial effects of tight-fitting hose and simian sexuality in "Chaucer's She-Ape (*PT*, 424)," *ChauR* 2 (1968): 159–65, while Biggins examines Chaucer's use of the simian metaphor as a way of conveying melancholy since apes were apparently melancholic when they were "under lunar influence" (p. 202). In "The Horsemen of the *Canterbury Tales*," *ChauR* 3:1 (1968): 29–36, Rodney Delasanta interprets the Parson's "disquisition on the prideful array of clothing" as a way to "undercut those 'in outrageous array' and by contrast exalt those who sartorially humble themselves" (pp. 33–34). For the Parson's "sharp sarcastic tongue for [contemporary fashion's] sexually titillating excesses" as part of Chaucer's

---

tion the *Tale* has recently enjoyed tends to ignore issues of gender and sexuality altogether.[14] This is not surprising when we consider that *The Parson's Tale* has rarely attracted scholars whose work interrogates forms of sexual identity in the *Canterbury* collection.[15] Although Glenn Burger's *Chaucer's Queer Nation* features a chapter on *The Parson's Tale*, his examination of confession's "complex and sometimes contradictory relationship to pleasure" reveals perversities not in questions of sexuality but in relationships of desire and authority between clerics and laity: although the confessor exercises ecclesiastical control during the sacerdotal dialogue, the penitent can use the sacrament as a means to activate and empower personal experience by giving voice to it.[16] Here the emphasis is on the power and pleasure generated by the penitent, who recalls past sins and their supposed delights.[17] Yet the instructional voice

---

satirizing of the Parson, see Finlayson, "The Satiric Mode and the *Parson's Tale*," pp. 114–15. Hartung suggests that the invective illustrates Chaucer's "profound personal involvement" (p. 72) in the penitential project, but he does not explore the reasons behind the involvement or the repercussions of it for the *Tale*. For a reading of the diatribe on dress as an example of a "gendered, class-specific understanding of sin . . . supported by . . . frequent recourse to social commentary," see Larry Scanlon, *Narrative, Authority, and Power* (Cambridge: Cambridge University Press, 1994), p. 16.

[14] Recent critical studies of the *Tale* tend to examine lay instruction, vernacular authority, and Wycliffite reform: Glenn Burger notes that "even as a call to spirituality (in opposition to the game of story-telling) that *Parson's Tale* seems slightly out of step with trends in lay piety and with ecclesiastical attempts to meet the spiritual needs of the laity," *Chaucer's Queer Nation* (Minneapolis: University of Minnesota Press, 2003), p. 194; see also Katherine Little, "Chaucer's Parson and the Specter of Wycliffism," *SAC* 23 (2001): 225–53; and Pitard, "Sowing Difficulty," pp. 299–330.

[15] Queer considerations of Chaucer that explore sexuality and gender have largely been preoccupied with the Pardoner. Especially noteworthy are Glenn Burger, "Kissing the Pardoner," *PMLA* 107 (1992): 1143–56; Carolyn Dinshaw, "Chaucer's Queer Touches / A Queer Touches Chaucer," *Exemplaria* 7:1 (1995): 75–92, as well as her *Chaucer's Sexual Poetics* (Madison: University of Wisconsin Press, 1989); and Steven F. Kruger, "Claiming the Pardoner: Toward a Gay Reading of Chaucer's Pardoner's Tale," *Exemplaria* 6:1 (1994): 115–39. Literary critics whose psychoanalytic work addresses pleasure and desire at play across the *Tales* also find no place for the Parson in their scholarship; see, for example, L. O. Aranye Fradenburg's *Sacrifice Your Love: Psychoanalysis, Historicism, Chaucer* (Minneapolis: University of Minnesota Press, 2002), and Paul Strohm's *Theory and the Premodern Text* (Minneapolis: University of Minnesota Press, 2000), pp. 165–81.

[16] Burger, *Chaucer's Queer Nation*, p. 191. Burger uses the term "queer" in relation to *The Parson's Tale* in order to signal "alternative, more inclusive and less knowable, ways of self-identifying" (p. x); the *Tale* becomes queer because it "constitutes something much more than the simple substitution of true ecclesiastic authority and eternal truth for false secular materiality and temporality" (pp. 196–97).

[17] Ibid., pp. 191–93. See also Karma Lochrie's *Covert Operations* (Philadelphia: University of Pennsylvania Press, 1999), p. 40, which examines the pleasures associated with articulating sin during confession.

of *The Parson's Tale* allows for additional reflection: it prompts us to consider the cleric's own participation in complex systems of satisfaction present in the text.[18]

I would argue that the Parson's interest in the potential erotic dangers of the male sartorial subject evinces pleasure on sexual, textual, and visual levels.[19] Textually speaking, the narrative of X.422–30 outlines the silhouette of the lower male torso and thereby creates sexual pleasures akin to those described by Carolyn Dinshaw and Roland Barthes, respectively: "The unfolding narrative is the site of bliss," and "extravagant repetition" illustrates textual erotics.[20] Yet it is the argument of this essay that these pleasures extend beyond the textual to the homoerotic when the Parson positions the fashionable male body as both subject and object of visual pleasure. Homoerotic scopophilia was first explored in response to Laura Mulvey's classic article, "Visual Pleasure and Narrative Cinema," yet literary critics have found relevant accounts of it in medieval texts—Burger notes the feminization of the male body when it is subjected to the male gaze in Chaucer's *Physician's Tale,* while

---

[18] Chaucerian scholars have tended to see the individual tales as either dramatized speech of their individual tellers or as fictions with a narratorial voice that is not always that of the teller. My argument depends on the former assumption and differs from that of Siegfried Wenzel, who asserts that *The Parson's Tale* exhibits more of Chaucer's beliefs because it is so closely followed by Chaucer's *Retraction;* see Wenzel, "*The Parson's Tale* in Current Literary Studies," *Closure in The Canterbury Tales: The Role of The Parson's Tale,* ed. David Raybin and Linda Tarte Holley (Kalamazoo: Medieval Institute Publications, 2000), pp. 1–10. Scholars who see ideas in *The Parson's Tale* diverging from Chaucer's own are Finlayson, "The Satiric Mode and the *Parson's Tale,*" 94–116; Carol V. Kaske, "Getting Around the *Parson's Tale:* An Alternative to Allegory and Irony," *Chaucer at Albany,* ed. Russell Hope Robbins (New York: Burt Franklin, 1973), pp. 147–77; and Donald R. Howard, *The Idea of the Canterbury Tales* (Berkeley and Los Angeles: University of California Press, 1976), p. 379.

[19] For some critics, the *Tale's* genre forestalls any potential pleasure that may be derived from the text. A. S. G. Edwards and Derek Pearsall have described literature as "formal writing that gives or purports to give pleasure" in "The Manuscripts of the Major English Poetic Texts," in *Book Production and Publishing in Britain, 1375–1475,* ed. Jeremy Griffiths and Derek Pearsall (Cambridge: Cambridge University Press, 1989), pp. 257–78, 271 n. 1. Pearsall, however, has noted in the *Canterbury Tales* that "the *Parson's Tale* is not, itself, literature" (p. 289), which suggests that the *Tale* cannot provide the same kinds of pleasure as literature.

[20] Dinshaw, *Chaucer's Sexual Poetics,* p. 41, and Roland Barthes, *The Pleasure of the Text,* trans. Richard Miller (New York: Hill and Wang, 1975), pp. 41–42. Dinshaw argues that the Parson approximates the narrator of *Troilus and Criseyde,* who experiences delight in telling his story: the "careful pacing" of the narrative's unfolding "reveals his progressively escalating personal interest, a growing emotional involvement. He skips over details, makes choices, and paces his reading, taking pleasure in the encounter with the very surface of the text" (p. 41).

Suzanne Akbari highlights the "phallic aspect of the gaze" and the implications of sodomy when Dante looks upon Brunetto Latini in the *Inferno*.[21] What is interesting about these observations in terms of *The Parson's Tale* is the suggestion of erotic pleasure existing in the look between active and passive men.

Medieval optical theorists tend to accord an active role to the visible object, while contemporary moralists often understand the sartorial subject as passive. However, I argue that the Parson establishes a complex situation in which the clothed figure oscillates between passive object and active subject. Drawing from the work on scopophilia of Sigmund Freud and Laura Mulvey, I demonstrate that the Parson creates a visual mechanism operating between men in which the sartorial subject exercises agency by indicting the viewer's desires; as a visual spectacle, the man clad in couture potentially urges spectators into the same sin.[22] While the penitential needs to provide moral guidance and to teach appropriate behavior, the *Tale*'s consideration of *Superbia* as manifested by excessive dress engages the concern that "the confession of sins could, paradoxically, become the occasion for sin."[23] The Parson's contempla-

---

[21] In "Visual Pleasure and Narrative Cinema," *Screen* 16:3 (1975): 6–18, Laura Mulvey posits a paradigm of spectatorship in which the active male gaze objectifies the female body in cinema. Mulvey does not consider the implications of a gaze between men because "man is reluctant to gaze at his exhibitionist like" (p. 12). For reactions to Mulvey that suggest ways of looking that position men as erotic objects, see Paul Willemen, who sees "the two looks distinguished by Mulvey . . . [as] varieties of one single mechanism: the repression of homosexuality" (pp. 212–13), in "Voyeurism, the Look, and Dworkin," *Narrative, Apparatus, Ideology: A Film Theory Reader*, ed. Philip Rosen (New York: Columbia University Press, 1986), pp. 210–18; Richard Dyer, "Don't Look Now: The Male Pin-Up," *The Sexual Subject: A Screen Reader in Sexuality* (London: Routledge, 1992), pp. 265–76; Steve Neale, "Masculinity as Spectacle: Reflections on Men and Mainstream Cinema," *Screen* 24:6 (1983): 2–16; and Kenneth MacKinnon, "After Mulvey: Male Erotic Objectification," in *The Body's Perilous Pleasures*, ed. Michele Aaron (Edinburgh: Edinburgh University Press, 1999), pp. 13–29. For scopophilia in medieval texts, see Burger, *Chaucer's Queer Nation*, p. 134, and Suzanne Conklin Akbari, *Seeing Through the Veil: Optical Theory and Medieval Allegory* (Toronto: University of Toronto Press, 2004), p. 150.

[22] Here I draw upon Richard Newhauser's work on St. Bernard of Clairvaux's rendition of spectacle and sin; see "The Sin of Curiosity and the Cistercians," *Erudition at God's Service*, ed. John R. Sommerfeldt (Kalamazoo, Mich.: Cistercian Publications, 1987): 71–95. In addition, Sarah Stanbury notes in "several of the *Canterbury Tales*, the operations of sight become not only a major thematic concern but also a structuring device" (*Seeing the Gawain-Poet* [Philadelphia: University of Pennsylvania Press, 1991], p. 133). See also her "Regimes of the Visual in Premodern England: Gaze, Body, and Chaucer's *Clerk's Tale*," *NLH* 28:2 (1997): 261–89.

[23] Allen J. Frantzen, *Before the Closet* (Chicago: University of Chicago Press, 1998), p. 116.

tion of the fashionable male is foremost a warning to and condemnation of those who dress ostentatiously. Yet I show that his sudden invocation of female attire remedies his fascination with men's clothing and thus bespeaks an emerging awareness of the transgressions associated with his momentary predilection for pleasure.[24]

Chaucer composed his *Parson's Tale* at the end of a century that witnessed a change in men's fashion from loose expansive garments to form-fitting clothing based on the cut of the fabric.[25] Although similar changes begin to appear two centuries earlier in women's fashion, the simple construction of twelfth-century garments demanded less fabric for the design and therefore allowed for less waste of costly fabric.[26] Archaeological discoveries reveal that it was customary to conserve fabric in garments made before the year 1340: rectangular and triangular shapes of cloth were sewn in patchwork-like fashion in order to create a "whole" piece of fabric from which a new article of clothing could be made.[27] The revolutionary fashion changes of the fourteenth century were based on complicated cuts that rendered the finished garment

[24] For views that consider the Parson as a strong moral authority, see Jane Cowgill, "Patterns of Masculine and Feminine Persuasion in the *Melibee* and the *Parson's Tale,*" *Chaucer's Religious Tales,* ed. C. David Benson and Elizabeth Robertson (Cambridge: D. S. Brewer, 1990), pp. 171–83; Laskaya, *Chaucer's Approach to Gender,* pp. 128–30; and Pearsall, *The Canterbury Tales,* p. 47. Scanlon addresses Chaucer's clerical authority in *The Parson's Tale,* pp. 1–26. Scholars have also considered morality in relation to storytelling; see Wenzel, "*The Parson's Tale* in Current Literary Studies," pp. 1–10; and Laurie A. Finke, " 'To Knytte Up Al this Feeste': The Parson's Rhetoric and the Ending of the *Canterbury Tales,*" in *Chaucer's Religious Tales,* ed. C. David Benson and Elizabeth Robertson (Cambridge: Cambridge University Press, 1990), pp. 171–83.

[25] Stella Mary Newton's *Fashion in the Age of the Black Prince* (Woodbridge: Boydell Press, 1980) is the key text on the development and reception of fashion in the fourteenth century. See, too, François Boucher, *Histoire du Costume* (Paris: Flammarion, 1963), pp. 191–97; Blanche Payne, *History of Costume from the Ancient Egyptians to the Twentieth Century* (New York: Harper and Row, 1965); and Doreen Yarwood, *English Costume from the Second Century B.C. to 1967,* 3rd ed. (London: B. T. Batsford, 1967), p. 70.

[26] The twelfth-century tunic and the heavier super-tunic were cut from a rectangular T-shaped pattern. For each side of the garments one continuous seam was sewn up the underside of the sleeve from the wrist to the underarm and then down the side of the body. A hole was subsequently cut at the top so that the head could pass through comfortably.

[27] Peter Spufford notes that garments were made from recycled fabric from old clothing in his "Trade in Fourteenth-Century Europe," *The New Cambridge Medieval History,* vol. 6, ed. Michael Jones (Cambridge: Cambridge University Press, 2000), p. 162. For archaeological evidence of geometric shapes of cloth sewn into "new" fabric, see Elisabeth Crowfoot, Frances Pritchard, and Kay Staniland, *Textiles and Clothing, c. 1150–1450,* 2nd ed. (Woodbridge: Boydell, 2001), p. 7.

form-fitting—a style unlike that of twelfth-century garments, which were fitted to the body by cinching the waist with a belt or securing excess fabric with buttons or laces.[28] No longer based on rectangular patterns, the inner and outer tunics, known respectively as a gypon or a paltock and a cotehardie or doublet, were transformed into snug garments. The tapered nature of the cotehardie resulted from several tailored pieces sewn to form.[29] Sleeves were cut separately, stitched into rounded armholes at the shoulder, and fitted to the arm with buttons that often had to be fastened by someone other than the wearer.[30] The tight garment was closed in the front by a row of buttons or laces running from the neck to the waist, where it then flared into a skirt with an opening at the front. The hemline of the cotehardie was on the rise throughout the fourteenth century: in 1360 it revealed most of the thigh, by 1380 it stopped at the hips, and by the turn of the fifteenth century the hem fell just below the waist.[31] The under-tunic for the cotehardie, known as a gypon circa 1327 and a paltock circa 1360, also underwent changes. Both the paltock and the cotehardie were waisted garments that buttoned or laced up the front center, but the hem of the paltock was shorter so that it would not be seen under the cotehardie. Along the hemline of the paltock were eyelets through which laces would pass to attach hose. The shorter the hem of the paltock, the longer the hose. In the first half of the fourteenth century, hose still

---

[28] Mireille Madou, *Le Costume Civil* (Turnhout: Brepols, 1986), p. 23. Madou notes that cutting did not become a part of the couturier's repertoire until the fourteenth century. Crowfoot et al. maintain that cloth—its color and quality, especially when draped on the body—is a preoccupation of the thirteenth century, whereas cut is a preoccupation of the fourteenth. They assert that the desire to cut fabric to fit the human form was "triggered off by developments in plate armour which demanded more closely-fitting padded garments underneath" (p. 7). For an explanation of the development of plate armor and its affect on contemporary fashions, see Anne Hollander, *Sex and Suits* (New York: Alfred A. Knopf, 1994), pp. 42–47.

[29] Françoise Piponnier provides a pattern of Charles de Blois's *pourpoint*, a jacket equivalent to a cotehardie or doublet, which dates from circa 1364, in "Une revolution dans le costume masculine au XIVe siècle," *Le Vêtement: Histoire, Archéologie et symbolique vestimentaires au Moyen Âge*, ed. Michel Pastoureau (Paris: Cahiers du Léopard d'Or, 1989), p. 237.

[30] For archaeological evidence of tight sleeves, see Crowfoot et al., p. 4; Newton, *Fashion in the Age of the Black Prince*, pp. 1–13; Piponnier, "Une revolution dans le costume masculine au XIVe siècle," pp. 225–42; and Susan Crane, *The Performance of Self: Ritual, Clothing, and Identity During the Hundred Years War* (Philadelphia: University of Pennsylvania Press, 2002), p. 14.

[31] Yarwood, *English Costume*, p. 70.

were two separate stockings drawn up over the entire leg, but as the hem of the paltock rose over time, the hose developed into tights and were attached to the paltock all around the body.[32] Tights that clung to the legs and lower torso accompanied the snug cotehardie, and by 1500 "a man could appear in public revealing, through his covering of clothing, the form of his genitals or even of his buttocks."[33] These "profoundly disturbing" fashion changes were thought to signify disruption in England's late medieval social order,[34] and it seems that the government enacted sumptuary legislation in order to maintain a sense of "social recognizability" among the population.[35] But select Acts of Apparel and certain religious commentaries ultimately reveal that legists and clerics were becoming increasingly concerned with the clothed body's sexuality.[36]

As a penitential manual, part of the project of *The Parson's Tale* is to provide instances of sinful bodies in need of correction so as to promote contrition and penance. The case of the proud fashionable body that partakes in material excesses of late fourteenth-century England serves

---

[32] Ibid., pp. 72–74.

[33] Newton, *Fashion in the Age of the Black Prince*, p. 110. Crane notes that innovative weaves resulted in the production of woolen fabrics with increased elasticity; see *The Performance of Self*, p. 14.

[34] Claire Sponsler, *Drama and Resistance* (Minneapolis: University of Minnesota Press, 1997), p. 3. Also pertinent is Sponsler's "Narrating the Social Order: Medieval Clothing Laws," *CLIO* 21:3 (1992): 265–83. See, too, Alan Hunt, *Governance of the Consuming Passions: A History of Sumptuary Law* (New York: St. Martin's Press, 1996).

[35] Hunt is wary of linking sumptuary legislation to the rise in fashionable dress circa 1340 in England. He notes that sumptuary statutes existed before 1340 and names instead "critique of luxury" and a desire to preserve existing social status as "the more pervasive roots of the sumptuary impulse" (p. 45).

[36] The Acts of Apparel passed by Parliament in the fourteenth and fifteenth centuries articulate the government's unease concerning fashion and sexuality. A 1482–83 entry reads, "And it is ordained and enacted by the Authority aforesaid, That no manner Person under the Estate of a Lord, shall wear from the said Feast any Gown or [Mantle] unless it be of such Length, that, he being upright, it shall cover his privy Members and Buttocks," *The Statutes of the Realm*, 11 vols. in 12 (1816; repr. London: Dawsons, 1963), 2:470. The statutes are predominantly concerned with men's fashion; regulations for women's and children's clothing appear as clauses at the end of the stipulations for men of a given rank in ordinances of 1363 and 1463. In the 1483 ordinance, the only dress stipulation for women is for female servants. There is no mention of the cut or style of women's clothing in any of the fourteenth- or fifteenth-century ordinances. See also Frances Baldwin, *Sumptuary Legislation and Personal Regulation in England* (Baltimore: Johns Hopkins University Press, 1926), and N. B. Harte, "State Control of Dress and Social Change in Pre-Industrial England," in *Trade, Government, and Economy in Pre-Industrial England* (London: Weidenfeld and Nicolson, 1976), pp. 132–65.

as one such example. Yet in the course of renouncing and condemning the fashionable male, the Parson creates a moment in which his intentions to curb lascivious behavior are temporarily overshadowed by his fascination with the spectacle. Fashionable clothing, by its very nature, uses "lines, shapes, and volumes . . . [to] produce a visual model of dynamic coherence and integrity."[37] Clothing invites us to look—just as it beckons the public's gaze as stylish bodies bustle along city streets or strut down fashion runways today, so did it lure the critical eye of clerics, who condemned sartorial changes in the later Middle Ages.[38] At this moment in *The Parson's Tale,* clothing broadcasts a body on display: the garment "notifies" the public of the stylish individual's tendency toward lechery and pride.[39] Like his contemporary chroniclers of English history, the Parson underscores the visibility of the fashion icon, but, unlike the chroniclers, our tale-teller suggests that wearing clothing is a kind of public performance that could affect and potentially indict the viewer.[40] By conveying prideful and lustful tendencies, the stylish individual threatens to promote a contagion that can "pass through visual rays and . . . encourage simulation."[41] This simulation is exactly what must be avoided. The purpose of the penitential manual—and, more specifically, the Parson's examination of the seven deadly sins—is to help the sinner internalize orthodox Christian teachings and register them in the actions

[37] Hollander, *Sex and Suits,* p. 5.
[38] For clothing inviting the regard of others, see Georges Bataille, *Erotism,* trans. Mary Dalwood (San Francisco: City Lights Books, 1986), p. 132.
[39] This particular act of display in *The Parson's Tale* runs counter to Augustine's description of lust, which "seeks privacy" and "shuns the public gaze." See Augustine, *City of God,* trans. Henry Bettenson (London: Penguin, 1984), bk. XIV, chap. 18, p. 579.
[40] I am suggesting a kind of performance where members of the audience are not considered "passive spectators," but respondents and participants in the display. See Crane, *The Performance of Self,* p. 142. Chronicles of English history that depict dress as spectacle include *Eulogium Historiarum Sive Temporis,* ed. Frank Scott Haydon, Rolls Series no. 9, vol. 3 (London: Longman, Green, Longman, Roberts, and Green, 1863), p. 231: those who wear the latest fashion "are judged scamps and idlers rather than barons, actors rather than soldiers, mimes rather than arms-bearers" [potius judicantur citherones et nebulones quam barones, histriones quam milites, mimi quam armigeri]. See also *Chronica Johannis de Reading et Anonymi Cantuariensis,* ed. James Tait (Manchester: Manchester University Press, 1914), p. 167. While these chronicles highlight the performative nature of dress, the appropriately skeptical narrative voice describes instances where the viewer is not endangered by the fashionable body.
[41] Michael Camille, "The Pose of the Queer: Dante's Gaze and Brunetto Latini's Body," *Queering the Middle Ages,* ed. Glenn Burger and Steven F. Kruger (Minneapolis: University of Minnesota Press, 2001), p. 59.

of the body.[42] Yet the emphasis on acts of display recurs throughout the passage: some show the bulge of genitalia ["somme of hem shewen the boce of hir shape" (X.423)], others show "swollen membres" through dress in latest fashion ["the wrecched swollen membres that they shewe thurgh disgisynge" (X.425)], and the buttocks are "ful horrible for to see" (X.428)—"that foule partie shewe they to the peple prowdly" (X.429). The Parson figures the sartorial subject in an economy of vision that not only establishes the sin of wearing excessively tight garments but also suggests that flaunting the body's contours "to the peple" is equally transgressive. The fear is that anyone witnessing "the horrible disordinat scantnesse" of loose outer coats cut short ["kutted sloppes"] or short jackets ["haynselyns"] may be encouraged "to wikked entente" (X.422).[43] The following lines wind up establishing a potentially seductive exhibitionism in their delineation of the size and shape of the male lower torso. As such, the moral integrity of the spectator becomes jeopardized, especially if he should choose to act upon such visual titilation.

Fourteenth-century homilists articulate similar positions: John Bromyard notes that women who wear revealing clothing are sinful, but equally culpable are "those who behold them" since looking at "wantonly adorned women" subjects the spectator to "lascivious and carnal provocation."[44] Likewise, Robert Rypon, a preacher contemporary with Chaucer, observes that men seek admiration from others and derive "sensuous pleasure" from dressing *en vogue:* "men wear garments so short that they scarcely hide their private parts (*et certe ut apparet ad ostendendum mulieribus membra sua ut sic ad luxuriam provocentur*)" [and certainly it appears that they do this for the purpose of exposing to view their members to women in order that likewise they are provoked to

---

[42] Scanlon, *Narrative, Authority, and Power*, p. 13.

[43] Rowland notes that the "'wikked entente' of those who adopt such figure-hugging garments" was particularly upsetting to the Parson, p. 163.

[44] John Bromyard's *Summa Praedicantium* exhibits a pervasive concern about women parading in sexually suggestive clothing and ultimately provoking the viewer. See Owst, *Literature and Pulpit*, p. 397. See also Ruth Karras, "Misogyny and the Medieval Exemplum: Gendered Sin in John of Bromyard's Summa Praedicantium," *Traditio* 47 (1992): 233–57. Although Owst dates the *Summa* in the mid-1380s, which would make it concurrent with the composition of the *Canterbury Tales,* Leonard Boyle has argued for a more precise date of 1346–48 for the completion of the *Summa,* six to eight years after the onset of the revolutionary fashion changes in men's dress. See "The Date of the Summa Praedicatium of John Bromyard," *Speculum* 48:3 (1973): 533–37.

lust].[45] Rypon's preaching echoes the Parson's understanding of individual motivations to dress fashionably. According to Rypon, men wear
tight hose and short jackets for two reasons: to reveal the form of their
genitalia and to encourage either themselves or those who behold them
to engage in lascivious behavior. In these ways, the homilist affirms the
potential indictment of the viewer suggested in the Parson's exposition
on prideful dress. Pride, the "sin of exaggerated individualism,"[46] is not
so individual; it affects those who look as well as the perpetrator of the
sin.

The idea that the observer plays at least as large a role as an object
in a paradigm of spectatorship accords with the medieval notion of vision that stipulates interaction between observer and object. Saint Augustine writes in *De Trinitate* that "vision is produced both by the visible
thing and the one who sees, but in such a way that the sense of sight as
well as the intention of seeing and beholding come from the one who
sees, while that informing of the sense, which is called vision, is im-
printed by the body alone that is seen, namely, by some visible thing."[47]
Visual perception, in Augustine's terms, happens when an object imprints an image of itself on someone who intends to see something.
Although Augustine stipulates that two entities are needed in order for
vision to occur, he privileges the person or thing that is viewed as the
entity responsible for sight.[48] Roger Bacon's *Opus Majus* affirms the visible object's activity by suggesting that the object generates images of

[45] Owst, *Literature and Pulpit*, pp. 404–5. See also Owst, *Preaching in Medieval England* (Cambridge: Cambridge University Press, 1926), p. 54. The syntax of Rypon's
verbal clause, *ut sic ad luxuriam provocentur*, leaves ambiguous the subject of "provocentur"; though the direct antecedent for the final clause is the women (*mulieribus*)
who behold the fashionable male, the subject of the verb—those who are provoked to
lust—could also be understood as the men who provoke themselves to lust in an autoerotic moment when they reveal their genitals (*membra sua*) through tight dress.

[46] Morton Bloomfield, *Seven Deadly Sins* (East Lansing: Michigan State College Press,
1952), p. 75.

[47] Augustine, *The Trinity*, trans. Stephen McKenna (Washington, D.C.: Catholic University of America Press, 1963), p. 318. "Quocirca ex uisibili et uidente gignitur uisio
ita sane ut ex uidente sit sensus oculorum et aspicientis atque intuentis intentio; illa
tamen informatio sensus quae uisio dicitur a solo imprimatur corpore quod uidetur, id
est a re aliqua uisibili," *De Trinitate*, ed. W. J. Mountain and Fr. Glorie, *Corpus Christian-
orum, series Latina*, vol. 50–50A (Turnhout: Brepols, 1968), XI.2.3. Richard Zeikowitz
quotes this excerpt and provides a summary of the differences between medieval and
modern theories of spectatorship in *Homoeroticism and Chivalry: Discourses of Male Same-
Sex Desire in the Fourteenth Century* (New York: Palgrave Macmillan, 2003), p. 87.

[48] Zeikowitz, *Homoeroticism*, p. 87.

itself along light rays emanating from its surface.[49] In this way, the object being viewed is the active agent that broadcasts itself to an audience of passive viewers.[50] Bacon, however, eventually concedes that "vision is active and passive. For it receives the species of the thing seen, and exerts its own force in the medium as far as the visible object."[51] While the object is responsible for conveying itself to the eye, the beholder does not remain completely passive. This theory of vision does not reserve the active position entirely for the spectator and the passive role for the object, which is how modern theories of spectatorship have tended to delineate the economy of looking.[52] Rather, it allocates a certain amount of agency to the viewed object.

The fashionably dressed man occupies such a twofold position in *The Parson's Tale*. On the one hand, the Parson figures that sartorial subject as an active agent who threatens to encourage simulation by "shewing" himself; on the other, the Parson betrays a concern about this same body's passivity when likening the posterior contours of the male body to "the hyndre part of a she-ape in the fulle of the moone" (X.424). At this moment, the implications of spectatorship converge with homoerotic tendencies: by witnessing a fashion-savvy man, the male spectator positions himself as one who potentially participates in a homoerotic dynamic. Beryl Rowland notes that simian sexuality is used as a means to address human sexual behavior in *The Parson's Tale:* "the man of fashion, like the ape, flaunts his posterior for the purpose of sexual gratification."[53] Rowland sees the imaginative simile working to highlight the "flagrantly provocative" nature of the clothed body. Yet, the simile also situates the well-dressed man as a submissive object of scrutiny. Having

[49] Katherine H. Tachau, *Vision and Certitude in the Age of Ockham: Optics, Epistemology, and the Foundations of Semantics, 1250–1345* (Leiden: E. J. Brill, 1988), p. 4.

[50] According to Tachau, Bacon's theory "carries a commitment to the activity of objects upon passive recipients," p. 16.

[51] Roger Bacon, *The Opus Majus of Roger Bacon,* trans. Robert Belle Burke (New York: Russell and Russell, 1962), 2:470. For the Latin, see Roger Bacon, *The "Opus Majus" of Roger Bacon,* ed. John Henry Bridges (Frankfurt am Main: Minerva, 1964), 2:pt. 5.1, dist. 7, chap. 4, p. 52: "visus est activus et passivus. Nam recipit speciem rei visae, et facit suam virtutem in medium usque ad visibile." Both English and Latin are quoted in Zeikowitz, *Homoeroticism,* p. 89. See Tachau for additional moments when Bacon shows the activity of the observer, p. 16 n. 43.

[52] Mulvey, "Visual Pleasure and Narrative Cinema," pp. 6–18.

[53] Rowland, "Chaucer's She-Ape," p. 163. By "specifying the full moon, Chaucer is alluding to . . . the period of estrus when the behavior of the she-ape, in the view of the moralist, is likely to be the most flagrantly provocative. At this time the she-ape shows sexual skin changes and enlarged pudenda and offers herself for copulation" (p. 165).

suggested a kind of sexual gratification in which the posterior functions as the locus of sexual pleasure, the Parson has created a moment which suggests that the fashionably dressed man becomes passive.[54] In Rowland's opinion, the simile points toward a natural coupling between the she-ape in estrus and the stimulated male ape, but it also endorses a more unnatural relation. The sartorial subject in *The Parson's Tale* is unambiguously male. If we understand that he occupies the same position as the fertile simian that awaits her stimulated male, then it seems as if the fashionable male would be available for penetration by a male suitor.

The proud sartorial subject thus functions not only as an example of sin but also as a figure in a complex system of erotic pleasure, which includes the Parson as the tale-teller, the reader as a penitential subject, and the penitential tradition as one that inadvertently expresses pleasure in the descriptions of erotic discourse it must include in its guidelines for confession. The repetitive description of men's couture reveals that desire and eroticism exist first in the narrative of the body's "shewing" and second within the paradigm of visual spectatorship established by figuring an erotic look between the Parson and his sartorial subject in the *Tale*. Of the ten lines devoted to the sinfulness of scanty dress, nine address men's fashion; while women's fashion prompted vituperative responses from clerics, *The Parson's Tale* is not preoccupied with women

---

[54] Owst notes the "reprehensible 'tendirnes' and perilous effeminacy" when men delight in soft clothing in fourteenth-century sermons; see *Literature and Pulpit*, p. 411. *Molles,* a derivative of the Latin word meaning soft (*mollities*), also characterizes effeminate men or those who take the passive role in sexual relations in an early penitential manual, the *Canon of Theodore.* Due to their submissive roles in sexual relations, these men receive the same punishment as women adulteresses; see Pierre Payer, *Sex and the Penitentials* (Toronto: University of Toronto Press, 1984), pp. 40–41 and 170 n. 110. Payer quotes the *Canons of Theodore* 1.2.6: "Sodomitae vilannos peniteant et molles sicut adultera" [Let the sodomites repent seven years and the effeminate ones just as adulteresses]. See also John Boswell, *Christianity, Social Tolerance, and Homosexuality* (Chicago: Chicago University Press, 1980), p. 157: "If those who suffer [the passive position in intercourse] really perceived what was being done to them, they would rather die a thousand deaths than undergo this. . . . For . . . not only [is he] made [by it] into a woman, but [he] also cease[s] to be a man." Boswell quotes Saint John Chrysostom's *In Epistolam ad Romanos,* 4.2.3, in appendix 2. The threat, then, is that men who dress or behave "like women" become passive, and the "effeminacy" of which these clerics speak describes the position of one man as submissive to another. Indeed, the *Eulogium Historiarum,* an anonymous fourteenth-century chronicle, echoes the vehement hostility church fathers have for man's passivity in sexual acts by stating that the concern that fashionable men are "judged rather like women than men" [potius mulieres quam mares judicantur] (p. 230). While this clerical text warns against men becoming objectified and therefore feminized, *The Parson's Tale* makes no such obvious caveat.

in the same way it is with men.[55] The text repeats an anatomical catalogue of the male body twice and thereby underscores its figural display:
some men "shewen the boce [bulge] of hir shap, and the horrible swollen membres, that semeth lik the maladie of hirnia" (X.423), "the buttokes of hem faren as it were the hyndre part of a she-ape in the fulle of
the moone" (X.424), and "wrecched swollen membres" covered with
mi-parti (bi-colored) hose "semeth that half hir shameful privee membres
weren flayne" (X.425). Whereas clothing is obviously a covering of the
body, this moment in the text figures the garment as the means to
expose the body further. Despite remaining fully clothed, the figural
uncovering of male sexual members prompts us to visualize the proud,
lustful body beneath the clothing. Moreover, just as we are invited to
examine the "flayed" fashionable male, the text accentuates his exterior
silhouette: a man's posterior "is ful horrible for to see," especially when
men "that foule partie shew . . . to the peple prowdly" (X.428–29).
The Tale's catalogue of anatomical fragments on display offers the exact
repetition with variation that Barthes describes as erotic in The Pleasure
of the Text: "The word can be erotic on two opposing levels, both excessive: if it is extravagantly repeated, or on the contrary, if it is unexpected, succulent in its newness."[56] The Parson's interest in the male
body permits him to experience delight in storytelling. Each succulently
new reiteration of the "swollen membres" reveals an increasing fascination with narrative—a fascination derived in part from the Parson's sexual desire.[57]

As the Parson dances figuratively around the body of the fashionable
male, his descriptive language becomes progressively infected with sexual suggestivity while maintaining an emphasis on "shewing."[58] The
narrative voice establishes pleasure in a paradigm of visual spectatorship,

---

[55] Owst quotes excerpts that denounce women's clothing in sermons by John Bromyard, Bishop Brunton of Rochester, Austin friar John Waldeby, and Robert Rypon; see
Literature and Pulpit, p. 392. Odile Blanc's study of manuscript illuminations of dress
indicates that even though women's bodies were considered lascivious by moralists, the
illuminations show that "vestimentary transformations of the time were the domain of
men" ("From Battlefield to Court: The Invention of Fashion in the Fourteenth Century," in Encountering Medieval Textiles and Dress: Objects, Texts, Images, ed. Désirée G.
Koslin and Janet E. Snyder [New York: Palgrave, 2002], pp. 157–72; see p. 170).

[56] Barthes, The Pleasure of the Text, p. 42.

[57] R. Howard Bloch, The Scandal of the Fabliaux (Chicago: University of Chicago
Press, 1986), pp. 89–90: "narrative fixation upon the partial object is at the origin of
sexual desire."

[58] For narrative engaging the subject in different positions of meaning and desire, see
Teresa deLauretis, Alice Doesn't (Bloomington: Indiana University Press, 1984), p. 106.

which emphasizes looking at the fashionable body and that same body's status as a visual object. While I have suggested that the Parson is a figure who represents clerical preoccupations with sexual regulation, the tale is not one "imposed on the collection from without, but spoken from within" in the voice of the Parson.[59] His character is intimately tied to narrative because he is defined as an "ensample," or exemplum, of moral behavior in the *General Prologue* (I.496–97). As such, the Parson's storytelling provides meaning for the moral concepts he illustrates: his "moral effect on the social world he inhabits is a narrative one, and this characterization circumscribes even the ostensibly non-narrative textual authority he exerts in his tale."[60] I argue, however, that the Parson's position as a character of moral authority is compromised during his diatribe on prideful dress because he controls the description of the sartorial subject. As he outlines rhetorically the contours of the male body, he participates in a pleasure derived from the image of the fashionable male created by his advancing narrative. This is not a case where we have a "confessor's diffidence [that] wavers slightly," as one scholar has previously noted,[61] but rather one in which the confessor is not diffident at all. The Parson is entirely (albeit momentarily) subsumed by visual and narrative pleasures. His consideration indicts him in the very practices of looking against which he warns his public.

Modern notions of spectatorship first formulated by Sigmund Freud and later reconsidered by Laura Mulvey in terms of cinema and gender may be helpful in elucidating the Parson's visual paradigm. According to Freud, visual impressions are the most frequent pathway to sexual arousal; sexual pleasure is derived from looking at something (scopophilia) and being looked at (exhibitionism).[62] For Freud, the scopophilic and exhibitionist instincts are autoerotic. Looking is first an activity directed toward an exterior object; however, at an undetermined moment, the spectator realizes that pleasure is generated from looking at something analogous to his own body. The individual therefore gives up the object and turns his visual pleasure toward himself. As such, the spectator who was once the active looker is transformed to a passive object

---

[59] Scanlon, *Narrative, Authority, and Power,* p. 7.
[60] Ibid., p. 8.
[61] Frantzen, "Disclosure," p. 455.
[62] Freud, "Three Essays on Sexuality," *Standard Edition of the Complete Psychological Works of Sigmund Freud,* vol. 7, ed. and trans. James Strachey (London: Hogarth, 1964), pp. 125–248, at 156.

who positions himself as an exhibitionist.[63] While Freud acknowledges that scopophilia involves another person as a desired sexual object, he emphasizes the autoerotic beginning of the drive: the instinct "has indeed an object, but that object is part of the subject's own body."[64] Laura Mulvey, on the other hand, predicates the scopophilic drive on the desire for another human being: visual spectatorship is an erotic relationship between an active male spectator and a passive female spectacle. There is "a separation of erotic identity of the subject [who looks] from the object [who is looked at]."[65] Such a separation is important to the goal of *The Parson's Tale* because the penitential wants the spectator to register the male fashionable body as other, feel repulsed, and reject identification. Medieval clerics would likely advocate such comportment because it curbs lasciviousness. Although penitential manuals provide guidelines of both salvific and sinful behavior, readers should recognize the fashionable male as an example of how not to act. But, as Freud shows, the scopophilic instinct winds up turning back on itself. Pleasure is rooted in narcissism and the constitution of the ego: the spectator identifies with the object-spectacle through his fascination with the object's likeness to the spectator. In terms of *The Parson's Tale,* the spectator's attention would turn from the fashionable male to himself. Pleasure, then, is generated from the sartorial subject but ultimately is turned toward the spectator himself. The erotics of the visual paradigm are registered in the body that looks, and *The Parson's Tale* features a male cleric—indeed all male clerics who consult the guide—observing a male sartorial subject.

Indeed, the visual pleasures derived from scopophilia reactivate the Parson's own narcissistic enjoyment, which eventually calls his own moral state into question because, as Boethius tells us, "Everything which is known is known not according to its own nature but according to the nature of those comprehending it."[66] If the Parson criticizes the tightly-clad male for encouraging lascivious tendencies, then it seems as if those same tendencies are within the Parson's reach. Sexual pleasure produced from the Parson's description of the fashionable male indicates

[63] Freud, "Instincts and Their Vicissitudes," *Standard Edition of the Complete Psychological Works of Sigmund Freud,* vol. 14, ed. and trans. James Strachey (London: Hogarth, 1964), pp. 109–40, esp. 129.

[64] Ibid., p. 130.

[65] Mulvey, "Visual Pleasure and Narrative Cinema," p. 10.

[66] Boethius, *The Consolation of Philosophy,* trans. S. J. Tester (Cambridge, Mass.: Harvard University Press, 1973), p. 423.

that the Parson, too, may be invested in this eroticism because his interest in the sartorial subject deflects the penitent reader's attention from the body clad in couture toward the moralist. Although the Parson showcases the proud man's deviant tendencies by elaborating on fears of contagion, vanity, lasciviousness, and passivity, his disgust oscillates between shame and the scopophilic pleasure that shame seeks to contain.[67] This illicit pleasure is not unproblematic, especially when considering that *mi-parti* hose renders "shameful privee membres" flayed, charred, or diseased. These descriptions evoke a scopophilia that is somewhat sadistic. In linking desire with disgust, the Parson's erotic fascination thereby becomes an important measure of how the moralist is implicated in what he disavows.

While narrative pleasure extends to the *Tale*'s genre (the rhetoric of the vernacular penitential manual exhibits bliss in varied repetition of the very acts it condemns and, as a result, each titillating new portrayal threatens to subvert the genre's moral end), the Parson's brutal description of corrupted male genitalia suggests something other than pure delight. His scopophilic act invites revulsion and rejection of the sartorial subject through an enunciation of shame. He articulates one of the notions of the penitential, which was to "demarcate what was deviant and . . . to awaken revulsion against the deviant" as stipulated by the Fourth Lateran Council in 1215.[68] But his *Tale* illustrates a complexity in such demarcation. For the Parson, there is a fine line between revulsion and arousal. His fascination with a revolting object becomes rhetorically indistinguishable from desire. His shame—and that which the penitential wishes to generate in the reader—should restrain the desire to look. It should become the "enforcer of proper behavior" because shame reorients the self toward morally-sound conduct.[69] Yet shame "operates only after interest or enjoyment has been activated and inhibits one or the other or both. The innate activator of shame is the incomplete reduction of interest or joy."[70] The Parson's move to identify "privee membres" that appear flayed as "shameful" bespeaks a pleasure in considering the rather sadistic image. We have a moment of what

---

[67] Freud, "Three Essays on Sexuality," p. 157.

[68] Edwin D. Craun, *Lies, Slander, and Obscenity in Medieval English Literature: Pastoral Rhetoric and the Deviant Speaker* (Cambridge: Cambridge University Press, 1997), p. 3.

[69] Eve Kosofsky Sedgwick, "Queer Performativity: Henry James's *The Art of the Novel*," *GLQ* 1 (1993): 1–16; pp. 5–7 are apposite here.

[70] Silvan Tompkins, *The Negative Affects* (New York: Springer, 1963), p. 123.

Eve Kosofsky Sedgwick calls "queer performativity"—"the name of a strategy for the production of meaning and being, in relation to the affect shame."[71] In terms of *The Parson's Tale,* it is not just that fashion is sinful. Fashion situates "the queer subject in relation to identity, shame, and interest in the world . . . [in such a way] that makes its queer performativity so necessary."[72] We might say that the Parson's attention to the fashionable subject explicitly encourages a rejection of such immoral sartorial behavior, but this same interest winds up conveying a desire that produces meaning in the narrative and visual registers of pleasure in the *Tale.*

The Parson's extended preoccupation with the fashionable male suggests that clerics, like their fellow laymen, can succumb to the weaknesses of the flesh. He, too, is "engendred of vile and corrupt mateere" (X.333) like everyone else. We have arrived at a moment that "focalizes fundamental problems about the status of claims made by those imprisoned in such corrupt matter."[73] During the discourse on clothing, the Parson's rhetoric of dress does more than just invite the reader to meditate on how moralists "may condemn and abuse what they actually ponder and may even enjoy in the act of negation."[74] It also illustrates the Parson as one who participates in such enjoyment. And though his invocation of women's extravagant dress at the end of the denunciation of men's fashion could be considered a knee-jerk clerical antifeminist remark, it seems more likely that his turn to women's attire tempers perverse pleasure and bespeaks a guilty recognition of the homoerotic enjoyment his diatribe creates. His shift to the fashionable female body therefore registers a shame that the Parson never explicitly announces and thereby challenges the idea that this cleric completely fails to recognize his imbrication in the very sins he condemns.[75]

---

[71] Sedgwick, "Queer Performativity," p. 11.

[72] I am indebted to Glenn Burger's formulation of shame, queer performativity, and pornography in *Chaucer's Queer Nation,* p. 13.

[73] Aers, *Chaucer, Langland, and the Creative Imagination,* p. 109.

[74] Ibid., pp. 109–10. Aers sees Chaucer disclosing "the very personal presence which the Parson tries to ignore" in *The Parson's Tale,* p. 112. More recently, Judith Ferster considers how the *Tale* "fits the Parson" because it articulates truths that are relative to his character in "Chaucer's Parson and the 'Idiosyncracies of Fiction,'" *Closure in "The Canterbury Tales,"* ed. Raybin and Holley, pp. 115–50.

[75] Aers makes the important point that while the Parson pronounces the body horrible and sinful, he "never pauses to reflect on the vital implications for his *own* vision. . . . Lacking all self-reflexivity [the Parson] totally fails to bring the grounds of his discourse, and his own fallen state, into consideration," *Chaucer, Langland, and the Creative Imagination,* pp. 109–10.

The turn to the fashionable female neuturalizes any homoerotic tendency by resolving what would have been an unnatural coupling between male spectator and male spectacle. After nine lines of prose that describe the scanty nature of men's clothing and channel both the Parson's and the spectator's gaze to men's sexual organs, the focus shifts to women's faces: "As of the outrageous array of women," what we see is a "chaast and debonaire" face, but we should not be deceived because her attire is marked with "likerousnesse and pride" (X.430). It is an anticlimactic moment given the preceding tirade on the immorality of men's attire, the homiletic tradition, which articulates vehement opposition against women and their fineries, and the lengthier treatment of women's dress in the French sermon of MS Bodley 90. The move from fashionable male to fashionable female is important because it serves as a corrective to the homoerotic moment that the Parson has unwittingly (or not) created by situating the male body as spectacle. While it has been suggested that "overabundant detail is the norm" in *The Parson's Tale*,[76] Chaucer's move from the fashionable male to the fashionable female is precisely calculated and quite telling. By replacing the male body-spectacle with a woman's figure at the end of the description, the Parson draws on clerical-antifeminism as a disguise for the homoerotic desire that is grounded in a perversion particular to the narrative frame of the *Tale*.

We may recall Harry Bailey's initial invitation to the Parson to "Unbokele and shewe us what is in [his] male" (X.26) in order to "knytte up wel" the tale-telling game (X.28). Although the common understanding of this request is that the Parson should "open the bag" or "tell a story"—the medieval equivalent to our "let's see what's in his bag of tricks"—Harry's inquiry may be read as a pun on male sexuality.[77] Given the host's interest in questions of sexuality as they pertain

[76] David Raybin, "'Manye been the weyes': The Flower, Its Roots, and the Ending of *The Canterbury Tales*," *Closure in "The Canterbury Tales*," ed. Raybin and Holley, pp. 11–44; see p. 30 n. 27.

[77] *The Middle English Dictionary* defines "male" as a bag or pouch, which is the common Chaucerian usage; see *GP* l. 694, *PardT* l. 920, *CYT* l. 566. The *MED* includes the idiomatic expression "unboklen (unclosen, unlasen) a male"—to "open the bag, display (one's) wares, tell a story, give information"—which is how it is used here in the *ParsT* as well as at *MilP* l. 3115 when Harry announces that the storytelling game has begun. The understanding of "male" as the male sexual principle, male sexuality, or masculinity is relatively new in Chaucer's time; a 1382 Wycliffite Bible seems to be the earliest citation, though Chaucer employs "male" as "man" in *WBP* l. 122 and *Bo* 4 pr.6.153. For "male" as a pun on male genitalia, see Eugene Vance, "Chaucer's Pardoner: Relics, Discourse, and Frames of Propriety," *NLH* 20 (1989): 723–45.

to narrative, it is perhaps not that surprising that Harry prompts the Parson with a homoerotically charged appeal to tell a tale that includes unbuckling and revealing the male body.[78] After all, Harry has already demonstrated an abiding interest in male clerical bodies: in denouncing the perversions of the Pardoner's false relics, he imagines enshrining the Pardoner's genitals in a hog's turd (VI.951–55); he suggests that the monk could copulate as prolifically as a barnyard rooster if given permission (VII.1945–47); and he begins the *Epilogue to the Nun's Priest's Tale* with a comical blessing of the said priest's buttocks and testicles (VII.3447–48). The Parson fulfills Harry's wish to "shewe us what is in [his] male" by delivering a homoerotic vision of masculine desire within an orthodox tale that outlines sinfulness in the excessive nature of contemporary fashion. But in providing moral counsel, the Parson winds up conveying his own errant dispositions as well as the pleasure the penitential generates in stipulating moral guidelines.

Penitential manuals were designed to transmit codes of morally acceptable sexual behavior, but the presentation of clothing in the *Tale* blurs the very opposition between morality and immorality. *The Parson's Tale* does not offer just two options for action, as Mulvey's theory of looking does (one looks with erotic desire and rejects difference or one looks with narcissism and embraces similarities), as critical scholarship of the *Tale* claims (it has a "double perspective,"[79] and the Parson himself is a "split" figure[80]), or even as medieval clerics postulate (either one is moral and behaves accordingly by feeling contrite, confessing, and satisfying one's penance, or one is not). The *Tale* rather explores the complicated nuances in stipulating moral behavior through narrative and visual paradigms. As a voice for the clerical tradition, the Parson does not simply argue against dressing in a particular fashion—he does precisely what he warns against. By creating a spectacle of the fashionable male, the Parson's goal of deterring his audience from adopting fashionable dress becomes compromised by the suggestive nature of the de-

---

[78] For a reading of Harry Bailey's interests in textuality and sexuality, see John Plummer, "'Beth Fructuous and that in Litel Space': The Engendering of Harry Bailey," in *New Readings of Chaucer's Poetry,* ed. Robert G. Benson and Susan J. Ridyard (Cambridge: D. S. Brewer, 2003), pp. 107–18. Though Plummer notes that Harry often uses language that connects narrative with sexuality, he does not cite this moment as an example.

[79] Kaske, "Getting Around the *Parson's Tale*," p. 168.

[80] Scanlon, *Narrative, Authority, and Power,* pp. 8–9, and Little, "Chaucer's Parson," p. 226.

scription itself: his pleasure serves as an example of the illicit enjoyment that should be avoided when watching the fashionably dressed male.

In the end, his "insistent and pervasive doctrinal emphasis," which reportedly makes the *Tale* "uninteresting or even repugnant to many,"[81] discloses instead an engagement with pleasure, especially in the *Tale's* most original chapters, that is neither doctrinal nor uninteresting. This pleasure is consistent both with sexual and social pleasures apparent in other tales of the collection and with the linguistic and visual pleasures invoked and ultimately embraced at the end of *The Parson's Tale*. As the Parson outlines how satisfaction of sins should be carried out, he notes that penance should be publicly visible so that "men seen it" (X.1035); "a pitous wyl" must be expressed "by word outward" (X.1039). These words and actions must in the end yield a kind of pleasure: though the penitent body may satisfy sin by "werynge of heyres [hairshirts], or of stamyn [coarse woolen cloth], or of haubergeons [coats of mail] on hire naked flessh" (X.1052), the individual is nevertheless advised to cast the penitential garments aside if such adornment makes the heart bitter, angry, or annoyed. The Parson instructs, "But war thee wel that swich manere penaunces on thy flessh ne make nat thyn herte bitter or angry or anoyed of thyself, for bettre is to caste awey thyn heyre, than for to caste awey the swetenesse of Jhesu Crist" (X.1053). Clothing's peniten-tial role should be that of satisfaction of sin, but when uncomfortable hairshirts and coarse woolen garments distract the individual's attention from the "swetenesse of Jhesu"—a sweetness that by definition appeals to the senses[82]—the exterior evidence of penance should be jettisoned in favor of spiritual bliss. The Parson's replacement of penitential cloth-ing with metaphoric garments of "misericorde, debonairetee, suffraunce, and swich manere of clothynge" (X.1054) endorses an enjoyment very much connected to the exteriorization of penance; what is worn on the body should indicate the merits or faults of the soul. "Swetenesse" and "plesaunce leefful" (X.41) often have metaphoric links to physicality through penitential or fashionable clothing that either screens or evokes

---

[81] Pearsall, *The Canterbury Tales*, p. 246.
[82] Several of the definitions for "swetenes(se)" in the *MED* refer to the senses: "swet-enesse" is (1) "the quality of being sweet or pleasant to the taste; also *fig.* spiritual sweetness"; (2) "a sweet smell, a fragrance"; (3) "melodiousness, harmoniousness, sweetness of sound"; (4) "delight, pleasure, enjoyment, bliss"; (5) "tenderness, gentle-ness, loving-kindness."

it, and though the ultimate pleasure derived from this *Tale* should be one of orthodox spirituality, the Parson shows that the visual paradigm created in the penitential can sometimes compromise the moral directive of his *Tale* through optical and linguistic pleasures generated by spectatorship.

Private Practices in Chaucer's *Miller's Tale*

María Bullón-Fernández
Seattle University

I N CHAUCER'S *GENERAL PROLOGUE*, we learn that Robyn, the Miller, is a champion at breaking doors and at lifting them off their hinges: "There was no dore that he nolde heve of harre / Or breke it at a rennyng with his heed" (lines 550–51).[1] In *The Miller's Tale*, another Robyn, the carpenter's servant, lifts a door easily. At the carpenter's request, Robyn goes to Nicholas's bedroom door and "by the haspe he haaf it of atones" (line 3470). This Hitchcock-like appearance of Robyn the Miller in his own story emphasizes his habit of breaking doors, a habit that is manifested more generally in the pattern of breaking boundaries, both material and immaterial, and entering private spaces in the tale. Indeed, the Miller tells a story that revels both in the construction of and transgression against private and public boundaries. The tale's exploration of spatial boundaries is further emphasized through the recurrent use of the word "pryvetee" and its derivatives "privee" and "pryvely"—words that, proportionately, and given the shortness of the tale, occur more frequently in *The Miller's Tale* than in any other Chaucerian work.[2]

I am grateful to Winthrop Wetherbee and Andrew Galloway for their detailed suggestions on early drafts of this essay. I also want to thank Frank Grady and the anonymous readers of *SAC* for their excellent suggestions.

[1] All quotations from Chaucer's work are taken from *The Riverside Chaucer*, 3rd ed., gen. ed. Larry D. Benson (Boston: Houghton Mifflin, 1987), with line references in parentheses.

[2] Proportionately, there is a much higher occurrence of the term and its derivatives in *The Miller's Tale*, where they occur a total of thirteen times, than in any other tale or even in any other Chaucerian work. Only in the much longer *Parson's Tale* do the words appear slightly more frequently, a total of fifteen times. Private spaces, houses and rooms, of course, figure prominently in *Troilus and Criseyde*, but the terms "pryvetee," "pryvee," and "pryvely" appear only fifteen times. Given the length of this work, the comparative frequency of their occurrence in *The Miller's Tale* is thus much higher. On

Due in part to this lexical density, a number of studies have examined the concept of privacy in the tale. Although the first sustained analysis of this concept, E. D. Blodgett's analysis of privacy in the First Fragment, did not appear until 1976, the last two decades have seen several interpretations, ranging from analyses of the theological implications of "pryvetee" to studies of its gender and sexual connotations.[3] While these interpretations illuminate some significant connotations of the term, there remains an unexplored link between the notion of privacy and the construction of urban space in late medieval England as it relates to merchants, artisans, and the market economy.[4] Set in Oxford, *The Miller's Tale* is one of the few stories in the *Canterbury Tales* that has a specific urban setting contemporaneous to Chaucer and that gives us a sense of urban life in late medieval England.[5] There is a "detailed

privacy in *Troilus and Criseyde*, see, for instance, Sarah Stanbury, "The Voyeur and the Private Life in *Troilus and Criseyde*," *SAC* 13 (1991): 141–58. Critics have paid less attention to the use of these terms in another lengthy Chaucerian text, *The Legend of Good Women*. In this work the terms appear a total of fifteen times as well.

[3] E. D. Blodgett, "Chaucerian *Pryvetee* and the Opposition to Time," *Speculum* 51 (1976): 477–93, emphasizes the philosophico-theological meaning of private space in *The Miller's Tale*, and sees "pryvetee" in the First Fragment as a space that tries to exist outside time, a space of "otium." Thomas J. Farrell, "Privacy and the Boundaries of Fabliau in the *Miller's Tale*," *ELH* 56 (1989): 773–95, has analyzed the notion of privacy in its relationship to the fabliau as a genre and to the issue of public versus private justice. William F. Woods, "Private and Public Space in *The Miller's Tale*," *ChauR* 29 (1994): 165–78, has written about the interplay between public and private spaces in the tale, arguing that Alison is "the most private space in the tale" (166). Fred Biggs and Laura Howes, "Theophany in the Miller's Tale," *MÆ* 65 (1996): 269–79, as well as Louise Bishop, "'Of Goddes pryvetee nor of his wyf': Confusion of Orifices in Chaucer's Miller's Tale," *TSLL* 44 (2002): 231–46, have focused on the theological and epistemological implications of "pryvetee" in the story. Karma Lochrie, *Covert Operations: The Medieval Uses of Secrecy* (Philadelphia: University of Pennsylvania Press, 1999), pp. 164–76, has examined the implications of "pryvetee" in terms of gender ideology and the husband's legal right of "coverture" over the woman, while David Lorenzo Boyd, "Seeking 'Goddes Pryvetee': Sodomy, Quitting, and Desire in *The Miller's Tale*," in *Words and Works: Studies in Medieval English Language and Literature in Honour of Fred C. Robinson*, ed. Peter S. Baker and Nicholas Howe (Toronto: University of Toronto Press, 1998), pp. 243–60, has explored the sodomitical trope implied by the "misdirected kiss" and the phrase "Goddes pryvetee."

[4] See R. W. Hanning, "Telling the Private Parts: 'Pryvetee' and Poetry in Chaucer's *Canterbury Tales*," in *The Idea of Medieval Literature: New Essays on Chaucer and Medieval Culture in Honor of Donald R. Howard*, ed. James M. Dean and Christian K. Zacher (Newark: University of Delaware Press, 1992), pp. 108–25, for a suggestive essay that mentions a link between the market economy and "pryvetee" but focuses on other tales than the Miller's.

[5] Although Oxford was not among the largest urban centers in the late fourteenth century, it still ranked as the sixteenth largest town in England according to the 1377 poll tax records. See Alan Dyer, "Ranking Lists of English Medieval Towns," in *The Cambridge Urban History of Britain*, vol. 1, ed. D. M. Palliser (Cambridge: Cambridge

concreteness" about the "urban, workaday milieu," as David Wallace has put it, that is particularly remarkable.[6] From the carpenter to his urban wife (we are told that Alison "was of town" [3380]) and his servants, to the student, the parish priest (who is also a barber-surgeon), the smith, and the neighbors who arrive at the end and laugh at the carpenter, the tale has an unmistakable urban flavor. As Wallace has also noted, "Chaucer's London readers would certainly have recognized the crowding together of artisanal, clerical, and ecclesiastical forces (of bedroom, workplace, and chancel) that is represented in Chaucer's Oxford."[7] Such a "crowding together" in medieval cities led to contests over space that made the demarcation of zones of "pryvetee" particularly important and also contributed to a heightened use of private practices beyond the mere physical marking of private spaces.[8] *The Miller's Tale* explores these practices of privacy and relates them to two characteristically urban groups: merchants and craftsmen.[9]

The concept of "practice" I use in this essay is based on Pierre Bourdieu's work.[10] Bourdieu defines practices as doings by agents that do not necessarily stem from a specific, conscious aim but constitute and are constituted by the *habitus:*

The conditionings associated with a particular class of conditions of existence produce *habitus,* systems of transposable dispositions, structured structures predisposed to function as structuring structures, that is, as principles which gen-

---

University Press, 2000), pp. 758–59. For recent studies of Oxford in comparison with other English medieval towns, see also Jennifer Kermode, "The Greater Towns, 1300–1540," in *The Cambridge Urban History of Britain,* pp. 441–65, and Derek Keene, "The South-East of England," in *The Cambridge Urban History of Britain,* pp. 545–82. For a classic study of medieval Oxford, see H. E. Salter, *Medieval Oxford* (Oxford: Clarendon Press, 1936). On Chaucer's familiarity with Oxford, see J. A. W. Bennett, *Chaucer at Oxford and Cambridge* (Toronto: Toronto University Press, 1974).

[6] See David Wallace, *Chaucerian Polity: Absolutist Lineages and Associational Forms in England and Italy* (Stanford: Stanford University Press, 1997), p. 128.

[7] Ibid., p. 129.

[8] My notion of the contest that takes place in fourteenth-century England and in which the *Canterbury Tales* takes part is similar to Peggy Knapp's notion as she develops it in *Chaucer and the Social Contest* (New York: Routledge, 1990), although my focus is different.

[9] While privacy is more explicitly at the center of *The Miller's Tale,* it is also relevant to the other tales of the First Fragment. Unsurprisingly, the "noble storie" of *The Knight's Tale* treats the theme differently than the *The Reeve's Tale* and *The Cook's Tale,* which are in part conditioned by the Miller's approach to the topic. I will return to the wider resonances of "privitee" in the First Fragment in my conclusion.

[10] See Pierre Bourdieu, *The Logic of Practice,* trans. Richard Nice (Stanford: Stanford University Press, 1990), for a full and detailed explanation of his theory of practice.

erate and organize practices and representations that can be objectively adapted to their outcomes without presupposing a conscious aiming at ends or an express mastery of the operations necessary in order to attain them.[11]

This does not mean that no one can strategize and adapt consciously to the *habitus*, but even those strategies depend on and are defined by the *habitus*. As Roberta Gilchrist has put it, writing of material practices: "The subject . . . is both active in interpreting material culture and complicit in being conditioned by it."[12] Thus the actual practices that distinguished between private and public spheres in late medieval England did not necessarily arise from a concerted effort by certain social groups to create a symbolic distinction between private and public. Merchants and artisans did not start creating private zones, such as private bedrooms or secretive guilds, in an organized, conscious way. Rather, the *habitus* was constituted through certain conditions that in turn generated actual practices.

One of the factors that conditioned the practices of privacy in the late Middle Ages was the crowding together of the population in urban spaces. This affected both the arrangement of private and public spaces in buildings and streets and the conception of the body as a private space, for cities, as Elizabeth Grosz has argued, interface with bodies: "The city is made and made over into the simulacrum of the body, and the body, in its turn, is transformed, 'citified,' urbanized as a distinctively metropolitan body."[13] In exploring "pryvetees" in an urban setting, *The Miller's Tale* associates the practice of "pryvetee" with cities and with bodies in cities. In addition to the negotiation over urban spaces in a physical sense, another factor that generated practices of privacy at the time had to do with the relationship between space and the economy. As Henri Lefebvre has argued, space "is not a thing but rather a set of relations between things (objects and products)."[14] It is

---

[11] Ibid., p. 53.

[12] Roberta Gilchrist, "Medieval Bodies in the Material World: Gender, Stigma, and the Body," in *Framing Medieval Bodies,* ed. Sarah Kay and Miri Rubin (Manchester: Manchester University Press, 1994), p. 46.

[13] Elizabeth Grosz, "Bodies-Cities," in *Sexuality and Space,* ed. Beatriz Colomina (Princeton: Princeton Architectural Press, 1992), p. 242. Although Grosz's study focuses on contemporary metropolitan cities, which are larger than medieval cities were, the latter still constituted spaces that differed from villages in their "crowding together" of people from different walks of life.

[14] Henri Lefebvre, *The Production of Space,* trans. Donald Nicholson-Smith (London: Blackwell, 1991), pp. 82–83. See also Barbara A. Hanawalt and Michal Kobialka, ed. *Medieval Practices of Space* (Minneapolis: University of Minnesota Press, 2000), for a collection of essays on medieval topics that draw from Lefebvre's theories.

"a social relationship . . . inherent to property relationships (especially of the earth, of land) and also closely bound up with the forces of production (which impose a form on that earth or land)."[15] Thus, economic developments and social class structure are intrinsically connected with space—how we conceive and produce it. In Lefebvre's view, significant changes in social class structure and in the economy produce a redrawing of spaces, and, at the same time, this redrawing affects social class structure and the economy. The distinction between private and public spaces in the late Middle Ages was increasingly made due, to a great extent, to the conditions of dependence on "pryvee" profit created by the market economy. This is not to argue that privacy was a new concept "invented" by the market economy and those most involved in it, merchants and artisans; privacy is a concept that preceded the market economy.[16] It is to argue that the practices of privacy in late medieval urban England were generated through both the sedimentation of historical practices and certain contemporaneous social and economic conditions.[17]

The concept of "pryvetee" in *The Miller's Tale* thus acquires a significant dimension when we examine the spatial practices in the tale through the consideration of its urban, economic, and class-specific connotations. All the main characters in the tale practice privacy in various ways. From John's careful division of his house into rooms or his desire to keep Alison "narwe in cage" (line 3224), to Nicholas's exploitation of "God's secrets" in order to gain access to Alison's "pryvetees," Alison's own willing collaboration with Nicholas's secretive plot, and Absolon's secretive acquisition of a coulter to get revenge after the "misdirected kiss," there is a constant emphasis in the tale on how the different characters both create their own private spaces and transgress against those of others. This is especially so in the case of the male characters, I will argue—Alison manages her "pryvetees" differently. Chaucer thus ascribes an obsession with privacy to those crowded in

---

[15] Lefebvre, *The Production of Space,* p. 85.
[16] For an overview of the notion of privacy in early medieval law, see Georges Duby, ed., *A History of Private Life: Revelations of the Medieval World,* trans. Arthur Goldhammer, vol. 2 (Cambridge, Mass.: Belknap Press of Harvard University Press, 1988), pp. 8–17.
[17] As Bourdieu, *The Logic of Practice,* argues, the *habitus* is constituted in time and practices are constituted both by historical practices and by new developments in the present: "[practices] can . . . only be accounted for by relating the social conditions in which the *habitus* that generated them was constituted, to the social conditions in which it is implemented" (p. 56).

cities and those engaged in commerce, the latter primarily men, but this obsession, *The Miller's Tale* shows, is ultimately futile because boundaries marking private spaces are inevitably unstable. More crucially, the tale also suggests, the impulse to practice privacy and thus to create zones of "pryvetee" is in a sense its own downfall, for it always provokes someone else's desire to break through that "pryvetee." In other words, as soon as something is defined as "privee," that very definition opens up the possibility of its violation: if the space were not "privee," it would not be susceptible to violation.[18]

Before turning to the analysis of *The Miller's Tale*, we need to review the range of meanings of "pryvetee" in Middle English. A primary definition of "prive" is "hidden" or "secret" with the implication of immoral, sinful, or selfish.[19] The phrase "prive membres" is a clear example of such a negative connotation—for example, the reference to "shameful privee membres" in *The Parson's Tale* (line 425). Such connotations play an important role in the tale and, as we will see below, in the depiction of merchants and artisans in some contemporary writings. Nevertheless, the entries for the words "privite" and "prive" in the *MED* suggest a wide range of meanings that would not have been necessarily negative.[20] More important, in order to understand the many levels at which privacy operates in *The Miller's Tale*, we need to consider space in Lefebvre's

---

[18] Lochrie, *Covert Operations*, makes a similar point about privacy and secrecy (p. 164).

[19] See the definitions of the nouns "private," "prive," and "privete," the adjectives "private," "prive," and the adverbs "private," prive," "privately," "priveli," and "priveement" in the *MED*. This negative sense is common in Chaucer's work. In addition to the examples in *The Miller's Tale*, which I will examine below, let me point, for instance, to *The Man of Law's Tale*, where the knight who kills Hermengyld "pryvely upon a nyght . . . crepte / In Hermengyldes chambre, whil she slepte" (lines 594–95); or to *The House of Fame*, where the concept is associated with falseness and duplicity in a line in which the narrator argues that, in order to get rid of a woman, a man will often accuse her of being "Or fals, or privy, or double" (I, line 285).

[20] Stephen Knight, *Geoffrey Chaucer* (Oxford: Basil Blackwell, 1986), has argued that in Chaucer, following medieval cultural norms, "private feelings, whether of love, vengeance, or despair, were consistently seen as being, however understandable, a threat to the common social good" (p. 12). While Chaucer, as this essay argues, sees privacy in more complex terms, we will see below that the discourse that associated privacy with merchants and artisans did portray their private practices in opposition to the common good. See H. Marshall Leicester Jr., "Of a fire in the dark: Public and Private Feminism in the *Wife of Bath's Tale*," *WS* 11 (1984): 157–78, for a positive interpretation of the notion of privacy in relation to the Wife of Bath. To Sarah Stanbury, "Women's Letters and Private Space in Chaucer," *Exemplaria* 6 (1994), the notion of privacy was "very much under negotiation in [Chaucer's] poetry—and the site of extraordinary issues of control" (p. 278).

sense, that is, in terms not merely of material but also of immaterial boundaries.

In Middle English, "privite" could thus have material and immaterial senses. A general definition of the word, "pertaining or belonging to oneself," "something not shared, individual," could be used in either sense. The immaterial sense of privacy, of what belongs to the self, refers to one's mind and soul, while the material sense can refer to one's private property and one's body. Spiritually and psychologically, then, privacy was often used in connection with confession and, generally, with one's thoughts and desires, as in the common phrase "hertes pryvete."[21] A broader definition of the sphere of the self, a definition including those close to a person, explains the phrase "prive conseil," which refers to a king's or a knight's closest advisers.[22] In a material sense, the connection between privacy and property probably grew out of the association of privacy with a secluded space, a house or a room to which others have restricted access, as evident, for instance, in the phrase "privee place."[23] Note Nicholas's words to John in lines 3493–94: "And after wol I speke in pryvetee / Of certeyn thing that toucheth me and thee." Finally, in a material sense as well, privacy was connected to the body. We should note in this respect that even if "prive membres" generally had negative connotations, the association between the body and privacy was not always negative, as it was sometimes seen in terms of rights. Records of the London Assize of Nuisance make this clearer, and as Diane Shaw has argued, reveal the development of a more positive identification between privacy and the body. The cases in the Assize show that sensory assaults against one's body residing in one's property, such as noises and smells coming from a neighbor's house, were considered illegal invasions of privacy: "Not only was property entitled to certain rights of inviolability, but so too was the body—as long as it was ensconced within its propertied bounds."[24]

[21] In his tale the Parson distinguishes between three types of penance: "solempne," "commune," and "privee" (lines 101–5). In *Troilus and Criseyde* 2.1396–97, Pandarus asks Troilus, "Which is this brother that thou lovest best, / As in thi verray hertes privetee?" See, further, Stanbury, "The Voyeur and the Private Life in *Troilus and Criseyde.*"

[22] The sultan in *The Man of Law's Tale* sends for his "privee conseil" (line 204), privy council, in order to confer with them about marrying Custance.

[23] This meaning is also evident, for instance, in the following lines from the "Complaint of Mars": "Sojourned hath this Mars of which I rede / In chambre amyd the paleys prively" (lines 78–79).

[24] See Diane Shaw, "The Construction of the Private in Medieval London," *JMEMSt* 26 (1996): pp. 447–66, at 461.

The material and immaterial senses of "pryvetee" are evident already in the "Miller's Prologue," which introduces the theme of "pryvetee." In his reply to the Reeve, who does not want the Miller to tell a story about a cuckolded carpenter, the Miller famously says: "An housbonde shal nat been inquisityf / Of Goddes pryvetee, nor of his wyf" (lines 3163–64). Through the story of the carpenter, the Miller will warn us about the consequences of trying to know "Goddes pryvetee." At the same time, he will warn husbands against trying to know their wives' "pryvetee." The first sense of "pryvetee" we are introduced to, then, is religious and spiritual, referring to God's secrets, his mysteries. But, as critics usually point out, a second, material sense arises immediately when we realize that "pryvetee" also refers to "wyf." As the argument between the Reeve and the Miller makes clear, "pryvetee" in reference to the wife has a bodily sense. But because the same word is applied to both God and the wife, its double meaning, as private thoughts and private bodily parts, applies to both.[25] Coupled with "Goddes pryvetee" in the same line, a wife's "pryvetee" acquires the first sense—her secrets, her intentions and desires—while the bodily sense of "pryvetee" also applies to "Goddes pryvetee."[26] These two types of meanings, an immaterial one (thoughts, desires) and a material one (for example, the body, the house), operate in the tale as well and are in constant interplay. In the following pages I will first focus on the immaterial sense and later on the material sense, but will keep the interplay between the two at the forefront of the discussion.

Private Practices in Immaterial Spaces

In late medieval England, merchants and artisans were often depicted as private both because of suspicions regarding their interest in private profits and because of guilds' association with secrecy. These depictions

---

[25] Lochrie, *Covert Operations,* reads "pryvetee" in connection with Alison in line 3164 and later on, via Catharine MacKinnon, as things that in medieval English culture women were not supposed to have (p. 167). As I argue here, "pryvetee" has another meaning that is equally relevant, especially in this line, since it is coupled with "Goddes pryvetee": secret designs, secret thoughts. Paula Neuss, *"Double-entendre* in 'The Miller's Tale,'" *EIC* 24 (1974): 325–40, points to this second meaning as well: "pryvetee" in the Miller's phrase "refer[s] to a wife's private parts as well as her private business" (p. 330). By hinting in the *Prologue* that Alison has her own thoughts, I will argue below, the Miller suggests that Alison is not just an object in this tale. She is also an agent.

[26] See Boyd, "Seeking 'Goddes Pryvetee,'" esp. pp. 245–48, and Bishop, "'Of Goddes pryvetee nor of his wyf.'"

had to do in part with the struggle over the control of the urban economy involving three recognizably different, but sometimes overlapping,
groups (gentry, merchants, and artisans).[27] Such representations were
articulated especially in the fourteenth century, particularly in estates
literature, and are likely connected to the increasingly evident changes
in the social and economic makeup of medieval cities, which were fueled
by the activities of the mercantile and artisanal classes.[28] Often, the authors of these depictions were members of the gentry who, in their attempt to preserve their power in cities, accused merchants and artisans
of focusing on private and selfish interests as opposed to the common
(public) profit.[29] It was not unusual for the gentry to cooperate with

[27] Scholars disagree about the exact makeup of the gentry. For the purposes of this
essay, I follow Caroline M. Barron's distinction between the gentleman and the merchant: "Whereas the gentleman lived off an income derived from rents (his livelihood),
the merchant still lived by barter and sale. Although the successful merchant might use
his wealth to buy country estates . . . yet the wealth was amassed not through landed
estates but by trade." See Caroline M. Barron, "London, 1300–1540," in *The Cambridge
Urban History of Britain*, 1:411–12. The role of the gentry in city government varied,
depending on the city and the time period. Jennifer Kermode, "The Greater Towns,
1300–1540," argues that rentier patricians were more powerful in larger English cities
before the Black Death (p. 457). According to Christopher Dyer, "Small Towns, 1270–
1540," in *The Cambridge Urban History of Britain*, "the landed gentry figured prominently in small-town society" (p. 514).

[28] While the growth of towns and the development of markets in medieval Europe
were not new phenomena in the fourteenth-century, nor did they happen in a progressively linear way—towns and markets went through periods of expansion and contrac-
tion. By the fourteenth century towns had produced a "social space" and social practices
that differed significantly from those of the rural world. See Richard H. Britnell, *The
Commercialisation of English Society, 1000–1500* (Manchester: Manchester University Pres,
1996), esp. pp. 155–70, for a discussion of the complex process of expansion and con-
traction in English towns before and after the plague. For studies of the rise of the
merchant and artisan classes, see Sylvia Thrupp's classic work, *The Merchant Class of
Medieval London* (Ann Arbor: University of Michigan Press, 1962). For more recent
works, see Christopher Dyer, *Standards of Living in the Later Middle Ages: Social Change
in England, c. 1200–1520* (Cambridge: Cambridge University Press, 1989); Jenny Kermode, *Medieval Merchants: York, Beverley, and Hull in the Later Middle Ages* (Cambridge:
Cambridge University Press, 1998); S. H. Rigby, *English Society in the Later Middle
Ages: Class, Status, and Gender* (London: Macmillan, 1995); Heather Swanson, *Medieval
Artisans: An Urban Class in Late Medieval England* (Oxford: Basil Blackwell, 1989).

[29] As Britnell, *The Commercialisation of English Society*, notes, "The dividing line between public interest and sectional interest was often hard to draw. Much of the local
economic regulation of this period suffered from a deficient concept of what the public
interest was. Burgesses—the acknowledged free men of each borough—invariably defined the public interest as the strengthening of their own privileges at the expense of
countrymen and merchants from other towns. Often, however, they turned against
particular groups of traders and craftsmen" (p. 176). According to Thrupp, "Such public
opinion as was represented in parliament and in the pulpit dreaded [the fraternities']
power for it was known to be exercised for selfish purposes" (p. 21).

merchants and powerful artisans in different governmental structures to the detriment of the less-powerful guilds.[30] Nevertheless, the gentry aimed at defining itself as a group separate and distinctively different from merchants and artisans, who, supposedly unlike them, had an excessive interest in their private profit. Due to these suspicions, merchants and artisans themselves, as Thrupp notes, needed to (and often did) couch their personal interests in the language of common profit in order to advance those interests.[31] But the gentry's accusations prevailed in many fourteenth-century texts.

Examples of these accusations can be seen in estates literature.[32] John Gower's *Mirour de l'Omme* criticizes both merchants and craftsmen for their use of fraud and thus illustrates how the gentry used this discourse.[33] Although Gower asserts that he is not against a merchant earning profit, "provided he earn it in moderation and without fraud," his allegorical figure Fraud is a merchant who "is clipping away the possessions of his neighbors, for he cares not in what guise (whether behind or before) he seeks his own lucre, disdaining the profit of the community."[34] In these lines Gower establishes an opposition between common

[30] For instance, Kermode, in *Medieval Merchants*, observes that in York the merchants fought the "rentier patricians," while in Beverley "it was a mixture of lesser merchants and craftsmen who were challenging the established oligarchy in the 1380s" (p. 25). In London the well-known example of the struggle for the mayoralty between John Northampton, who was backed by the lesser artisans, and Nicholas Brembre, a grocer, also manifests the complexity of the process. In this case, lesser artisans and merchants competed for power against each other. See Thrupp, *Merchant Class*, pp. 77–79. Thrupp notes that "aldermen were consistently drawn from the wealthiest men in the city and remained in office at pleasure for terms averaging a dozen years" (p. 81). For a more recent and brief account of this struggle, see Caroline M. Barron, "London, 1300–1540," pp. 405–6. To Swanson, in *Medieval Artisans*, the merchant class managed to subordinate the artisans politically and economically (p. 149). R. H. Hilton makes a similar observation in *English and French Towns in Feudal Society* (Cambridge: Cambridge University Press, 1992), pp. 76–77

[31] See Thrupp, *Merchant Class*, pp. 97–98.

[32] For the association of merchants and artisans with fraud, usury, and avarice, see Jill Mann, *Chaucer and Medieval Estates Satire: The Literature of Social Classes and the General Prologue to the Canterbury Tales* (Cambridge: Cambridge University Press, 1973), pp. 99–105.

[33] Our records on Gower are limited, but we know enough to assert that he did not belong to a major aristocratic family, that he had some landholdings, and that he may have been a lawyer. His social status, then, was closer to the gentry than to the aristocracy or the merchant class. See John Hines, Nathalie Cohen, and Simon Roffey, "*Iohannes Gower, Armiger, Poeta*: Records and Memorials of His Life and Death," in *A Companion to Gower*, ed. Siân Echard (Cambridge: D. S. Brewer, 2004), pp. 23–41, for a recent assessment of the evidence on Gower's life.

[34] John Gower, *Mirour de l'Omme*, trans. William Burton Wilson (East Lansing, Mich.: Colleagues Press, 1992), p. 331. In the original these lines are as follows: "Mais qu'il le face par mesure / Sanz fraude" (lines 25208–9); and "Les biens de ses voisins tondant, / Car il ne chalt par quelle guise, / Ou soit derere ou soit devant, / Son proper

profit and individual profit—and merchants are identified with the latter. In another section Gower also writes about craftsmen: "People who live from handicrafts, if they do their work well and justly, are necessary for the commonwealth. And God himself cherishes them. But if they cheat, it is a vice that is opposed to the commonwealth."[35] Fraud also associates with them and with his companion Avarice. Gower establishes again an opposition between excessive interest in private profit, in this case on the part of craftsmen, and the interests of the commonwealth. Interestingly enough, Gower ends this section by writing: "There is no trade of any sort in which Fraud (if he is so inclined) does not have twenty-four hirelings who have refused to do good; and this troubles us in the city—both burghers and officials."[36] It is significant that Gower distinguishes between burghers and officials, on the one hand, and merchants and craftsmen, on the other, setting up an opposition between the two groups, and insinuating that there exists a tension between both groups and the interests of the city. The gentry thus used the discourse of common profit to cast a suspicious light on both merchants and artisans on the basis of their allegedly selfish focus on their private profit.

Chaucer's *General Prologue,* of course, as Jill Mann has shown, was also written in the tradition of estates literature, even as it diverged from it in significant ways.[37] The association of fraud, usury, and avarice (sins that have to do with personal profit) with merchants and guildsmen is evident in Chaucer's portraits of the Guildsmen (lines 361–78) and the Merchant (lines 270–84). The Guildsmen and the Merchant are described separately, which may seem to discourage us from seeing similarities between them. The five Guildsmen, moreover—a haberdasher, a carpenter, a weaver, a dyer, and a tapestry-maker, or weaver of tapes-

---

lucre vait querant. Et le commun proufit despise" (lines 25255–60). See G. C. Macaulay, ed. *The Complete Works of John Gower,* vol. 1 (Oxford: Clarendon Press, 1899). Gower's explanation of what constitutes "good" profit was common in the Middle Ages—as Thrupp notes, "God approved of newly accumulated wealth, it was understood, only on condition that it was honestly won" (*Merchant Class,* p. 174).

[35] Gower, *Miroir de l'Omme,* p. 334: "Les gens qui vivont d'artefice, / Si bien le font solonc justice, / Au bien commun son necessaire, / Et mesmes dieu lour encherice, / Mais s'ils trichent, c'est une vice / Q'au bien commun est trop contraire" (lines 25501–6).

[36] Ibid., p. 341: "N'est un mestier d'ascun degré / Dont Triche, si luy vient a gré, / N'ait vingt et quatre soldoiers, / Qui le bienfaire ont refuse, / Et ce nou trouble en la Cité / Les burgois et les officiers" (lines 25963–68).

[37] Mann, *Chaucer and Medieval Estates Satire.* Mann sees similarities between Gower's and Chaucer's descriptions of merchants. However, she also notes similarities with Langland's Avarice and thus does not see either Gower or Langland as Chaucer's direct source. See pp. 99–103.

tries—belong to guilds of mid-to-low stature.[38] These guilds usually had weak mercantile ties.[39] Despite these differences, though, there are some significant similarities between their portraits.

A sense of mystery informs both portraits. The Guildsmen remain anonymous figures about whom the narrator points out not that they *were,* but that they *"semed* ech of hem a fair burgeys" (line 369). We are also told that they had property and rent as well as wives eager to vouch for that: "For catel hadde they ynogh and rente, / And eek hir wyves wolde it wel assente; / And elles certeyn were they to blame" (lines 373–75). These details, though, do not reveal much about them. Although they are individualized in terms of their trade, the five Guildsmen are otherwise indistinguishable: "they were clothed alle in o lyveree" (line 363). A similar anonymity is evident in the Merchant's portrait ("I noot what men hym calle," the narrator says in line 284). The narrator also mentions explicitly the merchant's need to hide something: "Ther wiste no wight that he was in dette, / So estatly was he of his governaunce" (lines 280–81). His behavior is "estatly," but we do not know his real financial situation—Mann has commented on the concealment of debts and on the possible suggestions of fraud and avarice in the Merchant's portrait, noting that money-exchange, such as the one mentioned in line 278 ("Wel koude he in eschaunge sheeldes selle"), was often associated with shady and illegal dealings.[40] Significantly too, both sets of portraits use the word "solempne," suggesting

[38] Peter Goodall notes "the general 'mediocrity' of the gilds they come from" in "Chaucer's Burgesses and the Aldermen of London," *MÆ* 50 (1981): 289. Of the five types of guildsmen in the *General Prologue,* only the haberdashers are classified by Sylvia Thrupp as one of the greater companies (p. 398). Various other articles on Chaucer's guildsmen have attempted to explain their significance by looking at contemporary historical records and at political events. See, especially, Ann B. Fullerton, "The Five Craftsmen," *MLN* 61 (1946): 515–23; Thomas Jay Garbáty, "Chaucer's Guildsmen and Their Fraternity," *JEGP* 59 (1960): 691–709; and Britton J. Harwood, "The 'Fraternitee' of Chaucer's Guildsmen," *RES,* n.s. 39 (1988): 413–17.

[39] This is not to argue that no member of any of these five guilds could have been as wealthy or as politically powerful as a merchant, but that such members were the exception rather than the rule. Writing about masons and carpenters, Swanson, in *Medieval Artisans,* observes that while some builders, such as masons, were independent contractors and became wealthy, these were a minority (pp. 83–84). In fact, Swanson continues, many master carpenters had to work on "wage rates"; hence, "the distinction between them and their servants was not great" (p. 85).

[40] See Mann, *Chaucer and Medieval Estates Satire,* pp. 99–103. Thrupp cites a passage from the tale of King Edward in which a merchant is seen as "a dominating and vaguely sinister figure": "He is a marchande of gret powere / Many man is his trespere / Men owe hym mony a pounde" (*Merchant Class,* p. 317). Merchants were accumulating powers that were not always transparent to others.

the pilgrim's self-conscious attempt to be more than they are and thus hide what they might be: while the Merchant "spak ful solempnely" (line 274), the Guildsmen belong to "a solempne and a greet frater-nitee" (line 364). Merchant and Guildsmen, then, are portrayed as sus-piciously secretive.

In line 613, moreover, the artisans' craft is referred to as a "myster." The use of the word "myster" is significant as well, pointing to another sense in which merchants and artisans were associated with privacy in the late Middle Ages. The word could have two different meanings in Middle English: it could refer to guild or craft (from Latin "minister-ium"), or to mystery (from Latin "mysterium"). The conflation of the two Latin words in Middle English is, curiously enough, more than or-thographical. Indeed, one of the reasons why guilds were associated with mysteries and secrecy had to do with the word "myster" and its implica-tions. As Karma Lochrie puts it, "[t]he intimate connection between the *misterium artis* 'skill of the craft' and the *mysteria* or 'secrets' of the guild fostered a sense of community founded on secrecy."[41] Guilds, whether parish guilds or craft guilds, were typically bound by vows of secrecy, vows that made them suspicious to the political authorities.[42] Guilds' secret and private practices stemmed in part from their need to protect their economic interests, a need that became increasingly acute because of the constant struggle for control over the economy in late medieval cities.[43] As both city councils and the state became gradually aware of, and troubled about, the economic independence of merchants and arti-sans, they developed new forms of control over them.[44] In turn, guilds

[41] Lochrie, *Covert Operations,* p. 160.
[42] For instance, the statutes of the Guild of St. Mary, Lynn, state: "who-so be-wreys þe counseyl of þis gilde to anny straunge man or woman sal pay, to amendement of þe lyght, a punde of wax." Quoted in Wallace, *Chaucerian Polity,* p. 92. Thrupp also notes that secrecy was often associated with fraternities. For instance, "The grocers forbade members to reveal any 'secretis' that had been discussed in meetings, on pain of expul-sion from the company" (*Merchant Class,* p. 21).
[43] Lochrie, *Covert Operations,* attributes this need for secrecy in part to the need "to protect guild monopolies over specialized crafts and to initiate the idea of intellectual property," and in part to "economic pressures," p. 107.
[44] In *Chaucerian Polity,* Wallace notes that the initial impulse behind the Westminster returns of 1389, which went as far as "ask[ing] not for an enquiry into, but rather for *the suppression of,* all guilds and fraternities" (p. 91), came from the Commons. According to Wallace, "The burgesses and knights of the shire who argued for this had doubtless been unsettled by the Rising of 1381" (p. 91). They also proposed that "the goods and chattels of the guilds should be sold off to pay for the war with France," but this was never accepted (p. 91). This incident illustrates one of the ways in which the gentry tried to control merchants and artisans at a national level. On regulation at a local level,

and merchants responded to governmental scrutiny and control by further extending the walls of secrecy and privacy around them. In other words, the logic laid down by the economic and political structures led merchants and artisans to generate more private spaces, while at the same time the creation of private spaces increased the governmental officials' desire and perceived need to enter them.[45] This paradox brings us to *The Miller's Tale*. In the tale Chaucer is interested not only in showing how his characters practice privacy, or in denouncing such practices, but also in examining the instability of private boundaries. Chaucer's tale shows that no boundaries are perfectly impermeable and that there is an inherent paradox in the notion of privacy: the act of creating private boundaries contains the seeds of privacy's own violation.

While in the tale John the carpenter is certainly neither an anonymous nor shady character, he shares some significant features with the Guildsmen and the Merchant.[46] As a carpenter, John is a lesser artisan, and, like the Guildsmen in the *General Prologue*, he is rich. In fact, unlike the Guildsmen in the *General Prologue*, he *is*, rather than simply seems, rich. The Miller tells us as soon as the second line in his tale that the carpenter is "A riche gnof" (line 3188). That he owns what J. A. W. Bennett has called "a commodious house" and rents a room to a student confirms both his wealth and his participation in some wise financial practices: it was not uncommon in the period for homeowners to rent out rooms as an additional source of income.[47] The carpenter's wealth is

see Britnell, *The Commercialisation of English Society*, esp. pp. 173–78. See also Stephanie Jed, *Chaste Thinking* (Bloomington: Indiana University Press, 1989), esp. chap. 3, "*In secretis penetralibus*: Mercantile Writing and the Construct of Privacy." Jed offers an insightful analysis of the merchants' use of secrecy in late fourteenth-century Florence that is aptly relevant to England as well.

[45] There is another mystery associated with the guilds in late medieval England. The guilds, or "misteries," primarily, were in charge of performing the *mystery* plays, plays that represented the mysteries of Christian history and doctrine. Although not apparent in the portraits of the guildsmen and the Merchant in the *General Prologue*, this connotation plays a role in the "Miller's Tale," where Absolon, a barber-surgeon as well as a priest, is said to play the role of Herod "upon a scaffold hye" (line 3384) and John the carpenter is fooled by Nicholas into playing the role of Noah, albeit not publicly.

[46] On carpenters' guilds, see B. W. E. Alford and T. C. Barker, *A History of the Carpenters Company* (London: Archon Books, 1969). Alford and Barker note that, although the evidence is fragmentary, "[a]s in the case of the older crafts, it is probable that the origins of the [Carpenters] Company are to be found in earlier, often secret, fraternities" (p. 13).

[47] See Bennett, *Chaucer at Oxford*, p. 31. *The Miller's Tale* is set at a time when the property market was booming in English towns, partly according to Britnell, in *The Commercialisation of English Society*, as a consequence of the Black Death (p. 171). For an analysis of the property markets, see Derek Keene, "The Property Market in English Towns," *D'une ville à l'autre: Structures matérielles et organisation de l'espace dans les villes*

also evident in the fact that he has servants—Robyn, his "knave," and Gille, his "mayde" (line 3556).[48] Although unlike most wealthy merchants, the carpenter seems neither educated nor very bright ("his wit was rude," line 3227), having servants and owning property puts him on a higher rung on the social ladder, closer to a merchant and further away from lesser craftsmen.[49] The carpenter's wealth, in fact, is one of the reasons some critics have argued that he is associated with Avarice.[50] While I would not agree that the carpenter is a figure for Avarice—even in his simplicity there is more to his characterization than a one-to-one allegorical correspondence would imply—the carpenter is tempted, in part, by Avarice. One can see his concern for saving Alison, his prized possession, whom/which he keeps "narwe in cage" (line 3224), as motivated in part by his desire to protect his riches—though he also seems motivated by a romantic strain as he almost swoons at the thought that Alison may drown (lines 3522–24). Not surprisingly, then, as a relatively rich urban inhabitant and as an artisan, John has a heightened sense of private boundaries, both material and immaterial.

It is this heightened sense that Nicholas exploits and that is particularly evident in the scene when Nicholas pretends that he has had a vision of an impending second flood. Nicholas's trick aims at tempting John to enter immaterial "pryvetees" (God's), and he uses "pryvetee" in both its material and immaterial senses to entice him. This scene, more-

---

européennes (XIIIe–XVIe siècle), ed. Jean-Claude Maire Vigueur (Rome: École Française de Rome, 1989), pp. 201–26. Keene notes a link between old age and investing in property: rents and houses could "provide security for a loan. . . . As old age approached, or if illness struck, property which was no longer needed as domestic or business accommodation could be exchanged for cash, for income, or for a regular allowance of food, drink, and clothing. Houses were very often divided for this purpose. . . . Even property holders on the smallest scale could use the property market in this way" (ibid. pp. 221–22). Although not particularly smart in other ways, as an old man, John the carpenter seems like a smart investor.

[48] Kermode, in *Medieval Merchants,* notes that it was common in urban society to hold a number of servants. Merchants in the three cities she studies usually had several servants (an average of two in York, more in Hull, fewer in Beverley). On merchants' servants, see also Thrupp, *Merchant Class,* pp. 151–52. Bennett, in *Chaucer at Oxford,* has also noticed that the carpenter's servants further emphasize his wealth (p. 30).

[49] According to Thrupp, "The merchant's craft demanded some degree of literacy" (ibid., p. 155). Kermode observes similarly that "[l]ong-distance commerce encouraged basic literacy as well as numeracy" (*Medieval Merchants,* p. 111).

[50] See D. W. Robertson Jr., *A Preface to Chaucer: Studies in Medieval Perspectives* (Princeton: Princeton University Press); W. F. Bolton, "*The Miller's Tale:* An Interpretation," *Mediaeval Studies* 24 (1962): 83–94; and Paul A. Olson, "Poetic Justice in the *Miller's Tale,*" *MLQ* 24 (1963): 227–36.

over, points to something paradoxical: there is a constant back-and-forth movement in it between creating zones of "pryvetee" and violating them. By locking himself up in his room and marking his private space, Nicholas makes John want to pry into his supposedly private affairs; Nicholas's supposed knowledge of God's "pryvetees" also makes John eager to know. In creating private spaces, in marking private boundaries, Nicholas invites their violation.

Notice John's reactions to Nicholas's ploy. When he realizes that Nicholas has not come out of his room for a couple of days, he sends his servant Robyn to find out if there is something wrong with him. One could argue at this point that John's actions show he is humane—he seems concerned for Nicholas's well-being—but it is significant that at the beginning of a scene that will be rife with boundary-crossing, John would ask Robyn to pry into Nicholas's private affairs. Even though John does not hesitate to cross Nicholas's private boundary, when Robyn reports that he has seen Nicholas sitting "evere capyng upright" (line 3444) in his room, the carpenter's response is, "Men sholde nat knowe of Goddes pryvetee" (line 3454). As an artisan who would have been aware of trade or guild secrets, John notes at this point that one should respect God's trade secrets, as it were. And yet, continuing to pry into Nicholas's private affairs, he asks Robyn to remove the student's door so that he can go into his private space, a foreshadowing of his own attempt to enter "Goddes pryvetee" shortly thereafter.

The carpenter's next action also reveals his strong sense of his own privacy: as he tries to wake up Nicholas, he says a charm on four sides of the house and on the threshold of the outside door, marking his private boundaries—the boundaries of both his house and his soul—to prevent any demonic spirits from entering (lines 3480–86). This tendency to create boundaries combined with his eagerness for crossing others' boundaries is cleverly exploited by Nicholas. When Nicholas says that he has something to tell John, but only "in pryvetee" (line 3493), and that what he has to tell him is "Christes conseil" (line 3504), John shows an immediate desire to cross the boundary he had previously reproved Nicholas for crossing, that of God's "pryvetee." Eager to know, he swears by Christ that he is no gossip and will not betray Nicholas (lines 3508–12). Nicholas, ever so slyly, continues to play on John's strong sense of boundaries. On the one hand, he suggests that there are certain limits to how much of God's private designs John may know—he tells him his servants cannot be saved: "Axe nat why, for though thou aske me, / I wol nat tellen Goddes pryvetee" (lines 3557–58). On the other hand, he does let him in on the main secret and makes him feel included by means of the pronoun "oure" when he orders John to hang the troughs in secret, "That no man of oure purveiaunce espye" (line 3566). John the carpenter is aware of private, immaterial boundaries and is at the same time eager to transgress against them. In doing so, he hopes to create a new space of privacy for himself (the "privee" knowledge of God's "pryvetees").

As Bourdieu argues, "Agents can adequately master the *modus operandi* that enables them to generate correctly formed ritual practices, only by making it work practically, in a real situation, in relation to practical functions" (90). Nicholas becomes such an agent in the tale. He generates a practice of privacy for the carpenter by enticing him to know and hide "Goddes pryvetee." But Nicholas, a student and an urban inhabitant, is not an outsider to the *habitus* and thus he can only adopt the practices that are made possible by the *habitus*. Indeed, Nicholas's ability to create immaterial zones of "pryvetee," that is, his possession of secret knowledge, owes much to his status as a student. As Peter Goodall has argued, there is a connection between privacy and the search for knowledge—or study as a "secretive pursuit"—that seems especially evident in his case.[51] The Miller's description of Nicholas emphasizes his secretiveness: he knew about "deerne love" (line 3200), and he was "sleigh and ful privee" (line 3201). Even the fact that he has his own private room, which, Goodall notes, was not common for late fourteenth-century students, underscores his secrecy.[52] As a student who is supposed to pursue secretive knowledge, Nicholas can generate secretive practices for the carpenter, and he does this as an insider to the *habitus*.

Nicholas, though, is ultimately more interested in material than in immaterial "pryvetees." While Goodall is right to note the references to secrecy in the description of Nicholas, we also need to notice the irony in the portrait.[53] Nicholas's room looks pristine. All his books and instruments are so perfectly organized that one wonders if he ever uses

---

[51] See Peter Goodall, "'Allone Withouten any Compaignye': Privacy in the First Fragment of the *Canterbury Tales*," *ELN* 29 (1991): 10. I should also note that students formed their own guilds in the Middle Ages.

[52] Goodall, "'Allone Withouten any Compaignye,'" pp. 7–8.

[53] Writing about Nicholas, Mann, in *Chaucer and Medieval Estates Satire*, has noted that students were often criticized for their laziness in estates literature (p. 245n).

them—the verb "longynge" in "His astrelabie, longynge for his art" (line 3209) may mean, as Benson's gloss suggests, "belonging to" or "necessary for," but it can also mean that the astrolabe is longing to be used. Nothing is said in this portrait about how much time he spends studying. As a student Nicholas is supposed to practice privacy in an intellectual search for uncovering secret knowledge, the unknown. John assumes that this is what he is interested in and Nicholas cleverly exploits such an assumption. But Nicholas is not interested in that kind of "prive" knowledge. He pursues "prive" knowledge in the carnal, not the intellectual, sense of the phrase.[54] Nicholas generates practices of privacy that have to do with its immaterial sense, but his main interest lies in material spaces. It is the material boundaries of "pryvetee" that he will violate and it is in a material sense that his own privacy will be violated. John and Absolon, the other main male characters in the tale, we will see, also experience a similar violation of their material "pryvetees," while Alison, the only female character, does not seem to experience the boundary-crossing as a violation against her will.

Private Practices in the Material World: Property and the Body

Even though material boundaries may seem more stable than immaterial ones, the tale shows that these are also intrinsically unstable. Walls and material boundaries are supposed to mark the physical separation between private property and public spaces. However, as Lefebvre puts it, these boundaries "give rise . . . to an appearance of separation between spaces where in fact what exists is an ambiguous continuity."[55] That walls and boundaries are unstable was particularly evident in medieval European cities, generally, and in English cities too.[56] According to Derek Keene, in medieval English towns private space encroached on public space and vice versa: "In areas of high demand for land and houses public space was converted for private use by encroach-

---

[54] For a biblical interpretation of the theme of knowledge in the tale, see Biggs and Howe, "Theophany in the Miller's Tale." Their analysis, however, does not take into account the carnal sense. For an analysis of the theme of knowledge as carnal knowledge, see Boyd, "Seeking 'Goddes Pryvetee.'"

[55] Lefebvre, *The Production of Space,* p. 87.

[56] See Howard Saalman, *Medieval Cities* (New York: George Braziller, 1968), pp. 28–35, for a general discussion of public and private spaces in medieval European towns. David Nicholas, *The Later Medieval City, 1300–1500* (London: Longman, 1997), has argued that "[t]he cities also began developing the notion of public space and buildings during the thirteenth century" (p. 13).

ment on to the street. Conversely, an increasing density of settlement created a need for access, so that private entries and passages leading to houses erected on former garden land set back from the street acquired a public status as new lanes or streets."[57] While increasing density led to the creation of private boundaries, the plague, which had the effect of depopulating the cities temporarily, also led to greater awareness of private boundaries. In post-plague England, spaces were renegotiated and their ownership changed as many towns saw first the abandonment and later the redevelopment of houses and markets.[58] Such changes could only have made urban inhabitants more conscious of space divisions in general, and of the boundaries of their own material spaces, their properties and their bodies, in particular. In other words, as Grosz has argued, bodies define cities, but cities also define bodies.[59]

Indeed, the material boundaries of privacy applied to both property and the body, as Diane Shaw's examination of cases in the London Assize of Nuisance suggests. In public life, Shaw argues, "Londoners accepted the physical aggravation of [the] urban confusion of human activity and spatial complexity. Within the bounds of their own property, however, acceptance of sensory encroachments lessened. Affronts that plagued body and property were taken to the Assize."[60] Landowners' and tenants' property complaints against their neighbors could refer to damage done to the property itself or to "sensory assaults" against their bodies, including smells, noises, or sight-related invasions, such as a neighbor's ability to watch through a window or other opening into the plaintiff's property. In 1341, for instance, Isabel Luter complained that "the stench from the neighbor's cesspit penetrated her tenement through their unlawful windows."[61] Shaw's study shows that one of the ways in which property and the body were identified was through the

[57] Keene, "The Property Market in English Towns," p. 222.

[58] According to Britnell, *The Commercialisation of English Society, 1000–1500*, "The abandonment of properties meant there was more empty space but did not always lead to unsightly ruins. Some sites were newly developed by speculators. Sometimes, too, wealthier townsmen constructed large houses or house rows across a number of former plots" (p. 171). Christopher Dyer, *Standards of Living in the Later Middle Ages: Social Change in England, c. 1200–1520* (Cambridge: Cambridge University Press, 1989), makes a similar point: "The wealthier townsmen kept gardens even in the centers, and as the built-up zone contracted in the later middle ages, gardens, orchards and yards expanded over the sites of decayed homes" (p. 191).

[59] See Grosz, "Bodies-Cities."

[60] Shaw, "The Construction of the Private in Medieval London," p. 448.

[61] Ibid., p. 453.

notion of privacy: "In a property-oriented court, the presence of complaints about the invasion of privacy suggests that no distinction was made between the prerogatives of the corporeal body and real estate: this would indicate, then, that the definition of bodily boundaries was property-based."[62] This association between property, privacy, and the body reminds us that bodies are intersected by space and at the same time create their own space.

The range of meanings of "estat" in Middle English further illustrates how property and the body were associated in medieval England. The same word could be used to refer to bodily form, physical health, and to social class and property.[63] "Estat" thus encapsulates the connection between one's property and one's body that is also evident in the complaints in the Assize of Nuisances. In fact, this connection is evident even in the word "property" itself. As Charles Donahue Jr. has noted,

Our word "property" comes either directly or through French *propriété* from Latin *proprietas* which means "the peculiar nature or quality of thing" and (in post-Augustan writing) "ownership." *Proprietas* is itself derived from *proprius*, an adjective, equally applicable to physical things or qualities meaning, "own" or "peculiar," as opposed to *communis*, "common," or *alienus*, "another's" . . . [E]ven before it comes to be a legal term "property" is an abstraction of the

---

[62] Ibid., p. 450.

[63] The first definition of "estat" listed in the *MED* is "State or condition," which is then subdivided into the following meanings: among others, a person's stature, bodily form, physical health, or the state of his/her soul. The second, third, and fourth definitions show that "estat" could refer to social, religious, and political rank. Finally, the fifth definition refers to one's property or possessions. See Howard Kaminsky, "Estate, Nobility, and the Exhibition of Estate in the Later Middle Ages," *Speculum* 68 (1993): 684–709, for an extensive analysis of the meaning of "estate" in various medieval European languages. Kaminsky focuses on two of its meanings, social class and property. Concentrating mostly on the nobility, he argues that estates in the Middle Ages were not simply private property: "An individual's estate was his private property in its public aspect" (p. 692). Kaminsky notes in passing that "estate" could refer to the state of one's health. Mann's *Chaucer and Medieval Estates Satire* also pays attention primarily to the meaning of estate as social class. In a more recent analysis of the semantic development of the word "estat" from Middle English to Early Modern English, Peggy Knapp, *Time-Bound Words: Semantic and Social Economies from Chaucer's England to Shakespeare's* (New York: St. Martin's Press, 2000), similarly emphasizes that the primary meaning of "estat" in Middle English refers to social class and notes "the ideological connection between the standing a person is granted and the property he or she can display" (p. 32). As I argue in this essay, there is a further connotation of "estat," one's body as well as soul, that also needs to be considered and that illuminates the other meanings.

idea of what distinguishes an individual or a thing from a group or from another.[64]

"Property" and "estate" denote not only "things" that are owned but also features characteristic of a person's body. In addition, there is another meaning of "estat," "the state of one's soul," that is also evident in "property" and plays an important role in estates literature. *Estates* literature often saw a continuity among one's physiognomy and moral characteristics. Chaucer's description of the Miller's red beard (line 552) illustrates this point. As Mann has noted, "The redhead . . . is a widespread figure of deceit and treachery."[65] The self had its own intrinsic "properties," its moral and bodily features, and, in addition, property in the sense of what one owns was seen as an extension of the self.

Because of the crowding together in cities, we might expect urban inhabitants like the carpenter, the student, the wife, and the parish clerk in *The Miller's Tale* to be particularly aware of private and public boundaries in connection with property and the body. The spatial arrangement of his house points to John's concern with private material boundaries. It is perhaps no coincidence, we should add, that John is a specific type of artisan, a carpenter, that is, someone who often would have been involved with building houses, or private spaces with material boundaries. John's house, moreover, reflects a fourteenth-century tendency identified by scholars. Shaw, for instance, notes that "the increasing number of separate bedrooms and chambers constructed within dwellings over the course of the fourteenth century indicates a growing desire for privacy and the ability to partition personal space."[66] Although Chaucer does not give us a detailed description of the house, nevertheless, it is significant that he does specify the existence of at least two separate rooms, one for Nicholas and another one for the carpenter and his wife (there is no explicit reference to a separate room for the two servants, Robyn and Gille, but it is clear that neither one of them sleeps

---

[64] Charles Donahue Jr., "The Future of the Concept of Property Predicted from Its Past," in *Property: Nomos XXII,* ed. J. Roland Pennock and John W. Chapman (New York: New York University Press, 1980), p. 31.

[65] Mann, *Chaucer and Medieval Estates Satire,* p. 162.

[66] Shaw, "The Construction of the Private," p. 449. Shaw also explains how the link between privacy and one's home was made: "The mediated resolutions of the conflict between neighbors reveal that the principle of the inviolability of private property included a surprising correlate of privacy" (p. 450).

in either Nicholas's or John's and Alison's room).[67] Nicholas's room is upstairs; it is clearly demarcated through several references (for example, "A chambre hadde he in that hostelrye / Allone, withouten any compaignye" [lines 3203–4]). John's and Alison's room is twice referred to as a "bour," which Larry D. Benson glosses as bed chamber (see lines 3367 and 3676–77).[68] The relative importance of private spaces for John becomes especially evident when contrasted with Symkyn's house in *The Reeve's Tale*, which only seems to have one bedroom where he, his wife, their daughter, and the baby sleep (for example, lines 4143–45). That John has a heightened awareness of material boundaries, moreover, influences Nicholas's choice of trick. Noah's ark, Kathryn Walls has shown, was often associated with secrecy in the Middle Ages and the three troughs—private, individual spaces meant to replicate the ark—embody privacy.[69]

The material sense of privacy also plays a crucial role in Absolon's development as a character. Initially, Absolon does not show much interest in private practices, but he comes to adopt them somewhat unconsciously, as a response to circumstances, to what Bourdieu calls "structured and structuring structures."[70] Absolon is both a parish clerk and a barber-surgeon. As a barber-surgeon, he is closer to John— barber-surgeons also had their own guilds. Although parish priests could also be involved with mystery plays, we may be meant to relate his role of Herod "upon a scaffold hye" (line 3384) to his job as a barber-surgeon. Nonetheless, Absolon's acting role in a mystery play and his possible affiliation with a "myster" or guild seems to be his only association with privacy at the beginning of the tale.

The "publicness" of Absolon's parish job appears to influence his practices more than his artisanal job. His description, unlike Nicholas's, suggests that there is no mystery or secret about him. He displays himself openly: his hair "strouted as a fanne large and brode; / Ful straight

---

[67] See Bennett's interesting attempt to draw the plan of the carpenter's house in *Chaucer at Oxford,* p. 28.

[68] The first definition of "bour" in the *MED* is dwelling or house and the second one is inner room, especially a bedroom. Larry D. Benson glosses "under our boures" in line 3367 as "next to our bed chambers."

[69] Kathryn Walls, "The Significance of *Arca* and *Goddes Pryvetee* in *The Miller's Tale,*" *N&Q* 240 (1995): 24–26. Walls cites a significant passage from John Trevisa's translation of Bartholomaeus Anglicus's *De Proprietabus Rerum,* in which he states, although not referring specifically to Noah's Ark, that from the word "archa" "comeþ þis word 'archanum', priuete þat is sliliche ykepte vnknowen to multitude of men" (p. 25).

[70] Bourdieu, *The Logic of Practice,* p. 53.

and evene lay his joly shode" (lines 3315–16). Unlike Nicholas also, he spends most of his time in public places, such as taverns and breweries (line 3334), or in the parish. His initial lack of a strong sense of "pryvetee" is especially evident when he goes to the carpenter's house to woo Alison for the first time (line 3356). Absolon's performance in front of Alison's window is public. He does not even pay attention to the fact that the carpenter is in the bedroom with Alison. He has no secrets, or, rather, he does not practice privacy in its immaterial sense; neither does he seem to think that others should, given that the carpenter is with Alison when he woos her. Blodgett has rightly pointed out that, "[j]ust as Nicholas is a 'private' character, Absolon is 'public'—he carries movement and the outside world into the tale and the carpenter's garden of marriage."[71] We need to notice, though, that Absolon is not a static character in the tale. When after this first scene he realizes that he needs to be "prive" if he is going to succeed, he changes and starts acting "priveli." Thus, in a moment that reminds us of John wondering about Nicholas's whereabouts before, when Absolon notices that the carpenter is not around (John is building the troughs), he asks a "cloisterer / Ful prively after John the carpenter" (lines 3661–62). Thinking that the carpenter is not around, he secretively approaches Alison's window. His private practice at this point, though, is only partly successful.

Significantly, the first time he tries to be secretive or "prive," his own "pryvetee" is actually invaded. Indeed, his reaction to kissing Alison's private parts suggests that he takes her joke on him as a sensory assault on his body: "Who rubbeth now, who froteth now his lippes / With dust, with sond, with straw, with clooth, with chippes, / But Absolon, that seith ful ofte, 'Allas!'" (lines 3747–49). It is this invasion of his body, his material boundaries, that makes Absolon finally and unequivocally replace his openness, or "publicness," by secretiveness or private practices in an immaterial sense. After the misdirected kiss, he goes secretly to Gervays the smith and refuses to tell him why he is up so early or why he needs the coulter (lines 3760–87). In contrast with the open and confident display of his self that we saw before—the Absolon who could "In twenty manere . . . trippe and daunce" (line 3328)—in lines 3760–87 we see an Absolon who walks softly and stealthily (for example, "a softe paas he wente over the strete" [line 3760], and "Ful softe out at the dore he gan to stele" [line 3786]). While initially Abso-

---

[71] Blodgett, "Chaucerian *Pryvetee*," p. 484.

lon does not have a strong sense of boundaries, then, he realizes its practical utility. Absolon's change shows the way the *habitus* conditions behavior, specifically the way in which, if we want to achieve a practical goal, spatial practices, material and immaterial, in a sense impose themselves on us.

The importance of privacy is also evident in the character of Alison, but in her case, we will see, we need to consider how gender makes a difference as well. The traditional association of female bodies with privacy and property plays out in a significant way in the tale.[72] As Lochrie has argued, the tale examines the identification of privacy with women.[73] Thus, John's concern with "pryvetee" also manifests itself in his relationship with his wife, the female body within the house. House and wife, as Woods has observed, become "analogous" in Chaucer's tale, as they were in medieval English law; both are men's private possessions.[74] Because John is jealous and old, we are told, while his wife is young and wild, he keeps her "narwe in cage" (line 3224). His preoccupation with Alison's "pryvetee" obviously has to do with taking control of her body, specifically, her "prive membres," one of his pieces of property. And it is this private, material space that Nicholas and Absolon want to invade.

The male characters' focus on conquering Alison has led some critics to see Alison as an object, while others, despite such focus, see her as an independent agent with her own desires.[75] Part of the reason for the

[72] One of the first studies that associated women and private property was Friedrich Engels, *Ursprung der Familie, des Privateigenthums und des Staats* [The Origin of the Family, Private Property, and the State], published in 1884. Among more recent works that examine this association in various historical periods as well as in contemporary times, see Dorothy O. Helly and Susan M. Reverby, eds., *Gendered Domains: Rethinking Public and Private in Women's History* (Ithaca: Cornell University Press, 1992); Joan Kelly-Gadol, "The Relation of the Sexes: Methodological Implications of Women's History," *Signs* 1 (1976): 809–23; and Joan B. Landes, ed., *Feminism: The Public and the Private* (Oxford: Oxford University Press, 1998). A fascinating and complex analysis of the gendering of domestic space, particularly in Leon Battista Alberti's work, can be found in Mark Wigley, "Untitled: The Housing of Gender," in *Sexuality and Space*, ed. Beatriz Colomina (Princeton: Princeton Architectural Press, 1992), pp. 327–89. For an analysis of women and privacy in Chaucer, see Sarah Stanbury, "Women's Letters and Private Space in Chaucer," *Exemplaria* 6 (1994): 271–85. For an analysis of privacy, property, and women in the Middle Ages, see Lochrie, *Covert Operations*.

[73] Lochrie, *Covert Operations*, p. 164.

[74] Woods, "Private and Public Space in the *Miller's Tale*," p. 166.

[75] Readings that argue for Alison's subjectivity tend to see her as a manifestation of sexual desire and thus as an agent to the extent that she acts upon her desires. See, for instance, Kolve, *Chaucer and the Imagery of Narrative*, p. 25, or Patterson, *Chaucer and the Subject of History*, p. 258. This view has been disputed by various feminist critics, who have argued that Alison is primarily an object of male desire. For examples of this view,

disagreements on this issue, I would argue, is that Alison is at the same time an agent and an object of private practices. She is an agent to the extent that, as Bourdieu would put it, one can adopt practices strategically, which she does, but she is an object to the extent that she is conditioned by existing practices that try to do away with woman's agency and treat her as the "privee" space, indeed the very material "privee" body, to be invaded. This ambiguity is evident in her portrait (lines 3233–70). The portrait, which has sometimes been interpreted as a titillating draw for the male audience, if not for the Miller and Chaucer himself, treats her as an object that can be easily known.[76] However, the allusion to her "purs of lether" (line 3250), which she holds by her belt and whose contents we know nothing about, suggests that Alison has her own private space, which we know nothing about.

There are other suggestions that Alison has a psychological sense of privacy and that she holds some control over her "pryvetees," both bodily and psychological. This psychological sense becomes clearer when we notice the use of the word "privee" in relation to Alison and when we realize that, after an initial rejection, she becomes a willing collaborator with Nicholas's plot. When the student approaches her and tries to convince her to sleep with him, at first she rejects him, but when he insists, it does not take her long to give in and start plotting with him. She then asks Nicholas, "That but ye wayte wel and been privee" (line 3295), because her husband is "ful of jalousie" (line 3294). The two of them together "Acorded been to this conclusioun, / That Nicholas shal shapen hym a wyle / This sely jalous housbonde to bigyle" (lines 3402–4), and we are told that "this was his desir and hire also" (line 3407). Alison is an active participant in the ploy; she is no "sely," or passive, woman in the tale but, like the men in the tale, practices privacy to her own advantage. At the same time, though, she shows a different sense of "pryvetee" than the male characters. Unlike the men in the tale, Alison turns out to be aware of the instability of private spaces.

Given the men's obsession with controlling Alison, it is ironic and also significant that hers, the only female body in the tale, is the one that remains in some control at the end. Nothing that happens to her

---

see Lochrie, *Covert Operations,* who contends that the tale denies Alison any subjectivity (p. 167), and Kara Virginia Donaldson, "Alisoun's Language: Body, Text, and Glossing in Chaucer's 'The Miller's Tale,'" *PQ* 71 (1992): 139–53.

[76] See, for instance, Woods, "Private and Public Space in the *Miller's Tale,*" pp. 168–69, and Lochrie, *Covert Operations,* pp. 171–72.

body happens against her will and calculations. In the tale, Alison has a choice of lovers, Nicholas and Absolon, and she exerts her power to choose. Moreover, the fact that she shares her "pryvetees" with Nicholas suggests something even more crucial. Writing about another Alison, the Wife of Bath, R. W. Hanning has argued that the Wife sometimes shows "unwillingness to buy into a culture of pryvetee, in the sense of private possession," although at other times she also shows the impulse to hide.[77] The Miller's Alison shows a similar unwillingness to try to guard her "pryvetees" absolutely. And this unwillingness contrasts with the men's more insistently secretive practices. In a sense, Alison recognizes the limits of her agency and, as it were, works with the limitations of any attempt to mark private spaces, that is, with the fact that private spaces are bound to be violated. The men in the tale, by contrast, do not recognize such limits and thus suffer the consequences.

The male characters are significantly the ones that in the end have their own bodies invaded against their will, thus losing control over their most private space even as they have been intent on transgressing against other people's private boundaries.[78] We have seen the invasion of Absolon's body above. In the case of John, not only does Nicholas transgress against his "pryvetee" by invading his wife's "prive membres," but the carpenter also receives a final lesson on his body: "For al his kepyng and his jalousye" (line 3851), for all his secrecy/privacy, he breaks his arm (his body/property is damaged) and becomes a public joke—his neighbors think he is mad (lines 3840–49). Even Nicholas, the most secretive of the male characters, has his own body violated in the end. When he puts his buttocks out "prvely" (line 3802), his own reward is to be invaded in his own body/privacy (his "towte") in a way, moreover, that suggests his involuntary "feminization."[79] The Miller's use of the adverb "pryvely" in this sense is significant. This is the only time Nicholas crosses, even if only in part, into a public space in the tale. The threshold symbolizes the continuity between public and private spaces and the violability of the boundaries that supposedly protect private spaces. Nicholas's private action invites its violation. Men's in-

---

[77] Hanning, "Telling the Private Parts," p. 122. See page 123 for his argument about her opposite impulse.

[78] I thus agree with Lorenzo Boyd, "Seeking 'Goddes Pryvetee,'" in his analysis of the tale, although my argument considers the social, in addition to the homosexual, implications of such an association

[79] See Boyd's analysis of the sodomitical connotations of this moment in the tale in "Seeking 'Goddes Pryvetee,'" esp. pp. 250–54.

ability to control their own bodies and those of their wives, then, and, more broadly, the impossibility of keeping one's "pryvetes" intact become the focus of the tale: male bodies, like female bodies and all private spaces, are susceptible to violation.

Chaucer's choice of a miller to tell this story is particularly apt. Many millers in the fourteenth century occupied in a sense an intermediate space on the borders between urban and rural communities.[80] While some of them lived in cities, many had their mills in rural areas and on the fringes of cities. Of those who lived in villages, many had frequent contact with city dwellers as they often did business with them.[81] This is the case, for instance, of Symkyn, the miller in *The Reeve's Tale,* as we will see below. The interspatial position of Robyn the Miller in between the rural and the urban worlds allows him in theory to be more easily aware and critical of the practices of privacy that pervade the lives of those who inhabit urban spaces, especially of merchants and artisans. Thus, unlike his thoroughly urban characters, one would expect the Miller, a "less" urban character, to be less prone to be "pryvee," or have something to hide. We should notice the contrast between the mystery and anonymity that characterize Merchant and Guildsmen in the *General Prologue* and the individuality and openness that characterize the Miller, whose name, Robyn, we learn in the Prologue to his own tale (line 3129). While in the *General Prologue* the portraits of the Guildsmen and the Merchant focus on what they wear, rather than on their physical features, the Miller's portrait gives us numerous details, primarily about his physique—including a wart with a tuft of hairs (line 555)—that individualize him and, more crucially, that indicate openness. His detailed physical description suggests that he has nothing to hide: what we see is what we get. No boundaries, physical or psychological, prevent us from "seeing" him. He does, however, as mentioned before, perceive other people's boundaries and is intent on breaking them: "There was no dore that he nolde heve of harre / Or breke it at a rennyng with his

---

[80] Mills were more typically found in rural areas, but there were significant numbers of mills in or close to urban communities. On Chaucer's Miller and the ambiguous social position of millers, see Patterson's thorough discussion in *Chaucer and the Subject of History,* chap. 5. For a historical examination of the milling industry that pays close attention to mills that were close to, or in, cities, see John Ambler and John Langdon, "Lordship and Peasant Consumerism in the Milling Industry of Early Fourteenth-Century England," *Past and Present* 145 (1994): 3–46.

[81] See Langdon and Ambler, "Lordship and Peasant Consumerism in the Milling Industry."

heed" (lines 550–51). He is also adept at marking and creating *narrative* boundaries around others, for example, carpenters, only to break them: he entices us to listen to his story of "pryvetees," paradoxically marking the secret borders of his story only to cross them. The Miller seems more interested in crossing other people's private boundaries than in protecting his own, giving the impression that he has nothing to hide. The Reeve, though, will uncover the Miller's own "pryvetees" and show us otherwise.

Private Matters in the Other Tales in the First Fragment

When considering the First Fragment as a whole in the light of *The Miller's Tale,* it becomes clear that privacy is one of the main threads that connects the Miller to the other three tales and that the practices of space in each need to be analyzed in social and economic terms. The Miller's notion of privacy competes with the Knight's and exposes the inner workings of the nobility's management of space, while the Reeve, and especially the Cook, in Chaucer's return to a decidedly urban milieu in the final, unfinished tale of the First Fragment, explores further the implications regarding privacy raised by the Miller.

Privacy matters differently in *The Knight's Tale* than in the other three tales. The contrast becomes especially evident when we compare it to *The Miller's Tale. The Knight's Tale* is set in the distant, classical past and all its characters are noble. Initially, privacy in the tale appears to conflict with the common profit and "noble" goals. The tale centers on Palamon and Arcite's individual desires, which threaten the common good because the desiring individual does not take anything into consideration except personal satisfaction—Palamon and Arcite, sworn brothers (line 1147), even break their bond to each other because of their love for Emily. But private desires are eventually made to work for public aims. Theseus, in typical noble fashion (as the discourse of common profit would have it), redirects these private desires toward the common good.[82] First, rather than letting Palamon and Arcite fight without any witnesses, as it were in "pryvetee," he organizes a public tournament in which they can fight for Emily without killing each other, and hence without causing any further public conflicts. Second, for political rea-

---

[82] Farrell, "Privacy and the Boundaries of Fabliau in the *Miller's Tale,*" has made a similar point: "The Knight makes room for private action, but tends ultimately to subsume those parts of his tale under more public business" (p. 786).

sons—to forge peace between Thebes and Athens—he asks Palamon to marry Emily at the end of the tale. Thus public, not private reasons, lead to their marriage. These public reasons, though, do more than merely bolster Theseus's power. Again and again in the tale, Theseus conflates the private and the public. Either he turns private desires into public acts, or, if we consider the very beginning of the tale, he makes what seem like public actions, the Greeks' war against and defeat of the Amazons, take on private connotations: Theseus marries Ypolita as a result of his victory. *The Knight's Tale* shows how the nobility's definition of space operates: private and public interests are made to overlap rather than border on, and compete with, each other.[83] Nevertheless, the Miller's response to the Knight through his own tale sheds a critical light on Theseus's management of space. The Miller's insistence on private motivations in his own tale encourages us to interrogate such an overlap and, specifically, the private motivations behind Theseus's public acts.

The world of *The Reeve's Tale* is obviously closer to that of *The Miller's Tale* and constitutes a response to the Miller, seeking to "quit" his tale in many ways. One of the fundamental ways it does so is through the theme of privacy, which the Reeve uses cleverly in order to turn the Miller's joke against him. Privacy in *The Reeve's Tale,* though, needs to be examined in relation to the rural/urban opposition that Wallace has observed in the tale and to the interspatial situation of millers mentioned above.[84] Symkyn is in between rural and urban spaces. His mill is located in a small village, Trumpington, near Cambridge (lines 3921–23), and he does business with city dwellers.[85] He is thus a borderline figure in terms of place. Accordingly, his concern with privacy is less sophisticated or multidimensional than that of the characters in *The Miller's Tale.* Where the Miller explores the many complex levels at which practices of privacy can operate in an urban world inhabited by craftsmen, the Reeve collapses all these levels into two main ones: his miller's main practice of privacy is fraud; his other practice is manifested

[83] For an analysis of the private/public overlap as it is evident in the notion of estate, see Kaminsky, "Estate, Nobility, and the Exhibition of Estate in the Later Middle Ages." Kaminsky argues that "estate . . . lay athwart the modern disjunction of 'public' and 'private' elements and comprised both of them" (p. 702).

[84] Wallace, *Chaucerian Polity,* sees *The Reeve's Tale* as an example of the interdependence of city and village as well as of the sometimes violent opposition between the two (pp. 130–36).

[85] On Trumpington as a small village in the fourteenth century, see Bennett, *Chaucer at Oxford,* p. 109.

in his jealousy and protectiveness of the boundaries around his wife (see lines 3956–62). Thus, while his deceptiveness and secrecy bring Symkyn closer to the traditionally negative depictions of "selfish" artisans and merchants, the lack of private rooms in his house and his seeming disregard of the dangers of letting the students sleep in his own private space suggests that he is less savvy about practicing privacy than John the carpenter. In this sense, his comment to the students when he offers them "herberwe" is significant:

> Myn hous is streit, but ye han lerned art;
> Ye konne by arguments make a place
> A myle brood of twenty foot of space.
> Lat se now if this place may suffise,
> Or make it rowm with speche, as is youre gise.
> (I.4122–26)

Basking in his initial victory over the students, his secretive stealing, the miller does not realize that in his private material space, inside his house, he needs to draw clear boundaries as well. While the students do not subsequently enlarge his room with words, they do play another trick on him: they violate his other private property, his wife's and his daughter's bodies. This violation, in a domino effect, leads to the daughter's revelation in lines 4240–46, which allows them to uncover the miller's secretive fraudulent practices. In taking the miller's "pryvetee," his wife's and daughter's bodies, the students perfectly mirror the miller's fraudulent taking of their own "pryvetee."

The Reeve's Tale then makes a point similar to the Miller's about the instability of "pryvetees," but it does so in a less complex way by exploring fewer dimensions of the concept. One reason it does this, I would argue, is that the Reeve seems impatient to get to his revenge—he does not have time for narrative complications because he wants to give the miller (as well as the Miller) his punishment. But another, more significant, reason, I would argue, is that in peeling away all the different layers of "pryvetee" that the Miller had identified in his tale, the Reeve zeroes in on the former's main practice of "pryvetee," stealing. The Miller's portrait in the *General Prologue* had already pointed to this practice: "Wel koude he stelen corn and tollen thries; / And yet he hadde a thombe of gold, pardee" (562–63). *The Reeve's Tale* emphatically reminds us of this, uncovering the practices of the jovial Miller, who in his tale poked fun at others' construction of private boundaries. Even if he may not seem to, Robyn the Miller also acts "pryveli." Breaking people's doors, which thieves might do literally, works as a metaphor in the Miller's case for his fraudulent practices. The Miller himself also practices privacy (he steals), and, like the characters in his own tale, he is ultimately "uncovered."

It is appropriate that the Reeve would be the one to uncover the Miller's fraudulent practices and break into his "pryvetee." After all, the Reeve, as his portrait points out, knows how to uncover secrets: "Ther nas bailliff, ne hierde, nor oother hyne, / That he ne knew his sleighte and his covyne" (lines 603–4). And, even more significant, the Reeve himself knows about private practices because of his former occupation as a carpenter. It is no coincidence that in the Reeve's portrait the line that describes how he can "yeve and lene hym [his lord] of his owene good" (line 611)—a line that suggests that the Reeve himself may also be stealing since it is unclear whether "owene good" refers to the lord's or the Reeve's—is immediately followed by, "In youthe he hadde lerned a good myster: / He was a wel good wrighte, a carpenter" (lines 613–14). The Reeve can easily match the Miller, because he also comes from the world of merchants and craftsmen.

The Cook's reaction immediately following *The Reeve's Tale* focuses significantly on the issues of "pryvetee" in the house. He spends five lines showing that he knows better than Symkyn, his immediate and implicit referent in lines 4330–34:[86]

> Wel seyde Salomon in his langage,
> "Ne bryng nat every man into thyn hous,"
> For herberwynge by nyghte is perilous.
> Wel oghte a man avysed for to be
> Whom that he broghte into his pryvetee.

The Cook, a Londoner who works for the Guildsmen, has a more heightened awareness of private practices and is thus more savvy about them than Symkyn. *The Cook's Tale* confirms and emphasizes the association of "pryvetee" with the practices, material and immaterial, of the urban mercantile and artisanal classes, and it shows more explicitly than *The Miller's Tale, The Reeve's Tale,* and the *General Prologue* that the concept of "pryvetee," even with its many holes, is not merely a characteristic but is a *sine qua non* for their business practices.

[86] These lines also make us think of John the Carpenter.

Critics have been puzzled by the different tone of the first and the second halves of this unfinished tale. The first half (I.4365–88) takes the point of view of an apprentice, Perkyn, who has dubious connections to London's lowlifes, while the second half (I.4689–4422), told from the point of view of the apprentice's master, takes a moralistic tone that reflects what V. A. Kolve has called "a bourgeois voice," the voice of those engaged in trade.[87] Kolve remarks on the contrast between the two voices and notes: "I think it likely Chaucer intended us to perceive the mercantile overtones of this *Cook's Tale* morality as differing, in some subtle ways, from other competing registrations of the goals of human life."[88] That is, the second half of the tale encourages us to judge the first half by the moral standards of the master victualler. What Perkyn does is bad for the master's "chaffare," for his business: "That fond his maister wel in his chaffare, / For often tyme he foond his box ful bare" (lines 4389–90).

But what is it that Perkyn does? The Cook uses the word "pryvetee" in a significant context in the tale. We learn in the first half that Perkyn wastes money, especially on others. He spends his time on the streets and he is far from thrifty: "he was free / Of his dispense, in place of pryvetee" (lines 4387–88). Benson's edition glosses "place of pryvetee" as "private place." In Middle English, though, the phrase "in place of" can mean "instead of," and thus, as V. J. Scattergood has argued, the meaning of these lines may be " 'and to that end (that is, dicing) he was generous in what he spent instead of keeping his money hidden.' "[89] "Pryvetee" in those lines is thus associated with keeping one's money private, with not wasting it and keeping it to oneself, which is precisely what Perkyn fails to do. As an apprentice to the artisanal class, Perkyn, it seems, should have begun to learn (as Absolon eventually does in *The Miller's Tale*) the importance of practicing "pryvetee" in all the senses we have examined. Perkyn would have been expected to practice the habit of keeping boundaries, material and immaterial, between public and private spaces, that is, keeping his private profit to himself, keeping a private dwelling, and making sure women's bodies are kept in private. Perkyn, however, practices the exact opposite. Not only does he waste his money and spend his time on the streets, but after the apprentice-

---

[87] Kolve, *Chaucer and the Imagery of Narrative*, p. 269.
[88] Ibid., p. 277.
[89] V. J. Scattergood, "Perkyn Revelour and the *Cook's Tale*," *ChauR* 19 (1984–85): 19.

master relationship breaks down, Perkyn takes up with a friend who does not privatize his wife's body: she "heeld for contenance / A shoppe, and swyved for hir sustenance" (lines 4421–22). Neither the husband, nor Perkyn, who associates with him, practices the privatization of women's sexuality.

Perkyn's disregard for privacy puts him on the fringes of the mercantile and artisanal world, that is, on the fringes of the *habitus*. Bourdieu argues that the *habitus* tends to generate what are seen as "common-sense" behaviors, "which are likely to be positively sanctioned because they are adjusted to the logic characteristic of a particular field." And, he continues, "[a]t the same time . . . it tends to exclude all the 'extravagances' ('not for the likes of us'), that is, all the behaviours that would be negatively sanctioned because they are incompatible with the objective conditions."[90] In *The Cook's Tale*, Perkyn's behavior is seen as an extravagance. The master's use of the "common-sense" saying "Wel bet is rotten appul out of hoord / Than that it rotie al the remenaunt" (lines 4406–7) makes precisely that point: Perkyns's extravagances are "not for the likes of us." The master's actions show that those who do not practice privacy become eventually marginalized in the world of commerce; they become identified with the margins of society, with inappropriate and low-life behavior. A good merchant practices privacy.[91]

As I mentioned at the beginning of this essay, in the late Middle Ages the gentry explicitly depicted privacy as a suspicious practice. Responding to this rhetoric, merchants, to an extent, tried to portray themselves as interested in the common profit. However, the structures of the urban market economy and the concentration of markets and bodies in cities conditioned their practices of privacy. The rhetoric of those merchants who praised the common profit did not (or could not) match their practices.

Chaucer's exploration of the practices of privacy in these texts, and particularly in *The Miller's Tale*, reproduces the gentry's denunciation of merchants' and artisans' private practices, and also goes beyond to examine the instability of private boundaries. Chaucer's exploration of pri-

[90] Bourdieu, *The Logic of Practice*, pp. 55–56.
[91] Perkyn's disregard of privacy also differs from Theseus's (or the nobility's) management of space. Theseus makes the private seemingly subordinated to the public and makes them coalesce; the public coincides with his private interests because both public and private are made to intertwine in the noble world. Perkyn's practices, then, differ from those of both the noble and the mercantile and artisanal classes: he gives the private away by turning it over to the public. The nobility does not give the private away. It constructs it as public.

vacy, moreover, does not stop at merchants and artisans, but also leads him to consider his own dependence on the practices of privacy as a writer. Chaucer himself is, after all, an insider to the *habitus* as well. Hanning has argued that "[t]he interaction between the impulses toward pryvetee and disclosure constitutes the basic transaction of Chaucer's storytelling society; words are finally that society's most important chaffare."[92] *The Miller's Prologue* exemplifies such impulses. By telling the story of the cuckolded carpenter, Chaucer (the ultimate narrator) is also creating and, at the same time, breaking the boundaries of a "pryvetee." In *The Miller's Prologue,* Chaucer the narrator entices us by saying and, supposedly, warning us in an aside and disclaimer that the Miller's and Reeve's tales are tales of "harlotrie" (line 3184). He notes that we do not need to read them if we do not want to (lines 3170ff.), significantly also introducing at this point the idea of private reading ("Turne over the leef and chese another tale," line 3177), thus dramatizing the practice of privacy. Chaucer the narrator creates a private space by marking its boundaries (this is a "prive" story about "prive membres") and reminding us that, if we are reading, we are in our own private space. Moreover, by reminding us of the private character of our act of reading, Chaucer is also enticing us to break boundaries—nobody will know; why not break the boundaries? As he creates private boundaries and simultaneously suggests their instability in his own narratives, Chaucer points to the dependence of his own poetics on the concept of "pryvetee." In Chaucer's poetics, fiction itself and the writer of fiction are similarly implicated in the practices of privacy that the gentry associates with the urban mercantile and artisanal classes.

Writing about *Troilus and Criseyde* (III.295–98), Hanning notes that those lines suggest that "it is unnatural, *agaynes kynde,* for a poet to protect pryvetee. To do so, the poet must be silent, must cease, in other words, to be a poet."[93] In the *Canterbury Tales* also, Chaucer recognizes that narrative interest depends to a great extent on the construction of and transgression against "pryvetee," that is, on what is not known. This dependence of Chaucer's poetics on private spaces may be one of the reasons that *The Cook's Tale* ends abruptly. At the end of the tale as we have it, Chaucer got himself into a space, Perkyn's "public" space, that was not productive for the narration of *The Cook's Tale.* And the rest is silence.

---

[92] Hanning, "Telling the Private Parts: 'Pryvetee' and Poetry in Chaucer's *Canterbury Tales,*" p. 123.

[93] Ibid., p. 109.

Images of Pity:

The Regulatory Aesthetics of John Lydgate's Religious Lyrics

Shannon Gayk
Indiana University

L ATE MEDIEVAL CLERICS did not underestimate the power of the image. They did, however, differ on how to assess and respond to the laity's increasing attachment to devotional artifacts.[1] In a lyric on the pietà, one of the most popular images of the period, the Benedictine monk and poet John Lydgate offers a brief explanation of the proper use of visual images in religious devotion:

> To suche entent was ordeynt purtreture
> And ymages of dyverse resemblaunce,
> That holsom storyes thus shewyd in fygur
> May rest with ws with dewe remembraunce.[2]

Images, for Lydgate, are *libri laicorum,* books for the laity. This statement might seem like a critical commonplace. What I will suggest in this essay, however, is that Lydgate's insistence on the mnemonic useful-

---

I am very grateful to Maura Nolan, Jill Mann, James Simpson, Frank Grady, and the anonymous reader for *SAC* for their many helpful comments and suggestions as I wrote and revised this essay.

[1] For example, Hans Belting, *Likeness and Presence: A History of the Image Before the Era of Art,* trans. Edmund Jephcott (Chicago: University of Chicago Press, 1994), p. 1, suggests that "[w]henever images threatened to gain undue influence within the church, theologians have sought to strip them of their power. . . . It was never easy to control images with words because, like saints, they engaged deeper levels of experience and fulfilled desires other than the ones living church authorities were able to address."

[2] "The Image of Pity," lines 37–40, in John Lydgate, *The Minor Poems of John Lydgate,* part 1, ed. Henry Noble MacCracken, EETS, o.s. 192 (London: Oxford University Press, 1934), pp. 297–99. Hereafter cited as MacCracken with line numbers of the lyrics inserted parenthetically after quotations in the text.

ness of images sets him apart from his contemporaries, who emphasized the affective and emotional content of images. For Lydgate, images are valuable insofar as they help one remember in an intellectual rather than an affective way.[3] In another lyric, Lydgate similarly urges the "folkys all, whyche haue deuociown" when viewing visual signs "[t]o haue memory of Crystes passioun, / As doctors remembre in theyr doctryne" (lines 1, 14–15).[4] Of this passage, we might ask: Is it reasonable for Lydgate to expect the unlearned laity to read complex visual figures with the exegetical skill of "doctors"? After all, his contemporary, Nicholas Love, explicitly tells his lay readers that he will "passen ouer" those matters "expownet by holy doctours."[5] For Love, the omission and suppression of such scholarly detail is an act of regulation. Lay piety, his *Mirror of the Blessed Life of Jesus Christ* suggests, is best kept "bodily," affective, and incarnational.[6] Indeed, vernacular devotional works of this period typically are affective and incarnational, mirroring and embodying the agendas of emergent forms of lay piety influenced by Franciscan and Bernardine theology that de-emphasized the function of images as *libri laicorum* and emphasized their ability to effect "the stirring of emotion rather than the imparting of knowledge."[7]

[3] Such an emphasis on relating images and memory is entirely consistent with Lydgate's monastic background. "Monastic art," Mary Carruthers writes, is "an art for *mneme*, 'memory,' rather than one for mimesis. . . . *Mneme* produces an art for 'thinking about' and for 'meditating upon' and for 'gathering.' . . . An art of tropes and figures is an art of patterns and pattern-making, and thus an art of *mneme* or *memoria*, of cognition, thinking" (*The Craft of Thought: Meditation, Rhetoric, and the Making of Images, 400–1200* [Cambridge: Cambridge University Press, 1998], pp. 3–4). Similarly Miriam Gill examines extant monastic wall paintings to suggest that unlike the *libri laicorum* found on the walls of parish churches, monastic art is figurally complex and intended to be an extension of monastic *lectio;* see "The Role of Images in Monastic Education: The Evidence from Wall Painting in Late Medieval England," in *Medieval Monastic Education,* ed. George Ferzoco and Carolyn Muessig (London: University of Leicester Press, 2000), pp. 117–35.

[4] "The Interpretation and Virtues of the Mass," in MacCracken, ed., *Minor Poems,* p. 87.

[5] Nicholas Love, *Mirror of the Blessed Life of Jesus Christ,* ed. Michael Sargent (New York: Garland, 1992), 45:8–10. This is just one of many references to the differing abilities of the laity and the clergy in spiritual understanding in Love's translation of the *Meditationes Vitae Christi.* For a brief discussion with additional examples, see Sargent's introduction, p. xxxv.

[6] Ibid., p. 10. See also Nicholas Watson, "Censorship and Cultural Change in Late-Medieval England: Vernacular Theology, the Oxford Translation Debate, and Arundel's Constitutions of 1409," *Speculum* 70 (1995): 854, and Watson, "Conceptions of the Word: The Mother Tongue and the Incarnation of God," *New Medieval Literatures* 1 (1997): 95.

[7] Rosemary Woolf, *The English Religious Lyric in the Middle Ages* (Oxford: Clarendon Press, 1968), p. 184. For representative studies of late medieval religious images and the production of affect, see Hans Belting, *The Image and Its Public in the Middle Ages: Forms and Function of Early Paintings of the Passion,* trans. Mark Bartusis and Raymond

Lydgate's insistence on clerical modes of "remembraunce" suggests both his unease with affective, unmediated visual experience and his desire to promote an altogether different devotional model for the laity—an application of the practice of monastic *lectio* and *memoria* to contemporary devotional images that uses the images only as prompts upon which are layered sets of complex theological figures.[8] This insistence is both conservative and innovative. On the one hand, it appeals to an older, monastic model, while on the other, it resists the period's dominant affective understanding of images by translating these traditional models into nontraditional vernacular verse. Lydgate's attitude toward images is most clearly manifested in a series of verse apologetics for contemporary images that attempt to regulate the images' affective (and potentially subversive) power by redirecting their veneration into a form of monastic *lectio*. This essay, then, examines what I will call the "regulatory aesthetics" of two of these lyrics and argues that Lydgate's choice of the most popular affective visual images of the period as his subjects demonstrates his desire to produce a clerically regulated vernacular alternative to current modes of affective piety that collapsed temporal boundaries in order to enable affective, participatory memory.

In translating Latinate, pre-Bernardine devotional practices and hermeneutics into vernacular poetry, Lydgate simultaneously authorizes the vernacular as a mode of theological instruction and reasserts the importance of clerical mediation of lay spirituality. Precisely because he translates monastic hermeneutics into vernacular religious verse, Lydgate's

---

Meyer (New York: Aristide D. Caratzas, Publisher, 1981), pp. 41–64; Kathleen Kamerick, *Popular Piety and Art in the Late Middle Ages* (New York: Palgrave, 2002); and Richard Marks, *Image and Devotion in Late Medieval England* (Thrupp: Sutton, 2004), pp. 11–37. For influential readings of the status of visual, affective piety in the period's literature, see Gail Gibson, *Theater of Devotion: East Anglian Drama and Society in the Late Middle Ages* (Chicago: University of Chicago Press, 1989); Caroline Bynum, *Holy Feast, Holy Fast: The Religious Significance of Food to Medieval Women* (Berkeley and Los Angeles: University of California Press, 1987); and Sarah Beckwith, *Christ's Body: Identity, Culture, and Society in Late Medieval Writings* (London: Routledge, 1993). See also Laurelle LeVert, "'Crucifye hem, Crucifye hem': The Subject and Affective Response in Middle English Passion Narratives," *Essays in Medieval Studies* 14 (1997): 73–90.

   [8] On the clerical interest in regulating devotional images, see M. R. James, "Pictor in Carmine," *Archaeologia* 94 (1951): 141–66; W. R. Jones, "Lollards and Images: The Defense of Religious Art in Later Medieval England," *Journal of the History of Ideas* 34:1 (1973): 27–50; Marks, *Image and Devotion,* p. 27. See also Michael Camille, "Seeing and Reading: Some Visual Implications of Medieval Literacy and Illiteracy," *Art History* 8 (1985): 26–49, and Vincent Gillespie, "Medieval Hypertext: Image and Text from York Minster," in *Of the Making of Books: Medieval Manuscripts, Their Scribes and Readers, Essays Presented to M. B. Parkes,* ed. P. R. Robinson and Rivkah Zim (Aldershot: Scolar Press, 1997), p. 216.

authorization of religious writing in English is fundamentally different from both Lollard assertions of lay spiritual autonomy and orthodox assumptions that the vernacular is unsuited for more complex or abstract theology. For this reason, his vernacular verse-theology also complicates recent scholarly paradigms that have sought to align the language politics of late medieval vernacular discourse with the period's "incarnational aesthetic."[9] Lydgate's shorter religious lyrics offer an alternative to this model by drawing on what James Simpson has recently termed "reformist textual practices": textual and figural accretion, subtle negotiations of competing authorities, and sometimes jarring juxtapositions of genres.[10] The sacred images that prompt these lyrics become textual *loci* where multiple histories, figures, traditions, and sources of authority intersect. Onto devotional images created and used as prompts of affective memory and personal identification, Lydgate attempts to map an alternative mode of remembrance that is indebted to ecclesiastically mediated history. Thus, the visual "remembraunce" that Lydgate evokes is referential rather than incarnational or phenomenal.

Lydgate's choice to write poems on the period's most popular devotional images, I suggest, is a considered intervention in the contemporary debates about the validity and proper use of religious images; however, his aesthetic choices and his appeals to variant sources of authority reveal a deep, if unarticulated, ambivalence about both the terms of those debates and popular lay religious practices. Just as he layers the narratives of Troy and Thebes with political propaganda to reassert the legitimacy of the Lancastrian regime, Lydgate layers his religious writing with forms of textual mediation in order to reassert the authority of historical discourse and ecclesiastical structures. The regulatory function of Lydgate's lyrics is revealed by his aesthetic choices. I read his religious lyrics as regulatory insofar as they are marked by their attempts to recover older devotional models, by their translation of Latinate, or aureate, rhetorical forms into vernacular discourse, and by their insistence on referential mediation and moral pedagogy rather than phenomenal (or incarnational) experience. On the one hand, they reject the affect and atemporality of contemporary devotional practice; on the other

---

[9] On the period's "incarnational aesthetic," see Gibson, *Theater of Devotion*, p. 6. On the conflation of this aesthetic with language politics, see Watson, "Conceptions of the Word," pp. 86–91.

[10] James Simpson, *Reform and Cultural Revolution*, Oxford English Literary History, vol. 2, 1350–1547 (New York: Oxford University Press, 2002), p. 62.

hand, they offer a clerically mediated alternative in the vernacular. In response to phenomenal and physical devotional practices, Lydgate attempts to reclaim monastic devotional practices and recapture a world in which lay piety was mediated by clerical authority.

Lydgate's unique commitment to versifying devotional images has been noted by several critics.[11] However, with the exception of the work of James Simpson, these discussions of Lydgate's propensity for writing about religious images fail to take into account the heightened interest in and controversy surrounding religious images at the time of the composition of the poems. While scholars have often overlooked Lydgate's interest in the relationship between images and texts, they have also been quite reluctant to deal with his even more massive corpus of religious writing largely because it has been assumed that he made his most interesting and important contributions through his politicized narrative histories and his attempts to establish himself as an inheritor of the Chaucerian tradition.[12] Yet even a cursory examination of Lydgate's religious writing reveals him to be as much "vernacular theologian" as

[11] Almost a century ago, Eleanor Hammond briefly considered Lydgate's curious habit of writing visual texts; see "Two Tapestry Poems by Lydgate: The Life of St. George and the Falls of Seven Princes," *Englische Studien* 43 (1910): 10–26. Derek Pearsall suggested in *John Lydgate* (Charlottesville: University of Virginia Press, 1970) that "Lydgate was particularly active in exploring the borderland of word and picture, though he did so quite unconsciously and would not have been aware of a borderland" (p. 179). Christine Cornell, " 'Purtreture' and 'Holsom Stories': Lydgate's Accommodation of Image and Text in Three Religious Lyrics," *Florilegium* 10 (1988–91): 167–78, argues to the contrary that Lydgate was fully aware of his actions and suggests that in these poems, "Lydgate increases or curtails the complexity of the poetic description and decoration, according to the purpose of the particular work of art" (p. 167). Rosemary Woolf also finds in Lydgate's propensity for poems on devotional images a central example of the increased allusion to external visual objects and decreased descriptive detail in fifteenth-century religious lyrics (*The English Religious Lyric*, p. 183). Most recently, James Simpson reads Lydgate's religious lyrics as characteristic examples of how fifteenth-century religious poetry works "wholly within traditions of the lay-directed, affective image" (*Reform*, p. 454).

[12] The overwhelming critical interest in Lydgate has been in reading his work within its political context or as an inheritor of the Chaucerian tradition. For representative political readings of Lydgate, see V. J. Scattergood, *Politics and Poetry in the Fifteenth Century* (London: Blandford Press, 1971), and Lee Patterson, "Making Identities in the Fifteenth Century: Henry V and Lydgate," in *New Historical Literary Study*, ed. Jeffrey Cox and Larry Reynolds (Princeton: Princeton University Press, 1993). For readings of Lydgate's relationship to Chaucer, see Paul Strohm, "Chaucer's Fifteenth-Century Audience and the Narrowing of the 'Chaucer Tradition,' " *SAC* 4 (1982): 3–32; Derek Pearsall, "Chaucer and Lydgate," in *Chaucer Traditions: Studies in Honor of Derek Brewer,* ed. Ruth Morse, Barry Windeatt, and Toshiyuki Takamiya (Cambridge: Cambridge University Press, 1990), pp. 39–53; and Seth Lerer, *Chaucer and His Readers* (Princeton: Princeton University Press, 1993).

courtly poet laureate, engaging in a number of the most controversial theological topics of his day in a uniquely literary way.[13] Such reluctance to see Lydgate as a "religious" writer is rooted in a persistent scholarly tradition of treating Lydgate's monastic background as a hindrance, rather than a help, to his literary aspirations. Indeed, even Lydgate's own jovial host in *The Siege of Thebes* demands that the pilgrim from Bury "leyn aside thy professioun" and "preche not of non holynesse."[14] Scholars have been even more determined to downplay Lydgate's monastic life, implicitly accepting the assumptions articulated half a century ago by H. S. Bennett, that "[h]is life in the cloister did nothing to bring out other qualities which may have been latent in him . . . the little he knew of life was colored by his ecclesiastical prejudices."[15]

In recent years, however, critics have been more receptive to exploring the poetic implications of Lydgate's religious vocation, though they remain primarily interested in its manifestations in Lydgate's major courtly and political works.[16] Christopher Cannon has noted that as Lydgate had the status of an "official" public poet, his poetry straddled "two worlds," but he remained essentially "a monastic versifier."[17] Simi-

---

[13] A. S. G. Edwards, "Lydgate Scholarship: Progress and Prospectus," in *Fifteenth-Century Studies: Recent Essays,* ed. Robert Yeager (New Haven: Yale University Press, 1984), pp. 29–47, found it surprising that Lydgate's shorter religious poems have been little studied. Since the publication of Edward's survey, there have been several essays treating Lydgate's religious poetry, but the subject is still awaiting full treatment.

[14] John Lydgate, *Siege of Thebes,* ed. Robert R. Edwards (Kalamazoo, Mich.: TEAMS, 2001), lines 132 and 167.

[15] Bennett, *Chaucer and the Fifteenth Century* (New York: Oxford University Press, 1961), p. 142. Similarly, in *English Literature at the Close of the Middle Ages* (New York: Oxford University Press, 1945), E. K. Chambers writes that Lydgate and other fifteenth-century lyric writers "read like the work of cloistered ecclesiastics who have mistaken religious fervor or conviction for literary inspiration" (p. 114). Although Pearsall has given one of the most comprehensive descriptions of Lydgate's religious poetry thus far in his monograph, *John Lydgate,* in a more recent article, "Lydgate as Innovator," *MLQ* 53 (1992): 5–22, he dismisses the possibility of reading Lydgate as a religious writer. Walter Schirmer, *John Lydgate: A Study in the Culture of the XVth Century,* trans. Ann E. Keep (London: Methuen, 1961), remains a useful overview of Lydgate's religious verse.

[16] Lydgate's religious poems frequently are given attention in volumes that do not fall within the standard definitions of "Lydgate scholarship." For example, Gail Gibson briefly discusses Lydgate's "Testament" in relation to the piety of the Clopton family in *Theatre of Devotion,* pp. 84–90. Rosemary Woolf compares the style and thematic interests of Lydgate's religious poetry to that of other fifteenth-century lyrics in *Religious Lyric,* pp. 198–202 and pp. 208–10.

[17] Christopher Cannon, "Monastic Productions," in *The Cambridge History of Medieval English Literature,* ed. David Wallace (Cambridge: Cambridge University Press, 1999), p. 342.

larly Scott-Morgan Straker has argued that Lydgate's use of his monastic background in the *Siege of Thebes* enables him to "redeem the authority of the monastic voice."[18] Other scholars, including Lois Ebin and Susan K. Hagen, have explored Lydgate's use of the monastic voice and tradition within his more didactic and homiletic poems to suggest that he viewed his poetic task as one of moral instruction.[19] Yet while this recent work seeks to redeem Lydgate's monastic background from the bad press it has received in the past, for the most part it continues to operate on the assumption that Lydgate's religious writing is an entirely orthodox articulation of late medieval official piety. This essay extends these arguments about Lydgate's moral and memorial aesthetic while suggesting the potential of Lydgate's relatively ignored religious writing to reveal complex negotiations among political ideologies, modes of clerical regulation, and lay devotional practices that both complement and complicate current scholarly paradigms of late medieval "vernacular theology."

"With Dewe Remembraunce": Memory, Affect, and Lydgate's *Pietà*

Both Lydgate's ambivalence and his mode of regulatory and homiletic amplification are evident in his lyric "On the Image of Pity," a poetic rendering of the extremely popular image of the pietà.[20] The image of the lifeless Christ stretched across his mother's lap was a relatively new devotional object, with the earliest versions appearing in Germany in the beginning of the fourteenth century.[21] These early versions of the

---

[18] Scott-Morgan Straker, "Deference and Difference: Lydgate, Chaucer, and the *Siege of Thebes,*" *RES* 52 (2001): 2.

[19] Lois Ebin, *Illuminator, Makar, Vates: Visions of Poetry in the Fifteenth Century* (Lincoln: University of Nebraska Press, 1988), pp. 19–48. Susan K. Hagen, *Allegorical Remembrance: A Study of "The Pilgrimage of the Life of Man" as a Treatise on Seeing and Remembering* (Athens: University of Georgia Press, 1990), argues that Lydgate's translation of *The Pilgrimage of the Life of Man* is an instruction manual in allegorical reading.

[20] MacCracken, ed., *Minor Poems*, pp. 297–99. All subsequent citations to "On the Image of Pity" will be given parenthetically in the text by line number.

[21] Woolf, *The English Religious Lyric,* p. 393. Woolf's book contains an extraordinarily helpful introduction to the history of the pietà in an Appendix (pp. 392–94), noting both the prevalence of the image in late medieval England and its ambiguous beginnings. As the extrabiblical pietà was apparently a particular favorite of the iconoclasts, there are few extant English versions. The popularity of the image, however, has never been disputed. On the status of the pietà in England, see Marks, *Image and Devotion,* pp. 121–43, and Nigel Morgan, "Texts and Images of Marian Devotion in Fourteenth-Century England," in *England in the Fourteenth Century: Proceedings of the 1991 Harlaxton Symposium,* ed. Nicholas Rogers (Stamford, Lincolnshire: Paul Watkins, 1993), pp. 51–57. For general background on the pietà, see Gertrud Schiller, *Iconography of Christian*

image represented a smiling young mother with a Christ child in her arms and seem to have been intended as nativity scenes foreshadowing the Passion. Within a century, however, Mary's gladness had given way to mourning, and the representation of her sorrow had become one of the most widespread and popular visual images in England.[22] The popularity of the image needs little explanation; it was an especially suitable object of devotion in an age of increasing Marian piety, emphasis on the passion and humanity of Christ, and affective meditation.[23]

Extra-biblical and atemporal, the affective potential of the image was easily exploited in both its visual and literary expressions. Makers of the image emphasized the pathetic qualities of the scene by adding affective details: in some versions of the image, the Virgin's tearful gaze is fixed on her son; in others, she looks sorrowfully outward, as if beseeching the viewer to participate in her agony and feel her pity.[24] The image's affective power, however, was also rooted in its relative freedom from the confining particularity of the historical narrative of the Passion.[25] Thus visual depictions of the pietà were doggedly atemporal and incarnational, skirting historical context and complex typological reference in order to resituate the figures of the passion within the viewer's memory as experientially present.

Contemporary literary depictions of the pietà also sought to make the image present to the reader in the same way that the visual image enabled experiential memory. In its literary manifestations, the image was often generalized and embellished with affective details (such as cries of lament) to heighten the emotional effect.[26] For example, one Middle

---

Art, vol. 2, trans. Janet Seligman (Greenwich, Conn.: New York Graphic Society, 1972), pp. 179–81.

[22] Woolf points out that the "Pietà grouping and complaint were not part of the traditional narrative meditation" and notes its absence in literary accounts as diverse as the mystery cycles, the *Cursor Mundi,* and the *Meditaciones Vita Christi (The English Religious Lyric,* p. 392).

[23] Marks concurs: "Our Lady of Pity was a subject whose primary appeal lay in emotional responses evoked by sight. The capacity of this particular image to embody a subtle range of meanings could be conveyed with greater effect visually than by means of the written word" (p. 143).

[24] Schiller, *Iconography,* p. 180.

[25] On this narrative isolation, see Woolf, *The English Religious Lyric,* p. 255.

[26] Along these lines, Rachel Fulton, *From Judgment to Passion: Devotion to Christ and the Virgin Mary, 800–1200* (New York: Columbia University Press, 2002), p. 197, has suggested that "praying to the Virgin . . . forced medieval Christians to forge new tools with which to *feel.* . . . [Mary] schooled religiously sensitive women and men in the potentialities of emotion."

English lyric on the pietà describes the author's intensely personal encounter with the weeping virgin, who calls out to the reader: "who can not wepe, com lerne of me."[27] As Émile Mâle suggests, "[n]othing in our ancient Pietàs distracts us from the thought of sorrow."[28] Indeed, pity is certainly the lesson of the image. Margery Kempe's tearful encounter with "owr Lady clepyd a pyte" in a church suggests that she has learned this lesson well.[29] When a priest requests that she hush, saying that Christ died long ago, she replies that Christ's death is as fresh to her as if it had just happened. For Margery, then, the image facilitates a collapsing of temporal boundaries; it makes the past present to her.[30] The way of seeing articulated here by both Margery and the weeping Virgin was not unfamiliar to Lydgate, but its affective intent and, more important, its insistence on the necessity of collapsing temporal boundaries is conspicuously absent in Lydgate's poetic depiction of the pietà.[31]

Lydgate's poem "On the Image of Pity" begins with a gesture toward the desired affective response, making an appeal to the reader's gaze and emotions, yet by its final stanza the poem has become a theological argument about the validity and right use of images that emphasizes their importance as mnemonic devices.[32] What Lydgate means by "remembrance" in this lyric, however, is quite different from Margery's understanding. Whereas Margery's memory is participatory and sug-

[27] "Who can not wepe, com lerne of me," in *Hymns to the Virgin and Christ: The Parliament of Devils and Other Religious Poems,* ed. Frederick Furnivall, EETS, o.s. 24 (London: N. Trübner & Co., 1867), pp. 126–27.

[28] Émile Mâle, *Religious Art in France: The Late Middle Ages, a Study of Medieval Iconography and Its Sources* (Princeton: Princeton University Press, 1986), p. 123.

[29] "And thorw þe beholding of þat pete hir mende was al holy ocupyd in þe Passyon of owr Lord Ihesu Crist & in e compassion of owr Lady, Seynt Mary, be which sche was compellyd to cryyn ful lowed & wepyn ful sor, as þeu sche xulde a deyd" (*The Book of Margery Kempe,* ed. Stanford Brown Meech and Emily Hope Allen, EETS, o.s. 212 [London: Oxford University Press, 1940], p. 148).

[30] This mode of experiential memory and affective identification is also evident in contemporary poetic representations of the pietà. A fifteenth-century lyric in Oxford, Bodleian Library, MS Ashmole 189, for example, represents the Virgin petitioning the reader to "wepe for my dere sone, which on my lap lieth ded."

[31] Lydgate's familiarity with Nicholas Love and reliance on the *Meditaciones* has been posited by Vernon Gallagher in John Lydgate, *Life of Our Lady,* ed. Joseph A. Lauritis (Pittsburgh, Pa.: Duquesne Studies, 1961), pp. 97–142.

[32] The poem is organized into five eight-line stanzas with the rhyme scheme ababbcbc. It is found in London, British Library, MS Additional 29729, and Oxford, Bodleian Library, MS Ashmole 59. A manuscript rubric to the copy of the poem found in the Ashmole manuscript reads: "Here foloweþe a devoute exortacon to moeve men to devoutely to þe ymage of pyte by orisounes and preyers."

gests a suspended atemporal moment, for Lydgate remembrance implies the recollection of a multilayered but distant history that may (but does not necessarily) enable contextualization of the present.[33] Nevertheless, Lydgate's poem begins in the present, condemning the reader's hardheartedness and directing his gaze to the "peyne" inflicted on the Virgin because of his "offence":

> O wretched synner! what so ever thow be,
> With hert endurat hardar than þe stone,
> Turne hidder in hast, knelle doun, behold and se
> The moder of Cryst, whose hert was woo begon
> To se her childe, whiche synne dide nevar non,
> For thyn offence thus wounded & arayd;
> Rewe on that peyne, remembringe here vpon,
> Pray to that quene, that moder is, and mayd.
>
> (lines 1–8)

The reader, identified as a hard-hearted "wretched synner" is commanded to turn and "behold and se" the image, thus mirroring the woeful gaze of the mother who beholds her son. Yet unlike other contemporary lyrics on the pietà, the reader here is not called to identify with or suffer alongside Mary but rather to see both Christ and the Virgin's agony as a direct result of "thyn offence." Mary suffers because of the reader's sin. For Lydgate, then, the image becomes a memorial and penitential device, intended to prompt feelings of personal guilt in its reader.

While guilt might be an affective response to the image, it is certainly not the one suggested by the visual image itself. Indeed it is more akin to pre-Bernardine forms of Marian devotion, for, as Rachel Fulton suggests, "early prayers to Mary focus more or less exclusively on the sufferings of the sinner—wretched and miserable and in desperate straits, his or her only hope the intervention of Mary or the mercy of her Son."[34] Even in the opening lines of the poem, Lydgate depicts Mary as a celestial queen rather than the weeping woman of most contemporary representations. Likewise, Lydgate's Mary is an exalted intercessor and mediator; she is not a figure with whom one is encouraged to identify

[33] Of the aesthetics of Lydgate's Marian poems, Pearsall suggests, "The heaping-up of invocation, epithet, image, and allusion is meant to overwhelm with excess, hardly to be comprehended. The aim is not to stir devotion, but to make an act of worship out of the elaboration of the artifact" (*John Lydgate,* p. 268).

[34] Fulton, *From Judgment to Passion,* p. 208.

too closely. Lydgate employs this appeal to "[r]ewe on that peyne, re-membringe here vpon" to remind the reader of the necessity of clerical and historical mediation. He does so by inscribing both the initial, af-fective image and the guilt it prompts in a versified discussion of forms of ecclesiastical authority and figural history. Intercession and clerical mediation are needed for the resolution of this guilt, Lydgate suggests, and Mary, rather than functioning as an atemporal model of sorrow, serves as the paradigmatic historical intercessor.

Moving away from the suggestively affective appeals to Mary's ma-ternal sorrow in the opening lines, Lydgate's second stanza turns to theological reflection on the fall of humanity as the requisite prehistory for the glorification of Mary. He makes a figural leap to the Garden of Eden, noting the *felix culpa* that led to the fall of Adam but also enabled the Virgin to assume her role as intercessor:

> With this conceyt, þat yf syne had not bene,
> Causynge our fadar Adam his grevous fall,
> Of heven had she not be crounyd quene,
> Ne ther ataynyd astate emperiall
>
> (lines 9–13)

Although the first stanza is a direct appeal for the reader to "behold and se" a pietà and "[r]ewe on that peyne," by the second stanza Lydgate has begun to specify how the reader should go about "remembringe here vpon" by adding layers of scriptural typology and contemporary Marian piety to supply this ahistorical image with a past and a future. In so doing, he suspends the figure of Mary between iconographic and textual worlds, using the initial image of the pietà as a foundation for monastic *lectio.* This way of reading, Jean Leclercq suggests, is a mode of "reminiscence whereby the verbal echoes so excite the memory that a mere allusion will spontaneously evoke whole quotations and, in turn, a scriptural phrase will suggest quite naturally allusions elsewhere in the sacred books."[35] Here Lydgate's poetic process mimics the referential layering and gathering of *lectio:* his introductory allusion to the pietà and human sin suggests a figural link to the Fall. The Fall necessitated

---

[35] Leclercq, *The Love of Learning and the Desire for God,* trans. Catharine Michari (New York: Fordham University Press, 1961), p. 73. For a more recent description of the gathering and layering mnemonic process of monastic *lectio* and *meditacio,* see Carruth-ers, *Craft of Thought,* pp. 19–21.

the incarnation, which, in turn, enabled the exaltation of Mary as queen and intercessor.[36]

The Virgin represented in the lyric's second stanza is an entirely different figure from "the moder of Cryst, whose hert was woo begon" with whom Lydgate began. While the pietà is meant to direct its viewer's attention to the compassion of Mary, Lydgate's representation of Mary as a queen who has "ataynyd astate emperiall" emphasizes religious power and authority rather than sorrow.[37] She is no longer earthly and human, but rather is now in heaven and thus is distant and impassive. Yet because she has been transformed from earthly mother to celestial queen, she is a powerful intercessor for penitent humans. To this effect, Lydgate instructs his reader:

> Besechyng her þat this memoriall
> Of very pitie wold meve hir for thy grace
> To pray þat lord, which may pardon all,
> To here her bone . . .
>
> (lines 13–16)

Lydgate returns to the theme of "pitie" here, but in an entirely different context. Instead of identifying with the pity of the weeping Virgin, the penitent reader uses this "memoriall / Of very pitie" to move the queen to intercede on his or her behalf. The goal of pity is not identification with the suffering mother of Christ, but rather pardon by "þat lord." To leave Christ nameless at this point is again to reject the affective intimacy inherent in the image of the pietà and choose instead a much older devotional model. Mary's intercessory power was emphasized in

---

[36] Lydgate makes this figural link explicit in another of his Marian poems, "Regina Celi Letare":

> O felix culpa! thus may we syng,
> Reioysyng in your ladyes high honour,
> So many a thousand to haue vndyr your wyng
> Thorough the byrthe of that blessed creatour
> That lyst to dy, that were dettour,
> So verrey God & man with good chere,
> Thy blessyd son thyn owne fygure,
> Resurrexit sicut dixit.
>
> (MacCracken, ed., Minor Poems, p. 293, lines 17–24)

[37] Lydgate's other Marian lyrics have a similar focus on Mary as queen and intercessor. See, for example, "Ave Regina Celorum," in MacCracken, ed., Minor Poems, pp. 291–92; and "Stella Celi Extirpauit," in MacCracken, ed., Minor Poems, pp. 294–95.

Offices of the Virgin in the period of the Benedictine Reform (the latter half of the tenth century); yet as we have already noted, it was certainly not the predominant depiction of the Virgin in the late Middle Ages.[38] In this earlier model, Mary's role as intercessor parallels the mediatory role of *ecclesia,* and indeed, the figural echoing of the mother of Christ and the mother church returns the poet to the regulatory necessities of his own historical moment.[39]

Yet it is not enough for the laity to seek intercession and pardon in Mary. Lydgate, perhaps responding to the Lollard critique of the clerical role in confession and absolution, insists that assurance of heavenly pardon remains under the jurisdiction of earthly ecclesiastical authority.[40] To emphasize this point, after instructing the reader to remember the fall of humanity and the glorification of Mary and then to pray for intercession, Lydgate next tells the reader "with hasty pace":

> Rene to a prest whill this is in thi mynd,
> Knelynge down lowly withe hert contryt,
> Tell out bothe croppe & rote, leve nought behynd—
> Thy synnes all, be they gret or lyte,
> Wher they were blake, then shall they wexe whyt.
>
> (lines 17–21)

Although the Virgin has the authority to intercede, the penitent must follow the proper ecclesiastical procedures to ensure pardon by running to a priest to make confession "whill this is in thi mynd." The "this" here is neither the "image of pity" nor a feeling of compassion. Rather, it is the series of figurally-linked textual images we have just seen un-

---

[38] See Mary Clayton, *The Cult of the Virgin in Anglo-Saxon England* (Cambridge: Cambridge University Press, 1990), pp. 61–88. Fulton also notes that "Marian prayers of the Carolingian and Anglo-Saxon period stress above all Mary's power as intercessor with her son" (*From Judgment to Passion,* p. 218).

[39] On the association of Mary with the church, see Nigel Morgan, "Texts and Images of Marian Devotion in English Twelfth-Century Monasticism, and Their Influence on the Secular Church," in *Monasteries and Society in Medieval Britain: Proceedings of the 1994 Harlaxton Symposium,* ed. Benjamin Thompson (Stamford, Lincolnshire: Paul Watkins, 1999), p. 128.

[40] The role of the earthly church in the absolution of sin was a central concern of the Lollards. In the "Twelve Conclusions," for example, "þe ix conclusiun þat holdith þe puple lowe is þat þe articlis of confessiun þat is sayd necessari to saluaciun of man, with a feynid power of absoliciun enhaunsith prestis pride, and Aeuith hem opertunite of priue calling othir þan we wele now say" (*Selections from English Wycliffite Writings,* ed. Anne Hudson [Toronto: University of Toronto Press, 1997], p. 27).

fold. It seems appropriate, then, that the stanza concludes with set of didactic instructions such as those that a confessor might give to the recently confessed penitent: "Continew in clennys, & then thow shalt be quyte, / And saffe fro fendes all that are in helle" (lines 23–24).

We might expect Lydgate to end his poem here. He has led the reader from a potentially affective experience with a pietà to participation in the ecclesiastically regulated act of confession. Yet he continues with two stanzas of commentary on his own "reading" of the image. He instructs the reader:

> Enprynt thes wordes myndly thy hert within,
> Thynk how thow sest Cryst bledyng on þe tre,
> And yf thow steryd or temptyd be to syne
> It shall sone sese and pase a-way from the.
> Remembre all so this dolorus pytie,
> How þat this blyssid ladye thus doth enbrace
> Her dere son ded, lygyng vpen her kne,
> And, payne of deth, thow shalt not fayll of grace.
>
> (lines 25–32)

Lydgate returns to the image of the pietà that spun off the subsequent figural threads we have traced and offers the first description of the visual image itself. But we must again note that even this description is entirely lacking in pathetic detail. There is neither weeping nor wailing in Lydgate's account, despite its description as "dolorus." The Virgin is as emotionless at the death of her son as she will be after her assumption and glorification. His descriptive austerity here again indicates that Lydgate's charge to "remembre . . . this dolorus pytie," is not a call to affective identification but a visual prompt of figural and textual remembrance.

This point is suggested by the opening lines of the stanza in which Lydgate asks the reader to "[e]nprynt thes wordes." Although he often associates the act of writing or printing with remembering, it is noteworthy that here Lydgate asks the reader to imprint *words*, not the visual image. Similarly, Lydgate's four-line apologetic for images at the conclusion of the poem blurs the distinctions between visual and textual remembrance and betrays his thinking about the proper use and limitations of images:

To suche entent was ordeynt purtreture
And ymages of dyverse resemblaunce,
That holsom storyes thus shewyd in fygur
May rest with ws with dewe remembraunce.

(lines 37–40)

As already noted, Lydgate's point in its simplest form is that the purpose of pictures is to remind. However, understanding the more subtle nuances of this short apologetic hinges, in part, on how the reader interprets the crucial, but slippery, word "fygur." A figure, the *Middle English Dictionary* reveals, can be a person, a material image or representation such as a visual pietà, a written character such as word, letter, or even poem, or a sign or symbol.[41] Lydgate could simply be reciting the orthodox argument that pictures teach through telling stories. Alternatively, he could be punning on the word "fygur" to indicate the "holsom storyes" he has just unveiled in verse that develops, as we have seen, by means of a series of figural associations.[42]

Further, to say that "purtreture" was established merely for "remembrance" is only a partial representation of the standard defense of images.[43] In the standard apologetic, images were held to be useful as *libri laicorum* for teaching moral lessons, portraying exemplary lives, and stimulating affective devotion.[44] Lydgate alters this defense here and elsewhere in his work. For example, as has been suggested by Michael Camille and Susan K. Hagen, the pilgrim in Lydgate's translation of the *Pilgrimage of the Life of Man* sets forth a threefold defense of images in which the affective use of images is conspicuously absent.[45]

[41] *MED*, s.v. "figure."

[42] It is not unprecedented for Lydgate to employ the term to describe a piece of writing. For example, Lydgate applies the term "fygure" to a psalm, in his introduction to his verse translation of De Profundis: "Thys psalme in viij David doth devyde, / A morall fygure of viij blyssidnessys" (MacCracken, ed., *Minor Poems*, p. 79, lines 41–42).

[43] By the mid-fifteenth century, however, clerical writers often emphasized the mnemonic function of images. Reginald Pecock, for example, frequently defends the usefulness of "seable rememoratijf signes," in *Repressor of Over Much Blaming of the Clergy*, ed. Churchill Babington, Rolls Series 19, 2 vols. (London: HMSO, 1860; repr., 1966), 1:209.

[44] There is a vast corpus of Latin and Middle English writing on this threefold apologetic. For a recent discussion and relevant bibliographical information, see Kamerick, *Popular Piety*, pp. 27–38.

[45] See Michael Camille, "The Iconoclast's Desire: Deguileville's Idolatry in France and England, in *Images, Idolatry, and Iconoclasm in Late Medieval England: Textuality and the Visual Image*, ed. Jeremy Dimmick, James Simpson, and Nicolette Zeeman, 151–71 (Cambridge: Cambridge University Press, 2002), p. 167, and Hagen, *Allegorical Remembrance*, p. 103.

This absence, I suggest, is also an especially conspicuous one in this poem, given the usual affective import of the pietà. Christine Cornell argues that the poem "depends upon a distinct division of labour. The picture stirs our emotions, and the poem instructs us in the use of these emotions."[46] While this is the case with similar complaints, it is my claim that Lydgate's poem not only regulates the emotion stirred by the image by inscribing it within texts, figures, and institutions, but also requires the rejection of any unmediated experience prompted by such emotion. Unlike other contemporary lyrics on the pietà in late medieval England that seek to complement and give a voice to the image of the suffering virgin in order to prompt affective devotion, Lydgate subordinates the image to his text by circumscribing the image within the realm of textuality. He does this in two ways: first, he minimizes its affective power by substituting figural exegesis for pathetic description; second, he undermines the image's ability to collapse temporal boundaries by situating it as only one of a series of figural images and emphasizing the textuality of "remembraunce." The image is rendered unnecessary by these poetic and theological manipulations because the text no longer requires the image to achieve its theological and didactic goals. As the poem's final lines suggest, the image is useful to prompt remembrance, but the complex workings of remembrance are only found in the "holsom storyes shewyd in fygur" when they are theologically appropriated and read as texts.

"Looke on thus ffygure": Typological Distance and Lydgate's *Imago Pietatis*

Such theological appropriation is evident in Lydgate's lyric, "The Dolerous Pyte of Crystes Passioun," a poetic treatment of another image, the *imago pietatis* or the "Man of Sorrows."[47] The *imago pietatis* was even more popular than the pietà in late medieval England and was an object of both private and public devotion, appearing in Books of Hours as well as in wall paintings and stained-glass windows.[48] Gertrud Schiller

---

[46] Cornell, "'Holsom Stories,'" p. 169.

[47] MacCracken, ed., *Minor Poems,* pp. 250–52. All subsequent citations to "The Dolerous Pyte of Crystes Passioun" will be given parenthetically in the text by line number. Like "On the Image of Pity," the poem is composed of eight-line stanzas with a rhyme scheme of ababbcbc. It is found in Oxford, Bodleian Library, MS Laud 683.

[48] Mâle, *Religious Art,* p. 81. For a short listing of the appearance of the image in England, see Duffy, *Stripping of the Altars: Traditional Religion in England, 1400–1580* (New Haven: Yale University Press, 1992), pp. 108–9.

writes that "the Man of Sorrows in its many artistic forms is the most precise visual expression of the piety of the Late Middle Ages."[49] Like the pietà, it is extra-biblical, atemporal, and intended solely to prompt pity.[50] In the image, Christ still seems to be suffering, although he is clearly dead; he appears to be standing upright, but his head is drooping and his arms are crossed in order to display the gaping wounds on his hands and in his side.[51] The image of Christ as the "man of sorrows" was often associated with Old Testament references used in the Good Friday Mass, such as Isaiah 53:3–5.[52] By the late fourteenth century the *imago pietatis* was linked with the eucharistic piety of the Mass of Saint Gregory and began to be widely disseminated throughout Europe, accompanied by extravagant indulgences.[53]

Like the Eucharist, the *imago pietatis* emphasized the brokenness of

[49] Schiller, *Iconography*, p. 197. Although the concept of Christ as "man of sorrows" would have been familiar through the liturgy, the roots of this particular visual representation lie in Byzantine art, since the probable prototype of the *imago pietatis* was a small thirteenth-century mosaic icon at the church of Santa Croce that was likely brought to Rome from the East. The classic study of the *imago pietatis* remains E. Panofsky, "Imago Pietatis," in *Festschrift für Max J. Friedländer* (Leipzig: E. E. Seemann, 1927), pp. 261–308. For additional background on the emergence and transmission of the *imago pietatis* and its relation to the Mass of Saint Gregory, see Belting, *Image and Its Public;* Schiller, *Iconography*, pp. 198–99; Mâle, *Religious Art*, pp. 95–100; and Carlo Bertelli, "The *Image of Pity* in Santa Croce in Gerusalemme," in *Essays in the History of Art Presented to Rudolf Wittkower*, ed. Douglas Fraser, Howard Hibbard, and Milton J. Lewine (London: Phaidon, 1967), pp. 40–55. Woolf also includes a concise overview of the *imago pietatis* in *Religious Lyric*, pp. 389–91, and Duffy includes a short synopsis in *Stripping of the Altars*, pp. 238–40.

[50] Like Woolf and Schiller, Hans Belting notes that since the image was "not limited to a particular biographical situation . . . [it] was able to symbolize the full range of the meditation on the passion" (*Image and Its Public*, p. 40).

[51] Mâle cites four variations of the image: (1) The nude Christ coming out of the tomb, (2) Christ in the tomb with two angels, (3) Christ with the Virgin and Saint John, and (4) the scene of the Mass of Saint Gregory, with the Man of Sorrows on the altar and his blood flowing into the eucharistic chalice (*Religious Art*, pp. 97–98).

[52] "Despised, and the most abject of men, a man of sorrows, and acquainted with infirmity: and his look was as it were hidden and despised, whereupon we esteemed him not. Surely he hath borne our infirmities and carried our sorrows: and we have thought him as it were a leper, and as one struck by God and afflicted. But he was wounded for our iniquities, he was bruised for our sins: the chastisement of our peace was upon him, and by his bruises we are healed." All translations of the Vulgate are taken from the *Douay-Rheims Version* (Rockford, Ill.: Tan Books and Publishers, 1899).

[53] This association with the Gregorian mass derived from the myth that Gregory had commissioned the first representation of the *imago pietatis* for the church at Santa Croce after a miraculous eucharistic vision in which Christ appeared to him on the altar with his blood running into the eucharistic chalice. The first appearance of the image of the Gregorian mass, however, is not until the beginning of the fifteenth century. See J. A. Endres, "Die Darstellung der Gregorius-Messe im Mittelalter," *Zeitschrift für christliche Kunst* 30 (1917): 155.

Christ's very human body and the immediacy of his suffering. Christ's wounds are always evident, and the instruments of his torture often encircle him, suspended over his bowed head or built into the image's frame. While the instructions of the accompanying indulgences often sought to mediate the viewer's experience of the image, redirecting a subjective emotional response into prescribed penitential formulas appealing to Christ's divinity, the image itself encouraged affective identification with the suffering man, for, as Schiller notes, "the Man of Sorrows [was] not only the divine image of the period but also the image of man."[54] Thus, the *image pietatis* was fundamentally incarnational in that it impressed both the physicality and accessibility of Christ's suffering body upon its viewer.

In addition to emphasizing the humanity of Christ, like the pietà, the image also derived its emotional efficacy from its detachment from spatial and temporal contexts. Woolf writes that "the particular emotiveness of the *imago pietatis* derives from the fact that it is a picture in which the figure of the suffering Christ is isolated from the historical sequence of the Passion. . . . Reference to historical time is deliberately evaded. . . . No historical or dogmatic purpose is served by this representation."[55] Other late medieval religious lyrics accentuate this atemporality and the suffering of the wounded body through several distinctive characteristics: they focus on the wounds and suffering of Christ; they are addressed to the individual reader; and they emphasize Christ's own emotion, suggesting most specifically that love is his motivation for enduring the passion.[56] The Christ of the popular fifteenth-century lyric "Wofully araide," for example, describes how he wears a crown of sharp

---

[54] Schiller, *Iconography,* p. 198.

[55] Woolf, *The English Religious Lyric,* pp. 184–85.

[56] In such lyrics, the wounded Christ often addresses the reader personally, as in the following excerpt from a lyric found in London, British Library, MS Harley 2339:

> Wiþ a spere scharp, þat was ful grill,
> Myn herte was persid—it was my wil-
> For loue of man þat was ful dere;
> Enuyous man, of loue þou lere.
>
> Arise up, vnlust, out of þi bed,
> And biholde my feet, þat are forbled
> And nailed faste upon þe tree;
> Þank me þerfore, al was for þee.

(*Religious Lyrics of the XIVth Century,* ed. Carleton Brown [Oxford: Clarendon Press, 1970], p. 227).

thorns and bleeds to death "for þi love" and asks, "What might I suffer more / Þen I have suffered, man, for þe?"[57]

Lydgate, however, wants nothing to do with either the suffering or the love-longing Christ central to many lyrics on the *imago pietatis*.[58] Meditation on Christ's crucified body in this poem is an opportunity to pray for salvation from the suffering of hell.[59] To this end, Lydgate's Christ is not represented as a static artifact designed to arouse love and pity but rather as a complex poetic web of figurally linked visual and textual images slowly revealed by a dynamic layering of sources and designed to rewrite the simplicity and atemporality of the initial "dolorous pyte." This translation from the initial affective image to the complex text representing a multifaceted image of Christ is effected, as in "On the Image of Pity," by Lydgate's insistence on the gathering and layering of typological images and orthodox religious practices.

Like "On the Image of Pity," "The Dolerous Pyte" begins with a reference to the material image, which prompts the verse meditation:

> Erly on morwe, and toward nyght also,
> First and last, looke on this ffygure;
> Was ever wight suffred so gret woo
> For manhis sake suych passioun did endure?
> My bloody woundis, set here in picture,
> Hath hem in mynde knelyng on your kne,
> A goostly merour to euery Cryature,
> Callid of my passioun the dolerous pyte.
>
> (lines 1–8)

These lines seem, in many ways, to encourage an affective response to the image. However, they also foreshadow a redirection of that emotion

---

[57] *Religious Lyrics of the XVth Century*, ed. Carleton Brown (Oxford, Clarendon Press, 1939), p. 157. Woolf notes that "Wofully araide" remained well known into the sixteenth century (*The English Religious Lyric*, p. 206).

[58] Pearsall similarly sees Lydgate's poems on the Passion as penitential rather than devotional. He writes, "Lydgate wrote comparatively few poems on the Passion, and those that he did write have little to do with the tradition of intimate, passionate attachment to the body of Christ which plays so large a part in medieval lyric-writing" (*John Lydgate*, p. 265).

[59] Rachel Fulton has suggested that after Anselm, Christians could no longer "look upon the crucified body of their Lord and see primarily an opportunity to pray for help in their adversity and for liberation from the torments of hell" (*From Judgment to Passion*, p. 190). This pre-Anselm model, however, is precisely the religious model that Lydgate wishes to revive in his poetry on the Passion.

into a typologically complex meditation on how such a "figure" should be read. The image becomes a text to be interpreted, using all of the available exegetical tools.

As in "On the Image of Pity," the ambiguity of the initial term "ffygure" is suggested by Lydgate's use of the visual figure to prompt a series of figural interpretations of the passion. The *imago pietatis* is certainly a figure, when the term is understood as meaning a material representation or a likeness as in a statue or painting, but, as we have noted, the term "figure" can also apply to texts, words, and allegorical modes of reading. Thus, from the opening lines of the poem, the reader is forced into the ambiguous borderland between image and text. The ambiguity continues throughout the first two stanzas as Christ describes his bloody wounds as "set here in picture." However, the term "picture" is somewhat ambiguous as it is also used frequently in exegetic and homiletic writing for rhetorical description.[60] The second stanza employs additional polysemous terms, as easily applicable to words as to images, urging the reader: "Set this lyknesse in your remembraunce, / Enprenteth it in your Inward sight" (lines 9–10).

But "this lyknesse" or "ffygure" implied as the object of the reader's gaze is soon traded for a decisively nonvisual figure as Lydgate adds to the *imago pietatis* an image of Christ as warrior and champion who promises to defend the reader "Ageyn the fend, þe flessh, þe world" (line 14). This is not the Christ of the *imago pietatis;* it is more akin to the Christ of the early Middle Ages, who, as Rachel Fulton suggests, "was a god far more comfortable on the battlefield than in the heart, a war-leader rather than a lover, an all-powerful warrior and king of heaven rather than a pitiable victim of human sin, his Cross not so much an instrument of torture as a weapon of victory."[61] This *imago pietatis* commands its viewer:

> Make me your pavis, passith not your boundis,
> Ageyn al wordly Trybulacioun,
> In ech temptacioun, thynk on my blody woundis,
> Your cheeff saffcondyt, and best proteccyoun,

---

[60] In her influential study of the literary production of English friars, *English Friars and Antiquity in the Early Fourteenth Century* (Oxford: Blackwell Press, 1960), Beryl Smalley notes that several of the "classicizing friars" call short, exemplary descriptions "pictures" (p. 112). See also Judson Boyce Allen, *The Friar as Critic* (Nashville: Vanderbilt University Press, 1971), pp. 102–10.

[61] Fulton, *From Judgment to Passion,* p. 54.

Your coote armure, brest plate & habirioun,
Yow to dyffende in al adversyte,
And I schal be your Trusty champioun
Whan ye beholde this dolerous pite.

(lines 17–24)

Woolf and Schirmer have noted that the introduction of the Christ-knight image creates a rather infelicitous juxtaposition with the *imago pietatis*.[62] Cornell explains the knight imagery as part of Lydgate's dependence on "the painting to depict the suffering Christ and on the allusive nature of the imagery to add greater depth to his description."[63] While the theme of "Christ as champion" certainly is part of the poem and emerges as a central, nonvisual image by the conclusion of the poem, I find it likely that in the second and third stanzas Lydgate is envisioning a different, though closely related, visual image that clarifies the figural relationship between the *imago pietatis* and the warrior Christ: the wound-marked shield.[64]

In the second stanza, Lydgate's Christ speaks of his "hertys wounde, percyd with a launce. . . . Yow to dyffende in your treble ffyght" (lines 11, 13). The third stanza opens with Christ asking the reader to "Make me your pavis" (line 17) against worldly tribulations and calls himself "Your . . . best proteccyoun / Your coote armure, brest plate & habirioun" (lines 20–21) and your "Trusty champioun" (line 23). Asking the reader to make Christ into his or her shield and protection suggests Lydgate's awareness of the popular fifteenth-century image of the shield in which Christ's wounds appear as the crest.[65] The frequent visual asso-

---

[62] Schirmer, *John Lydgate*, p. 185; Woolf, *The English Religious Lyric*, p. 202.

[63] Cornell, " 'Holsom Stories,' " p. 172.

[64] See Woolf, *The English Religious Lyric*, p. 202.

[65] The representation of the wounded shield is perhaps best known now from its depiction in the illustrated Carthusian manuscript, London, British Library, MS Additional 37049, where it is portrayed with substantial variations seven times. See folios 20r, 24r, 46v, 58v, 60v, 61v, and 63v. The *imago pietatis* also appears in this manuscript. Black-and-white photo reproductions of the illustrations from the manuscript are available in James Hogg, ed., "An Illustrated Yorkshire Carthusian Religious Miscellany, British Library London Addition MS. 37049," *Analecta Carthusiana* 95:3 (1981). Devotion to the five wounds, viewed separately from the suffering body of Christ, spread in the fourteenth century. By the time of the composition of Lydgate's poem they were commonplace, appearing in Books of Hours, meriting their own special mass, and serving as the object of devotion for confraternities established in the name of the wounds; see Mâle, *Religious Art*, p. 102. On the emergence of the "Mass of the Five Wounds," see R. W. Pfaff, *New Liturgical Feasts in Later Medieval Britain* (Oxford: Clarendon Press, 1970), pp. 84–115.

ciation of the five wounds in paintings of the *imago pietatis* with the image of the wounded shield, or "pavis," provides for Lydgate the means of a rhetorically subtle transition to the image of Christ as conqueror. The third stanza of the poem begins with the shield image and expands into the image of the entire warrior by layering on the image of the "pavis" the other knightly accoutrements: the "coote armure, brest plate & habirioun" (line 21). Only after these images have been added does Christ say he will be the reader's "Trusty champioun / Whan ye beholde this dolerous pite" (lines 23–24). While the link between Christ as champion and Christ as the man of sorrows might seem awkward and infelicitous to modern readers, the incorporation of the shield image facilitates a fluid transition from image to text and demonstrates Lydgate's poetic technique of layering image upon image, text upon text. Just as Lydgate layers pieces of armor on the initial image of the "pavis" in order to transform the picture, so his act of poetic making is a method of layering. The move to representing Christ as conqueror is simultaneously a move to the realm of the textual; the Christ-knight image is a poetic and homiletic image and not easily translated into a visual form.[66]

In the next segment of the poem, Lydgate superimposes additional layers of figural imagery onto the "dolorous pite." The image of Christ, now identified as the "Trusty champioun," exhorts the reader:

> Beth not rekles whan ye forby passe,
> Of myn Image devoutly taketh heede,
> Nat for my-silf, but for your trespace
> In Bosra steyned of purpil al my [weede].
>
> (lines 25–28)[67]

---

[66] The Christ-knight image, though commonplace in early religious writings such as *Ancrene Wisse,* was not frequently used in late medieval religious writing. On this image, see Rosemary Woolf, "The Theme of Christ the Lover-Knight in Medieval English Literature," *RES* 13 (1962): 1–16. Other than Lydgate's attempt to revive the image, the most notable exception in late medieval writing is William Langland's incorporation of the Christ-Knight theme into Passus XVIII of *Piers Plowman.* There has been some critical attention given to the appearance of this conquering Christ figure in relationship to the allegorical and figural development of Langland's poem. See, for example, Wilbur Gaffney, "The Allegory of the Christ-Knight in *Piers Plowman,*" *PMLA* 46 (1931): 155–68; James Weldon, "Sabotaged Text or Textual Ploy? The Christ-Knight Metaphor in *Piers Plowman,*" *Florilegium* 9 (1987): 113–23; and Lawrence Warner, "Jesus the Jouster: The Christ-Knight and Medieval Theories of Atonement in *Piers Plowman* and the 'Round Table' Sermons," *YLS* 10 (1996): 129–43.

[67] MacCracken has emended the manuscript's "blood" to "weede" to maintain the rhyme with the following line's "meede."

By having the image instruct its viewer to pay attention to it "Nat for my-silf, but for your trespace," Lydgate once again emphasizes that devotional images should not prompt intimate identification with Christ, but rather should remind their viewers how their "trespace" has caused their alienation from Christ and their need for reconciliation. This reconciliation is explained by the introduction of yet another christological figure: the "mystic winepress," suggested by the conflation of Isaiah 63:1–6 and Numbers 13.[68] The passage from Isaiah was read as an allegory for the wrath of Christ at the final judgment; Christ treads the grapes as the mighty conqueror and worker of salvation.[69] In "The Dolerous Pyte," however, Lydgate layers on this image of the conquering Christ a typological image of his suffering and passion. The thirteenth chapter of Numbers recounts the story of spies sent to Canaan who brought back a cluster of grapes hanging from a pole to dem-

---

[68] "Who is this that cometh from Edom, with dyed garments from Bosrah? this beautiful one in his robe, walking in the greatness of his strength. I, that speak justice, and am a defender to save. Why then is thy apparel red, and thy garments like theirs that tread in the winepress? I have trodden the winepress alone, and of the Gentiles there is not a man with me: I have trampled on them in my indignation, and have trodden them down in my wrath and their blood is sprinkled upon my garments, and I have stained my apparel. For the day of vengeance is in my heart, the year of my redemption is come. I looked about, and there was none to help: I sought, and there was none to give aid: and my own arm hath saved for me, and my indignation itself hath helped me. And I have trodden down the people in my wrath and have made them drunk in my indignation, and have brought down their strength to the earth." On this image, see A. Thomas, *Die Darstellung Christi in der Kelter: Eine Theologische und Kulturhistorische Studie* (Düsseldorf, 1936; facsimile reprint 1981); A. Weckworth, "Christus in der Kelter: Ursprung und Wandlungen eines Bildmotives," in *Beitrage zur Kunstgeschichte: Eine Festgabe für Heinz Rudolf Rosemann zum 9. Oktober 1960,* ed. Ernst Guldan (Munich and Berlin: Deutscher Kunstverlag, 1960), pp. 95–108.

[69] Lydgate also draws on this image in his translation of the hymn "Vexilla Regis Prodeunt," where he again collapses the images of conqueror and mystic winepress:

> Royal Banerys vnrolled of the kyng
> Towarde his Batayle, in Bosra steyned reede,
> The Crosse his standart Celestyal of schynyng
> Wyth purple Hewe depeynt, I tooke good heede
> (1–4)

Christ marches into battle to redeem his people with his blood-painted cross as his resplendent standard proclaiming his preordained victory and its red and purple hues prefiguring the eucharistic conflation of blood and wine (MacCracken, ed., *Minor Poems,* p. 25). William Herebert (d. 1333) also translated "Vexilla regis prodeunt," but his version supplies the personal, affective appeal lacking in Lydgate's translation. See *The Works of William Herebert,* ed. Stephen Reimer (Toronto: Pontifical Institute of Medieval Studies, 1987).

onstrate the abundance of the Promised Land.[70] This image became a widely recognized figure of Christ hanging on the cross. In this figuration, Christ himself becomes the "tendre clustris" of grapes that will be crushed to avenge the wrath of God. Indeed, Lydgate's Christ describes the crushing of the grapes in some of the most striking lines of poetry in the sequence:

> The vyne of Soreth railed in lengthe & brede,
> The tendre clustris rent doun in ther rage,
> The ripe grapis ther licour did out shede,
> With bloody dropis bespreynt was my visage
>
> (lines 33–36)

This image of the tender cluster of grapes complicates the *imago pietatis* by recalling and reimaging the eucharistic element latent in the initial image of the wounds of Christ. Although the figure of the "mystic winepress" was common in hymns and sermons, it only began to be represented in visual art at the beginning of the fifteenth century in France. It is possible that Lydgate would have encountered a visual depiction of the mystic winepress in his years in France, but regardless, he certainly would have been familiar with its figural implications from textual sources.[71]

However, Lydgate does not linger on the agony of Christ bearing "the bront allone of this ventage" (line 39), but rather returns to the realm of the textual and nonvisual in the sixth stanza by turning once again to the image of Christ as knight:

> My deth of deth hadde þe victorye,
> Fauht with Sathan a myhty strong batayl,

---

[70] Numbers 13:18–20, 24: "And Moses sent them to view the land of Chanaan, and said to them: Go you up by the south side. And when you shall come to the mountains, view the land, of what sort it is: and the people that are the inhabitants thereof, whether they be strong or weak: few in number or many: The land itself, whether it be good or bad: what manner of cities, walled or without walls. . . . And going forward as far as the torrent of the cluster of grapes, they cut off a branch with its cluster of grapes, which two men carried upon a lever. They took also of the pomegranates and of the figs of that place." Mâle notes that Augustine was among the first to bring together these two images (*Religious Art*, p. 112).

[71] It is worth noting that these two images are not easily represented in visual form, though there is evidence of visual representation of the "mystic winepress" in fifteenth-century France. For a description of the visual representation of the image in France, see Mâle, *Religious Art*, pp. 102–14. The image would have been known in England during this time, however, primarily from textual sources.

Grave this trivmphe depe in your memorie,
Lik þe pellican perced myn Entrayl,
Myn herte blood maad abrood to rayl,
Best restoratif geyn old Inyquyte,
My platys seuered, to-torn myn aventail,
Lik as witnesseth this dolorous pite.

(lines 41–48)

This is the dominant representation of Christ in Lydgate's corpus: the knightly king-warrior who has battled Satan and death and triumphed, thus attaining redemption for his followers/subjects. As in his *Life of Saint Alban and Saint Amphibal,* where the model of *imitatio christi* is the knight who is able to overcome and destroy idols, thus purifying his nation and leading many to the Christian faith, here Christ is a triumphant champion and restorer of righteousness "abrood." He is not a localized, regional king and champion; rather, his triumph sets him as authority over and restorer of all nations.

As we can see, Lydgate's religious poetry does not conform to the affective model, though it certainly bears affinities to it. The "Man of Sorrows" and "dolorous pite" are replaced over the course of the poem with the pre-Bernardine image of Christ the champion. Although he initially asked readers to "enprente" the image of Christ's wounds in their inward sight, he brings his poem to a close by asking them to "grave this *trivmphe* depe in your memorie" (my emphasis), just as Christ's own side was engraved with the pelican-like lance.[72] The act of piercing Christ's body becomes a metaphor for a translation from images to texts, for writing on the memory, and the poem comes full circle, returning to insistence on memory and allusion to its tools: the lance (the metaphorical pen) and the blood (the ink). Inscribing the image in texts enables the reader to experience the full typological resonance of "remembraunce of Crystys passioun" (line 55) and mediates the image's affective power. Lydgate's choice of layering heterogeneous and nonvi-

---

[72] The figure of the pelican is traditionally associated with the Passion; see Willibrordus Lampen, "'Pie Pelicane, Iesu Domine,'" *Antonianum* 12 (1946): 68–92, and *MED* s.v. "pellican." However, Lydgate, instead of drawing on the bestiary notion of a pelican feeding her children with her own blood, prompts the allusion but uses the image in a slightly different way, having the pelican pierce Christ's "entrayl" to provide a comparison ("Lik") with the way the reader's heart should be engraved "depe" with this triumph. For further background on the figural and artistic use of the pelican in the Middle Ages, see Francis Bond, *Dedications of English Churches: Ecclesiastical Symbolism, Saints, and Emblems* (Oxford: Oxford University Press, 1914), pp. 256–57.

sual depictions of Christ suggests that his version of the *imago pietatis* is not intended to produce weeping or passionate identification; instead, it seeks to arm its reader/viewer for spiritual battle by drawing on a series of loose figural associations normally restricted to religious texts and derived from scriptural exegesis.

It is also striking that the poem does not represent the image of the "dolorous pyte" as speaking, but rather represents Christ as instructing the "viewer" of the image how to read it from *outside* the image. His is a disembodied voice, speaking of a representation of himself without speaking from the vantage point of the image. The image itself is dead and voiceless. The effect of Christ's disembodied voice, I suggest, is to add one additional layer of distance. It is essential for Lydgate that an encounter with a material image must not be interpreted as an encounter with the person depicted by the image, but rather that it be read as a "goostly merour."[73] Lydgate maintains distance by framing his complaint in the more objective refrain, "whan ye beholde this dolerous pite" (line 24). The verses themselves show Christ discussing his passion in the first person, but by referring the reader to "this" pity instead of "my" pity, Lydgate suggests an awareness of the importance of not giv-

---

[73] Such distancing also protects Lydgate from the logical quandaries inherent in many of the period's lyrics in which a dead Christ speaks from the image, instructing the viewer to behold his wounds and suffering. For example, Christ's voice is indistinguishable from the image of the crucifix in the late fourteenth-century lyric "Abide, Ye Who Pass By:

> Abyde, gud men, & hald yhour pays
> And here what god him-seluen says,
> Hyngand on þe rode.
> Man & woman þat be me gase,
> Luke vp to me & stynt þi pase,
> For þe I sched my blode.
>
> Be-hald my body or þou gang,
> And think opon my payns strang,
> And styll als stane þou stand.
> Bihald þi self þe soth, & se
> How I am hynged here on þis tre
> And nayled fute & hand.
>
> Behald my heued, hi-hald my fete,
> And of ma mysdedes luke þou lete;
> Behald my grysely face
> And of þi syns ask aleggance,
> And in my mercy haue affyance
> And þou sall get my grace.
> (Brown, *Religious Lyrics of the XIVth Century,* pp. 59–60)

ing voice and agency to "dead" images. Thus, in refusing to collapse the distinction between an image and what (or who) it signifies, Lydgate makes a historicizing move that rejects an aesthetic that is unmediated, atemporal, or incarnational.

This point is highlighted in the final stanza of the poem. After the complex layering of images over the initial *imago pietatis,* Lydgate concludes with a stanza that reasserts his deference to the established orthodox use of the image by versifying the indulgence that was traditionally attached to the *imago pietatis:*

> From yow avoideth slouthe & necclygence,
> With contrit herte seith, meekly knelyng doun,
> O Pater-noster and Auees in sentence,
> A crede folwyng, seyd with devossioun,
> xxvi thousand yeeris of pardoun,
> Over xxx dayes, ye may the lettre see,
> In remembraunce of Crystys passioun
> Knelyng be-fore this dolorous pite.
>
> (lines 49–56)

As J. A. Endres has noted, indulgences such as this often circulated with or were attached to the *imago pietatis.*[74] Lollard critiques of images highlighted their association with extravagant indulgences such as this one. It is perhaps in light of these critiques that this final stanza is attached as a direct appeal to ecclesiastical and documentary authority ("ye may the lettre see")—the image is efficacious when accompanied by the prescribed observances because it has been given value by the church. While reading the image through the lens of the indulgence is a much less imaginative and a much more reductive way of "seeing" than the complex layers of figures and histories in the previous stanzas, Lydgate's translation of the indulgence draws out the poem's latent insistence on textuality. Ending with such an explicit reference to an ecclesiastical document suggests the increasing importance of texts in explaining and regulating lay religious practice in the fifteenth century.

Reclaiming the Past, Revising the Present

While Lydgate's poems on the pietà and *imago pietatis* never explicitly address the period's debates surrounding religious images, in their care-

---

[74] Endres, "Die Darstellung der Gregorius-Messe," pp. 152–54.

fully constructed *amplificatio,* their resistance to prompting a purely affective response, and their insistence on maintaining the complexity of figural hermeneutics, they suggest a "reformist" alternative to both Lollard literalism and iconoclasm and dangerously subjective forms of affective piety. At the same time, however, Lydgate's unique mode of regulation might also be read as "reactionary" or "nostalgic" in its frequent reliance on and attempt to revive monastic hermeneutics and mnemonics. It is also undeniably conservative in its goal of resurrecting traditional devotional models.

It could be said that traditionalism offers an alternative to participation in a present that one cannot understand or accept. Its very incongruity with its own historical moment disrupts the status quo and blurs the boundaries between what is reactionary and what is radical. However, when lodged as an accusation, the charge of traditionalism implies the outdated, backward-looking, and dull. Such has been the case with the religious writing of Lydgate, whose aesthetic practices are frequently dismissed as inescapably passé for his time. Derek Pearsall long ago suggested that "the whole direction of [Lydgate's] mind is medieval."[75] However, as I hope to have shown, in his insistence on the reclamation of old-fashioned models of devotional practice, Lydgate's appropriation of a distant past challenges the affective, and in the Monk of Bury's eyes, subjective, influence of fifteenth-century forms of piety. In bringing these old models into the new vernacular discourse, Lydgate seeks to control the emphasis on phenomenal experience inherent in the period's "incarnational aesthetic" by constructing a model in which traditional referential aesthetics more typical of monastic *lectio* and homiletics might be translated into the vernacular. In this situation, the conservative or reactionary position becomes, rather paradoxically, radical and innovative in its very alterity within an incongruous cultural situation.

The project of this essay might be seen as analogous to Lydgate's reclamation efforts. The current scholarly interest in recovering and celebrating what has been marginalized in past readings of late medieval religious writing—the bodily, the female, the heterodox, the affective—has fostered a new model of the late Middle Ages that is fundamentally incarnational. Ironically, recent critics writing within this paradigm have, in turn, often marginalized the conservative or traditional elements of this society. For this reason, the desire to reclaim Lydgate as a

---

[75] Pearsall, *John Lydgate,* p. 15.

monastic poet may seem to some readers outdated and irrelevant to contemporary scholarly conversations on late medieval religious writing. However, I would like to suggest that just as Lydgate revitalizes traditional monastic thought by deploying a new medium of expression—the vernacular—so too critics might begin to recognize the richness of "conservative" medieval devotion by attending to the forms and modes through which it was expressed—in this case, the lyric.

To this end, any recovery of late medieval religious experience must rely less on the assertion of or contribution to a unifying model such as that of "vernacular theology" or the "incarnational aesthetic" and more on an awareness of the period's religious culture and literature as dialogic, marked by the constant dialectical interaction of theological models and discourses. In the terms of this essay, such an awareness of the dialogic quality of late medieval literature enables us to acknowledge that while the period is certainly characterized by an "incarnational aesthetic," such an aesthetic was not universally endorsed. Indeed, the "regulatory aesthetic" of some clerical writers, like Lydgate, who seek to negotiate between forms of lay piety mediated by visual and sacramental signs and an emerging literate piety deriving its authority from texts, represent important reformist responses to the changing religious environment of late medieval England. This "regulatory aesthetic" is a fundamentally historical phenomenon, not only because it can be identified with a particular historical moment but also, and more importantly, because it takes up a particular position in relation to history and to tradition. That position is made manifest through the formal habits of writers like Lydgate, who turn away from the dominant aesthetic of the fifteenth century in order to capture and redeploy an aesthetic of the past—here, monastic modes of imagistic devotion. This combination of old forms with new modes, of the monastic with the vernacular, demands that we devise a reading practice adequate to its subtlety if we are to match the efforts of the very poets we are just now beginning to reclaim.

A New Fragment of the *Romaunt* of the Rose

Simon Horobin
University of Glasgow

MONG THE NINETEENTH-CENTURY PAPERS of the Reverend Joass, part of the Sutherland collection housed in the National Library of Scotland in Edinburgh, an envelope was recently discovered that contains a single vellum leaf folded in half.[1] The leaf measures 185mm x 170mm and contains twenty-four lines of text in single columns on both recto and verso, written in a professional secretary hand of the mid-fifteenth century. The envelope reads "?Lydgate c.1460" in a nineteenth-century hand, though the text preserved in this fragment is in fact lines 2403–50 of the Middle English translation of the *Roman de la Rose*, known as the *Romaunt of the Rose*. This text survives in a single manuscript, now Glasgow University Library Hunter 409 (V.3.7), and the discovery of a single leaf testifying to the earlier existence of a further copy of this work is therefore of considerable interest.

The text of the *Romaunt* is traditionally divided into three separate fragments, and the current scholarly consensus is that Chaucer was responsible for only fragment A.[2] The section of text in the NLS fragment derives from fragment B. It is impossible to determine for certain whether this single folio was originally part of a complete copy of the *Romaunt*, though there seems no reason to doubt this. The Hunter manuscript now contains 151 folios, although a further eleven leaves are missing, and the text is left incomplete. The leaves of the Hunter

---

[1] The fragment was discovered by Anna Tindley and Helen Brown of the Scottish History department, Edinburgh University. The identification of the text as the *Romaunt of the Rose* was made by Dr. Sally Mapstone of Oxford University. I am very grateful to each of them for allowing me to carry out my study of this fragment.

[2] For a recent summary of the extensive literature concerning the authorship of the *Romaunt*, see Charles Dahlberg, ed., *A Variorum Edition of the Works of Geoffrey Chaucer, Volume VII: The Romaunt of the Rose* (Norman: University of Oklahoma Press, 1999).

manuscript are larger than the NLS fragment, yet the writing space is of a similar size and each folio carries twenty-four lines. So it seems likely that the NLS fragment represents the sole survivor of a book originally comprising at least 160 folios.

No justification is provided for the date of 1460 given on the envelope in which the leaf is found, though it would seem to be supported on the basis of a study of the handwriting. The majority of the palaeographical features are characteristic of the secretary script, including the use of single compartment *a*, kidney-shaped *s* in final position, single-compartment *g* with horns and a tail that loops back and upward, and unlooped *w*.[3] Ascenders have small rounded loops characteristic of secretary, rather than the more exaggerated looped ascenders found in anglicana and early secretary hands. Two-shaped *r* is regular after round letters, such as *e, o*, while secretary *r* is found in most other environments, with an exceptional occurrence of anglicana long *r* in *desire* (fig. 2, line 15). The hand shows only modest use of the horns that commonly appear at the tops of letters and at points of breaking in secretary hands, especially of the first half of the fifteenth century, with horns appearing regularly on *g*, but not on *e* or *s*. These features, combined with the lack of letter forms characteristic of anglicana, point to the mid-fifteenth century as the approximate date of copying of this fragment.

The text is in black ink throughout, with a single decorated initial appearing at the beginning of line 17 of figure 1. The initial is in blue ink decorated with red penwork and has been used to indicate the beginning of a new paragraph in the text. The fragment is too short for an analysis of the dialect and spelling to be particularly revealing, though certain potentially diagnostic forms do occur. The spelling *eyghen* "eyes" has a patchy distribution and is limited to occurrences in East Anglia and the Home Counties in the *Linguistic Atlas of Late Mediaeval English {LALME}*.[4] The equivalent spelling in the Hengwrt manuscript of the *Canterbury Tales* [National Library of Wales, Peniarth 392D],

---

[3] For the palaeographical terminology used here and the significance of these features for dating, see M. B. Parkes, *English Cursive Book Hands, 1250–1500* (Oxford: Clarendon Press, 1969).

[4] Angus McIntosh, Michael Samuels, and Michael Benskin, eds., *A Linguistic Atlas of Late Mediaeval English {LALME}*, 4 vols. (Aberdeen: Aberdeen University Press, 1986), 4:164.

Figure 1. Reproduced by permission of Lord Strathnaver.

thought to be closest to Chaucer's own spelling, is *eyen;* though *eyghen* is found in Corpus Christi College Cambridge 61 of Chaucer's *Troilus and Criseyde.* The form *schull* is quite widespread in ME dialects and has a scattered distribution, though the highest concentration is in Ely, Essex, and Norfolk. Similarly, the form *or* "ere" occurs widely in large numbers, though it too is particularly concentrated in the East Midlands, East Anglia, and the Home Counties.[5] This evidence is thus hardly con-

[5] Ibid., 4:68.

Figure 2. Reproduced by permission of Lord Strathnover.

clusive, though it does indicate a possible connection with the counties surrounding London or with East Anglia. However, given that the London dialect was continually adopting forms found in these areas throughout the fourteenth and into the fifteenth centuries, it may be that the scribe's dialect represents a type of London English of this period.[6]

[6] For a discussion of the development of London English during this period, see Simon Horobin, *The Language of the Chaucer Tradition,* Chaucer Studies 32 (Cambridge: D. S. Brewer, 2003), chap. 2.

Transcription of the NLS fragment[7]

recto:

ffor often tymes [..] shall fall	2403
In love among thy paynes all	
[. . .] thou thy self all hoolly	2405
ffor yeten shalt so [.]tter[..]	
That mony tymes thou shalt [..]	
[..]ille as	
[.]omm *with* out	
Of f[. . .] oute	2410
Than so[..] [.]ft[..] all thy p[. . .]	
To memorie shalt thou come ageyne	
As man abaysshed wonder soore	
[. . .] after sighen more and moore	
ffor [. . .] thou well *with* outen wene	2415
haue bene	
That haue the euell of loue assaiede	
so dis[. . . . ..]	
After a thought shal take the soo	
That thy loue is to feer the froo	2420
Thou shalt seye god what may this be	
That I ne may my lady see	
Myn herte allone is to hire goo	
And I abide all soole in woo	
myn owene thought	2425
And with myne eyghen see [. . . . .] nought	

verso:

Allas myn eyghen sende I ne may	
My carefull herte to convey	
Myn herte guyde but they bee	
I preyse nothyng what euere they see	2430
Schull they abide than*n*e nay	

---

[7] The text on the recto is badly faded, although the use of digital images has enabled me to transcribe more of the text than can be read with the naked eye. Where the number of unreadable letters can be estimated, I have indicated the number using full stops in square brackets. Where it is not possible to determine the number of unreadable letters, I have left a gap in the transcription. I have expanded abbreviations and indicated all such expansions through the use of italics.

But goon and visiten with oute delay
That myn herte desireth soo
ffor certeynly but yf they goo
A foole my self I may well hoolde   2435
Whan I ne see that myn herte wolde
Wherfore I wole goon here to seen
Or esede shal I neuere ben
But if I haue some tokenyng
Than goost thou forth *with*oute dwellyng   2440
But ofte thou faylest of thy desire
Or thou maist come hire eny nere
And wastest in veyn thy passage
Than*n*e fallest thou in a newe rage
ffor want of sighte thou gynnest morne   2445
And homward pensyf doost thou reto*u*rne
In grete myschef than*n*e shalt thou bee
ffor than*n*e agayne schull come to thee
Syghes and pleyntes with newe woo
That noon yrchon ne pryketh soo   2450

By a strange coincidence, the leaf carrying lines 2395–442, overlapping considerably with the lines covered by the fragment, is missing from the Hunter MS. This means that editions of the *Romaunt* have had to rely on the text of the poem printed by William Thynne in his *Collected Works* of 1532 for this, as well as other missing portions of text.[8] The Thynne edition used the Hunterian MS as its copytext, as has been shown conclusively by James E. Blodgett, and it therefore provides a useful witness to the missing text.[9] However, as no other witness to the text survives, it has not been possible to test the accuracy of the Hunterian manuscript by comparison with another copy. Thus, even though it preserves only a small portion of the text of the *Romaunt,* the NLS fragment provides valuable evidence with which we may check the accuracy of the Hunter MS, and Thynne's edition where text is missing in the Hunter MS.

    Comparison of the text of the fragment with that of the Hunter MS, and with Thynne's text where Hunter is out, shows considerable agree-

[8] William Thynne, ed., *The Workes of Geffray Chaucer newly printed, with dyuers workes whiche were neuer in print before* (London: Thomas Godfray, 1532), *STC* 5068.
[9] James E. Blodgett, "Some Printer's Copy for William Thynne's 1532 Edition of Chaucer," *The Library,* 6th ser. 1 (1979): 97–113.

ment, suggesting a close relationship between their texts. There are, however, a number of substantive differences, some of which make only comparatively minor difference to the text. For instance, line 2436 in Thynne's edition reads, "Whan I ne se what myne hert wolde," where the NLS fragment has *that* instead of *what*. At line 2439 the NLS fragment adds *if*, where Thynne's edition reads, "But I haue."[10] Another minor difference appears at line 2446, where the subject and verb appear in a different order in the two witnesses. The Hunterian version of this line is "And homewarde pensyf thou dost retorne."

However, despite the general similarity between the two texts, there are several differences where the NLS fragment preserves better readings. For instance, at line 2427 Thynne's text reads, "Alas myne eyen sene I ne may," a reading emended by the *Riverside* editor to *sende*, citing the French *envoier* as support. The reading *sende* in the NLS fragment provides further support for this emendation, and indicates the superiority of its text. At line 2413 the NLS fragment begins the line with "As," missing in Thynne's edition but added by the *Riverside* editor following the French "Aussi come." The most important substantive difference between the two manuscripts is found in the final line of the fragment, where the Hunterian MS reads, "That no yecchyng prikketh soo." In this case the NLS reading *yrchon*, "hedgehog," is clearly the preferred reading, as may be gleaned from the sense of the immediate context and a comparison with the text of the French original: "Qui poignent plus que heriçons" (line 2328).[11] Future editors of this text should therefore use the reading of the NLS fragment to correct the version of this line found in the Hunter MS. It is possible that the first two examples show errors introduced by Thynne that were not present in the Hunter manuscript, though it is also possible that Thynne was simply transmitting errors that he encountered in his copytext. In the final example the error is found in both witnesses, showing that here the NLS fragment clearly preserves a more accurate text than that of the Hunter MS.

The importance of this fragment for the editing of the poem extends beyond the individual readings discussed above. As well as using the

---

[10] The Hunter MS and the Thynne edition are quoted from the digital facsimiles edited by Graham D. Caie. See http://www.memss.arts.gla.ac.uk/html/samples.htm. Line numbers refer to the lineation of the text printed in *The Riverside Chaucer*, gen. ed. Larry D. Benson (Oxford: Oxford University Press, 1988).

[11] The text of the *Roman* is quoted from Ronald Sutherland, ed., *The Romaunt of the Rose and Le Roman de la Rose, A Parallel-Text Edition* (Oxford: Blackwell, 1967).

Hunter MS as his copytext, Thynne also made a number of changes to his text of the *Romaunt*. Some of these changes affect minor details of orthography, such as Thynne's preference for the more archaic form of the past participle with the *y*- prefix. However, other changes are more substantial and include filling gaps of complete lines left blank in the Hunter MS, or correcting erroneous readings in his base text. The source of these improvements has been the cause of considerable editorial debate. It is now generally assumed that Thynne turned to a copy of the French original to correct obvious errors in the Hunter MS, though the possibility that he used another manuscript of the English work cannot be ruled out. This possibility is admitted by Alfred David in his textual notes to the edition of the *Romaunt* printed in the *Riverside Chaucer*, though it is swiftly rejected in favor of the view that Thynne consulted a manuscript of the French *Roman:* "It is of course possible that Thynne had access to a second manuscript of the Romaunt, which he used to emend G [the Hunter MS]. A far likelier explanation of the differences between the two texts, however, is that Thynne edited G, just as modern editors have done, with the aid of the French original and according to his notions of Chaucerian usage."[12] It is not clear why this is the far likelier explanation of the differences between the Hunter MS and Thynne's edition, though the fact that the only surviving manuscript was Thynne's copytext has no doubt contributed to the sense that no other manuscripts were available. The survival of a single leaf, testifying to another complete manuscript of the poem that preserves several readings closer to the French version than those found in the Hunter MS, is a salutary reminder that such manuscripts did circulate and could have been used by Thynne. It is worth recalling in this context Francis Thynne's report that his father was given a commission to "serche all the liberaries of Englande for Chaucers Workes," as well as William Thynne's own claim in his preface to have collected "trewe copies or exemplaries" of Chaucer's works with which he planned to correct the many errors found in earlier editions.[13] This raises the possibility that better readings in Thynne that have been rejected by editors could stem from another witness to the poem, such as that represented by the fragmentary text preserved in this single leaf.

---

[12] *The Riverside Chaucer*, p. 1198.
[13] For the quotation from Francis Thynne and extracts from the preface to Thynne's edition, see "William Thynne (d. 1546)," in *Editing Chaucer: The Great Tradition*, ed. Paul G. Ruggiers (Norman, Okla.: Pilgrim Books, 1984), pp. 35–52.

As a result of his view that Thynne's changes were based upon the French text, David rejected complete lines added by Thynne to fill gaps in the Hunter MS, preferring to leave blank lines in the *Riverside* text. But if Thynne's additions stemmed from another copy of the poem, then they could be genuine lines omitted by the scribe of the Hunter MS or missing from his exemplar. While consultation with a French copy is a plausible explanation of certain changes carried out by Thynne, it also creates a number of difficulties. For instance, the majority of the complete lines that are missing from the Hunter MS but found in Thynne have close parallels in the French text and so could stem from the French source. However, one such line supplied by Thynne, "That al to late cometh knowynge" (line 6318), is not closely related to the French: "Que trop est grief l'aparcevance."[14] Perhaps more compelling evidence for Thynne's use of another manuscript of the ME work are the changes he introduced that have no parallel in the French text, many of which are improvements on the text found in the Hunter MS. For instance, line 688 of the *Riverside* text reads, "But of song sotil and wys." The reading *But* derives from Thynne's edition, as the Hunter MS reads *For*. Thynne's reading cannot, however, derive from the French version as there is no equivalent for this line in the *Roman*. It is interesting to note that, despite his view that Thynne emended his text against the French and that "his efforts should not be taken as authentic," David adopts a number of readings from Thynne against the evidence of the Hunter MS, as in the previous example.[15] Another example is found at line 4208, where the *Riverside* text reads: "The keyes kepte of the utter gate," though the word *kepte* is found only in Thynne. David claims that "when the reasons for the variants in Th[ynne] are not obvious, attempts have been made to account for them."[16] However, no explanation is provided as to the authority for Thynne's emendation of his copytext in this instance, nor why it has been adopted for the *River-*

---

[14] James Blodgett suggests that this line could translate a French version that read *tart* rather than *fort*, though he concedes that no such variant is recorded in Langlois's edition of the *Roman*. See "William Thynne," p. 50. Charles Dahlberg posits another scenario, in which he sees Thynne using the synonymous *knowyng* to avoid repeating *aperceyvyng*, while *al to late* is a more specific rendition of the French *trop . . . grief*. See Dahlberg, *A Variorum*, p. 268.

[15] Alfred David has suggested to me that *But* makes better sense than *For* and need not require the authority of another manuscript. It seems more likely to me that Thynne's emendation was prompted by comparison with another source rather than through dissatisfaction with *For*, which is an otherwise acceptable reading.

[16] *The Riverside Chaucer*, p. 1199.

side edition. The reading in the French text is *porte* and it is not obvious why Thynne should choose to render it *kepte*.[17]

One potential objection to the possibility that Thynne collated the Hunter MS with another copy is the sporadic and irregular distribution of the changes Thynne introduced.[18] There is no reason, however, why Thynne's collation of his witnesses could not have been equally erratic, as is assumed for his consultation of his French source, showing the same decline in interest about 1,300 lines into the job. The systematic and comprehensive collation of manuscript witnesses is a modern rather than a Tudor editorial practice. In fact this sporadic consultation of other witnesses is precisely what Blodgett found in Thynne's establishment of his texts of other works in his collected edition.[19] For instance, for his text of *La Belle Dame sans Merci*, Thynne used Pynson's text of 1526 as his copytext. However, a group of variant readings that appear in a cluster between lines 189 and 206 suggests that this section of the text was emended through consultation with the text in Longleat House MS 258. Collation between manuscripts and printed witnesses is evidenced in parts of a number of works printed by Thynne, including *The Parliament of Fowls*, *Troilus and Criseyde*, *The Canterbury Tales*, and *The Assembly of Ladies*.

Blodgett claims that, where a work is a translation, Thynne's method of correcting his text was to turn to the original rather than another witness of the Middle English work. The basis for this claim is a single reading found in Thynne's edition of the *Physician's Tale*, and his editorial practice as witnessed by his text of the *Romaunt*. The single instance from *The Physician's Tale* is the reference to Claudius as a *client*, where other extant manuscripts read *cherl* or *clerk*. Thynne's reading appears to derive from Chaucer's Latin source, where the reading *clienti* is found. This is certainly an interesting reading, though hardly sufficient to establish an editorial practice based upon consultation of sources rather than other manuscript witnesses. The reading *client* could have appeared in another copy of *The Physician's Tale* available to Thynne but no longer extant, or perhaps in a marginal gloss. Alternatively it may simply rep-

---

[17] Alfred David has suggested that the choice of "kepte" was inspired by alliteration with "keyes." This is a possible explanation, although the introduction of alliteration is not generally a feature of Thynne's editing procedure.

[18] David discusses the distribution of Thynne's emendations and notes that 11 percent of the lines before 1300 show variation, while after 1300 only 4.7 percent of the remaining lines contain variant readings. See *The Riverside Chaucer*, p. 1198.

[19] See the discussion in "William Thynne," pp. 42–50.

resent Thynne's own knowledge of this particular text. Whichever explanation is adopted for this reading, it is clear that it alone is not sufficient to establish that Thynne habitually consulted original sources when editing Chaucer's works.

The principal support for the theory of consultation of original sources is Thynne's treatment of the text of the *Romaunt,* though, as we have seen, the evidence of the NLS fragment serves to cast some doubt on the editorial theory, now hardened into fact, that Thynne's emendations of the Hunter MS derived from collation of the manuscript with a copy of the French *Roman.* The survival of a single leaf containing readings closer to the French version than the Hunter MS is an important reminder that at least one such manuscript was extant and could have provided Thynne with readings with which to correct his copytext. We have seen that the theory that Thynne consulted original sources rests almost exclusively on the text of the *Romaunt,* and it seems necessary that this theory be reviewed in the light of this discovery. Given that sporadic comparison of manuscript witnesses is found in many of the other texts edited by Thynne, this seems a possible explanation of the variation between the Hunter MS and Thynne's text of the *Romaunt.* The survival of a single leaf of a manuscript of the *Romaunt* that preserves readings closer to the French source shows how Thynne could have obtained such readings without recourse to a text of the French *Roman.* So, while this fragment preserves only a small section of the poem, it does have considerable importance as the sole surviving witness to a lost copy of this important ME work.

Colloquium: The Afterlife of Origins

Introduction

Arlyn Diamond
University of Massachusetts Amherst

CHAUCER, WITH HIS TRICKSTER PRESCIENCE, seems to have anticipated our fascination with his sources. The essential link between his life as a reader and his life as a poet is made for us over and over in his poetry. For example, in *The Parliament of Fowls* he tells his audience,

> Of usage—what for lust and what for lore—
> On bokes rede I ofte, as I yow tolde.
>
> .   .   .   .
>
> For out of olde feldes, as men seyth,
> Cometh al this newe corn from yer to yere,
> And out of olde bokes, in good feyth,
> Cometh al this newe science that men lere.
> (lines 15–16, 22–25)[1]

Throughout the course of his career, he names the texts that matter to him: "Virgile, Ovide, Omer, Lucan and Stace" (*TC* V. 1792), or "Fraunceys Petrak, the lauriat poete . . . whos rethorike sweete/Enlumyned al Ytaille of poetrie" (*CT* IV.31–33). Being Chaucer, he also gives us false clues: "As writ myn auctour called Lollius" (*TC*, I. 394). He makes fun of pedants anxious to show off their education, like the monk with his hundred tedious tragedies, or Chauntecleer, wielding learned authorities like weapons. In significant part Chaucer's characters, like the poet, are defined by their sources, their textual communi-

---

[1] All quotations are from *The Riverside Chaucer*, gen. ed. Larry D. Benson (Boston: Houghton Mifflin, 1987).

217

ties and the use they make of them. The Clerk reads Aristotle and his philosophy, the Wife of Bath is taught proverbial wisdom by her dame. For the cozening Friar of *The Summoner's Tale,* or the Pardoner, old books are simply another means to profit. Our Chaucer too is shaped by our reading of his "essential texts" and the uses he has made of them, although we cannot always agree on what these are. We have had the courtly young French Chaucer, the serious and ambitious Italian Chaucer, the Augustinian Chaucer. A concern with origins, understood not as simple fact but as shifting literary history, is not anachronistic, or a sign of our distance from the poet, but is part of our complicated connection to him.

When Nancy Bradbury and I proposed a symposium on Chaucer's sources for the 2004 Glasgow Congress of the New Chaucer Society, we were in part inspired by the recent appearance of the first volume of the revised *Sources and Analogues,* and in part by the challenges we had encountered in our own efforts to understand the formation of the texts we studied.[2] The title, "Afterlife of Origins," was meant to suggest the malleability (or slipperiness) of the concept of "source," as well as the centuries-old lure of the quest for a beginning, what Kenneth Bleeth refers to in his witty account of the history of Chaucerian scholarship as the search for "the *fons et origo*" of a passage. We began with a set of questions, not about particular sources, but about how to think of "source study" in an age of postmodern Chaucer studies. What constitutes a source, for us, for Chaucer, for earlier scholars? What epistemologies are involved in his and our understanding of the term? Is there a hierarchy of sources, privileging textual over visual, written over oral, Latin over English, "hard" over "soft"? What does it mean, as Peter Beidler demonstrates, that we prefer a nonexistent French source to an available Dutch one? Does source study lead us to a more fractured, heterogeneous image of the Middle Ages, or does it help us build a more cohesive sense of Chaucer and his culture? What theoretical models help us understand our practice, and Chaucer's?

Looking for sources is a very conservative enterprise in many senses, which is perhaps why it has come to seem old-fashioned. It links us to those early modern scholars who first began annotating Chaucer, hoping

---

[2] *Sources and Analogues of the Canterbury Tales,* ed. Robert M. Correale and Mary Hamel, vol. 1 (Cambridge: D. S. Brewer, 2002).

to preserve him through recovering his world. It requires of us very traditional linguistic, codicological, archival, and historical skills. It saves otherwise devalued texts, like popular romances or hagiography, because they were important to Chaucer. It is also shaped, as Amy Goodwin makes clear, by particular academic and publishing realities. Looking at the complex ways in which participants responded to the topic of Chaucer and source study, what strikes me now is that everyone seems to have taken for granted the skills necessary to do such work. Everyone also seems to have taken for granted the pleasures that attract us to the search: the challenge of the obscure reference, of the unknown manuscript, and, most important, of the ever-elusive Chaucer. Who wouldn't like to find the man of great authority, or Wade's boat, unsophisticated as such a scholarly fantasy might seem in the twenty-first century? And, in finding the boat, we might find, as Carolyn Collette has done with alchemical references, or Nancy Bradbury with proverbs, a thriving culture of practice and citation.

In the discussion at Glasgow in 2004, it became clear that to do source study under the aegis of Chaucer, that father of English poetry whom even Harold Bloom acknowledges to be of the first rank, is to be constantly resisting a teleological narrative of origins. It is too easy for the sources to be occluded by the "masterpiece," like the so-called primitive masks that inspired Picasso, and became fixed as part of the history of modernism, generically "African" and timeless, lacking their own particularities of time and place and artistic influence. The romances of the Auchinleck Manuscript are given a place in surveys of literature as the source of *Sir Thopas,* undifferentiated as interesting and complex narratives in their own right. Those of us who find value in these romances would like to think of a source as a point of connection between our text and the world it inhabits. In this light, what seems to offer a way out of the dilemma, at least for a number of contributors, is a turn to culture itself as the object of inquiry, a turn to a map of communicative practices understood synchronically rather than a linear history that progresses from simple beginnings to achieved genius. In this willingness to look beyond written exemplars, we are following what Chaucer does, rather than what he says.

Chaucer himself distinguishes reading from life, texts from observation. Jove's eagle in *The House of Fame* mocks his student for being completely unaware of what goes on around him:

> . . . also domb as any stoon,
> Thou sittest at another book
> Tyl fully daswed ys thy look.
>   (656–58)

But of course, and this is in large part the matter of our discussion, it is not as simple as that easy division of authority and experience, as Dolores Frese shows in her analysis of the complex layering of inspiration, borrowed metaphor, and "hard source" in *The Clerk's Tale*.

This symposium moves in a very general sense from attempts to provide histories and definitions of source study to examinations of less conventional kinds of sources to more theoretical considerations of the practice of source study, asking, as Betsy McCormick proposes, not what a source is, but how a source does. The answers are, not surprisingly, Chaucerian. Just as the poet seeks appropriate representations for his own artistic stimulation, talkative eagles or statues of noble predecessors or a spinning house of rumors or even a random group of irrepressible travelers, so the members of the symposium offer concrete examples and intellectual metaphors, "thick description," or "intertext" or "rhizome" or "habitus," to suggest the ways in which source study might be practiced now. Our hope was to be provocative rather than definitive. Therefore, as we moved our symposium from oral presentation to print, Nancy Bradbury and I asked our contributors for essays that are brief, informal, and suggestive, so that they may serve as textual embodiments of the lively exchange of ideas in which they originated.

The Physician's Tale and Remembered Texts

Kenneth Bleeth
Connecticut College

I
N A 1915 ARTICLE ENTITLED "Chaucer's Bed's Head," Frederick
Tupper, contemplating the so-called maidenly virtues of Virginia in *The
Physician's Tale*, tells us that he "cannot resist the thought that Chaucer
. . . had 'read them in a book'"—but not in the *Roman de la Rose,*
Chaucer's immediate source for the tale; nor in Livy, the story's ultimate
source; nor in Gower's retelling of the Appius and Virginia anecdote.
"Keen in his quest," Tupper writes, "the seeker" (as Tupper styles himself) turns to the Fathers of the Church. Jerome and Augustine fail to
supply sufficiently compelling parallels. But what about Ambrose,
whose *De Virginibus* is quoted with approval by both Jerome and Augustine? "And there the search," Tupper informs us, "came happily to
an end."[1]

We can recognize in Tupper's comments two characteristics of the
First Age of Chaucerian source study. First is the assumption that Chaucer's sources were necessarily to be found "in a book." Second, Tupper
embraces the belief that the questing scholar's task is to hack his way
through the textual underbrush, undeterred by false trails, to uncover
the *fons et origo* of a Chaucerian passage or work. (The flip side of these
assumptions is the scholar's frustration when definitive sources prove
elusive—you can hear this tone, I think, in Root's observation in 1906
that Chaucer may have assembled *The Squire's Tale* from "such scraps of
knowledge about Tartary and the Far East as he had picked up in reading or conversation.")[2] Evidently persuaded by Tupper's parallels, Edgar
Shannon included the Ambrose material in *The Physician's Tale* chapter

[1] Frederick Tupper, "Chaucer's Bed's Head," *MLN* 30 (1915): 5–7.
[2] Robert Kilburn Root, *The Poetry of Chaucer* (Boston and New York: Houghton
Mifflin, 1906), p. 270.

of the first *Sources and Analogues*.[3] But other, more plausible possibilities were subsequently proposed. In the second volume of the new *Sources and Analogues,* Ambrose does not make the cut. In his place are excerpts from the chapters on the education of children and the proper behavior for young women in John of Wales's *Communiloquium,* the late thirteenth-century preacher's manual that includes citations from the very passages in *De Virginibus* that had initially attracted Tupper's attention.[4]

But even the *Communiloquium,* which, as Robert Pratt has demonstrated, the poet certainly knew in some form, does not provide any eureka moments for the student of *The Physician's Tale*.[5] The tale's set pieces on virginity and female conduct demonstrate with particular clarity the truth of C. S. Lewis's observation that medieval authors "hardly ever attempt to write anything unless someone has written it before."[6] When texts are layered with citations and paraphrases of earlier authorities, it frequently proves impossible to isolate a specific source for an often-cited anecdote or piece of doctrine. Moreover, the desire to pin down the precise point of origin for topoi with widespread currency misrepresents both the rich intertextuality of medieval discourse and the manner in which Chaucer's extensive but unsystematic reading made its way into his poems.

Nature's monologue (VI.11–29), for example, has been quarried for allusions to Ovid, Cicero, Juvenal, the *Ovidius moralizatus,* and, in particular, Jean de Meun, whose Nature, like Chaucer's, identifies herself as God's "vicaire" (*Roman de la Rose,* lines 16752, 19477), and who describes the goddess in hyperbolic language reminiscent of Nature's account of Virginia's beauty in Chaucer.[7] But Jean inherited the trope of

---

[3] Edgar F. Shannon, "The Physician's Tale," in *Sources and Analogues of Chaucer's Canterbury Tales,* ed. W. F. Bryan and Germaine Dempster (Chicago: University of Chicago Press, 1941), pp. 407–8.

[4] Kenneth Bleeth, "The Physician's Tale," in *Sources and Analogues of the Canterbury Tales,* ed. Robert M. Correale and Mary Hamel, vol. 2 (Woodbridge, Suffolk, and Rochester, N.Y.: D. S. Brewer, 2005), pp. 558–63.

[5] Robert A. Pratt, "Chaucer and the Hand That Fed Him," *Speculum* 41 (1966): 619–42.

[6] C. S. Lewis, *Studies in Medieval and Renaissance Literature* (Cambridge: Cambridge University Press, 1966), p. 37.

[7] See the notes to lines 9–29 and 31–39 in *The Physician's Tale, A Variorum Edition of the Works of Geoffrey Chaucer,* vol. 2, part 17, ed. Helen Storm Corsa (Norman: University of Oklahoma Press, 1987). For Juvenal, see William Kupersmith, "Chaucer's Physician's Tale and the Tenth Satire of Juvenal," *ELN* 34 (1986): 20–23. Chaucer references are to *The Riverside Chaucer,* gen. ed. Larry D. Benson (Boston: Houghton Mifflin,

Nature as *vicaria Dei* from Alanus de Insulis's *De planctu naturae,* which itself has been proposed as a source for Chaucer's lines.[8] Karl Young, making a case in 1941 for the *De eruditione filiorum nobilium* of Vincent of Beauvais as a model for the account of Virginia's virtues, cites a passage, in which Vincent condemns the use of cosmetics, that he believes to be closer to the essential significance of the description of Nature's "painting" of Virginia's figure than the lines in the *Roman.*[9] And Carolyn Collette, quoting part of a Wycliffite treatise, suggests that Nature's language of painting and counterfeiting is best understood in relation to the late medieval discourse on the power of images.[10] Each of these glosses adds something to our comprehension of Nature's speech. But they do so not by identifying material that Chaucer was directly imitating or even (except in the case of Ovid and the *Roman*) that he had necessarily read. Rather, they direct our attention to what Michael Riffaterre, in an important essay entitled "The Mind's Eye: Memory and Textuality," calls "a vast terra incognita of . . . mythologemes, ideologemes, [and] descriptive systems" that link themselves to—Riffaterre's phrase is "feed into"—any given text, and that a medieval audience would have brought to bear on its experience of a literary work.[11] These intertexts, Riffaterre argues, exist in a memorial relation to the primary text; it is as if they had lost their written materiality and survive solely in the mind's eye. Especially when dealing with subjects as ubiquitous as virginity or the relation of Nature and Art, we need to expand our notion of a source beyond written texts, to that "unwritten component [that] is vastly more developed than the written."[12] Instructed by Mary Carruthers, V. A. Kolve, and other scholars of medieval memory, students of Chaucer's sources must now consider as possible evidence not

---

1987). Citations from *Le Roman de la Rose* are to Guillaume de Lorris and Jean de Meun, *Le Roman de la Rose,* ed. Félix Lecoy. 3 vols. (Paris: Honoré Champion, 1965–70).

[8] Barbara Bartholomew, *Fortuna and Natura: A Reading of Three Chaucer Narratives* (The Hague: Mouton, 1966), pp. 52–53; Geraldine Sesak Branca, "Experience versus Authority: Chaucer's Physician and Fourteenth-Century Science," Ph.D. diss. (University of Illinois, Champaign-Urbana, 1971), pp. 91–92.

[9] Karl Young, "The Maidenly Virtues of Chaucer's Virginia," *Speculum* 16 (1941): 340–49.

[10] Carolyn P. Collette, " 'Peyntyng with Greet Cost': Virginia as Image in the *Physician's Tale,*" *Chaucer Yearbook* 2 (1995): 49–62.

[11] Michael Riffaterre, "The Mind's Eye: Memory and Textuality," in *The New Medievalism,* ed. Marina S. Brownlee, Kevin Brownlee, and Stephen G. Nichols (Baltimore: Johns Hopkins University Press, 1991), p. 33.

[12] Ibid., p. 44.

only those volumes that the poet might have kept "at his beddes heed" (I.3211) but also remembered texts, semantic fields, and pictorial images—the cultural topics stored in the mental retrieval systems of both author and audience, and ready to be activated by what the poet's readers and hearers discover in the primary text.[13]

[13] Mary Carruthers, *The Book of Memory: A Study of Memory in Medieval Culture* (Cambridge: Cambridge University Press, 1990); V. A. Kolve, *Chaucer and the Imagery of Narrative: The First Five Canterbury Tales* (Stanford: Stanford University Press, 1984).

New Terminology for Sources and Analogues:

Or, Let's Forget the Lost French Source for *The Miller's Tale*

Peter G. Beidler
Lehigh University

WE HAVE GROWN SLOPPY in our use of the terms *source* and *analogue,* sometimes even using them as if they were synonyms. In an earlier essay,[1] I urged that Chaucerians should refine our use of the terms by agreeing on definitions of three terms: *source* for a work that we are sure Chaucer knew and used; *hard analogue* for a work that would have been available to Chaucer, that has strong plot and character connections with the Chaucerian tale under consideration, but that lacks the verbal parallels that would let us be sure it was a source; and *soft analogue* for a work that, either because of its late date or because of its narrative distance from the Chaucerian tale, Chaucer almost certainly did not know. In this essay I want to propose a further refinement of our terminology and then lay to rest the notion of a lost French source for *The Miller's Tale.*

Whatever our reasons for wanting to identify the various models for Chaucer's work, we need to be more precise than most of us have often been in the past. Different scholars, of course, have different reasons for wanting to identify the specific antecedents for a Chaucerian work. Some of us who seek to locate sources are driven by a desire to know more about Chaucer's biography: where he traveled, what languages he knew, how widely he had read, how well he remembered what he had read, and even whether a given work can be dated to what might be

---

[1] "Just Say Yes, Chaucer Knew the *Decameron:* Or, Bringing the *Shipman's Tale* Out of Limbo," in *The Decameron and the Canterbury Tales,* ed. Leonard Michael Koff and Brenda Deen Schildgen (Teaneck, N.J.: Fairleigh Dickinson University Press, 2002), esp. pp. 41–42.

called his "French period," his "Italian period," or his "English period." For most of us, the interest is less in Chaucer's life than in his literature. Whatever our theoretical orientation, we seek to establish what Chaucer's most likely sources were, or at least what the closest analogues were, so that we can attempt to measure the distance from them of Chaucer's own work. We seek to identify patterns in the kind and number of changes that Chaucer made in transferring old literary wine to a new bottle: his purposes, for example, in adding a scene or a character, or in cutting the first hundred lines of a narrative, or in making a certain character less likable, or more independent, or more full of pride. Sometimes we seek only to identify what elements Chaucer chose not to change.

Volume 2 of the Boydell and Brewer *Sources and Analogues* contains my chapter on *The Miller's Tale*. While working on that chapter, I found myself frustrated by the limitation that the two standard terms *source* and *analogue* gave me. There were, after all, lots of analogues for *The Miller's Tale*, but none of them had yet emerged as an undisputed source. There had been talk about a lost source, but I concluded that such a source, if it ever existed, could not help us because we could not know what it might have been like or how Chaucer might have changed its characters or its narrative line. I found myself needing a refined terminology to do what I thought was my duty in helping Chaucerians talk about the antecedents to the *The Miller's Tale*. In the end, I decided that only one of the various analogues is both old enough and close enough to *The Miller's Tale* in plot and language that it could have been Chaucer's actual source: the Middle Dutch *Heile van Beersele*. The story of Heile is not precisely a source, since we cannot be sure that Chaucer knew it, but it is surely more than an analogue, at least in the sense that the other, post-Chaucerian tales are analogues. The term that works best for *Heile van Beersele* is hard analogue with near-source status.

Amending my earlier list, I therefore propose the following five terms and definitions:

hard source: a specific work for which we have an extant copy and that we know, from verbal similarities, character names, and plot sequences, that Chaucer used. An example would be Boccaccio's *Teseida* as a hard source for *The Knight's Tale*.

soft source: a literary, historical, philosophical, classical, religious, mythological, biographical, anecdotal, proverbial, musical, or artistic work that Chaucer almost certainly knew and probably remembered (consciously or not) as he wrote and that provided at least a general or distant influence upon some elements in his own work. Examples would be Boethius's *Consolation of Philosophy* and Statius's *Thebaid* as soft sources for *The Knight's Tale,* the biblical account of the Annunciation for *The Miller's Tale,* and *The Knight's Tale* itself as a soft source for *The Miller's Tale.*

hard analogue: a literary work that is old enough in its extant form that Chaucer could have known it and that bears striking resemblances, usually more narrative than verbal, to a Chaucerian work. We should normally speak of a hard analogue when we do not have a hard source. If it is an especially strong candidate, we might use terminology like *hard analogue with near-source status.* Examples would be *Decameron VIII, 1* for *The Shipman's Tale* and *Heile van Beersele* for *The Miller's Tale.* On this last, see my argument below.

soft analogue: a literary work that, because of its late date or its remoteness from its Chaucerian counterpart, Chaucer almost certainly did not know, but that may provide clues to another work that Chaucer may have known. Examples might be Sercambi's *De avaritia et luzuria* for *The Shipman's Tale* and a nineteenth-century Portuguese tale that sounds a bit like *The Merchant's Tale* and that may even have derived from it.

lost source: a literary work that is not extant but that may have existed at one time and that Chaucer may possibly have known, if indeed it ever did exist. The concept of a lost source should be advanced only with the greatest caution. Any argument for such a source will be strengthened by manuscript or historical evidence that it once existed. Positing such a work should be done only with the full knowledge that if such a work did exist, we have almost no idea what it was like.

The idea of a lost source has featured prominently in discussions of *The Miller's Tale.* These discussions have often demonstrated considerably less caution than the case warrants. In the rest of this short essay I want to argue specifically against this once-prevalent notion that there was such a source.

We know that Chaucer knew at least some French fabliaux. There is no question, for example, that the most likely source for *The Reeve's Tale* is the Old French *Le meunier et les .ii. clers.* Since Chaucer probably knew that fabliau, it seems quite possible that he knew other thirteenth-century French comic tales as well. There is not a scrap of manuscript evidence, however, that a French source for *The Miller's Tale* ever actually existed. I have read widely in the Old French fabliaux to see whether I could find French counterparts to three of the physical properties of *The Miller's Tale* that are fundamental to its story line: (1) the suspended tubs, (2) the bedroom window, and (3) the hot poker. So far as I can tell, none of these properties plays in any extant French fabliau a role parallel to the one it plays in *The Miller's Tale*.

1. *The suspended tubs.* At Nicholas's urging, old John hangs three tubs from the beams in his house. These are variously described a "tubbe," a "knedyng trogh," and a "kymelyn" (I.3564, 3620–21).[2] To be sure, we do find the occasional tub in the French fabliaux, where it typically serves for bathing with one's lover or for hastily hiding a wife's lover from a suspicious or suddenly returned husband. In none of the French fabliaux, however, is a tub suspended from above, and in none is one used as an ark to escape a predicted flood. Never, indeed, in any of the French fabliaux is there a predicted flood.

2. *The bedroom window.* The window in *The Miller's Tale* plays an important role in the plot. It appears three times, first when Absolon serenades Alison, next when Absolon kisses Alison's buttocks, and finally when Absolon returns with his hot coulter and gets his revenge, not against Alison, but against Nicholas. I have found no French fabliau in which a window plays any important role. I find passing references to a few windows here and there, but in none of these does a man serenade a woman on the other side of her bedroom window or ask for a window-kiss from such a woman, and in none of them does anyone present her or his buttocks out the window for a kiss.

3. *The hot poker.* After being insulted by Alison, Absolon rushes to the shop of his friend the blacksmith Gerveys and borrows a hot coulter. We do find a couple of references to a hot poker in the Old French fabliaux, but there it is quite different from the one we find in *The Miller's Tale*. *De l'aventure d'Ardenne* is a tale about a man too stupid to know how to make love to his wife and who has to be shown how by his mother-in-law. Near the end of the tale is an absurd sequence in which the stupid husband finds an awl with which he thinks to puncture

---

[2] Quotations are taken from *The Riverside Chaucer,* gen. ed. Larry D. Benson (Boston: Houghton Mifflin, 1987).

a wine-bag to collect some wine to take to his wife. He stirs the fire with the awl to make some light. In the faint light he sees the exposed bottom of a sleeping knight and strikes, thinking he is puncturing a wineskin. The only other hot poker in an Old French fabliaux appears in *De la dame escoilliee,* in which a woman insists on bossing her husband. She is eventually "castrated" by a count who has his knights hold her face-down on the ground and then makes incisions and pretends to remove the testicles from her buttocks. Near the end of that troubling scene, the count threatens that he will cauterize the roots of her testicles so the testicles do not grow back, and he tells one of his retainers to go and heat up an iron coulter. No such mission is necessary, however, because the newly gelded lady swears that she will henceforth be fully obedient to her husband. In neither of these tales is the hot poker similar in function to the one we find in *The Miller's Tale,* where Absolon purposefully goes to a blacksmith, asks to borrow a hot coulter, then runs with it through the streets to punish someone for an insulting humiliation.

It does not appear, then, that the suspended tub, the window, and the hot iron used as a weapon of punishment can be found in the Old French fabliaux or that these three props are in any important way associated with French fabliaux. Wouldn't it be nice if we could locate a medieval comic tale about a woman who is accosted at her night-window by successive lovers and who hides one of them in a tub suspended from the roofbeams? Wouldn't it be nice if that tale included an ass-kissing at that window and, later, a man's buttocks stuck out that same window? Wouldn't it be nice if in that same tale the one who did the kissing then avenged himself by burning someone at that window with a hot iron? And wouldn't it be nice if that tale was old enough that Chaucer could have known it, was in a language that Chaucer probably recognized, and was available in a country he is known to have had connections with?

There is, of course, such a tale: the Middle Dutch *Heile van Beersele,* dating probably from the third quarter of the fourteenth century. That is the only tale that I include in the chapter on *The Miller's Tale* in the new *Sources and Analogues.* It has been known to us for more than eighty years, but has been largely ignored as Chaucer's likely source because A. J. Barnouw, the man who brought it to the attention of the scholarly world, claimed that he had found not Chaucer's probable source but merely a Middle Dutch adaptation of a lost French original that Chaucer would have known.[3]

Why have scholars been so reluctant to take seriously the idea that *Heile van Beersele* was, of all of the analogues to *The Miller's Tale,* Chaucer's most likely source, preferring to chase after the chimera of a lost French source? Perhaps they were reluctant to challenge the experts, the scholars who stated with such assurance that there must have been such a source. Perhaps they wanted to posit a French fabliau with ass-kissing and farting so they could blame the scatological elements of *The Miller's Tale* not on Chaucer but on one of those "primitive" French entertainers famous for their fascination with the lower body parts. Perhaps they assumed that no Dutch writer was clever enough to invent such a plot, but instead must have been merely copying something from French. Or perhaps they assumed that Chaucer, despite his having had a wife from Hainault and a patron born in Ghent, and despite the likelihood that in his various diplomatic or commercial functions he would have had dealings with the nearby Low Countries, just across the channel from Dover, never learned enough Middle Dutch to read the tale.

We cannot know now why scholars have chosen to bypass the analogue that we have in order to imagine a source that we do not have. I would like to think, however, that if they had had access to the terminology that I suggest above, they would have been more careful to distinguishing among the various analogues and to describe them, and that my words of caution about when to posit a lost source would have made them more reluctant to drag the red herring of such a possibility across the trail of those who sought to discover what was most original in *The Miller's Tale.* And I would like to think that they might even agree with me that we should read *Heile van Beersele* as a hard analogue with near-source status when we seek to discover what is most distinctively Chaucerian in *The Miller's Tale.* In any case, I suggest that, at least until some real evidence is discovered, we forget about that "lost" French source.

---

[3] "Chaucer's 'Milleres Tale,'" *MLR* 7 (1912): 145–48. Barnouw admitted that "no trace" of a French fabliau of *The Miller's Tale* type had ever been found. Barnouw's opinion was picked up by Stith Thompson, who presented the antecedents to *The Miller's Tale* in the original 1941 *Sources and Analogues.* Thompson notes that "the argument for a lost French fabliau as Chaucer's immediate source is strengthened by the presence of a fourteenth-century fabliau in Flemish." See Stith Thompson, "The Miller's Tale," in *Sources and Analogues of Chaucer's Canterbury Tales,* ed. W. F. Bryan and Germaine Dempster (Chicago: University of Chicago Press, 1941), p. 106. For my chapter on *The Miller's Tale,* see *Sources and Analogues of the Canterbury Tales,* vol. 2, ed. Robert M. Correale and Mary Hamel (Woodbridge, Suffolk: D. S. Brewer, 2005), pp. 249–75.

Chaucer's *Clerk's Tale:* Sources, Influences, and Allusions

Amy W. Goodwin
Randolph-Macon College

Chaucer's DISCLOSURE AND CONCEALMENT of the sources for his *Clerk's Tale,* allied with the extensive scholarship tracing the transmission of the Griselda story in the fourteenth, fifteenth, and sixteenth centuries, present us with some of the complicated problems involved in source studies. How we define a source and what sources we attend to are influenced by the form of argument we wish to make about Chaucer's *Clerk's Tale* and the values guiding and coloring scholarship in any given period.

J. Burke Severs defined a source as a text Chaucer had before him as he composed *The Clerk's Tale,* and his practice was generally to look for significant verbal parallels and close translations of words and phrases. Using these kinds of evidence, *The Literary Relationships of Chaucer's Clerkes Tale* established beyond dispute Chaucer's use of Petrarch's *Historia Griseldis* and the anonymous French *Le Livre de Griseldis.* Severs followed Occam's razor in defining a source as he did and in giving little weight to correspondences between Chaucer's *Clerk's Tale* and other versions of the Griselda story if the evidence was not textual or if textual not plentiful. In part, he valued clear lines of transmission, and the limitations of this approach are perhaps most evident in his treatment of textual details in *The Clerk's Tale* that appear to derive from the adaptation of Philippe de Mézières's *Le miroir des dames mariees* by the compiler of *Le Ménagier de Paris* and of rhetorical similarities between Chaucer's and Boccaccio's Griselda stories.[1] The image of Chaucer composing *The*

---

[1] The historical context of Severs's argument is important; his argument was not set against a late twentieth-century increased willingness to recognize Boccaccio's influence on the *Canterbury Tales.* One of his aims was to disprove W. E. Farnham's case for Boccaccio's Griselda story and A. S. Cook's case for *Le Ménagier de Paris* as Chaucer's sources in addition to Petrarch. See Willard Edward Farnham, Chaucer's *Clerkes Tale,"*

Clerk's Tale with Petrarch's *Historia Griseldis* to one side and the anonymous *Livre de Griseldis* to the other is thus neater than it should be, not just because it leaves out Chaucer's use of Philippe's and Boccaccio's Griselda stories, copies of which he may not have had as he composed *The Clerk's Tale,* but also because these versions surely influenced him beyond the details or features he imitated.

The distinction between a source that Chaucer had before him in written form and a source that he had stored in his memory seems moot to me when we are trying to identify texts that influenced Chaucer's invention in composing *The Clerk's Tale.* These two different kinds of sources—a source text and, let us say, a source of invention—may nonetheless have very different values with respect to the insights they provide into Chaucer's poetic process or other issues. There have been practical reasons for distinguishing between them for projects such as Robert M. Correale and Mary Hamel's *Sources and Analogues of the Canterbury Tales* (I was a contributor to volume 1).[2] In projects such as this one, working definitions of sources and analogues—exclusive rather than expansive—develop with a mind to the project, and once a project is completed these provisional definitions do not have to take on an absolute status or universal acceptance. Criteria informing working definitions include more than just the kinds of evidence that will allow us to identify or exclude a text as a source. They are also informed by the purpose of the project and its audience.

MLN 33 (1918): 193–203, and Albert Stanburrough Cook, "Chaucer's *Clerk's Tale* and a French Version of His Original," *Romanic Review* 8 (1917): 210–22. Severs's argument against Chaucer's use of Boccaccio was actually stronger than his argument against the use of *Le Ménagier* because Severs showed in comparing the different contestants that some of the correspondences Farnham had found between Chaucer's and Boccaccio's Griselda stories could also be found in Philippe de Mézières's *Le miroir des dames mariees,* which the compiler of *Le Ménagier* adapted for his work on domestic conduct. Severs suggested that Philippe might have know *The Decameron,* giving Boccaccio the status of a source within a source. See J. Burke Severs, *The Literary Relationships of Chaucer's Clerk's Tale* (1942; Hamden, Conn.: Archon Books, 1972), pp. 37, 135–76, for Severs's comparisons of the correspondences among Petrarch's and Chaucer's and the French Griselda stories; for Severs's discussion of Boccaccio's influence on the French versions, see 126 n. 4 and 176 n. 8. Helen Cooper in "The Frame," *Sources and Analogues of the Canterbury Tales,* ed. Robert M. Correale and Mary Hamel, vol. 1 (Cambridge: D. S. Brewer, 2002), pp. 1–22, has clinched the case for Boccaccio's influence on the *Canterbury Tales.* On Chaucer's indebtedness to Boccaccio's Griselda story, see John Finlayson, "Petrarch, Boccaccio, and Chaucer's *Clerk's Tale," SP* 97 (2000): 255–75; and Thomas J. Farrel's response to this essay, "Source or Hard Analogue, *Decameron* X,10 and *The Clerk's Tale," ChauR* 37 (2003): 346–64.

[2] Thomas J. Farrell and Amy W. Goodwin, "*The Clerk's Tale,*" pp. 102–67.

Neither the preface to Bryan and Dempster's 1941 *Sources and Analogues of Chaucer's Canterbury Tales,* nor that to Correale and Hamel's 2002 *Sources and Analogues of the Canterbury Tales,* nor the draft "Guide for Contributors to the Sources and Analogues Project," which was issued in the early 1990s, defines what a source is. Rather, they all assume a stereotypical definition. The absence of a clearly stated definition makes it possible for a source to be defined variously by the kinds of evidence each chapter on a particular tale provides. Both prefaces explain the inclusion or exclusion of material in terms of the purpose of the volumes, purposes that are identical in important respects: W. F. Bryan writes, "The purpose is to present in so far as possible the sources of the *Canterbury Tales* as Chaucer knew these sources or, where the direct sources are not now known, to present the closest analogues in the form in which Chaucer presumably may have been acquainted with them."[3] Because the volume aims to provide material "significant in the study of Chaucer's use of his sources, remote analogues and late derivative versions have not been included." The contributors have kept "comment and discussion to the barest necessary minimum" because "the primary intent has been not to present a series of studies on Chaucer's sources but to present texts and thus to make readily accessible the material for the study of sources and influences."[4] Robert Correale writes that the purpose of the new *Sources and Analogues of the Canterbury Tales* "is essentially the same as that of its distinguished predecessor." The presentation of texts—updated editions, newly discovered manuscripts, newly discovered sources, and English translations—is its aim, "leaving questions of how [Chaucer] adapted [sources] for his own artistic purposes to be answered by literary critics."[5] In some sense, the new *Sources and Analogues,* like its predecessor, aims, generally, to present source texts that will themselves provide the evidence of Chaucer's indebtedness to them.

Some important pragmatic concerns guided the editorial practice of the new *Sources and Analogues.* All contributors were aware that the length of chapters would affect the cost of publication and the attractiveness of the project to a publisher. Until the meeting of the New Chaucer Society at the Sorbonne in July 1998, the question of who

---

[3] W. F. Bryan and Germaine Dempster, eds., *Sources and Analogues of Chaucer's Canterbury Tales* (Chicago: University of Chicago Press, 1941), p. vii.
[4] Ibid., pp. vii, viii.
[5] Correale and Hamel, *Sources and Analogues of the Canterbury Tales,* pp. vii, viii.

would publish the project was still somewhat up in the air. In the early 1990s progress reports on the chapters included word-count estimates on introductions, texts, and translations, although no limits were set for the chapters. At the New Chaucer Society Biennial Congress in Los Angeles in 1996, the contributing editors briefly discussed the possibility of publishing the work on the Internet and creating hypertexts. Although discarded, this idea sought a way to avoid the space limitations imposed by books. Another consideration had to do with the reception of the publication. From the beginning, the new sources and analogues project was conceived with the intention to create *"the* standard reference work on Chaucer's sources"; contributors, therefore, were to "be guided in their selection of sources and analogues by what they believe our specialized and general audiences would want and expect to find" in such a reference.[6] This general guide required some negotiations over assumptions about shared values among Chaucer scholars, but its aim was to advise caution in including texts whose relationship was contested in Chaucer studies.

Although the definition of a source in the new *Sources and Analogues of the Canterbury Tales* varies, in general, the work privileges source texts—texts from which Chaucer closely adapted or translated material for his own rendering of a tale—over sources of Chaucer's invention— texts that may have inspired Chaucer to inflect a tale in a particular way. Viewed with this distinction in mind, Boccaccio's and Philippe de Mézières's Griselda stories might be considered as sources of invention—though we might also assign these two works a more intermediate status, comparable to source understudies awaiting a particularly compelling argument that marshals more rhetorical and textual evidence of Chaucer's indebtedness to them. The category sources of invention may always have a marginal status because the more precise one can be about how a particular work influenced Chaucer's composition, the more likely it is that the particular work in question will jump categories into source texts—as Boccaccio's *Decameron* has done as a result of Helen Cooper's argument in "The Frame."

But sources of invention can also be a permanent category for some kinds of texts. For example, Aristotle's influence on Chaucer's rendering of *The Clerk's Tale*—if such an influence could be shown—might always

---

[6] "Guide for Contributors to the Sources and Analogues Project (Draft Only)," item 12, p. 3.

be a source of invention rather than a source text. Although there seem to be no passages in *The Clerk's Tale* that Chaucer translated from any of Aristotle's works, the Clerk's portrait linking the Clerk with the study of logic and twenty books of Aristotle invites us to look for an Aristotelian influence. How such an influence might be detected and what it might signify are questions that have been explored but not fully answered.[7] One obvious place to look would be in Chaucer's additions, specifically, the Clerk's commentary, to see if his judgments and observations reflect some kind of pattern of deliberation identifiably Aristotelian. Boccaccio's allusions to the *Nicomachean Ethics* in the frame of his Griselda story and Petrarch's elimination of them in his own Latin rendering make the pursuit of Chaucer's reference to Aristotle significant for our understanding not just of how the works of Aristotle were transmitted in the vernacular but also of how Chaucer may have read his source texts. Our definitions of sources—source texts and sources of invention—need to be flexible enough to capture the nimbleness with which they were used.

---

[7] Some scholars have identified works by Aristotle taught in the Oxford curriculum to argue that the tale represents a logician's rebuttal to *The Wife of Bath's Prologue*. See, for example, Joseph Grennen, "Science and Sensibility in Chaucer's Clerk," *ChauR* 6 (1971–72): 81–93; and Jerome Taylor, "Frounceys Petrak and the Logyk of Chaucer's Clerk," *Francis Petrarch, Six Centuries Later*, ed. Aldo Scaglione (Chapel Hill: University of North Carolina Press, 1975), pp. 364–83. Glending Olson has argued that the *Nicomachean Ethics* sheds light on the notion of appropriate play within the *Canterbury Tales* and specifically in *The Clerk's Prologue*. See his "Rhetorical Circumstances and the Canterbury Storytelling," *SAC: Proceedings* 1 (1984): 211–18.

Proverb Tradition as a Soft Source for the *Canterbury Tales*

Nancy Mason Bradbury
Smith College

THE ORIGINAL CALL FOR PAPERS posed to this panel a series of questions, among them, whether our discipline sustains "a hierarchy of sources, privileging textual over visual, written over oral, Latin over English, 'hard' over 'soft.'" In this brief essay, I use the example of proverb tradition to reflect on the largely unexplored potential of the "soft source" to serve as a middle term between, at one extreme, the privileging of empirically demonstrable "hard sources" over all other kinds of textual relations, and, at the other, the rejection of traditional source study altogether on the postmodernist grounds that one vast intertext connects all texts equally. As the first new *Sources and Analogues* volume and the contributions to this symposium demonstrate, between these poles lies a whole spectrum of fresh approaches to the study of Chaucer's raw materials.[1]

In the second paper of this symposium, Peter G. Beidler suggests that we distinguish between a *hard source,* "a specific work for which we have an extant copy and that we know, from verbal similarities, character names, and plot sequences, that Chaucer used," and a *soft source,* for which Chaucer's knowledge of the material is not in question, but where the influence on his work may be more "general" or "distant." Beidler's hard source is familiar to us all from centuries of source study: a traditional source text must be temporally prior, accessible to the writer in question, and demonstrably influential on his or her work, the ideal form of evidence being close and extended verbal parallels. Boccaccio's *Teseida* is a recognized hard source for *The Knight's Tale.* As I propose to use the term, however, what best distinguishes a soft source is not that

---

[1] Robert M. Correale and Mary Hamel, eds. *Sources and Analogues of the Canterbury Tales,* vol. 1 (Woodbridge, Suffolk, and Rochester, N.Y.: D. S. Brewer, 2002).

its influence on Chaucer's work is general or distant, but rather that it need not be a single written text. A soft source might be a pictorial image, cultural practice, oral tradition, set of conventions, or real event, but the soft source as I conceive of it leaves a distinct verbal imprint on the work in question to indicate its special relevance. In the absence of this distinct imprint, I see little benefit in treating the material as a *source* at all, as opposed to a context or background or other "general" or "distant" influence. By admitting that it is not hard, my proposed soft source acknowledges the traditional criteria for source study, but, as a source, it nevertheless takes its place among the identifiable materials out of which Chaucer crafted his work.

In answer to the question with which I began—do hard, single-text sources stand in hierarchical relation to soft in contemporary Chaucer studies?—I can only say that for myself and a number of other participants in this symposium, it is the so-called soft sources that at this moment seem to present the freshest and most promising new ways of thinking about the poet's raw materials. Traditional source study has been devoted disproportionately, it now seems, to mapping Chaucer's reception of major literary texts. Rather than pitting soft against hard or traditional sources, however, or debating about terminology, I want instead to sketch out the case for the importance of a particular source. Soft sources are often ill-suited to representation in *Sources and Analogues* volumes; the tale-by-tale organization of both the old and the new editions makes it hard to register even so vastly influential a soft source as medieval proverb tradition, the example to which I devote my essay.

Why proverb tradition? Proverbs play a variety of important roles in the *Canterbury Tales*.[2] They are affirmed, denied, revered, ridiculed, and ignored at one's peril; they occur in nearly every tale, and even their absence can be significant. Many scholars regard the *Thopas-Melibee* pair-

---

[2] Studies of individual proverbs in Chaucer are not uncommon, but efforts to generalize about their literary and cultural work are scarce. A dramatic plea for the centrality of proverbs to premodern thought is Betsy Bowden, "A Modest Proposal, Relating Four Millennia of Proverb Collections to Chemistry Within the Human Brain," *Journal of American Folklore* 109 (1996): 440–49. Two recent articles that attempt a larger perspective on proverb use in Chaucer appeared in *Oral Tradition* 17 (2002): Betsy Bowden, "Ubiquitous Format? What Ubiquitous Format? Chaucer's *Tale of Melibee* as a Proverb Collection, " 169–207, and Nancy Mason Bradbury, "Transforming Experience into Tradition: Two Theories of Proverb Use and Chaucer's Practice," 261–89. See also Barry Taylor, "Medieval Proverb Collections: The West European Tradition," *Journal of the Warburg and Courtauld Institutes* 55 (1992): 19–31; Stephen D. Winick, "Proverbial Strategy and Proverbial Wisdom in *The Canterbury Tales*," *Proverbium* 11 (1994): 259–81; and Cameron Louis, "The Concept of the Proverb in Middle English," *Proverbium* 14 (1997): 173–85.

ing as somehow indicative of Chaucer's central literary concerns, and thus it is striking that *Sir Thopas*, arguably the one tale with no proverbial wisdom whatsoever, is balanced against *Melibee*, which is made up of little else. In *The Nun's Priest's Tale*, also regularly cited as a key to Chaucerian poetics, proverbs are plentiful, playful, and highly significant. Throughout the *Canterbury Tales*, the poet-narrator and his fellow pilgrims not only use but call attention to proverbs, and from the earliest extant manuscripts onward, copyists and editors have further emphasized them by inserting such marginalia as attributions to sources, Latin equivalents, pointing hands, and annotations that include *nota*, *proverbe*, and *proverbium*. The difference between our view of the proverb and that of Chaucer and his audiences is thrown into relief when we read that John Lydgate admired Chaucer's skill in amplifying his works "With many proverbs diverse and unkouthe."[3] Lydgate's delight in "unkouthe" proverbs reminds us that one of the pleasures of literature for premodern audiences was the discovery of unfamiliar proverbial expressions. In the preface to his 1598 edition, Thomas Speght apologized for his failure to mark Chaucer's "sentences," which consequently "must be left to the research of the Reader," a telling remark about what he assumed readers would *do* with Chaucer's text.[4] If we are interested in how Chaucer's contemporaries might have thought about sources, it is worth noting that the large majority of his readers and listeners would never have encountered Boccaccio's *Teseida*, let alone placed it beside *The Knight's Tale* for parallel reading. These contemporaries have, however, left us the tangible marks of their exceptional interest in a particular type of cultural material that existed long before *The Knight's Tale* and left a distinct and recognizable verbal imprint on it—the tale's many proverbs.

Few contemporary Chaucerians remain interested in source hunting for its own sake, and what interests me is how different kinds of raw materials are reshaped and interact within Chaucer's texts. In *The Knight's Tale*, to stay with the same example, Palamon escapes from prison and finds himself "by aventure" in the same shrubbery with one

---

[3] John Lydgate, *Siege of Thebes,* ed. Robert R. Edwards (Kalamazoo: Western Michigan University, 2001), Prologue, 51.
[4] The title page of Speght's second edition (1602) advertises that he has remedied the omission: "Sentences and Prouerbes noted." See Derek Pearsall, "Thomas Speght," in Paul G. Ruggiers, ed., *Editing Chaucer: The Great Tradition* (Norman, Okla.: Pilgrim Books, 1984), pp. 73, 85.

of the very few persons in Athens he knows, his cousin and now bitter rival, Arcite (I.1462–527). The Palemone of Boccaccio's *Teseida* simply goes to that particular grove because he has been told that Arcita will be there.[5] Thus our knowledge of the hard source, the *Teseida*, shows us that Chaucer created this extraordinary coincidence deliberately, presumably to further the tale's powerful questioning of the forces that control human events and the degree to which a mortal can believe those forces to be benevolent. It is interesting to me that Chaucer rushes into the gap created by this deliberate departure from Boccaccio's plot line with four traditional English proverbs, all spoken by the narrating Knight. Three of them ostensibly apologize for the coincidence[6]: "al day meeteth men at unset stevene"(I.1524), "Selde is the Friday al the wowke ylike"(I.1539), and "Yet somtyme it shal fallen on a day / That falleth nat eft withinne a thousand yeer"(1668–69).[7] Yet even as these pieces of familiar proverbial wisdom appear to normalize the coincidence and to reassure the reader about the "unset stevene" that brings these knights together, they in fact make its implications all the more unsettling by revealing that what is "normal" for mortals is instability and total ignorance of the working of cosmic forces. A fourth expression, "feeld hath eyen and the wode hath eres"(I.1522), also warns of a deeply hostile world; in this case, one in which spies watch us in the open and eavesdroppers overhear us if we take cover.[8] This kind of rapid shift, from hard to soft sources, from one discourse to another, from Boccac-

---

[5] *Teseida delle nozze d'Emilia*, ed. A. Limentani, in *Tutte le opere di Giovanni Boccaccio*, ed. Vittore Branca (Milan: Mondadori, 1964–83), 2:384–89 (book 5, stanzas 6, 22).

[6] In " 'Sentence' and 'Solaas': Proverbs and Consolation in the *Knight's Tale*" (*ChauR* 22 [1987]: 100–101), Thomas Luxon notes that the proverbial expressions in I.1539 and I.1668–69 seek to normalize what appear to be extraordinary coincidences. Winick (see note 2 above) assigns the same function to those in I.1466 and 1524 (p. 267). Luxon and Winick stress the value of "conventional wisdom" in apologizing for what might otherwise seem a defect in Chaucer's plot, but neither relates this dense outbreak of English proverbs to his deliberate and problematic deviation from the plot of the *Teseida*.

[7] Bartlett Jere Whiting and Helen Whiting index the expression in I.1524 as M210 in *Proverbs, Sentences, and Proverbial Phrases Mainly Before 1500* (Cambridge, Mass.: Harvard University Press, 1968). Whiting cites an earlier instance of this expression (c. 1350) and one that is roughly contemporary (c. 1390). Chaucer's is the only medieval instance cited for the expression in I.1539 (Whiting F622), but *The Riverside Chaucer* (I.1539n) offers a reference in support of the idea that Fridays were held to be unpredictable in "proverbial and folk wisdom." For the English expression in 1668–69, Whiting offers a related expression from c. 1250 and a citation from a proverb collection of 1450 (D56).

[8] A citation in English and Latin from a proverb collection of c. 1300 attests to the proverbial status of the expression in I.1522 (Whiting F127).

cio's epic-philosophic poem of chivalry to homely English proverb tradition, is everywhere in the *Canterbury Tales,* a vital part of its larger dynamic of juxtaposing rival discourses and traditions.

Even if we grant its importance as an influence, why treat proverb tradition as a *source?* Many of Chaucer's fictional tellers, including the Man of Law, the Wife of Bath, and the Clerk, imply or insist that where the story comes from is part of the story. The same may be true for some of the smaller and less well-documented genres represented in the *Canterbury Tales,* including proverbs, riddles, charms, local legends, and folktales. Scholars have spent centuries mapping Chaucer's reception of his hard sources—the majority of them prestigious canonical texts. Yet one of the ideas that energizes the *Canterbury Tales* is that these received literary models can give only an incomplete picture of life in the body and in the world; old books become even richer and more rewarding when their representations are complemented or contested by other, less authoritative, kinds of cultural materials. Although many of these preexisting verbal forms cannot be traced to single hard literary sources, these soft materials are also recognizable as having led a separate life outside and prior to their appropriation into the *Canterbury Tales,* and, by the very logic of the work itself, merit our attention as well. Proverbs are a crucial instance of Chaucer's quoting behavior. Their influence is readily apparent in innumerable individual lines; it is neither general nor distant. Finally, as this symposium's title reminds us, traditional source study has been the object of a vigorous critique that charges it with a nostalgic desire for origins that are alleged to be ultimately illusory.[9] Including medieval proverb tradition among Chaucer's sources is one kind of response to this too-sweeping dismissal: proverb tradition is a huge, international, and now only partially extant complex of widely circulating expressions, and no scholar is likely to be accused of believing that the mystical originary moment of the *Canterbury Tales* can be found there. Although I recall hearing at a New Chaucer Society Congress about ten or twelve years ago that Chaucerian source study was dead, in fact the informal contributions to this panel and the vast scholarship in the new *Sources and Analogues* volumes demonstrate that sources still have a significant role to play in Chaucer studies—source study still has a life, not just an afterlife.

---

[9] Allen J. Frantzen provides an overview of the postmodern critique of the myth of origins drawn mainly from the works of Derrida, Foucault, and Said in the first chapter of his *Desire for Origins: New Language, Old English, and Teaching the Tradition* (New Brunswick, N.J.: Rutgers University Press, 1990).

In the flurry of electronic messages that preceded our session at the 2004 Glasgow Congress, a fellow panelist confessed her inability to dissociate the adjectives *hard* and *soft* from the boiling of eggs. The image of eggs led me to think in turn of the bitter religious controversy in *Gulliver's Travels* between those who break their eggs at the big and at the small ends. To privilege traditional hard sources over other kinds is to risk siding with the Big-Endians, who held without reflection to the ancient traditions of their fathers. By rejecting as illusory any search for origins, the Little-Endians have created wars and schisms, and, for once, Gulliver hardly exaggerates when he reports that "Many hundred large volumes have been published upon this controversy"(Bk. I, chap. 4). Swift has Gulliver opt for religious pluralism: in his view, the choice of ends should be left to the individual conscience. My argument is similar: in source study, pluralism, both of methods and of materials, has more to offer us than polarization.

The Alchemy of Imagination and the Labyrinth of Meaning:

Some Caveats About the Afterlife of Sources

Carolyn P. Collette
Mount Holyoke College

I N *THE NAME OF THE ROSE*, Umberto Eco constructs the library at the heart of the monastery as a labyrinth, a structural symbol of his theory of literary semiotics. The labyrinth, a figure he explicates in *A Theory of Semiotics* and in *Postscript to the Name of the Rose*, represents the tortuous and essentially independent paths that individuals trace in their apprehension and creation of meaning in response to verbal signs: "Like a large labyrinthine garden, a work of art permits one to take many different routes, whose number is increased by the criss-cross of its paths."[1] In the *Postscript*, he distinguishes among types of labyrinths, identifying the rhizome pattern as the one William of Baskerville (like the reader) encounters: "The rhizome is so constructed that every path can be connected with every other one. It has no center, no periphery, no exit, because it is potentially infinite."[2] He goes on, "The space of conjecture is a rhizome space . . . the world in which William realizes he is living . . . has a rhizome structure: that is, it can be structured but is never structured definitively."[3]

The rhizome labyrinth's indefinite structure is the labyrinth Vincent DiMarco and I entered when we began our research on the sources and analogues of *The Canon's Yeoman's Tale*. The tale is famously one without known sources, but it exists within a tradition of Chaucer's close familiarity with alchemy and a plenitude of contemporary alchemical materi-

---

[1] Umberto Eco, *A Theory of Semiotics* (Bloomington: Indiana University Press, 1976), p. 275.
[2] Umberto Eco, *Postscript to the Name of the Rose,* trans. William Weaver (New York: Harcourt, Brace, 1983), p. 57.
[3] Eco, *Postscript,* p. 58.

als that provide a contextual labyrinth of the sort Eco describes: one that can be structured, but never structured definitively. To compound the difficulty, the discourse of alchemy is without a center or a periphery; endlessly self-reflexive, it correlates to no clear external signifiers or interpretants. For Chaucer to use such a discourse means that he engaged in the dual conversation that, Eco maintains, all authors who work with source materials create. A writer creating a work creates two conversations. First, the text that is being written is in dialogue with "all other previously written texts" and, second, the author is in dialogue with a model reader.[4] Chaucer's work seems to offer a textbook example of these precepts. *The Canon's Yeoman's Tale* is indeed in dialogue with multiple previously written texts, and, at the same time, Chaucer alludes to, draws on, and hints at his sources in a way that assumes a model reader, one adept enough to grasp the structure of his labyrinth with its copious verbal crisscrossing paths.

The difficulty, of course, is in our coming "after." The afterlife of the sources and the analogues the poet alludes to is shadowy at best; trying to track them, we enter a labyrinth where even the paths are not clear, the location of a center unsure, and all conclusions are debatable. We know that Chaucer drew on material for the tale, that he did not create it wholly from his imagination. We know from the way that the tale is composed that he plays with the discourse of alchemy, as Lee Patterson and others have shown, and that the cadencing, the lists, the rhythms of the tale bring poetry and meaning out of arcane materials and conventions.[5] Yet neither Part 1 nor Part 2, as a whole, has been linked to definitive antecedents. A strong modern critical tradition holds that the tale is Chaucer's disparagement of an art that he found false. A more venerable tradition of Chaucer as an alchemical adept began as early as the fifteenth century, when Thomas Norton cited Chaucer's alchemical wisdom in the *Ordinal*; this tradition flourished in the seventeenth century in conjunction with the story that Gower, whose alchemical writings are extensive and informed, served as Chaucer's teacher in the art.

What Vince DiMarco and I discovered is that "sources" for the tale indeed abound in the literary and cultural milieu of Chaucer's world, but that they do not fit neatly into categories like "hard" or "soft" sources or analogues. We discovered a host of alchemical references in

---

[4] Ibid., p. 47.
[5] Lee Patterson, "Perpetual Motion: Alchemy and the Technology of the Self," *SAC* 15 (1993): 25–57.

the English literature of the fourteenth and fifteenth centuries, as well as many textual antecedents/sources for parts of the first part of the tale, in various languages. More unexpectedly, we discovered that Chaucer's roots in the city of London are reflected in the tale, both in the casual mention of assaying the "silver" found in the bottom of the crosslet at a local goldsmith's shop and in a series of injunctions the goldsmiths of Chaucer's time had promulgated in order to maintain their reputation for honesty. Dorothy Waley Singer's early twentieth-century work documents a thriving trade and interest in alchemy in London.[6] Christine de Pizan and Bernard of Treves both refer—with different degrees of approbation—to Christine's father, close adviser to Charles V, and his interest in alchemy. Finally, Chaucer's French contemporary Philippe de Mézières used alchemical metaphors as the major structural figures of his *Songe du Vieil Pelerin*, a work of social criticism.[7] None of these is a source, or even an analogue, but all help us to trace the labyrinthine paths that lead to understanding the tale. In this case the cultural matrix in which the tale was created and to which it contributed emerges as an essential heuristic tool.

Synchronic models of "source study" using theories of semiotics and discourse communities to identify the *sociolect* of a group or subculture may be much more useful than the more diachronically-based models of originary paradigms. In *Interpretation and Overinterpretation*, Eco observes,

when a text is produced not for a single addressee but for a community of readers—the author knows that he or she will be interpreted not according to his or her intentions but according to a complex strategy of interactions which also involves the readers, along with their competence in language as a social treasury . . . the whole encyclopedia that the performances of that language has implemented, namely, the cultural conventions that that language has produced and the very history of the previous interpretations of many texts, comprehending the text that the reader is in the course of reading.[8]

[6] Dorothea Waley Singer, *Catalogue of Latin and Vernacular Alchemical Manuscripts in Great Britain and Ireland Dating from before the XVI Century*, 3 vols. (Brussels: M. Lamertin, 1928–31).

[7] On the thematic connections between this text and Chaucer's work, see Carolyn Collette, "Reading Chaucer through Philippe de Mézières: Alchemy, the Individual, and the Good Society," *Courtly Literature and Clerical Culture*, ed. Christoph Huber and Henrike Lähnemann (Tübingen: Attempto Verlag, 2002), pp. 177–94.

[8] *Interpretation and Overinterpretation: Umberto Eco with Richard Rorty, Jonathan Culler, Christine Brooke-Rose*, ed. Stefan Collini (Cambridge: Cambridge University Press, 1992), pp. 67–68.

Understanding the reception of Chaucer's tale within such a paradigm of successive and continual interpretation is crucial to identifying the field of its sources and analogues. The problem lies in being sure that in the textual labyrinth with all its crisscrossing, we can determine the right way to hear Chaucer's own conversation with his sources.

In this matter a degree of caution is always in order, no matter how definite a source may be. We may be able to identify a particular source, but we will never be able to read it in the context of the labyrinth of Chaucer's culture. We create approximations, inferences, and likely contexts. In the oral version of this essay at the 2004 NCS conference, I tried to make this point by using the following anecdote. In the spring of 2003, after the invasion of Iraq, and after a year and a half of national anxiety about terrorism, President George W. Bush landed a jet on the deck of the aircraft carrier USS *Abraham Lincoln*, off the coast of California, and, welcomed enthusiastically as a hero, strode across the flight deck to address the nation under a banner proclaiming "Mission Accomplished." Such a staged performance undoubtedly drew on sources. We could speculate on what might have influenced him and his advisers to create such a theatrical moment and arrive at very different conclusions. Watching the movie *Independence Day* on July 4, 2004, I developed a sense of certainty that the movie is one of the best "sources" for understanding that moment on the aircraft carrier, although the film probably had nothing to do with that staging. Or did it? The movie *Independence Day* appeared late in the first Clinton administration, and featured a young president, an aviator by training, who dons a flight suit and flies out to defeat the aliens threatening to destroy the earth. His victorious return, represented in the film by a brief shot of him striding down the tarmac of a landing strip dressed in his flight suit, bears an uncanny relationship to Bush's moment of triumph on the deck of the aircraft carrier.[9] Is it a source? Not really. Might it become a "source," say, in a hundred years or so? Yes, I think so. Although it is a visual not a textual source, the semiotic dimension of the event on the *Abraham Lincoln* draws on the "encyclopedia of performances," the "cultural conventions" of heroism, victory, and leadership that provide both a common store of signs and a store of shared interpretants for our culture. While neither Bush nor his advisers may have even thought of

[9] On the politics of the film and the Clinton administration, see Michael Rogin, *Independence Day, or How I Learned to Stop Worrying and Love the Enola Gay* (London: British Film Institute Publishing, 1998).

Independence Day during their planning, the film helps place the event on the *Abraham Lincoln* within the context of late twentieth-century American popular culture. In a similar way Chaucer's imagination may have created, and his audience may have received, *The Canon's Yeoman's Tale* in response to a series of popular "sources" lost to us in another culture that lacks the "social treasury" of his time.

Reading sources this way constructs a Chaucer quite different from the figure who has dominated Chaucer studies for the last hundred years. No longer the isolated genius, the seminal father-figure who saw further and more clearly than any of his contemporaries the potential of the English language, he emerges as less solitary in his genius, more social, communal, shaped by and shaping the cultural paradigms of his time and later. It also means that we must add a third dialogue to Eco's list: in addition to the conversation an author may have with his sources and his readers, we add the conversation he is part of in the intellectual world he inhabits.

The broader implications of what we found and the questions raised by this particular tale go to the reshaping of the concept of sources and analogues. At an editorial meeting for the new sources and analogues project in Boulder, Derek Brewer observed that each generation of Chaucerians will make its own sources and analogues. The new volumes reflect our current interest in what a previous generation may have termed *analogues*, the verbal echoes, structural parallels, similarities of theme and phrase that occur within a range of time that does not necessarily predate the composition of Chaucer's work. Serious efforts to ensure that representation of the field of thought in which the tales take their place has produced a new concept of sources and analogues that hearkens back to Eliot's notion of tradition and the individual talent: each new work is shaped by and in turn shapes the tradition into which it enters. As critics, we will live with a more open conception of connections and affinities than a previous generation of Chaucerians felt comfortable with or needed.

In addition, this new way of thinking about sources opens a space for considering the role of the critic in establishing connections. We know that Chaucer frequently made use of specific texts that he identifies as his sources. But he often makes subtle changes in the tone or content of such sources, as with *The Clerk's Tale* and its ending, or in his re-creation of Criseyde. As a result, even when we think we are certain, we find ourselves laboring to trace the labyrinthine paths of Chaucer's literary imagination. Although we can make informed, shrewd, and sometimes inspired guesses, we cannot know for sure how Chaucer's imagination worked in adapting, echoing, and answering the texts he encountered. Trying to do so inevitably privileges the critic as the *vates*, the mediator. When we talk about identifying Chaucer's sources, are we not talking about tracing the roots of imagination? And do not our own imaginations become surrogates for Chaucer's? Constructing evanescent links, recording the firing of synapses is impossible. And we are dealing with the world of semiotics—where signs evoke both shared and idiosyncratic series of signifieds. That means we must live with indeterminacy and uncertainty about sources. Somewhere in the background of *The Canon's Yeoman's Tale* for an artist like Chaucer, living in the city of London, the city and its inhabitants, his reading, his colleagues and their shared culture all become part of the sources of his art. There is no way to trace or document this fact. And so we say the tale has no sources.

The "Buried Bodies" of Dante, Boccaccio, and Petrarch:

Chaucerian "Sources" for the Critical Fiction of Obedient Wives

Dolores Warwick Frese
University of Notre Dame

V ERIFYING A SOURCE, as Peter Beidler's useful taxonomy of terms makes clear, can sometimes resemble the vain attempt that seeks "in a net . . . to hold the wind."[1] In the present argument for an archaeology of sources explicitly and implicitly conserved in Chaucer's *Clerk's Tale,* where the "afterlife of origins" can be seen to disclose at least three levels of textual substrate,[2] I suggest a way in which we might move beyond the narrator's explicit naming in *The Clerk's Prologue* of his ("hard") Latin source—"Fraunceys Petrak, the lauriat poete" of Italy (IV.29, 31).[3] Behind the linguistic screen of Petrarch's Latin translation of the *Decameron*'s final fiction[4] and—after his aggressive[5] linguistic

---

[1] For Beidler's taxonomy of terms, see the second paper in this symposium. The metaphoric analogue is from Wyatt's Petrarchan sonnet #7.

[2] A much earlier version of my ensuing argument for Petrarch (explicit), Boccaccio (implicit), and Dante (subliminal) as operative "source" texts for Chaucer's *Clerk's Tale* was presented as "Three Men and a Baby: Boccaccio, Petrarch, Chaucer, and the Making of Patient Griselda," the Grellet-Simpson Lecture in Medieval Literature, Mary Washington College, Fredericksburg, Virginia, 1995.

[3] All quotations from the *Canterbury Tales* are taken from *The Riverside Chaucer,* 3rd ed., gen. ed. Larry D. Benson (Boston: Houghton Mifflin, 1987).

[4] For the Italian text of *Decameron* X.x, with facing page text of Petrarch's Latin translation, see *La novella di Griselda fra Boccaccio e Petrarca,* ed., Luca Carlo Rossi (Palermo: Sellerio editore, 1991); for the Modern English translation, see Giovanni Boccaccio, *Decameron, The John Payne Translation Revised and Annotated by Charles S. Singleton* (hereafter, *Decameron*) (Berkeley and Los Angeles: University of California Press, 1982), vol. 2.

[5] David Wallace, *Chaucerian Polity: Absolutist Lineages and Associational Forms in England and Italy* (Stanford: Stanford University Press, 1997), pp. 277 and 467 n. 74, notes Petrarch's telling characterization of his Latin translation as an "attack" or act of aggression against Boccaccio's work: *"ystoriam ipsam tuam scribere sum aggressus."*

move against a tale that celebrates and valorizes the Italian vernacular—on through Chaucer's brilliant "re-veiling" of the vernacular bride
in rime-royal English stanzas for his version of the Griselda story, we
can still detect the warm breath of Boccaccio.[6] In this brief essay, I try
out a conception of source study broad enough to encompass not just
influential texts by Dante, Petrarch, and Boccaccio, but also radical cultural ideas—including, in the case of *The Clerk's Tale,* the idea of choosing the vernacular as a medium for literature of lasting value.

This process of linguistic and epistemological rerouting constitutes a
move, I suggest, that Chaucer implicitly acknowledges, knowingly
adopts, poetically interrogates, and conclusively subverts through the
winding course of *The Clerk's Prologue* and *Tale.* Peaking in the final
rime-royal stanza (lines 1170–76), which bridges the tale proper to the
Lenvoy de Chaucer with which it playfully concludes—noting that "Gris-
ilde is deed, and eek hire pacience, / And both atones buryed in Ytaille"
(lines 1177–78)—*The Clerk's Tale* finally gives up one of its carefully
guarded "underground" sources by the surprising disclosure of an influential name: not that of Boccaccio, but the Wife of Bath (1170). For
English Alys and Italian Griselda, expressly paired in this revealing act
of poetic *bravura,* both claim descent from Dante's influential treatise
on vernacular eloquence,[7] which sets forth with striking specificity the
terms for their respective fictional instantiations as exemplars of the
Mother Tongue.[8] Although many examples could be adduced in support
of my proposition, I shall limit myself to two: the source as metaphorical
underground spring, and the elegant clothing of the word as well as the
bride, along with her "surrendered" and "restored" progeny.

---

[6] For the growing consensus that Boccaccio's Italian *Decameron* is a text that Chaucer
must, in fact, have known, see, for example, Helen Cooper, "The Frame," in *Sources and
Analogues of the Canterbury Tales,* vol. 1, ed. Robert M. Correale and Mary Hamel (Cambridge: D. S. Brewer, 2003), pp. 7–13; John Finlayson, "Petrarch, Boccaccio, and Chaucer's *Clerk's Tale*," *SP* 97 (2000), 255–75; Wallace, *Chaucerian Polity,* pp. 277–94;
Warren Ginsberg, *Chaucer's Italian Tradition* (Ann Arbor: University of Michigan Press,
2002), esp. chaps. 4, 6, and 7.

[7] *De vulgari eloquentia,* a cura di Pier Vincenzo Mengaldo, "Introduzione e Testo"
(Padua: Editrice Antenore, 1968). For English translation and commentary, see Mari-
anne Shapiro, *De vulgari eloquentia: Dante's Book of Exile* (Lincoln: University of Nebraska
Press, 1990).

[8] For the Wife of Bath as "Mother Tongue," see R. W. Hanning, "'And countrefete
the speche of every man / He koude, whan he sholde telle a tale'": Toward a Lapsarian
Poetics for *The Canterbury Tales*," *SAC* 21 (1999): 56. I had earlier employed the same
nomenclature, making the same connection to *De vulgari,* in "Dante in Drag," a paper
presented to the Biennial Chaucer Congress, Los Angeles, 1996, in a session on "Cross
Dressing in the Middle Ages."

Source, Spring, Stream, and River

What, then, constitutes a source for Chaucer? To begin answering this question, we could do worse than approaching his own account of "sources" inscribed into the *Clerk's Prologue,* where the above noted textual genealogy of Petrarch's *Insignis obedientia et fides uxoria,*[9] cited as a "hard source" for the tale of Griselda, merges with a fluid description of the River Po's course through the Italian landscape: "Where as the Poo out of a wele smale / Taketh his firste spryngyng and his sours" (lines 48–49), thence to be swollen, in its "estward" movement toward the rising sun (line 50), by tributaries that combine to form the great watercourse whose masculine naming by Virgil as "the King of rivers" [*a Virgilio rex dictus*] Petrarch approvingly cites.[10] But this description of territory delineated by the Po, which the Clerk identifies as Petrarch's own "prohemye" (line 43) to the tale of the "obedient and faithful wife" translated into Latin, reproduces a highly specific terrain memorialized previously by Dante as he maps, admires, sifts, mocks, praises, and rejects a proliferating variety of Italian dialects in his search for truly eloquent vernacular usage, the language, as he notes, that we take in as eagerly and easily as our mother's milk, which marks the time of its effortless infant acquisition.[11]

Accordingly, when Petrarch revisits the Dantesque course of the Po to authorize his retranslation-into-Latin of Boccaccio's supreme fiction valorizing the vernacular's patient and enduring triumph, that decision considerably complicates the Clerk's subsequent one to redact—and then dismiss—this "prohemye" (line 43) or "proem" as "a thing impertinent" (line 54). While the Italian landscape certainly does "not pertain" to the Canterbury itinerary of Chaucer's English vernacular project, the Clerk's choice words simultaneously pronounce an implicit judgment of "impertinence" on Petrarch's attempted erasure of Boccaccio's undertaking, along with Dante's status therein as the never-named but clearly discernable source of inspiration for the narrative plot and governing tropes of *Decameron* X.x, several of which I examine below.

---

[9] For Petrarch's Latin text, including accompanying letters (*Epistolae Seniles* XVII.3) sent to Boccaccio in connection with the translation of *Decameron* X.x into Latin, see Thomas J. Farrell, ed. and trans., "The Griselda Story in Italy," in Correale and Hamel, *Sources and Analogues of the Canterbury Tales,* pp. 108–39.

[10] Ibid., pp. 110–11.

[11] *De vulgari,* I.i, 1–2 and I.x, 3–7.

Chaucer's adoption and critique of Petrarch's "source study" of the River Po thus forms a blazon for contested vernacular turf whose linguistic and literary course, as mapped by Dante, undergirds the original "making" and subsequent "taking" of Boccaccio's Griselda as an instantiation of the Mother Tongue, and also governs core issues of contention in the Chaucerian making of Alys of Bath.

Metaphorically and metonymically, Boccaccio's originary fiction— the "small, springing well and source"—has been swallowed by the swelling tributaries that constitute Petrarch's and Chaucer's confluent versions of the story. The Clerk's bold critique of Petrarch's "impertinent" geomythic move thus supplies an initial gesture implying knowledge and understanding of "vernacular source" as fundamental to the meaning of the tale he tells, whether or not he appreciates Dante's treatise as the deep "welle" whose hidden streams continue to course through the Latin redaction of Petrarch's proem that he puts into English rhymed couplets.[12] Note as well that Boccaccio's own concluding *Decameron* fiction never rises to the explicit naming of Dante as its imaginative source, though that tale's inventive virtuosities follow the luminescent trace of *De vulgari* closely in bringing forth Gris-elda / "Old Grey" / the ancient mother tongue, "tried" and proven "true," likewise animating Chaucer's rejuvenated "Old Hag," who repeatedly names Dante as the "source" of her sermonizing on "true nobility" in *The Wife of Bath's Tale* (lines 1125–64, esp. 1125–27).[13] This "nobility," as we will shortly see, has been assigned linguistic as well as moral grounds in Dante's poetic theorizing. Accordingly, *De vulgari*'s pungent insights concerning the "noble" mother tongue—like the elusive creature Dante claims metaphorically to be tracking throughout the opening chapters of this theoretical text—form an absent presence and present absence standing in for "that vernacular we have been hunting" throughout "the

---

[12] Chaucer's acquaintance with this same mythopoetic landscape is attested by its ingenious reinscription from Boccaccio in *The Knight's Tale* where the confluence of Italy and the Po [YPOLITA]; the "eastward" move "Emele-ward" to Emelia [EMELYE]; and the further path leading on to "Venyse" [VENUS] generate names for the fictional female presences. I have explored these and other cognate instances of nominal concealment, and the underlying poetics of indirection, in "The Names of Women in *The Canterbury Tales:* Chaucer's Hidden Art of Involucral Nomenclature," in Juliette Dor, ed., *A Wyf Ther Was: Essays in Honour of Paule Mertens-Fonck* (Liège: Liège Lang. and Lit., Dept. d'anglais, University de Liège, 1992), pp. 155–66.

[13] Although *Convivio* 5.15.19–38 supplies the direct "source" for the hag's "sermon" on nobility, Dante's valorization of the "mother tongue" as "the nobler" linguistic instantiation lies beneath, I am suggesting, as an operative textual substrate.

Italian woods."[14] This iterative trope of elusive hunting with which Dante opens the *De vulgari* thus constrains the signate behavior of inveterate "hunting" introduced at the outset of each writer's telling of this tale to characterize the "yonge lorde" Walter, Griselda's gratuitously "testing" husband.

"Marrying Up" and "Dressing Down"

Dante's treatise, written in Latin and valorizing eloquent vernacular usage, is dedicated to the proposition that a successful "marriage" of the "humble" mother tongue to the "noble" textual traditions of *Latinitas* is both possible and highly desirable. With a series of metaphoric installations—many of them quite striking and some of them, as I will show, ingeniously recuperated by Boccaccio, who appropriates these metaphors and then recasts their theoretical notions as fictionalized narrative events—Dante insists in *De vulgari* that mutual accommodation mandated for such "marital success" requires that the former *patois* of localized usage submit to the disciplinary strictures of grammatical study whose achievement of a stabilized linguistic medium, for example, Latin, has enabled the brilliant creation of classical exemplars. At the same time, learned exponents of *Latinitas* must acknowledge and incorporate into their own creative performance the native genius of the mother tongue, here made akin to divine inspiration by virtue of its effortless acquisition in infancy.[15]

After discriminating and characterizing grammatical Latin and native vernacular usage, Dante defends his intention to deal with "the nobler" vernacular, asserting that "of the two the nobler is the vernacular: first because it is the first language ever spoken by mankind; second because the whole world uses it though in diverse pronunciations and forms; finally because it is natural to us while the other is more the product of art. And I intend to deal with the nobler."[16] However surprising at first glance, it would appear that Dante's *De vulgari* first issues the "marriage license" for Walter's strict testing of Griselda, even as her absolute spousal compliance with this disciplinary regime is meant to certify linguisti-

---

[14] For Dante's sustained metaphorics of "hunting," see Shapiro trans., *De vulgari eloquentia*, pp. 58, 63–65, and 219 n. 68.

[15] *De vulgari* I.1.1 posits an association *ab initio* for the vernacular and "the heavenly Word" [*verbo aspirante de celis*]. See Mengaldo, ed., "Introduzione e Testo," p. 3, and Shapiro, trans., *De vulgari eloquentia*, p. 47.

[16] Shapiro, *De vulgari eloquentia*, pp. 47–48.

cally what most readers after Petrarch have always grasped as a core moral and/or psychological truth, to wit: the "worthiness" of peasant Griselda and her allegorically modeled "superiority" as the "nobler" partner in this surprising alliance.

Dante's "sourcebook" on vernacular eloquence not only supplies Boccaccio, and through him Petrarch and Chaucer, with essential tropes like "the hunt" and "the marriage" discussed above, and of Griselda's divestiture, nudity, and "reclothing" in "nobler" garb, to be noted below, but it also furnishes the overarching rationale for those extenuated trials and—in the case of Petrarch and Chaucer—the explicit thematics of "maternal suckling" that the Latin and English authors intrude consciously as a specific Dantesque embellishment[17] to mark the wrenching surrender of infant progeny, demanded by Walter and agreed to by Griselda at the precise moment of their weaning: "When the child had stopped nursing" [*cum iam ablactata infantula*] and "When the child stopped nursing after two years" [*quo nutricis ab uberte post biennium subducto*] for Petrarch; followed by Chaucer's equally lactic markers for the removal of the daughter and son ("Whan that this child had souked but a throwe" [450] and "Whan it was two yeer old, and fro the brest / Departed of his norice" [617–18]). As the offspring of this vexed marriage are given over to seeming death, we may thus note that the first, a ("vernacular") daughter, had been quickly conceived ("[n]at longe tyme after that this Grisild / Was wedded" [lines 442–43]), while the ("latinizing'") son's conception requires more time for its accomplishment ("In this estaat ther passed been foure yeer / Er she with childe was [lines 610–11]). In each instance, Walter's concealed patriarchal project will prove to have involved their aristocratic nurture at Bologna, preparing for the tale's final apotheosis of return and restitution to the belatedly honored maternal source. Indeed, at the outset of Griselda's marriage to Walter, Boccaccio signals that the vernacular stands as a source of inspiration for his inventive tale when the bride is stripped, then exhibited nude to the audience of nobles and peasants alike, prior to her wedding. This startling move is cognate with the one by which

---

[17] See Gary P. Cestaro, "The Primal Scene of Suckling in Dante's De vulgari eloquentia," *Dante Studies* 109 (1991): 121, where the icon of "a babe suckling at his mother's breast" is identified as lying at "the heart of metaphoric agency" in *De vulgari,* where "the several linguistic and historical propositions put forward in the treatise can all be shown to point to the powerful presence of this originary vignette in the poet's mind." See also Cestaro's *Dante and the Grammar of the Nursing Body* (Notre Dame: University of Notre Dame Press, 2003).

he puts the *Teseida* under the patronage of the "naked Muse" [*le Muse nude*], noting this "new age" of vernacular performance as the era when "the Muses began to walk unclothed before men's eyes."[18]

Petrarch, however, arguably aware of these linguistic and textual tropes in play between Dante's theorizing and Boccaccio's fictionalizing, but not supportive of the vernacular praxis they instantiate, declines absolutely to endorse, or promulgate without fundamental modification, an allegorical representation valorizing the ultimate triumph of the mother tongue, as the tale of Patient Griselda, installed as the culminating insignia of the *Decameron*'s cento of vernacular fictions, had done with such brilliance. The project of *Latinitas*[19] thus supplies the motive force for Petrarch's aggressive revisions that rechannel the signifying streams of Boccaccio's allegory of perfected vernacular emergence into the more rigid mold of traditional personification allegory. Newly sealed with a highly conventional *moralia* concerning "the soul's obedience to God under trial," Petrarch's "lord" [*dominus*], who is *Walterus,* becomes "Our Lord /God" [*deo nostro / deo*], and the "country wife/little woman" [*coniuge rusticana/ muliercula*], who is Griselda, becomes the reinscribed insignia for "the most steadfast of men" [*constantibus viris asscripserim*]. Boccaccio's Mother Tongue, cloaked in Latin, regendered as an emblem for the most steadfast of men [*constantibus viris*],[20] and returned to sender, dramatizes Petrarch's devastating resistance to Boccaccio's enthusiasm for Dante's project of cultivated vernacular eloquence. His specific reference to Boccaccio's tale "in the mother tongue" and his textually knowing act of "redress," whereby he sends Griselda back to her maker stripped of the vernacular and rewrapped in Latin with a mandated value judgment—["Whether the change of vestment has disfigured it or perhaps adorned it, you be the judge"][21]—indirectly convey Petrarch's awareness of Dante's theoretical work on the mother tongue, cognizance of its influential impression on Boccaccio, and a deliberate decision to contest that influence.

[18] For the "nude muse," see Giovanni Boccaccio, *Teseida XII,* 84–85, edizione Critica per cura di Salvatore Battaglia (Florence: G. C. Sansoni, Editore, 1938), p. 370; Bernadette Marie McCoy, trans., *The Book of Theseus: Teseida delle Nozze d'Emilia by Giovanni Boccaccio* (New York: Medieval Text Association, 1974), p. 328. Chaucer's "naked text in English to declare" (*The Legend of Good Women,* G Prol. 86) thus involves its vernacularity, not just its commonly assumed "unglossed" status.

[19] Wallace, *Chaucerian Polity,* pp. 262–67.

[20] Farrell, in Correal and Hamel, *Sources and Analogues of Chaucer's Canterbury Tales,* pp. 128–29.

[21] Ibid., pp. 110–11.

These running reflections on the "afterlife of origins" in Chaucer's *Clerk's Tale* do not propose to follow strictly in the steps of traditional "source study," attempting to "prove" with precision that Chaucer did, indeed, "know" and/or "use" any given text of the *Decameron* or of the *de Vulgari*, as "hard" or "soft" "source" or "analogue" while creating his own version of that collection's terminal tale for the Canterbury Clerk. In the end, such an undertaking, in effect, might well constitute an act of aesthetic exhumation uncomfortably similar to the Clerk's own ultimately dismissive gesture toward his named source, "Fraunceys Petrak, the lauriat poete," who "is now deed and nayled in his cheste" (*Clerk's Prologue*, line 31). Rather, in following the shadow of Dantesque meaning cast from between-the-lines of *Decameron* X, x, and in tracking the prey of sequent textual strands that continue—consciously or unconsciously—to bind these serial fictions to that surprisingly theoretical point of origin, I hope to have verified both the acuity of Chaucer's own aesthetic discernment and the continuing inventiveness with which his remarkable art maintains the play of spume between "hard" theory and creative praxis, between the commonality of residual source and the *sui generis* forms of poetic originality.

A Feel for the Game:

Bourdieu, Source Study, and the *Legend*

Betsy McCormick
Mount San Antonio College

S INCE CHAUCER INVARIABLY TRANSFORMS his literary sources as part of his "makyng," our reception history of those sources is as necessary to consider as is that of Chaucer and his audience. Do we as contemporary readers, or as critics, have the kind of knowledge and ease with Chaucer's sources to fully grasp the rhetorical play invoked in his "makyng"? Such ease lies in the realm Pierre Bourdieu has termed cultural capital, a form of intellectual currency that underwrites our *habitus*, which he defines as the ability to effectively (or one could say affectively) function within any given field—in this instance the literary/cultural field. Bourdieu's theory has been described as one of "radical contextualization," which seems a particularly apt way to approach source studies.[1] To apply Bourdieu's ideas to source study would allow us to go beyond the matter of "what a source is" to the question of "how a source does." How does the cultural capital underlying any source interact and play with the main text? How do we as contemporary readers differentiate between "how the source did" in the *habitus* of the medieval reader and in our own: How did a source make meaning then and how does it make meaning now? Source study approached as a *recuperation* of cultural capital would allow for a more expansive—and self-reflexive—understanding of Chaucer's "makyng" and its participation in the cultural fields of the late fourteenth century.

I first came to Bourdieu through my interest in game theory, since the analogy of game underlies his theories, particularly descriptions of central concepts like field, habitus, and capital. A field (*champ*)—

[1] Randall Johnson, "Editor's Introduction," pp. 1–25 in Pierre Bourdieu, *The Field of Cultural Production: Essays on Art and Literature,* ed. Randall Johnson (New York: Columbia University Press, 1993), p. 9.

comprising any spectrum of human experience, from the political and economic to the cultural and the literary—is a structured space with its own fundamental laws and relations; in simpler terms, we could say that it constitutes a game space. Entering into any field requires habitus (or *sens pratique*), which Bourdieu describes as a "kind of practical sense for what is to be done in any given situation—what is called in sport a 'feel' for the game."[2] This feel for the game emerges via the acquisition of capital, the specialized knowledge of a field. Possession of capital means knowing the rules of the game and acquiring such knowledge is a life-long process, derived from a matrix of familial, educational, and social structures and institutions. Bourdieu defines cultural capital as an internalized code that enables the deciphering of cultural fields, relations, and objects. While all forms of capital are individually internalized, cultural capital itself is both multivalent and dynamic.[3] Consequently, "a work of art has meaning and interest only for someone who possesses the cultural competence, that is the code, into which it is encoded."[4] Cultural capital is the knowledge necessary to play the game of culture, and without it the game loses all meaning.

Perhaps the most significant aspect of Bourdieu's theory within the context of source study is his notion of "interest." In this adaptation of Johann Huizinga's *illusio,* Bourdieu argues that those entering into a field are required not only to have the cultural capital necessary to play, but they must take the game seriously—in his terminology, they must be "interested" rather than "disinterested."[5] As he explains it, "games which matter to you are important and interesting because they have been imposed and introduced in your mind, in your body, in a form called the feel for the game."[6] If "your mind is structured according to the structures of the world in which you play, everything will seem

---

[2] Pierre Bourdieu, *Practical Reason: On the Theory of Action* (Stanford: Stanford University Press, 1998), p. 25.

[3] The dynamic character of cultural capital is readily apparent to anyone who has taught more than one generation of college students. Our cultural capital may stay the same, while that of our students has—to put it euphemistically—diverged from ours in many areas.

[4] Pierre Bourdieu, *Distinction: A Social Critique of the Subject of Taste,* trans. Richard Nice (Cambridge, Mass.: Harvard University Press, 1984), p. 2.

[5] See "Is a Disinterested Act Possible?" pp. 75–91, in *Practical Reason,* where Bourdieu also suggests the terms *investment* and *libido* as synonyms. See also "Illusion and the *Illusio,*" in *The Rules of Art: Genesis and Structure of the Literary Field,* trans. Susan Emanuel (Stanford: Stanford University Press, 1992), pp. 331–36.

[6] Bourdieu, *Practical Reason,* p. 77.

obvious and the question of knowing if the game is 'worth the candle' will not even be asked."[7] By being interested in the game, we are, necessarily, its willing participants; in fact, he argues that we embody the very game itself. Bourdieu further delineates this spectrum of engagement as ranging among positions of interest, disinterest, and indifference on the part of any field's participants. Those in the position of disinterest are still directly involved in the game; after all, opposition itself means that one is still invested in the game itself. Consequently, the disinterested participants are as involved in the game as the interested. Rather, it is indifference that signals nonparticipation in a game or field. For the indifferent, who refuse to play at all, the game has no meaning, no engagement.

This spectrum of interest/disinterest/indifference offers an instructive way to consider our own problematic reception of Chaucer's *Legend of Good Women* as well as its source study. As many contemporary readers might attest, sometimes it is a difficult task to be "interested" in the *Legend*. After all, what Chaucer asks the reader of the *Legend* to do is enter into one late medieval cultural field: the literary-rhetorical debate over the nature of Woman. That the *Legend*'s intertextual play is so dependent upon knowledge of its medieval cultural capital and context confirms Chaucer's "interest" in this game. However, since our contemporary *habitus* operates quite differently from that of the late medieval reader, our "interest" often wanes. As we possess different capital, and a differing *habitus,* when entering this cultural field, we tend to be disinterested in the Bourdieuian sense. Some are, perhaps, not so much disinterested as indifferent to the game; there is certainly a strain of indifference running throughout the modern critical reception of the *Legend*—where not only Chaucer the author is "bored" by his text, but so is his critic. It would seem that we lack the interest, often literally as well as theoretically, to enter into the cultural field of the text's game; and, consequently, we have a hard time playing Chaucer's game seriously.

But Bourdieu's version of radical contextualization might allow us to engage seriously, and with "interest," in the *Legend*'s game. Consider Robert Frank's astute observation of reading the *Legend*: "For every name on the first list [the Prologue's balade] there is a story which even in fragmentary form flashes across the memory and illuminates the name."[8] Indeed, part of our critical apparatus must become the question of exactly what is the story being illuminated in our cultural capital and how "does" it affect our reception, in addition to asking what and how the story "did" for Chaucer and his audience. The *Legend*'s list of good women is, in fact, a highly conventional one when considered within the late medieval context. Like so many of his predecessors, including Guillaume de Machaut, Jean le Févre, and Christine de Pizan, Chaucer uses the stories of Cleopatra, Medea, and Dido as *exempla* for a profeminist representation of female constancy. However, a concept often lost on the contemporary reader is that the structure of the medieval debate allowed these same *exempla* to be used in support of anti-feminist depictions of female inconstancy. While seemingly antithetical to the contemporary reader—after all, how could the same example be both "good" and "bad"?—those *exempla* whose contemporary interpretation seems to allow only for antifeminist interpretation could occupy either position in medieval cultural capital. The medieval habitus had to consider not necessarily who an author chose as *exempla*, or even why, but instead *how* he used them in order to prove his side and "win" the game. An examination of "how the source does" in the *Legend*, especially how the various debate texts play within and among themselves, could allow our own reading of Chaucer's game to move away from the indifference/disinterest spectrum toward a reading that is not only more serious, more interested, but also more playful.

Since the individual habitus is grounded in history—Bourdieu calls it "embodied history"—we cannot ignore the habitus, the history, that we bring to any text.[9] Nor can we ignore the habitus within which Chaucer lived and wrote—one that comprises so much more than the sources he uses and transforms. In her application of Bourdieu's ideas to feminist theory, Toril Moi has argued for performing a true Bourdieuian analysis—a process she terms (following Geertz) "thick analysis."[10] Such a

---

[8] Robert Worth Frank Jr., "The *Legend of Good Women:* Some Implications," in *Chaucer at Albany*, ed. Rossell Hope Robbins (New York: Burt Franklin, 1975), p. 72.

[9] Pierre Bourdieu, *The Logic of Practice*, trans. Richard Nice (Stanford: Stanford University Press, 1990) p. 56.

[10] Toril Moi, "The Challenge of the Particular Case: Bourdieu's Sociology of Culture and Literary Criticism," pp. 300–311, in *What is a Woman? And Other Essays* (Oxford: Oxford University Press, 1999). She warns against the more usual piecemeal approach of applying only parts of Bourdieu's theories since "the only way to understand the concept of symbolic capital is to link it to a specific cultural field . . . to remove these concepts from each other's company and from any actual social and human context is to miss the close, concrete relationship between subjectivity, institutions and the social

method—one that encompasses as many fields as possible to understand literary texts—would be ideal for source study because it would allow us to see "the way in which certain texts enter into field-related intertextual relations with other texts."[11] As Moi rightly points out, doing such thick analysis is time-consuming, detailed work, but I would argue that it provides a more expansive understanding of how an author like Chaucer "does" sources as well as a more "thick" understanding of the larger cultural field within which he, and we, operate. Bourdieu's version of radical contextualization could allow us to engage seriously, with "interest," in the medieval habitus. Such a method moves beyond and beneath the catalogue of sources into the structures that underlie the creation of texts, intertexts, and contexts. And certainly, any enlargement of our knowledge of that habitus in turn enlarges our own cultural capital and allows us to read such texts in more interested, and interesting and playful, ways.

---

field that constitutes the original and powerful intellectual contribution of Bourdieu's sociology of culture to contemporary thought" (pp. 309–10).

[11] Ibid., p. 296.

The Afterword of Origins: A Response

Ruth Evans
University of Stirling

Introduction: Textual Forensics

I N 1973 THE LITERARY CRITIC HAROLD BLOOM famously dismissed source study as a "wearisome industry . . . that will soon touch apocalypse anyway when it passes from scholars to computers."[1] Scholars may wince, but Bloom's put-down long held sway in many humanities departments. Source hunters—the opposites, Bloom presumes, of lithe and vigorous literary critics—are not only mere drones in the archive but also aggressively bent on destroying themselves together with the very objects they work with: literary texts.

Yet professional academics of all stripes regularly "do" source study—every time they detect plagiarism in a student essay. Ironically employing the same computer technology that Bloom so presciently fingered as the key to ratcheting up the success of the whole "allusion-counting" enterprise, teachers can now Google suspect phrases to locate an essay's "hard sources": in Nancy Bradbury's definition, "temporally prior, accessible to the writer in question, and demonstrably influential on his or her work, the ideal form of evidence being close and extended verbal parallels." Academics must then carefully differentiate these "hard" sources from the "soft" ones: those that the student, in Peter Beidler's words, "almost certainly knew and probably remembered (consciously or not) as he wrote." Finding a plagiarized essay's "hard analogue" (Beidler again: "a literary work that is old enough in its extant form that

---

[1] Harold Bloom, *The Anxiety of Influence: A Theory of Poetry* (New York: Oxford University Press, 1973), p. 31.

[the student] could have known it and that bears striking resemblances, usually more narrative than verbal, to a [student essay]") may be more difficult. After all, what is "resemblance" in the context of plagiarism? A further instance: our suspicions may be aroused by an essay's odd shifts of tone or a sophistication that belies previous performance, and yet the source eludes us. Do we have a case for prosecution if this "lost source" cannot be produced as evidence?

Within certain institutional contexts, then, a precise calibration of the relationship between a text and its raw materials matters rather urgently. Bloomian critics should not be so sniffy. But my point is rather that source study has been figured primarily—and to its detriment—in forensic terms. Even "hard" and "soft" suggest not so much boiled eggs (Bradbury) as degrees of punishment. And yet in the case of literary texts we may suppose that readers are in pursuit of something other than "evidence" with which to arraign the author. But what? And how might source study reclaim the attention of literary critics? The excellent set of papers in this symposium argues in diverse and compelling ways that we need to rethink entirely the relationship between Chaucer's poetry and its sources. The forensic model no longer holds. Nor does Bloom's dismal view of "allusion-counting" as self-consuming pedantry. These papers use source study not to perform a positivist return to origins but rather to address the very difficulty of seeking origins in a world where, I would argue, technology inflects the status of "knowledge" in new ways. These papers also engage with Chaucerian "invention" in its rhetorical sense: not only what is discovered but also what is created. In the words of Carolyn Collette: "When we talk about identifying Chaucer's sources . . . we [are] talking about tracing the . . . labyrinthine paths of Chaucer's literary imagination."

This revival of source study comes about, I would argue, for two reasons: on the one hand, through the redefining of textuality by philosophers and cultural critics (especially those who invoke the influence of the new media: Derrida, Alan Liu, George Landow, Jean-Louis Lebrave), and, on the other, through the rethinking of the nature of origins that is taking place across both the sciences and humanities (Foucault, Michel Serres, Deleuze and Guattari). These papers beautifully complicate the traditional notion of an origin. Nevertheless, as Amy Goodwin argues, there are clear-cut political and institutional differences between a definite source and the potentially infinite weave of language and cultural practices out of which Chaucer constructed his poetry: "The distinction between a source text and what we might call a source of Chaucer's invention takes on importance when determining their different values, and it takes on an urgency of a different sort when figuring out what to include in a project such as Robert M. Correale and Mary Hamel's *Sources and Analogues of the Canterbury Tales*." So we need in some sense to go back to origins and ask: What is a source?

The Taxonomic Urge, or Information Versus Noise?

Neither Bryan and Dempster's monumental *Sources and Analogues* project of 1941 nor the preface to Correale and Hamel's revised (2002) version of the project, nor the draft, "Guide for Contributors to the Sources and Analogues Project," issued in the early 1990s, defines what a source is. Rather, in Goodwin's words, "they all assume a stereotypical definition," namely, an identifiable literary work that is directly imitated by Chaucer. But the problematic of source study, as these papers recognize, is part of a much larger set of questions about how we conceive of a text's relationship to the culture that produced it and to the culture within which it is read. Bradbury puts this very well: "[A]t one extreme, [there is] the privileging of empirically demonstrable 'hard sources' over all other kinds of textual relations, and, at the other, the rejection of traditional source study altogether on the postmodernist grounds that one vast intertext connects all texts equally."

At one end of the spectrum is Beidler, who proposes that we refine our existing taxonomy by adding "soft source" and "lost source" to the current three (hard source, hard analogue, and soft analogue). At the other end is Collette, boldly declaring that *The Canon's Yeoman's Tale* has "no sources," because everything in Chaucer's cultural and geographical milieu feeds into his "art." And there are positions in between. Goodwin adds another category to Beidler's five: "a source within a source." Collette hints at a seventh: the "source" that "does not necessarily predate the composition of Chaucer's work." I am tempted to suggest that this evokes Bloom's point about the final stage of poetic influence: that it "involves the ultimate victory available to modern poets, a victory, achieved by only a few of the greatest poets of the last few centuries, in which, as in the poetry of Yeats and Wallace Stevens, the impression is created that they (the modern poets) are being *imitated by their precursors*."[2] Thus Chaucer "imitates" Milton or Spenser—or T. S. Eliot.

[2] Ibid., p. 141.

Sources can also include virtual and nonlinguistic materials: those stored in the memory (Kenneth Bleeth, Goodwin) or "a pictorial image, cultural practice, oral tradition, set of conventions, or real event, . . . [that] leaves a distinct verbal imprint on the work in question" (Bradbury). And Frese wants to incorporate "subliminal" sources and "radical cultural ideas—including . . . the idea of choosing the vernacular as a medium for literature of lasting value."

Where do these much broader definitions of "source" come from? Collette's understanding of origins as a swirl of possibilities is very close to Michel Serres's argument that an origin is not a single point but rather a form of "noise"—the originary hubbub out of which all things come. Resisting the notion of knowledge as a tree with a single root, these papers all play with different metaphors to describe this nonsimple understanding of origins: the labyrinth and the rhizome (Collette); intertextuality (Bleeth); Michael Riffaterre's notion of "the mind's eye" (Bleeth); "habitus" and "radical contextualization" (Betsy McCormick); "a map of communicative practices understood synchronically" (Arlyn Diamond).

The metaphor of the rhizome, derived ultimately from Deleuze and Guattari's *Mille Plateaux*, is especially apt. To see "origins" as a network with multiple nodes is also to recognize the difficulty of using conventional interpretive categories to describe what it contains. Even armed with Beidler's taxonomic Baedeker, in Collette's words, "[W]e enter a labyrinth where . . . the paths are not clear, the location of a center unsure, and all conclusions are debatable. . . . '[S]ources' for [*The Canon's Yeoman's Tale*] indeed abound in the literary and cultural milieu of Chaucer's world, but . . . they do not fit neatly into categories like 'hard' or 'soft' sources or analogues." In Collette's paper, as in Goodwin's, I hear familiar echoes of Barthes's textuality: "a tissue of quotations drawn from the innumerable centers of culture." But in Bleeth's and Goodwin's highlighting of sources that Chaucer and his audience had stored, perhaps imperfectly, in their memory, I hear a less familiar (more suggestive?) version of textuality: that of genetic criticism (*la critique génétique*).[3] Genetic criticism stresses the multiple temporalities of the writing process. It sees a text not as a stable end product but as a series of staging posts, composed of various authorial "avant-textes" (drafts, revi-

---

[3] See "Introduction: A Genesis of French Genetic Criticism," in *Genetic Criticism: Texts and Avant-textes,* ed. Jed Deppman, Daniel Ferrer, and Michael Groden (Philadelphia: University of Pennsylvania Press, 2004), pp. 1–16.

sions, remembered texts) that are received by the reader in a kind of retroactive loop. Both author and readers move backward and forward between material and virtual texts, activating processes of living memory and challenging readers' conditioning by the relative fixity of print.

Collette and McCormick isolate another important facet of the debate: the difficulties of reading historically. To identify a particular source does not mean that we can ever fully understand how that source "did" (McCormick) in the habitus of the medieval reader. Yet sources are not simply there to be discovered: we find only what our categories will allow us to find. As the information theorist Geoff Bowker observes, if "[i]nformation, in [Gregory] Bateson's famous definition, is about differences that make a difference," then "[d]esigners of classification schemes constantly have to decide what really does make a difference."[4] Goodwin's demand for "working definitions" of sources and analogues that "develop with a mind to the project" is a plea for just such a reader-oriented classificatory system: provisional, localized, nonuniversal. But at what point in staring into the vast textual weave of texts, images, and practices that Chaucer might have drawn on do we start to descry "information" rather than simply a blur of con-texts? Is it to keep at bay that deafening roar that we try to impose order on it by making categories appear? What about *our* relation to sources?

What Source Study Tells Us About Ourselves

If there is a kick to be had in identifying some of Chaucer's most teasing references—the man of great authority, Wade's boat—then we cannot, as Diamond reminds us, take the nature of that kick for granted. Source hunting, it is sometimes argued, uses desire for the past as a way of consoling ourselves for our own being-in-lack. But our relation to origins is historically complex. In *The Order of Things*, Foucault argues that modern thought, from the beginning of the nineteenth century, wrestles with "a problematics of the origin at once extremely complex and extremely tangled."[5] On the one hand, it attempts to insert man's chronology within that of things, so that "man's origin would be no more

[4] Geoffrey C. Bowker, "Lest We Remember: Organizational Forgetting and the Production of Knowledge:" http://epl.scu.edu:16080/~gbowker/pubs.htm. Last accessed December 28, 2005.

[5] Michel Foucault, "The Retreat and Return of the Origin," in *The Order of Things: An Archaeology of the Human Sciences,* trans. not given (London: Tavistock, 1970), pp. 328–35, at 333.

than a date, a fold, in the sequential series of beings": the beginnings of culture and of civilizations, biological evolution. On the other hand, it seeks "to align the experience man has of things, the knowledge he has acquired of them, and the sciences he has thus been able to constitute, in accordance with chronology (so that though all man's beginnings have their locus within the time of things, his individual or cultural time makes it possible . . . to define the moment at which things meet the face of their truth for the first time)."[6] There is thus something of a contradiction in our thinking about origins. Recognizing ourselves as mere blips in the evolutionary fold, we also demand that Chaucer's texts "meet the face of their truth" in their origins. My sense that MY origins belong to another time and are never wholly recoverable is not aligned with my sense that *things* have knowable origins. To attempt to see ourselves as inhabiting a historical moment in which "one vast intertext connects all texts equally" (Bradbury) is the inverse of the attempt to categorize things less sloppily. I think these papers honestly reflect that irreconcilability.

They also wonderfully describe how the search for origins has supported normative nationalist and political agendas. That search has reproduced Chaucer's own view of himself as a sophisticated savorer of Continental European culture and been blind to his dependence on the "homely" English proverbial tradition (Bradbury). The reason why scholars refuse to give up on the "lost French source" of *The Miller's Tale* and to acknowledge *Heile van Beersele* as its obvious "source," Beidler argues, is because of the belief that no Dutch source could be as clever as a French one. But Beidler also sees this blindness as the fault of taxonomic systems that are too blunt: "if [scholars] had had access to the terminology that I suggest above, they would have been more careful to distinguish among the various analogues and to describe them." Scholars have long refused to recognize Boccaccio's last tale of the *Decameron* as a source for *The Clerk's Tale,* despite their rhetorical similarities, because "assessments of rhetorical effects vary historically" (Goodwin). Chaucer himself explicitly draws our attention to the politics of sources. The Wife of Bath's injunction to listeners of her tale not to accept the surface antifeminism of the tale of Midas's ears but to return to the Ovidian source—and to learn something about the dynamics of antifeminism in the process—asks its audience to be alive to how sources might be (mis)-

---

[6] Ibid.

read.[7] All of this recalls Derrida's two orders of the archive: "sequential" (to do with commencement) and "jussive" (to do with commandment). What we find in the storehouse of the past are both the origins of things *and* the principles that govern their conservation, because not everything is deemed worthy of keeping—or worthy of being found.

But What About the Poetry?

Will cataloguing sources actually tell us anything meaningful about Chaucer's poems? Correale sees the purpose of the new *Sources and Analogues* to make available Chaucer's ur-texts—"updated editions, newly discovered manuscripts, newly discovered sources, and English translations," but to leave "questions of how [Chaucer] adapted them for his own artistic purposes to be answered by literary critics" (cited by Goodwin). However, Correale's absolute distinction between source study and literary interpretation (which ironically recapitulates Bloom's distinction) is everywhere contested in these papers, largely because they conceive of authorship, influences, and the literary in more complex ways than do either Correale or Bloom. Several contributors explore the question of invention, picking up on the way that Chaucer and his audience would have understood sources in rhetorical terms: as *topoi,* or memory places. Frese's sensitivity to the ways in which Chaucer authorizes himself as a writer in the vernacular through taking over various tropes from Dante, Petrarch, and Boccaccio acts as a valuable reminder that Chaucerian source study cannot be divorced from the politics of translation in the later Middle Ages. However, in rightly positing a Chaucer who draws his material from "the innumerable centers of culture," these papers nevertheless do not perhaps do enough to demonstrate that Chaucer's poetry is everywhere stamped with what Derek Attridge calls "authoredness": a mark of the singularity of his writing.

But what of technology? What of the computer and its apocalyptic threat—or promise? Strangely, none of these papers mentions the ease with which we can now track down sources and allusions on the Internet. Is there perhaps a reluctance to recognize that although source study requires exceptional "linguistic, codicological, archival, and historical skills" (Diamond), it can also be as mechanical as clicking a mouse?

[7] See Lee Patterson, " 'For the Wyves Love of Bathe': Feminine Rhetoric and Poetic Resolution in the *Roman de la Rose* and *The Canterbury Tales*," *Speculum* 58 (1983): 656–95.

Digital technology has changed the way we think about "knowledge." "Knowledge" now is "information," often decontextualized, de-authorized, and presented (for example, in hypertextual form) in non-narrative modes. How then might we conceive of source study in relation to the changing status of knowledge? That these papers cannot agree on what a source is strikes me as instructive in itself. So although on the one hand we want and need more flexible definitions of sources, on the other we understand that we must live with what Collette describes as "indeterminacy and uncertainty about sources." These papers reflect that impasse—but also suggest important new ways in which we can reconceptualize the study of Chaucer's sources.

REVIEWS

Suzanne Conklin Akbari. *Seeing Through the Veil: Optical Theory and Medieval Allegory.* Toronto: University of Toronto Press, 2004. Pp. x, 354. $65.00.

This learned, stimulating, and uncommonly well-written book pursues an essentially new approach to medieval literary allegory through the application of medieval optical theory. The book's title alludes to a vocabulary typical of medieval writers who speak of allegory. Since to read an allegory is to see beneath or around or through or under or behind what first meets the eye, it proves highly instructive to examine in some detail what medieval scientists and their popularizers, some of whom were widely read poets like Jean de Meun and Dante, actually believed about the mechanics and physiology of human vision.

There is, of course, a fairly large body of medieval optical writings, which the author succinctly reviews in her second chapter. The ideas were varied. Was the human eye a mirror or a lamp? For Akbari the key distinction is between optical theories tending toward "intromission" on the one hand and "extramission" on the other: "Although both mechanisms facilitate the purpose of vision—the meeting of subject and object—intromission stresses the primacy of the object, extramission the primacy of the subject" (pp. 23–24). As this statement implies, "subjectivity" is among the author's principal interests. From the point of view of modern science, the most impressive of medieval opticians was the Arab Alhazen, whose book is explicitly cited by Jean de Meun (under the suggestive title *Livre des Regards,* and whose technical vocabulary remains standard among ophthalmologists still).

It is impossible in brief compass to suggest either the copiousness or the complexity of the book's argument. If the implicit attempt to formulate a general field theory of medieval allegory is not finally successful, neither is it less successful than some previous explicit attempts. Medieval literary allegory is too varied in its compositional ambition, and above all in its artistic achievement, to invite any but a capacious and rhetorical definition. In my opinion, that of Isidore of Seville remains the most satisfactory. Allegory is *alieniloquium,* saying one thing to mean another. The most urgent task of literary historians with regard to medieval allegory is in my opinion not the synoptic panorama, in which the most devilish and interesting details of individual works invariably fade away in horizontal depth, but the specific and if necessary even microscopic examination that can, when deftly performed, genuinely advance our understanding of ever much studied poems. Professor Akbari has identified a fruitful "optical" species of the allegorical genus, and the most important parts of her important book are her specific "readings" of important works in several vernaculars.

The authors of the *Roman de la Rose* are the first and most apt of the important vernacular writers (the others being Dante and Chaucer) subjected to Akbari's illuminating lens. Guillaume de Lorris placed at the very center of his garden an Ovidian emblem of ambiguous vision, the mirror of Narcissus. That Jean de Meun fully appreciated that Guillaume had reshaped his Ovid to construct an allegory of the operations of the human eye is attested to by his exegetical reprise of the garden setting at the end of his poem. At the moment when Jean sees through the veil of the poem inherited from his predecessor, it is revealed to be not a veil but a retina.

The *Roman de la Rose* is the indispensable text for any attempt at a synoptic account of late medieval literary allegory, and the two chapters devoted to it in *Seeing Through the Veil* are the best and strongest parts of a good and strong book. The analysis devoted to Dante and to Chaucer, both of whom claim two chapters, while no less learned or spirited, perhaps inevitably lacks the thickness of the discussion of the French allegorists. The fifth chapter takes up the *Vita nuova* and the *Convivio,* the sixth the *Commedia.* Many dantisti have attempted to describe an artistic trajectory that in one way or another reveals the mature poet of the *Commedia* moving away from, or even more forcefully rejecting an earlier and tentative commitment to idealism variously identified as courtly love, Platonism, or crypto-pagan Boethianism. Akbari's "optical" analysis is quite helpful in finding one important ground of stable continuity linking works of very different conception and genius. I find the two Chaucerian chapters (one devoted to the dream visions, a second to the *Canterbury Tales*) are somewhat thinner in this regard. Though the *Canterbury Tales* are clearly allegorical in an Isidorian sense, and though they are thick with allegorical imagery and situations, the terms adopted by the author probably justify the phrase "Vestigial Allegory" in her chapter title.

There has been a great deal of earlier scholarship devoted to the topics taken up by Professor Akbari, and it would be impossible for her to have consulted all of it. Still, there are serious gaps. I shall indulge a personal grievance in noting that she has not consulted two essays of mine devoted to optics in the *Roman de la Rose,* one of which ("The Garden of the *Roman de la Rose:* Vision of Landscape or Landscape of Vision?" 1986) explicitly anticipates several strands of her argument. Of course vernacular literary allegorists were not the first medieval writers to appropriate optical science for literary ends. Hence one lacuna in Akbari's bibliography is sufficiently surprising to merit the adjective "alarming": to wit, the author's neglect of Robert Javelet's *Image et ras-semblance au 12è siècle* (1967), the massive French *thèse* devoted to the exploration of "visionary" themes in the vast genre of scriptural exegesis. Indeed the greatest of medieval allegories, Holy Writ, is at times culpably neglected in this study. In one place (p. 94), for example, where Professor Akbari is discussing an idealized portrait of Blanche in the "Book of the Duchess," she says that the "comparison of the lady's body to a tower [*round tour of yvoyre,* l. 946] is quite conventional, found in several examples of courtly poetry including the *Roman de la Rose.*" The image is in fact an explicit reminiscence of the Canticle (7:4), one detail in a complex pattern of the scriptural "apotheosis" of Blanche noted in an essay (*JEGP* 66 [1967]) by the premier expert on Chaucer's early debt to French allegory, James Wimsatt, whose name appears nowhere in her book.

JOHN V. FLEMING
Princeton University

ELIZABETH ALLEN. *False Fables and Exemplary Truth in Later Middle English Literature.* New York: Palgrave Macmillan, 2005. Pp. viii, 225. $65.00.

The title of Elizabeth Allen's work will result in its inevitable comparison to Larry Scanlon's *Narrative, Authority, Power: The Medieval Exemplum and the Chaucerian Tradition* (Cambridge, 1994), and Allen acknowledges the importance of his work early in her text. However,

while the two books discuss some of the same works of literature, nota-
bly Chaucer's *Pardoner's* and *Clerk's Tales,* Gower's *Confessio Amantis,* and
Lydgate's *Fall of Princes,* Allen's approach to exemplary literature complements Scanlon's. He examined the "political and ideological significance of the exemplum" as a "narrative enactment of cultural
authority," concentrating on exempla from sermons and the *Fürstenspiegel* ("Mirror of Princes") tradition (p. i). Allen focuses on exemplum not
as a form or a genre (indeed, Scanlon also rejected the possibility of a
formal definition) but as a *mode* of literature that "express[es] an aspiration toward exact alignment among authorial purpose, narrative form,
and audience response" (p. 2). Should this alignment occur, the audience
will respond by imitating (in the case of virtue) or avoiding (in the case
of vice) the action represented in the exemplum, but Allen also points
out that "exemplary discourse is itself a form of moral activity" (p. 16).
While Scanlon traces the history of the exemplum as an evolving rhetorical construction of literary power from the Latin tradition to the vernacular, Allen limits her scope to Middle English literature and what she
calls "a poetics of exemplarity," though readers might quibble that
much of her analysis is based more upon what medieval writers would
have called "rhetoric" than "poetics," inasmuch as exemplary literature
is meant to be persuasive.

   In her introduction Allen sets up an analytic framework for the exemplum, discussing the ways in which these texts must balance narrative
specificity with interpretive generality, though that generality led to
medieval anxieties about misinterpretation of sermon exempla, particularly among "a potentially various and unpredictable lay audience" (p.
12). She deploys such Aristotelian concepts as "phronesis," the principle
of practical wisdom based on an individual's good judgment, and "ais-
thesis," the sense of perception upon which readers must rely in order
to make choices among a multiplicity of possible interpretations. She
also discusses the latter term's etymological relation to aesthetics. The
introduction provides a useful overview of the conceptual terrain that
Allen plans to cover and could stand on its own as a helpful introduction
to exemplum as literature.

   Allen could have used the broadly applicable methodology set out in
her introduction in relation to any number of texts, so inasmuch as she
purports to limit herself to late Middle English literature, it is surprising
that she first turns to William Caxton's translation of *Le Livre du Cheva-*

lier de la Tour Landry. According to Allen, Caxton's response to the French original in his *Book of the Knight of the Tower* "glosses over the internal divisions in the Knight's narration, claiming the *Book* as a tool for the education of disparate audiences brought under the exemplary wing of his royal patroness [Elizabeth Woodville, Queen of Edward IV]" (p. 31). While Allen's analysis of the differences between the French and English texts is deft, it is noteworthy that the occasion for the stalwartly exemplary translation bears a significant resemblance to Scanlon's "narrative enactment of cultural authority," with Caxton taking advantage of royal patronage to exercise authoritative control over the text.

Allen devotes two chapters to the differences between Gower's, Chaucer's, and Lydgate's handling of Livy's narrative of Virginia and Virginius. She asserts that in the *Confessio Amantis,* Gower "argu[es] for an imaginative use of example instead of Livy's historical facticity," while Chaucer's *Physician's Tale* "uses the narrative to call into question the very nature of the exemplary impulse" (p. 54). Lydgate's two very brief retellings of the story in *The Fall of Princes* attempt to "stabilize the desperate oscillations of Chaucer's Physician and the unpredictable political fiction-making of Gower" (p. 99). Allen's readings focus on the unreliable narrators of Gower's and Chaucer's versions versus Lydgate's contextually appropriate focus on the evil judge Appius in his *Fürstenspiegel.* The discussion of Gower and Lydgate are useful, but the analysis of *The Physician's Tale* is basically another rehearsal of the topos of Chaucerian indeterminacy, here viewed through the lens of exemplarity.

In her chapter on Chaucer's Pardoner and his reappearance in the fifteenth-century *Canterbury Interlude,* Allen uses the apocryphal continuation to interrogate the severity of the Host's violent response to the Pardoner after his *Tale;* she reaches the conclusion that the *Interlude* poet engages in a *lectio facilior* whereby "the Host's verbal violence in *The Pardoner's Tale* is deflected off the Host and blamed completely on the Pardoner" (p. 125) because of his dishonest and licentious behavior in Canterbury. This conclusion leads Allen to speculate about the *ordinatio* of the *Canterbury Tales* and *Interlude* in the only manuscript of the latter, the Northumberland manuscript.

Allen's final chapter examines Henryson's *Testament of Cresseid* in relation to *Troilus and Criseyde,* discussing the ways in which Criseyde's behavior at the end of Chaucer's poem remains largely unreadable, thus showing again that Chaucer "depicts the exemplary mode itself as a conceptual failure" (p. 140). Enter Henryson, whose poem presents a painfully exemplary Cresseid. Again Allen makes helpful points about the mechanics of foisting "exemplarity" upon a narrative, but her conclusion—that Henryson "pulls the story back from the brink of indeterminacy to reinvest Cresseid with the vivid and emblematic power of an exemplary figure" (p. 156)—is not strikingly original.

Allen's *False Fables and Exemplary Truth* is not as far-reaching or ambitious as Scanlon's *Narrative, Authority, Power*, and therefore it may not be as useful to medievalists seeking a fully historicized analytic overview of exemplum as a mode of discourse. However, within its more limited scope, Allen's book offers insight into the exemplary impulse in fourteenth- and fifteenth-century British literature, and therefore it provides a suitable pendant to Scanlon's work.

EDWARD WHEATLEY
Loyola University

JOHN H. ARNOLD and KATHERINE J. LEWIS, eds. *A Companion to "The Book of Margery Kempe."* Cambridge: D. S. Brewer, 2004. Pp. xxiv, 246. $90.00.

SIÂN ECHARD, ed. *A Companion to Gower.* Cambridge: D. S. Brewer, 2004. Pp. x, 286. $110.00.

The past decade has seen a striking proliferation of companions and introductory guides. Among the causes for this proliferation one would certainly want to cite such entirely salutary developments as the expansion of the canon and the sharp growth in new approaches combined with the renewal of some older ones. But more worrying ones need to be acknowledged as well: the apparently permanently soft market for scholarly books and the continual economic pressures on academic and scholarly presses. Most of us would be happier in a publishing environment where more of the money currently going into companions and other introductory anthologies was going into monographs. Nevertheless, the profusion of companions offers intellectual benefits of its own. It provides for a consolidation of some of the best and most innovative scholarly work in recent decades, a stocktaking of our now impressively expanded canon, and a concerted means for suggesting the direction of future work. These two collections respond mainly to the more positive developments, especially the expanding canon. The current centrality of Margery Kempe constitutes one of feminism's most notable triumphs in Middle English scholarship, while a critically sophisticated historicism has pried Gower out of his perennial status as Chaucer's also-ran.

These two companions form early contributions to a new initiative by Boydell and Brewer, a cluster of companions on topics from the *Ancrene Wisse* to the Lancelot-Grail cycle. The publishers do not classify these companions as a separate series, nor was I able to find anything on their web sites regarding the general aims or range of this initiative. The dust jacket to the Kempe *Companion* explains that its "authors both survey existing work and present new arguments, insights and ideas," and it seems safe to infer that as the more general goal, with emphasis especially on making original contributions to current scholarship. Both of these read as collections of scholarly essays written mainly for other Middle English scholars. The Gower *Companion* advertises itself as aimed at "the advanced undergraduate or graduate student," but it makes no concession even to the most advanced of undergraduates. (Price will be an additional barrier: like all Boydell and Brewer books, these volumes are beautifully, but expensively, produced.) The overview these volumes provide must largely be inferred mainly from the topics of their essays taken as a whole, although Arnold and Lewis mitigate this problem with a Preface and an Afterword. Without sacrificing specialized rigor, this austere approach will provide the novice, given enough persistence, with the general picture of the field that any introduction should offer. But the approach also puts considerable pressure on editorial selection and requires every contribution to make good on the claims to originality. Arnold, Lewis, and their contributors meet these challenges brilliantly, while the results for Echard's volume are more mixed.

A Companion to Gower follows three excellent Gower anthologies edited by R. F. Yeager between 1989 and 1998, and it simply lacks much of their range and daring. Where they concentrated on Gower's politics, the narrative complexity of his didacticism, and gender and sexuality, this *Companion,* though it includes Diane Watt's exemplary "Gender and Sexuality in *Confessio Amantis,*" concentrates on more traditional topics: manuscript studies and history of the book, language, especially Gower's trilingualism, and Gower's *nachleben*. This turn toward the traditional might not in itself have been a problem had it not licensed weaker contributions to ignore what has been most vital in recent Gower studies. There is also some outright hostility. The collection's first essay, a thorough if uninspired account of Gower's tomb in Southwark Cathedral by John Hines, Nathalie Cohen, and Simon Roffey, declares, "We have, fortunately, now passed beyond the short and negative phase of critical fashion in which the Barthes-derived 'death of the author,' a hangover of the Parisian egoism and nihilism of 1968, meant a blanket refusal to take any scholarly interest in the historical circumstances from which texts derived, least of all the biographies of their authors" (p. 23). Dearie me!—1968 was a while ago. If Barthes is now out of fashion— not a particular cause for celebration, in my view—one would have thought that the sell-by date had also long since elapsed on fatuous (and xenophobic!) theory-bashing. Two other essays seem caught in a similar time warp, though without this hostility: Russell A. Peck's "The Politics and Psychology of Governance in Gower: Ideas of Kingship and Real Kings" and John Burrow's "Gower's Poetic Styles." Ignoring almost everything that has been recently written on Gower's politics, Peck opts for the older view of Gower as a "single-minded" idealist (pp. 216– 17)—a view not so much wrong as incomplete. It yields a Gower incapable of either poetic ambiguity or political complexity. Burrow offers some fairly random thoughts on Gower's style, by which he means not the medieval sense made famous by Dante, but rather the narrower senses assumed by formalist criticism of the mid-twentieth century, specifically prosody and diction.

Fortunately, the rest of the essays are better than this, some of them much better. Jeremy J. Smith's "John Gower and London English," Derek Pearsall's "The Manuscripts and Illustrations of Gower's Works," and R. F. Yeager's "John Gower's French" are models of their kind. All three will become indispensable reference tools. Yeager surveys the *Miroir de l'Omme,* the *Cinkante Balades,* and the *Traitié Pour Essampler les Amantz Marietz,* and also offers a variety of convincing suggestions for further work on these neglected texts. That is less true of A. G. Rigg and Edward S. Moore's "The Latin Works: Politics, Lament, and Praise." They punctuate their serviceable account of Gower's Anglo-Latin context with Pecham-like complaints about Gower scholarship's inadequate Latinity. The two essays on Gower's *nachleben,* Helen Cooper's " 'This worthy olde writer': *Pericles* and Other Gowers, 1592–1640" and Echard's "Gower in Print," are lucid and concise. Robert Epstein's "London, Southwark, Westminster: Gower's Urban Contexts" is workmanlike. That leaves the only two extended accounts of Gower's poetic practice, both of them first-rate: Ardis Butterfield's *"Confessio Amantis* and the French Tradition" and Winthrop Wetherbee's "Classical and Boethian Tradition in the *Confessio Amantis."* Butterfield's essay builds on the pioneering work she has done elsewhere regarding French literary culture's ongoing influence on Middle English tradition. Here she gives real intertextual heft to the figure of Amans, convincingly locating him in dialogue with "the lover-figures that dominate medieval French love narratives" (p. 172). Wetherbee offers Boethius as the origin of a tradition extending to Gower through the Cosmographia, *Complaint of Nature,* and *Romance of the Rose,* a tradition that explains not the stability of Gower's didacticism, but precisely its ambiguities and complexity.

In contrast to this uneven volume, *A Companion to "The Book of Margery Kempe,"* seems everything a companion should be. As the editors explain in their Preface, the volume sets out to provide a more fully historicized account of Margery's book, and in that it certainly has succeeded. Taken together, these essays present an extremely rich and detailed account of the work's complicated relation to previous contemplative tradition, to fifteenth-century literary culture, to local, regional, and national politics, to late medieval gender roles, and to contemporary ecclesiological disputes. Barry Windeatt's magisterial and accessible Introduction opens the volume, guiding the reader from Hope Emily Allen's discovery of *The Book of Margery Kempe* in the 1930s to the explosion of scholarly interest in the text in the 1980s to the present. The essays that follow are strong, some very strong indeed. My two favorites were Jacqueline Jenkins's "Reading and *The Book of Margery Kempe"* and Sarah Salih's "Margery Bodies: Piety, Work, and Penance." Jenkins surveys current scholarship on late medieval literacy, then exhaustively reexamine the *Book* itself to demonstrate how fully self-conscious and literate its "trope of illiteracy" (p. 128) actually is. Salih, with a similar survey of late medieval asceticism, offers an important new reading of Margery's theology, arguing (1) that Margery opposes contemplation to "bodily piety" even as "her visionary experiences are insistently vivid in physical detail" (p. 2) that she continually refers "to the idea of asceticism whilst not performing it," with the result that (3) her spiritual autobiography "substitutes slander for bodily suffering" (pp. 168–72). Five other essays, while narrower in focus, were equally compelling. Isabel Davis's "Men and Margery: Negotiating Medieval Patriarchy," suggestively sketches Margery's notions of masculinity, while Kate Parker's "Lynn and the Making of a Mystic" provides a concise and authoritative account of the local political and social context for Margery's career as a contemplative. In *"A Shorte Treatyse of Contemplacyon: The Book of Margery Kempe* in Its Early Print Contexts,"* Allyson Foster returns to the short excerpts by which the world knew Margery from Wynkyn de Worde's 1501 redaction until Allen's modern edition, convincingly noting their Early Modern juxtapositions with accounts of Catherine of Siena. Diane Watt, in "Political Prophecy in *The Book of Margery Kempe,"* argues that Margery occasionally pursued the politically prophetic role carved out by predecessors like Saint Bridget, but "was probably constrained by a widespread fear of heresy" (p. 159); while Katherine J. Lewis, in "Margery Kempe and Saint Making in Later Medieval English," convincingly suggests that the hagiographical impulse in the production of the *Book* responded to nationalist aspirations.

The four remaining essays, while equally useful, raise quibbles. Kim M. Phillips's "Margery Kempe and the Ages of Woman," relies too much on a conceit of the "life cycle" borrowed from the eternal present of social science, a model that as Phillips concedes in her conclusion does not fit Margery particularly well. John H. Arnold, while ably rehearsing the relevant issues in "Margery's Trials: Heresy, Lollardy, and Dissent," takes Lynn Staley, Ruth Nisse, and others to task for their notion of dissent without providing a viable alternative of his own. Claire Sponsler's "Drama and Piety: Margery Kempe" convincingly suggests that the communal occasion for Margery's bargain with her husband on midsummer's eve was "the annual performance of the great York biblical cycles" (pp. 129–30), but Sponsler's understanding of drama is so inclusive that its specific relevance to Margery never really emerges. And P. H. Collum provides a careful account of Margery's works of mercy in "'If lak of charyte be not ower hynderawnce': Margery Kempe, Lynn, and the Practice of the Spiritual and Bodily Works of Mercy," except that she routinely describes these works as "charity" in the modern sense without ever once noting the difference between the predominant medieval and modern meanings of the term.

These objections do not detract from the overall contributions these essays make to this very strong volume. The volume is so strong, in fact, that I found very puzzling its one false note. It strikes an unaccountably pugnacious pose toward literary scholarship and one literary scholar in particular, Lynn Staley. In both their Preface and Afterword, Arnold and Lewis accuse literary scholars of failing to recognize "that historicizing Margery provides a *better* reading of the *Book*" (p. 217; emphasis in original), and a number of contributors dismiss as antihistorical Staley's interpretive distinction between "Margery" as character and "Kempe" as author. Phillips is even impelled to declare, "There was a real Margery Kempe" (p. 17), as if that has ever been in doubt. While there are some literary scholars, even some literary medievalists, who are not particularly interested in history, they are a distinct minority, and to my knowledge they do not include anyone who has ever written on Margery Kempe. These attacks, then, seem a backhanded and particularly ungracious way of acknowledging (1) that it has been literary scholars rather than historians who have been primarily responsible for Margery Kempe's current popularity; and (2) that Lynn Staley's book has been and remains the single most authoritative treatment of the topic. The structural division she locates in the *Book*'s narratorial voice applies a standard technique of narrative analysis, one that goes at least as far back as Wayne Booth's "implied author," and is even arguably implicit in Percy Lubbock's older distinction between showing and telling. Anyone who thinks its effect in *Margery Kempe's Dissenting Fictions* is to deny the importance of history—much less the existence of Margery herself—has badly missed the point.

LARRY SCANLON
Rutgers University

CHRISTOPHER CANNON. *The Grounds of English Literature.* New York: Oxford University Press, 2004. Pp. xi, 237. $65.00.

Christopher Cannon's study of early Middle English follows quite naturally from his first book, *The Making of Chaucer's English* (Cambridge, 1998). Not only is this volume virtually prophesied there (p. 218), but both studies implicitly adopt the same critical moves. Cannon is preeminently engaged with positionality, posture or stance; he most readily situates himself at the margins of current critical ken and adopts as his field of study what he perceives as the currently ignored and unseen.

The strength of Cannon's current study is a series of closely analytical chapters taking up (I hesitate to say, given his overall argument, the canonical masterpieces of) early Middle English writing. These studies emphatically do not form a sequence (cf. the promise of "radial rather than progressive" argumentation [p. 13]). But, however isolated, they present significant swaths of provocative local readings. I was particularly impressed, for example, by the discussions of *Laȝamon*, land, and law (pp. 65–77); of misogyny and protofeminism in *The Owl and the Nightingale* (pp. 121–34); and of the workings ("the spirit") of early romance (pp. 182–93).

The first chapter indicates why Cannon must present these as isolative readings. Cannon's "Ground(s)" are generated from a Marxian-inflected Aristotelian hylomorphism. In his presentation, each text forms a fragment, what survives "The Norman Yoke" (which Cannon construes throughout as quite literally an appropriate historical narrative, see 19, 23ff.). There are considerably more supple and nuanced historical accounts, such as, for example, Hugh M. Thomas's *The English and the Normans: Ethnic Hostility, Assimilation, and Identity, 1066–c. 1220* (Oxford, 2003). Hylemorphism enables Cannon's "topical" emphasis, each work instantiating a single literary focus or "idea" conjoined with a single place, alternatively a localized foundation put into dialogue with a field of ideas (pp. 12–13). Insofar as Cannon presents an overarching argument, it joins his first and final chapters (the latter on romance). There Cannon adopts a stance (one to which I am quite sympathetic) antipathetic to the notion of an English canon; for him, this forms a linked and concatenated "spiritualization" of literature. It shuts down the "grounded" possibilities of earlier centuries.

Thus, a great deal here rides on Cannon's conception of the "fragment," with its attendant ideas of detachment and isolation. The argument always presupposes his exhibits' "isolation from vernacular models and examples" (p. 2). But a substantial grounding for this view is Cannon's own inattention (as was, in his first book, the description of Chaucer's English as a matter merely of lexis).

The most provocative exhibit here is that Cannon presents as his argument's ground, a discussion of "The First Worcester Fragment" ("Sanctus Beda was iboren") (pp. 34–41). In the first place, although the source, Worcester Cathedral Library, MS F.174, is fragmentary (and we do not know when cut down and transformed into book covers), and the last three words (as well as odd readings around the edges) nineteenth-century conjectures, "Sanctus Beda" is a substantially complete statement, as plate 10 in Christine Franzen's facsimile, *The Tremulous Hand of Worcester: A Study of Old English in the Thirteenth Century* (Oxford, 1991), illustrates. Given the page format, and the continuous texts on this leaf, no more than two or three written lines could have followed the surviving conclusion of "Sanctus Beda." Moreover, it is scarcely isolated. MS F.174 is a quite substantial book, perhaps copied c. 1240, sixty-six folios in all and thoroughly continuous except at head and end. "Sanctus Beda" adjoins its other two texts, the following one (now legitimately fragmentary) a much more extensive alliterative effort contemporary with it, as Douglas Moffatt's *The Soul's Address to the Body: The Worcester Fragments* (East Lansing, 1987) demonstrates. The preceding text, a further substantial rebuff to the notion of "vernacular isolation" or of "cataclysm of 1066," is a copy of Ælfric's Grammar and Glossary. And F.174 is far from isolated; it sits within an oeuvre of more than twenty manuscript books, in the main Anglo-Saxon ones, that this Worcester Cathedral writer annotated, in the interests precisely of ensuring the continuity of pre-Conquest traditions (enshrined, for example, in his presentation of both poems *saxonice*, as prose and not lined verse). (See Franzen's survey of the scribe's oeuvre, pp. 29–83.)

Such an (attenuated) analysis indicates what we (as Cannon would say) here cannot be/have not been allowed to see. Cannon's isolative argument ("loss of literature") follows only from what he chooses here to exclude or ignore. The "tremulous hand" of F.174 is not alone, and more than sixty substantial "Anglo-Saxon" manuscripts (a great many, like Worcester F.174, communicating Ælfric) were copied after the Conquest, steadily down to and after 1200. (For a quick sketch, see N. R. Ker, *Catalogue of Manuscripts Containing Anglo-Saxon* [Oxford, 1957], pp. xv–xix.)

Similarly, Cannon uses *Wace* effectively in his discussion of *Laȝamon*, and once (p. 20) in passing refers to Anglo-Norman and Latin. He fails ever to address the implications. Without exception (even Ormm used Latinate exegetical tools), every text discussed here is engaged in some form of interlingual negotiation, either as receptor from another (insular) text or integrally, as part of its transmission (cf. Cannon's further exclusionary gestures, things he vaguely knows are worthy of someone's serious investigation, at pp. 12, 19). What if—a prospect Cannon cannot entertain—there are only "early insular literary things," not a linguistically bounded category? What if "English," with all its centralist and nationalist overtones, did not program his argument?

Or again, in spite of a very interesting association of inner and outer in *Ancrene Riwle* with the permeable Herefordshire March (pp. 143–54), Cannon fails to notice the regionalism of his exhibits. Different selective procedures could well have thrown up other things ("The Vices and Virtues," Trinity Homilies, and "Poema Morale" are generally southeastern, for example). But all the texts Cannon treats cluster in either the area around the Wash or in Hereford/Worcestershire and might be seen as locally engaged with some range of the others. A final example of what Cannon does not allow to attain visibility concerns past laborers with early Middle English; the bibliography shows minimal attention to important studies by such scholars as Bella Millett, Jocelyn Wogan-Browne (including as Jocelyn Price, a fine essay prefiguring most of Cannon's discussion of *Ancrene Riwle*), or Elaine Treharne.

Cannon generously provides translations of all his citations. These need to be used with considerable care, since he encounters difficulty in reproducing the texts accurately in modern English. The most striking (and argumentatively central) example would be his impossible identification of Ormm's form "laefe" as a reflex of Old English "līf," rather than of Old English "(ge)læfa" (p. 92; see, among many others, "norþ and ek south," to be translated "everywhere" [p. 180]). One should be thankful for deliberatedly isolated crisp and provocative readings, but Cannon's effort to reduce things seen ensures that his account will remain as advertised, marginally grounded and fragmentary indeed.

RALPH HANNA
Keble College, Oxford

DAVID R. CARLSON. *Chaucer's Jobs*. New York: Palgrave Macmillan, 2004. Pp. 168. $65.95.

The relation of Chaucer's various "day jobs" to his poetic "moonlighting" is a topic ripe for reconsideration, especially as critics are attempting to define a possible place for biographical criticism in the post–New Historicist, post-biopolitical landscape. David Carlson marshals salient facts about Chaucer's many bureaucratic and royal appointments in a concise way and then engages in a broad-ranging discussion of the poetry. How successful you find this discussion will depend largely on whether or not you agree with Carlson's central (and often repeated) thesis: that "serving and keeping the dominant order is what Chaucer did" in his administrative as well as his poetic life (p. 39).

The slim book—one hundred pages exclusive of notes—contains three chapters. The first discusses Chaucer's various occupations: his youth spent in service in royal and noble households; his work in the 1380s as controller of customs in London and, later, as a justice of the peace in Kent; and finally, his two-year stint as clerk of the king's works. Reading the poet's literary work through the lens of the life is of course a familiar approach, one on display in the many comprehensive biographies of Chaucer (such as those by Donald R. Howard and Derek Pearsall), as well as the literary criticism of such scholars as David Aers, Lee Patterson, and Paul Strohm. Carlson's conclusions differ in degree rather than in kind from those of previous critics, since he argues that the poet was first humiliated and then co-opted by the succession of mercantile and royal interests that employed him.

On this view, the type of early work that Chaucer undertook in royal and noble households was "punitive" (p. 3), and would thus have made the poet acutely aware of his servile status. Chaucer's later spell as controller is read in light of contemporary complaints to parliament in 1376 about the misbehavior of certain collectors of customs, such as Richard Lyons, who was accused of graft and extortion. Like Lyons, Chaucer's interests as controller were aligned with those of the merchant oligarchy, which benefited greatly from an admittedly imperfect system. In the 1380s, Chaucer's service on the Kent peace commission would have found him hearing cases involving labor violations, theft, brawling, breaking and entering, and other offenses deemed deleterious to the community's welfare. For Carlson, this appointment meant that "Chaucer was employed at repressive (specifically, counterrevolutionary) police-work" (p. 20). The author argues that Chaucer's most important position, both for his administrative career and his imaginative life, was his appointment as clerk of the king's works. In the course of building royal lists, renovating the St. George Chapel at Windsor Castle, and rebuilding Tower Wharf, Chaucer would have been enlisted in the Ricardian project of, on the one hand, shoring up the tenuous relation of crown to nobility and, on the other, reassuring London's merchant oligarchy that the municipal wool trade was a priority for the king.

The author's conclusions about the material presented in Crow and Olson's *Chaucer Life-Records* may occasionally seem overstated, even to a sympathetic reader, without more context. When describing Chaucer's early domestic service, for instance, Carlson does not acknowledge that household apprenticeship was undertaken by all classes of society (including the nobility), and, therefore, to be in service was not necessarily to feel "servile." Similarly, evidence that may have nuanced or tempered the biographical picture sketched here is sometimes left unconsidered. While Chaucer's time as a JP saw him enforcing the admittedly unpopular labor laws, during this same period, he acted (on at least one occasion) as surety for a labor violator. His willingness to do so meant that he understood the limitations of these laws and so was not merely enforcing them as an unthinking, "counterrevolutionary" factotum.

The argument of the book's next chapter, "Writing," is neatly summed up at the outset: "Chaucer's writing did the same kind of work in the cultural sphere as he had contributed by his other employments to the concrete, less mediated work of social management" (p. 33). The early complaints intentionally fashion a world without work where the lover's preoccupation with loss masks the actual economic and political considerations that govern the aristocratic marriage market. Like the complaints, *Troilus and Criseyde* eschews labor in favor of a new, "unproductive" idea of sexual pleasure that validates the erotic at the expense of the everyday. The *Canterbury Tales* is considered to be "an incipient disciplinary machine" (p. 54), a conclusion that has much to recommend it but that is, regrettably, argued here too briefly (in ten pages). Instead of an extended engagement with the notions of work presented in the tales, we are offered generalizations, such as "class conflict is all but invisible" (p. 55) in the poem, but when it does arise, it is always resolved in favor of the dominant ideology.

The final chapter, "Reception," argues that Chaucer finds himself the father of English poetry not on account of the sublimity of his verse nor the topicality of his subject matter, but because he produced an apolitical, "servile vernacular literature" (p. 97), obsequious to the interests of the great if not the good. Evidence of how compelling Chaucer's lack of political vision was to his earliest reader-writers is to be found in the works of Deschamps, Usk, Gower, Clanvowe, Scogan, and Hoccleve. These writers represent Chaucer as an erotic rather than a political poet and attempt to trade on the social value of the Chaucerian name, a commodity whose worth stems not only from poetic work but also from connections made through royal and bureaucratic appointments. Carlson thus explores at some length the paradoxical problem of "making writing pay" (p. 90), in both cold cash and cultural capital. My concern with this section is again with what is missing. In arguing that Chaucer's immediate legacy was exclusively one of political disinterest, Carlson neglects to account for the simultaneous emergence of the "radical" Chaucer: the ostensible author of *The Plowman's Tale*, whose works were marshaled as evidence in fifteenth-century heresy trials and who was later notoriously deemed by John Foxe to be a "right Wycliffian."

The image of the medieval author and his audience that emerges from this book is a proto-capitalist one in which "the reader-consumer is almighty" and "the writer-producer . . . becomes a virtual wage slave" in the vineyards of bastard feudalism (p. 44). Yet like the idea of bastard feudalism itself, the notion of what work may have meant to a pre-industrial author and his audience remains largely unexplored; in fact, the book never discusses what notions of work—whether intellectual, spiritual, or manual—would have been available to a fourteenth-century person at all. Despite this shortcoming, the book will be salutary for its polemical tone, perhaps stirring many devils to advocate. In the end, what Carlson says of Chaucer—that he was "a useful poet, rather than a good one" (p. 64)—could be said, *mutans mutandis*, of this book about Chaucer's poetry as well.

KELLIE ROBERTSON
University of Pittsburgh

THERESA COLETTI. *Mary Magdalene and the Drama of Saints: Theater, Gender, and Religion in Late Medieval England.* Philadelphia: University of Pennsylvania Press, 2004. Pp. xiii, 342. $59.95.

The play of *Mary Magdalene,* preserved in a single copy in MS Bodleian Digby 133, is one of the most remarkable artifacts of late medieval English theater. At more than 2,000 lines, 40 speaking parts, and multiple geographic locales—including some purely psychic ones—it is a daunting play to consider staging, and we can only imagine how the grand spectacle of the saint's life, derived from Jacobus de Voragine's *Legenda Aurea,* occupied the East Anglian community that originally performed the work. Its subject, sometime called the "Apostle to the Apostles," is of course a source of perpetual fascination in European culture, up to the current best seller, *The Da Vinci Code.* Theresa Coletti's exhaustively researched *Mary Magdalene and the Drama of Saints* sets out to explore this intriguing play from every possible angle of its sources, location, and performance. Among her central arguments is that medieval drama, often overlooked as canonical literature, is important precisely for what it can tell us about more popular and public forms of devotion.

Coletti's introduction and first chapter deal with the Digby play's immediate historical context with particular reference to the material culture of fifteenth-century East Anglia. By examining the records of Norfolk religious institutions, Coletti arrives at a new proposal for the site of the play's original production, Saint Giles's hospital in Norwich. She presents a convincing circumstantial argument about the hospital's overall devotional culture, which includes both a "religiomedical discourse" (42) about two of the play's major themes, death and charity, and also a record of liturgical spectacles and processions. Coletti thus locates the *Mary Magdalene* play squarely within an intellectual world familiar to readers of Julian of Norwich and Margery Kempe, in which there were frequent contacts between clerics and laypersons, and female authors like Catherine of Siena and Bridget of Sweden had an encouraging impact on the spiritual lives of local women. Indeed, as Coletti points out, St. Giles was, like other medieval hospitals, staffed by "chaste" women "of good life" (52) who exemplify the informal lay religious "orders" that thrived at this time.

The second and third chapters both focus closely on the figure of Mary Magdalene herself in East Anglian texts and visual art. As Coletti shows in readings of Julian's *Showings,* Kempe's *Book,* Walter Hilton's *Scale of Perfection,* and Osbern Bokenham's *Legendys of Hooly Wummen,* Mary Magdelene comes to represent the authority of experiential knowledge; as an eyewitness of both the passion and resurrection of Jesus' body, she is the ultimate figure of mediation between the human and the divine. The saint's sexual sin becomes the mark of both her physicality and transcendence. For late medieval theologians, especially the heterodox beguine Marguerite Porete (who likely influenced Julian via the Middle English translation of her *Mirror of Simple Souls*), Mary Magdalene exemplifies the possibility of a dynamic female spirituality, the progress of a sinful soul to perfection in contrast to the static perfection of the Virgin Mary. Coletti finds an exemplary use of Mary Magdalene's unique character in Bokenham's prologue to the *Legendys,* written for his patroness, the Countess of Eu; her devotion to the "apostylesse" licenses the Augustinian canon to critique a courtly culture dominated by masculine ideals. Coletti also briefly considers the Digby play of *Mary*

Magdalene against the background of the East Anglian Lollards' arguments in favor of women preachers, concluding that the play comes close to unorthodox positions in its portrayal of Mary's activities even as it firmly advocates the sacraments being administered only by men.

Unfortunately, Coletti only discusses the Digby play itself in depth in the final chapters of her book, which gives the entire work a somewhat lopsided feel. Peculiarly, she also introduces one of the play's major intertexts, the Pseudo-Origen *De Maria Magdalena,* only pages from the end of the study; while she emphasizes both this twelfth-century work's immense popularity and its theological importance in its insistence on Mary Magdalene's corporeal spirituality, she does not consider its possible impact on the rest of the East Anglian religious culture that informs her book. Despite these problems of organization, the last chapters are the richest in the book. The fourth, entitled "Gender and the Anthropology of Redemption," deals with the Digby play's fascinating conflations of Mary Magdalene with the Virgin Mary, tracing how the two often mirror each other in medieval theologies of the feminine. Overall, Coletti provides an excellent reading of the Digby play as depicting a world dominated by the destructive "masculine eros" (161) of tyrants, which Mary Magdalene is able to control through the prostitute-saint's potent combination of promiscuity and chastity. Like the male saints who circulate Christian doctrine in their missionary travels, Mary's former sexual life enables her transformation into a kind of "masculine" traveling and preaching apostle.

Coletti concludes her account of the Digby play with a wonderful final chapter on theatricality. Here she deals with the play's most crucial aspects, its uses of the nature of theater itself to convey the saint's fusion of the carnal and spiritual realms. As Coletti puts it, the stagecraft of the Digby *Mary Magdalene* is "medieval English theatricality at its flamboyant best" (191), and she does a fine job of explaining how the work draws on earlier theatrical idioms, especially the great urban Mystery Cycles. In a short Conclusion, Coletti gives an overview of what happened to the "medieval" Magdalene—a composite of various New Testament women—under the scrutiny of humanists in the Early Modern period. Coletti's tantalizing observations about the visionary Anne Barton's political uses of Mary Magdalene under Henry VIII will hopefully spark some further scholarship on this figure. *Mary Magdalene and the Drama of Saints* does much to illuminate the culture that produced as bizarre a work as the Digby play; it will be welcomed by anyone interested in medieval views of sanctity and gender as well as by students of medieval English theater.

RUTH NISSE
University of Nebraska–Lincoln

LAURIE A. FINKE and MARTIN B. SHICHTMAN. *King Arthur and the Myth of History.* Gainesville: University Press of Florida, 2004. Pp. xiii, 262. $59.95.

King Arthur and the Myth of History reads Arthurian pseudohistory through poststructuralist and postcolonial theory, focusing on three periods of cultural upheaval—twelfth-century Britain, the Wars of the Roses, and the period of twentieth-century fascism. The authors state that the book is the result of twenty years of teaching, and it provides a fascinating measure of the changes in perception and approach to Arthurian literature over that time. The core of the book is a strong and theoretically inclusive examination of the tradition of Arthurian historiography from Geoffrey to Hardyng and Malory. Chronicle histories are indeed "disciplinary orphans" and this study persuasively challenges disciplinary boundaries between history and literature, fact and fiction. Approaching medieval historiography in its own terms by investigating the ways in which Arthurian legend was accepted as history opens up the spectrum of Arthurian writing from the historical through to the fantastical. The authors offer a telling challenge to current thinking about medieval national identity with an analysis of the problematic semantic range of medieval legal and political terminology. Other convincing readings are of Merlin as Bloch's "powerful image of the writer," of the patron-client relationships in the trading of history as symbolic capital, and of the effects of primogeniture on historical narrative and gender roles. The chapter on Hardyng's *Chronicle* faces the question of what may be learned from "a serious consideration of such bad history"; the answer being an in-depth account of the use of history to create legitimacy for a shaky regime. An equally careful analysis of Caxton's Malory demonstrates how his preface negotiates the tricky propaganda potential of Arthurian history. But the concern with Arthur as a signifier of feudal-dynastic expansion leads to a selectivity of material that may be disappointing for readers of the literature—at times the authors seem to be envisaging a static iconic Arthur, as in the Nine Worthies tapestry, rather than the central figure of a narrative sequence leading ineluctably to betrayal and death, and there is little acknowledgment that the best writers of the Arthurian legend go beyond the sycophantic service of current rulers. It is an approach that also requires an understanding of the historical and cultural context that chimes with postcolonial theory and modern constructions of identity. While it is recognized that the material is often resistant, the discussion here shows that we have yet to find a way to describe the cultural and political scene in the three centuries following the Conquest. Wace, a Jerseyman, is not himself Anglo-Norman, nor is there any evidence for the claim that he was of mixed birth. He is not a "French historian writing English history" (103), but a Norman historian writing British history; the differences are significant. The post-Conquest English are English, not "Saxon," and it seems regressive to call Layamon "a Saxon priest" or, worse, a "minor Anglo-Saxon poet"; moreover, that the Anglo-Normans also considered themselves English from at least the reign of Henry I creates further resistance when it comes to trying to distinguish between different ethnic groups. Wider use of recent work by historians like Hugh Thomas, John Gillingham, and Rees Davies would solve some of the problems apparent here with identifying labels. There is also a tendency to adopt the later conflation of British and English history when discussing these early texts. Writers including Layamon are constructing the "Brut" tradition, which may be the history of England but is not the history of the English; Arthur is not called an English king until the Auchinleck "Arthour and Merlin."

The most engaged and provocative chapter in this study is the final one with its claim that a fascist aesthetic is the "darkness at the heart" of Arthurian history, evident in the romanticized self-image of Nazis and neo-Nazis as chivalric warriors. The issue this raises about the use and abuse of mythical history is valid, but the relationship to the Arthurian histories of Geoffrey and his successors occupying the rest of the book is little more than guilt by association: "There may be an unsavory kinship between the armored warriors of medieval Europe—even the romanticized armored warriors of King Arthur's court—and the armored divisions of Nazi blitzkrieg" (198). The Grail always occupies a marginal and fantastical place in Arthurian history, if it enters it all, and this has now been fully contextualized and put in perspective in Richard

Barber's *The Holy Grail: History of a Legend* (2004). The focus here is on two works of occult "history" by which the Grail legend contributes to a pernicious fascist myth, Jean-Michel Angebert's *The Occult and the Third Reich* (New York, 1974) and Trevor Ravenscroft's *Spear of Destiny* (New York, 1973). Again, the comparison does not convince—these are not texts central to their culture as were Geoffrey, Wace, or Malory. They batten on Nazi chic and a popular fashion for conspiracy theory— the latter recently more successfully mined by *The Da Vinci Code*—and despite all assertions of a link, this chapter rather demonstrates the differences between the medieval and the modern. This "paranoid history" with its obsession with Atlantis, the Aryan race, and all the rest excises the Matter of Britain in favor of cosmic spiritual conflict. As thus described (and I depend on their description, as life is too short to consult the originals), it owes less to legendary history than to Jessie Weston, perhaps Charles Williams (neither of whom are cited) and from thence the wilder shores of twentieth-century fantasy. The authors are concerned to demonstrate how their theoretical approaches expose the dangers inherent in such fascist fantasy and an Afterword defends poststructuralist readings of history from association with Holocaust denial. The best antidote to conspiracy theories is the careful reading of the textual tradition and the awareness of its exploitation across the centuries; this book demonstrates and encourages this. It will find its place on the reading lists for Arthurian courses and serves as a useful reminder of one justification for our teaching of such literature: to encourage the well-read and skeptical exercise of scholarship in the service if not of truth, then at least of fiction.

ROSALIND FIELD
Royal Holloway University of London

RALPH HANNA. *London Literature, 1300–1380*. Cambridge: Cambridge University Press, 2005. Pp. xxi, 359. $95.00.

In the field of Middle English, palaeographers and codicologists for the most part stick to palaeography and codicology. They provide an invaluable service industry, but themselves eschew the translation of their findings into literary criticism and cultural history. Ralph Hanna is an accomplished palaeographer and codicologist who, by contrast, actively develops his codicological observations into their literary critical and literary historical consequences. He is also at the forefront of *Piers Plowman* scholarship. In this book he promises a "topical" approach, in the etymological sense: an approach to place (here London), set within the years 1300–1380 (that is, almost all "Edwardian" writing). This book promises, then, different sets of connections, of urgently required kinds. On the one hand, we should expect links between the more empirical, material minutiae of given books and classes of book with larger interpretative histories. And on the other, we should expect the notoriously unconnected masterpiece of *Piers Plowman* to be given more of a local habitation and a name. Does the book deliver on these high expectations?

Chapter 1 provides a survey of the evidence, within these guiding persuasions: that London was pretty well without an English literary culture before 1300 (p. 5); that the ten fourteenth-century manuscripts listed on pages 5–7 offer a far-reaching conspectus of pre-1380 London textual production, within whose context *Piers Plowman* can be situated; and that, even within the period 1300–1380, London had nothing much in the way of book production to show for itself between c. 1340 and 1365. This chapter also offers a brief conspectus of other London "literary" textualities.

This survey achieved, Hanna divides his detailed presentation of London book production and intellectual culture into different discursive areas. Chapter 2 investigates London legal texts. He underlines the cardinal role of Statute books, and brings to light authors and texts that in turn illuminate vernacular literature, especially Andrew Horn, Chamberlain of the City (fl. 1310–25); Thedmar, from a German immigrant family and author of *Liber de antiquis legibus;* and John Walwyn, author of the *Vita Edwardi Secundi*. The argument in this chapter that the legal texts are focused on "gaining a heritable locale and exercising jurisdiction within it" (p. 96) also points to the discussion of Romance (especially the Auchinleck manuscript) in Chapter 3. For romances also "describe a frontier, a locale open to be crafted into family properties" (p. 107). Once more, "new" authors (new to me at any rate) surface, such as the royal clerk Walter de Milemete, and new sets of connections, as between the "mercantile-industrial City and royal Westminster" (p. 124).

This excellent chapter is followed by the real gem of the book, Chapter 4, which is devoted to discussion of Anglo-Norman audiences and London biblical texts, in particular texts in Pepys 2498. This chapter is full of revelations about a vibrant, self-confident London spiritual culture that points directly forward to *Piers Plowman*. The remarkable *Mirror* by Robert Gretham, its even more trenchant Middle English translation, the prose *Apocalypse*, the *Early English Prose Psalter*, and the interpolated version of the *Ancrene Riwle*—cumulatively these reveal a cultural mobility from Latin and Anglo-Norman to English, from previously vibrant centers of textual production in, say, the West, to London, and from regular religious consumption to secular, urban consumption. These are striking texts and Hanna deserves great credit for bringing them to light so lucidly.

A brief account of the death of Anglo-Norman literature, marked by the Chandos Herald's memorial *Vie du Prince Noir* (1385) in Chapter 5, is a prelude to discussion of the one canonical text (*Piers Plowman*) discussed in Chapter 6. An epilogue underscores the end of Edwardian literary culture.

Readers wishing to connect *Piers Plowman* with an Edwardian London culture will already have seen how Chapters 2 and 4 in particular lead directly into that poem. Readers wishing to see Hanna himself capitalize, on the basis he has laid in those chapters, to render the connections explicit will, however, be disappointed. Faced with the challenge of developing his fertile suggestion that *Piers* is an Edwardian rather than a Ricardian poem, one might expect Hanna to isolate grand themes of law and lay spiritual authority that have emerged in the previous chapters and apply them broadly to Langland's poem. Instead, he chooses to attempt a close, sequential reading of segments of *Piers Plowman*, much of which has no obvious relevance to London.

Some of the argument is inevitably familiar to readers who know the scholarship on *Piers Plowman*. Some of it is also a little baffling: Hanna argues that "any putative dialogue between Chaucer and Langland . . . is at best a monologue," since Langland's "career had, in the main, ended in autumn 1377" (p. 247). This does not square with the pushing forward of the C-Text composition to at least 1388, a more recent dating that Hanna has himself supported elsewhere ("Given the evidence for the poet's reliance on the 1388 promulgation of the Statute of Labourers, Langland may have worked on the C Version throughout the 1380s" (Ralph Hanna III, *William Langland* [Aldershot, Hants.: Ashgate, 1993], pp. 16–17). Neither does it square with the description of the C-Text, in the book currently under review, as "much the most intellectually demanding form of the poem" (pp. 289–90). Some of the argument is flawed: the king's desire to prohibit tax evasion is described as a questionable desire to equate "lawe" with the king's "private financial profit" (p. 270); this argument implies a fundamental misunderstanding about taxation and the seriousness of its evasion. Above all, however, the chapter unaccountably fails to connect seriously with those preceding it: the best it can do is to gesture to those chapters in occasional asides. In short, this book reached its remarkable climax in Chapter 4; the expected climax, so carefully prepared, for the most part misses its opportunity.

The book is marred by many technical and presentational failings: (1) Professor Hanna is a master of many skills, but the humble comma eludes his grasp. Very often he sets an appositional word or phrase off only by a comma, when it needs more than one take for the reader to understand that the comma marks an apposition (for example, p. 37/ 15; p. 56/15–16; p. 86/11; p. 89/1; p. 106/20; p. 136/19 etc.). (2) Hanna is also, sometimes, far too close to the material to offer illuminating broader perspectives to readers coming to the topic for the first time; a good deal of the prose in Chapters 1 and 2 is what I call "bibliographer shelf-mark mash" (prose crammed with shelf marks to the point of bare intelligibility [for example, p. 47]). (3) Further, a good deal of the book is written for the *cognoscenti*. Thus the phrase "of course" occurs frequently: "The uniqueness of this document of course testifies to the normal use of anglicana for Latinate or Anglo-Norman scribal use" (p. 45). (4) Most frustrating by far, there are no images, which render frequent discussion of *mise-en-page,* let alone of manuscript illuminations, very hard going. (5) The Introduction's promise to maintain "bonhomie" by "not feeling compelled to cite, much less offer a critique of, works I have found generally unhelpful" (p. xviii) looks to me like self-indulgence; the maintenance of *bonhomie* has no place in scholarship, as Hanna has himself demonstrated so frequently. (6) For "Edwardian period (1270–1370)" (p. 149), read "Edwardian period (1272–1377)"; (7) for "Apocalyse" (p. 170), read "Apocalypse." (8) For "seduceat" (p. 173), read "seducent."

JAMES SIMPSON
Harvard University

RALPH HANNA and DAVID LAWTON, eds. *The Siege of Jerusalem.* Early English Text Society, o.s. 320. Oxford: Oxford University Press, 2003. Pp. xcix, 224. $85.00.

Hanna and Lawton's critical edition of *The Siege of Jerusalem* is designed to replace that of Eugen Kölbing and Mabel Day (EETS 188 [1932]). As is the case with both the earlier editions of *The Siege* (the Kölbing/Day edition and the partial edition by Thorlac Turville-Petre), this edition is based on Bodleian Library, MS Laud Misc. 656 (L). The Hanna and Lawton edition does, however, differ from that of Kölbing and Day in that it makes use of Princeton University Library, MS Taylor Medieval 11 (P), a witness of which Kölbing and Day were unaware, and isolated P readings are sometimes adopted as emendations. Hanna and Lawton's account of the relationship between the manuscripts nevertheless basically agrees with earlier opinions offered by Hulbert and Day, although they do provide more detail and, in particular, clarification of the problematic affiliations of British Library, MS Cotton Caligula A.ii, part 1 (C).

There is evidence of a certain amount of carelessness in this edition. It is, for instance, difficult to have much faith in the glossary when so many past-tense verbs appearing under the very first letter are recorded as *pr.* ("present") (see glosses for *apered, assembleden, assented, assenteden, auntred, availed*). Emendations, too, are sometimes problematic. The editors accept Hoyt Duggan's findings regarding the metrical constraints on the b-verse, and they emend the text accordingly, but not all such emendations are convincing. Infinitives in *-e,* for instance, are often emended to *-en metri causa* in noneliding position on the grounds that pronounced final *-e* must have been absent from the author's dialect, whereas the evidence suggests that infinitive *-e* was syllabic: infinitives in *-en* are normally only used in the *Siege* manuscripts in positions where they are necessary to prevent elision. Hanna and Lawton's approach here appears to result in part from *a priori* assumptions about the language of alliterative poets, but their view is doubtless reinforced by their localization of the *Siege* author's dialect in the area of Barnoldswick, West Yorkshire. Unfortunately this localization is unreliable. In particular, the use of forms of "shall'" in /s/ (*sall* etc.) for diagnostic purposes, something that sets a firm southern limit on any possible placement, is based on unconvincing evidence: that such forms occur three times in positions where initial /s/ would make it possible for this auxiliary to provide a third metrical stave in the a-verse. Since the number of these examples is so small, since such staves are not a metrical requirement, and since the editors themselves admit that such evidence is ambiguous, it seems unwise to place quite so much reliance on it. Once this particular form is discounted, the evidence suggests a more southerly placement.

Because this localization is suspect, the material on likely sites of composition and possible patrons (both to a large extent based on this localization) must also, for the moment, be suspect, as must some of the arguments concerning the relationship with *The Destruction of Troy,* since the editors suggest that similarities of diction in the two poems may simply reflect the fact that the two poets lived in close geographical proximity and were making use of a specific local tradition of alliterative verse.

Emendations are also sometimes problematic for other reasons. For example, Hanna and Lawton's determination to interpret lines 718ff. as direct speech (and a series of verbs with *–n* endings as imperatives), a decision resulting in various emendations, is quite simply peculiar, especially since indirect rather than direct speech is employed in the source at this point. Hanna and Lawton also fail to make sufficient use in their treatment of the a-verse of evidence available from the b-verse. For example, at 1.560 the expected form of the verb, given the gloss of "hammered, pounded," would be *malleden* rather than *mallen* (the glossary records this as a preterite), and the form *mallen,* in addition, gives an extremely short a-verse. The evidence from b-verses does indeed suggest that *-eden* endings were regularly subject to scribal reduction, either to *-ed* or to *-en* (see, for example, Hanna and Lawton's emendation of the b-verse at 1.793).

The recording of variants is in some ways disappointing. Metrically significant variants are recorded for the b-verse (where they affect editorial decision-making) but not for the a-verse, a "double standard" (the editors' term) that makes this edition of less use to those interested in a-verse meter than is the Kölbing/Day edition (the latter do at least record such a-verse variants as *suþ/sithen*). It is also a pity, given the importance of the Thornton manuscripts, that certain variants which may throw light on Thornton's scribal practice are no longer recorded. The apparatus of the Kölbing/Day edition, for instance, shows that the oblique form of the third person plural pronoun consistently appears in the Thornton manuscript with initial *th-/þ-*, but in all remaining manuscripts with initial *h*- (the latter being the form required by alliteration). This information is no longer available in the present edition.

Nevertheless, in many respects Hanna and Lawton offer the reader considerably more information than do Kölbing and Day. The position or nonoccurrence of the caesura is recorded in the variants, as are paraphs present in Lambeth Palace Library, MS 491, part 1 (D), as well as all b-verse variants affecting metricality. This last is only one example of the considerable care taken to make editorial practice transparent. Not only "positive emendation" but also materials that have been deleted are signaled in the text, while the introduction and, where necessary, the notes provide detailed accounts of editorial decision-making.

In addition, and perhaps most important, the Hanna/Lawton edition represents a major advance on Kölbing/Day in its identification of sources. Three sources were identified by Kölbing and Day: the *Vindicta salvatoris*, Ranulph Higden's *Polychronicon*, and Jacobus de Voragine's *Legenda aurea*, and a further source, the *Bible en françois*, by Phyllis Moe. Hanna and Lawton now identify a fifth source, the translation of Josephus's *Jewish Wars* usually attributed to Rufinus of Aquileia, which contains, as they conclusively demonstrate, close verbal and narrative parallels to substantial portions of *The Siege*, including not only passages unparalleled in previously identified sources but also sections interwoven with passages drawn from those sources. The identification of the sources of *The Siege* now therefore appears to be complete.

JUDITH A. JEFFERSON
University of Bristol

ALFRED HIATT. *The Making of Medieval Forgeries: False Documents in Fifteenth-Century England.* London and Toronto: The British Library and University of Toronto Press, 2004. Pp. xiv, 226. $60.00.

The title of Alfred Hiatt's *The Making of Medieval Forgeries: False Documents in Fifteenth-Century England* is slightly misleading on two counts. For a book that modestly proclaims its subject to be *Fifteenth-Century England*, it displays a conspicuous wanderlust: back in time as far as the famous Donation of Constantine (probably a product of the eighth century), and forward to the textual criticism of Papenbroeck and Mabillon, both of whom lived into the early eighteenth. This is a small quibble of course, but the second way this title misleads is somewhat more significant: although we are told that we are to hear about the *Making of Medieval Forgeries,* we do in fact learn rather more about their consumption—in reality, Hiatt's study proves to be more a kind of medieval forgers' *Rezeptionästhetik* than a guide to their techniques.

Early in the book, Hiatt argues that the debate between Giles Constable and Elizabeth Brown (over the degree to which medieval forgery grew out of a more fluid attitude to truth in an earlier period) has run its course, and that now what is needed is a reconception of the subject—a move away from the study of context and function, and toward "the fundamental questions of how and why forgeries were identified, discussed, and repudiated" (p. 8). Despite, as I have said, substantial sorties into earlier and later periods, Hiatt uses three fifteenth-century case studies to exemplify this approach: the *Chronicle of Pseudo-Ingulf,* a document produced in mid-fifteenth-century Croyland Abbey and intended to fill in gaps in its muniments resulting from a fire in 1091; the *De antiquitate et origine alme et immaculate universitatis Cantebrigie,* a highly fanciful history that attributes the founding of Cambridge University to a Spanish prince called Cantaber, who apparently visited Britain after a spell of study in ancient Athens; and the *Chronicle* of John Hardyng, a major plank in the author's extended campaign to justify and encourage the invasion of Scotland by, first, Henry VI and, later, Edward IV. Each of these texts prompts the author to extend his study to analogous cases: from Croyland, for instance, he moves on to St. Augustine's, Canterbury, and Bury St. Edmunds; from Cambridge, to Oxford, and Bologna; and from Hardyng to William of Worcester. All three texts have one important feature in common: each presents us with a historical narrative that includes, or accompanies, forged charters, and thus offers us a historiographical context in which to interpret and theorize medieval forgery. The subjectivity of historical narrative (*à la* Hayden White) has become an article of faith among many literary critics nowadays, and by setting medieval forgeries in such a narrative context Hiatt makes their reception appear no longer a simple matter of separating truth from falsehood: from his perspective, forged charters take their place next to genuine ones along a sliding scale where all truths (or falsehoods) are made to appear relative. This is a world where even textual criticism can masquerade as a species of forgery.

The Making of Medieval Forgeries is a handsomely produced volume, supported by dense scholarship and illustrated with a wealth of fascinating plates. Its argumentation is ingenious and often entertaining, and it has much to teach even those well versed in the period. I was particularly intrigued by its account of Hardyng's back-to-front diagram (Hiatt flatters it by calling it a map) of Northern Scotland; it conjures up the Pythonesque image of a Yorkist army, armed with Hardyng's directions, getting itself hopelessly lost in the Scottish Highlands—an opportunity for speculative reception that Hiatt wisely resists. Since *The Making of Medieval Forgeries* does not set out to be a comprehensive survey of its subject, it is perhaps rather churlish to complain about the topics it does not cover, but readers should be warned that this is very much a study of intellectual forgery—forgery, as it were, from above. They will search in vain for the grubbier manifestations of the forger's vocation—the erasures, the interlinings, the overwritings, that form part of the stock in trade of men like the Chancery clerk William Brocket, who tampered with an *Inquisition post mortem* in 1432. My only serious complaint is that there is an occasional slipperiness in Hiatt's use of terminology. The word *antiquarian*, for instance, is frequently used to describe the historical researches of men seeking to bolster the legal interests, the prestige, or the political advantage of institutions with which they were associated, yet *antiquarian* surely suggests research that is driven primarily by a disinterested passion for the past—naive and uncritical certainly, but not, as here, grossly partisan. By this definition, William of Worcester (or John Leland, William Lambarde, and John Stowe) are antiquarians, but John Hardyng is certainly not. Even more crucially, the word *forgery* itself is used in a wide variety of meanings—a facsimile, a speculative re-creation, or a creative embellishment, are quite as likely to be labeled forgery as full-blown documentary fraud. But that, I suppose, when one comes to think of it, is Hiatt's whole point.

RICHARD FIRTH GREEN
The Ohio State University

LAURA F. HODGES. *Chaucer and Clothing: Clerical and Academic Costume in the General Prologue to the "Canterbury Tales."* Cambridge: D. S. Brewer, 2005. Pp. xiv, 316. $90.00.

This second of two volumes on Chaucer's use of clothing in his *General Prologue* to the *Canterbury Tales* provides invaluable information about how the attire worn by Chaucer's pilgrims might have been understood by Chaucer and his contemporaries. The earlier volume, published by D. S. Brewer in 2000, offered a thorough and illuminating contextualization of the secular pilgrims' clothing, and in so doing challenged certain long-standing critical notions, such as the transgressive nature of the Wife of Bath's scarlet hose and the Miller's blue hood and weapons. This book resumes the discussion—and the critical dismantling—in the context of the pilgrims associated with holy orders and universities, a list that comprises, in the order in which Hodges addresses them, the Prioress, the Monk, the Friar, the Clerk, the Physician, the Pardoner, the Summoner, and the Parson. It also inhabits the same methodological space as the earlier volume, as Hodges scrutinizes what she calls Chaucer's "costume rhetoric" (p. 3), or his manipulation of the intricate code of late fourteenth-century costume signs and their associations, through her own systematic investigation of that code in historical and legal documents, visual art and artifacts, literature, and religious rules. In its critical and bibliographical scope, rigor, and substance, this book, along with the first installment of *Chaucer and Clothing*, makes a considerable contribution to both Chaucer studies and costume studies.

The author begins her study with a discussion of the discrepancy between the ideal attire of religious orders and their actual dress practices. Surveying religious rules, sumptuary laws, literary complaints, and historical records, Hodges's first chapter finds much evidence supporting the idea that transgressions of religious attire were a growing problem, but one that in practice seems to have enjoyed a certain amount of tolerance. While religious rules concentrate on the proper level of expense, appropriateness to climate and occupation, and craftsmanship of religious attire, sumptuary laws and ecumenical council records indicate that these rules were regularly ignored, and often with full knowledge of spiritual authorities. This contextual material directly shapes the argument of Hodges's next two chapters, in which she maintains that the Prioress's clothing in the *General Prologue* does not mark her as the "scandalous" figure some critics would like her to be. Rather, her controversially high headdress, her "ful fetys" habit, and the gold pendant on her coral rosary all seem to be in keeping with other descriptions of respectable and even saintly religious figures. Chapter 4 reconsiders the Monk's attire in a similar way, comparing it to other descriptions of sartorial misbehavior in satires and Church documents, and finding that his garments—even his "bootes souple"—are more ordinary than flamboyant.

Whereas Hodges's careful undoing of established criticism and readers' assumptions reveals normative dress where one least expects it, it also finds possible transgression in heretofore little-explored corners. As we learn in Chapter 5, for example, the Friar's duplicity and lechery can be found not only in his notorious tippet filled with phallic knives, but also in his "semycope," which, say Hodges, "would fall short on the Friar's body as it falls short of propriety" (p. 152). Furthermore, the "double worsted" fabric of his cope is appropriate to Chaucer's Friar not because it is worldly and luxuriant, as some critics have supposed, but because of its association with fraudulent mercantile practices in this period. The following chapter contains one of Hodges's most interesting and potentially provocative arguments, as it greatly complicates the idea that Chaucer's threadbare Clerk is an "ideal" figure in the *General Prologue*. Citing contemporary debates over proper clerkly attire, the problematic symbolism of "thredbar" garments (worn at times by both Avarice and Coveitise), and the Clerk's potential for the vice of *curiositas,* or excessive desire for knowledge, Hodges comes to the conclusion that his garment displays the precarious balance of his current life situation.

The last four chapters might be said to deal with the concept of vestimentary advertising. The Physician's fabric and color schemes, we learn in Chapter 7, not only put him in the running for "the most lavishly dressed of any of the pilgrims" (p. 219), but also show that "the Doctor knows and practices the principles of effective public presentation" (p. 201). Chapter 8 more overtly discusses the subject of advertising in its examination of Chaucer's pairing of the inappropriate headdresses worn by the Pardoner and the Summoner. Both the Pardoner's cap with vernicle and the Summoner's curious garland and cake-buckler, according to Hodges, broadcast the discontinuity between their sartorial performance and their inner characters. In contrast, the opposite can be said about the sartorial representation discussed in Hodges's final chapter, "The Parson Has No Clothes." In describing no clothes for the Parson, the one pilgrim who voices his own philosophy of dress in his sermon on pride, says Hodges, Chaucer signifies the Parson's complete lack of pride; rather than clothe himself in material goods, he clothes himself in his good works. In its title, this chapter skirts the issue of Chaucer's own sartorial advertising: for if the Parson wears "no clothes," then it is Chaucer the "swindler," so to speak, who has woven the invisible suit for him to wear and for us to ponder. Hodges's conclusion offers her final deductions regarding this process of Chaucer's "costume rhetoric." While the restricted scholarly lens of this book—Hodges's self-pronounced commitment to analyzing only the costume, and not the accompanying gestures, actions, or words of the pilgrims—helps enable the book's extended clothing analysis and confident historical pronouncements, it also underscores the relative analytical economy of the book. Entrenched as it is in costume history and references, the book has very little room to explore some of the more extensive literary and cultural implications of its findings. And while the author makes very clear that she is aware of such extenuating questions, that awareness did not always lessen the force of their absence for this reader. Hodges's impressive quantity of evidence provides new readings of these pilgrims' garments, but of sheer necessity often leaves open what this means for the pilgrims (and the texts) themselves. Thus, despite (or because of) the enormity of scholarly information offered in this two-volume set, and Hodges's own determination to set the critical record straight regarding Chaucer's pilgrims' attire, *Chaucer and Costume* seems to me to open as many doors as it closes. In the end, however, perhaps this is also its finest attribute.

ANDREA DENNY-BROWN
University of California, Riverside

CONOR MCCARTHY. *Marriage in Medieval England: Law, Literature, and Practice.* Woodbridge, Suffolk, and Rochester, N.Y.: The Boydell Press, 2004. Pp. viii, 185. $80.00.

Conor McCarthy's study of texts dealing with the wide "variety in marital ideology and practice" (p. 18) in medieval England provides useful syntheses of scholarship on the legal and socioeconomic contexts of marriage and applies that scholarship to a range of fourteenth- and fifteenth-century literary texts. McCarthy organizes his material along an arc that roughly parallels the natural course of marriage in human experience, starting with two substantial chapters on the role of consent in marriage and on the relation of marriage and property, and then moving on to shorter discussions of marriage as an alliance between

303

families or nations, marital affection, marital sexuality, gender roles and children, and finally widowhood.

Most of the chapters begin with a fairly extensive review of scholarship dealing with ecclesiastical and secular legal perspectives on these "thematic" dimensions of marriage, often incorporating theological and moral discourse (for example, the writings of Jerome and Augustine on marriage and sexuality) as applicable. The chapters then turn to representations of marriage in literary, hagiographical, and epistolary texts, including *Troilus,* the *Legend of Good Women,* the *Knight's, Merchant's,* and *Franklin's Tales,* and the *Wife of Bath's Prologue; Piers Plowman* (the Meed episode); *The Book of Margery Kempe;* the Paston Letters; the lives of Mary d'Oignies, Christina of Markyate, and Bridget of Sweden; and brief discussions of passages from selected Old English texts. Although McCarthy's syntheses of legal, historical, and theological contexts will be familiar to scholars who have studied medieval marriage in depth, they should provide nonspecialists and students with a helpful overview of the field at large, enriched and concretized by the literary and epistolary manifestations of attitudes and practices sketched out more abstractly in the normative texts.

While the individual chapters of *Marriage in Medieval England* present specific theses about the literary works he discusses therein, McCarthy's introduction highlights several broader arguments of the book: in particular, the multiple, often competing ideologies underlying a similar multiplicity of practices involved in medieval English marriages. In addition to the tensions and contradictions within the theory and experience of medieval marriage, McCarthy also notes the importance of continuities in marriage across the period, including the significance of property, the role of familial or national alliances in some marriages, the recognition of affection as an element in marriage, and so on. Other points that he emphasizes in his introduction are the fluidity of the rhetorical boundaries between medieval legal and literary texts and the broad array of medieval texts that can be classified as literary, including fictional, (auto)biographical, and epistolary writings. These reasonable observations about medieval forms of discourse do not mean that McCarthy views the fluidity he sees among these forms and genres as absolute. By organizing his chapters so that they move from normative texts (ecclesiastical and secular laws, court documents, moral writings) to fictional and nonfictional treatments of individual marital relationships, he implicitly suggests that the texts he explores are best viewed as residing on a spectrum rather than being in completely free, omnidirectional play with each other.

McCarthy's interest in continuities in the medieval English experience of marriage, as well as the changes in that experience, is reflected in his occasional glances back at Anglo-Saxon marriage practices as seen in legal and literary texts. This is an unusual and intriguing extension of the more familiar and more studied Middle English material, but I am not finally convinced that the Anglo-Saxon texts are as illuminating as, say, the inclusion of marital practices as represented in the medieval drama, later medieval chronicle writing, or court spectacle might have been. The discussions of Old English texts are too brief to allow detailed comparisons with the fourteenth- and fifteenth-century texts that are McCarthy's main literary examples and do not sufficiently address the watershed between Anglo-Saxon and post-Conquest legal practices, whether ecclesiastical or secular.

McCarthy is more successful in his discussion of later medieval texts. As he himself observes, his selection complements earlier book-length treatments of marriage in Middle English literature, such as Neil Cartlidge's *Medieval Marriage: Literary Approaches, 1100–1300* (1997), Henry Ansgar Kelly's *Love and Marriage in the Age of Chaucer* (1975), and my own *Kindly Similitude: Marriage and Family in Piers Plowman* (1995). The range of texts that he discusses necessarily limits the depth he can achieve on the work of individual writers, perhaps with the exception of Chaucer, selections from whose writings are addressed in four of McCarthy's seven chapters. He also pays detailed attention to the Meed episode in *Piers Plowman,* helpfully refining my discussion of that part of the poem by suggesting a more precise interpretation of the enfeoffing of Meed and False by Favel as a jointure rather than a *maritagium.*

In general, McCarthy's book is written clearly and for the most part carefully. Nonetheless, a number of typographical errors remain in the text, and some diction and orthography will raise readers' eyebrows (for example, "Augustine's ambiguity about marital intercourse" [p. 13], where "ambivalence" seems a more accurate way to describe the saint's attitude; "suppositious children" [p. 65], where "supposititious" must be the intention). More substantive is the mischaracterization of the *De bono coniugali*'s defense of the biblical patriarchs' marital practices, described as "defend[ing] the Church fathers against the charge of unchastity" (p. 10). Since McCarthy's surrounding discussion refers to Old

Testament models of marriage, it seems more likely that this is a faulty use of the phrase "Church fathers" than a misunderstanding of Augustine's point, but it should nonetheless have been caught and corrected in the copy-editing process.

In the conclusion to the book, McCarthy briefly considers the interesting question of how legal and social practices relating to marriage might be influenced by literary representations, while acknowledging that such influence is inevitably "subtler" and "more difficult to trace" than influences in the opposite direction (p. 162). He also returns to the important theme of the simultaneous continuities, tensions, and outright contradictions within medieval marital norms and practices. Indeed, this may be the most valuable lesson, whether new or simply a refresher course, that readers can take away from *Marriage in Medieval England:* those who seek to understand medieval marriage fully must take into account a very wide variety of source material, *auctoritees,* and expressions of *experience,* and must listen most carefully to the many voices that "speke of mariage" in the period.

M. TERESA TAVORMINA
Michigan State University

MARK MILLER. *Philosophical Chaucer: Love, Sex, and Agency in the "Canterbury Tales."* Cambridge: Cambridge University Press, 2004. Pp. x, 289. $75.00.

In *Philosophical Chaucer,* Mark Miller takes the familiar—Chaucer's indebtedness to Boethius's *Consolation of Philosophy* and Jean de Meun's *Romance of the Rose,* the role of sex, gender, and sexuality in some of the best known of the *Canterbury Tales,* as well as the problem of agency and normativity more generally—only to re-present it in profoundly defamiliarizing and challenging ways. In particular, Miller argues that Chaucer's interest in love is fundamentally an interest in the structures of practical reason, agency, and the drive to autonomy, not so much the abstract articulation of philosophical problems as the ways people inhabit "what we might call the affective and political life of philosophical problems." In the process, Miller forces a revaluation of how and why we should think of Chaucer's poetry as philosophical by focusing our attention on how Chaucer uses the forms of literary representation to investigate the dialectical structure of thought and desire.

Chapter 1 begins *in medias res* with a powerful and compelling close reading of "the natural" in *The Miller's Tale*. The Miller may seek to "quite" the Knight (and his emphasis on a deliberative rationality) by making the normativity of "the natural" seem self-evident and adequate such that there can be no practical function left for reason to play. But while this argument for a normative naturalism targets the Knight, it also, paradoxically, implies that the actions represented by the Knight and his characters are either impossible or not perverse, since if they did exist they would be part of nature. The Miller's way of addressing the problem of ethical normativity is to wish that it could never have arisen, a nostalgic longing for an "animal" or "childlike" condition, which, from the Miller's own point of view, never was and never could have been. Moreover, his nostalgic way of holding to such a theory does as much to undermine his own sense of normative gender and sexuality as to support it, for

a worry about secrecy, however muted by the Miller's loud avowals of careless-ness, is a structural product of the way he responds to the problem of normati-vity. . . . One powerful form that the Miller's longing for a state of carefree animality takes, then, is something like a phenomenology of the closet, a rela-tionship to a territory of secrecy which he is committed to saying does not exist and cannot matter, and which has the hold it does on him precisely by virtue of the way he seeks to deny it. (pp. 55–56)

The chapter concludes with a brilliant analysis of the effeminizing conse-quences of the Miller's identification with Alisoun—perfect exemplar of the human even as she also serves as the purely passive object of male desire—and the interpenetration of such a shameful and desirable ef-feminacy with a wish for mortification on the Miller's part.

Chapter 2 argues that in the Knight's ideal of a Thesean deliberative rationality, Chaucer "lays out the contours of a theory of autonomy that is about as good as he thought it was possible to produce" (p. 101). What makes an action, reason, or desire autonomous in this theory is its "reflective endorsability"; while a person's rational capacities play a central role in this activity, it is finally the person, not his or her reason, that determines what is endorsable and does the endorsing. Nonethe-less, Chaucer remains interested in "what further thoughts about agency this theory cannot accommodate and, more ambitiously, he wants to understand why autonomy resists grounding in any comprehensive theory" (p. 101). Thus, because Thesean deliberative rationality is predicated on the renunciation of erotic passion, it cannot accommodate either the Knight's "glamorization of Palamon and Arcite's erotic suffering or his identification with a formalist ethical and erotic ideal whose clearest embodiment is Emily" (p. 32).

Chapter 3 provides a direct analysis of why normativity resists grounding in a comprehensive theory by means of a provocative and original close reading of Boethius's *Consolation of Philosophy*. Carefully attending to that text's dialectical method, Miller reads the dialogue between the Prisoner and Philosophy (herself a figure for the Prisoner's reflective capacities) as outlining an interior argument arising from conflicts in his most basic intuitions concerning action and desire, conflicts that are paradigmatic for a rational creature. Their source "lies in an antinomy that structures practical rationality, and that ensures that an investment in having a coherent agency and identity is necessarily inflected by an investment in self-dissolution and self-punishment. In this sense, agency and identity are constitutively masochistic, even as masochism becomes a name for a condition of agentive and psychic life rather than an avoidable or aberrant psychosexual condition" (p. 33).

In a close reading of the *Roman de la Rose*, Chapter 4 returns this discussion of the philosophical account of repression and fetishism, and its understanding that agency is constitutively masochistic, to a sexual context. Miller's focus here on the poem's representation of the courtly lover, whose desire depends on the interpenetration of sadomasochistic structures with a longing for utopian sociality, as in the previous chapter, lays bare the deep history of psychological phenomena that we often think of as distinctively modern and associated with psychoanalysis. Yet as Miller shows in his analysis, such structures organizing medieval concepts of agency and normativity are in fact derived from the ancient and medieval intellectual traditions most important to Chaucer.

Chapter 5 expands earlier discussions of the incoherences of normative masculinity by examining the turn in *The Wife of Bath's Prologue* and *Tale* to a feminine subjectivity for which a similarly utopian intimacy is a central value and through which is developed a fuller account of a masochistic erotics. Miller argues that the Wife provides Chaucer with an occasion for exploring the myth of the subject, not only to subject that myth to critique but also to understand what gives it ideological power.

Chapter 6 concludes the book with a discussion of what would be required to constitute oneself and one's desires in relation to an ideal of love that is incompatible with such naturalist, instrumentalist, and subjectivist fantasies as have been raised by the *Miller's, Knight's,* and *Wife of Bath's Tales.* Miller argues that the Clerk intends a divided response of admiration and repulsion at Griseldan unconditionality because our divided response to Griselda is a sign of an irresolvable split in love's conceptual and affective structure.

One of the most useful and interesting features of the book is its careful and thoughtful consideration of methodology, especially as it attempts to find a *via media* between the often polarized modes of critical theory and historicism. Miller's approach to this question is an interesting and instructive balancing act. While interested in many of the same questions animating recent queer and psychoanalytic accounts of medieval gender and sexuality, Miller chooses not to employ the conceptual frameworks of, say, modern psychoanalysis in order to begin to understand how Chaucer and his main intellectual interlocutors might have conceptualized an interest in these topics. Similarly, in theorizing Chaucerian agency and autonomy, Miller balances the more familiar accounts of normativity as the drive toward ideological normalization (by Foucault, Butler, Sedgwick, and others) with an account "very much alive in Chaucer's time, and the one still dominant in contemporary philosophical ethics, in which 'normativity' refers to the authority rational and ethical considerations have for agents, and in which an internalization of that authority is understood not in terms of 'subjection' but rather as essential to the pursuit of autonomy, or a good life, or happiness" (p. 13). The result is a book that not only provides fresh and provocative readings of the Canterbury tales that have become central texts for recent feminist, queer, and psychoanalytic Chaucer criticism, but that also suggests new ways to forge links between theory and history, and the postmodern and the premodern.

GLENN BURGER
Queens College and the Graduate Center,
The City University of New York

RUTH NISSE. *Defining Acts: Drama and the Politics of Interpretation in Late Medieval England.* Notre Dame, Ind.: University of Notre Dame Press, 2005. Pp. x, 226. $40.00 cloth, $23.00 paper.

Ruth Nisse argues in *Defining Acts* that late medieval English theater, by the very fact of vernacular textual performance, was deeply invested in the practices of interpretation of authoritative religious texts and especially in the contested problems of translating and conveying meaning with truth and clarity. In these carefully conceived and persuasive chapters, form follows argument; in Nisse's sure hands, this religious theater becomes extraordinarily compelling and cogent and clear. That this is so, despite the notorious elusiveness and silences, the complex manuscript and performance histories, and the vexed scholarly speculations regarding this theater, is no small tribute both to what she calls medieval drama's "desire for legibility" (p. 8) as well as to her own skill, learning, and tact. But it is also tribute to the bold and successful effort made here to engage with this theater in an informed context of other kinds of lay, vernacular late medieval texts—ranging from *The Miller's Tale* to sermons and chronicles—that confront, critique, and interrogate the "dangers and pleasures of theatrical representation" (p. 5).

Chapter 1 begins with Chaucer's fabliau gaming with the instability of exegetical categories in and through the "shot-window" stage of *The Miller's Tale,* which Nisse reads as "an architecture of the imagination" (p. 16) through which parodic enactments of Incarnation are outrageously performed. That all ends crashing in disorder at the end of the tale not only rebuts the idealism of ancient Athenian tournament in *The Knight's Tale,* but offers, Nisse argues, Chaucer's own awareness of the mystery play challenges and contests to staged Scripture. In constructing her argument, Nisse invokes a fascinating passage in Thomas Walsingham's *Historia Anglicana,* in which the scornful puppet show jesting by rebels of 1381 with the heads of the chief justice John Cavendish and the hapless, assassinated prior of Bury becomes a perverse performance of mystery play tyrants with what the chronicler calls "absurdly improper action" (*cum maxima ineptia*). As Nisse puts it, Bury St. Edmunds did indeed stage this performance "literally over the prior's dead body" (p. 15). But the furious contest between clergy and laity over how to interpret and translate sacred texts and bodies would take a wide range of forms, she argues, over the course of the next century.

The York Plays, the subject of Chapter 2, belong to what Nisse, fol-

lowing Anne Hudson, calls the turn-of-the-century "window of opportunity" for the relatively free exchange of Wycliffite reformist ideas (p.
25), especially from the pulpit. In this chapter, she demonstrates that
the York Plays draw on far more heterodox ideas about translation and
interpretation that has been previously assumed; indeed, the insistent
preoccupation with the "full clere," open, plain sense of Scripture in a
play like the skinners' "Entry into Jerusalem" identifies scriptural understanding and authority with civic rule itself. It is in the courts and
temples of tyrants that sacred text dissolves into interpretative chaos,
giving a play like *The Judgement of Christ before Pilate* the force of lay
Lollard polemic.

In Chapter 3, perhaps the most provocative chapter of this lively
book, Nisse reads the York cycle pageants as skeptical, however, of female lay authority, especially female visionary authority to interpret
Scripture, and she suggests that a play like the York *Dream of Pilate's
Wife* reveals antagonism to female visionary claims. Through its repudiation of Procula and the Devil's misleading visions, the play enacts both
warning about the discernment of spirits and labels women's mysticism
as a "dangerously excessive form of knowledge and writing" (p. 49).
Although Nisse probably goes too far in calling the York *Nativity* play
"a dramatization of St. Bridget of Sweden's vision" (the Marian speech
she cites as Bridgetine example is, in fact, right out of the ubiquitous
Franciscan *Meditationes vitae Christi*) and in calling Mary's prayer at the
manger the cycle's "inaugural moment" for raising the problem of
women's contemplation and meditation (pp. 47, 48), she is certainly
correct in seeing the York Plays as deeply reticent about the kind of
Briggitine spirituality that animates the Marian pageants in the *N-Town
Plays*. In the conclusion to her third chapter, Nisse reads the *N-Town
Mary Play* as drama that "advances the idea that after the Incarnation,
all writing must involve a female element" (p. 74), even suggesting that
the expositor *Contemplacio* is not just a female-gendered noun and name
but a celebratory allegorical figure of "women's devotion and visionary
authority within the frame of salvation history" (p. 66).

The "modernity" of the Wakefield Master's translation of the theme
of labor into plays wittily interrogating writing, exegesis, and language
itself makes those plays of the Towneley manuscript utterly different
from the urban, lay drama of the York Plays, Nisse argues in Chapter
4. Focusing especially on the *First Shepherd's Play* and its production of
feast from a rustic "pastor's" empty bag, this chapter makes the surpris-

ing claim that the Wakefield Master, by the very pyrotechnics and wit of his verbal display, attempts, as did contemporary antitheatrical polemic, to "direct the audience's vision away from the stage and into an interior condition." The Wakefield Master of the Towneley manuscript, she ends by arguing, "pens a theatrical art that succeeds in its representations only when the visible finally disappears inward and the stage, like the beggar's bag, is perfectly empty" (p. 98).

It is the exegesis of the entire Christian community, clerical as well as lay, that is dramatically challenged, Nisse claims, in the Croxton *Play of the Sacrament,* by the community of contesting diasporic Jews, who seek "to recover and represent the lost origins of both Jewish Scripture and—by extension—English Jewish history" (p. 113). Nisse sets this challenge in the "thinly disguised prosperous urban mercantile world of Bury and Norwich" (p. 114) as well as in the dimly glimpsed apocalypse heralded by the final conversion of the Jews, for, she says, given the new wandering expulsion of the baptized Jews at the end of the play, it is only at the End of Days that history, sacrament, and meaning "can be fully restored to Christian hands" (p. 123).

The final demonstration of the way that late medieval theater performed the instability of translation of devotion and Scripture comes in Chapter 6 with discussion of the East Anglian play of *Wisdom,* which Nisse assumes, following Alexandra Johnston, to have been "a professional production for the court of a great East Anglian magnate, intended for an audience of gentry and clergy alike" (p. 131). Nisse skillfully reads the play as a critique of the mixed life, of, that is, the social and political dangers for readers, both clerical and lay, of interpretation of mystical texts like those of Richard Rolle and Bridget of Sweden. "*Wisdom* rebukes a gentry who not only misinterpret such texts but willfully read allegory in the most literal sense to advance specific political ends" (p. 131). "*Wisdom* warns all of us," Nisse writes, "how easily the figural language of the spirit can be transformed into the slogans of a misruled ruling class" (p. 7), arguing instead for its own conservative devotional program and invoking profane pageantry only to redirect the audience's eye from riotous sensuality and theatrics to the serene certainties of Wisdom Himself. In this chapter, as in all the thoughtful and imaginative readings in this book, the vernacular late medieval performance of text is seen to be fraught with both peril and possibility.

In *Defining Acts: Drama and the Politics of Interpretation in Late Medieval*

England we see the challenges and problems of theatrical exegesis played out in a theater of remarkable range and urgency. Ruth Nisse ably persuades in this thoughtful, illuminating book that, as her epigraph from Beckett's *Endgame* extolls, "Ah the old questions, the old answers, there's nothing like them!"

GAIL MCMURRAY GIBSON
Davidson College

LINDA OLSON and KATHRYN KERBY-FULTON, eds., *Voices in Dialogue: Reading Women in the Middle Ages*. Notre Dame, Ind.: University of Notre Dame Press, 2005. Pp. xvii, 508. $50.00.

This substantial volume of essays is notable for its content, which is consistently valuable and interesting, but still more notable for the form in which that content is presented: essays are presented in pairs, with the second essay being a response to the first—and, in some cases, giving rise to a third piece by one or both of the original writers. The format is useful in so many ways that one hopes it will create a new subgenre in the admittedly crowded category of essay collections.

As a whole, the book offers a medievalists' corrective to Jane Austen's mocking description of history (or at least historiography): "the men all so good for nothing, and hardly any women at all." The injustice of both parts of this characterization, at least as it relates to women's access to and participation in intellectual culture in the Middle Ages, is amply demonstrated in pieces that range, chronologically, from the patristic era to the Reformation and, geographically, from Bohemia to France, North Africa to England, although English topics play a larger role than those of any other single area. The authors, too, range from scholars early in their careers to distinguished senior academics, though the eminences of the field are especially well represented. The collection's examination of hierarchies, debates, and gender politics in medieval culture, and its attention to modern assumptions and blind spots on these topics, inevitably draws our attention to similar questions about modern culture, making it intriguing to consider the gender, status, and style of the authors of these pieces and how they formulate their arguments and responses. The wide-ranging introductory essay by Olson emphasizes the usefulness of "collegiality" and collaborative authorship as ways of thinking about not only the volume's medieval subjects but its modern creators, male and female. This introduction, along with Kerby-Fulton's lucid account of the issues surrounding female preaching and the contrapuntal discussion of Alcuin Blamires and Barbara Newman on the perception and depiction of women's relationship to intellectual creativity in (for the most part) secular literature, are the most broadly "thematic" pieces in the book and provide useful points of contact for the essays on more specific topics.

Rather than attempting to do justice to each essay's argument—an attempt that could only do a disservice to a collection this extensive and varied—this review will aim to suggest some of the many resonances that emerge from a reading of the whole book. The thematic coherence of the volume and its consistent emphasis on response and context make it both easier and more compelling for a reader to follow the links that bind these varied essays to one another. The fact that in a number of pairings the valuable close study of the first essay is given a wider background and/or further methodological implications by the second—as, for instance, in the pairings of Catherine Conybeare and Mark Vessey on the letters of Augustine, Alison Beach and John Van Engen on the sermonic compositions of the nuns of Admont, Mary Jane Morrow and David N. Bell on the manuscript context of certain Anselmian prayers, or Katherine Zieman and Margot E. Fassler on Brigittine liturgical practice—promotes a big-picture approach that links all the essays and continually reworks the reader's sense of what has gone before.

The effect is amplified in cases where two pairings are combined to make a quartet. Thus Fiona Somerset's contextualization of the Lollard Walter Brut's attitude toward women's intellectual role, which shows his relative lack of interest in a pro-feminist stance, is given a broader background by Kathryn Kerby-Fulton's account of Brut's links to continental traditions, with their greater room for women teachers. This pairing is followed by Alfred Thomas's discussion of attacks on Bohemian Wycliffite women (in a sense mirroring Kerby-Fulton by raising the question of Wyclif's reception on the continent), which sees these portrayals as indebted more to polemic than to actual practice. Dyan Elliott's brief response elegantly concludes the series with an overview of Bohemian and English characterizations of women teachers and their political contexts. Four essays that consider Birgitta of Sweden and her order have a similarly cumulative effect: Katherine Zieman and Margot

E. Fassler examine Birgitta's liturgical compositions, considering how both the form of liturgical practice and its intersection with clerical and visionary discourse might inflect our sense of the kinds of speech and doctrinal positions available to medieval religious women, while Elizabeth Schirmer and Steven Justice consider the reading practices of the nuns of Syon in the context of vernacular theology and Archbishop Arundel's *Constitutions*. And the discussion between Nicholas Watson and Felicity Riddy on Margery Kempe's authorship of her book is complemented by Genelle Gertz-Robinson's consideration of how both Margery and the Protestant Anne Askew occupied the rhetorical space of preaching even as they ostentatiously avoided its physical space, carrying the discussion of the location of voice into a new realm and the collection forward into the Reformation. David Wallace's response to Gertz-Robinson both returns to the issues raised by Watson and Riddy and brings the evidence of visual culture to bear on the question of women's access to the pulpit; he also provides a concluding grace note on community and collegiality that echoes Olson's introductory remarks.

All the essays, moreover, reach beyond their immediate contexts to other pieces in the book, often in unexpected and illuminating ways. Indeed, one of the great rewards of this volume is the way in which it works against academic overspecialization by pushing readers to follow the connections it provides in such abundance. Many of the collection's recurring themes touch on methodological or otherwise widespread concerns for many medievalists: the problem of evidence (Olson, Jaeger and Constable, Somerset and Kerby-Fulton); the shifting meanings of literacy (Olson, Conybeare and Vessey, Morrow and Bell, Zieman, Schirmer and Justice); the issue of modern biases and blind spots (Beach and Van Engen, Kerby-Fulton, Fassler, Justice). Also central, though less explicitly noted than most of the above, is the role of religion both as a major area of current inquiry and as a challenge and resource for medieval women and men.

The effect of paired essays is to highlight assumptions, contexts, and omissions, an effect that is, inevitably, most striking in the two most contentious exchanges in the volume, those between Stephen Jaeger and Giles Constable on the *Epistolae duarum amantium,* the possible "lost love letters" of Abelard and Heloise, and between Watson and Riddy on the nature of the authorship of Margery Kempe's *Book.* A clash of disciplinary approaches is clear in Jaeger's and Constable's differing assessments of what can be claimed in the absence of what Constable calls "positive evidence," as opposed to circumstantial "argument." Jaeger's compelling but often aggressively stated argument in favor of the letters' attribution to Abelard and Heloise lays him open to Constable's "gentlemanly skepticism" (as Jaeger puts it in his counter-response), but as Jaeger points out, Constable does not so much refute his argument as suggest that, given the absence of "positive evidence," it may derive from wishful thinking or emotional involvement. For Watson and Riddy, the interpretive divide is a similarly troubled one, between a reading that requires crediting Margery with deliberate authorship and one that emphasizes the text itself without particular regard to its historical or authorial origins, regarded as essentially irretrievable (in an echo of the Jaeger-Constable disagreement). Each of these pairs offers a kind of test case of a major debate in the field of medieval studies.

The collection's variety is not without its costs: a reader new to a given topic might become somewhat lost among the names of Augustine's female correspondents, for example, or the chaotic chronology of Margery Kempe's text. But the confusion thus occasioned is outweighed by the value of being introduced to, for example, late-antique epistolary conventions, or the culture of the eleventh- and twelfth-century schools, or the practices of monastic scriptoria. Any useful essay collection can probably be said to be more than the sum of its parts, but the work that the writers and editors have done to enter fully into their dialogues on every level makes this one especially rewarding. One can only hope it will receive the compliments both of attentive reading and then of imitation.

CLAIRE M. WATERS
University of California, Davis

LISA PERFETTI, ed. *The Representation of Women's Emotions in Medieval and Early Modern Culture.* Gainesville: University Press of Florida, 2005. Pp. vii, 222. $65.00.

Emotions as they are represented in medieval sources have recently generated a significant amount of critical interest. Jill Mann, in a session of the New Chaucer Society some years ago, was one of the first to raise the issue. This year, the International Medieval Congress held at the University of Leeds has set emotions and gesture as the focus of its entire conference, and the New Chaucer Society has organized sessions devoted to emotions for this summer's meetings. The topic is necessarily interdisciplinary and inspires multiple avenues of research in areas as varied as medical understandings of emotion, legal constructions and curtailments of emotions, emotions as guides to meditations on Christ's Passion, and the manifestations of emotions as personified abstractions closely linked to the Seven Deadly Sins, all necessary contexts when considering any literary treatment of emotions. Each of these domains has its own specialized contours, terminologies, and archives. And if you explore representations of emotions from the fifth to the seventeenth centuries in countries as different as England, Iceland, France, and Spain, each period and place has its own distinct history and culture. How, then, do you begin to explore such a vast topic?

Lisa Perfetti's timely collection of essays chooses gender as its entry point. More specifically, she focuses on women, a choice that brings to the foreground the medieval medical and theological assumption that women are particularly prone to emotional displays of certain kinds. Perfetti justifies the choice to focus on women because she suggests that enough work has been done on emotions in general to justify a more narrow focus on women and emotions alone. However, very little work has been done on emotions in general. We still do not have a clear understanding of what emotions were understood to be in the Middle Ages, let alone what forms of discourse especially associated women with emotions and why. Before beginning a study of representations of emotions in texts by or about women, it might have been helpful if the medieval association of women with emotion was more clearly established at the outset of the volume rather than in partial accounts scattered throughout the essays. Finally, the collection includes consideration of a number of literary representations, but its understanding of the specific kind of work this representation performs in relationship to other cultural discourses is never clarified.

In her introduction, Perfetti suggests that the essays to follow are united by their concern with four areas: (1) Emotions in relationship to constructed ideas about the body. (2) Class and ethnicity as they influence representations of emotion. (3) The ways that emotions disrupt or form communities. (4) The way women authors respond to stereotypes that associate them with emotion. While the essays do at times touch on these topics, they consider these issues (and, for that matter, the topic of emotions and women in general) with varying degrees of comprehensiveness and depth. The two theoretical essays that follow Perfetti's introduction might have served to set up the concerns of the essays that follow, but they end up leading the reader down two completely different paths. Exploring the significance of philosophical theories of the passions and humors along with their strong distinctions between male and female essences, Ann Matter's essay historicizes emotions by demonstrating the progressive interiorization of emotions from the medieval to the Early Modern period. Then, continuing his work on the theory of allegory and gender, James Paxson explores the implications of the tendency in the Middle Ages to personify emotions as female in relationship to Hildegard of Bingen's use of female personification in the *Ordo Virtutem.*

The "case studies" that follow these two theoretical essays consider representations of a wide range of emotions, from anger to grief to shame, in a variety of genres. From the drama to the poetry of the trouvères to the romance to mystical texts produced in different countries, including France, Germany, and England, these representations span the early Middle Ages (at times reaching back to classical sources) to the Early Modern period. Each essay, with varying degrees of success, clears the ground of discussion by summarizing the theological and historical contexts within which any given text is situated. In a particularly strong essay, Ellen Carrera explores the role of emotions as opposed to intellect in the meditations of Mechtild of Magdeburg, Angela of Foligno, and Teresa of Avila. She deconstructs the assumption that strong emotions were specific to female mystics by showing how several strands of religious thought encouraged affective meditation for men and women alike. At the same time, she demonstrates how restrictions on women's education and preaching reinforced the tendency of female mystics to express themselves in terms of emotions rather than intellect. Katherine Goodland's interesting consideration of female lamentation and mourning in four dramatic cycles demonstrates the different ways the cycle plays responded to displays of grief. She first demonstrates the origin of excessive lamentation in pagan ritual, then explores the manner in which these plays either reinforce or seek to contain such displays. Wendy Pfeffer's essay on women's emotions in the poetry of the trouvères provides fascinating glimpses into an array of emotions expressed by women poets (for example, grief at being forced into an undesired

marriage), but it is laden with unsupported claims and is undercontextu-
alized to the point that it reads as notes rather than an argument. Kristi
Gourlay's essay, "A Pugnacious Pagan Princess," is the first of the essays
to consider race and ethnicity; it rather too broadly surveys attitudes
toward male and female anger in a variety of sources, from court records
to literary texts, then turns to an interesting study of the Saracen romance heroine Floripas, showing how exceptional are her displays of
emotion. Sarah Westphal's theoretically sophisticated and exceptionally
well-argued analysis looks at the intersection of law and gender in Middle High German texts. It carefully delineates forms of anger (for example, the socially approved heroic form of anger), then turns to a
consideration of female anger in the *Sachsenspiegel*, showing how representations of Calefurnia's excessive bodily rage in the courtroom contributed to the historical diminishment of female legal agency and
ultimately to female silencing. Westphal furthermore demonstrates how
ethical negativity is ascribed to the dark skin of other female characters
when their anger is not contained. Valerie Allen's intelligent essay concerning the *Ancrene Wisse* and Chaucer within a well-focused context of
works by Aristotle, Augustine, and Aquinas shifts attention to an entirely different area of discourse, shame and sexuality, and demonstrates
how shame that arises from bodily experience is specifically feminized in
medieval texts. The collection rather abruptly ends here and could have
been improved with a bibliography.

A collection that initiates discussion of a large but badly neglected
topic will inevitably cohere with difficulty. It is bold of Perfetti to begin
a crucially important investigation into a pervasive cultural trope. As
society continues to associate women with excessive displays of emotion
and casts such displays in a negative light, it is all the more crucial that
we investigate the origins of these views. This collection of essays provides ample avenues for further discussion.

ELIZABETH ROBERTSON
University of Colorado at Boulder

TISON PUGH. *Queering Medieval Genres.* New York: Palgrave Macmillan,
2004. Pp. x, 226. $65.00.

Tison Pugh's *Queering Medieval Genres* is a rich and careful book: rich in
the breadth of engagement with queer studies from classical to post-

modern, with literary criticism from Bakhtin to Derrida, and with medieval texts and scholarship, English and Franco-Latin; and careful in framing the investigated texts as "resistance" and "subversion," and not as rejection or short-circuit of sexual and gender hegemony. The dominant ideological edifice within which these texts practice their subverting *bricolage* remains intact. Pugh states: "On the whole, I see little evidence to indicate their interest in subverting Christianity. . . . Rather, through their queering authorial play, they resist, expand, and subvert Christian constructions of queerness while affirming a commitment to salvation and to Christ" (p. 15). By contrast, some queer theorists would perceive conflict and opposition where Pugh sees resistance and subversion. The concentration of power in the institutions of which the authors were dependent members, and in relation to which, as Pugh shows, they acted as acculturated contributors, amplifies any trace of insubordination, however feeble. (By the way, thanks to Pugh's insightful readings, the traces appear far from feeble.) In a queer theoretical framework different from Pugh's, the opposition voiced by these texts would be seen as witnesses of an irreconcilably different consciousness. In that different framework, the texts would mark the onetime presence and subsequent maintenance and/or clever clandestine subsistence of a parallel culture. The texts' "little . . . interest in subverting Christianity" (p. 15) would be seen either as a survival strategy or as the trace of a mute (and thus the more disturbing) breakdown testifying to the violence exerted by the dominant culture.

By focusing on genre as the means of analyzing queerness, Pugh's investigation is, much of the time, equally interested in same-sex desire as in subversions or differences of many kinds; for example, the play between the anticipated genre projected by the narrative frame versus the genre of the imbedded narratives in *Canterbury Tales,* in his incisive discussion of "Alison of Bath, the fabliau speaker of an Arthurian romance" (p. 16). This enables Pugh's discussion of Alison's queering of heteronormativity, especially marriage. The question arises: If Alison's desire queers heterosexuality, is there a desire for a same-sex relationship in the offing? In other words, how queer is this queering? Is any sexual "resistance, expansion, and subversion" queer, or is only same-sex desire queer? If not an opposition, is there a continuum between sexual resistance/subversion and same-sex desire in the medieval period, and if so, how can we apprehend it theoretically and in reading practice? If this question is irrelevant, why? And whose interests are best served by asking it? Pugh's answer may be the utopian image that closes the book: when same-sex is an aspect of the social norm, is it still different? Or, "how will queer signify, if and when it is comfortably ensconced in the suburbs?" (p. 158; I say utopian because I am just back from Poland, where All Poland party members throw stones at pro-gay rallies; but I could take an example closer to home, the lawsuit against Miami University's partners' benefits policies, which—I have it on good authority—is expected to survive us all).

The point of departure of *Queering Medieval Genres* is the genre, that unfashionable and conservative category, rendered hip by the long-standing awareness that the play of genres allows the representation of unorthodox desires and subject positions, from political queer camp to parody, as the particular relationship to genre that defines modern and postmodern art and literature (this is my take on the issue, informed by camp theory and Hutcheon, and does not represent Pugh's account in the Introduction). The operative theory in *Queering Medieval Genres* is the queer genre theory, "the intersections of genre, gender, and sexuality" (p. 158). Genre play, or, in Pugh's terms, queering genres, chips away at the hegemonies and institutions in power. *Queering Medieval Genres* focuses on the unsettling of the heteronormative hegemony of religion, friendship, love, marriage, and desire. This focus allows Pugh to substantiate (without explicitly articulating it) his warrant that *genre play is queer,* that is, altering literary *genres* has primarily sexual and not primarily aesthetic or other functions. *Queering Medieval Genres* analyzes specific texts that manifest subversions within four historically situated genres: the eleventh- to twelfth-century Franco-Latin lyric (Marbod of Rennes, Baudri of Bourgueil, Hildebert of Lavardin), fabliaux (the *Canterbury Tales*), tragedy (*Troilus and Criseyde*), and romance (*Sir Gawain*). The chronological, language, and genre breadth of *Queering Medieval Genres* is a pleasure in itself, but it is also a logical and much appreciated choice for a book on queering the medieval, since Latin lyric is the vehicle for the most flagrant and abundant expression of same-sex desire and anxiety, and the twelfth century, its heyday. And while we speak of breadth, many elegant and insightful references to related work are stowed away in fifty pages of footnotes, to one's regret.

A ticklish issue, for me, is the constant emphasis on Christianity, in relation to which the texts and their subversive queering movements are situated: "the focus on queering the individual against an overarching Christian background provides the unity of interpretation for the chapters of this monograph" (p. 17). Yet, Christianity is almost always an unexamined category in *Queering Medieval Genres* (symptomatically, Christ, Christianity, and God are absent from the index), and it is not historically situated in terms of institutional practices.

Queering Medieval Genres delivers extensive, innovative readings, and I particularly appreciated the writing. Two examples: Gawain is a "reluctant masochist" (p. 130), tempted by "pleasures that [he] both enjoys and enjoys denying himself" (p. 138); the ending of *The Wife of Bath's Tale* spins out of control into a different genre: "Alison speaks in two voices here, the mellifluous (if not saccharine) tones of romance and the strident tones of fabliau" (p. 75). Last but not least, the readings evolve in constant dialogue with other analyses, especially of Chaucer. The abundance and the elegance of that dialogue is just one of the book's great pleasures.

Anna Klosowska
Miami University

Virginia Chieffo Raguin and Sarah Stanbury, eds. *Women's Space: Patronage, Place, and Gender in the Medieval Church*. Albany: State University of New York Press, 2005. Pp. x, 261. $85.00 cloth, $24.95 paper.

Medievalists reading Foucault's "In Other Spaces" are likely to find themselves in a familiar place. His first "other space" is medieval, the space of "emplacement"—that is, of fixed hierarchies and topographies of power—in contrast to the post-Galilean space of "extension" and the modern orientation of the "site." But medieval space is of course both produced and contested, not fixed, as different discourses map the world and the communities that inhabit it. Recent work has illuminated such contests, for example, between the way that notaries and artisans defined medieval Marseille and as they register in the substitution of Nuremberg for Jerusalem in a late medieval chronicle (Daniel Smail and Kathleen Biddick, both in *Medieval Practices of Space*, ed. Hanawalt and Kobialka). *Women's Space*, edited by Virginia Chieffo Raguin and Sarah Stanbury, contributes to the growing body of scholarship on medieval space by investigating the place of gender systems and women's practices in parish churches and monasteries.

The editors have long collaborated on the *Mapping Margery Kempe*
Web site (www.holycross.edu/kempe), an important resource and pedagogical tool for thinking about the spaces of *The Book of Margery Kempe:*
the towns of late medieval East Anglia, their parish churches and cathedrals, routes and sites of pilgrimage abroad. This work seems to inspire
many of the central concerns of *Women's Space:* the gendered spaces of
the parish church, the place of lay patronage, the conceptual association
between the female body and sacred space, the material, visual, and
narrative resources for constructing—and now reconstructing—the
space of medieval devotion. It is no coincidence, I think, that this
groundbreaking work is prompted by *The Book of Margery Kempe,* which
offers a probing analysis not only of the way space organizes and is
organized by social identity but also of the surprising fragility of this
organization, readily undone by those who abandon key aspects of that
identity—Margery in madness or devotion, or her incontinent husband,
who "spares no place" in his dotage.

The lead essay by Ruth Evans on the York cycle takes the relationship
between the body and space as its central focus. Her provocative analysis
begins with the claim that the Fall instantiates spatial, as well as sexual,
difference: the undifferentiated world of Paradise gives way to the binary of Eden and exile at the same moment that Adam and Eve become
aware, and ashamed, of their sexed bodies. This underwrites Evans's
reading of both the York Plays and the city itself. Gender play or crossing, Evans claims, threatens the social meaning and organizing function
of space. The performance of the York Plays encodes this threat, not
only thematically but in its very form: the dangerous mobility of exilic
sexuality is reproduced by the mobility of a play cycle performed on
pageant wagons. If Evans's bracing argument does not always slow
enough to work through its logic and evidence in detail, it offers a new
way to think about urban theater as a spatial practice, one sure to be
controversial but also richly productive for future explorations of Beatriz
Colomina's question: "How is the question of space already inscribed in
the question of sexuality?" (*Sexuality and Space,* 1992).

Other essays in the volume provide good examples of two ways space
can be used as an analytical category: as the object of representation and
the place of social practice. Virginia Blanton's essay on the representation of Saint Æthelthryth in the *Liber Eliensis* shows how the saint's

body, enclosed in its shrine, figures Ely abbey and its monastic community. The virgin's body was a flexible symbol, an image of the monastery's purity and its vulnerability, which allowed the abbey to address its precarious position during the Norman Conquest and subsequent political crises. Blanton does not pursue the implications of the symbolic equation of female saint and male community for our understanding of medieval gender and sexuality, but she provides a strong analysis of the institutional concerns that inform it. Katherine French uses churchwardens' accounts to investigate gendered seating arrangements in parish churches. Her fine-grained comparative analysis of parishes in Westminster and Bridgewater shows that the gendering of space was a very local phenomenon, informed but not determined by discourses about women's place. She makes a compelling argument that the organization of church space by sex could make women visible as a group and so establish the ground for other forms of gendered association and activity.

The editors both offer essays that extend our understanding of Margery Kempe's gestural vocabulary by reading its reference to the space of the parish church. Stanbury argues that Kempe's self-representation in key visions is influenced by the donor portraits in contemporary devotional art. The *Book* presents a sort of ekphrasis of images that represent the lay donor in close proximity to the object of her devotion, a strategy Stanbury reads as Kempe's effort to establish her place among Lynn's mercantile elite. Her argument is well supported by Raguin's suggestion that Margery's body, prone at the altar, imitates the position of brass memorials of prominent citizens found there. Raguin's wide-ranging essay provides especially valuable attention to the way the parish church was defined by sensory experience—the sounds and smells, as well as the sights, it affords. Although not all of the specific claims are convincing—for example, that Margery's weeping is a "reasonable" imitation of clerical recitation of the liturgy—Raguin shows how attention to the spaces Margery inhabits can teach us more about her devotion as a bodily practice.

The volume widens its focus from England to other European places in the last three essays. Ena Giurescu Heller provides a corrective history of a specific place—the sacristy of Santa Maria Novella in Florence—by uncovering the important role of Monna Andrea Acciaiuoli in its decoration. She shows how this history has been obscured by medieval gender protocols, which subordinate Monna Andrea to her husband, Mainardo Cavalcanti (who originally commissioned the chapel) and by the assumptions of modern historiography. Jane Tibbetts Schulenberg offers a series of hagiographic anecdotes about the miraculous exclusion of women from male monastic churches. They predictably represent women as temptresses and threats to sanctified space, but the argument that they therefore served to warn women from violating sacred space is unconvincing without a discussion of the likely audiences of the Latin *vitae,* which must often have been the monks themselves, not women. Similarly, the reading of these accounts as evidence that women resisted such restrictions grants them the status of transparent fact without investigating the contexts of their production and circulation—that is, the conditions that might help us understand the local purpose they served.

The final essay provides perhaps the clearest evidence of how complicated medieval space could be. Corine Schleif investigates the gendered logic and practice of distinguishing between left and right, directions determined in religious iconography not by the viewer but by the image. The essay works toward a fascinating exploration of the difference between this embodied, positional sense of moral significance (in which the right was privileged over the left) and an abstract geographic one (in which south was privileged over north), both used to map male priority. While the first structured the relations in devotional art, the second determined the position of congregation and some of the gendered decoration (images of saints) in the nave of the church. The two ways of reckoning space could thus sometimes complement, sometimes complicate, each other. Schlief's nuanced exploration of different, often overlapping, systems of gendered space is a strong conclusion to this thought-provoking volume.

CATHERINE SANOK
University of Michigan

KELLIE ROBERTSON and MICHAEL UEBEL, eds., *The Middle Ages at Work: Practicing Labor in Late Medieval England.* New York: Palgrave Macmillan, 2004. Pp. vi, 267. $65.00.

The title doesn't work. These essays do not in fact give an account of medieval people at work or, as the editors prefer to euphemize it, practicing labor. When they approach work, the essays are about its intellectual margins—how legislators tried to control workers, how preachers thought about work, how intellectuals themselves might have worked, what happened to the concept of labor.

What the collection does not discuss is the actual presence of labor in the medieval period or the medieval consciousness. One brief passage (pp. 146–47) deals with manuscript illuminations, but only to note that peasants are depicted as wearing clothes inappropriate to their status. It does not wonder why this is—aesthetics or politics, or both?—or consider the common visual bestialization of labor, turning peasants into grotesques and part-animals. Similarly, the recurrent partial presence of labor in literature is not discussed seriously: Langland's prologue, with its density of work detail, is treated as a generic exercise by Andrew Cole in an essay proclaiming its flight from labor reality in the title "Scribal Hermeneutics." The collection offers no discussion of Chaucerian labor, from the occupants of the House of Rumour and the low-class birds to the old women and dazed peasants who form a substratum of the *Canterbury Tales*. The York essay collection, *The Problem of Labour in Fourteenth-Century England*, which emphasizes the actual activities and representations of medieval labor, though mentioned in a few footnotes, has not been used as a source, nor has the rich empirical detail of Christopher Dyer's research engaged the authors' attention.

Not all of this collection is without value. Those who eschew the curiously assertive semi-theory approach that seems to infect modern academe (with the required brief reference to Foucault, Butler, or Žižek) and just get on with some descriptive work do provide useful material. Brian W. Gastle's account of the varying uses of the category of "femme sole" shows that this legal role was not only, and perhaps not much, for brave proto-feminists, but that the rich used it to dodge the embarrassments of wealth. Kate Crassons's study of a major sermon by the Wycliffite, and martyr, William Taylor outlines both his Lollard sympathy for the poor and his distaste for unearned charity, marking both a telling contrast and then a more telling comparison with the archconservative FitzRalph. Mark Addison Amos's account of the affairs of the Carpenters' Company is a sound piece of exposition, deserving future footnotes and even the attention of Chaucerians interested in the *Prologue*'s curiously recessive account of the guildsmen.

None of these is actually about "the Middle Ages at work"—but a least they do relate to the topic. The quite separate domain of literary labor is where other papers prefer to operate: Andrew Cole's shift from the workplace to the writing desk has been noted, and Ethan Knapp deploys the same process, also advertised in his title—"Poetic Work and Scribal Labor in Hoccleve and Langland." Catherine Batt restricts her para-laboring to the iconic symbolism of women's spinning in a piece focused on Hoccleve but departing from, and also demasculinizing, the revolutionary jingle "When Adam delved and Eve span." The focus on intellectual idealism in these essays perhaps explains part of the mysterious modern vogue for Hoccleve, but offers little else of interest, especially on real labor.

The editors' labor is also somewhat deficient. The essay titles need work: Amos on the Carpenters hardly deserves the excitable title "The Naked and the Dead," while those of Cole and Knapp, quoted above, sound like successful parody. The editorial dividing of the ten essays into five sections seems entirely unnecessary: it suggests anxiety about the coherence of the contents (quite justified) and in any case wavers between the slack "Gender Trouble" and the obscure "Producing Poetics." More oddly, Kellie Robertson's own essay, itself excitably entitled "Branding and the Technologies of Labor Regulation," seems quite unaware (or perhaps unconcerned) that the adjacent essay, Anthony Musson's somewhat dry account of antilabor legislation, states on branding that "there is no evidence that this punishment was ever ordered or indeed carried out" (p. 121). An equally odd editorial feature is that Michael Uebel, though signatory to the Introduction, and (collation with Robertson's essay suggests) perhaps author of its more labile paratheory sequences, does not in fact provide an essay for the collection.

That Introduction entitles itself "Conceptualizing Labor in the Middle Ages." The most useful of the essays described above never even try to do that, but just pass on some handy facts; the others discussed above use a *soi-disant* theorization as a means of eluding the realities of labor and their implications, then and now. But there is grace. Two essays do show that "conceptualizing labor" is in fact a viable maneuver, and that there is more to offer on this topic than Anglo-Saxon empiricism. It will not surprise readers of medieval criticism that Britton Harwood's is one: his essay crisply titled "The Displacement of Labor in *Winner and Waster*" traces the tensions of the text back to a coded source in real labor troubles of the real Middle Ages. He is able to do this in part through good scholarship, but he also has the necessary equipment for his job—a well-understood and practiced skill in the valuable and still seriously underrated mode of Pierre Macherey. Not just mentioning a theorist once or twice and then darting back to trivia and smartness, Harwood shows how to develop a position, offer a new reading, and then actually present an account of the role and the representation of labor in the period. The collection could have done much more like this, using the real strengths of theory on the topic of labor: it is surprising that there is no "postcolonial" piece on workers as exploited social— even Saxon—indigenes, or indeed a piece on how laborers are so often "queered" as animals.

Something at the appropriate theoretical level is offered in the final essay by William Kuskin. Occasionally slipping into elusive glibness, this is nevertheless a lively and interesting piece on how labor itself, especially in Caxton's ambience, has diminishing visibility in the economically and representationally transitional stage of the late Middle Ages. This account helps to clarify that Marx's allegorical treatment of the forces of economic politics in *Capital* is not just para-religious discourse, but a way of identifying what ideology had obscured.

Curiously, Kuskin's title, "The Erasure of Labor," refers to what has happened in most of these essays, and in a number of ways that is for reasons related to the forces that he shows operating at the interface of social and technological change. Caxton's printing press and the modern MLA are both sites of dissemination and obfuscation, both equally possessed by and productive of ideology.

And just like the modern academic winter festival, this collection is full of detailed work (amazingly the footnotes occupy more than twenty percent of the book), a lot of unfocused rhetoric, some whispers of professional ambition; and yet there are, if you stick around and keep your concentration, a couple of pieces really worth your effort.

STEPHEN KNIGHT
Cardiff University

CORINNE SAUNDERS, ed. *Cultural Encounters in the Romance of Medieval England.* Woodbridge, Suffolk, and Rochester, N.Y.: D. S. Brewer, 2005. Pp. x, 193. $75.00.

The biennial conference series "Romance in Medieval England" is fast approaching its tenth anniversary (in York in March 2006) and *Cultural*

Encounters, derived from the eighth conference held in Durham in 2002, is the sixth installment of what has become a regular series of essays on insular romance; a seventh volume, from the 2004 Dublin conference, is in production. The conference remit is wide—conventionally excluding Chaucer and Arthurian romances, including the *Gawain*-poet and Malory, in favor of the vast and rich corpus of noncanonical romance (metrical, alliterative and prose, in manuscript and print, in Middle English and Anglo-Norman)—and the research it promotes (like the volumes that it produces) is correspondingly diverse.

Work on manuscripts, including textual variants and editorial practice, medieval and modern; on audience; on sources and recurrent motifs; on Anglo-Norman texts; and on long-forgotten best sellers figure prominently in essays that are unabashedly specialized and often resistant to current critical trends. Some of the very best work in previous volumes in this series have justifiably become classics in the field—Jocelyn Wogan-Browne on romance and hagiography, Carol M. Meale on audiences, John J. Thompson on the medieval anthologizing process, Judith Weiss on wooing women—but the kind of theoretical pyrotechnics that have characterized recent American forays into English romance (in the work of Jeffrey Jerome Cohen, Geraldine Heng, and Vance Smith, for instance) is notable for its absence. Indeed it is not too much of an overstatement to suggest that the series bears witness to an increasingly entrenched continental divide. Not all contributors are British or even UK-based (although the majority are), but almost all (generalizations always invite refutation) favor a brand of scholarship that, despite the most recent volume's up-to-the-minute title, is self-consciously old-fashioned. Derek Brewer's antipathy to the "bizarre attempt[s]" of "feminists such as Dinshaw" to "sexualise all human relationships" (in this volume's "Some Notes on 'Enobling Love,'" a discursive tour of English romance in response to Stephen Jaeger's recent book), much like his professed distaste for current fashion ("that modern sensibility, which consciously cultivates . . . dirty, slovenly clothing"), is an extreme example of a kind of critical self-fashioning that purposefully eschews what it identifies as trendy.

That said, there is much to be celebrated in (broadly) old-fashioned scholarship. Perhaps most important is the space it allows for rigorous analysis of individual motifs across a range of texts (Robert Rouse on representations of the law in *Havelok, Horn Childe,* and *Bevis;* Rosalind Field on the "king over the water" in a cluster of seven Anglo-Norman exile-and-return romances and their English offspring; Judith Weiss on the ineffectual monarch in the Anglo-Norman *Ipomadon* and continental French *Robert le Diable* and *Octavian*) and for close reading of the mechanics of key and discrete textual episodes (Ivana Djordjević on the poetics of translating Bevis of Hampton's mother from the Anglo-Norman *Boeve* to the Middle English *Bevis*) without demanding that they be subservient to overarching, rigid extra-textual frameworks. Rouse, Field, and Weiss are sensitive to the medieval political dimensions of their romance motifs and Djordjević is conversant with current debates in translation theory, but they speak primarily (as they do at the conferences) to an audience whose own main interest is in the nitty gritty of a vast and imperfectly understood genre that flourished in England in at least two languages for over three hundred years.

"Defining romance," as Helen Cooper pithily reminds us in the current volume, "is one of the more time-wasting activities"—notoriously fluid medieval uses of the term repeatedly stump modern scholars in search of neat generic paradigms—and a persistent strength of this series is its probing at the peripheries of the genre, at the various textual cultures that inform and are informed by it. Tony Davenport's short essay on the Ine and Æthelburgh story (a pre-Alfred, Wessex king and his wife, whose trajectory, which appears in chronicles from the Anglo-Saxons through to Robert Mannyng, resembles, in fits and starts in the fragments that remain, those of Havelok and Guy of Warwick) is a provocative case in point. There is no extant romance of Ine and no evidence suggests that one was ever written; what Davenport explores in this "missed opportunity" (an "embryonic" romance whose "impulses" were "never fulfilled") is, rather, the processes by which chronicle (the alter ego of so many "historical" romances) morphs into something else, even though this time that something else is not romance. Likewise, Cooper's own contribution on Thomas of Erceldoun exposes the ambivalence inherent in what James Murray entitled Thomas's "romance and prophecies" (which he edited from the Thornton manuscript). Thomas, or so he tells us, meets and has sex with an elf queen, is transported into Elf-land, and on his release receives a series of prophecies that go on to have a lively postmedieval life independent of Thomas and his otherworldly romance. Cooper simultaneously challenges Murray's assumption that Thomas's text is a "romance" (despite its exploitation of one of romance's *ur*-motifs) while demonstrating the suggestive proximity of prophecy to, in particular, ancestral romance.

And Neil Cartlidge too, in what is one of the best essays in the collection, highlights, in a cogent dialogue between *Sir Gowther* and the Latinate clerical culture of demonology that the text itself promotes ("thereof seyes clerkus"), what romance is not and why that matters.

Three other essays exemplify the series' commitment to promoting lesser-known texts—Hardman on *Tristrem and Isoude*, Bradbury on *Athelston*, and Dalrymple on *Torrent of Portyngale*—all effectively demonstrating the particularities and peculiarities of material that should be at the forefront of the current critical agenda. And, finally, what is the volume's party piece: Elizabeth Archibald's lively tour of the provocative absence of baths or any other evidence that courtly lovers ever had a good scrub in English romance. The genre, it seems, offers disappointingly little challenge to modern assumptions about the incivility of the Middle Ages in matters of personal hygiene and underscores the provocative alterity of our own cultural encounter with the medieval past. "Romance in Medieval England" serves an invaluable function in its promotion of texts and traditions, English and Anglo-Norman, that are elsewhere marginalized or ignored, but as it faces its anniversary encounter with its own past, it sits at a crucial juncture. Whether it will embrace the impulse to theorize, whether it will refine its own distinctive approaches to textual scholarship, or whether it will use those approaches to shape and inform what is criticism's dominant trends remains to be seen.

NICOLA MCDONALD
University of York

LYNN STALEY. *Languages of Power in the Age of Richard II.* University Park: Pennsylvania State University Press, 2005. Pp. xiv, 394. $45.00.

This is an immensely informative and stimulating guide to a field that Staley essentially defines as well as excavates: the "languages" of argument about royal power and political authority in England c. 1380–99, as deployed especially by Chaucer, Gower, Richard Maidstone, Thomas Usk, and Richard II himself. The book's central historical argument is also its best: like Nigel Saul (for example, *Richard II* [New Haven: Yale

University Press, 1997], pp. 238–39), Staley views Richard and his supporters as responding to the crisis of the "Merciless Parliament" with a self-conscious amplification of his claims to royal power, emphasized in the face of growing evidence of its unacceptability. Staley ingeniously defines this posture as a turn to a "sacramental" mode of kingship, drawn from contemporary French versions of anointed kingship because English traditions did not supply the necessary terms. This strategy was advanced and supported by at least Roger Dimmock and Philippe de Mézières, but it elicited a range of resistance and criticism by many English writers. Richard's posture was particularly ill-timed not only because of the challenges by the Lords Appellant, but also because of the Wycliffite challenges to "sacrality" as such, which Staley brilliantly generalizes to political as well as religious realms.

The corollary to all this is that poets and potentates both realized that language, rhetoric, and imaginative literature were as important politically as direct power. Thus Staley advances a further, more openly speculative treatment of how "languages" of social power might have been shaped by Richard's disapproving uncles, John of Gaunt and Thomas of Woodstock, especially by means of the *Pearl*-poems, for which, she proposes, they served as major patrons. Finally, Staley presents a range of French fourteenth-century prose political writings and their English "responses" (or rather, contrasts), which she proposes are all ultimately related to Virgil's *Georgics,* the *ur*-model, in her view, of capacious late medieval economic and household narratives.

This book presents a large and absorbing landscape, whose materials and scholarly bases Staley has clearly pondered deeply. The readings of all the materials are sensitive, highly informed critically, and, especially with Chaucer, sometimes brilliantly compelling. Sometimes the details of the textual expositions claim too much attention without enough sharp edges or provable historical connections, or they move too far from key assertions (the tours of the French advice writings near the end of the book seem long; the historical importance of Philippe de Mézières's views remains speculative; and the most succinct and complete assertion of the book's main historical claim does not appear until page 78). Understandably, not all explications can live up to the promise of showing both how the works possess "great beauty and subtlety" as well as "constitute the fragments of a conversation about the terms of lost languages of power by those commissioned to figure powers they at once elaborated and scrutinized" (p. 261). Gower, for instance, is aptly positioned as advocating a kind of constitutionalism and as generally suggesting ambiguity about authoritative interpretation; but none of his poetic narratives is examined, and little of his writing receives the kind of insight, ingenuity, and evident pleasure that Staley displays in treating Chaucer (and the *Pearl*-poems, too, although those are scrutinized within very particular and speculative historical hypotheses).

But the combination of so many materials, and the potential for a kind of endless inquiry into them, is as satisfying as it is provocative and seminal. The term that orients the inquiry, "language," is elusive, perhaps usefully so. It can mean a kind of generic discourse, as in the language of love-poetry; usually it means a conscious position in social theory and the nature of authority expressed in terms that seem strange to us but would be comprehensible to contemporaries (this follows, without citation, Antony Black's usage, in, for example, *Political Thought in Europe, 1250–1450* [Cambridge: Cambridge University Press, 1992]). It can also mean something like social mode, especially treating the "mercantile" and the "sacramental" (as in comparing those in Chaucer's original form of Fragment VII—as speculatively reconstructed—with the chronicler Henry Knighton's account of the Merciless Parliament [pp. 335–36]). This last sense of "languages" and "conversations" has some (undeclared) relation to recent Marxist analyses of "class-debate," by which, as Fredric Jameson says, "the individual text will be [treated] as a *parole*, or individual utterance, of that vaster system, or *langue*, of class discourse . . . the individual utterance or text is grasped as a symbolic move in an essentially polemic and strategic ideological confrontation between the classes" (*The Political Unconscious: Narrative as a Socially Symbolic Act* [Ithaca: Cornell University Press, 1981], p. 85). Yet Staley is far more interested in elucidating complex contemporary social visions than narrowly specified social locations, and in writers' "conversations," in which positions may be dialectically combined, than direct polemical confrontations.

One might indeed quibble that there is not enough show of direct confrontation, that the metaphor of a "conversation" promises more interaction than the study actually locates. Thus we are told that the materials "suggest" or that we can "postulate" such a "conversation" (pp. 136, 176), or that the poets' use of the language of love to discuss politics "may indicate that such language was current among favor seekers at court" (p. 55); or, as noted above, that we can examine only the "fragments of a conversation about the terms of lost languages of power." Undoubtedly true. But there seem to be missed opportunities of discussing writers' evident debates with one another, using the not-insubstantial evidence of their intertextual citations for what those might imply about their interactions on the matters of royal and religious authority.

Yet this study presents a magisterial tour of late fourteenth century literature written within the ambit of the royal court, approached through a fascinating new paradigm for the period's political and religious tensions. Staley displays a capacity to move deftly from the details of literary form and plot and of intricate political and aristocratic history to a compelling thematic or modal level of "sacrality" and its antithesis (contractualism?). This constitutes a major and original synthesis of the entire Ricardian period, and also of our own last decade's most important scholarly approaches to this material.

On the later claims of Gaunt's and Woodstock's uses of the *Pearl*-poet to define their prestige and power and advice to the king, readers will have to decide for themselves, since Staley is explicitly speculative. The argument is interesting and the circumstantial evidence edifying. It is a stretch, perhaps a good one, to imagine the Pearl as Woodstock's living daughter passed in infancy to a London house of Franciscan Minoresses. It is also intriguing to consider Staley's portrayal of Woodstock as "a cultured and intelligent man" who would immediately appreciate the ironies in *Sir Gawain* (p. 222), against Froissart's depiction of an intemperate warmonger who despises the "smooth and flowery language" that the French use in negotiations. Staley, however, is aware of such contemporary images (see, for example, page 219), providing there, as throughout, a well-founded provocation for further extensions of this many-sided, continually instructive, and certainly enduring project.   .

ANDREW GALLOWAY
Cornell University

ROBERT M. STEIN and SANDRA PIERSON PRIOR, eds. *Reading Medieval Culture: Essays in Honor of Robert W. Hanning.* Notre Dame, Ind.: University of Notre Dame Press, 2005. Pp. xii, 505. $37.50.

Twenty of Robert W. Hanning's friends, students, colleagues, and associates (many of whom fall into more than one of these categories) have written essays for this impressive collection covering literature from the early Middle Ages through the Renaissance. Given the long historical range of this anthology, the editors are to be commended for organizing the commissions into coherent groupings that also provide honorific signposts to some of the primary fields Professor Hanning has cultivated in his own academic career, namely, "The Place of History and the Time of Romance," "Chaucer's Texts and Chaucer's Readers," and "Italian Contexts." Moreover, in the Introduction, the editors further explain the volume's relevance to Robert Hanning's work by spending time outlining the ways in which the essays depend upon, or allude to, their honoree's writings. In short, one of the most remarkable virtues of this collection is the seriousness with which the editors have engaged in their task of delivering to readers a volume that makes sense.

The essays in the section entitled "Chaucer's Texts and Chaucer's Readers" are the ones most relevant to the interests of subscribers to this journal, so in this review I will concentrate on those, beginning with Peter Travis's "The Body of the Nun's Priest, or, Chaucer's Disseminal Genius." Travis argues that Harry Bailly's focus on the male sexuality of the Monk and the Nun's Priest gives Chaucer a chance to enter the twelfth-and thirteenth-century debates about whether or not language, especially in its stylistic registers, is "effeminate" and in need of a "masculine semiotics" (p. 241), symbolized often by the figure of Genius, to rescue it from shifting, destabilizing "feminine" influences. Chaucer, as Travis argues, does not actually take a strong position on this issue, choosing instead simply to diagnose the problem that his forebears saw and then to play with its implications in the language surrounding his sexy, but presumably celibate, Nun's Priest. In another essay taking gender as its subject, "'Raptus' and the Poetics of Married Love in Chaucer's *Wife of Bath's Tale* and James I's *The Kingis Quair*," Elizabeth Robertson notes that both of these late medieval texts meditate on how rape denies its victims agency and subjectivity. In their representations of situations experienced by male characters (the knight in the Wife's story and the first-person narrator in James I's effort), both texts take a strong stand against the social formations that prevent people from having any choice in their sexual, and marital, partners. In an essay similarly focused on agency, Laura Howes, in "Chaucer's Criseyde," sensitively accounts for Criseyde's gender-based social victimization, showing how her attempts to be a "good girl" by obeying the men in her life serve to govern her choices and her actions, thus contributing to her sad fate as an icon of faithlessness in love.

Margaret Aziza Pappano's "'Leve Brother': Fraternalism and Craft Identity in *The Miller's Prologue and Tale*" and William Askins's "All That Glisters: The Historical Setting of the *Tale of Sir Thopas*" bring new historical information to bear on Chaucer's texts. Pappano delineates the complex use of the language and the mentalities of the artisanal guilds in *The Miller's Prologue and Tale*, showing how the themes of brotherhood and "shared risk" are lampooned by the Miller and violated by the Reeve. Askins reads *The Tale of Sir Thopas* with its Flemish connections in mind, noting a number of fascinating and poorly understood details in the poem that speak to Chaucer's familiarity with Anglo-Flemish trade goods, textile production, and currency exchange.

Rounding out the section devoted to Chaucer are essays covering the critical history and postmedieval reception of the poet's works: George Economou, John Ganim, Sealy Gilles, and Sylvia Tomasch contribute significantly to our understanding of Chaucer's works as they have been addressed by Victorian and modern critics. Economou, in "Chaucer and Langland: A Fellowship of Makers," intelligently analyzes the latest scholarship dealing with the relationship between Chaucer and Langland. He illuminates, for example, the kinds of controversies that have arisen, and must inevitably arise, when these two poets are placed in dialogue with each other. John Ganim, in "Chaucer and Free Love," finds in William Morris and Virginia Woolf two of Chaucer's most engaged readers, each of whom cultivated a distinctive "private" medievalism that spoke to their own needs as they struggled to invent their public and private selves. Morris, for instance, saw in Chaucer a combination of "innocence and fatalism" (p. 351) that seemed to be characteristic of his own life, and Woolf—who wrote about Chaucer through the imagined perspective of John Paston—strove to capture the experience of a "modern self" looking backward to a past much brighter than the time in which she found herself. In "Professionalizing Chaucer: John Matthews Manly, Edith Rickert, and the *Canterbury Tales* as Cultural Capital," Gilles and Tomasch outline the ways in which the editorial and critical work of Manly and Rickert embodied the prevailing American values of the 1920s and 1930s. Using original archival research, the authors also show how these scholars struggled to justify their new methodologies (the use of scientific, especially evolutionary, principles driven by sophisticated technology, to establish Ur-texts) in a climate slowly becoming antagonistic to expensive and time-consuming projects involving British, rather than American, authors. Their desire to depict Chaucer as a plain-speaking, democracy-loving, all-American sort of guy emerges from their published work and their correspondence, even though Manly, at least, denied that he was seeing Chaucer in this way. As universities began focusing more on American literature, and as on-going work on the Manly-Rickert edition of Chaucer's works failed to come up with the promised Ur-text, the scholarship and the personal careers of these two Chaucerians tragically lost whatever prestige they may have originally enjoyed.

Readers of this journal will also be interested in some of essays in this collection that lie outside the grouping concerned with Chaucer alone. Warren Ginsberg, working closely with Boccaccio's *Filocolo,* provides a detailed comparison of it to *The Franklin's Tale.* Christopher Baswell offers a superb and complex analysis of authenticating devices in the Arthurian chronicle tradition which demonstrates how they were shaped by linguistic, political, and readership concerns. Monika Otter subtly treats the subject of futurity in medieval historical narrative, cleverly showing us how authors deployed prophecy to extend the relevance of their work through time. Finally, Joan Ferrante, in a deeply researched essay, recovers the meaning behind some of Dante's ghostly allusions in the *Commedia* to powerful thirteenth-century queens.

Writers of the other essays in this collection will forgive me, I hope, for not having the space in which to address their contributions and for focusing, as I have done, on those essays that most immediately bear on Chaucer, his readership, or his immediate literary community. But it must be said, both about the essays I have covered and those I have not, that the high quality of the contributions in this collection persuasively and movingly attests to their authors' great respect and deep affection for Robert W. Hanning.

LISA J. KISER
The Ohio State University

JOANNA SUMMERS. *Late-Medieval Prison Writing and the Politics of Autobiography.* Oxford: Clarendon Press, 2004. Pp. x, 229. $110.00.

This study concerns seven texts from late medieval England that purport to have been written from prison: Thomas Usk's *Testament of Love,* the *Kingis Quair* of James I of Scotland, the English *Book of Love* by Charles of Orleans, the *Testimony* of William Thorpe and the *Trial* of Richard Wyche (two Lollards), George Ashby's *A Prisoner's Reflections,* and Thomas Malory's *Morte Darthur.* Such varied writings can hardly be said to constitute in any strict sense a "genre," as Summers rather reluctantly admits, but they do have in common the feature that interests her: "Each of the authors I discuss inscribes himself and his imprisoned situation within his text. I examine, therefore, how far each text invites a reading as autobiography with discussion incorporating the available modes of self-construction and the varying types of first-person narrators at this time" (p. vii).

Summers shows herself well aware that "autobiography" is a contested issue in medieval studies, and she discusses the theoretical problems at some length in her Introduction. It is clear that all the authors in question did in fact suffer imprisonment, under a variety of circumstances and for a variety of reasons, either political or (in the case of the two Lollards) religious; they all also, with one exception, "inscribe themselves" accordingly. The exception is Charles of Orleans. Charles did indeed remain as a prisoner in England for no less than twenty-five years, but Summers rightly insists that, unlike the others, he does not make anything of the fact in his poems. His writings, she says, are "pseudo-autobiographical," representing the narrator on occasion as a prisoner of Love, but never as a prisoner of the English king. In this respect, she suggests, they belong rather with Gower's *Confessio Amantis* than with her other texts: "Charles does not construct a politically favourable autobiographical identity in order to persuade his audience, but rather an ironic pseudo-autobiographical lover in order to entertain" (p. 107).

It is the construction of "a politically favourable autobiographical identity" that chiefly interests Summers in her other texts. She has included Malory, whose colophons speak of him as a "knyght presoner," but her discussion (confined here to an Epilogue) does not attempt to press a political reading on the rest of the *Morte:* "while the text conveys a view of Malory as a man writing out of and during the experience of suffering imprisonment, these elements do not seem sufficiently central, elaborated, or petitionary to suggest a political self-presentation" (p. 183). The heart of her book lies in readings of the remaining five authors— Usk, Ashby, James I, Thorpe, and Wyche. The chapter on Thorpe and Wych, both men writing as Lollard heretics under interrogation, finds their texts easy enough to characterize: "Both texts construct textual identities whose exemplary behaviour in the face of imprisonment and persecution is designed to encourage other Lollards in the firmness of their beliefs, and convince of the corruption of the Church" (p. 112). Usk and Ashby make more personal and party-political appeals, addressed respectively, Summers argues, to the royalist and Lancastrian parties of their day. The turbid prose of Usk's *Testament* makes exact interpretation difficult, but Summers gives a convincing account of the author's self-portrayal as a faithful lover and loyal political servant, combining the two roles in his appeals to "Margarete of Virtw." In this connection, she suggests that the figure of Margaret alludes, among other things, to Richard II himself, appealing to the mercy of the pearl-loving monarch. Less persuasive to me is the author's discussion of that other elusive text, *The Kingis Quair*. James was indeed a prisoner and, unlike Charles, he does represent himself as literally such in his poem. Summers argues that the king, writing at a time between his release from captivity and his return to Scotland, intended the poem to persuade the awaiting Scottish nobility of the virtues that would commend him to them: "his self-rule and maturity acquired through incarceration" (p. 72). But this is a rather speculative interpretation of a royal poem that, like Charles's *Book of Love,* seems hardly to condescend to any mundane political appeal, even by implication.

A recurring theme of the book is intertextuality, and above all the influence of that other prison book, the *Consolatio* of Boethius, especially in the writings of Usk, James, and Ashby. Summers wisely does not treat autobiographical and Boethian readings as alternatives between which she has to choose. She argues that "the authors redeploy the *Consolation* as an autobiographical model, motivated in varying degrees by political interests, primarily to persuade the audience of their moral worth" (p. 191). These writers, that is, fashion themselves upon the Boethian model, but the moral worth in question is specifically their own. Summers handles these awkward issues intelligently. Occasionally she makes a weak concession to anti-autobiographical opinion, as when she speaks of Thorpe's *Testimony* as "a highly embellished fictional account of an experience which may or may not have actually occurred" (p. 127), but overall she steers her way skillfully through what are at present troubled waters. This is a judicious and original study, which illuminates its prison texts by comparison without attempting to minimize the differences between them.

J. A. BURROW
Bristol University

CINDY L. VITTO and MARCIA SMITH MARZEC, eds. *New Perspectives on Criseyde.* Asheville, N.C.: Pegasus Press, 2004. Pp. 336. $17.95, paper.

The essays in this generally worthwhile collection make one thing clear: the poem that Chaucer refers to in his Retractions as "the book of Troilus" has evolved, over its long critical history, into something more like "the book of Criseyde." One has to wonder, in fact, whether a volume devoted to the comparatively static Troilus could ever invite the broad range of topics found here: everything from gendered reading practices, to manuscript studies, to exemplarity, to aesthetics, to codependency. It must be said, however, that the title of the collection, *New Perspectives on Criseyde,* is a bit misleading, or perhaps just overly optimistic. For whatever their other virtues, none of the perspectives adopted here strikes me as being particularly new. Some, indeed, are going on fifteen, twenty, or even thirty years old, and the wear, I am sorry to report, is starting to show. For this reason, *New Perspectives on Criseyde* will probably appeal more to those looking for a handy compilation of well-established critical positions than to anyone searching for the next leap forward in Chaucer studies.

The anthology's first section, "Historical Contexts for Understanding Criseyde," starts off with an overview of twentieth-century interpretations of Criseyde by Lorraine Kochanske Stock, who deftly traces Criseyde's critical journey from a woman whose "slydynge . . . corage" must be either attacked or defended, to a symbol of idolatry, to a "charming enigma," to a feminine subject shaped by, or struggling against, cultural and historical forces largely beyond her control. Stock's account leaves little doubt that Criseyde is as much a product of criticism as of Chaucer's text, and it does an excellent job of teasing out the genealogies from which most of these essays descend. Its comprehensiveness is rendered somewhat ironic, however, by the fact that two readings in particular, David Aers's "Chaucer's Criseyde: Woman in Society, Woman in Love" and Carolyn Dinshaw's "Reading Like a Man: The Critics, the Narrator, Troilus, and Pandarus," cast shadows across these pages so long and imposing that they threaten to blot out new growth. The two essays that round out this first section, Laura F. Hodges's "Criseyde's 'widewes habit large of samyt broun' in *Troilus and Criseyde*" and Kathryn Jacobs's "Mate or Mother: Positioning Criseyde Among Chaucer's Widows," are each as helpful and informative, in their own way, as Stock's. Neither one, though, does much to dispel the impression that this kind of historical "contextualizing" is but another means, to paraphrase Dinshaw, of containing the desire that Criseyde embodies.

The three essays gathered together under the rubric "Concerns of Gender and Power" are linked by what the editors describe as a shared interest in "concepts of reading and/or writing, both internal and external to the text itself" (p. 5). Kara A. Doyle's argument in "Criseyde Reading, Reading Criseyde," for example, is that Chaucer tries to coerce even his female readers into identifying with Troilus and objectifying Criseyde. From as early as the sixteenth century, however, Chaucer's female readers have been resisting his efforts. Indeed, as Doyle shows through the example of a letter written (presumably) by Margaret More Roper, the eldest daughter of Sir Thomas More, they have been identifying with Criseyde as a figure not of victimization or betrayal but of agency. Doyle's essay is subtle and multifaceted, repeatedly calling our attention to the fact that readers have the power to make and unmake the meanings of texts and that a character like Criseyde can assume something like an independent existence. Missing, though, is any consideration of the Palinode, where the reader is enjoined to identify neither with Troilus nor Criseyde, but with Christ. Identification is likewise at stake in Martha Dana Rust's " 'Le Vostre C': Letters and Love in Bodleian Library Manuscript Arch. Selden. B.24," only this time it is Criseyde's forced identification with the material properties of one particular witness to Chaucer's poem. Turning a sharp eye upon the manuscript's physical details, Rust notes, in the first place, how a small illustration equates the black-clad widow Criseyde with the black letters of the text. She then shows how the manuscript's marginal glosses force a literal reading of Criseyde's metaphoric displacement, over the course of Book V, by her increasingly ambivalent letters to Troilus. Eventually reduced to "a sign of her absence—her last letter," Criseyde is made to stand for the "variance" found not only in the emotional content of the letters she writes but also, Rust argues, in the manuscript tradition itself (p. 131). Finally, Rust calls attention to the fact that a scribe has mistakenly prefaced Criseyde's signature with the masculine article Le. Seizing on the figurative implications of this slip, Rust makes the intriguing suggestion that the authors of the letter are, ultimately, the various men who have manipulated the terms of Criseyde's representation. Holly A. Crocker pursues a similar argument in "How the Woman Makes the

Man: Chaucer's Reciprocal Fictions in *Troilus and Criseyde*." "An icon of feminine virtue," Criseyde gets pressed into service not simply as Troilus's mirror, a surface reflecting and confirming "his general worth in Troy," but as the partner in a larger system of "idealized complementarity" (pp. 146, 145, 144). What Criseyde betrays is thus not Troilus, not a person, but an image of virtue necessary to the maintenance of both civic and chivalric fantasies.

The book's third section, "Postmodern Prisms," while arguably its weakest overall, includes what may be its single best piece. Peggy A. Knapp's "Criseyde's Beauty: Chaucer and Aesthetics" is one of the few essays in the collection to dwell at length on Criseyde's status as a made thing: a figure in a text. Drawing on Gadamer's description of the hermeneutic circle, Knapp reminds us that Criseyde's beauty matters not only because it determines her fate within the text, but because it largely determines our responses to her. And since the meanings we attribute to beauty change, sometimes radically, from era to era, so too our responses to Criseyde's beauty change, over time, the meanings we attribute to Chaucer's text. As the poem *devises* Criseyde, so we, in turn, *devise* the poem. This is not, however, an innocent operation, as Knapp demonstrates in her reading of Book II (among the highlights of the collection). Criseyde's beauty derives at that point, Knapp argues, from the intimate details of her portrait: her blushes, her downward glances, her humming. If those details tempt us into mistaking Criseyde for an actual person, they also call into question the ethics of reading her as not-human, as a symbol. Criseyde is never more mysteriously beautiful than when she resists allegorization. If she is a victim of anything, it is our own impulse to attribute meaning to her beauty, to turn enigma into sign. The other essays in this section are "Re-reading / Re-teaching Chaucer's Criseyde," Susannah Chewning's heartfelt meditation on the peculiar challenges presented to feminist scholars by "*all* of Chaucer's women," and by Criseyde in particular (p. 165); Marcia Smith Marzec's and Cindy L. Vitto's "Criseyde as Codependent: A New Approach to an Old Enigma"; and Jean E. Jost's "The Performative Criseyde: Self-Conscious Dramaturgy."

For the volume's final section, "Revisioning Criseyde," the editors invited three prominent critics to revisit earlier interpretations of *Troilus and Criseyde,* two of which turn out to be their own. Although Peter G. Beidler's " 'That I was born, alas': Criseyde's Weary Dawn Song in *Troilus and Criseyde*" and John V. Fleming's "Criseyde's Poem: The Anxieties of the Classical Tradition" both rise to the occasion, the most successful of these revisions proves to be Winthrop Wetherbee's "Criseyde Alone," largely because its self-styled "Criseydean" point of view allows it to raise one of the anthology's more provocative questions. Why, the essay wants to know, should not Criseyde betray Troilus, when it is obvious that he embodies a moribund code of chivalric ethics? Could we not even go so far as to read Criseyde's rejection of Troilus as expressing Chaucer's own rejection of "a failed ideal"? (p. 302). Wetherbee's is also the one essay in the collection to offer an extended treatment of Henryson's *Testament of Cresseid*.

None of the essays in *New Perspectives on Criseyde* actually manages anything genuinely new. But they do something every bit as valuable: they clear the ground on which we might encounter another Criseyde altogether, untimely and unexpected, patiently awaiting our arrival.

GEORGE EDMONDSON
Dartmouth College

Books Received

Barr, Helen, and Ann M. Hutchison, eds. *Text and Controversy from Wyclif to Bale: Essays in Honour of Anne Hudson.* Medieval Church Series, 4. Turnhout: Brepols, 2005. Pp. xxii, 448. $113.00.

Butterworth, Philip. *Magic on the Early English Stage.* New York: Cambridge University Press, 2005. $85.00. Pp. xxii, 295. $85.00.

D'Arcy, Anne Marie, and Alan J. Fletcher, eds. *Studies in Late Medieval and Early Renaissance Texts in Honour of John Scattergood.* Portland, Ore.: Four Courts Press, 2005. Pp. 416. $75.00.

Cox, Catherine S. *The Judaic Other in Dante, the "Gawain" Poet, and Chaucer.* Gainesville: University Press of Florida, 2005. Pp. x, 239. $65.00.

Davenport, Tony. *Medieval Narrative: An Introduction.* New York: Oxford University Press, 2004. Pp. viii, 304. $29.95.

Gadd, Ian, and Alexandra Gillespie, eds. *John Stow (1525–1605) and the Making of the English Past.* Toronto: University of Toronto Press, 2004. Pp. xiv, 192. $60.00.

Ganim, John M. *Medievalism and Orientalism.* New York: Palgrave Macmillan, 2005. Pp. x, 156. $69.95.

Glaser, Joseph, trans. *Geoffrey Chaucer: "The Canterbury Tales" in Modern Verse.* Indianapolis: Hackett, 2005. Pp. vi, 348. $9.95 paper, $34.95 cloth.

Grady, Frank. *Representing Righteous Heathens in Late Medieval England.* New York: Palgrave Macmillan, 2005. Pp. ix, 214. $65.00.

Hilmo, Maidie. *Medieval Images, Icons, and Illustrated English Literary Texts from the Ruthwell Cross to the Ellesmere Chaucer.* Burlington, VT.: Ashgate, 2004. Pp. xxv, 236. $99.95.

Johnson, David, and Elaine Treharne, eds. *Readings in Medieval Texts: Interpreting Old and Middle English Literature.* New York: Oxford University Press, 2005. Pp. xi, 400. $29.95 paper.

Kabir, Ananya Jahanara, and Deanne Williams, eds. *Postcolonial Approaches to the European Middle Ages: Translating Cultures.* New York: Cambridge University Press, 2005. Pp. xii, 298. $80.00.

Lupack, Alan. *The Oxford Guide to Arthurian Literature and Legend.* New York: Oxford University Press, 2005. Pp. xiv, 496. $90.00.

McCarthy, Conor, ed. *Love, Sex, and Marriage in the Middle Ages: A Sourcebook.* New York: Routledge, 2004. Pp. xii, 292. $24.95 paper.

Machan, Tim William, ed. with the assistance of A. J. Minnis. *Sources of the "Boece".* The Chaucer Library Series. Athens: University of Georgia Press, 2005. Pp. xiv, 311. $85.00.

Milner, Stephen J., ed. *At The Margins: Minority Groups in Premodern Italy.* Medieval Cultures, 39. Minneapolis: University of Minnesota Press, 2005. Pp. ix, 283. $24.95 paper.

Minnis, Alastair, and Ian Johnson, eds. *The Cambridge History of Literary Criticism. Volume 2: The Middle Ages.* New York: Cambridge University Press, 2005. Pp. xvi, 865. $160.00.

Mortimer, Nigel. *John Lydgate's "Fall of Princes": Narrative Tragedy in Its Literary and Political Contexts.* Oxford: Oxford University Press, 2005. Pp. vx, 360. $110.00.

Nicholson, Peter. *Love and Ethics in Gower's "Confessio Amantis."* Ann Arbor: University of Michigan Press, 2005. Pp. x, 461. $80.00.

Nolan, Maura. *John Lydgate and the Making of Public Culture.* Cambridge Studies in Medieval Literature, 58. New York: Cambridge University Press, 2005. Pp. ix, 276. $85.00.

Richmond, E. B., trans. *The Parliament of Birds: Geoffrey Chaucer.* London: Hesperus Press, 2005. Pp. xv, 151. $15.95 paper.

Simpson, James. *Reform and Cultural Revolution*. Oxford English Literary History, Volume 2, 1350–1547. New York: Oxford University Press, 2002. Pp. 680. $74.00.

Soergel, Philip M., ed. *Studies in Medieval and Renaissance History: Sexuality and Culture in Medieval and Renaissance Europe*. 3rd ser., vol. 2. New York: AMS Press, 2005. Pp. xv, 281. $89.50.

Sponsler, Claire. *Ritual Imports: Performing Medieval Drama in America*. Ithaca: Cornell University Press, 2004. Pp. viii, 235. $35.00.

Stahuljak, Zrinka. *Bloodless Genealogies of the French Middle Ages: "Translatio," Kinship, and Metaphor*. Gainesville: University Press of Florida, 2005. Pp. xi, 242. $65.00.

Stohm, Paul. *Politique: Languages of Statecraft Between Chaucer and Shakespeare*. Notre Dame: University of Notre Dame Press, 2005. Pp. 299. $55.00 cloth, $27.50 paper.

Warren, Nancy Bradley. *Women of God and Arms: Female Spirituality and Political Conflict, 1380–1600*. Philadelphia: University of Pennsylvania Press, 2005. Pp. 264. $55.00.

Watt, Diane, ed. *The Paston Women: Selected Letters*. Woodbridge, Suffolk, and Rochester, N.Y.: D. S. Brewer, 2004. Pp. x, 178. $27.95 paper.

Watt, Mary Alexandra. *The Cross That Dante Bears: Pilgrimage, Crusade, and the Cruciform Church in the "Divine Comedy."* Gainesville: University Press of Florida, 2005. Pp. xii, 227. $59.95.

Wenzel, Siegfried. *Latin Sermon Collections from Later Medieval England: Orthodox Preaching in the Age of Wyclif*. New York: Cambridge University Press, 2005. Pp. xxiv, 713. $170.00.

Whitelock, Jill, ed. *The Seven Sages of Rome (Midland Version)*. EETS, o.s. 324. New York: Oxford University Press, 2005. Pp. lxxx, 182. $85.00.

Williams, Deanne. *The French Fetish from Chaucer to Shakespeare*. New York: Cambridge University Press, 2004. Pp. xiv, 283. $75.00.

An Annotated Chaucer Bibliography, 2004

Compiled and edited by Mark Allen and Bege K. Bowers

Regular contributors:

Bruce W. Hozeski, *Ball State University* (Indiana)
George Nicholas, *Benedictine College* (Kansas)
Marilyn Sutton, *California State University at Dominguez Hills*
David Sprunger, *Concordia College* (Minnesota)
Winthrop Wetherbee, *Cornell University* (New York)
Elizabeth Dobbs, *Grinnell College* (Iowa)
Teresa P. Reed, *Jacksonville State University* (Alabama)
William Snell, *Keio University* (Japan)
Denise Stodola, *Kettering University* (Michigan)
Brian A. Shaw, *London, Ontario*
William Schipper, *Memorial University* (Newfoundland, Canada)
Larry L. Bronson, *Mt. Pleasant, Michigan*
Martha Rust, *New York University*
Warren S. Moore, III, *Newberry College* (South Carolina)
Amy Goodwin, *Randolph-Macon College* (Virginia)
Erik Kooper, *Rijksuniversiteit te Utrecht*
Cindy L. Vitto, *Rowan College of New Jersey*
Anne Thornton, *San Antonio College* (Texas)
Richard H. Osberg, *Santa Clara University* (California)
Brother Anthony (Sonjae An), *Sogang University* (South Korea)
Margaret Connolly, *University College, Cork* (Ireland)
Juliette Dor, *Université de Liège* (Belgium)
Mary Flowers Braswell and Elaine Whitaker, *University of Alabama at Birmingham*
Stefania D'Agata D'Ottavi, *University of Macerata* (Italy)
Gregory M. Sadlek, *University of Nebraska at Omaha*
Cynthia Ho, *University of North Carolina, Asheville*
Richard J. Utz, *University of Northern Iowa*

Rebecca Beal, *University of Scranton* (Pennsylvania)
Mark Allen and R. L. Smith, *University of Texas at San Antonio*
Joerg O. Fichte, *Universität Tübingen* (Tübingen, Germany)
John M. Crafton, *West Georgia College*
Robert Correale, *Wright State University* (Ohio)
Bege K. Bowers, *Youngstown State University* (Ohio)

Ad hoc contributions were made by the following: Stephanie Amsel (University of Texas at San Antonio) and Terri Pantuso (University of Texas at San Antonio). The bibliographers acknowledge with gratitude the MLA typesimulation provided by the Center for Bibliographical Services of the Modern Language Association; postage from the University of Texas at San Antonio Department of English, Classics, and Philosophy; and assistance from the library staff, especially Susan McCray, at the University of Texas at San Antonio.

This bibliography continues the bibliographies published since 1975 in previous volumes of *Studies in the Age of Chaucer*. Bibliographic information up to 1975 can be found in Eleanor P. Hammond, *Chaucer: A Bibliographic Manual* (1908; reprint, New York: Peter Smith, 1933); D. D. Griffith, *Bibliography of Chaucer, 1908–1953* (Seattle: University of Washington Press, 1955); William R. Crawford, *Bibliography of Chaucer, 1954–63* (Seattle: University of Washington Press, 1967); and Lorrayne Y. Baird, *Bibliography of Chaucer, 1964–1973* (Boston: G. K. Hall, 1977). See also Lorrayne Y. Baird-Lange and Hildegard Schnuttgen, *Bibliography of Chaucer, 1974–1985* (Hamden, Conn.: Shoe String Press, 1988); and Bege K. Bowers and Mark Allen, eds., *Annotated Chaucer Bibliography, 1986–1996* (Notre Dame, Ind.: University of Notre Dame, 2002).

Additions and corrections to this bibliography should be sent to Mark Allen, Bibliographic Division, The New Chaucer Society, Department of English, Classics, and Philosophy, University of Texas at San Antonio 78249-0643 (Fax: 210-458-5366; E-mail: mallen@utsa.edu). An electronic version of this bibliography (1975–2004) is available via The New Chaucer Society Web page <http://artsci.wustl.edu/~chaucer/> or at <http://uchaucer.utsa.edu>. Authors are urged to send annotations for articles, reviews, and books that have been or might be overlooked.

Classifications

Abbreviations of Chaucer's Works

ABC	*An ABC*
Adam	*Adam Scriveyn*
Anel	*Anelida and Arcite*
Astr	*A Treatise on the Astrolabe*
Bal Compl	*A Balade of Complaint*
BD	*The Book of the Duchess*
Bo	*Boece*
Buk	*The Envoy to Bukton*
CkT, CkP, Rv–CkL	*The Cook's Tale, The Cook's Prologue, Reeve–Cook Link*
ClT, ClP, Cl–MerL	*The Clerk's Tale, The Clerk's Prologue, Clerk–Merchant Link*
Compl d'Am	*Complaynt d'Amours*
CT	*The Canterbury Tales*
CYT, CYP	*The Canon's Yeoman's Tale, The Canon's Yeoman's Prologue*
Equat	*The Equatorie of the Planetis*
For	*Fortune*
Form Age	*The Former Age*
FranT, FranP	*The Franklin's Tale, The Franklin's Prologue*
FrT, FrP, Fr–SumL	*The Friar's Tale, The Friar's Prologue, Friar–Summoner Link*
Gent	*Gentilesse*
GP	*The General Prologue*
HF	*The House of Fame*
KnT, Kn–MilL	*The Knight's Tale, Knight–Miller Link*
Lady	*A Complaint to His Lady*
LGW, LGWP	*The Legend of Good Women, The Legend of Good Women Prologue*
ManT, ManP	*The Manciple's Tale, The Manciple's Prologue*
Mars	*The Complaint of Mars*
Mel, Mel–MkL	*The Tale of Melibee, Melibee–Monk Link*
MercB	*Merciles Beaute*
MerT, MerE–SqH	*The Merchant's Tale, Merchant Endlink–Squire Headlink*

353

MilT, MilP, Mil–RvL	*The Miller's Tale, The Miller's Prologue, Miller–Reeve Link*
MkT, MkP, Mk–NPL	*The Monk's Tale, The Monk's Prologue, Monk–Nun's Priest Link*
MLT, MLH, MLP, MLE	*The Man of Law's Tale, Man of Law Headlink, The Man of Law's Prologue, Man of Law Endlink*
NPT, NPP, NPE	*The Nun's Priest's Tale, The Nun's Priest's Prologue, Nun's Priest's Endlink*
PardT, PardP	*The Pardoner's Tale, The Pardoner's Prologue*
ParsT, ParsP	*The Parson's Tale, The Parson's Prologue*
PF	*The Parliament of Fowls*
PhyT, Phy–PardL	*The Physician's Tale, Physician–Pardoner Link*
Pity	*The Complaint unto Pity*
Prov	*Proverbs*
PrT, PrP, Pr–ThL	*The Prioress's Tale, The Prioress's Prologue, Prioress–Thopas Link*
Purse	*The Complaint of Chaucer to His Purse*
Ret	*Chaucer's Retraction {Retractation}*
Rom	*The Romaunt of the Rose*
Ros	*To Rosemounde*
RvT, RvP	*The Reeve's Tale, The Reeve's Prologue*
Scog	*The Envoy to Scogan*
ShT, Sh–PrL	*The Shipman's Tale, Shipman–Prioress Link*
SNT, SNP, SN–CYL	*The Second Nun's Tale, The Second Nun's Prologue, Second Nun–Canon's Yeoman Link*
SqT, SqH, Sq–FranL	*The Squire's Tale, Squire Headlink, Squire–Franklin Link*
Sted	*Lak of Stedfastnesse*
SumT, SumP	*The Summoner's Tale, The Summoner's Prologue*
TC	*Troilus and Criseyde*
Th, Th–MelL	*The Tale of Sir Thopas, Sir Thopas–Melibee Link*
Truth	*Truth*
Ven	*The Complaint of Venus*

WBT, WBP, WB–FrL	*The Wife of Bath's Tale, The Wife of Bath's Prologue, Wife of Bath–Friar Link*
Wom Nob	*Womanly Noblesse*
Wom Unc	*Against Women Unconstant*

Periodical Abbreviations

AdI	*Annali d'Italianistica*
Anglia	*Anglia: Zeitschrift für Englische Philologie*
Anglistik	*Anglistik: Mitteilungen des Verbandes deutscher Anglisten*
AnLM	*Anuario de Letras Modernas*
ANQ	*ANQ: A Quarterly Journal of Short Articles, Notes, and Reviews*
AraA	*Arbeiten aus Anglistik und Amerikanistik*
Archiv	*Archiv für das Studium der Neueren Sprachen und Literaturen*
Arthuriana	*Arthuriana*
BAM	*Bulletin des Anglicistes Médiévistes*
BJRL	*Bulletin of the John Rylands University Library of Manchester*
C&L	*Christianity and Literature*
CarmP	*Carmina Philosophiae: Journal of the International Boethius Society*
CE	*College English*
Chaucer Yearbook	*Chaucer Yearbook: A Journal of Late Medieval Studies*
ChauNewsl	*Chaucer Newsletter*
ChauR	*Chaucer Review*
CL	*Comparative Literature* (Eugene, Ore.)
CLS	*Comparative Literature Studies*
CML	*Classical and Modern Literature: A Quarterly* (Columbia, Mo.)
CollL	*College Literature*
Comitatus	*Comitatus: A Journal of Medieval and Renaissance Studies*
Comparatist	*The Comparatist: Journal of the Southern Comparative Literature Association*
CRCL	*Canadian Review of Comparative Literature/Revue Canadienne de Littérature Comparée*
Crossings	*Crossings: A Counter-Disciplinary Journal* (Binghamton, N.Y.)

DAI	*Dissertation Abstracts International*
Disputatio	*Disputatio: An International Transdisciplinary Journal of the Late Middle Ages*
DR	*Dalhousie Review*
ÉA	*Études Anglaises: Grand-Bretagne, États-Unis*
ÉC	*Études Celtiques*
EHR	*English Historical Review*
EIC	*Essays in Criticism: A Quarterly Journal of Literary Criticism*
ELH	*ELH*
ELN	*English Language Notes*
ELR	*English Literary Renaissance*
EMS	*English Manuscript Studies, 1100–1700*
Encomia	*Encomia: Bibliographical Bulletin of the International Courtly Literature Society*
English	*English: The Journal of the English Association*
Envoi	*Envoi: A Review Journal of Medieval Literature*
ES	*English Studies*
ESC	*English Studies in Canada*
Exemplaria	*Exemplaria: A Journal of Theory in Medieval and Renaissance Studies*
Expl	*Explicator*
Fabula	*Fabula: Zeitschrift für Erzählforschung/Journal of Folktale Studies*
FCS	*Fifteenth-Century Studies*
Florilegium	*Florilegium: Carleton University Papers on Late Antiquity and the Middle Ages*
FMLS	*Forum for Modern Language Studies*
Genre	*Genre: Forms of Discourse and Culture*
GRM	*Germanisch-Romanische Monatsschrift*
HLQ	*Huntington Library Quarterly: Studies in English and American History and Literature* (San Marino, Calif.)
InG	*In Geardagum: Essays on Old and Middle English Language and Literature*
Italica	*Italica: Bulletin of the American Association of Teachers of Italian*

JAIS	*Journal of Anglo-Italian Studies*
JEBS	*Journal of the Early Book Society*
JEGP	*Journal of English and Germanic Philology*
JELL	*Journal of English Language and Literature* (Korea)
JEngL	*Journal of English Linguistics*
JEP	*Journal of Evolutionary Psychology*
JGN	*John Gower Newsletter*
JHiP	*Journal of Historical Pragmatics*
JMEMSt	*Journal of Medieval and Early Modern Studies*
JML	*Journal of Modern Literature*
JNT	*Journal of Narrative Theory*
JournalX	*Journal x: A Journal in Culture and Criticism*
JRMMRA	*Quidditas: Journal of the Rocky Mountain Medieval and Renaissance Association*
L&LC	*Literary and Linguistic Computing: Journal of the Association for Literary and Linguistic Computing*
L&P	*Literature and Psychology*
L&T	*Literature and Theology: An International Journal of Religion, Theory, and Culture*
Lang&Lit	*Language and Literature: Journal of the Poetics and Linguistics Association*
Lang&S	*Language and Style: An International Journal*
LeedsSE	*Leeds Studies in English*
Library	*The Library: The Transactions of the Bibliographical Society*
LRB	*The London Review of Books*
MA	*Le Moyen Age: Revue d'Histoire et de Philologie* (Brussels, Belgium)
MÆ	*Medium Ævum*
M&H	*Medievalia et Humanistica: Studies in Medieval and Renaissance Culture*
Manuscripta	*Manuscripta* (St. Louis, Mo.)
Mediaevalia	*Mediaevalia: An Interdisciplinary Journal of Medieval Studies Worldwide*
Mediaevistik	*Mediaevistik: Internationale Zeitschrift für Interdisziplinäre Mittelalterforschung*
MedievalF	*Medieval Forum* <http://www.sfsu.edu/~medieval/index.html>

MedPers	*Medieval Perspectives*
MES	*Medieval English Studies*
MFN	*Medieval Feminist Newsletter*
MichA	*Michigan Academician* (Ann Arbor, Mich.)
MHJ	*Medieval History Journal*
MLN	*Modern Language Notes*
MLQ	*Modern Language Quarterly: A Journal of Literary History*
MLR	*The Modern Language Review*
ModA	*Modern Age: A Quarterly Review*
MP	*Modern Philology: A Journal Devoted to Research in Medieval and Modern Literature*
N&Q	*Notes and Queries*
Neophil	*Neophilologus* (Dordrecht, Netherlands)
NFS	*Nottingham French Studies*
NLH	*New Literary History: A Journal of Theory and Interpretation*
NM	*Neuphilologische Mitteilungen: Bulletin of the Modern Language Society*
NML	*New Medieval Literatures*
NMS	*Nottingham Medieval Studies*
NOWELE	*NOWELE: North-Western European Language Evolution*
OT	*Oral Tradition*
PAPA	*Publications of the Arkansas Philological Association*
Parergon	*Parergon: Bulletin of the Australian and New Zealand Association for Medieval and Early Modern Studies*
PBA	*Proceedings of the British Academy*
PBSA	*Papers of the Bibliographical Society of America*
PLL	*Papers on Language and Literature: A Journal for Scholars and Critics of Language and Literature*
PMAM	*Publications of the Medieval Association of the Midwest*
PMLA	*Publications of the Modern Language Association of America*
PoeticaT	*Poetica: An International Journal of Linguistic Literary Studies*
Postscript	*Postscript: Publication of the Philological Association of the Carolinas*

PQ	*Philological Quarterly*
Prolepsis	*Prolepsis: The Tübingen Review of English Studies*
ProverbiumY	*Proverbium: Yearbook of International Proverb Scholarship*
RCEI	*Revista Canaria de Estudios Ingleses*
Reinardus	*Reinardus: Yearbook of the International Reynard Society/Annuaire de la Société Internationale Renardienne*
RenD	*Renaissance Drama*
RenQ	*Renaissance Quarterly*
RES	*Review of English Studies*
RMSt	*Reading Medieval Studies* (Reading, England)
Romania	*Romania: Revue Consacrée à l'Étude des Langues et des Littératures Romanes*
RSQ	*Rhetoric Society Quarterly* (University Park, Pa.)
SAC	*Studies in the Age of Chaucer*
SAF	*Studies in American Fiction* (Boston, Mass.)
SAP	*Studia Anglica Posnaniensia: An International Review of English*
SAQ	*South Atlantic Quarterly*
SB	*Studies in Bibliography: Papers of the Bibliographical Society of the University of Virginia*
SCJ	*The Sixteenth-Century Journal: Journal of Early Modern Studies* (Kirksville, Mo.)
SEL	*SEL: Studies in English Literature, 1500–1900*
SELIM	*SELIM: Journal of the Spanish Society for Medieval English Language and Literature*
ShakS	*Shakespeare Studies* (Baltimore, Md.)
ShY	*The Shakespeare Yearbook*
SIcon	*Studies in Iconography*
SiM	*Studies in Medievalism*
SIMELL	*Studies in Medieval English Language and Literature*
SMART	*Studies in Medieval and Renaissance Teaching*
SN	*Studia Neophilologica: A Journal of Germanic and Romance Languages and Literatures*
SoAR	*South Atlantic Review*
SP	*Studies in Philology*
Speculum	*Speculum: A Journal of Medieval Studies*
SQ	*Shakespeare Quarterly*
SSF	*Studies in Short Fiction*

SSt	*Spenser Studies: A Renaissance Poetry Annual*
TCBS	*Transactions of the Cambridge Bibliographical Society*
Text	*Text: Transactions of the Society for Textual Scholarship*
TLS	*Times Literary Supplement* (London, England)
TMR	*The Medieval Review* <http://www.hti.umich.edu/t/ tmr/>
Tr&Lit	*Translation and Literature*
TSLL	*Texas Studies in Literature and Language*
UCrow	*The Upstart Crow: A Shakespeare Journal*
UTQ	*University of Toronto Quarterly: A Canadian Journal of the Humanities* (Toronto, Canada)
Viator	*Viator: Medieval and Renaissance Studies*
WS	*Women's Studies: An Interdisciplinary Journal*
YER	*Yeats Eliot Review: A Journal of Criticism and Scholarship*
YES	*Yearbook of English Studies*
YULG	*Yale University Library Gazette*
YWES	*Year's Work in English Studies*
YLS	*The Yearbook of Langland Studies*
ZAA	*Zeitschrift für Anglistik und Amerikanistik: A Quarterly of Language, Literature and Culture*

Bibliographical Citations and Annotations

Bibliographies, Reports, and Reference

1. Allen, Mark, and Bege K. Bowers. "An Annotated Chaucer Bibliography, 2002." *SAC* 26 (2004): 443–535. Continuation of *SAC* annual annotated bibliography (since 1975); based on contributions from an international bibliographic team, independent research, and *MLA Bibliography* listings. 315 items, plus listing of reviews for 95 books. Includes an author index.

2. Allen, Valerie, and Margaret Connolly. "Middle English: Chaucer." *YWES* 83 (2004): 194–224. A discursive bibliography of Chaucer studies for 2002, divided into four subcategories: general, *CT, TC,* and other works.

3. Boswell, Jackson Campbell, and Sylvia Wallace Holton. *Chaucer's Fame in England: STC Chauceriana, 1475–1640.* New York: Modern Language Association of America, 2004. xxx, 390 pp. Tallies 1,378 "references to, allusions to, and echoes of Chaucer and his works in printed books published between 1475 and 1640," updating and correcting a portion of Caroline Spurgeon's landmark bibliography. Entries are arranged chronologically by date of publication and, within years, alphabetically; they provide bibliographical information, including Short Title Catalog (STC) numbers, and (where appropriate) quote the source and identify subsequent editions. Headnotes indicate who discovered the references. The work includes several appendices and indexes: STC books, a general index, an index of Chaucer's life and reputation, an index of Chaucer's works, and a list of works cited.

4. Oizumi, Akio. *A Lexical Concordance to the Works of Geoffrey Chaucer.* 5 parts. *A Complete Concordance to the Works of Geoffrey Chaucer,* vol. 13, parts 1–5. Supplement series, vol. 13, parts 1–5. Hildesheim, Zurich, and New York: Olms-Weidman, 2003. Parts 1–2: xx, xiii, 1478 pp.; parts 3–5: xii, xiii, xii, 1718 pp. A lemmatized concordance, arranged alphabetically, based on the text and corpus of *The Riverside Chaucer.* Each entry includes a headword, part of speech, references to standard dictionaries (*MED, OED,* and others), definitions, frequency of occurrence, a list of attested spellings (with frequencies specified), occasional cross-references, information about collocations and uses in phrases

(where appropriate), and a list of occurrences, with the headwords quoted in the context of the lines in which they appear. Volume 1: A–D; 2: E–L; 3: M–R; 4: S–T; 5: U–Z and numerals.

Recordings and Films

5. Forni, Kathleen. "A Cinema of Poetry: What Pasolini Did to Chaucer's *Canterbury Tales*." *Literature/Film Quarterly* 30 (2002): 256–63. Not a realization of *CT*, Pasolini's *I racconti di Canterbury* is a subversive parody, providing a critical model different from many contemporary approaches.

See also no. 40.

Chaucer's Life

6. Ackroyd, Peter. *Chaucer*. London: Chatto & Windus, 2004. xvi, 175 pp. 21 b&w illus.; 18 color illus. A biography of Chaucer that records his career as a courtier and diplomat and explores how it may have affected his personality and shaped his poetry. Designed for a general audience, with translations of quoted material, suggestions for further reading, and a brief index. See also no. 219.

7. Brook, Lindsay L. "The Ancestry of Sir Paon de Ruet, Father-in-Law of Geoffrey Chaucer and of John 'of Gaunt.'" *Foundations* 1.1 (2003): 54–56. Brook suggests that Sir Paon de Ruet may have been "a cadet of the family of the Lords of Roeulx" and part of the entourage of Philippa of Hainaut. He was probably born about 1309.

8. Carlson, David R. *Chaucer's Jobs*. The New Middle Ages. New York: Palgrave Macmillan, 2004. 168 pp. Chaucer's occupations—domestic servant, customs agent, justice of the peace, and clerk of the King's Works—shaped his literature, and his "servility" enabled him to become the "father" of English poetry. His biography and his works alike reveal "submersion in the interests of power," so that the early complaints mythologize the "ideal of the aristocratic good life"; *TC* is an "apology for the good life of erotic preoccupation"; and *CT* gives voice to some dissidence, only to police and suppress it. Admirers and imitators of Chaucer emulated his servility and, in doing so, shaped his critical legacy.

9. Hughes, David. *The Hack's Tale. Hunting the Makers of Media:*

Chaucer, Froissart, Boccaccio. London: Bloomsbury, 2004. xiv, 205 pp. Hughes combines travelogue and appreciative criticism as he traces the lives and footsteps of Chaucer, Froissart, and Boccaccio, exploring what each author contributed to growth in popular literature. Focuses on Chaucer's life and *CT.*

10. Lerer, Seth. "Chaucer's Sons." *UTQ* 73 (2004): 906–15. Comments on Thomas and Lewis as Chaucer's sons and explores *Astr* as a didactic treatise, part of Chaucer's "Macrobean" development from "literary study to moral inquiry."

11. Wallace, David. "Chaucer and Deschamps, Translation and the Hundred Years' War." In Rosalynn Voaden, René Tixier, Teresa Sanchez Roura, and Jenny Rebecca Rytting, eds. *The Theory and Practice of Translation in the Middle Ages* (*SAC* 28 [2006], no. 91), pp. 179–88. Wallace considers Eustace Deschamps's attitudes toward the English occupation of Calais and reads Deschamps's ballade 285 (which praises Chaucer) as a "spirited act of reverse or returned colonization." Identifies parallels in the careers of Deschamps and Chaucer, plus the two writers' relations with Oton de Granson.

See also nos. 39, 46, 82, 86, 187.

Facsimiles, Editions, and Translations

12. Brewer, Charlotte. "Critical, Scientific, and Eclectic Editing of Chaucer." In Richard Firth Green and Linne R. Mooney, eds. *Interstices: Studies in Middle English and Anglo-Latin Texts in Honour of A. G. Rigg* (*SAC* 28 [2006], no. 71), pp. 15–43. Examines several key terms in textual/editorial theory, exploring their application to various editions of Chaucer—Skeat's edition, Pollard's Globe edition, and editions by Zupitza, Koch, Manly and Rickert, and Robinson. The terms are used inconsistently, but Skeat's "best-text method tempered with a slight sprinkling of eclecticism" and common sense has proved most influential.

13. Caie, Graham D. " 'New Corn from Old Fields': The *Auctor* and *Compilator* in Fourteenth-Century English Literature." *RCEI* 47 (2003): 59–71. Caie argues that modern editions of medieval texts ought to be accompanied by the glosses that accompany them in the manuscripts. He discusses Chaucer's glosses to *CT,* as well as his use of the humility

topos. The glosses to *CT* may be Chaucer's own, and electronic editions can make them readily available.

14. Dane, Joseph A. "In Search of Stow's Chaucer." In Ian Gadd and Alexandra Gillespie, eds. *John Stow (1525–1605) and the Making of the English Past: Studies in Early Modern Culture and the History of the Book* (*SAC* 28 [2006], no. 17), pp. 145–55. Traces Stow's declining reputation among eighteenth- and nineteenth-century editors of Chaucer as well as a gradual revival of appreciation of Stow's edition, first among bibliophiles and later with modern Chaucerians. Dane examines the variants in imprints of Stow's edition and how these variants are cataloged in the STC. Includes facsimiles of two different title pages from the 1561 edition.

15. Driver, Martha. "Stow's Books Bequeathed: Some Notes on William Browne (1591–c. 1643) and Peter Le Neve (1661–1729)." In Ian Gadd and Alexandra Gillespie, eds. *John Stow (1525–1605) and the Making of the English Past: Studies in Early Modern Culture and the History of the Book* (*SAC* 28 [2006], no. 17), pp. 135–43. Driver assesses "Stow's pervasive intellectual influence on two later antiquarian readers of Chaucer." To Browne and Le Neve, Stow's edition was "a highly regarded and trusted exemplar, used to supply omissions, correct errors, and add notes."

16. Edwards, A. S. G. "John Stow and Middle English Literature." In Ian Gadd and Alexandra Gillespie, eds. *John Stow (1525–1605) and the Making of the English Past: Studies in Early Modern Culture and the History of the Book* (*SAC* 28 [2006], no. 17), pp. 109–18. Considers the texts Stow used in his career. His 1561 edition of Chaucer is marked less by its engagement with Chaucer than by the inclusion of Lydgate's *Siege of Thebes*. The evidence of Stow's annotations suggests interest in Lydgate but a surprising lack of "sustained interest" in Chaucer.

17. Gadd, Ian, and Alexandra Gillespie, eds. *John Stow (1525–1605) and the Making of the English Past: Studies in Early Modern Culture and the History of the Book*. London: British Library, 2004. 192 pp. Fifteen essays explore the life and legacy of John Stow, the sixteenth-century author of *Survey of London* (1598) and the editor of the 1561 edition of Chaucer. For four essays that pertain to Chaucer, see nos. 14–16 and 19.

18. Needham, Paul. "*The Canterbury Tales* and the Rosary: A Mirror of Caxton's Devotions?" In Takami Matsuda, Richard A. Linenthal, and John Scahill, eds. *The Medieval Book Collector and a Modern Collector: Essays in Honour of Toshiyuki Takamiya* (*SAC* 28 [2006], no. 78), pp. 313–56.

Needham documents the prominence of beads in nineteen of the twenty-three woodcuts in Caxton's second edition of *CT*. Suggests that the illustrations were influenced by the "expanding cult of rosary devotions" in Caxton's time and describes the history of such devotions. Reproduces all of the woodcuts.

19. Pearsall, Derek. "John Stow and Thomas Speght as Editors of Chaucer: A Question of Class." In Ian Gadd and Alexandra Gillespie, eds. *John Stow (1525–1605) and the Making of the English Past: Studies in Early Modern Culture and the History of the Book (SAC* 28 [2006], no. 17), pp. 119–25. Despite his expertise, Stow was not associated directly with Speght's 1598 edition. Speght "was able to ornament the edition with the names of his eminent friends," while Stow, lacking class, continued behind the scenes, providing "barrowloads of facts."

20. Robinson, Peter, ed., with Barbara Bordalejo and Orietta Da Rold, and contributions by Lorna Stevenson, Elizabeth Solopova, and Daniel W. Mosser. *The Miller's Tale on CD-ROM.* The *Canterbury Tales* Project. Leicester: Scholarly Digital Editions, 2004. 1 CD-ROM. Includes interlinked images and transcriptions of all fifty-eight pre-1500 versions of *MilPT,* with complete collations (linked to variant maps), commentaries on family relationships of the versions, and stemmatic commentary on key readings. The search engine enables comparisons by spelling, word, line, witness, and complex combinations. Includes full descriptions of all witnesses and scribes (by Mosser), fully lemmatized databases of all spellings and words, and a bibliography.

21. Serrano Reyes, Jesús, and Antonio R. León Sendra, trans. *Cuentos de Canterbury.* Biblioteca Universal Gredos, no. 24. Madrid: Editorial Gredos, 2004. 646 pp. Spanish translation of *CT,* with introduction and explanatory notes.

22. Tomasch, Sylvia. "Editing as Palinode: *The Invention of Love* and *The Text of the Canterbury Tales.*" *Exemplaria* 16 (2004): 457–76. Comments on the critical reception of Manly and Rickert's *The Text of the Canterbury Tales* (1940), exploring underlying assumptions about textual theory and gender politics. Uses Tom Stoppard's play *The Invention of Love* (1997) to reveal perspectives that underlie the praise of Manly's work and the occlusion of Rickert's.

23. Wheeler, Bonnie. "Leaning on Chaucer." In Takami Matsuda, Richard A. Linenthal, and John Scahill, eds. *The Medieval Book Collector and a Modern Collector: Essays in Honour of Toshiyuki Takamiya (SAC* 28 [2006], no. 78), pp. 461–66. Wheeler reproduces and describes two

versions of a sketch by Edward Burne-Jones, representing Chaucer embracing Burne-Jones and William Morris (the producers of the Kelmscott Chaucer). Includes an 1890 photograph of the Kelmscott duo and related materials.

24. Windeatt, Barry, ed. *Troilus and Criseyde*. London: Penguin, 2003. lxx, 561 pp. An edition of *TC*, with on-page glosses, explanatory notes at the end of the text, a glossary, and a selected bibliography. Includes a table of correspondences between *TC* and Boccaccio's *Filostrato*, plus a chronology of Chaucer's life and writings. The introduction considers source relations, dating, genre and structure, implied audience, and themes of freedom, gender, and epistemology.

See also nos. 29, 79, 112, 169.

Manuscripts and Textual Studies

25. Aita, Shuichi. "The Text of Chaucer's Parson's Tale in Bodleian Library MS Arch. Selden B.14: A Comparison of the Variants with B. L. MS Lansdowne 851." *SIMELL* 19 (2004): 37–49. Aita compares textual variants of *ParsT* in the Selden MS with British Library MS Lansdowne 851, showing how scribes attempted to clarify meaning by altering vocabulary and syntax.

26. Bowers, John M. "Two Professional Readers of Chaucer and Langland: Scribe D and the HM 114 Scribe." *SAC* 26 (2004): 113–46. Bowers describes the habits and activities of the two scribes, assessing what such factors can tell us about the scribes' careers and early fifteenth-century book production. Scribe D reflects "commercial opportunism" in producing works by prestige poets (Chaucer and Gower); the HM 114 scribe anticipates a later tendency to serve a civic rather than an aristocratic clientele. The article also comments on fifteenth-century readership of Chaucer and Langland and on the role of HM 114 in the textual tradition of *TC*.

27. Edwards, A. S. G. "Gower in the Delaware Chaucer Manuscript." In Takami Matsuda, Richard A. Linenthal, and John Scahill, eds. *The Medieval Book Collector and a Modern Collector: Essays in Honour of Toshiyuki Takamiya* (*SAC* 28 [2006], no. 78), pp. 81–86. Edwards comments on several features of Takamiya MS 32, which "provides the only significant narrative conjunction of the works of Chaucer and Gower": quire numbering and arrangement of materials indicate that the Gower

material was "selected by the prospective purchaser" and that the production of the manuscript was "unsystematic."

28. Erler, Mary C. "Fifteenth-Century Owners of Chaucer's Work:
Cambridge, Magdalene College MS Pepys 2006." *ChauR* 38 (2004):
401–14. Pepys MS 2006 contains a unique grouping of *Mel, ParsT,
Truth,* and *Scog.* Written by two scribes, it displays the names of John
Kyriell (gentry) and William Fettyplace (London mercer). The two social classes of Kyriell and Fettyplace indicate either a broadening of the
readership of Chaucer's works or a decline in the status of his readers.

29. Gardham, Julie, comp., and David Weston, introd. *The World
of Chaucer: Medieval Books and Manuscripts. Catalogue and Exhibition of
Manuscripts and Early Printed Books from Glasgow University Library, Held
at the Hunterian Museum 15 May to 28 August 2004.* Glasgow: Glasgow
University Library, 2004. 52 pp. Color illus. Brief discussion of six
Chaucerian books and twenty-five related works, with a highly selective
bibliography. For an expanded version, see http://special.lib.gla.ac.uk/
exhibns/chaucer/index.html (May 19, 2005).

30. Horobin, Simon, and Linne R. Mooney. "A *Piers Plowman* Manuscript by the Hengwrt/Ellesmere Scribe and Its Implications for London
Standard English." *SAC* 26 (2004): 65–112. Attributes Trinity College,
Cambridge, MS B.15.17 (which includes the B-text of *Piers Plowman,*
Richard Rolle's *Form of Living,* and a devotional poem) to the Hengwrt/
Ellesmere scribe (Scribe B), summarizing and illustrating the graphetic
features of his hand. Spelling features of the manuscript parallel those
of Hengwrt and Ellesmere, indicating that such features are idiosyn-
cratic rather than evidence of a rising standard. The scribe (like Scribe
D) was probably a "full-time" textwriter or a freelance scribe.

31. Mooney, Linne R. "A New Scribe of Chaucer and Gower." *JEBS*
7 (2004): 131–40. The scribe of British Library MS Harley 1758 (a
copy of *CT*) also executed London, Society of Antiquaries 134, which
includes Gower's *Confessio Amantis* and works by Lydgate, Hoccleve, and
John Walton. The two manuscripts were produced in the West Midlands, the result of "provincial production." The scribe is the fifth to be
identified as copyist of works by both Chaucer and Gower.

32. ———, and Daniel W. Mosser. "Hooked-g Scribes and Takam-
iya Manuscripts." In Takami Matsuda, Richard A. Linenthal, and John
Scahill, eds. *The Medieval Book Collector and a Modern Collector: Essays in
Honour of Toshiyuki Takamiya (SAC* 28 [2006], no. 78), pp. 179–96.
Offers a "new listing of the hooked-g group of scribes" and attributes

Takamiya MS 24 and two Takamiya fragments (MS 30 and single leaf from Plimpton MS) to the more specific "slanted hooked-g scribe," also responsible for Cambridge, Trinity College R.3.3; Oxford, Bodleian Library, Lyell 31; London, Lambeth Palace Library MS 256; and other portions of the Plimpton MS. Other distinctive features include violet ruling and frame, large format, gothic minuscule headings and running titles, and an identifiable spelling system.

33. Mosser, Daniel W. "The Scribe of Takamiya MS 32 (formerly the 'Delamere Chaucer') and Cambridge University Library MS Gg.I.34 (Part 3)." *JEBS* 7 (2004): 121–30. Mosser argues that the same scribe executed both manuscripts; the Cambridge manuscript is of *Mandeville's Travels.*

34. Nakao, Yoshiyuki, Akiyuki Jimura, and Masatsugu Matsuo. "A Project for a Comprehensive Collation of the Hengwrt and Ellesmere Manuscripts of *The Canterbury Tales:* The General Prologue." In Junsaku Nakamura et al., eds. *English Corpora Under Japanese Eyes* (an anthology commemorating the tenth anniversary of the Japan Association for English Corpus Studies). Language and Computers, no. 51. Amsterdam: Rodopi, 2004, pp. 139–50. Project proposal for a computer-assisted comparison of the Hengwrt and Ellesmere manuscripts of *CT,* focusing on how the manuscripts represent compound words, the use of double and single letters, the omission and addition of letters, the use of abbreviations and expanded forms, and the use of capital or noncapital letters.

See also nos. 12, 20, 50, 96, 99, 111, 160, 168, 174, 182, 210, 217.

Sources, Analogues, and Literary Relations

35. Hagedorn, Suzanne C. *Abandoned Women: Rewriting the Classics in Dante, Boccaccio, and Chaucer.* Ann Arbor: University of Michigan Press, 2004. xii, 220 pp. Hagedorn emphasizes the variety of versions of classical stories of abandoned women (Statius, Virgil, and Ovid) and the ways they were adapted in medieval tradition (e.g., Dante's *Inferno;* Boccaccio's *Teseida, Fiammetta,* and *Amorosa Visione;* and Chaucer's *KnT, TC,* and *LGW*). In Statius's *Thebaid,* Boccaccio's *Teseida,* and Chaucer's *KnT,* Theseus tries to correct and channel the aggressions of the Theban royal family, despite hints of corruption in his past. In *LGW* (Ariadne), Theseus reflects his dubious past; in *Anel,* the amorous past of Arcite parallels Theseus's. Hagedorn explores relationships with *Heroides* elsewhere in

LGW, arguing that the Dido account indicates more than one way to tell a story. *TC* reads *Heroides* subversively, since its tales of abandoned women in *TC* underly the abandonment of Troilus, a man. See also no. 251.

36. Heffernan, Carol Falvo. "Chaucer's *Miller's Tale* and *Reeve's Tale*, Boccaccio's *Decameron*, and the French *Fabliaux*." *Italica* 81 (2004): 311–24. Several motifs and verbal echoes among *MilT*, *RvT*, and *The Decameron* strengthen the case for "memorial borrowing" and invite the invention of a new critical term for Chaucer's poems: "*metrical* novellas."

37. Honegger, Thomas. "The Legacy of the Bestiaries in Chaucer and Henryson." *Reinardus* 12 (1999): 45–65. Chaucer and Henryson use the bestiaries in different ways. Chaucer only hints at the allegorical potential of his animals in *CT* and *PF*, although he does capitalize on familiar allegorizations in his similes and symbols. More directly, Henryson "applies the technique of allegorical interpretations of animals" that is found in bestiaries.

38. Mann, Jill. "Newly Identified Quotations in Chaucer's *Tale of Melibee* and the *Parson's Tale*." In Takami Matsuda, Richard A. Linenthal, and John Scahill, eds. *The Medieval Book Collector and a Modern Collector: Essays in Honour of Toshiyuki Takamiya* (*SAC* 28 [2006], no. 78), pp. 61–70. Mann identifies sources for *Mel* 7.1178–79, 1184, and 1186–88; and for *ParsT* 10.144, 261–63, 274, 331–32, 382–84, 630, 657, 694, and 822.

39. Olivares Merino, Eugenio M. "Juan Ruiz's Influence on Chaucer Revisited: Survey." *Neophil* 88 (2004): 145–61. Surveys scholarship pertaining to Chaucer's contact with Spain and suggests several routes of transmission for the influence of Juan Ruiz's *Libro de buen amor* on *TC* and *PardT*. Chaucer was probably aware of Ruiz (and other Spanish literature) through the library of Constanza of Castile, wife of John of Gaunt.

See also nos. 11, 94, 98, 103, 115, 118, 123, 132, 133, 135, 136, 141, 144, 146, 165, 167, 173, 180, 193–95, 203, 213.

Chaucer's Influence and Later Allusion

40. Blandeau, Agnès. "*A Knight's Tale:* La très noble histoire d'une comique imposture." *BAM* 65 (2004): 19–35. Assesses Brian Helge-

land's movie *A Knight's Tale* (2001), including its allusion to *KnT* and its inclusion of Chaucer as a character.

41. Boffey, Julia, comp. *Fifteenth-Century English Dream Visions: An Anthology.* New York and Oxford: Oxford University Press, 2003. x, 284 pp. Texts, notes, and introductions to Lydgate's *Temple of Glass;* James I of Scotland's *The Kingis Quair;* Charles of Orleans's *Love's Renewal; The Assembly of Ladies;* and Skelton's *The Bouge of Court.* The general introduction and the introductions to individual poems clarify textual issues and Chaucer's influence. Includes a selective bibliography. See also no. 224.

42. Carlson, David R. "The Chronology of Lydgate's Chaucer References." *ChauR* 38 (2004): 246–54. Lydgate's references to Chaucer's poetry help scholars date the writings of the later poet.

43. Kalter, Barrett Dean. "Modern Antiques: Imagination, Scholarship, and the Material Past." *DAI* 65 (2004): 2211A. Chapter 2 examines two views of *CT* in eighteenth-century England: as a philologist's "historical foundation in need of preservation" and as "merchandise facilitating social refinement."

44. Lerer, Seth. "Paul Bush and the Chaucer Tradition." *MÆ* 73 (2004): 103–7. Paul Bush's dream vision, *The Extripacion of Ignorancy,* was influenced by Chaucerian models and coins the phrase "lycour laureate" to describe Chaucer.

45. Nakao, Yoshiyuki. "Henryson's Cresseid." In Masahiko Kanno and Yuko Tagaya, eds. *Words and Literature: Essays in Honour of Professor Masa Ikegami.* Tokyo: Eihosha, 2004, pp.105–28 (in Japanese). Discusses ambiguity in the character of Henryson's Cresseid from a lexical and semantic point of view, with a comparative note on Chaucer's Criseyde and Shakespeare's Cressida.

46. Prendergast, Thomas A. *Chaucer's Dead Body: From Corpse to Corpus.* New York and London: Routledge, 2004. vii, 180 pp. Invoking a medieval association of book and body, Prendergast examines the cultural history of Chaucer's remains. The study assesses fifteenth-century attempts to mourn Chaucer's death, traces early modern ambivalence toward the poet's body-as-relic, and discusses the restored tomb as a symbol of nineteenth-century British nationalism. Prendergast argues that this restoration project and certain editing practices share a totalizing impulse. Modernists opposed a disembodied Chaucer to a continued popular interest in the body as signifier of genius. An appendix presents

Laurence Tanner's previously unpublished "Chaucer's Tomb and Nicholas Brigham."

47. Pugh, Tison. "Chaucerian Fabliaux, Cinematic Fabliau: Pier Paolo Pasolini's *I racconti di Canterbury*." *Literature/Film Quarterly* 32 (2004): 199–206. Assesses Pasolini's film as a series of medieval fabliaux, not as an attempt to capture all the genres of *CT*.

48. Wheatley, Edward. "Spike Lee's *Get on the Bus:* Mr. Chaucer Goes to Washington." *Film & History Annual* [n.v.] (2001–2): 1–9. Similarities between Lee's *Get on the Bus* and *CT* include the following: a pilgrimage motif, shifting narrative levels, the figure of a Host, a similar cast of characters, and themes such as inconclusiveness and complicated Christian resolution.

See also nos. 8, 65, 110, 112, 145, 191, 192, 200.

Style and Versification

49. Li, Xingzhong. "A Central Metrical Prototype for English Iambic Tetrameter Verse: Evidence from Chaucer's Octosyllabic Lines." In Anne Curzan and Kimberly Emmons, eds. *Studies in the History of the English Language II: Unfolding Conversations.* Topics in English Linguistics, no. 45. Berlin and New York: Mouton de Gruyter, 2004, pp. 315–41. Statistical evidence—including stress patterns, line divisions, pauses, missing and extrametrical syllables, and syntactical inversion—from Chaucer's octosyllabic lines corroborates a proposed prototype of iambic tetrameter and encourages us to regard Chaucer's lines as "gradient-based iambic tetrameter."

Language and Word Studies

50. Balhorn, Mark. "The Rise of the Epicene *They.*" *JEngL* 32 (2004): 79–104. Traces usage of generic *they* following an epicene antecedent (such as *anyone* or *everyone*) to the late fourteenth century. The Hengwrt manuscript of *CT* shows an eighteen percent occurrence of *euery, ech,* and *euerich* as antecedents to *they, hem,* and *hir(e)*. This and other texts indicate augmented use over time and suggest a correlative preference for the generic pronoun with a gradual increase of female social agency.

51. Burrow, J. A. "Nonverbal Communication in Medieval England:

Some Lexical Problems." In Richard Firth Green and Linne R. Mooney, eds. *Interstices: Studies in Middle English and Anglo-Latin Texts in Honour of A. G. Rigg* (*SAC* 28 [2006], no. 71), pp. 44–54. Burrow comments on several scenes in *TC* while exploring the limited vocabulary with which medieval English poets could convey nonverbal communication. Considers words such as *cheere* and *countenance*.

52. Kendrick, Laura. "Chaucer and the Nouvelle."*BAM* 66 (2004): 79–94. Examines the origins of the *nouvelle* in "news" and Chaucer's interest in *tydynges*.

53. Knapp, Peggy A. "Chaucer Imagines England (in English)." In Kathy Lavezzo, ed. *Imagining a Medieval English Nation* (*SAC* 28 [2006], no. 76), pp. 131–60. Knapp historicizes several terms (*ymaginacioun, fantasye, resoun, imaginatyf, engyn*) representing the role of language in national fantasy, exploring how Chaucer uses them throughout his poetry to construct ways of imagining. In *CT, PrT* demonstrates Chaucer's commitment to the expressive potential of English, and the understanding of time by several of the pilgrim-citizens (Knight, Monk, Miller, and Pardoner) affects their unhistoricized storytelling.

54. Nakao, Yoshiyuki. *The Structure of Chaucer's Ambiguity.* Tokyo: Shohakusha, 2004 (in Japanese). xiv, 451 pp. Describes ambiguity in Chaucer, focusing on *TC* and textual ambiguities (scribal/editorial variation, intertextuality, macrostructure-theme, character, plot, speech presentation, cohesion); interpersonal ambiguities (speech acts, modality); and propositional ambiguities (syntax, words, voice).

55. Pakkala-Weckström, Mari. "Discourse Strategies in the Marriage Dialogue of Chaucer's *Canterbury Tales*." *NM* 105 (2004): 153–75. Pakkala-Weckström analyzes the power struggles within male/female couples, examining politeness strategies and providing brief analyses of speech size, topic, control, distribution of flow, and turn-taking. Considers *MilT, MerT, ShT, WBT, FranT, Mel,* and *ClT*.

56. Rothwell, W. "Henry of Lancaster and Geoffrey Chaucer: Anglo-French and Middle English in Fourteenth-Century England." *MLR* 99 (2004): 313–27. Henry of Lancaster is usually treated in the context of medieval English history; Chaucer, of medieval English literature. Better understanding of the Anglo-French language and culture familiar to both men helps us appreciate Anglo-French and assess the *Livre de seyntz medicines,* Henry's penitential work rooted in the French of a small group of the religious elite.

57. Rudanko, Juhani. " 'I wol sterve': Negotiating the Issue of a

Lady's Consent in Chaucer's Poetry." *JHiP* 5.1 (2004): 137–58. As speech acts, threats are usually both conditional and commissive; i.e., they depend on an inferred promise, and they commit the speaker to some future course of action. Threats in Chaucer's works are usually modulated by the additional element of playfulness. Rudanko examines the presentation of threat in wooing scenes from *PF, KnT, MilT,* and *TC,* arguing that coercive wooing often depends on the threat of the speaker's own death, modulated by some degree of playfulness.

58. Schooler, Victoria D. "Prayer in Chaucer's Poetry." *DAI* 65 (2004): 1773A. Schooler examines *WBPT, KnT,* and *TC,* using speech-act theory to reveal Chaucer's attitudes toward prayer as personal utterance rather than rote activity.

See also nos. 4, 120, 142, 153, 207.

Background and General Criticism

59. Akbari, Suzanne Conklin. *Seeing Through the Veil: Optical Theory and Medieval Allegory.* Toronto: University of Toronto Press, 2004. xii, 354 pp. Tracks developments in the theory and practice of personification allegory in medieval literature (especially the *Roman de la Rose,* works by Dante, and works by Chaucer) in relation to optical theory and epistemology. As confidence in the epistemological reliability of vision and language diminishes historically, allegory becomes a less confident genre. According to Akbari, there is a "distinct progression in Chaucer's use of faculty psychology," particularly his "use of vision as a metaphor for knowing." Reliance on allegorical vision in his early works (*BD, SNT, Bo*) gives way to dependence on sound (*PF, HF, LGWP*) and eventually to abandonment of personification and allegory in *CT* (*Mel* and *MerT*), although vestiges remain.

60. Amtower, Laurel, and Dorothea Kehler, eds. *The Single Woman in Medieval and Early Modern England: Her Life and Representation.* Medieval and Renaissance Texts and Studies, no. 263. Tempe: Arizona Center for Medieval and Renaissance Studies, 2003. xxii, 242 pp. Eleven essays by various authors on topics ranging from Anglo-Norman literature to early modern portraiture and drama. For two essays that pertain to Chaucer, see nos. 131 and 181.

61. Astell, Ann W. "On the Usefulness and Use Value of Books: A Medieval and Modern Inquiry." In Scott D. Troyan, ed. *Medieval Rheto-*

ric: A Casebook (*SAC* 28 [2006], no. 89), pp. 41–62. Assesses medieval notions of the utility of books, comparing modern and medieval theoretical discussions. Astell's essay focuses on the symbolic exchange value of books and the "antisacrificial rhetorical strategies" for offering books as gifts to God and to others. Includes discussion of *GP* as an accessus to *CT* and of *Ret* as the place where Chaucer "assumes responsibility for the *utilitas* of his poetry."

62. Barasch, Frances K. "Shakespeare and the Puppet Sphere." *ELR* 34.2 (2004): 157–75. Barasch traces puppetry from Socrates to the Renaissance, arguing that Elizabethan puppet theatre conveyed popular learning. Chaucer's descriptions of the pilgrim Geoffrey as a "popet" (7.701–2) and of Alison as a "popelote" (*MilT* 1.3254) may reflect puppet entertainment in the fourteenth century.

63. Børch, Marianne, ed. *Text and Voice: The Rhetoric of Authority in the Middle Ages.* Odense: University Press of Southern Denmark, 2004. 272 pp. Ten essays by various authors on medieval verbal and visual rhetoric, with recurrent attention to authority, glossing, and vernacularity. For three essays that pertain to Chaucer, see nos. 81, 104, and 117.

64. Camargo, Martin. "Time as Rhetorical Topos in Chaucer's Poetry." In Scott D. Troyan, ed. *Medieval Rhetoric: A Casebook* (*SAC* 28 [2006], no. 89), pp. 91–107. Camargo explores how time functions rhetorically in Chaucer's works, discussing duration as a feature of style (amplification and abbreviation), time as an attribute of action (time as cause) and person (time of birth as character), and several examples of specious argument from opportunity. Draws examples from *CT* and *TC*.

65. Cooper, Helen. *The English Romance in Time: Transforming Motifs from Geoffrey of Monmouth to the Death of Shakespeare.* New York and Oxford: Oxford University Press, 2004. xvi, 542 pp. The motifs of medieval romances continued to be familiar in Tudor-Stuart England, although their meanings and the ways they were understood changed in time. Cooper traces a broad variety of romance motifs—quest, pilgrimage, encounters with fairies, the "Fair Unknown," threats to virginity, monstrous birth, magic and nonfunctioning magic, troth-plighting, etc.—documenting their availability to the English Renaissance in black-letter editions of medieval works and discussing their development and appropriation in Renaissance drama and narratives. References to Chaucer and his works recur throughout, particularly to *TC* and the romances of *CT* (*KnT, MLT, WBT, FranT,* and *Th*). Includes an appendix on medieval romance in English after 1500.

66. Dalrymple, Roger, ed. *Middle English Literature: A Guide to Criticism.* Blackwell Guides to Criticism. London: Blackwell, 2004. xviii, 264 pp. An introduction to critical approaches to Middle English literature, featuring twenty-two reprinted examples of critical methods by various authors. Chapters include authorship; textual form; genre; language, style and rhetoric; allegory; historicism; gender; and identity. Each chapter includes examples (mostly excerpts), a historical critical introduction, and suggestions for further reading. Discussion of Chaucer and his works (especially *CT* and *TC*) is important—often central—to nearly every chapter.

67. Davenport, Tony. *Medieval Narrative: An Introduction.* Oxford: Oxford University Press, 2004. x, 305 pp. Davenport describes several categories of medieval narrative, focusing on English literature, particularly Chaucer. Discusses didactic narratives (exempla and fables), historical accounts (chronicle, epic, romance), comic tales (fabliaux and novella), fantasies (otherworldly voyages and dream visions), tragedies, and compilations, as well as prologues and narrative personae. Assesses the development of each category out of classical and vernacular traditions and into late medieval England, commenting on how medieval notions of narrative helped shape later views. Pays sustained attention to *CT* and *TC*, with recurrent comments on Chaucer's other works and a wide range of other medieval stories.

68. Fradenburg, L. O. Aranye. "Simply Marvelous." *SAC* 26 (2004): 1–27. Fradenburg contemplates medieval romance as a product of desire and a producer of *jouissance.* Considers the functions and values of wonder; the enjoyment and signification of romance; and the relationships of wonder to "vernacularity," technology, weariness, and realism. Comments on *SqT, Th, TC,* and a number of other texts: *Sir Gawain and the Green Knight,* the *Tain bo Cuailinge, Culhwch & Olwen,* and other narratives.

69. Graßnick, Ulrike. *Ratgeber des Königs. Fürstenspiegel und Herrscherideal im spätmittelalterlichen England.* Europäische Kulturstudien, no. 15. Köln, Wien, Weimar: Böhlau, 2004. xii, 471 pp. A New Historicist assessment of Middle English mirrors for princes: Chaucer's *Mel* and works by Trevisa, Hoccleve, Lydgate and Burgh, Hays, Ashby, and Gower. These texts construct an ideal king and normative social values and—set against the reign and deposition of Richard II—disclose much about contemporary society. Graßnick explores topics such as counsel, virtue, and strategies of transmission and includes an appendix that lists

owners of mirrors for princes in fourteenth- and fifteenth-century England.

70. Gray, Douglas. "'Lat be thyne olde ensaumples': Chaucer and Proverbs." In Richard Firth Green and Linne R. Mooney, eds. *Interstices: Studies in Middle English and Anglo-Latin Texts in Honour of A. G. Rigg* (*SAC* 28 [2006], no. 71), pp. 122–36. Gray comments on the cultural value and functions of proverbs and their kin (adages, aphorisms, etc.), focusing on two "clusters" of proverbs: the "proverb war" of *WBP* and the complex and intricate uses of proverbs by Pandarus, Criseyde, and the narrator in *TC*.

71. Green, Richard Firth, and Linne R. Mooney, eds. *Interstices: Studies in Late Middle English and Anglo-Latin Texts in Honour of A. G. Rigg.* Toronto: University of Toronto Press, 2004. xxii, 219 pp. Ten essays by various authors, a forward and an introduction, a bibliography of Rigg's publications, and a subject index. Three essays pertain to Chaucer; see nos. 12, 51, and 70.

72. Hoffman, Frank G. "The Dream and the Book: Chaucer's Dream-Poetry, Faculty Psychology, and the Poetics of Recombination." *DAI* 65 (2004): 2194A. Examines medieval notions of poetics and faculty psychology as approaches to *BD, HF, PF,* and *LGWP.*

73. Kern-Stähler, Annette. *A Room of One's Own: Reale und mentale Innenräume weiblicher Selbstbestimmung im spätmittelalterlichen England.* Tradition—Reform—Innovation, Studien zur Modernität des Mittelalters, no. 3. Frankfurt am Main: Peter Lang, 2002. xvi, 358 pp. 1 color illus.; 77 b&w illus. Examines interior space in late medieval English architecture, manuscript illumination, and literature, focusing on homes, churches, and their imagery as they helped to shape feminine identity. Topics include Margaret Beaufort and her circle, Richard Rolle, Margery Kempe, cycle plays, "The Mirror of the Blessed Life of Jesus Christ," and works by Chaucer, Gower, Lydgate, and others. Recurrent attention to *CT, LGW,* and especially *TC.* See also no. 263.

74. Kline, Daniel T., ed. *Medieval Literature for Children.* New York and London: Routledge, 2003. xii, 353 pp. Sixteen essays by various authors, most of them addressing individual texts as literature written for children—for example, *The Babees Book, Sir Gowther,* Aelfric's *Colloquy,* and selections from the *Gesta Romanorum* and from Gower's *Confessio Amantis.* In his introduction, Kline assesses "the history and definition of medieval children's literature." Two essays pertain to Chaucer, with many references throughout; see nos. 155 and 169.

75. Klitgård, Ebbe. "Chaucer as Performer: Narrative Strategies in the Dream Visions." *RCEI* 47 (2003): 101–13. Klitgård assesses the "linguistic, communicative and narrative markers of performativity" in *BD, HF,* and *PF,* arguing that Chaucer composed the works for live performance but also with an eye to repeated performance or reading.

76. Lavezzo, Kathy, ed. *Imagining a Medieval English Nation.* Minneapolis: University of Minnesota Press, 2004. xxxiv, 353 pp. An introduction by the editor and ten essays by various authors consider the presence and nature of nationalism in medieval England. Medieval scholarly tradition and political structures anticipate the nation state and the nationalist discourses of modernity. For two essays that pertain to Chaucer, see nos. 53 and 177.

77. Lynch, Kathryn L. "Team Teaching the Literature of the European and Islamic Middle Ages: The European Perspective." In Richard F. Gyug, ed. *Medieval Cultures in Contact.* Fordham Series in Medieval Studies, no. 1. New York: Fordham University Press, 2003, pp. 213–22. Lynch describes how a team-taught, cross-cultural course in European and Islamic literatures discovers dimensions in the literatures, including *SqT, FranT,* and *MLT.*

78. Matsuda, Takami, Richard A. Linenthal, and John Scahill, eds. *The Medieval Book Collector and a Modern Collector: Essays in Honour of Toshiyuki Takamiya.* Cambridge: Brewer; Tokyo: Yushodo, 2004. xx, 530 pp.; b&w and color illus. Thirty-eight essays and two commemorations celebrate the sixtieth birthday of Takamiya, focusing on "medieval manuscripts and early printed books, Arthurian literature, and nineteenth- and twentieth-century medievalism." Many of the essays pertain to volumes in the honoree's collection. The book includes a bibliography of Takamiya's publications. Seven essays pertain to Chaucer; see nos. 18, 23, 27, 32, 38, 111, and 217.

79. McCarthy, Conor, ed. *Love, Sex and Marriage in the Middle Ages: A Sourcebook.* London and New York: Routledge, 2004. xii, 292 pp. Anthology for teaching medieval ideas about love, sex, and marriage; includes modern translation of portions of Chaucer's works: *PardT, WBP,* and *Buk.*

80. Mieder, Wolfgang. *Proverbs: A Handbook.* Greenwood Folklore Handbooks. Westport, Conn.: Greenwood, 2004. xvi, 304 pp. An introduction to the study of proverbs (paremiology), covering definition and classification, several examples over time, scholarly approaches, and analyses of the contexts in which proverbs appear (e.g., song, advertis-

ing, cartoons, and literature). Traces "first come, first served" to *WBP* and discusses the development and disappearance of the association of millers with gold thumbs.

81. Minnis, A. J. "Absent Glosses: A Crisis of Vernacular Hermeneutics in Late-Medieval England." In Marianne Børch, ed. *Text and Voice: The Rhetoric of Authority in the Middle Ages* (*SAC* 28 [2006], no. 63), pp. 138–67. Considers the lack of extensive glosses and commentaries on late Middle English literature, including Chaucer, arguing that in England, unlike on the Continent, the concern with *translatio studii* (transferring the authority of the ancients to the present) was "tainted by the Lollards" and their promotion of the vernacular.

82. Oliver, Clementine. "A Political Pamphleteer in Late Medieval England: Thomas Fovent, Geoffrey Chaucer, Thomas Usk, and the Merciless Parliament of 1388." *NML* 6 (2003): 167–98. Explores the identity and political career of Thomas Fovent (Favent), author of the polemical treatise on the Merciless Parliament—*Historia Mirabilis Parliament*—arguing that the treatise is best regarded as a "pamphlet," an index to the public opinion of the age, not partisan propaganda. Oliver compares and contrasts Fovent's political savvy and caution with those of Chaucer and Usk. See also no. 265.

83. Palmer, James Milton. "Narratives of Healing: Emotion, Medicine, Metaphor, and Late-Medieval Poetry and Prose." *DAI* 64 (2004): 2479A. Explores medieval attitudes toward the medical foundations of the emotions in *MerT, TC,* Gower's *Confessio Amantis,* and Diego de San Pedro's *Cárcel de Amor.*

84. Sadlek, Gregory. *Idleness Working: The Discourse of Love's Labor from Ovid Through Chaucer and Gower.* Washington, D.C.: Catholic University of America Press, 2004. xii, 298 pp. Bakhtinian analysis of the discourse of love's labor in classical and medieval love literature, focusing on two traditions: one, rhetorical, playful, and concerned with the labor of courtship; the other, serious, philosophical, and concerned with the labor of reproduction. The two combine in the later love poetry, including Chaucer's, in a steady "embourgeoisement de l'eros" [a making bourgeois of love]. Constructed by means of a rich array of labor vocabulary and imagery, "work" is presented as a necessary but fulfilling component of human existence, a foreshadowing of the Protestant Work Ethic. The final chapter focuses on Chaucer, particularly *PF* and *TC.*

85. Schoff, Rebecca Lynn. "Freedom from the Press: Reading and Writing in Late Medieval England." *DAI* 65 (2004): 1773A. Examines

the works of Chaucer, Langland, and Margery Kempe in the context of the standardization of textual discourse that accompanied the development of printed books.

86. Simms, Norman Toby. *A New Midrashic Reading of Geoffrey Chaucer: His Life and Works.* Studies in British Literature, no. 89. Lewiston, N.Y.: Mellen, 2004. x, 486 pp. Reads details of Chaucer's life and works as evidence that he can be viewed as a "fuzzy Jew," who acquired some kabbalistic knowledge through his travels and contact with Jews in London and who disguised this knowledge in ways that anticipate the writings of fifteenth-century Spanish Marranos. Discusses cryptic aspects of Chaucer's life and the ironies of his works, assessing *CT,* especially *PrT* and *WBPT.* Argues that *BD* was "inspired by kabbalistic letter combinations."

87. Stanbury, Sarah. "EcoChaucer: Green Ethics and Medieval Nature." *ChauR* 39 (2004): 1–16. Depicting nature as an "active force," Chaucer encourages the reader to explore nature's "effects on social institutions and human drives." In so doing, he balances "a dis-enchanted skepticism about nature's benevolence" with "a canny understanding" of how institutions invoke "'the natural' to justify their own privileges."

88. Steinberg, Theodore L. *Reading the Middle Ages: An Introduction to Medieval Literature.* Jefferson, N.C.: McFarland, 2003. viii, 188 pp. An introduction to the study of medieval literature, with chapters on *Beowulf,* Chrétien de Troyes, the *Lais* of Marie de France, *The Romance of the Rose, The Tale of Genji,* Jewish literature, sagas, Dante, *Pearl, Sir Gawain and the Green Knight,* and Chaucer. Includes general discussion of Chaucer's travels, use of language, sources, and primary themes of love and common profit, as well as manuscripts. Focuses on *CT,* with brief discussions of *HF, PF,* and *TC.*

89. Troyan, Scott D. ed. *Medieval Rhetoric: A Casebook.* Routledge Medieval Casebooks, no. 36. New York and London: Routledge, 2004. viii, 262 pp. Ten essays by various authors, addressing topics such as rhetorical tradition, accessus, and handbooks, especially their influence on Middle English literature. For six essays that pertain to Chaucer, see nos. 61, 64, 158, 196, 203, and 215.

90. Vitz, Evelyn Birge. "The Liturgy and Vernacular Literature." In Thomas J. Heffernan and E. Ann Matter, eds. *The Liturgy of the Medieval Church.* Kalamazoo, Mich.: Medieval Institute, 2001, pp. 551–618. Vitz surveys the influences and echoes of liturgical wording and practice in a range of medieval literature—English, French, Italian, narrative, lyrical,

parodic, etc. Includes focused treatments of *La Queste del Saint Graal,* *The Roman de la Rose,* *The Divine Comedy,* and *CT,* particularly *PrT* and *Ret.* Characterizes Chaucer's uses of the liturgy as "complex and ambiguous" and "probably ambivalent as well."

91. Voaden, Rosalynn, René Tixier, Teresa Sanchez Roura, and Jenny Rebecca Rytting, eds. *The Theory and Practice of Translation in the Middle Ages.* The Medieval Translator/Traduire au Moyen Age, no. 8. Turnhout: Brepols, 2003. xxvi, 350 pp. Twenty-eight essays by various authors selected from the Seventh International Conference on the Theory and Practice of Translation in the Middle Ages, July 2001, Santiago de Compostela, Spain. Topics range from cook books to Lollard arguments. For four essays that pertain to Chaucer, see nos. 11, 112, 180, and 192.

92. Wallace, David. *Premodern Places: Calais to Surinam, Chaucer to Aphra Behn.* Malden, Mass., and Oxford: Blackwell, 2004. x, 342 pp. 30 b&w illus. Wallace contemplates and reconstructs historical understanding of several locations, using visual and verbal texts to recapture perspectives of medieval and early modern witnesses or visitors. Explores Calais as an English outpost and Flanders as its neighbor, drawing upon *Th, ShT,* and *PardT,* as well as works by Deschamps, Hakluyt, and others. Also considers the early modern reception of Dante at Wells in Somerset, medieval slave trade in Genoa, Italian humanist imagining of the Canary Isles as the classical Fortunate Isles, and the letters of Héloïse and Abélard and the works of Aphra Behn in the colonial representation of Surinam.

93. Waters, Claire M. *Angels and Earthly Creatures: Preaching, Performance, and Gender in the Later Middle Ages.* Philadelphia: University of Pennsylvania Press, 2004. xi, 282 pp. Conflicted cooperation between authority and authorization is a manifestation of the fundamentally hybrid nature of the preacher's calling, one recognized in medieval handbooks as standing between earth and heaven. Significantly, women's preaching was a formative influence on ideas of men's preaching, particularly because theorists' discussions of women preachers raise and examine questions about personal authority and the body's role in that authority without directing those questions toward male preachers. Chapter 2 argues that Chaucer's *CT,* with its intense emphasis on speech, embodiment, and authority, illuminates central issues in preaching theory by presenting them in concentrated and personified forms. The Parson and the Pardoner encapsulate a central ethical and moral

issue: the appropriate relationship between the preacher's human body and his spiritual task.

94. Williams, Deanne. *The French Fetish from Chaucer to Shakespeare.* Cambridge: Cambridge University Press, 2004. xiv, 283 pp. Traces the "representations of, and responses to" France and Frenchness in *BD* and Chaucer's Prioress, the Corpus Christi plays, Caxton's publishing career, the poetry of Stephen Hawes and John Skelton, and Shakespeare's history plays. English identity is marked throughout this literature by efforts to "emulate French culture" in conflict with a desire to "articulate a distinctively English voice." *BD* is Chaucer's meditation on his earlier imitations of French poetry—an English manifesto and a nostalgic elegy. The *GP* Prioress and *PrT* reveal a desire to identify with French culture and a simultaneous inability to read cultural codes accurately. Williams also discusses the role of Chaucer in Caxton's output.

The Canterbury Tales—General

95. Crépin, André. "Chaucer's *Subtil Engyn.*" *ÉA* 56 (2003): 403–11. Crépin sketches the range of Chaucer's diversity in *CT* and suggests that Chaucer abandons artistic diversity for the Parson's warning against sinful excess.

96. Dawkins, Richard. *The Ancestor's Tale: The Dawn of Evolution.* Boston and New York: Houghton Mifflin, 2004. xiv, 672 pp. Dawkins uses the frame-and-tale structure of *CT* to organize a series of excurses on evolution and the development of biological life. Recurrent references to Chaucer and *CT,* with brief discussion on evolutionary biology as a model in the *Canterbury Tales* Project.

97. Ellis, Jerry. *Walking to Canterbury: A Modern Journey Through Chaucer's Medieval England.* New York: Ballantine, 2003. 309 pp. A personal travelogue of a walking trip from Canterbury to London following the Pilgrims' Way—interspersed with brief summaries of portions of *CT* and musings on medieval social history and folk wisdom, the United Kingdom and the United States, contemporary spirituality, and people met along the way.

98. Higgins, Iain Macleod. "Tit for Tat: *The Canterbury Tales* and *The Flyting of Dunbar and Kennedy.*" *Exemplaria* 16 (2004): 165–202. Higgins explores the "incidental affiliations" between *CT* and *The Flyting of Dunbar and Kennedy,* demonstrating how flyting tradition informs *CT,* especially Part 1 and the debate between the Wife of Bath and the Clerk.

The tale-telling contest is related both to flyting and to the debate tradition of *Wynnere and Wastoure*.

99. Hilmo, Maidie. *Medieval Images, Icons, and Illustrated English Literary Texts: From Ruthwell Cross to the Ellesmere Chaucer*. Burlington, Vt.: Ashgate, 2004. xxvi, 236 pp. 76 b&w illus. Six related essays on the interaction of words and images in English literary tradition: a theoretical introduction, plus essays on the Ruthwell Cross, Anglo-Saxon art, the Auchinleck and Vernon manuscripts, the manuscript of *Pearl*, and the Ellesmere manuscript of *CT*. The latter essay (pp. 160–99) shows how Ellesmere illustrations "advance concepts of good government" and encourage viewers to regard the real goal of pilgrimage as spiritual, expanding their "aristocratic space" in ways that imply "celestial space."

100. Lucotti, Claudia. "El tema del matrimonio en *The Canterbury Tales* de Geoffrey Chaucer." *AnLM* 11 (2002–3): 47–52. Summarizes medieval attitudes toward gender relations in marriage and comments on the diverse range of representations of marriage in *CT*.

101. Mitchell, J. Allan. *Ethics and Exemplary Narrative in Chaucer and Gower*. Chaucer Studies, no. 33. Cambridge: D. S. Brewer, 2004. Examines the ethics of exemplarity in *Confesso Amantis* and in *CT*, arguing that reading for the moral—deliberating ethically—is improvisatory and reflexive and aims at practice rather than theory. Exemplarity involves the reader in its moral rhetoric, inviting a taxonomic practice of considering similar cases and an act of reduction to make a decision. Chapters 1 and 2 consider the intuitive recognition of a moral, the reader's extracting of meaning from exempla, the use of example in classical rhetoric, and the rise of homiletic compilations in the Middle Ages. Chapters 3 and 4 argue that Gower, like Chaucer, challenges univocal meaning by offering readers contrary exempla—the morals of which readers determine according to their personal circumstances and conscience. Chapters 5–7 examine *WBP, FrT, SumT, PardP, PardT, ClT, Mel,* and *ParsT*, arguing that Chaucer critiques the misuse of exemplarity (but not the genre) and analyzing how readers derive morals from the tales and tales within tales, the teller, or a combination of these features.

102. Nakao, Yoshiyuki. "Travels in *The Canterbury Tales:* Their Structure and Meaning." In Noboru Harano et al., eds. *Travels Through Space and Time in Medieval Europe*. Hiroshima: Keisuisha, 2004, pp. 97–140. Nakao discusses traveling as physical movement through space and mental movement through time. A dual space-time scheme is central to

the structure of *CT* and contributes to the rise of dualistic interpretations of such words and phrases as *licour* (1.3), *engendred* (1.4), and *nature* (1.11) in *GP* and *Bobbe-up-and-doun* in *ManT* (9.2).

103. Peck, Russell A. "St. Paul and the *Canterbury Tales.*" *Mediaevalia* 7 (1984 for 1981): 91–131. Biblical Pauline notions of pilgrimage recur throughout *CT*, evident in imagery drawn from Paul's letters, although often in "parody and travesty": old men and new men, doctrine amidst enigma, iconography of wells, vessels, widows, musical instruments, and various concepts of time, heritage, and the "search for grace."

104. Spearing, A. C. "Textual Performance: Chaucerian Prologues and the French *Dit.*" In Marianne Børch, ed. *Text and Voice: The Rhetoric of Authority in the Middle Ages* (*SAC* 28 [2006], no. 63), pp. 21–45. Critiques "dramatic" or Kittredgean readings of the prologues in *CT*, especially those "newly oiled by Lacan," and considers the prologues in light of the French *dit*—loosely defined as "speech imitated in clerkly writing" or the "illusion of speech created in writing." Spearing comments on *GP, RvP, MLP, FranP,* and *PardP* and discusses *WBP* as an extended "textual performance" by "Chaucer in drag."

105. Tovey, Barbara. "Chaucer's Dialectic: How the Establishment Theology Is Subjected to Scrutiny in Five *Canterbury Tales.*" *Interpretation* 31 (2004): 235–99. *ManT* reflects Chaucer's awareness of the dangers of challenging authority, yet he repeatedly challenges Christian and Boethian orthodoxies concerning evil. *KnT* does not reconcile the existence of evil, and the orthodoxy of Christian Providence in *MLT* is "exceedingly crude and naïve," immediately rejected through the Wife of Bath's assertion of experience. *ClT* raises again the question of why evil exists, and in *FranT* human agency is sufficient to maintain truth. Tovey also discusses belief and skepticism in the opening lines of *LGWP*.

106. Utz, Richard. "Gender and Time in Chaucer's *Canterbury Tales.*" In Zygmunt Mazur and Richard Utz, eds. *Homo Narrans: Texts and Essays in Honor of Jerome Klinkowitz.* Kráków: Jagiellonian University Press, 2004, pp. 193–206. Chaucer's male narrators and characters are obsessed with ideas of linear/finite time, progression, arrival, and teleology. His female characters either silently subscribe to the male obsession or are dominated by cyclical/monumental and transcendent time. The Wife of Bath is the antithesis of the allegorical figure of *Temperantia.*

107. Ward Mather, Lisa Jeanette. "'Lat us werken thriftly': Rethinking Identity and Social Organization in Chaucer's Fabliaux." *DAI* 64 (2004): 2503A. Discussing *MilPT, ShT, WBP,* and *SumT,* Ward

Mather argues that "Chaucer engages with the medieval genre of fabliau" to "develop a new theory of identity and social order."

108. Wetherbee, Winthrop. *Geoffrey Chaucer: The Canterbury Tales.* 2nd ed. Landmarks of World Literature. New York: Cambridge University Press, 2004. vi, 125 pp. Re-issue of the 1989 edition, with a revised guide to further reading. See also no. 290.

109. Zangen, Britta. "Women in Chaucer's Male Universe: Literary Critics Coping with Misogynism." In Britta Zangen, ed. *Misogynism in Literature: Any Place, Any Time.* Frankfurt am Main: Peter Lang, 2004, pp. 39–58. Antifeminism is prevalent throughout *CT* in depictions of women, assumptions about them, and attitudes toward female-male relations. Nevertheless, *CT* is still considered a "master-piece" of literature, evidence that critics have not completed the work of feminist intervention.

See also nos. 5, 8, 9, 18, 21, 34, 43, 47, 48, 53, 55, 64, 66, 67, 73, 86, 88, 90, 135, 157.

CT—The General Prologue

See nos. 34, 61, 104, 126, 151.

CT—The Knight and His Tale

110. Bowers, John M. "Three Readings of *The Knight's Tale:* Sir John Clanvowe, Geoffrey Chaucer, and James I of Scotland." *JMEMSt* 34 (2004): 279–307. Three variants of *KnT*—Sir John Clanvowe's reading of the story of Palamon and Arcite, Chaucer's *KnT,* and *The Kingis Quair* of James I—provide insight into the shifting ideologies of chivalric performance and the establishment of Chaucer as a literary author during the Ricardian and Lancastrian periods.

111. Cooper, Helen. "Textual Variation and the Alliterative Tradition: *Canterbury Tales* I.2602–2619, the D Group and Takamiya MS 32." In Takami Matsuda, Richard A. Linenthal, and John Scahill, eds. *The Medieval Book Collector and a Modern Collector: Essays in Honour of Toshiyuki Takamiya* (*SAC* 28 [2006], no. 78), pp. 71–80. Examines manuscript variants in *KnT* 1.2616–17 in relation to Chaucer's awareness of alliterative tradition and its lexicon, suggesting that "hurtleth"

is preferable to "hurteth" at 2616 and that "born" (D Group) for "hurt" at 2617 may have been influenced by the preceding line.

112. Greenwood, Maria K. "What Dryden Did to Chaucer's *The Knight's Tale,* or Translation as Ideological Input." In Rosalynn Voaden, René Tixier, Teresa Sanchez Roura, and Jenny Rebecca Rytting, eds. *The Theory and Practice of Translation in the Middle Ages (SAC* 28 [2006], no. 91), pp. 189–200. Dryden's translation of *KnT* "tidies, clarifies, and modernizes" the text for its eighteenth-century readers, turning Chaucer's "subversive parodies back into the illusory heroic idealizations" of Statius and Boccaccio. Greenwood focuses on the characterizations of Theseus and Emelye.

113. Hamaguchi, Keiko. "Domesticating Amazons in *The Knight's Tale." SAC* 26 (2004): 331–54. Explores the "postcolonial uneasiness visible" in *KnT,* particularly in Hippolyta's subversive mimicry in the face of efforts by Theseus and the Knight to westernize her "Amazonness." Emelye's powerful gaze upon the victorious Arcite reveals similar slippage.

114. Piñeiro, Aurora. "Lo solemne y lo festivo: Contrastes y paralelismos en le primer ciclo de historias *Los cuentos de Canterbury." AnLM* 11 (2002–3): 23–34. Compares and contrasts the plots, characters, and themes of *KnT* and *MilT.*

115. Thompson, Jefferson M. *"Ratio Amoris* and *Amor Rationis:* The Struggle for Supremacy Between Love and Reason in *The Romance of the Rose* and *The Knight's Tale."* In Piotr Fast and Wacław Osadnok, eds. *From Kievan Prayers to Avantgarde: Papers in Comparative Literature.* Warsaw: Wydawnictwo Energeia, 1999, pp. 83–98. Thompson traces parallels among several dichotomies—*eros* and *agape, cupiditas* and *caritas,* love and reason—arguing that Chaucer was unsatisfied with the simple dichotomies he found in the *Roman de la Rose.* In *KnT,* love is "reprimanded" as folly, but the supremacy of reason is challenged as well.

See also nos. 35, 40, 57, 58, 65, 105, 130, 164.

CT—The Miller and His Tale

116. Beidler, Peter G. " 'Now Deere Lady': Absolon's Marian Couplet in the *Miller's Tale." ChauR* 39 (2004): 219–22. In *MilT,* John is not jealous of Absolon's song to Alison because he hears in it a song to the Virgin, asking her for mercy.

117. Børch, Marianne. "Geoffrey Chaucer and the Cosmic Text: Rejecting Analogy." In Marianne Børch, ed. *Text and Voice: The Rhetoric of Authority in the Middle Ages* (*SAC* 28 [2006], no. 63), pp. 97–120. Assesses Nicholas's manipulation of language and signs in *MilT* as Chaucer's embedded analysis of typological or analogical thinking. The references to mystery plays in *MilT* counterpoint the "poetics of a trickster clerk" whose manipulations embody a challenge to analogical thinking.

118. Finlayson, John. "Chaucer's Absolon and Boccaccio's *Decameron*." *NM* 103 (2002): 403–7. The "basic conception and function" of Absolon in *MilT* were inspired by *Decameron* 8.2, which also influenced *ShT*.

119. Muñoz G., Adrián. "A Little Chat on Chaucer's 'The Miller's Tale.'" *AnLM* 11 (2002–3): 47–52. A fanciful conversation between Chaucer and the author about *MilT*, touching on questions of genre and theme. Chaucer's portion of the dialogue is in mock Middle English.

See also nos. 20, 36, 57, 62, 65, 80, 105, 107, 114, 121.

CT—The Reeve and His Tale

120. Allman, W. W. "Sociolinguistics, Literature, and the *Reeve's Tale*." *ES* 85 (2004): 385–404. In light of sociolinguistic categories such as register, distance-solidarity, and dialect, Allman contends, *RvPT* and the Reeve's portrait in *GP* stand as sustained examinations of failed sociality and unsatisfied desire at both dramatic and narrative levels.

121. Silberman, Lauren. "*The Faerie Queene*, Book V, and the Politics of the Text." *SSt* 19 (2004): 1–16. Introduces the 2002 Kathleen Williams Lecture on the sexual politics of *FQ* with an anecdote about a Smith College professor's delicacy with language in *MilT* and *RvT;* connects *RvT* with acquaintance rape.

122. Woods, William F. "Symkyn's Place in the *Reeve's Tale*." *ChauR* 39 (2004): 17–40. *RvT* is "concerned with breaking the ranks of social hierarchy" and what causes individuals to desire such breaks. The clerks, the women, Bayard, and especially Symkyn all experience "frustrated desire," which leads Symkyn "to expand into outer or inner space, because he is unable to accept the nature of his own small space."

See also no. 36.

CT—The Cook and His Tale

See no. 217.

CT—The Man of Law and His Tale

123. Barefield, Laura D. "Women's Patronage and the Writing of History: Nicholas Trevet's *Les Cronicles* and Geoffrey Chaucer's *Man of Law's Tale.*" In Laura D. Barefield. *Gender and History in Medieval English Romance and Chronicle.* New York: Peter Lang, 2003, pp. 37–72. Barefield contrasts the characterizations of Constance in *Les Cronicles* and *MLT,* focusing on how female patronage (by Mary of Woodstock) may have encouraged the character's active role in Trevet's version.

124. Cooper, Christine F. *"Mirabile Translatu:* Translating Women and the Miraculous in the Later Middle Ages." *DAI* 65 (2004): 1772A. Considers *MLT* and *SqT* in a study of female xenoglossia (the ability to use or comprehend foreign tongues) in the later Middle Ages.

125. Delany, Sheila. " 'Loi' and 'Foi' in *The Man of Law's Introduction, Prologue,* and *Tale.*" *Mediaevalia* 8 (1985 for 1982): 135–49. The various parts of *MLPT* "cohere around the multiple meanings of 'law,' " although the "Introduction" was still being shaped.

126. Fichte, Joerg O. "Rome and Its Anti-pole in the *Man of Law's* and the *Second Nun's Tale: Cristendom* and *Hethenesse.*" *Anglia* 122 (2004): 225–49. Fichte explores Rome in *CT,* both as an actual place and as a symbol. Focuses on Rome versus Syria in *MLT* and Christianity versus paganism in *SNT,* with comments on the Wife of Bath's and the Pardoner's connections with Rome, as well as orientalism in *GP, SqT,* and *Th.*

127. Heng, Geraldine. "Beauty and the East, a Modern Love Story: Women, Children, and Imagined Communities in *The Man of Law's Tale* and Its Others." In Geraldine Heng. *Empire of Magic: Medieval Romance and the Politics of Cultural Fantasy.* New York: Columbia University Press, 2003, pp. 181–237. Heng assesses *MLT* as an account of a "feminized crusade" that involves "sexual martyrdom" on the part of Custance and reveals the power of her "reproductive sexuality." The fusion of hagiography and romance in *MLT* is also evident in *C/T,* but while both *Tales* show how the "politics of emotion undergirds the nationalist imaginary," *MLT* also indicates how (as in *King of Tars*) race challenges ideas of community. See also no. 254.

128. Millersdaughter, Katherine Elizabeth. "The Geopolitics of Incest in the Age of Conquest: Gerald of Wales Through Geoffrey Chaucer." *DAI* 64 (2003): 1245A. English political claims to Wales depended in part on claims of Welsh incest; Millersdaughter discusses various texts (including *MLT*) in which this "heterogeneous, colonialist discourse" is evident.

See also nos. 77, 157.

CT—The Wife of Bath and Her Tale

129. Black, Merrill. "Three Readings of the Wife of Bath." In Diane P. Freedman and Olivia Frey, eds. *Autobiographical Writing Across the Disciplines: A Reader*. Durham, N.C.: Duke University Press, 2003, pp. 85–95. An autobiographical reading of *WBPT* by a woman who was for a time an abused wife. Black records three different responses to Chaucer's materials at three different stages in her life, focusing on the Wife's responses to abuse by her husbands.

130. Lambert, Anne H. "The Wild Woman and Her Sisters in Medieval English Literature." *DAI* 64 (2004): 4456A. Considers various tamed and untamed wild women in medieval literature, including two of Chaucer's characters: the Wife of Bath, and Emelye of *KnT*.

131. Moore, Jeanie Grant. "(Re)creations of a Single Woman: Discursive Realms of the Wife of Bath." In Laurel Amtower and Dorothea Kehler, eds. *The Single Woman in Medieval and Early Modern England: Her Life and Representation* (*SAC* 27 [2005], no. 60), pp. 133–46. As an often-married single woman, the Wife of Bath confronts and eludes the "binarisms that contained married women": married/not married, male/female, experience/authority, etc. In the fantasy of *WBT*, she succeeds partially in creating a "world of experience"—a theme of *WBP*—by establishing a link between herself as a single woman and the knight of her tale.

132. Revard, Carter. "The Wife of Bath's Grandmother: or How Gilote Showed Her Friend Johane That the Wages of Sin Is Worldly Pleasure, and How Both Then Preached This Gospel Throughout England and Ireland." *ChauR* 39 (2004): 117–36. An Anglo-Norman piece in BL MS Harley 2253 copied about 1340 is analogous to *WBP* in tone, wit, and "outrageousness." Chaucer might have known this

story of two women discussing the virtues of chastity versus sexual license. Includes text and translation.

133. Ziolkowski, Jan. "Old Wives' Tales: Classicism and Anti-Classicism from Apuleius to Chaucer." *Journal of Medieval Latin* 12 (2002): 90–113. Traces the tradition of characterizing stories as "old wives' tales" from Plato through Apuleius and Jerome to Chaucer's *WBT*, showing how the genre draws power from the paradox that "old women were the least powerful members of society and yet the most feared and reviled because of their seemingly uncontrolled speech and behaviour." The genre is relatively highly regarded in periods when the vernacular is esteemed.

See also nos. 58, 65, 70, 79, 80, 86, 101, 104, 106, 107, 126, 154, 181, 196, 200.

CT—The Friar and His Tale

See no. 101.

CT—The Summoner and His Tale

134. Eaton, R. D. "More 'Groping' in *The Summoner's Tale.*" *ES* 85 (2004): 615–21. Although erotic and homosexual elements are undoubtedly evident in *SumT*, certain words and gestures, particularly the friar's ill-fated grope, do not unambiguously have the homosexual charge that has been claimed.

135. Geltner, G. "*Faux Semblants:* Antifraternalism Reconsidered in Jean de Meun and Chaucer." *SP* 101 (2004): 357–81. Reexamines antimendicancy in Jean de Meun's *Roman de la Rose* and in *CT,* suggesting that Jean's portraits of friars should be seen primarily as portraits of hypocrisy and that Chaucer's portrayals of friars (especially in *SumT*) are mediated by the opinions of narrators. Like Jean, Chaucer depicts hypocrisy in individualized portraits that are not merely antifraternal.

136. Rand, Thomas. "'The Summoner's Tale' and Proverbs 21:14." *ANQ* 17.2 (2004): 18–20. Read in the context of Proverbs 21:14 ("a gift in secret pacifieth anger; and a reward in the bosom, strong wrath"), Thomas's gift is comic and condemns Friar John.

137. Travis, Peter W. "Thirteen Ways of Listening to a Fart: Noise in Chaucer's *Summoner's Tale.*" *Exemplaria* 16 (2004): 323–48. In light

of medieval commentary on sound, the fart at the end of *SumT* allows a wide range of "physical, political, social, clerical, and intellectual" reverberations, particularly ones associated with the Peasants' Uprising of 1381. Travis also comments on the hermeneutic range of the references to sound in *HF,* the debate in *PF,* and the chase scene in *NPT.*

See also nos. 101, 107, 151.

CT—The Clerk and His Tale

138. Bodden, M. C. "Chaucer's *Clerk's Tale:* Interrogating 'Virtue' Through Violence." In Mark D. Meyerson, Daniel Thiery, and Oren Falk, eds. *'A Great Effusion of Blood'? Interpreting Medieval Violence.* Toronto: University of Toronto Press, 2004, pp. 216–40. Bodden reads *ClT* as Chaucer's deconstruction of the violence of hagiography. Plot and purported allegory clash in the *Tale,* and Walter is concerned not with Griselda's obedience but with her outward show. Virtue without will is no virtue at all. The Envoy repudiates *ClT,* which is rife with the stuff of torture: spectacle, pain, and ritualized time.

139. Scanlon, Larry. "Poets Laureate and the Language of Slaves: Petrarch, Chaucer, and Langston Hughes." In Fiona Somerset and Nicholas Watson, eds. *The Vulgar Tongue: Medieval and Postmedieval Vernacularity.* University Park: Pennsylvania State University Press, 2003, pp. 220–56. Scanlon considers contemporary ideas of vernacular literature and its potential for "subversiveness" through incompleteness, focusing on the concept of "poet laureate" as introduced into English by Chaucer in *ClT* and on the interdependence of tradition and the African-American vernacular in Langston Hughes's *Ask Your Mama.* See also no. 284.

140. ———. "What's the Pope Got to Do with It?: Forgery, Didacticism, and Desire in the *Clerk's Tale.*" *NML* 6 (2003): 129–65. Scanlon reads *ClT* against a historical tension between aristocratic arranged marriage and canonist marriage of consent, focusing on the espousal scene, the papal letter forged by Walter, and the conclusion and Envoy of the *Tale.* Didactic or exemplary, rather than allegorical, *ClT* is less ideological or ironic than it is expressive of a desire to celebrate—despite its costliness—a feminine spirituality located in the domestic sphere. The

unhistorical nature of the papal dispensation signals the desire. See also no. 265.

See also nos. 101, 105, 127.

CT—The Merchant and His Tale

141. Kohler, Michelle. "Vision, Logic, and the Comic Production of Reality in the *Merchant's Tale* and Two French Fabliaux." *ChauR* 39 (2004): 137–50. In *MerT* and two French fabliaux (*Les perdris* and *Le prestre qui abevete*), the "victims' justifiably skeptical search for visual proof" paradoxically results in deceptive "visual confirmation." Examining how this process takes place may elucidate both "the force of language" in the works and "the absurdity that is central to their humor."

See also nos. 59, 83.

CT—The Squire and His Tale

142. Ambrisco, Alan S. "'It lyth nat in my tonge': *Occupatio* and Otherness in the *Squire's Tale*." *ChauR* 38 (2004): 205–28. The Squire's "bad use of *occupatio* and his self-conscious admissions of rhetorical inadequacy" preserve the foreign, "acknowledging Mongol cultural differences but failing to clarify the terms on which such differences rest." Through "this rhetoric of failure," *SqT* suggests the limitations of the Squire's English and of the English language itself. *SqT* is "unified not by its narrative elements but . . . by the way its linguistic anxieties are revealed and processed."

See also nos. 68, 77, 124, 126.

CT—The Franklin and His Tale

143. Bodden, M. C. "Disordered Grief and Fashionable Afflictions in Chaucer's *Franklin's Tale* and the *Clerk's Tale*." In Jennifer C. Vaught, ed., with Lynne Dickson Bruckner. *Grief and Gender: 700–1700*. New York: Palgrave Macmillan, 2003, pp. 51–63. In *FranT* and *ClT*, masculine grief is aligned with courtly ideals of gentility; feminine grief, with courtly suffering. By complicating these associations and disallowing

consolation of grief, Chaucer intervenes in the "discursive practices" of the fraudulence of the values that society attributes to grief.

144. Fumo, Jamie C. "Aurelius' Prayer, *Franklin's Tale* 1031–79: Sources and Analogues." *Neophil* 88 (2004): 623–35. Chaucer modeled the prayer for the removal of the rocks on a cluster of literary precedents, from Boccaccio to Boethius, Ovid, and Marian lyrics. Chaucer was as interested in the works' interpenetration as in the ironic tensions among them.

145. Knopp, Sherron. "Poetry as Conjuring Act: The *Franklin's Tale* and the *Tempest*." *ChauR* 38 (2004): 337–54. *FranT* and the *Tempest* share not only similarities in plot, character, and theme but also an engagement with the "status of poetry as allusion and conjuring act." The sense of "fiction dissolving into real life, and the voice of the narrator becoming the voice of the poet, may itself be the crowning illusion of fiction." Shakespeare "paid tribute" to Chaucer.

See also nos. 65, 77, 105.

CT—The Physician and His Tale

146. Farber, Lianna. "The Creation of Consent in the *Physician's Tale*." *ChauR* 39 (2004): 151–64. Chaucer's changes to source material emphasize what shapes a person and how she comes to understand and experience the world. If Virginia had continued to refuse her father and Virginius had cut off his daughter's head despite her protests, the *Tale* would have been one of tyranny. Because she agrees that there is no other choice, it is clear that he educated her and taught her to understand reality.

CT—The Pardoner and His Tale

147. Benson, C. David. "Chaucer's Pardoner: His Sexuality and Modern Critics." *Mediaevalia* 8 (1985 for 1982): 337–49. The Pardoner should be read not as a real person but as an allegorical figure. Modern discussions overemphasize the Pardoner's sexuality and distort the fact that hints about his sexuality prepare for the more important concern with his ecclesiastical abuses. The Prologue to the *Tale of Beryn* indicates that the Pardoner was a womanizer.

148. Cox, Catherine S. "Water of Bitterness: The Pardoner and/as

the Sotah." *Exemplaria* 16 (2004): 131–64. The discourse of *PardPT* "disrupts binary structures and exposes the fallacy of essentialist ideologies"; it "interrogates the literary and social consequences of identity categories" assumed in "christological exegesis." The Pardoner's relics recall various aspects of the Jewish Sotah ritual.

149. Green, Richard Firth. "Further Evidence for Chaucer's Representation of the Pardoner as a Womanizer." *MÆ* 71 (2002): 307–9. Details from a Latin flyting poem indicate that the Pardoner in *GP* is presented as an example of "effeminizing heterosexuality."

150. ———. "The Sexual Normality of Chaucer's Pardoner." *Mediaevalia* 8 (1985 for 1982): 351–58. The Pardoner is characterized not by signs of homosexuality, but by indication of effeminacy, thought in the Middle Ages to indicate carnality. Green offers parallels in works by Gower and Lydgate.

151. Grigsby, Bryon Lee. *Pestilence in Medieval and Early Modern English Literature.* Studies in Medieval History and Culture, no. 23. New York and London: Routledge, 2004. xiv, 206 pp. Grigsby considers leprosy, bubonic plague, and syphilis, focusing on how they were constructed as moral phenomena and how literary depictions contributed to historical developments in our (mis)understandings of them. Examines a range of texts, including *PardT,* in which false oaths are connected to the plague; and the *GP* description of the Summoner, through which Chaucer condemns lechery and the failure of ecclesiastical supervision.

152. Minnis, Alastair. "Chaucer and the Queering Eunuch." *NML* 6 (2003): 107–28. Argues against specifying the Pardoner's sexuality, on the grounds that historical evidence discourages such specification and that specification can only render the character less enigmatic and thereby less queer. Sexual characteristics ascribed to the Pardoner support a wide range of possibilities, uncanny in light of any single notion of normativity. In *GP, PardPT,* and the Prologue to *Beryn,* treatments of the Pardoner's sexuality provide an "effective if crude way of expressing disapproval." See also no. 265.

153. Pearcy, Roy J. "Chaucer's Amphibologies and 'The Old Man' in *The Pardoner's Tale.*" *ELN* 41.4 (2004): 1–10. Pearcy traces the history and literary use of amphibology—in Chaucer, a statement capable of two interpretations, uttered by a speaker with supernatural or oracular powers to a listener who can perceive only a meaning at variance with the true intent of the message (*TC* 4.1406, *MkT, NPT, KnT*). In

PardT, the Old Man uses amphibology to punish the rioters; the trickster Saint Martin of Jean Bodel's fabliau speaks similarly.

See also nos. 39, 79, 92, 93, 101, 126.

CT—The Shipman and His Tale

154. Dane, Joseph A. "The Wife of Bath's Shipman's Tale and the Invention of Chaucerian Fabliaux." *MLR* 99 (2004): 287–300. During the nineteenth-century construction of the fabliau as a distinct genre, scholars grouped *ShT* with other "coarse" tales and theorized that Chaucer had reassigned it from the Wife of Bath to the Shipman, assuming that the fabliau form was not expansive enough to accommodate the Wife's complex psychological character. The logical and aesthetic assumptions underlying the reassignment need scrutiny.

See also nos. 92, 107, 118, 157, 168, 216.

CT—The Prioress and Her Tale

155. Acker, Paul. "A Schoolchild's Primer (Plimpton MS 258)." In Daniel T. Kline, ed. *Medieval Literature for Children* (*SAC* 28 [2006], no. 74), pp. 143–54. Considers the Plimpton primer (written in English) in relation to the Latin education depicted in *PrT;* includes an edition of the primer.

156. Heffernan, Carol F. "Praying Before the Image of Mary: Chaucer's *Prioress's Tale,* VII 502–12." *ChauR* 39 (2004): 103–16. Heffernan considers the clergeon's devotion to Mary's image in relation to historical medieval religious images and the "affective piety" they were produced to evoke among the unlearned.

157. Lampert, Lisa. *Gender and the Jewish Difference.* The Middle Ages Series. Philadelphia: University of Pennsylvania Press, 2004. 277 pp. Lampert decenters Christianity and releases the study of Jews and Judaism from a "restricted economy of particularism." She shows how representations of Jews go beyond representations of the "Other" in a range of English texts by revealing fundamental understandings of reading, interpretation, and identity that form the basis of these texts. In *PrT,* the Virgin Mary's body symbolizes the contact between Judaism and Christianity, representing the limits of Christian ideology and identity.

In the broader context of *CT, PrT* reacts directly to *ShT,* in which chaos stems from unspoken sins of usury. *SNT* draws upon the dichotomies between blindness and sight, used in *PrT* to invoke an opposition "to Jewish perfidy" (13). Lampert also considers *MLT, Th-MelL, ParsT,* and *Ret.* The representation of Jews shapes *CT* because what it means to be Christian is negotiated in relationship to Jews and Judaism.

158. Spence, Timothy L. "The Prioress's *Oratio ad Mariam* and Medieval Prayer Composition." In Scott D. Troyan, ed. *Medieval Rhetoric: A Casebook (SAC* 28 [2006], no. 89), pp. 63–90. The Prioress's prayer to Mary shares characteristics with the "genre of prayer known as *pura oratio.*" Spence identifies features of this genre in rhetorical tradition, shows where they are evident in *PrP,* and suggests that they extend into *PrT,* undercutting claims that the *Tale* is satiric.

159. Zieman, Katherine. "Reading, Singing and Understanding: Constructions of the Literacy of Women Religious in Late Medieval England." In Sarah Rees Jones, ed. *Learning and Literacy in Medieval England and Abroad.* Utrecht Studies in Medieval Literacy, no. 3. Turnhout: Brepols, 2003, pp. 97–120. Zieman examines the "liturgical literacy" of medieval nuns, exploring the extent to which they may have understood Latin texts that they performed. *PrT* presents "singing explicitly characterized as illiterate" as "the purest form of piety"; *SNT* presents vernacular translation as an extension of singing, preaching, and proclaiming faith.

See also nos. 53, 86, 90, 94, 215.

CT—The Tale of Sir Thopas

160. Porcheddu, Fred. "Edited Text and Medieval Artifact: The Auchinleck Bookshop and 'Charlemagne and Roland' Theories, Fifty Years Later." *PQ* 80 (2001): 463–500. Critical review of two applied textual theories, exposing their weaknesses in light of recent theory and revealing their ongoing utility. Includes discussion of Laura Hibbard Loomis's arguments that *Th* indicates Chaucer's firsthand knowledge of the Auchinleck MS.

See also nos. 62, 65, 68, 92, 126, 157.

CT—The Tale of Melibee

161. Griffith, John L. "Anger with God and Man: The Social Contexts of Melibee's Anger." *MedievalF* 3 (2003): n.p. Reads *Mel* as a narrative of anger and anger management in which Prudence's "transformative" advice helps Melibee resolve his personal and political anger, even though his fundamental anger against God is not reconciled.

162. Kennedy, Kathleen E. "Maintaining Love Through Accord in the *Tale of Melibee*." *ChauR* 39 (2004): 165–76. Events depicted in Chaucer's French source "mirror a popular English legal remedy, the loveday or accord," and Chaucer uses the occasion to comment on the importance and role of "maintenance" (the "exchange of money and influence between a lord and high-level servants, kinsmen, and friends"). Chaucer's translation reveals the "limitations of out-of-court settlement: informal conflict resolution could be compromised by powerful retainer lords," just as it often was in the courts and Chancery.

See also nos. 28, 38, 59, 69, 101, 157, 163.

CT—The Monk and His Tale

163. Cowgill, Bruce Kent. "Chaucer's 'Myghty Men' and 'Wommanes Conseil.'" *Mediaevalia* 8 (1985 for 1982): 151–69. *Mel, MkT,* and *NPT* are related by their concern with spiritual perception or its lack: *Mel* deals with the failure to listen to Prudence and the return of Sophia; *MkT* shows "the consequence of sacrificing both prudence and *sapientia*"; *NPT* reasserts the message of *Mel* and encourages "movement from sin to salvation."

164. Czarnowus, Anna. "'My cours, that hath so wyde for to turne, / Hath moore power than woot any man': The Children of Saturn in Chaucer's *Monk's Tale*." *SAP* 40 (2004): 299–310. Suggests a link between *KnT* and *MkT:* Saturn's "children" can be either individuals born under the sign of Saturn or societies suffering the effects of the "Age of Saturn." The predicament of the Monk's Hugelyn and his children can be read in light of these traditions.

165. Wurtele, Douglas. "Reflections of the Book of Job and Gregory's *Moralia* in Chaucer's 'Monk's Tale.'" *Florilegium* 21 (2004): 83–93. Despairing in his sin, the Monk ignores the providential aspect of the

story of Job, and so his tragedies emphasize only death. He particularly ignores the conventionally exegetical readings of Adam and Sampson as examples of Providence.

CT—The Nun's Priest and His Tale

166. Field, P. J. C. "The Ending of Chaucer's *Nun's Priest's Tale.*" *MÆ* 71 (2002): 302–6. At *NPT* 7.3445, the referent for "my lord" is Christ.

See also nos. 137, 163, 209.

CT—The Second Nun and Her Tale

See nos. 126, 157, 159.

CT—The Canon's Yeoman and His Tale

[No entries]

CT—The Manciple and His Tale

167. Fumo, Jamie. "Thinking upon the Crow: The *Manciple's Tale* and Ovidian Mythography." *ChauR* 38 (2004): 355–75. Chaucer's use of the Ovidian source of *ManT,* insisting on the tale of the crow—and not the connecting tale of the raven—allows him to argue for the "potentially treacherous nature of language" and to lead smoothly into *Ret.* The influence of Ovid is more pervasive than has been previously argued.

See also no. 105.

CT—The Parson and His Tale

168. Pitard, Derrick G. "Sowing Difficulty: *The Parson's Tale,* Vernacular Commentary, and the Nature of Chaucerian Dissent." *SAC* 26 (2004): 299–330. Considers *ParsT* in light of Lollard concern with the use of English, the themes and drama of *MLE* and *ParsP,* and the inclusion of *ParsT* in MS Longleat 29. Longleat indicates that lay readers

used *ParsT* for private devotional purposes, although the original Latin material was intended to be used by priests to aid their parishioners. In the context of *CT, ParsT* is orthodox; yet, it reflects Chaucer's awareness of the value of the vernacular in shaping individual identity. The Parson's antagonist in *MLE* is the Shipman.

See also nos. 25, 28, 38, 93, 95, 101, 157.

CT—Chaucer's Retraction

See nos. 61, 90, 157, 167.

Anelida and Arcite

See no. 35.

A Treatise on the Astrolabe

169. Eisner, Sigmund, and Marijane Osborn. "Chaucer as Teacher: Chaucer's *Treatise on the Astrolabe.*" In Daniel T. Kline, ed. *Medieval Literature for Children* (*SAC* 28 [2006], no. 74), pp. 155–87. An introduction to *Astr* by Eisner that emphasizes Chaucer ability to write clear instructions for a child, followed by Osborn's Modern English version of the treatise.

See also no. 10.

Boece

[No entries]

The Book of the Duchess

170. Taylor, Mark N. "Chaucer's Knowledge of Chess." *ChauR* 38 (2004): 299–313. The chess metaphor in *BD* shows that Chaucer's knowledge of the game, while not extraordinary, was adequate for his purpose. His knowledge could have come from being an actual player, from studying medieval chess puzzles, from knowledge of the "didactic uses of chess in literature," or from chess metaphors. Chaucer's use of

the motif serves to express the depth of the Black Knight's love for his wife.

171. Wilcockson, Colin. "The Puppy in Chaucer's *Book of the Duchess.*" In Joanna Burzyńska and Danuta Stanulewicz, eds. *PASE Papers in Literature and Culture: Proceedings of the Ninth Annual Conference of the Polish Association for the Study of English. Gdańsk, 26–28 April 2000.* Gdańsk: Wydawnictwo Uniwersytetu Gdańskiego, 2003, pp. 431–36. The puppy in *BD* is not only a guide, but also a complex symbol of psychological and literary connectivity.

See also nos. 59, 72, 75, 86, 94, 175.

The Equatorie of the Planetis

[No entries]

The House of Fame

172. Cawsey, Kathy. "'Alum de glas' or 'Alymed glass'? Manuscript Reading in Book III of *The House of Fame.*" *UTQ* 73 (2004): 972–79. Cawsey suggests an emendation to *HF* 1124 and argues that the image of an "ice mountain limned in light, illuminated with gold, covered with melting writing" indicates Chaucer's concerns about literary transmission.

173. Kerr, John. "The Underworld of Chaucer's *House of Fame:* Virgil, Claudian, and Dante." In Stephen Gersh and Bert Roest, eds. *Medieval and Renaissance Humanism: Rhetoric, Representation, and Reform.* Leiden and Boston: Brill, 2003, pp. 185–202. In *HF,* Chaucer poses "epistemological instability" as a condition of the sublunar realm, which he characterizes as hellish through associations with Proserpina in her triple manifestation, references to Claudian, and allusions to Virgil and Dante.

174. Scattergood, John. "Chaucer's Joke Against the Egle: *The House of Fame,* 1011–1017." *N&Q* 51 (2004): 233–34. Argues for the adoption of "thy selven" instead of "they shynen" (line 1015) as the *lectio difficilior* and as the reading supported by Oxford, Bodleian Library MS Fairfax 16, the copy-text for most editions of *HF.*

See also nos. 59, 72, 75, 88, 137.

The Legend of Good Women

175. Gilbert, Jane. "Becoming Woman in Chaucer: 'On ne naît pas femme, on le meurt.'" In Nicola F. McDonald and W. M. Ormrod, eds. *Rites of Passage: Cultures of Transition in the Fourteenth Century.* York: York Medieval Press, 2004, pp. 109–31. Gilbert's anthropological reading of *BD* and *LGW* emphasizes how in *BD* Blanche is represented as having successfully left the land of the living for the land of the dead. In *LGW,* the female protagonists resist this rite of passage and, in doing so, resist the social conventions that underlie it.

See also nos. 35, 59, 72, 73, 105, 181.

The Parliament of Fowls

176. Cadden, Joan. "Trouble in the Earthly Paradise: The Regime of Nature in Late Medieval Christian Culture." In Lorraine Daston and Fernando Vidal, eds. *The Moral Authority of Nature.* Chicago: University of Chicago Press, 2004, pp. 207–31. Cadden traces the "persistent association of nature with moral conduct and social order" in various late medieval texts, from commentaries on Aristotle's *Nicomachean Ethics* to vernacular poetry. Focuses on *PF* as an example in which both desire and necessity are presented as part of Nature's realm.

177. Davis, Kathleen. "Hymeneal Alogic: Debating Political Community in *The Parliament of Fowls.*" In Kathy Lavezzo, ed. *Imagining a Medieval English Nation* (*SAC* 28 [2006], no. 76), pp. 161–90. Parallels between the sex/gender system and establishing medieval English identity indicate that the perceived doubleness of woman echoes that of the nation. *PF* does not fantasize about a unified nation, but it does produce "England" as a site of social contestation.

178. Matlock, Wendy Alysa. "Irreconcilable Differences: Law, Gender, and Judgment in Middle English Debate Poetry." *DAI* 65 (2004): 924A. Discusses how *PF, The Assembly of Ladies,* and *The Owl and the Nightingale* reflect late medieval court proceedings, gender issues, and eschatology.

179. Steiner, Emily. "Commonality and Literary Form in the 1370s and 1380s." *NML* 6 (2003): 199–221. Steiner assesses political "clamor," "appeal," and "voice," using them to discuss the Prologue to *Piers Plowman* as a work in which "commonality" is "the poem's ideolog-

ical subject *and* poetic process." Suggests briefly that the same is true of *PF*. See also no. 265.

See also nos. 57, 59, 72, 75, 84, 88, 137.

The Romaunt of the Rose

[No entries]

Troilus and Criseyde

180. Alexander, Michael. "Dante and *Troilus*." In Rosalynn Voaden, René Tixier, Teresa Sanchez Roura, and Jenny Rebecca Rytting, eds. *The Theory and Practice of Translation in the Middle Ages* (*SAC* 28 [2006], no. 91), pp. 201–13. Identifies ways Dante influenced the invocations in *TC*, as well as *TC*'s depictions of love and hell. Also explores the words that Chaucer invented to rhyme with "Troie" and with "Criseyde."

181. Amtower, Laurel. "Chaucer's Sely Widows." In Laurel Amtower and Dorothea Kehler, eds. *The Single Woman in Medieval and Early Modern England: Her Life and Representation* (*SAC* 27 [2005], no. 60), pp. 119–32. Surveys Chaucer's treatments of widows, which reveal an "awareness of their excluded social status and how it affects their assertions as individuals." Focuses on Dido and Cleopatra of *LGW*, the Wife of Bath, and, especially, Criseyde. In *TC*, Chaucer gives Criseyde an "elaborate subjectivity," although later tradition returns her to her earlier "reductionism or gendered willfulness."

182. Baker, Alison Ann. "Writers as Readers: The Scribes of Chaucer's *Troilus and Criseyde*." *DAI* 64 (2004): 2481A. Baker compares medieval and modern theories of textual production and examines the development of characters in *TC* by means of textual variants among the work's manuscripts.

183. Behrman, Mary. "Heroic Criseyde." *ChauR* 38 (2004): 314–36. Far from viewing herself as a "passive pawn," Criseyde sees herself as actively fleeing from an unhealthy relationship with Troilus to a healthy one with Diomedes. At the end of *TC*, she is no longer the cynical widow of Book 2, but instead a more "interesting" individual who has learned to liberate her own desires and hopes to do so once again with a more worthy partner.

184. Beidler, Peter G. " 'That I was born, alas': Criseyde's Weary

Dawn Song in Chaucer's *Troilus and Criseyde*." In Cindy L. Vitto and Marcia Smith Marzec, eds. *New Perspectives on Criseyde* (*SAC* 28 [2006], no. 212), pp. 255–76. Challenges R. E. Kaske's argument that Criseyde's *aube* is appropriate for a male speaker and suggests that her words indicate anxious weariness, perhaps even a death wish.

185. Bergquist, Carolyn Jane. "Fictions of Belief in the Worldmaking of Geoffrey Chaucer, Sir Philip Sidney, and John Milton." *DAI* 64 (2004): 2898A. As in the worlds of Sidney's *Arcadia* and Milton's *Paradise Lost*, the fictive world of *TC* is grounded in a key ethical concept. According to Bergquist, "*Kynde* or nature is the making and undoing of both Criseyde and the fiction that contains her."

186. Boitani, Piero. "Da Lollio a Bochas, Boccace e Boccaccio: Boccaccio in Inghilterra." *Rassegna Europea di Letteratura Italiana* 18 (2001): 29–39. Traces the knowledge and recognition of Boccaccio in English literary tradition from his obscured status as "Lollius" in Chaucer's *TC* to clearer acknowledgment in Lydgate and Dryden.

187. Burrow, J. A. "Another Proverb for Pandarus?" *ChauR* 38 (2004): 294–97. Burrow recommends repunctuating *TC* 2.255 as "Nece, alwey lo to the laste," suggesting that it means "look to the last," a phrase that might have been inspired by Chaucer's experiences as a "diplomat and negotiator."

188. Chewning, Susannah. "Re-reading/Re-teaching Chaucer's Criseyde." In Cindy L. Vitto and Marcia Smith Marzec, eds. *New Perspectives on Criseyde* (*SAC* 28 [2006], no. 212), pp. 165–80. To alleviate disappointment at Criseyde's lack of agency, readers should appreciate her not as a "real" woman but as an embodiment of the medieval masculine imagination. Criseyde follows the pattern of many of Chaucer's female characters: caught in a moment of crisis, faced with a crucial decision.

189. Crocker, Holly A. "How the Woman Makes the Man: Chaucer's Reciprocal Fictions in *Troilus and Criseyde*." In Cindy L. Vitto and Marcia Smith Marzec, eds. *New Perspectives on Criseyde* (*SAC* 28 [2006], no. 212), pp. 139–64. Seen in light of external texts that establish the medieval rhetoric of feminine virtue, Criseyde's betrayal reflects betrayal of the patriarchal culture that sets up expectations for feminine conduct and that uses a woman such as Criseyde for its own purposes.

190. Diller, Hans-Jürgen. "'Betwixen hope and drede': Predestination and Suspense in Chaucer's *Troilus and Criseyde*." In Raimund Borgmeier and Peter Wenzel, eds. *Spannung: Studien zur Englischsprachigen Literatur: Für Ulrich Suerbaum zum 75. Geburtstag*. Trier: WVT Wissen-

schaftlicher Verlag Trier, 2001, pp. 36–47. Explores crossing patterns of suspense in *TC:* the "maximal audience suspense and minimal participants' suspense" of the early books are reversed in Books 4 and 5. Attitudes toward predestination complicate the patterns. See also no. 225.

191. Doyle, Kara A. "Criseyde Reading, Reading Criseyde." In Cindy L. Vitto and Marcia Smith Marzec, eds. *New Perspectives on Criseyde* (*SAC* 28 [2006], no. 212), pp. 75–110. In Book 2 of *TC,* Criseyde gains subjectivity as a "reader" of Antigone's song. Although the narrator encourages female readers to "read like men" by identifying with Troilus, Margaret More Roper, in a letter to her father Sir Thomas More, aligns herself with Criseyde at a narrative moment without any connotation of betrayal.

192. Duncan, Thomas G. "Calculating Calkas: Chaucer to Henryson." In Rosalynn Voaden, René Tixier, Teresa Sanchez Roura, and Jenny Rebecca Rytting, eds. *The Theory and Practice of Translation in the Middle Ages* (*SAC* 28 [2006], no. 91), pp. 215–22. Considers Henryson's *Testament of Cresseid* as an extension of Chaucer's *TC* and a transformation of it—two different senses of "translation." Duncan examines the characterization of Calkas and other means of creating compassion for Cresseid.

193. Edmondson, George Thomas. "Troilus and Criseyde Between Two Deaths." *DAI* 64 (2004): 2880A. Considers the relations both between *TC* and Boccaccio's *Filostrato* and between *TC* and Henryson's *Testament of Cresseid,* examining them, not as sources or descendants, but as psychoanalytic "neighbors," fraught with "unsettling desires."

194. Fleming, John V. "Criseyde's Poem: The Anxieties of the Classical Tradition." In Cindy L. Vitto and Marcia Smith Marzec, eds. *New Perspectives on Criseyde* (*SAC* 28 [2006], no. 212), pp. 277–98. Against the backdrop of two of his own studies exploring the classical roots of *TC,* Fleming argues that Chaucer subverts gender stereotypes and the force of literary tradition as much as he can by giving Criseyde a measure of agency and by depicting Deiphoebus as betrayed not by Helen but by Pandarus.

195. Giancarlo, Matthew. "The Structure of Fate and the Devising of History in Chaucer's *Troilus and Criseyde*." *SAC* 26 (2004): 227–66. Considers issues of causality in *TC* as an aspect of the poem's structure and assesses the relationships of causation and structure to history and historicism. *TC* is more clearly recursive than its sources and is recurrently marked by the "Oedipus effect," in which knowledge of the fu-

ture causes present harm. In its multiple, circumscribing endings, the poem is an ancestor of "Marxist-influenced historicisms," despite the effort to replace Boethianism that underlies such historicisms.

196. Guidry, Marc. "Advice Without Consent in *Troilus and Criseyde* and *The Canterbury Tales*." In Scott D. Troyan, ed. *Medieval Rhetoric: A Casebook* (*SAC* 28 [2006], no. 89), pp. 127–45. In *TC*, "Chaucer explores the cultural function of counsel as a key mode of power distribution in chivalric society," examining Pandarus's advice, Criseyde's impersonations of him, and parallels between personal counsel and the Trojan Parliament. In both *TC* and *CT*, Chaucer depicts the effects of male counsel on female agency, showing that both Criseyde and the Wife of Bath attempt to appropriate traditional discourse of counsel.

197. Hill, Thomas Edward. "'Preserve me, oh Lord, as the pupil of thine eye': Perception and Cognition in Chrétien de Troyes' *Le Conte du Graal* and Geoffrey Chaucer's *Troilus and Criseyde*." *DAI* 64 (2004): 3287A. Like Perceval and Gawain in Chrétien's work, Troilus, Pandarus, and Criseyde in *TC* "embody various aspects of perception," vision, and knowledge; "they do so particularly through their portrayal as perceivers or readers" of their respective worlds.

198. Hines, John. "Medieval Medievalism and the Onset of the Modern." In *Voices in the Past: English Literature and Archaeology*. Cambridge: D. S. Brewer, 2004, pp. 105–36. Discusses the use of space and physical objects in *TC*, arguing that the poem's movements among exterior and interior spaces reveal how characters manipulate such spaces—and even furniture—to negotiate relationships with one another and to chart their courses through life.

199. Hodges, Laura F. "Criseyde's 'widewes habit large of samyt broun' in *Troilus and Criseyde*." In Cindy L. Vitto and Marcia Smith Marzec, eds. *New Perspectives on Criseyde* (*SAC* 28 [2006], no. 212), pp. 37–58. Hodges analyzes Criseyde's costume rhetoric, comparing details of her dress (and how it changes throughout the work) with mourning customs of late fourteenth-century England.

200. Jacobs, Kathryn. "Mate or Mother: Positioning Criseyde Among Chaucer's Widows." In Cindy L. Vitto and Marcia Smith Marzec, eds. *New Perspectives on Criseyde* (*SAC* 28 [2006], no. 212), pp. 59–74. Chaucer resists the prevailing "lusty widow" stereotype in his depictions of the Wife of Bath and Criseyde, paving the way for more positive images of widows on the Renaissance stage.

201. Jost, Jean E. "The Performative Criseyde: Self-Conscious Dra-

maturgy." In Cindy L. Vitto and Marcia Smith Marzec, eds. *New Perspectives on Criseyde* (*SAC* 28 [2006], no. 212), pp. 207–30. Jost applies performance theory to key points in the narrative at which Criseyde seems to manipulate her words and her behavior self-consciously to achieve a desired effect.

202. Knapp, Peggy A. "Criseyde's Beauty: Chaucer and Aesthetics." In Cindy L. Vitto and Marcia Smith Marzec, eds. *New Perspectives on Criseyde* (*SAC* 28 [2006], no. 212), pp. 231–54. Knapp examines how Chaucer makes Criseyde beautiful to his audience (then and now) and how critical readings of her character rely on cultural constructs of aesthetic beauty.

203. Mack, Peter. "Argument and Emotion in *Troilus and Criseyde*." In Scott D. Troyan, ed. *Medieval Rhetoric: A Casebook* (*SAC* 28 [2006], no. 89), pp. 109–26. Mack examines public and private oratory in Book 4 of *TC*, exploring the emotional emphases that Chaucer adds to Boccaccio and focusing on the relationship between emotion and argument in rhetorical theory. Mack's essay tallies Chaucer's various ways of depicting the "conflict and collaboration between argument and emotion" throughout *TC*.

204. Marzec, Marcia Smith, and Cindy L. Vitto. "Criseyde as Codependent: A New Approach to an Old Enigma." In Cindy L. Vitto and Marcia Smith Marzec, eds. *New Perspectives on Criseyde* (*SAC* 28 [2006], no. 212), pp. 181–206. Modern psychological analysis of the codependent personality reveals the enigmatic nature of much of Criseyde's behavior. Her drive to please and the absence of healthy boundaries in relationships with others indicate that she lacks a clear sense of self.

205. Meecham-Jones, Simon. "The Invisible Siege—The Depiction of Warfare in the Poetry of Chaucer." In Corinne Saunders, Françoise Le Saux, and Neil Thomas, eds. *Writing War: Medieval Literary Responses to Warfare*. Cambridge: D. S. Brewer, 2004, pp. 147–67. In *TC*, Chaucer avoids focusing on war, revealing his awareness of its importance in perpetrating the aristocratic culture of his day, as well as his need to evade the expectations imposed on him as a writer. Conflict and the psychological disjunction caused by war are granted a potent but implicit significance in the poem, indicating Chaucer's conviction that writers are responsible for the ethical effect of their writing on future audiences.

206. Mitchell, J. Allan. "Dressing and Redressing the Male Body: Homosocial Poetics in *Troilus and Criseyde*." *Postscript* 5.2 (2000): 1–19.

Deeply engaged with literary tradition and the dynamics of translation, *TC* resists "the patriarchal biases of the founding myth the narrator transmits to us." It "denaturalizes the masculine literary corpus" by revealing the "radical contingency of textuality" and the "homosocial orchestration of identity through exchange."

207. O'Brien, Timothy. "*Sikernesse* and *Fere* in *Troilus and Criseyde.*" *ChauR* 38 (2004): 276–93. Throughout *TC,* the words *sikernesse* and *fere* are repeated and echoed in other words that "complicate their apparently stable meaning." Thus, the "characters' fear of circumstances" cannot be separated from the "narrator's fears about the slipperiness of the verbal realm in which he operates." Verbal play operates as a "deterministic undercurrent" as well as a mode of knowing in the poem.

208. Olsen, Corey. "Earthen Vessels: Pedagogy, Authorship, and the Endings of *Piers Plowman* and *Troilus and Criseyde.*" *DAI* 65 (2004): 507A. Olsen argues that *TC* is an effort to "use poetry as a spiritual instrument," specifically in an attempt to link "celestial and earthly loves."

209. Ronquist, Eyvind. "Chaucer's Provisions for Future Contingencies." *Florilegium* 21 (2004) 94–118. Chaucer's interest in future contingencies (a problem raised by Aristotle) in part shapes the narratives in *TC* and *NPT*. The musings of Troilus and Criseyde about the future rely on Boethian principles (among others). Chaunticleer's theory—that dreams of the future create an inevitable destiny—allows for an exploration of his fatalism.

210. Rust, Martha Dana. "'Le Vostre C.': Letters and Love in Bodleian Library Manuscript Arch. Selden. B.24." In Cindy L. Vitto and Marcia Smith Marzec, eds. *New Perspectives on Criseyde* (*SAC* 28 [2006], no. 212), pp. 111–38. Rust describes medieval epistolary protocol and assesses three features of *TC* in Bodleian Library Manuscript Arch. Selden. B.24: an appended colophon, a female figure dressed in black drawn inside the first letter of the poem, and the scribal signature "Le vostre C."

211. Stock, Lorraine Kochanske. "'Slydynge' Critics: Changing Critical Constructions of Chaucer's Criseyde in the Past Century." In Cindy L. Vitto and Marcia Smith Marzec, eds. *New Perspectives on Criseyde* (*SAC* 28 [2006], no. 212), pp. 11–36. A decade-by-decade evaluative overview of critical perspectives on Criseyde throughout the twentieth century.

212. Vitto, Cindy L., and Marcia Smith Marzec, eds. *New Perspectives*

on Criseyde. Asheville, N.C.: Pegasus Press, 2004. 336 pp. Thirteen essays by various authors assess Criseyde in historical context, consider issues of gender and power, and apply postmodern approaches. Several essays revisit earlier scholarship on Criseyde (including the authors' own) and comment on current views. See nos. 184, 188, 189, 191, 194, 199–202, 204, 210, and 211.

213. Wetherbee, Winthrop. "Criseyde Alone." In Cindy L. Vitto and Marcia Smith Marzec, eds. *New Perspectives on Criseyde* (*SAC* 28 [2006], no. 212), pp. 299–332. Revisiting his own *Chaucer and the Poets: An Essay on* Troilus and Criseyde, Wetherbee argues that Criseyde is in many ways a more complex, mature, and heroic character than is Troilus. Troilus, the narrator of *TC,* and especially the narrator of Henryson's *Testament of Cresseid* exhibit wounded masculine vanity by refusing to acknowledge Criseyde as an individuated self or to understand the precarious nature of her plight.

214. Zeikowitz, Richard E. *Homoeroticism and Chivalry: Discourses of Male Same-Sex Desire in the Fourteenth Century.* The New Middle Ages, no. 35. New York: Palgrave Macmillan, 2003. x, 216 pp. Examines homoerotic acts between knights (kissing, expressions of love, and forming of lifelong bonds) in a variety of late medieval texts: *Amys and Amylion,* the *Prose Lancelot, Sir Gawain and the Green Knight,* the *Stanzaic Morte Arthur,* and *TC.* Provides backgrounds on friendship from classical and medieval precedent and explores the sexual reputations of several medieval kings, including Edward II and Richard II. Considers how the friendship between Pandarus and Troilus in *TC* competes with the love of Troilus and Criseyde, channels homoerotic impulses, and is dramatized in "sodomitical discourse." Also discusses the autoeroticism of Criseyde's gaze. See also no. 292.

See also nos. 8, 24, 26, 35, 39, 51, 54, 57, 58, 64–68, 70, 73, 83, 84, 88, 153.

Lyrics and Short Poems

[No general entries. See individual poems.]

An ABC

215. Donavin, Georgiana. "Alphabets and Rosary Beads in Chaucer's *An ABC.*" In Scott D. Troyan, ed. *Medieval Rhetoric: A Casebook*

(*SAC* 28 [2006], no. 89), pp. 25–39. *ABC* is intended not for private prayer but as a pedagogical "English-teaching" text. The poem's manuscript illuminations, visual imagery, and rosary-like structure reinforce the general medieval association of the Virgin with the education of youth (also reflected in *PrT*).

The Envoy to Bukton

See no. 79.

The Envoy to Scogan

See no. 28.

Truth

See no. 28.

Chaucerian Apocrypha

216. Adams, Jenny. "Exchequers and Balances: Anxieties of Exchange in *The Tale of Beryn*." *SAC* 26 (2004): 267–97. Adams argues that the "discourse of gaming" underlies *Beryn* and its Prologue (a.k.a. *The Canterbury Interlude*), which offer "centralized regulation as a solution to the inequalities inherent in exchange and commerce." Less optimistic about mercantile trust and goodwill than is Chaucer in *CT* (especially *ShT*), the *Beryn* author is nevertheless a good deal less distrustful of commerce than is Langland in *Piers Plowman*.

217. Blake, N. F. "Chaucer, Gamelyn and the Cook's Tale." In Takami Matsuda, Richard A. Linenthal, and John Scahill, eds. *The Medieval Book Collector and a Modern Collector: Essays in Honour of Toshiyuki Takamiya* (*SAC* 28 [2006], no. 78), pp. 87–98. Considers the inclusion of *Gamelyn* in early manuscripts of *CT* and the relative confidence with which scribes placed the tale. Given the possibility that some manuscripts predate Chaucer's death, he may have experimented with including the tale, even if he did not compose it.

218. Symons, Dana M., ed. *Chaucerian Dream Visions and Complaints*. Kalamazoo, Mich.: Medieval Institute, 2004. vii, 293 pp. Edits four works ("The Boke of Cupide, God of Love," "A Complaynte of a Lovers

Lyfe," "The Quare of Jelusy," and "La Belle Dame sans Mercy"), all except the "Quare" once attributed to Chaucer. Includes for each an introduction; the text, with obscure terms defined in the margins; explanatory notes; and textual notes. The volume also contains a glossary and bibliography. Seeks to bring these works out from Chaucer's shadow.

See also nos. 41, 147, 152.

Book Reviews

219. Ackroyd, Peter. *Chaucer* (*SAC* 28 [2006], no. 6). Rev. Ad Putter, *TLS*, Nov. 19, 2004, pp. 4–5.

220. Amtower, Laurel. *Engaging Words: The Culture of Reading in the Later Middle Ages* (*SAC* 24 [2002], no. 131). Rev. Deborah McGrady, *TMR* 03.12.06, n.p.

221. Barr, Helen. *Socioliterary Practice in Late Medieval England* (*SAC* 25 [2003], no. 89). Rev. Maura B. Nolan, *SAC* 26 (2004): 358–60.

222. Benson, Robert G., and Susan J. Ridyard, eds. *New Readings of Chaucer's Poetry* (*SAC* 27 [2005], no. 90). Rev. Aidan Conti, *N&Q* 51 (2004): 434–35; Anita Obermeier, *TMR* 04.04.06, n.p.

223. Black, Nancy B. *Medieval Narratives of Accused Queens* (*SAC* 27 [2005], no. 190). Rev. Rosalind Brown-Grant, *MÆ* 73 (2004): 354–55.

224. Boffey, Julia, comp. *Fifteenth-Century English Dream Visions: An Anthology* (*SAC* 28 [2006], no. 41). Rev. Kathryn L. Lynch, *N&Q* 51 (2004): 435–36.

225. Borgmeier, Raimund, and Peter Wenzel, eds. *Spannung: Studien zur Englischsprachigen Literatur: Für Ulrich Suerbaum zum 75. Geburtstag* (*SAC* 28 [2006], no. 190). Rev. Uwe Meyer, *Archiv* 241 (2004): 395–97.

226. Borroff, Marie. *Traditions and Renewals: Chaucer, The Gawain-Poet, and Beyond* (*SAC* 27 [2005], no. 94). Rev. Laura Howes, *TMR* 04.02.46, n.p.; Margaret Lamont, *Comitatus* 35 (2004): 189–91.

227. Braswell, Mary Flowers. *Chaucer's "Legal Fiction": Reading the Records* (*SAC* 25 [2003], no. 93). Rev. Cynthia Gravlee, *TMR* 03.02.16, n.p.

228. Brown, Sarah Annes. *The Metamorphosis of Ovid: From Chaucer to Ted Hughes* (*SAC* 23 [2001], no. 230). Rev. *FMLS* 40 (2004): 97; Amanda Kolson, *TLS*, Jan. 19, 2001, p. 26.

229. Burger, Glenn. *Chaucer's Queer Nation* (*SAC* 27 [2005], no. 143). Rev. Graham N. Drake, *TMR* 03.10.03, n.p.

230. ———, and Steven Kruger, eds. *Queering the Middle Ages* (*SAC* 25 [2003], no. 97). Rev. Michael O'Rourke, *SoAR* 68 (2003): 149–52.

231. Burrow, J. A. *Gestures and Looks in Medieval Narrative* (*SAC* 26 [2004], no. 120). Rev. William Ian Miller, *TMR* 3.01.34, n.p.; Sarah Stanbury, *SAC* 26 (2004): 367–69.

232. Cohen, Jeffrey J., ed. *Medieval Identity Machines* (*SAC* 27 [2005], no. 171). Rev. Tison Pugh, *Arthuriana* 14.2 (2004): 88–89.

233. Correale, Robert M., and Mary Hamel, eds. *Sources and Analogues of the "Canterbury Tales."* Vol. 1 (*SAC* 26 [2004], no. 47). Rev. N. F. Blake, *MLR* 99 (2004): 454–55; Peter Brown, *MÆ* 73 (2004): 122–23; Stephen Knight, *Speculum* 79 (2004): 1057–59; Helen Phillips, *SAC* 26 (2004): 372–75.

234. Crane, Susan. *The Performance of Self: Ritual, Clothing, and Identity During the Hundred Years War* (*SAC* 26 [2004], no. 126). Rev. Seth Lerer, *CL* 56 (2004): 262–66; Claire Sponsler, *SAC* 26 (2004): 375–78; Lorraine Kochanske Stock, *Speculum* 79 (2004): 158–61.

235. Curran, S. Terrie. *English from Caedmon to Chaucer: The Literary Development of English* (*SAC* 26 [2004], no. 100). Rev. Agnieszka Pysz, *SAP* 40 (2004): 367–72.

236. Dane, Joseph A. *The Myth of Print Culture: Essays on Evidence, Textuality, and Bibliographical Method* (*SAC* 27 [2005], no. 33). Rev. William Proctor Williams, *N&Q* 51 (2004): 452–53.

237. Delany, Sheila, ed. *Chaucer and the Jews: Sources, Contexts, Meanings* (*SAC* 26 [2004], no. 129). Rev. Lawrence Besserman, *Speculum* 79 (2004): 166–67; Catherine Cox, *SoAR* 69.2 (2004): 128–31; Steven F. Kruger, *SAC* 26 (2004): 378–81; Brenda Schildgen, *TMR* 04.12.04, n.p.

238. Dimmick, Jeremy, James Simpson, and Nicolette Zeeman, eds. *Images, Idolatry, and Iconoclasm in Late Medieval England: Textuality and the Visual Image* (*SAC* 26 [2004], no. 161). Rev. Glending Olson, *Speculum* 79 (2004): 169–71.

239. Dyas, Dee. *Pilgrimage in Medieval English Literature, 700–1500* (*SAC* 25 [2003], no. 155). Rev. Cynthia Ho, *TMR* 03.02.04, n.p.

240. Edwards, Robert R. *Chaucer and Boccaccio: Antiquity and Modernity* (*SAC* 26 [2004], no. 49). Rev. Piero Boitani, *MP* 102 (2004): 95–97; Warren Ginsberg, *SAC* 26 (2004): 381–85; Nick Havely, *MLR*

99 (2004): 455–56; James H. McGregor, *Speculum* 79 (2004): 474–76; Hanneke Wilson, *RES* 55 (2004): 115–17.

241. Eisner, Sigmund, ed. *A Treatise on the Astrolabe*. Vol. 6, The Prose Treatises, pt. 1, of *A Variorum Edition of the Works of Geoffrey Chaucer* (*SAC* 26 [2004], no. 25). Rev. Andrew Cole, *SAC* 26 (2004): 385–88; Edgar Laird, *TMR* 03.01.22, n.p.

242. Erler, Mary C., and Maryanne Kowaleski, eds. *Gendering the Master Narrative: Women and Power in the Middle Ages* (*SAC* 27 [2005], no. 277). Rev. Sam Sloane, *WS* 33 (2004): 344–45.

243. Farmer, Sharon, and Carol Braun Pasternack, eds. *Gender and Difference in the Middle Ages* (*SAC* 27 [2005], no. 193). Rev. Anne F. Harris, *TMR* 03.10.07, n.p.; Kathleen Coyne Kelly, *Arthuriana* 14.4 (2004): 84–86.

244. Finley, William K., and Joseph Rosenblum, eds. *Chaucer Illustrated: Five Hundred Years of the "Canterbury Tales" in Pictures* (*SAC* 27 [2005], no. 105). Rev. Charlotte C. Morse, *JEBS* 7 (2004): 169–72.

245. Forni, Kathleen. *The Chaucerian Apocrypha: A Counterfeit Canon* (*SAC* 25 [2003], no. 292). Rev. N. F. Blake, *MLR* 99 (2004): 455–56; Julia Boffey, *Speculum* 79 (2004): 479–81; Anne Hudson, *ES* 85 (2004): 261–63.

246. Foster, Edward E., and David H. Carey. *Chaucer's Church: A Dictionary of Religious Terms in Chaucer* (*SAC* 26 [2004], no. 4). Rev. Rose Arnold, *L&T* 18 (2004): 119–20; Guy Trudel, *N&Q* 51 (2004): 187–89.

247. Fowler, Elizabeth. *Literary Character: The Human Figure in Early English Writing* (*SAC* 27 [2005], no. 230). Rev. Louise M. Bishop, *TMR* 04.07.06, n.p.; Alfred David, *SAC* 26 (2004): 391–94; Liam Felsen, *Comitatus* 35 (2004): 217–19; Sherron E. Knopp, *MÆ* 73 (2004): 335–36.

248. Fradenburg, L. O. Aranye. *Sacrifice Your Love: Psychoanalysis, Historicism, Chaucer* (*SAC* 26 [2004], no. 133). Rev. Norm Klassen, *MÆ* 73 (2004): 336–38.

249. Ginsberg, Warren. *Chaucer's Italian Tradition* (*SAC* 26 [2004], no. 50). Rev. Henry Ansgar Kelly, *SAC* 26 (2004): 394–97.

250. Gray, Douglas, ed. *The Oxford Companion to Chaucer* (*SAC* 27 [2005], no. 5). Rev. Dieter Mehl, *Archiv* 241 (2004): 477–78.

251. Hagedorn, Suzanne C. *Abandoned Women: Rewriting the Classics in Dante, Boccaccio, and Chaucer* (*SAC* 28 [2006], no. 35). Rev. Alessia Ronchetti, *TMR* 04.06.15, n.p.

252. Harding, Wendy, ed. *Drama, Narrative and Poetry in the "Canterbury Tales"* (*SAC* 27 [2005], no. 114). Rev. Dieter Mehl, *Archiv* 241 (2004): 478.

253. Heffernan, Carol F. *The Orient in Chaucer and Medieval Romance.* (*SAC* 27 [2005], no. 115). Rev. Donald L. Hoffman, *Arthuriana* 14.3 (2004): 100–02.

254. Heng, Geraldine. *Empire of Magic: Medieval Romance and the Politics of Cultural Fantasy* (*SAC* 28 [2006], no. 127). Rev. John Block Friedman, *Speculum* 79 (2004): 1092–93; Michelle Warren, *TMR* 04.07.11, n.p.; Judith Weiss, *N&Q* 51 (2004): 431–32.

255. Hirsh, John C. *Chaucer and the "Canterbury Tales": A Short Introduction* (*SAC* 27 [2005], no. 151). Rev. C. David Benson, *Speculum* 79 (2004): 205–6.

256. Horobin, Simon. *The Language of the Chaucer Tradition* (*SAC* 27 [2005], no. 74). Rev. Julie Coleman, *N&Q* 51 (2004): 186–87; Wendy Harding, *TMR* 04.10.01, n.p.; Seth Lerer, *MÆ* 73 (2004): 121–22; John Thompson, *JEBS* 7 (2004): 180–82.

257. Hughes, Alan. *Signs and Circumstances: A Study of Allegory in Chaucer's "Canterbury Tales"* (*SAC* 27 [2005], no. 152). Rev. Ann Dobyns, *TMR* 04.12.11, n.p.

258. Jacobs, Kathryn. *Marriage Contracts from Chaucer to the Renaissance Stage* (*SAC* 25 [2003], no. 157). Rev. Ruth Morse, *Archiv* 241 (2004): 476–77.

259. Johnston, Andrew James. *Clerks and Courtiers: Chaucer, Late Middle English Literature, and the State Formation Process* (*SAC* 25 [2003], no. 111). Rev. N. F. Blake, *ES* 85 (2004): 263–65; Karen Smith, *MLR* 99 (2004): 458; Emily Steiner, *JEGP* 103 (2004): 134.

260. Jones, Terry, Robert Yeager, Terry Dolan, Alan Fletcher, and Juliette Dor. *Who Murdered Chaucer? A Medieval Mystery* (*SAC* 27 [2005], no. 14). Rev. Andrew James Johnston, *Anglia* 122 (2004): 690–92; Peter Nicholson, *JGN* 22.2 (2004): 7–8; Alexander Rose, *TLS*, Jan. 16, 2004, pp. 24–25.

261. Jones, Timothy S., and David A. Sprunger, eds. *Marvels, Monsters, and Miracles: Studies in the Medieval and Early Modern Imaginations* (*SAC* 26 [2004], no. 139). Rev. David Williams, *TMR* 04.01.08, n.p.

262. Kerby-Fulton, Kathryn, and Maidie Hilmo, eds. *The Medieval Professional Reader at Work: Evidence from Manuscripts of Chaucer, Langland, Kempe, and Gower* (*SAC* 25 [2003], no. 28). Rev. Andrew Taylor, *SAC* 26 (2004): 400–03.

263. Kern-Stähler, Annette. *A Room of One's Own: Reale und mentale Innenräume weiblicher Selbstbestimmung im spätmittelalterlichen England (SAC* 28 [2006], no. 73). Rev. Joerg Fichte, *Archiv* 241 (2004): 400–01; Andrew James Johnston, *Anglia* 122 (2004): 308–11.

264. Knapp, Ethan. *The Bureaucratic Muse: Thomas Hoccleve and the Literature of Late Medieval England (SAC* 26 [2004], no. 73). Rev. Howard Kaminsky, *TMR* 03.02.24, n.p.; Robert J. Meyer-Lee, *Archiv* 241 (2004): 402–4.

265. Lawton, David, Wendy Scase, and Rita Copeland, eds. *NML* 6 (*SAC* 28 [2006], nos. 82, 140, 152, and 179). Rev. Andrew James Johnston, *Anglia* 122 (2004): 692–97.

266. Lenz, Katja, and Ruth Möhlig, eds. *Of dyuersitie & chaunge of langage: Essays Presented to Manfred Görlach on the Occasion of His 65th Birthday (SAC* 27 [2005], no. 232). Rev. Aidan Conti, *N&Q* 51 (2004): 65–66; Thomas Honegger, *ES* 85 (2004): 569–71; Ingrid Piller, *Anglia* 122 (2004): 292–95.

267. Lynch, Kathryn L., ed. *Chaucer's Cultural Geography (SAC* 26 [2004], no. 144). Rev. Jeffrey J. Cohen, *SAC* 26 (2004): 409–11; H. L. Spencer, *RES* 55 (2004): 263–64.

268. Machan, Tim William. *English in the Middle Ages (SAC* 27 [2005], no. 77). Rev. Ivana Djordjević, *MÆ* 27 (2004): 330–31; Thorlac Turville-Petre, *EHR* 119 (2004): 501–2.

269. Matthews, David. *The Making of Middle English, 1765–1910 (SAC* 23 [2001], no. 102). Rev. Renate Haas, *Anglia* 122 (2004): 504–6.

270. ———, ed. *The Invention of Middle English: An Anthology of Primary Sources (SAC* 24 [2002], no. 173). Rev. Renate Haas, *Anglia* 122 (2004): 504–6.

271. Minnis, A. J., ed. *Middle English Poetry: Texts and Traditions. Essays in Honour of Derek Pearsall (SAC* 25 [2003], no. 121). Rev. Susanna Fein, *Speculum* 79 (2004): 251–54.

272. Orme, Nicholas. *Medieval Children (SAC* 25 [2003], no. 124). Rev. James A. Schultz, *M&H* 30 (2004): 156–59.

273. Osborn, Marijane. *Time and the Astrolabe in the "Canterbury Tales" (SAC* 26 [2004], no. 176). Rev. Sigmund Eisner, *TMR* 03.01.36, n.p.; Edgar Laird, *SAC* 26 (2004): 414–18.

274. Perkins, Nicholas. *Hoccleve's Regiment of Princes: Counsel and Constraint (SAC* 26 [2004], no. 81). Rev. Antony Hasler, *SAC* 26 (2004): 418–20.

275. Pfister, Manfred, ed. *A History of English Laughter: Laughter from Beowulf to Beckett and Beyond* (*SAC* 26 [2004], no. 193). Rev. Alwin Fill, *ArAA* 29 (2004): 130–33; Elizabeth Freund, *Archiv* 241 (2004): 393–95.

276. Rhodes, Jim. *Poetry Does Theology: Chaucer, Grosseteste, and the "Pearl"-Poet* (*SAC* 25 [2003], no. 129). Rev. Michael W. Twomey, *Speculum* 79 (2004): 261–62.

277. Robertson, Elizabeth, and Christine M. Rose, eds. *Representing Rape in Medieval and Early Modern Literature* (*SAC* 25 [2003], no. 130). Rev. Robin Norris, *N&Q* 51 (2004): 434; Corinne Saunders, *Arthuriana* 14.3 (2004): 104–5; Stephanie Trigg, *TMR* 04.01.36, n.p.

278. Rosenthal, Joel T. *Telling Tales: Sources and Narration in Late Medieval England* (*SAC* 27 [2005], no. 15). Rev. Peter Coss, *EHR* 119 (2004): 1044–46; Ad Putter, *TLS*, Nov. 19, 2004, pp. 4–5.

279. Salisbury, Eve, Georgiana Donavin, and Merrall Llewelyn Price, eds. *Domestic Violence in Medieval Texts* (*SAC* 26 [2004], no. 149). Rev. Elizabeth Robertson, *SAC* 26 (2004): 421–24.

280. Scala, Elizabeth. *Absent Narratives, Manuscript Textuality, and Literary Structure in Late Medieval England* (*SAC* 26 [2004], no. 150). Rev. Sheila Delany, *Speculum* 79 (2004): 271–73; Gergely Nagy, *Arthuriana* 14.3 (2004): 106–7; Larry Scanlon, *SAC* 26 (2004): 424–26; Andrew Taylor, *TMR* 03.02.03, n.p.

281. Shippey, Tom, and Martin Arnold, eds. *Film and Fiction: Reviewing the Middle Ages*. Studies in Medievalism, no. 12. Woodbridge, Suffolk; and Rochester, N.Y.: D. S. Brewer, 2003. Rev. Andrew James Johnston, *Anglia* 122 (2004): 692–97; Suzanne Lewis, *TMR* 04.01.20, n.p.

282. Shoaf, R. Allen. *Chaucer's Body: The Anxiety of Circulation in the "Canterbury Tales"* (*SAC* 25 [2003], no. 166). Rev. Marion Turner, *RES* 55 (2004): 114–15.

283. Simpson, James. *Reform and Cultural Revolution, 1350–1547* (*SAC* 26 [2004], no. 152). Rev. Thomas Herron, *SCJ* 35 (2004): 915; Dieter Mehl, *Archiv* 241 (2004): 200–05.

284. Somerset, Fiona, and Nicholas Watson, eds. *The Vulgar Tongue: Medieval and Postmedieval Vernacularity* (*SAC* 28 [2006], no. 139). Paul Cohen, *RenQ* 57 (2004): 1449–50.

285. Strohm, Paul. *Theory and the Premodern Text* (*SAC* 24 [2002], no. 191). Rev. Alan J. Fletcher, *SAC* 26 (2004): 430–33.

286. Treharne, Elaine, ed. *Writing Gender and Genre in Medieval Liter-*

ature: Approaches to Old and Middle English Texts (SAC 26 [2004], no. 156). Rev. Keiko Hamaguchi, *SIMELL* 19 (2004): 77–84; Eva Parra Membrives, *TMR* 04.02.07, n.p.

287. Trigg, Stephanie. *Congenial Souls: Reading Chaucer from Medieval to Postmodern (SAC* 26 [2004], no. 157). Rev. Clare R. Kinney, *MP* 101 (2004): 590–93; Camille La Bossière, *CollL* 31 (2004): 193–96; Seth Lerer, *JEGP* 103 (2004): 524; Karen Smyth, *TMR* 03.05.14, n.p.

288. Watt, Diane. *Amoral Gower: Language, Sex, and Politics (SAC* 27 [2005], no. 51). Rev. Jonathan H. Hsy, *MÆ* 73 (2004): 338–40.

289. Webb, Diana. *Medieval European Pilgrimage, c. 700–c. 1500 (SAC* 26 [2004], no. 180). Rev. Elizabeth Makowski, *Historian* 66 (2004): 411–12.

290. Wetherbee, Winthrop. *Geoffrey Chaucer: The Canterbury Tales.* 2nd ed. (*SAC* 28 [2006], no. 108). Rev. Andrew James Johnston, *Anglia* 122 (2004): 689–90.

291. Yeager, Robert F., and Charlotte C. Morse, eds. *Speaking Images: Essays in Honor of V. A. Kolve (SAC* 25 [2003], no. 147). Rev. Jim Rhodes, *SAC* 26 (2004): 433–36.

292. Zeikowitz, Richard E. *Homoeroticism and Chivalry: Discourses of Male Same-Sex Desire in the Fourteenth Century (SAC* 28 [2006], no. 214). Rev. John Arnold, *TMR* 04.02.15, n.p.; Donald L. Hoffman, *Arthuriana* 14.1 (2004): 120–22.

Author Index—Bibliography

INDEX